The Complete Writer's Guide to

HEROES

HEROINES

SIXTEEN MASTER ARCHETYPES

Tami D. Cowden, Caro LaFever, Sue Viders

 lone eagle
PUBLISHING COMPANY

An imprint of Watson-Guptill Publications/New York

THE COMPLETE WRITER'S GUIDE TO HEROES & HEROINES
SIXTEEN MASTER ARCHETYPES
Copyright © 2000 by Tami Cowden, Caro LaFever and Sue Viders

WATSON-GUPTILL PUBLICATIONS, an imprint of the Crown Publishing Group,
A division of Random House, Inc., New York
www.crownpublishing.com
www.watsonguptill.com

Cover design by Lindsay Albert
Book design by Carla Green
Edited by Linda J. Cowgill

Library of Congress Cataloging-in-Publication Data
Cowden, Tami.
    The complete writer's guide to heroes and heroines : sixteen master archetypes /
by Tami Cowden, Caro LaFever, and Sue Viders.--1st ed.
        p.   cm.
    ISBN 1-58065-024-4
    1. Authorship. 2. Characters and characteristics in literature. I. LaFever, Caro.
II. Viders, Sue. III. Title.

PN218.C69 2000
808.3'97--dc21   00-058184

Printed in the United States of America
    8 9 10 / 10 09

CONTENTS

ACKNOWLEDGMENTS

To Steve, my favorite husband and personal hero, for Alex and Kate, my favorite daughters, who are growing up to be bright, beautiful young heroines, and for Martin, as fine a son as one could want.

—Tami Cowden

To Dan, who spent endless hours at breakfast discussing characters, who rarely griped about watching classic black and white movies instead of *Rambo* or kickboxing, and who believes in my writing more than I do.

—Caro LaFever

To Jack, my long suffering hero and best friend, who listened to all my harebrained ideas, helped me with finding the right words and took me out to many dinners after long days at the computer.

—Sue Viders

The authors gratefully acknowledge the insight, support, contribution, advice and comments of Brenda Beagley, Sally Prince Davis, Karin Story Dearborn, Patti DeGroot, Carolyn Greene, Su Kopil, Betsy Norman, Roger Reid, Nancy Warren and our many friends on the RWA, BIAW and HODRW list-serves. We appreciate all you have done for us.

NOTES FROM THE EDITOR

Why is a book about Hero and Heroine Archetypes important to screenwriters? Because creating believable characterizations that connect with the audience is probably one of the most difficult aspects of writing an author faces. The weakest component of many screenplays and novels—not to mention numerous produced films and television shows—is characterization, especially in the inner life of individual. Why is this so? The creation of rich characterizations defies easy codification, making it very hard to understand, let alone teach. Sometimes an author creates a great character, other times characters just fall flat. When a book comes along that provides new insight into understanding characters and how they function, all writers should take notice.

In *The Complete Writer's Guide to Heroes & Heroines*, authors Tami D. Cowden, Caro LaFever and Sue Viders offer not a reductive theory on how to create complex characters, but a broad analysis of the basic male and female archetypes populating the vast field of literature and film. Through the use of numerous examples from films and books, they show how the archetypes operate beneath the faces of the most original characters to forge a link with the audience based in shared human experiences.

Writers and screenwriters alike will find this book an invaluable tool to understanding their characters at deeper levels. All good writers have to be psychologists who must understand their characters' actions and motivations. Through the description of the sixteen archetypes, authors Cowden, LaFever and Viders provide ample material to help writers know their creations. They present a cohesive method for organizing biographical information to aid the writer in clearly seeing a character in conflict, which is essential to the plot of every story. They show how the identification of the archetype at work in a character sheds light on the meaning of his inner conflict and the direction of his solution. They illustrate the advantage of combining archetypes to create more complex characters. In their discussion of the antagonism inherent in archetypal relationships between the opposite sexes, pairs and ensembles, they offer patterns of growth and reconciliation. All of these serve to broaden and deepen characters' dimension, which can only make for more authentic, more believable characters.

Linda J. Cowgill is a produced screenwriter who has also written for prime-time television. She has taught screenwriting seminars for the American Film Institute at the Kennedy Center in Washington, D.C., and at the Boston Film Institute. Currently, she teaches screenwriting at Loyola Marymount University. Ms. Cowgill is the author of the popular film school textbooks *Writing Short Films* and *Secrets of Screenplay Structure.*

INTRODUCTION

Stories have been told since the dawn of language. The focus of these tales has always been the people who inhabited them; events were recounted only as a backdrop to the exploits of the heroes and heroines. From the earliest days, storytellers have known a simple truth: strong characters may carry a weak plot, but weak characters cannot be hidden by a strong plot.

Since those primitive times to the present day, writers have woven tales about heroes and heroines, spun webs and built mazes through which protagonists must find their way to truth and happiness, and to their destiny. Sometimes these fictional men and women have been larger than life, but they also have been regular people who became heroic when faced with adversity. But high or low, brilliant or average, characters whose stories survive through the ages are those heroes and heroines that ring true to the human spirit. Their personalities, tragedies and triumphs, their decisions made in the heat of battle—strike a chord of recognition in all who hear the tale.

Why does this happen? Why do some characters reach into the collective heart and pluck the heartstrings of every reader, while others are immediately discarded into the dustbin of memory?

Great heroes and heroines have emerged from literature through the ages. These universal characters are instantly recognized by the audience. Their motives are clear, their personalities unclouded. Times, settings, actions and events may vary, but these protagonists shine like diamonds among rubble, the

> Strong characters may carry a weak plot but weak characters cannot be hidden by a strong plot.

audience immediately connecting and empathizing with their journey.

Carl Jung named these recurring and universal characters from the Greek word *archetypos*... which means *first of its kind.*

Carl Jung theorized that humans have a collective unconscious, "deposits of the constantly repeated experiences of humanity . . . a kind of readiness to reproduce over and over again the same or similar mythical ideas . . ." This shared memory of experiences has resulted in a resonance of the concepts of hero and heroine that transcends time, place and culture. Jung called these recurring personalities ARCHETYPES, from the Greek word *archetypos*, meaning "first of its kind."

A true hero or heroine is one who taps into these universal emotions and feelings. A writer who learns how to use archetypes can more easily create a hero or heroine who jumps off the pages and grabs the heart and head of the reader. These characters live in the minds of the audience long after the last page is turned or the last film clip is viewed.

Characters who fall within these archetypes have starred in story after story, entertaining and informing the human experience for millennia. A review of myths, legends, fairy tales, epic poems, novels and film reveals that the protagonists who recur in these stories fall into sixteen distinctive categories, eight each for the heroes and heroines. These are the sixteen heroic archetypes.

In the pages that follow, we explain these sixteen archetypes, show ways to use archetypal characters in fiction writing and explore how the archetypes interact with each other.

Section I: The Hero Archetypes

Section II: The Heroine Archetypes

Section I sets forth the eight HEROES and Section II the eight HEROINES.

Each archetype is discussed in detail. First, we provide a short sketch of the archetype's demeanor and attitudes. Patterns of viewing and responding to the world emerge. Discussion of the common dominant qualities, both positive and negative, found in each archetype comes next. Often, there is a relationship between these flaws and virtues. An archetype's strength frequently proves a weakness as well.

Next, the archetype's likely family background and childhood are reviewed. Of course, nothing is set in stone, but a character's motivation is generally traceable to an experience or series of experiences. Upbringing, family life and relationships with childhood peers are often pivotal in the development of the archetypal structure of the character. Again, we are not saying that each example of a character within an archetype has exactly the same background. We merely suggest that certain similarities in back story are likely.

Next we examine the two *styles* of each archetype. A style is the pattern of behavior in which the archetype is made manifest. Each style shows the basic characteristics of the archetype, but presents those patterns in slightly different ways. Mr. Spock of *Star Trek* and Lieutenant Columbo of *Columbo* are both members of the same archetype, but Spock's precise and direct manner is very different from Columbo's roundabout method.

Style:
The style of an archetype is…
the pattern of behavior in which the archetype is made manifest.

Finally, there is a review of typical occupations the archetypal character might pursue. Again, no occupation is outside the scope of any archetype—in fact, an atypical occupation might be the source of conflict with a character's story. But examples are given to demonstrate how the inherent personality traits frequently lead a character to certain types of professions.

Throughout the discussion, we provide examples from literature, television and film of characters within the archetype. These examples demonstrate one very clear point—archetypal characters are not carbon copies of each other. Mary Richards and Rhoda Morgenstern of *The Mary Tyler Moore Show* were both members of the same archetype, but very different women. Writers need not fear that use of the archetypes will result in cookie cutter characters.

In Section III, the different ways in which archetypes may be used in fiction writing are explored. First, the use of a *core* archetypal character is examined. A *core* archetype is a character who, through the course of the entire story, stays within a single archetypal model.

Section III:
Creating Characters
• Core
• Evolving
• Layered

Next, the use of *evolving* archetypal characters are explored. An *evolving* archetype is a character who begins the story as one archetype but, through the course of the heroic journey, has been transformed into another archetype by the conclusion of the story.

Finally, the use of a *layered* archetypal character is discussed. A *layered archetype* is a character who has attributes of more than one archetype combined together.

In Section IV, we discuss the ways in which the archetypes interact with each other. The inherent methods and motivations present within one archetype automatically create conflict when that archetype is confronted with the methods and motivations of another archetype. This section shows how to develop the internal conflicts between characters necessary for any story.

Section IV:
Archetype Interactions

The Appendix lists all the films, television programs and books used as examples.

We believe that this exploration of the universal archetypes will help the writer create dynamic heroes and heroines. These characters will tap into the universal subconscious and thus will live in the hearts of the audience long after the story has been told.

SECTION I
THE HERO ARCHETYPES

What is a hero? The word has its origins in ancient Greek, where it referred to a mythological or legendary figure, often with divine ancestry or awesome strength and powers. Tales told in the forum, like those myths and legends told around fires, spoke of great deeds of bravery, exciting journeys and noble sacrifices by these heroes. At times, these men might be wounded or flawed, but their acts of courage and gallantry excused their sins.

But as time progressed, and the love of fiction spread, the writers of stirring tales no longer limited their talents to the adventures of the bravest of the brave. A different type of hero emerged—an anti-hero, of sorts. No longer perfect, no longer the most noble of all men, heroes developed the flaws of mere mortals. At times, heroes were even men who were less than admirable, destined by their own defects of character to a tragic fate.

In addition to the sagas of demigods and the legends of gallant champions, accounts of more ordinary men began to emerge. Men who lived next door or in the next village began to star in their own fables and yarns. Their heroism consisted not of facing fantastic monsters, but in overcoming the everyday adversities of life.

In today's connotation, the term HERO means the male lead in a dramatic work

Today, we do not limit the term hero to its epic connotation. Instead, we use the term to mean a male protagonist—the male lead in a dramatic work.

Patterns have emerged in fiction. The common journey traveled by the hero over the course of a tale is well documented by the analysis of storytelling. Myths, fairy tales, novels and films replay the timeless passage. These same myths, fairy tales, novels and films tell and retell the stories of the eight archetypal heroes. These heroes are:

- The CHIEF—a dynamic leader, he has time for nothing but work.
- The BAD BOY—dangerous to know, he walks on the wild side.
- The BEST FRIEND—sweet and safe, he never lets anyone down.
- The LOST SOUL—a tormented being, he lives in solitude.
- The CHARMER—a smooth talker, he creates fantasies.
- The PROFESSOR—coolly analytical, he knows every answer.
- The SWASHBUCKLER—Mr. Excitement, he's an adventurer.
- The WARRIOR—a noble champion, he acts with honor.

There are eight male archetypes that have been used throughout literary history

At his core, every well-defined hero is one of these eight archetypes. The archetype tells the writer about the most basic instincts of the hero: how he thinks, how he feels, what drives him and how he reaches his goals. In turn, the skillful writer conveys these instincts to the readers or audience, who, immediately recognizing the personality of this hero, settle down to read or watch the tale retold anew.

This doesn't mean, of course, that in all literature, there are only eight heroes. Members of the same archetypal family aren't mere photocopies of each other. Heroes within a single archetype share a similar psyche, but they are not, nor should they be, clones of each other.

For example, Captain Kirk of *Star Trek* is a CHIEF. He gives his orders, never doubting his loyal crew will jump to follow him. His ship is his mistress, his one and only true love. He does, indeed, boldly go forth into the universe and presents the very picture of a leader.

But Henry Higgins, of *My Fair Lady,* is also a CHIEF. He, too, blithely announces his will, knowing his commands will be obeyed. He has no doubt that his opinion is correct, and anything he wishes to be done is, in fact, the correct thing to do. But *Star Trek* would have been a very different program had

Henry Higgins sat in the captain's chair on the *Enterprise* instead of James T. Kirk.

In the pages that follow, we provide the basic framework for crafting a dynamic, believable and recognizable hero. Each hero archetype is described in detail, beginning with an overview of the general demeanor and attitude of each archetype.

Next, we discuss the personal attributes, or qualities, of each archetype. These are the personality traits that appear in all characters within a single archetype. We describe the virtues that make the characters heroic, as well as the flaws they must overcome.

Then, for each hero, we discuss background. A story might start with the birth of the hero, but more typically he appears in the opening scene fully grown. But no adult, not even one forged from imagination, comes into being without a childhood. The hero's personality developed during his youthful experiences, so even if no precise mention of childhood events is made in the story, the writer should know and understand the hero's background.

A boy who grew up as the beloved son matures into a much different man than the one who spent his youth dodging parental blows. Did the hero grow up living in one house, or did his family move every year because of military transfers? Did both parents work or could neither hold a job? Was he popular with other children or was he the object of ridicule? Was he a teacher's pet or the class clown? Members of the same archetype do not have exactly the same childhood, but patterns of common experiences will be found in their backgrounds.

Next, we explore the subtypes, which we call styles, of each archetype. There are two ways in which the underlying psychological makeup of the hero may be manifested. For example, compare Johnny Castle, as portrayed by Patrick Swayze in *Dirty Dancing*, with Snake Plissken, played by Kurt Russell in *Escape from New York*. Both of these characters are BAD BOYs, yet present themselves in very different ways. Johnny is painfully aware of his need to dance for his dinner, and resentfully submits to the resulting disrespect. Snake, on the other hand, gives as good as he gets. He returns contempt in full measure. Both of these BAD BOYs will have similar gut feelings when faced with a specific situation, but may act on these feelings in somewhat different ways.

Do you remember plots or characters?

3

We conclude each archetype with a discussion of the occupations to which members of the archetype are likely to be drawn, and the ways in which the archetype's personality may manifest itself within this occupation are explored. Of course, there is an overlap of occupations among the archetypes. The writer's job is to determine how different archetypes might perform within a specific field. For example, a WARRIOR police officer might focus on capturing criminals. In contrast, a BEST FRIEND police officer would more likely be a visible and helpful presence welcomed by the respectable citizens on the block.

As you read through these hero archetypes, try to visualize your own hero—one who taps into the universal emotions all humans share, but has your particular stamp. This blending of age-old appeal with your own experiences, beliefs and emotions will create a living, breathing man who embodies the archetype he's based on, but will also include your very unique view of the world, and what you think it means to be a hero.

Writers today have many story options. Heroes may hark back to demigods of old, may be the man in the next cubicle, or they may be every man in between. But always, the hero should be a man the audience recognizes and understands.

Throughout our lives, we've grown up with stories of knights in shining armor, wounded souls in need of healing and charming seducers. We instantly know what drives these men, what motivates them. Each knight will be a unique character, each seducer will have his own tale, but the underlying archetype provides a solid foundation from which to begin.

What type of hero do you most enjoy reading or writing about?

THE CHIEF

The CHIEF is a leader. People instinctively look to this man for their answers. He is a man who seizes control whenever possible. Active, dynamic and strong-willed, he urgently needs to fix problems and produce results. He rarely takes time to build consensus or garner support—not unless he is forced to in order to achieve his goals. He expects people to line up and follow his directives unquestioningly.

Awesome challenges never discourage him. In fact, he relishes defeating the obstacles and enemies blocking his path. This man exudes confidence in every area of his life.

His motto is "do something or get out of the way." He charges off before thinking everything through. But his powerful personality often forces others to align themselves with his plan, and he usually wins the day even if all the details have not been pinned down and discussed.

The CHIEF appears unemotional and harsh, but this is absolutely not true. This guy has a fiercely protective side. What is his, he keeps. His loved ones are safely wrapped in a cocoon of cotton-wool that sometimes stifles them. He rarely takes time away from the pursuit of his goals to connect or bond with others. Independence is vitally important to him and the thought of relying on another person never crosses his mind.

Think about... Rex Harrison as Henry Higgins in My Fair Lady or William Shatner as Captain James T. Kirk in Star Trek

QUALITIES

Once the CHIEF locks his eyes on the prize, nothing stops him from grasping the golden ring.

VIRTUES

- *Goal Oriented*—Give the CHIEF something to aim for and he keeps going until he reaches the target. Always focused on what needs to be achieved, he plows through projects faster than most people, zeroing in on what is important and discarding the rest.
- *Decisive*—Bring a dilemma to the CHIEF and within minutes he has come to a conclusion about the best way to handle it. Almost always right about how to solve the problem, he never needs a helping hand to accomplish the task.
- *Responsible*—When he accepts a task, he follows through until it is completed. He never doubts that he can accomplish the

The CHIEF:
- *organizes everything well*
- *is concerned with function, not fluff*
- *is motivated and*
- *is confident*

job. The CHIEF often shoulders more than his share of the load in order to complete the mission to his satisfaction.

FLAWS

But he also can:
- come on too strong
- lack tolerance for mistakes and
- be inflexible

- *Stubborn*—The CHIEF sometimes becomes so focused on the mission before him that he loses track of when a cause is lost. Obstinate to a fault, even when someone points out that the battle is over, he continues to fight.
- *Unsympathetic*—He never asks for help, so he cannot understand why others seem to need so much of it. The CHIEF is impatient with tales of woe. Unsentimental, he expects people just to get over it.
- *Dominating*—Being right can be a burden, especially when no one listens. Irritated when decisions are not made right away, the CHIEF responds by trying to yank everyone into his corner. He sometimes bullies people into following him. After all, he is the one going in the right direction.

BACKGROUND

The CHIEF has always needed to control his environment

Think about...
Michael J. Fox
as Alex P.
Keaton in the
TV series
Family Ties

From childhood, he tried to hold the reins of his family. Whether he was the eldest child, the high school quarterback or the class president, responsibility was his at an early age. He took his assignments seriously.

Disciplined and sure of where he wanted to go, this child set his goals and moved forward. Achievement was his top priority and no one could dissuade him from whatever path he chose. Nothing and no one stood in his way for long.

In school, he quickly dominated playtime. This child learned to get what he wanted using the "system." He was never a rule breaker. Smart and savvy, he sized up his teacher within the first day and figured out the best way to get what he wanted. He did well in school subjects, but was more interested in leading the other children during recess. He not only had his own newspaper route, he had several other routes he'd signed up for and hired other kids to run. A budding entrepreneur, he may well have been making almost as much money as his father did.

The CHIEF would rather lead than communicate

In high school, he knew how to play the game and therefore, he was invariably successful. He was well liked, but truly close friends were few and far between. There was no reason to spend time away from his goals—or so he thought. He was smart enough to keep his relatives in the dark about anything of which they might disapprove—such as speculating his college savings on the stock market or sneaking out to work a second job.

The CHIEF was a realist. He took whatever opportunities came his way. But education, purely for learning sake, did not keep his interest for long, unless he clearly saw what this education would do for him in the working world. This is the kind of guy who started a business in his spare time and built it in to a million-dollar enterprise before his twenty-first birthday.

If his father was also a CHIEF, did this child live up to his family's expectations? Or was his father a drunk? Did this boy have to become a man too early?

STYLES

The CHIEF might be a BORN LEADER . . .

This CHIEF was born to assume his leadership position. He is a nobleman, trained from birth to shoulder the responsibility after his father dies; or the son of the company founder, who doubles the stock value once he is in charge. He naturally assumes the mantle of control, never doubting in his ability to get the job done. It is both his right and his privilege and he is pleased to finally be in charge. Think of the King of Siam in *The King and I*. Proud and stubborn, he ruled his kingdom with an iron hand. But he was also protective of his family and willing to explore new ways of improving his country.

Yul Brynner as The King of Siam in The King and I

Only loss of control scares the Born Leader

Remember Michael Corleone in *The Godfather II*? His father's Mafia empire was handed down to this man who had been groomed from birth to assume the leadership of his family. This CHIEF eagerly accepted the obligations given to him, and was ready to show all that his prowess would exceed his father's. He more than fulfills the family tradition of success.

Al Pacino as Don Michael Corleone in The Godfather II

The Born Leader has always been aware of his destiny

King Arthur grew up under Merlin the wizard's influence, not knowing his exact fate, but believing he would be able to handle anything put before him. Unlike some, he is not cowed by the heavy load placed upon him. Rather, it is all he has ever wanted or dreamed about. He keeps his duties as a leader at the front of all his other priorities.

The Born Leader is more conservative than his counterpart. After all, he is part of the establishment and it has always worked for him. Pride is a central trait for this man. When challenged,

King Arthur of the Camelot legend

7

Fitzwilliam
Darcy in *Pride
and Prejudice*
by Jane Austen

he exhibits disbelief and then a ruthless anger; this hero is the type to go down with the ship, never admitting he might lose the battle. Think of Darcy from Jane Austen's *Pride and Prejudice*. When his marriage proposal is rejected by a woman far beneath his social standing, his incredulity and chagrin clearly show that his pride has been wounded.

STYLES
. . . or else he is the CONQUEROR

This is a CHIEF who has had to fight for everything. His sense of destiny does not come from his family's position, but rather, from deep within himself. Perhaps it evolved from a childhood spent in the slums or from ridicule he endured. Whatever the cause, his past built an intense desire to succeed, to never be at the bottom of the ladder again. Always trying to better himself, he does not stop working towards his goals until he is totally in command of his surroundings. Don Vito Corleone in *The Godfather* is just such a man. Growing up in the slums of New York, this man learned early that he must seize control in order to live. Making offers others can't refuse became his calling card.

Marlon Brando
as Don Vito
Corleone in
The Godfather

The Conqueror demands respect

Marc Antony in
*Antony and
Cleopatra* by
William
Shakespeare

Think of Shakespeare's *Antony and Cleopatra*. A brash and defiant Roman leader, Antony gains control of Egypt and its queen, but in the end falls pray to shifting principles and muddled ideals.

This man takes care of his land or his soldiers because doing so honors his accomplishments. His sense of responsibility is toward his achievements, not his family. Think of General George Patton in *Patton*. This Conqueror leads his men against the hated Nazis with all the strength and guile a general might possess. He fights against restrictions to his power, but whatever the obstacles, he never loses sight of his ultimate goal: to win the war.

George C. Scott
as General
George Patton
in *Patton*

The Conqueror uses the establishment

He will go outside the parameters of the acceptable if that is what is required in order to achieve his aim. If challenged, he is amused rather than chagrined. He has always won before and he is sure to win this time. This is a dog-eat-dog world and only the strong survive. Remember *Jerry Maguire*? Once he set his course,

Tom Cruise as
Jerry Maguire in
Jerry Maguire

he is determined to win—at any cost. His pride and determination overcome all enemies and he triumphs in the end.

OCCUPATION

The CHIEF is drawn to professions that let him lead.

CEO

This man loves to be in charge and has no trouble telling people what to do. Being a CEO places the CHIEF in a position where he thrives. He is happy in his work, enthused about what he does and excited about where he is going.

Whichever corporation is lucky enough to get this man as top dog grows quickly and is on the cutting edge of the industry. Employees who are the "cream of the crop" are required; he delegates easily and needs to know his people can do the job.

SURGEON

He possesses the power of life and death and accepts this responsibility without a qualm. The CHIEF takes his Hippocratic Oath seriously, but does not let it overwhelm him.

Long hours, difficult decisions that need to be made quickly, and being in control of a team of doctors and nurses does not faze this man. But being a surgeon can cause him to develop a god complex—he thinks he can do no wrong. It is not unusual for his bedside manner to be brusque.

NOBLEMAN

He is the ideal nobleman. When the CHIEF leads an army in his king's service or manages a vast estate, he does his duty with decisiveness and courage. Protecting his vassals and holdings comes first.

Whether he inherited a time-honored title or earned his coronet through valor, he deserves his exalted status. He wears the mantle of duty and obligation with grace and ease, and he does not take kindly to having his will challenged.

CHIEFs:
• delegate willingly
• are impatient with slow or poor work
• are demanding and
• accomplish enormous amounts of work in very short periods of time

Other occupations CHIEFs might have:
• newspaper editor
• pilot
• sheriff
• stockbroker
• principal
• movie director
• bank president
• general
• oil tycoon
• football quarterback

THE BAD BOY

The BAD BOY struts into every room, daring one and all to knock the chip from his shoulder. It may seem that he cares nothing for the opinion of others, but in fact, the reverse is true. All his life, he has been pointed out as a bad example, so he does his best to maintain that reputation. As far as he is concerned, it is not his fault other people cannot—or will not—see the man beneath the image.

Think about...
Elvis Presley as
Vince Everett in
Jailhouse Rock

No woman forgets the BAD BOY in her life, no matter how hard she tries. His allure is irresistible. Women are attracted to this cool, wild and moody man like moths to a forbidden flame. The leader of the pack, he never follows the rules.

The BAD BOY covers up his smoldering passions with a leather jacket and a cocky smirk. A reckless man, he feels he has

James Dean as
Jim Stark in
*Rebel Without
a Cause*

nothing to lose. Behind his insolent stare lies a disappointed idealist—a man who wants to believe in honor and integrity, but cannot quite do it. He keeps his secrets deep inside himself, trusting no one. Beware. If pushed, he can show a dark and angry side.

Life either dealt him a lousy hand or changed the rules when he was holding four of a kind. Unwilling to play the game society expects of him, he follows his own code of conduct. There are lines he will not cross, but only he decides where those lines are drawn. If he does give his word—a rare occurrence!—he keeps it.

QUALITIES

The BAD BOY is every schoolgirl's fantasy and every father's nightmare.

The BAD BOY:
• is Joe Cool
• makes good
  use of his wits
• always knows
  a short-cut or
  a friend in the
  business and
• falls deeply in
  love

VIRTUES

• *Charismatic*—The BAD BOY can be tough and mean, but is also filled with devil-may-care charm. The twinkle in his eye lures the unwary into his web. He might be trouble, but, oh, what fun trouble can be! He inspires fervent loyalty and devotion in his few friends.

• *Street Smart*—A graduate of the school of hard knocks, the BAD BOY is wise beyond his years. This is the guy to have around when walking down a dark alley or when confronting a con artist.

• *Intuitive*—His instincts are finely tuned. Childhood beatings or schoolyard fights taught the BAD BOY that survival hinges on being constantly aware of the people around him. He is quick to assess someone's motivation and is not afraid to go with his gut. After all, his sixth sense might well have saved his life in the past. He trusts his instinct before trusting anything else.

FLAWS

• *Pessimistic*—He has learned the hard way that most people tend to be selfish. The BAD BOY expects the worst from everyone; it is safer than letting his guard down and being hurt. He is leery about trusting anyone with his heart.

• *Bitter*—The BAD BOY never forgets. His idealism has been crushed and only resentment and animosity remain. He carries his grudge with pride.

• *Volatile*—On the surface, this man may appear to be in control, but he is very emotional, and the seething rage deep inside him erupts if he is pushed into a corner. The BAD BOY tries to bury his emotions, but cannot always master the volcano of pain bubbling beneath the surface.

But he also can:
• break the rules
• let his bitterness get in the way of making good decisions and
• burn his bridges

BACKGROUND
Secrets from his past formed the BAD BOY
A BAD BOY grew up on the streets, even if he lived in a mansion. Families have provided nothing but pain and hurt for the BAD BOY. Perhaps they merely ignored him, but more likely his family abused or abandoned him. He might have been a runaway; living on the streets was a better alternative to what awaited him at home.

The BAD BOY never had to go looking for trouble
Bad luck found the BAD BOY wherever he went. Even if he tried to keep his nose clean, someone came around to push him back into the mire. He soon gave up trying to please anyone but himself. He thumbed his nose at any kind of authority. From kindergarten on, he never fit it at school. Always the scapegoat, he saw the principal more often than he saw his parents.

In high school, every girl had a crush on him. He was not above capitalizing on his wicked allure, but to tell the truth, he preferred women twice his age. Young high school girls could

Think about…
Macaulay Culkin as Kevin McCallister in *Home Alone*

11

never bring him home to meet mother, but that never bothered him.

The BAD BOY always got the blame

Did he have a tough home life? Was he rejected? Or did he reject life? Is this the guy that every girl hoped would look at her in high school, but when he did, she ran scared?

Broken windows, stolen hubcaps, drag races in the street—no matter what the mischief, he often took the rap for other kids' crimes. He learned early on not to expect anyone to listen to his side of the story. Justice was something given to others. Adults in town expected the worst from him, so that is what they got.

He was the rebel caught with marijuana or the kid who got kicked off the basketball team because he was not interested in following the coach's advice. Or maybe he was thrown out of school altogether. Even when he did well in school, the teachers just thought he had cheated. He wore his cynical attitude like armor to protect his still-vulnerable heart. By manhood, the world had crushed his hopes and expectations time and time again. He decided never to trust anyone but himself.

STYLES

A BAD BOY might be the BOY FROM THE WRONG SIDE OF THE TRACKS . . .

Patrick Swayze as Johnny Castle in *Dirty Dancing*

This BAD BOY fights tooth and nail to escape his past circumstances. Whether because of his family's poverty, his lack of education, or something that schoolyard bullies could simply sense, he was not accepted as a child. The memory of that rejection never fades entirely. He leaves his past behind, but remains distrustful of those who thought he would never make it or who tried to keep him down. Like Johnny Castle in *Dirty Dancing*, he expects to have the worst expected of him.

He never lets anyone inside his skin

Matt Damon as Will Hunting in *Good Will Hunting*

Consider Will Hunting in *Good Will Hunting*. His past created a streak of anger within him so deep and dark, he finds it impossible to trust the good fortune and opportunities presented to him. No one is allowed inside his skin, least of all his rich and loving girlfriend or the concerned and understanding counselor. Even his best friend from childhood is left in the dark about Will's feelings and his experiences. Only when he has come to understand the enduring power of love, do we see this man make an attempt to walk out of his shadows.

His pride is an integral part of his character and he does just about anything to protect it. He strains against the rules and regulations, disagreeing with society's phony attitudes. Jack Mayo from *An Officer and a Gentleman* also carried the scars of his father's betrayal. He could play along if that would get where he wanted to go, but only a stronger man could force him to lay down that emotional baggage and move on.

Richard Gere as Jack Mayo in An Officer and a Gentleman

He became a man early

Take a look at Mark Twain's *The Adventures of Huckleberry Finn*. Most adults have really let poor Huck down, one way or another. He flees his drunken, selfish father, heading down river to live his own life. His friendship with the runaway slave Jim, one of the few adults in the novel who displays responsible and non-judgmental behavior towards the young man, results in Huck's rejection of society's racist and hypocritical attitudes.

Mark Twain's The Adventures of Huckleberry Finn

STYLES

. . . or else he is a REBEL WITHOUT A CAUSE

Lashing out, this BAD BOY adamantly refuses to play by other people's rules, insisting on making his own. Pushing the envelope, he provokes "authorities" to gain the attention he craves. Think of Hud Bannon in *Hud*. Rebelling against a strict father with stern rules, this young man turns to hard driving, hard drinking and chasing women—all of it an attempt to gain his father's love instead of punishment. He thinks he has been mistreated, and vows to never trust again. Using this bad attitude to keep others away, he has a chip on his shoulder as big as Texas and he dares everyone to knock it off.

Paul Newman as Hud Bannon in Hud

The Rebel's bad attitude is a form of protection

Take a look at J.D. Salinger's *The Catcher in the Rye*. Holden Caulfield has just been expelled from his prep school for academic failure. Bright and sensitive, he narrates his story in a cynical, jaded voice. Holden longs for a beautiful and innocent world. He cannot bear the hypocrisy of the those around him; his attitude is an attempt to protect himself from pain and disappointment.

Holden Caulfield in The Catcher in the Rye by J.D. Salinger

The Rebel hides his inner goodness

This man is not a reprobate. Instead, he hides his light under a bushel of bad temper and sarcastic bravado. Robert Dupea in *Five Easy Pieces* is a talented musician who gave up a promising career and now works on an oil rig. Returning home to be with

Jack Nicholson as Robert Dupea in Five Easy Pieces

13

his dying father, he struggles with his fear of failure and yearns for what he has lost. But his dark view of the world lurks behind every sentence. No playing the game of "being nice" for this man.

Snake Plissken, from *Escape From New York* seems a most unlikely choice to save the world. A hard-edged criminal, he accepts his mission only for the sake of reward. But his own sense of what is right and wrong prevents him from handing over the computer program that will perpetuate the status quo—he slays the governmental dragon and becomes a hero.

Kurt Russell as Snake Plissken in *Escape from New York*

OCCUPATION

The BAD BOY pushes the envelope, gets on the boss' nerves and breaks all the rules.

BAD BOYs:
- like to be their own bosses
- do not enjoy being told what to do
- won't do a job that goes against their principles and
- are not the easiest guys to get along with

MOTORCYCLE MECHANIC

The BAD BOY was made for the biker lifestyle. The lack of petty rules and pompous customers satisfies his desire for independence and unpretentious surroundings.

He is a great salesman when he believes in the product. Selling motorcycles allows him to sell freedom—something he believes in with all his heart. But he is not someone you will find at the Chamber of Commerce meeting. Instead, he is on his Harley, cruising down the road.

COMPUTER HACKER

He might have begun as a programmer, but somewhere along the line the establishment made him angry. Maybe it was the rules and regulations. Maybe he felt he was misused by his employer. Whatever the reason, this man now likes to throw a wrench in the works.

The BAD BOY does not mind the long hours alone or the amount of patience it takes to crack into a network. If he feels justified, no laws stop him from doing what he wants to do. Better back up those systems—he might be looking at the files right now.

OUTLAW

The BAD BOY enjoys sticking it in the eye of authority, and is grimly amused by the law's attempts to hunt him down. But he will never be caught because he always stays one step ahead of the posse. Living outside of the law fits his self-image.

This "occupation" requires skill, timing and discernment. It is a challenge, and this man loves to use all his faculties to win the game. That it also gives him a bad reputation and a certain cachet is not something that bothers him at all.

Other occupations BAD BOYs might have:
• actor
• cowboy
• artist
• photographer
• cop
• mercenary
• chauffeur
• writer
• basketball star
• factory worker
• gang leader

THE BEST FRIEND

Everyone needs a best friend, a pal with broad shoulders to cry on, a guy with a sympathetic ear ready to hear about the latest catastrophe. Decent, kind and responsible, the BEST FRIEND is a buddy who can be counted on whether the chips are down or things are looking up.

He is also very good in a crisis. While others are hysterical, this man's calm, capable presence often soothes the troubled waters. He finds the solution, negotiates the peace and provides the buffer between warring parties. People instinctively trust him to be fair and he never disappoints.

The BEST FRIEND is the ultimate team player. Winning is not why he joins in, he really believes that playing the game is what matters. He fits in everywhere and is universally liked. Whether he operates out of a sense of duty or genuinely enjoys giving of himself, he is always there in a pinch and sticks by friends or lovers through thick and thin.

But the BEST FRIEND may find it difficult to assert himself. He tries to avoid hurt feelings or create difficulties, so he tends not to step forward and make a fuss. This proclivity can cause him to be overlooked in love and in the workplace. Which is a shame, because no woman could chose a more loving man and no employer could pick a more loyal employee. But an emotional earthquake is needed to dislodge this man from his desire to keep the peace.

QUALITIES

The BEST FRIEND is there to lend a hand, but sometimes he fails to realize that he needs to take the lead.

VIRTUES

- *Stable*—Old Faithful has nothing on the BEST FRIEND. He is consistently dependable and is always there when called for. When a crisis hits, this is the guy everyone wants to have around. And he sticks with it until the emergency passes and things return to normal.
- *Supportive*—Leaning on this man is easy because he will never disappear or waver. The BEST FRIEND's steady, calm demeanor does not change for good news—or bad. All those years of learning about the problems of others have given him a lot of experience in dispensing suitable and practical advice.

Think about...
Tom Hanks
as Joe Fox in
You've Got Mail

Kevin Kline
as Dave Kovic
in *Dave*

The BEST
FRIEND:
- is a gentleman
- is comfortable
  with himself
  and
- is easy to get
  along with

• *Tolerant*—The BEST FRIEND is not easily offended. He understands that people are individuals and appreciates their differences. He values teamwork and allows all the players to do their own work in their own way.

FLAWS

• *Complacent*—Often willing to go along to get along, the BEST FRIEND is not usually terribly ambitious. He can be a little too content with himself and the status quo.

• *Myopic*—While capable of seeing the bigger picture, he may not like the view. Afraid of getting hurt, he protects himself by focusing in on the details. His deliberately nearsighted outlook makes him treat only the symptoms, not the disease.

• *Unassertive*—The BEST FRIEND is accustomed to letting others go first. It is hard for him to step forward, even when he knows he should. The center of attention is not where he wants to be and he hates confrontation.

But he also can:
• make unnecessary sacrifices
• lack self-motivation and
• fail to stand out in a crowd

BACKGROUND

The BEST FRIEND has always been there to lend a helping hand

His personality has been defined by the importance he places on the needs of those around him. Even as a child, he risked the censure of others to befriend the underdogs and champion their causes.

Think about... Christopher Robin in *Winnie the Pooh* by A.A. Milne

The BEST FRIEND kept the peace

Easy going and undemanding, this boy remained untroubled regardless of his home environment. His parents probably fit into any '50s sitcom, but if the family was dysfunctional, he put his energy into mediating disputes. He was the dependable son who kept track of his little sister and made sure the bikes were put away at night.

Well-liked and popular with both girls and boys because of his optimistic personality, he joined in all the games. He never got into fights or picked on any outsiders. Teachers relied on him to help other students, and he easily earned his reputation as a responsible member of the school community.

Was this boy holding a dysfunctional family together at home? How often did his family members ask him to relinquish his dreams for their benefit? Or did his family always accept him for what he was, never expecting more?

The BEST FRIEND never rebelled

His adolescence was smooth, and he felt no need to defy parental authority. For this boy, success was not about good grades or top positions. He was content with his Bs and Cs and never yearned to be captain of the baseball team. He was more likely to play in the band or spend time with his friends and family. Having lots of friends was more important to him than being number one.

As a young man, the BEST FRIEND continued his lifetime patterns of contentment and complacency. He eased into whatever friends and family expected of him—college, the family business, buying the house next door to Mom and Dad. This guy tended to let a career "happen" to him, rather than pursuing one with single-minded determination.

STYLES

The BEST FRIEND might be a MR. NICE GUY . . .

Everyone can count on this BEST FRIEND, so everyone does. The expectations of family and friends rule him. Think of Robbie Hart in *The Wedding Singer*. He hides his love for the heroine because he believes she is happy with her selfish dolt of a fiancé. Robbie is only willing to reveal his own feelings when he discovers he can do so without risking her happiness.

Adam Sandler as Robbie Hart in The Wedding Singer

Mr. Nice Guy follows the course society sets for him

He never learned how to think of what he needed or wanted. But if pushed beyond his limits, he might finally break out of his iron cage. Remember Lester Burnham in *American Beauty*? Driven beyond endurance, he breaks out of his role and demands recognition as his own man. The reactions of his wife, employer and friends make for a wildly funny movie, filled with bittersweet yearnings and hidden pain.

Kevin Spacey as Lester Burnham in American Beauty

Mr. Nice Guy is torn between friends and his dreams

What about George Bailey in *It's a Wonderful Life?* His dream of traveling the world is constantly put on hold because of the needs of his family. He is aware of the pressure put upon him and tries to break free, but is always drawn back to his role of dependable son, husband and father. George does not need to change to live his life to the fullest, he only needs to recognize how his sacrifices have benefited others, and made him so rich in friends.

Jimmy Stewart as George Bailey in It's a Wonderful Life

Mr. Nice Guy's ability to empathize also frees him from the self destruction to which selfishness often leads. Think of Jake Barnes in *The Sun Also Rises*. Jake's war injury has removed him from participation in the battles drawn over the woman he and the other male characters love. Instead, he often tries to calm the tension between his friends during their conflicts. Although Jake is castrated, he proves to be the one complete man in the story—the one best able to achieve peace within himself.

Jake Barnes in *The Sun Also Rises* by Ernest Hemingway

STYLES
. . . or else he is the CONFIDANT
People matter to this BEST FRIEND. And not because of any misplaced sense of duty. He genuinely likes them and enjoys helping out. Always accepted and valued for the person he is, he accepts others in the same fashion. One classic example is *The Andy Griffith Show,* which placed Sheriff Andy Taylor amongst a strange group of friends and family. But his amiable personality gave Opie security, soothed Aunt Bee's ruffled feathers and tolerated Barney's constant mistakes.

Andy Griffith as Andy Taylor in the TV series *The Andy Griffith Show*

The Confidant brings out the best in others
The Confidant's self-confidence is infectious. Hang around him for awhile and anything seems possible. He never puts others ahead of himself unless they fit into his plans. But he encourages all around him to be the best they can be. Consider Harry in *When Harry Met Sally.* What you see is what you get. He offers advice, but never judgment, and always sympathy and support.

Billy Crystal as Harry Burns in *When Harry Met Sally*

The Confidant is secure about himself
Remember Mr. Knightly from Jane Austen's *Emma?* Smooth and polished, but no heartbreaker, he is a terrific real-world hero. Neither dragonslayer nor sycophant, he is just the right dose of easy-going acceptance and eyes–open understanding young Emma needs. Stern, practical, but always respectful, he offers an understanding shoulder and good advice as well as love.

Mr. Knightly in *Emma* by Jane Austen

Or, look at William Thacker in *Notting Hill.* Dealing with a nervous movie star and all the attendant hoopla, this man never loses his kind concern for others. He shows patience with both his bizarre roommate and paranoid movie-star girlfriend. Emotionally grounded, this man know himself. He acknowledges the pain he might endure if he falls in love with Anna. And in typical fashion, he is unsure about love being worth the risk to his calm, low-key life.

Hugh Grant as William Thacker in *Notting Hill*

BEST FRIENDs:
- have a real talent for mediating problems
- never offend
- are quietly observant and
- know what makes people tick

Other occupations BEST FRIENDs might have:
- counselor
- barber
- teacher
- optometrist
- therapist
- policeman
- carpenter
- baker
- small business owner

OCCUPATION

A BEST FRIEND is drawn to professions that help others.

VETERINARIAN

This job allows his natural affinity for loyal companions to be expressed every day. He takes pleasure in reassuring anxious owners and soothing the pets he treats. He is cool and calm in an emergency.

Though his patients may snap and claw at him, working long hours does not really bother him. Focusing on the needs of those unable to help themselves comes naturally to the BEST FRIEND.

PSYCHOLOGIST

Listening to other people's problems is something he's been doing all his life. Getting paid for it is an added bonus. He loves the satisfaction of helping people.

By focusing on the troubled lives of others, the BEST FRIEND is able to avoid looking at his own shortcomings. Establishing the distance necessary to maintain a proper and healthy relationship with his patients is sometimes difficult for him.

VICAR

Who better than the BEST FRIEND to put the needs of his flock first? He will never be rich—except in the number of lives he touches. To him, that is wealth beyond his wildest dreams. The ministry offers an honorable way for this unassuming man to satisfy his need to put others ahead of himself.

Kind words and gentle rebukes, not fire and brimstone, are found in his sermons. Nonjudgmental, he looks for the best in everyone. No one asks him when he will finally do something for himself. Everyone is too busy accepting his unquestioning generosity.

THE CHARMER

Ah, the CHARMER. He is sparkle and glitz, allure and appeal. Exuding enormous charisma, he showers the people in his life with gifts of laughter and happiness. He is always fun, often irresistible and frequently unreliable. Gathering companions and friends along the way, he spins a web of fascination around everyone he touches. But when the going gets tough, this man generally gets going.

He creates magical illusions without seeming to try and many are drawn under his spell. He can seduce anyone out of their souls and delights in charming the birds from the trees.

His motto is "live and let live." The CHARMER never judges anyone and it only seems fair that no one judge him. In fact, he never has cared much for any restrictions or rules. Life should be a party, not a job. Why can't everyone just have fun?

The CHARMER tries to get by on his personality and wit. Hard work is not in his vocabulary. If someone does try to get beyond the enchantment to the real man, he becomes nervous. Why would anyone want to talk about emotional pain and hurt? Why would anyone want to spend time on something that does not offer instant gratification? Better to keep everything light and easy.

> Think about...
> Bill Murray as Dr. Peter Venkman in *Ghostbusters*

> James Garner as Bret Maverick in the TV series *Maverick*

QUALITIES

The CHARMER makes you believe in fairy tales and happily-ever-after. Unfortunately, he is not always there in the ever-after.

VIRTUES

- *Creative*—Give the CHARMER a ball of twine and a few pieces of bread, and he magically creates a party. This man is always ready with a new and imaginative idea. Being with him is just plain fun. And romance? Wow! This man is an original.
- *Witty*—Smiles and laughter follow this man wherever he goes. Few can resist the CHARMER's banter. His sense of humor is one of his best assets and he knows it. No matter how bleak the situation, he makes light of it.
- *Smooth*—Capable of sizing up a situation in a matter of seconds, the CHARMER finds a way to persuade almost everyone that his solutions are the best. And what is even more

> The CHARMER:
> - is dramatic
> - makes friends easily
> - is always "on" and
> - has terrific enthusiasm

remarkable, everyone ends up pleased that he made the suggestion.

FLAWS

But he also can:
• be egotistical
• be fickle and capricious and
• refuse to grow up

• *Manipulative*—He does not usually see it this way, but many times the CHARMER uses his appeal to get want he wants no matter who gets hurt. He cloaks his real agenda behind his friendly overtures and does not notice the pain he leaves behind. He has never learned that sometimes hard work really is the only solution.

• *Irresponsible*—When the baby needs diapering, do not expect the CHARMER to be around, no matter what he promised. His behavior is erratic. He cannot be counted on because he follows his own game plan, and his strategy is rarely obvious to anyone but himself.

• *Elusive*—The CHARMER is the perfect chameleon. He is magic and dreams and fantasy. This moving target adapts to get what he wants, rarely showing his true feelings in the process. He refuses to be pinned down.

BACKGROUND

Think about…
Matthew Broderick as Ferris Bueller in *Ferris Bueller's Day Off*

The CHARMER needs everyone to love him. Smart, he quickly learned to manipulate the people around him without raising any hackles. Confrontation was never on his agenda. Rather, he sweet-talked people into doing what he wanted.

The CHARMER knew how to please

He was the apple of his mother's eye. Life was a bowl full of cherries and he meant to taste every one. In school, he was a popular favorite of teachers and children alike. Making friends came easily to him and he also cut a swath through all the little girls' hearts. He was clever enough to keep well ahead of the teacher's expectations. Why did it matter if he got his best friend to do his homework?

As soon as he strolled into high school, he had everyone figured out—from the principal down to the lowliest hall monitor. With an easy smile and a laughing slap on the shoulder, he set out to win all hearts to his side. Within a few weeks, he accomplished the task. Voted most popular in his class, he was the star of the school play or the class comedian. And he dated all the cheerleaders while inspiring countless teenage fantasies.

The CHARMER was the quintessential golden boy

His parents usually were as enraptured as everyone else. After all, this guy knew how to play to people's fantasies. They might have worried a bit about his easy dismissal of problems, but by this time he was so good at his "show," it was hard to decipher where the real boy ended and the illusion began.

He likely found his career by chance. Long term goals and plans were never his forte. But his star power was so great, he was the sort to be approached by a businessman who recognized excellent people skills or a director who wanted him for his next Broadway play. It seems as if life was always a smooth and easy ride for this guy and he began to believe his own press.

STYLES

The CHARMER might be the PLAYBOY . . .

He has lived his illusion for so long, he cannot imagine any other path. His life is filled with elegance, wit and style. Consider John Robie in *To Catch a Thief.* No man can carry off a tuxedo like he can. Smooth and cultivated, this CHARMER skims through life, never venturing into the depths of love or pain. He has learned to use his skills at captivating people to create a life and image that is suave and debonair.

The Playboy never looses his cool

Remember *Remington Steele?* No matter what the case, no matter what the danger, he invariably looks cool and collected. With a sly joke, he breaks the tension, but with his quick and clever mind he often wins the day. Everything this man does seems to turn out in his favor. Women flock to him because he knows how to treat them well. Men surround him hoping that some of his sparkle will rub off on them.

With a light touch, a sly joke and, of course, a winsome smile, this Playboy nearly always gets his way. He has long forgotten how to pull the curtain down on the show and stop playing his cherished role. Think of Tom Bowen in *Royal Wedding.* Part of a brother-sister dancing team, he comes to London to seek the limelight. Falling in love, he finds it hard to break out of the role he has defined for himself.

The Playboy is the star of his own show

If his wiles fail to produce what he wants, he immediately decides he never wanted it in the first place. He is a different

---

Did he learn early to use a grin to get his way?

But…what if his father ridiculed his charm?

What if the teachers didn't fall for his smiling face?

Cary Grant as John Robie in *To Catch a Thief*

Pierce Brosnan as Remington Steele in *Remington Steele*

Fred Astaire as Tom Bowen in *Royal Wedding*

23

Count Alexey
Kirilich Vronsky
in *Anna
Karenina* by
Leo Tolstoy

person on the outside than his is on the inside, but he does not want anyone to meet the "real" him. That might ruin the fantasy and spoil the fun.

In *Anna Karenina,* Count Alexey Kirilich Vronsky dazzles Anna with his handsome looks and courtly manner. He falls in love with her, but is so involved in playing his romantic, sophisticated role, he is unaware of the pain and hurt he inflicts. Though he loves her, he values his freedom even more.

STYLES
. . . or else he is the ROGUE
This CHARMER is not quite as smooth as the Playboy, but has a subtle way about him that is all his own. A boyish appeal, a lazy smile and a fascinating allure come together to produce a man that is hard to resist.

Gordon MacRae
as Curly in
Oklahoma!

Think of Curly in *Oklahoma!* He courts his girl by painting vivid pictures of what their life would be like, down to what kind of surrey he would drive her around in. His joking ways and smiling face make him a favorite with everyone.

Any man, woman or child in this man's company laughs constantly and enjoys every moment, even if they are on a sinking ship or an out-of-control train. Jack Dawson in *Titanic* is this kind of hero. His attractive smile and ready wit wins over a table of his social "betters." Jack's confidence rubs off on the girl he saves from certain death. His joy of life survives and flourishes in her long life and wonderful memories.

Leonardo
DiCaprio as
Jack Dawson
in *Titanic*

The Rogue's smile hides his cleverness
He is very smart and willing to take a few hard knocks, provided that in the end, he is a winner. Shakespeare's Petruchio in *The Taming of the Shrew* is just such a man. Behind his grin, this guy is intent on getting his woman. Why not crack a few jokes and have a few laughs along the way? And if he can steal a kiss or two to persuade the lady . . . so much the better.

Petruchio in *The
Taming of the
Shrew* by
William
Shakespeare

The Rogue's people-skills serve him well
He is often able to manipulate people around him into doing his work. And this Rogue makes them glad they volunteered. A modern day Tom Sawyer, he might even make them pay for the privilege. Like alchemists of old, he turns leaden defeat into golden success. He hides his quick mind behind an "aw, schucks" appeal and delights in surprising all those around him

when things turn out well. Remember, Axel Foley in *Beverly Hills Cop*? Axel delights in defeating the villain, but finds it hard to resist having some fun along the way.

OCCUPATION

The CHARMER is attracted to fields where a smile goes farther than hard work.

SALESMAN

With this job, he is in his element. He makes any purchase a delight and sends people off with the sure knowledge they made the right choice. Customers clamor to buy from him, and he enjoys using his wits to gain new business.

The CHARMER is probably the top producer in his company and he makes it look easy. He is well-liked by his co-workers, even though they end up doing the grunt work. On the other hand, he rarely lasts long at any one job. Either he gets bored or he uses up his credits.

CHARMERs
• are loaded with people skills
• ride a magic carpet of style
• are very smart and clever and
• are adept at changing to meet new circumstances

NEWSCASTER

He dominates the others on the set, even without the standard good looks. His smile is broader, his wit is livelier and he thrives on the attention this job brings.

A rising star in his field, he has enormous confidence in his own abilities. The CHARMER prefers the newscast be filled with lighter topics, funnier pictures. Dismal news is boring. He thinks he is the most popular person in the studio and is probably right.

Other occupations CHARMERs might have:
• tennis player
• advertising executive
• cafe piano player
• politician
• real estate agent
• public relations specialist
• jewel thief

GAMBLER

He uses his good looks to bluff his way through the game of life. His easy personality serves him well. Good at keeping secrets, he can figure out other people's hands in a matter of moments. Poker is more than this man's recreation, it is a job, and he is the best.

This man has learned to play his cards close to his chest. Willing to break the rules when necessary, he never lets his opponents know they're being cheated. When the CHARMER walks away a winner, the losers still think the game was well-played.

THE LOST SOUL

A tormented man filled with angst and passion, the LOST SOUL drifts through life with a heavy heart and a wounded spirit. He is dramatic, intriguing and secretive. This misfit has never adapted to society. A tremendous physical or emotional injury has produced a baffling puzzle of a man. Mystery and solitude surround him and he cannot find a way to rid himself of the pain he carries with him wherever he goes. A man with a past who yearns for love and acceptance, he never seems to find the key that opens the door to happiness.

This man has a poet's voice, an artist's creative genius and a writer's grasp on emotions. Never finding solace from his aching torment, he tries to distract himself by creating a sanctuary of peace. He is attuned to every nuance, be it a someone's expression or the flight of a bird. And he always remembers.

The LOST SOUL loves fiercely and hates just as passionately. Every wrong done to him is experienced intensely. Every word of love spoken to him is remembered for eternity. He suffers the slings and arrows of outrageous misfortune that have pricked his skin. He seems unable to find his way back to a land of promise and hope, so instead, he lurks in his cave, reliving the slights against him.

He wants things set right, but is unwilling to risk being vulnerable in order to make it happen. This man seems stuck in a perpetual cycle of pain. He spends far more time in the valleys of life than on the mountain top.

QUALITIES

The LOST SOUL endlessly relives his mistakes, but still dreams of a better life.

VIRTUES

- *Devoted*—The LOST SOUL gives everything to what he believes in, holding back nothing. He is intense and idealistic, and has a strong distaste for the superficial. When he makes a commitment, he gives his all. He is attentive and ardent in the pursuit of what he loves.
- *Vulnerable*—The LOST SOUL is easily hurt, easily touched. He guards his heart carefully because he intuitively knows it can be his greatest weakness. He feels deeply, whether he

Think about...
Nicolas Cage as
Ronny
Cammareri in
Moonstruck

Mel Gibson as
Martin Riggs in
Lethal Weapon

The LOST SOUL:
• is creative
• is complex
• is a man of
  few words and
• is appreciative
  of beauty

admits it or not. Criticism and censure slash deep wounds into his soul.

- *Discerning*—There are no secrets kept from the LOST SOUL. He is able to see beneath the surface, straight to the core. Because he sits apart from the world, watching and listening, he can often judge people's motivations with astounding accuracy.

FLAWS

- *Brooding*—Brows knitted and face unsmiling, the LOST SOUL sits on the outside, contemplating the unfairness of life. While his mystery and tragedy may intrigue people, his pessimistic view of life drives them away.
- *Unforgiving*—His idealism trips him up, with others and even with himself. He expects perfection and has a hard time grasping that everyone has faults. The LOST SOUL cannot seem to forget the slights he has suffered. He can rarely forgive himself when he fails. Frustration and guilt fill his life.
- *Fatalistic*—He hopes for the best, but the LOST SOUL anticipates that things will probably turn out for the worst. He immediately sees the negatives in people and knows they will not change. Catastrophe is around every corner and he resigns himself to the whims of fate.

But he also can:
- be highly critical
- be peculiar and eccentric and
- be introverted

BACKGROUND

An isolating event in his past defined the LOST SOUL

He might have been a normal child to begin with—maybe slightly solemn and given to introspection, but willing to smile and play with others. But a defining event isolated him from society, shaping this boy into the man he would become. Illness or injury kept him apart, or maybe it was the jeering prejudice of the other kids. Either way his response was to remove himself, withdrawing to an inner refuge where no one could touch him . . . or hurt him.

Think about... Charlie Brown in the comic strip *Peanuts* by Charles Schultz

The LOST SOUL never joined in any of the reindeer games

Separated from his peers by circumstances outside his control, he walked the hallways of childhood alone. He never fit in and oh, how cruel children can be. The strong, stubborn part of him refused to bow down to the playground bullies, so he often came home with a bloody lip or a black eye. But this boy was no complainer. He endured the painful ridicule with a hardened stare.

The LOST SOUL was a loner

Since he had little interest in team sports or any other typical school activity, he never found an avenue to make friends and fit in. He would easily score straight As if his interest was caught, but if the teacher or the subject were boring, he was likely to skip class. If he attended the prom at all, he did not dance or bring a date, but stood in the parking lot pretending not to care.

Once he was out of school, he probably hitched a ride out of town, a pack on his back and no real plan of what he would do next. He drifted from place to place, looking for that indefinable "something" that would ease the ache inside him. Eventually, separation and loneliness become a way of life for him. His isolation grew, his mistrust deepened. Because he was so perceptive, he noticed every lie, every betrayal. And he could not let go of any of the slights or forgive any of the deceptions. His tender heart shied away from putting down any roots. Distance is the only protection he knew.

STYLES

The LOST SOUL might be the WANDERER . . .

This LOST SOUL walks outside of mainstream society. Unwilling or unable to fit in, he has resigned himself to a life of endless drifting. Adam and Eve's son, Cain, is the quintessential example of this man. Driven out of the family and cursed by God, he spent the rest of his life roaming the earth, trying to find peace.

The Wanderer never finds contentment in one place

He might hold a job, may even function fine in day-to-day activities, but he always stands apart, holding himself back from any meaningful involvement with other people. Think of Crash Davis in *Bull Durham*. This itinerant catcher moves from ball team to ball team, from one town to another. He holds himself apart from the others. Not completely part of the team, nor yet wholly separate, he's seen it all. Been there, done that, bought the souvenirs. This man dreams of a beautiful relationship, but is not willing to stick his neck out to make it happen.

Perhaps it was a witch's spell? Does he carry the curse of generations? Or did an accident leave him disfigured?

Cain from the Old Testament

Kevin Costner as Crash Davis in Bull Durham

This Wanderer cannot seem to "attach"

Unsettled and restless, he often jumps from one dark place to another. He has no real ties with his family, and what friends he has look at him askance. Think of Angel from *Buffy, The Vampire Slayer*. The realization of the dreadful deeds he performed molded a man determined to stand apart. Buffy's inclusion of him as part of the team tries his will too hard. He cannot let go of his detachment.

He shuns involvement and protects his heart. It has become such a habit, he cannot imagine it any other way. Fox Mulder in *The X-Files* operates effectively as a FBI agent, but solving the riddle of his past is his hidden agenda—one he will not even share fully with his partner. He takes every setback to heart and consistently allows himself to be sidetracked. But his need to find the truth that is out there never lets him go, and he continues on his solitary hunt for redemption.

STYLES

. . . or else he is the OUTCAST

This LOST SOUL creates his own kingdom, either literally or inside himself. The outside world is too painful to deal with and he decides never to let anyone close to him again. Think of Charlie Allnut in *The African Queen*. He has isolated himself on his ship, his misery masked by alcohol and an acid wit. He wants nothing more than to be left alone to nurse his loneliness.

The Outcast wants to be left alone

Bruised and beaten by the constant ridicule and hatred directed at him from every corner, he swears to always rule his domain, to make sure no one reaches his troubled heart. It is his understanding that he is not lovable. And so he retreats, licking his wounds, reliving every injury. Heathcliff in *Wuthering Heights* is just such a man. Deserted by his one true love, first by marriage to another, then by death, he spends his life grieving for his Catherine.

The Outcast aches for what he cannot have

Think of Beast from *Beauty and the Beast*. Cursed, he yearns for the touch of Beauty, but is scared to reach out and accept the gift of her love. He longs for love and tenderness, but is unable to discover the key to getting what he desires. Only Belle's

David Boreanaz as Angel in the TV series *Buffy, the Vampire Slayer*

David Duchovny as Fox Mulder in the TV series *The X-Files*

Humphrey Bogart as Charlie Allnut in *The African Queen*

Heathcliff in *Wuthering Heights* by Emily Brönte

Beast in Walt Disney's *Beauty and the Beast*

29

courage in the face of his wrath releases him from the evil spell cast upon him.

This Outcast hides his warm and sensitive side behind his cloak of mystery. Resigning himself to his lonely fate, he stays apart, waiting for someone to rescue him from his desolation and anguish.

Remember Quasimodo in Walt Disney's *The Hunchback of Notre Dame*? Shunned by all because of his appearance, he still finds the compassion and strength to save Esmeralda. Even knowing he cannot win her love, he loves her still and is willing to sacrifice his life in order to save her. Beneath the ugly facade lies a true hero with a heart of gold.

OCCUPATION

LOST SOULs:
• function well amidst chaos
• pay attention to details
• take their jobs seriously and
• are detached from co-workers

The LOST SOUL looks for jobs where his skills are more important than his personality.

UNDERCOVER COP

He sticks with a case until it is solved, and he is unconcerned if that puts him in harm's way. His job is his life and home is any couch. Nothing gets in the way of completing his job, not even his conscience.

Good with details, the LOST SOUL remembers the obscure fingerprint or the offhand gesture that solves the mystery. His skill in fading into the woodwork is why he is assigned to all the toughest cases. He is the invisible man, even after a successful arrest is made.

PHOTOGRAPHER

What better place to watch the world than from behind a camera? The job demands emotional distance and he delivers. Photography allows the LOST SOUL to capture and present elemental emotions without his own immediate involvement.

He has a good eye and is dedicated to going after a story. He is not bothered by the long hours, the constant travel, the physical demands; they keep him busy and distracted from his loneliness. His work is his weapon and also his catharsis.

GUNFIGHTER

The world is a savage and unforgiving place, and only those who take care of themselves survive. Used to being alone and trusting no one, the LOST SOUL refuses to be part of a society riddled with hypocrisy and corruption.

He is good at slipping in and out of towns undetected. His cool eyes and steady hand hide his emotions and make him the odds-on favorite to win any fight, but he picks and chooses his battles, protecting only himself.

Other occupations LOST SOULs might have:
• artist
• musician
• singer
• bounty hunter
• cook
• gardener
• welder
• cab driver
• travel writer
• fishing guide

THE PROFESSOR

Is there a mystery that needs to be solved? Are your tax forms inexplicable? The PROFESSOR has all the answers. He takes the time to examine every aspect of an issue. This guy is logical, introverted and faithful. No fast breaks or hurried decisions for him. When he makes a commitment, he invariably follows through, but he will do it in his own time, and only after all the facts are in. No urgency will keep him from analyzing a problem from all angles.

The PROFESSOR's strength is his intellect or special skills. Expert in one field or many, he has turned his life into one big science project. Every experience, every emotion, every physical sensation has been the subject of objective observation. He is thoughtful, but not necessarily considerate.

He is used to being the smartest man in the room. His genius has set him apart from others for most of his life. However, this experience does not make it any easier for him to remember to communicate on levels understood by the less gifted. The inability of other people to keep up with him intellectually is a constant source of frustration for him. As a result, his social skills may not be up to par. His book-lined study is far more comfortable to him than any sports bar or basketball court. A PROFESSOR exercises his mind constantly, but only exercises his body if he realizes the connection between good health and strong reasoning skills.

QUALITIES

Trust the PROFESSOR to find the solution, but do not expect any explanations. They would be too hard to understand anyway.

VIRTUES

- *Expert*—Not just smart, the PROFESSOR also is educated. Perhaps he studied on his own or sailed through Harvard on a full academic scholarship. Either way, he knows about the subjects that interest him. Whatever his chosen field, he is the recognized authority.
- *Analytical*—This is a man who thinks before he acts. The PROFESSOR methodically takes apart a problem, assessing each piece of the puzzle until he finds the perfect way to put

Think about...
Jeff Goldblum as David Levinson in *Independence Day*

Gene Wilder as Dr. Frankenstein in *Young Frankenstein*

The PROFESSOR:
- is a genius, particularly in at least one field of expertise
- does the *New York Times* crossword puzzle in ink
- is persistent and thorough and
- thinks "outside of the box"

them back together. He refuses to be rushed and his conclusions are invariably correct.

- *Genuine*—The PROFESSOR has not developed the disguises others have. When he gives his heart, he is painfully vulnerable. True to his commitments, he never pretends something he does not actually feel. Hypocrisy and lies are foreign to him, and he is astonished when others use these weapons against him.

FLAWS

- *Insular*—He inhabits his own world and is unwilling to make room for others. The PROFESSOR knows everything about his field of choice, but nothing at all about other aspects of life. Devoting one's life to building that better mousetrap does not leave much time for socializing.
- *Inhibited*—He has not spent a lot of time building up his experience with women. Urges he felt in that direction have been pretty much ignored. He is either frantically trying to think of something to say, or he does not want to take the time to say hello. The PROFESSOR is never the life of the party.
- *Inflexible*—The PROFESSOR is definitely set in his ways, and he is not enthusiastic at the prospect of change. He is convinced that his way is the only way and can list fifteen reasons why he is right about it.

BACKGROUND
The PROFESSOR's special gifts rule his life
When you are a prodigy, it is generally apparent at an early age. His parents might have been pleased as punch at the genius in their midst, or maybe they viewed him as odd. Either way, he was set apart from other children at an early age. The feeling of isolation stays with him throughout his life.

Academics were the PROFESSOR's forte
He astounded teachers with his precocious abilities. Being surrounded by adults undoubtedly shaped his personality. If left unchallenged, he could all too easily be tempted to coast effortlessly through school. Praised and pushed to succeed even more, he might have developed an arrogance that raised the hackles of other children. Conversely, if his parents viewed him as odd, shyness or a sense of guilty shame over the ease of his accomplishments might have resulted.

But he also can:
- hate change
- be judgmental
- be nitpicky and fussy and
- lack spontaneity

Harry Potter in *Harry Potter and The Sorcerer's Stone* by J. K. Rowling

33

The PROFESSOR was the Nerd

Adolescence was probably a difficult time for the PROFES-SOR. His high I.Q. could not spare him those awkward teenage years. Understanding the biological reason and effect of hormones did not make it any easier to live through the experience. In fact, he may have been all the more miserably aware of his gawky shortcomings and rampaging hormones.

He got on well with most of his teachers, but being president of the chess club did not get a guy a lot of dates. Chances are that sports played only a small role, if any, in his school life—a disadvantage when the girls gravitated toward jocks. But sometimes he learned early to take advantage of his skills. He might have sold homework on the high school black market, or more respectably, hired himself out as a tutor.

Higher education was a given for him. If his family could not afford to pay for schooling, he found another route to the best college in the land. If scholarships were unavailable, he likely found a way to educate himself. Books have always been his closest companions.

STYLES

The PROFESSOR might be ABSENTED-MINDED . . .

This PROFESSOR is a lovable klutz. His hair is often a mess or his glasses are askew. His bow tie has a large mustard stain from the last office party, an event he attended by accident, after he stumbled upon it while working late. He can never remember where he put his pocket protector. Oh, wait, there it is—in his pocket!

The Absented-Minded Professor is at the top of his field

Those who work with this man recognize and appreciate his genius, but the uninitiated tend to take him much less seriously. Unable to understand or follow his thought processes, the general public is likely to discount him. Consider *Columbo*. The poor unsuspecting murderer is often relieved to see the shambling, cigar-ash-spilling detective assigned to the case. But a few, "Oh, just one more thing, Sirs," later, and the hapless villain's plot has been exposed.

Ellery Queen is a mystery writer, not a detective, but he solves many a tangled mystery from amidst the spillage from his desk. His father, Inspector Queen, is the professional police officer, but he and his sergeant routinely step aside to allow the

Were his parents awed by or complacent about his abilities? Did his family discount his academic achievements or worship them?

Peter Falk as Lt. Columbo in *Columbo*

The Ellery Queen mysteries

"Maestro" do the job by putting the pieces of the puzzle together.

The Absented-Minded Professor may chance upon the solution

He is not all knowing and all seeing. Sometimes, a bit of educated luck plays a role in his success. Phillip Brainard in *Flubber* was looking for a new energy source, not flying rubber. But he was able to see the possibilities of his discovery, even if the day of his wedding flew right out of his head.

In *Honey, I Shrunk the Kids*, inventor Wayne Szalinski's shrinking machine did not work until a baseball found its way into the energy path. But of course, distracted Wayne wholly fails to notice that his own children have been made into miniatures thanks to his device, and are in the pile of trash he takes out to the garbage.

Robin Williams as Phillip Brainard in Flubber

Rick Moranis as Wayne Szalinski in Honey, I Shrunk the Kids

STYLES

. . . or else he is MR. ORGANIZED

This PROFESSOR not only knows where his pocket protector is, he has one for each day of the week. Nicely labeled, too. His desk is immaculate, his home is immaculate and he is always immaculate.

Mr. Organized is a slave to logic

Linear thinking governs every aspect of this man's life. If an activity has no observable benefit, he is not interested. He wastes time on the nonessentials, but will take all the time he needs to think a problem through. *Star Trek*'s Mr. Spock works tirelessly to understand the universe, but makes no effort whatsoever to find out what makes Nurse Chapel tick.

No intuitive leaps for Mr. Organized. He makes decisions based on good sound deductive reasoning. Paying careful attention can yield a wealth of information, and he never makes a move without a solid rationale, even if that explanation is not clear to others. Sir Arthur Conan Doyle's *Sherlock Holmes* may seem to leap to wild conclusions in his solutions to the mysteries, but in fact, he can invariably point to the exact clue that revealed all to him.

Leonard Nimoy as Mr. Spock in Star Trek

The Sherlock Holmes stories by Sir Arthur Conan Doyle

35

Mr. Organized wants things just so

A place for everything and everything in its place. Frasier Crane, of *Frasier*, has a very clear idea of how his world should be. For the most part, he manages to maintain his cultured, orderly existence. Frasier's prissy attitudes constantly result in his own frustration, as an untidy world intervenes in his plans. The lonely intellectualism shared by Frasier and his brother Niles reveals the isolation experienced by the super intelligent.

Alvy Singer, in *Annie Hall*, is so regimented in his needs that he is unable to even enter a movie theater after a movie has already started. And, of course, it is the very contrast of Annie's nature from his that draws him to her. The allure of chaos can be strong for this man, if only for the sake of fascinated observation.

Kelsey Grammer as Dr. Frasier Crane in Frasier

Woody Allen as Alvy Singer in Annie Hall

OCCUPATION

The PROFESSOR is willing to follow paths that offer a mental challenge and the opportunity to work alone.

PROFESSORs
• are schedule-oriented
• are creatures of habit
• are not people-oriented and
• are absorbed and dedicated to their work

ENGINEER

He likes the clear-cut guidelines and expectations. Even more, he likes not having to deal with people. Machines are so much more understandable and they follow directions precisely. Graphs, columns and a continuing series of problems are waiting to be figured out.

The PROFESSOR's work is precise and accurate. Always. Given a riddle, he persists until he figures it out. He dislikes change and prefers to stay in the same office with the same assistants.

COMPUTER PROGRAMMER

The isolation does not bother him. Neither do the extended hours poring over complex codes. The PROFESSOR puts in overtime because he enjoys the work more than anything else. The boss has to kick him out of the office before he thinks of his social life.

He spends a lot of time inside his head, so he often comes up with intriguing computer programs and much needed improvements to old databases. He is always one step ahead of the competition.

SCHOLAR

Books were his solace as a child and they provide him a road map to live by. He might be digging up dinosaur bones or writing the history of the Renaissance, but his library offers him that comfortable hiding place away from the rough-and-tumble present world.

The PROFESSOR might be a lord living alone in his mansion, always working and studying, giving back to society in his own way. He might be first in the county to install gas lighting or to try a new farming technique, but he baffles his neighbors with his eccentric ways. The PROFESSOR is unconcerned; he is too busy working on his next experiment.

Other occupations PROFESSORs might have:
• math teacher
• scientist
• dentist
• air traffic controller
• accountant
• economist
• loan officer
• pharmacist
• astronomer

THE SWASHBUCKLER

The SWASHBUCKLER is always on the go. His motto is, "Action, action and more action." He is physical, daring and colorful. Figuring out how to scale a dangerous wall or finding a way to save the day is easy for this man. He loves to leave his mark on every exploit, so he chooses the most rash and flamboyant method of achieving his aim.

Think about...
Antonio
Banderas as
Zorro in *The
Mask of Zorro*

Impulsive and creative, this man lives for the next adventure. He is too restless for a boring desk job, too impetuous for long term commitments. But if his imagination is fired with stories of treasure and romance, he quickly joins the team and is an asset in any endeavor.

This man leaps before he looks. Taking enormous risks to achieve his purpose, the SWASHBUCKLER keeps pushing forward even when everyone around him is fainting from exhaustion. He is too caught up in the action to take stock of his surroundings. Most people would rather watch him from a distance, for if they venture too close they take the risk of being pulled into his whirlwind. The chances that he takes with life and limb scare those who love him. But his supreme confidence and joy of life allow him to escape any tragedy.

Michael Douglas
as Jack Colton
in *Romancing
the Stone*

Always in pursuit of the next adrenaline rush, the SWASH-BUCKLER might be completely sincere when he makes a promise, but promptly forgets it when the swordplay begins.

QUALITIES

The SWASHBUCKLER roller-coasters through life, and he rarely stops to let dizzy riders off.

VIRTUES

The SWASH-
BUCKLER:
• lives for today
• is enthusiastic,
  inspiring and
  dashing
• is adventurous
  and
• is fun-loving

- *Fearless*—The SWASHBUCKLER does not hesitate when faced with danger. He never freezes when confronted with a gun or runs away from an attacker. He delights in finding creative ways to outsmart his opponent. When trouble appears, he is the man to call.
- *Exciting*—Life is never dull with this man. The SWASH-BUCKLER thrives on action, and if there is none around, he creates it. He provokes, he stimulates, he electrifies. No matter what he does, he turns it into a riveting experience.
- *Capable*—The SWASHBUCKLER provides a quick unconventional solution to any problem. If the door lock cannot be

picked, he takes off the hinges. If the airplane is going down, he improvises his own parachute. He is competent and skilled in any emergency.

FLAWS

- *Unreliable*—The SWASHBUCKLER sometimes becomes so focused on the action around him, he forgets to pick up his paycheck. His need for excitement can make him seem uncaring and forgetful. If someone is in jeopardy, he happily saves the day, but count him out for the routine jobs.
- *Foolhardy*—When a new adventure beckons, the SWASH-BUCKLER rushes in where angels fear to tread. Imprudent in his boldness, he does not stop to weigh the danger before taking off for the next feat of derring-do.
- *Selfish*—He puts the challenge before everybody and everything. The SWASHBUCKLER is not concerned about the impact his priorities might have on others around him. The restless energy surging through him is more important than anything else.

But he also can:
- refuse to grow up
- be rash, reckless and irresponsible and
- be impulsive

BACKGROUND

The SWASHBUCKLER loved excitement

This child kept his parents on their toes. Whether from a settled environment or following an adventurous family tradition, from a very early age he was fearless in his pursuits. His family would often have to tie him down in order to ensure his safety. But he invariably escaped, not wanting to miss the next great escapade.

Peter Pan in *Peter Pan* by James M. Barrie

The SWASHBUCKLER had to see over the next horizon

His warm, sunny personality served him well in any environment. Many boys idealized his nonchalant manner in the face of danger and many girls kissed him in the back hall. He was the kid who climbed the highest tree and skated over the thinnest ice. Feeling invincible, he played truth and dare, and always took the dare. His teacher despaired of him ever sitting still, but if the subjects were about far-off lands and exhilarating quests, then this boy's interest was caught.

As he grew older, he grew bored with school and homework. He dreamed of sailing the seven seas. This boy founded the mountaineering club, signing up dozens of buddies who had no real interest in perilous heights or strenuous activity, but were swept away by his enthusiastic stories. He spent Friday nights hot-rodding, relishing the chance to do some joy-riding.

No commitments stood in the SWASHBUCKLER's way

As soon as he could, he escaped the dry, dusty classrooms to see the thrilling, exhilarating world. He packed his bags and joined the army or toured through Europe, intent on creating the life he had dreamed of for years.

Did he grow up with a fearful mother? Or does he come from a long line of adventurers?

He might spend years pursuing his dreams before settling down enough to hold a regular job. But even then, he will still be planning his next trip across Siberia, or researching the Pharaoh's tomb he is bound to discover. His eyes are always on the horizon, dreaming of what tomorrow will bring.

STYLES

The SWASHBUCKLER might be the DAREDEVIL . . .

He courts danger and embraces excitement. A rebellious chord sounds deep in this SWASHBUCKLER. He climbs the mountain because it is there, he races cars for the thrill and he kidnaps the heiress because he can.

Tom Cruise as Pete Mitchell in *Top Gun*

Think of Pete Mitchell in *Top Gun*. This Navy pilot hot-dogs with his pals, chases the ladies and enjoys every minute of his high-flying life. He rarely slows down to contemplate his actions or the consequences. He is too busy enjoying the endless blue skies spread before him and the fantastic aerial stunts he performs in his state-of-the-art jet. This fighter pilot does not even contemplate crashing.

The Daredevil knows no fear

Will Smith as Agent J in *Men in Black*

Risking his life is all in a day's work, and he shrugs his shoulders when scolded for the chances he takes. Always intrepid, he brings poise and self-confidence to every escapade. Remember Agent J in *Men in Black*? Given just a few hours to make a choice, he joins the game, relinquishing his past with barely a thought. Brow arched, he greets every new alien with a witty joke and a wry grin.

Nothing fazes the Daredevil

The Seven Voyages of Sinbad the Sailor by John Yeoman

This SWASHBUCKLER is in it strictly for the action and the challenge. If the task before him is nearly impossible, it makes him that much more excited and determined. Sinbad is just such a man. In *The Seven Voyages of Sinbad the Sailor*, we experience his seven voyages, visit exotic lands, and see strange, terrifying monsters. No wild sea or demon of destruction is too great for him to overcome.

Remember *Austin Powers: International Man of Mystery*? Austin has enormous fun chasing Dr. Evil, as well as chasing all the girls. This groovy '60s spy has no doubts he will bag his man, but why not have a bit of adventure on the way? Austin may be viewed as a fool by some, but he ends up winning.

Mike Myers as Austin Powers in *Austin Powers: International Man of Mystery*

STYLES
. . .or else he is the EXPLORER
Unlike his counterpart who lives for the race, this man loves the finish line. This SWASHBUCKLER has a personal commitment to the task before him. Remember the myth of *Jason and the Argonauts?* This young prince sets out on a voyage, intent on claiming the Golden Fleece for his own. His wild and dangerous adventures do not discourage him from reaching his goal.

The myth of Jason and the Argonauts

The Explorer never contemplates losing
He takes risks without blinking an eye, but he only does it in pursuit of his aim. There is a greater cause behind the foolhardy chances he takes. Whether rescuing the heroine or finding the buried treasure, he has a purpose. Think of Indiana Jones in *The Raiders of the Lost Ark*. He dives under trucks, fights simultaneously with an airplane and a hulking opponent, and escapes a pit of snakes. But these obstacles fail to stay his pursuit of the power held in the Ark. His success is never in doubt.

Harrison Ford as Indiana Jones in *The Raiders of the Lost Ark*

The Explorer knows where he is headed
Robin of Locksley in *The Adventures of Robin Hood* is a good example of this kind of man. Determined to defeat the Sheriff of Nottingham and stand against King John, he still takes time to court the lady and revel with his merry band of thieves. Able to control his energy and channel it into specific objectives, he is more serious, and can be more ruthless. Fun is important to him and he enjoys the journey. But the final goal must be achieved before he can call it day and be satisfied with his accomplishments.

Errol Flynn as Robin of Locksley in *The Adventures of Robin Hood*

He is a man of action, intense and passionate about his life and endeavors, but he has learned the value of thinking ahead and taking only calculated risks. The Explorer wants to be sure he is still alive and able to collect the prize he has won. Think of Bill

Bill Paxton as Bill Harding in *Twister*

Harding in *Twister*. Labeled the "Extreme" by his friends, this man wants to solve the riddle of tornadoes, but has no trouble enjoying the thrill of the chase.

OCCUPATION

Thrills and chills must be a part of any career the SWASH-BUCKLER chooses.

SWASH-BUCKLERs:
• have enormous energy and courage
• have the ability to fix problems without needing help and
• inspire others to action

ARCHEOLOGIST

He loves the travel, the excitement of the new discovery, and the challenge of putting the pieces together. This job is rarely boring and that is a big selling point for the SWASHBUCKLER. He does not enjoy paperwork or teaching, but the lure of the next expedition keeps him going.

He dares to go to the deepest jungle or into the darkest cave. Being uncomfortable does not faze him, and facing jeopardy only makes him that much more enraptured with the hunt. However, he also does not take orders well, and whoever supervises his digs is in for a long journey.

Other occupations SWASH-BUCKLERs might have:
• body guard
• safari guide
• jockey
• investigative journalist
• astronaut
• smoke jumper
• race car driver
• emergency doctor

BUSH PILOT

The man is not bothered by being alone much of the time, as long as there is adventure mixed in the job. Whether dropping off fire fighters or flying in medical supplies, this man enjoys the freedom of being his own boss and the challenge of this occupation.

He volunteers to take the worst flights and the most dangerous assignments. If the SWASHBUCKLER gets in a jam, he finds a way to rescue himself and the cargo, but the plane might go down in flames.

PIRATE

Suspense, danger, fun and freedom! What more could this man ask for? Either privateering for Good Queen Bess or in it for his own enrichment, the pirate role suits this man to perfection. He is gallant with the ladies, inspiring to his crew and happy to pick up a sword anytime a fight breaks out.

The SWASHBUCKLER's daring raids against his enemies have made him rich and powerful, and he has wisely stored his treasure where no man can get to it. But he secretly hopes someone tries.

THE WARRIOR

Dark and dangerous, justice is this man's watchword. He is remote, driven, and controlled. The WARRIOR's standards of conduct are high, and heaven help those who fail to meet them. Including himself. He sees everything in black or white, right or wrong. Shades of gray are an anathema to him. In his opinion, they are only excuses. He is the judge and the jury, and if necessary, the hangman, too.

Think about...
Bruce Willis as
John McClane in
Die Hard

The WARRIOR believes evil cannot go unpunished. He cannot allow the bad guys to walk away, so trouble seems to follow him wherever he goes. His commitment to righting wrongs can lead him into dark alleys and seedy side streets. But it is impossible for him to lay down his sword of honor. He will fight the good fight until justice has won, or he is dead.

Merciless with enemies, with friends he is loyal unto death. He is the ultimate protector, the defender of all who are weak and vulnerable. Once he has given his word—his commitment—he can always be counted upon to come through. He chooses his friends and lovers carefully, but once his heart is offered, he will always come through for them.

Clint Eastwood
as Harry
Callahan in
Dirty Harry

He often feels that only he can make a difference, only he can perform the task. It is difficult for this man to accept himself as human or consider asking for help. The WARRIOR believes in his cause and will always put it first. He uses whatever tools are before him to accomplish his goal—whether brute strength or quick thinking.

QUALITIES

The WARRIOR is a man of mettle who carries a sword of justice, but that sword cuts both ways.

VIRTUES

The
WARRIOR:
• must correct
  wrongs
• is chivalrous
  and
  lionhearted
• is focused and
  resolute and
• is idealistic

- *Tenacious*—The WARRIOR does not give up. He is tough-minded and well-motivated. He believes in his heart that what he is doing is right. Often he feels that only he can right this wrong, so he does not accept the possibility of defeat. Failure is unthinkable.
- *Principled*—This man personifies honor, duty and integrity. While others compromise their beliefs in order to get ahead, the WARRIOR never bends if what is being proposed does

43

not fit his moral code. No matter what it costs him, he does not go back on his word.

- *Noble*—He goes down with his cause, never betraying his friends or his commitments. The WARRIOR is self-sacrificing, incorruptible and never plays his comrades false. *Semper Fi*—always faithful—is the way he lives. And dies.

But he also can:
- be austere
- be obsessed and obstinate and
- demand too much of others

FLAWS

- *Self-righteous*—The WARRIOR knows his cause is virtuous and is willing to break laws to achieve the right outcome. Grimly determined to administer justice, he convinces himself that the end justifies any means.
- *Relentless*—The WARRIOR finds it impossible to give up his quest. He is pitiless, harsh and cruel to his enemies and, sometimes, even to his friends. When death is imminent or others around him are being harmed, this man presses forward until the last breath leaves his body. He will not be denied.
- *Merciless*—Because his is the side of truth and justice, no excuse stands in his way. Pardoning or excusing a sin never crosses his mind. The WARRIOR does not allow himself excuses, so why should he let others off easy?

BACKGROUND

The WARRIOR needed to see justice done

From an early age, this boy saw the injustice around him and made a determination to change it when he had the power to do so. He was fiercely protective of those who were unable to defend themselves, be it a litter of kittens, the school underdogs, his little sister or his abused mother. A strong sense of purpose was burned into him as a young child. No parent or teacher could dissuade him once he had made his decision about who was good and who was evil.

Jake Lloyd as Anakin Skywalker in *Star Wars: Episode I - The Phantom Menace*

The WARRIOR stepped in when others were afraid to

The tendency to be a loner made it hard for him to join a school team. His social skills were adequate enough to keep him in the mainstream, but his stubborn judgment of the actions of others kept him from reaching the pinnacle of social success. Truth, justice and the American way were far more important to him than being voted Mr. Popularity.

His willingness to fight for the weak may have gotten him a bad reputation. He might not look for trouble, but he never walked away from it and he did not care if that made the authorities angry. But unless there were a noble cause for the WARRIOR to pursue, he kept to himself.

His relationship with his family depended on the judgments he had made about them. If his father was a wife beater, than this boy became a fighter and a courageous defender of his women. But if his family life was normal, than he held warm regard for his siblings and parents. His loyalty to them was never questioned.

Money and power did not hold appeal for the WARRIOR

Lucrative job offers or shining diplomas were not the prize he was interested in. This young man looked for meaning in his life and hunted until he found the niche that provided him with that. He wanted a career worthy of his devotion and sacrifice. A WARRIOR needed to know his work made a difference in the world.

STYLES

The WARRIOR might be the AVENGER . . .

This man wants nothing more than to live his own life free from the cares of an unjust world. But that unjust world seeks him out, forcing this WARRIOR to take action to redress wrongs. Think of William Wallace in *Braveheart*. Forced to defend his homeland against the hated English, he leads his army in a desperate and gallant attempt at freedom. His bravery and defiance show the Scots what true courage means.

The Avenger is a reluctant hero

He tries to find the reasonable solution, a nonviolent way to settle the score, but when sweet reason fails, he is fully prepared to fight on any terms. In fact, because he knows all too well that bad guys rarely listen, his fighting skills are honed to a sharp edge. Tang Lung in *Return of the Dragon* exacting revenge on the gangsters who menaced his employer's business is a good example of a WARRIOR.

The Avenger enters the fray because no one else can get the job done, but his heart is not in his task. He acts efficiently and cold-bloodedly, but he wishes his skills were not needed. Remember Casey Ryback in *Under Siege?* Content to stay in his kitchen baking pies, this man is inevitably drawn into the battle. When bad men play games, only this man can save the day.

Was he a child witness to a violent crime? Did his commitment to truth cost him dearly?

Mel Gibson as William Wallace in *Braveheart*

Bruce Lee as Tang Lung in *The Return of the Dragon*

Steven Seagal as Casey Ryback in *Under Siege*

45

The Avenger believes in an eye for an eye

He is quite familiar with the evil people can do. His experiences have led to a cynical view of people, and while his standards are high, his expectations are low.

Edmond Dantas in *The Count of Monte Cristo* by Alexandre Dumas'

In Alexandre Dumas' *The Count of Monte Cristo*, Edmond Dantes is falsely accused of treason. This tale of imprisonment, daring escape and ultimate revenge shows how this man never forgets the wrongs done to him. Each step of his plan was carefully calculated. Every contingency was foreseen. He does not rest until his revenge is complete against those who plotted against him.

STYLES

. . . or else he is the KNIGHT

This WARRIOR embraces his destiny, accepting his mission in life with pleasure. He raises a banner of patriotism or social justice and fights a battle of principle, never outrage. Remember Jack Traven in *Speed?* A young cop, he willingly risks his life to save an elevator full of people and a busload of strangers. It was his job and he was determined to save the day no matter what the risk to himself. He had committed himself and there was no turning back.

Keanu Reeves as Jack Traven in *Speed*

The Knight is a savior

When Sir Percy Blakeley from *The Scarlet Pimpernel* deems the cause worthwhile, he becomes its most ardent supporter. Nothing stands in the way of his duty to the king, his country or the cause. No king could ask for a more devoted servant, no country could ask for a more faithful soldier. He willingly puts his life on the line to ensure victory. Repeatedly, he returns to France to save the helpless victims of the Terror.

Sir Percy Blakeley in *The Scarlet Pimpernel* by Baroness Emmuska Orczy

Honor is paramount to the Knight

Ruled by dogma, this man must follow the righteous path. Only he can do the job, only he can make the difference. *Superman* is just such a hero. Metropolis depends on him to keep the city safe. Nothing stops him from righting the wrongs and capturing the bad guys. His whole life is devoted to the role of protector. Vanquishing evil is all in a day's work for him.

Christopher Reeve as Clark Kent in *Superman*

He views the world as one of black and white, and if he strays into the gray, he is lost. Once committed, he does not look back. His zeal carries him through the roadblocks, and he never loses his focus on the ultimate goal: justice. Think of Atticus Finch in *To Kill a Mockingbird.* One of the few people of his town who believes in equality between the races, he agrees to defend a black man charged with raping a white woman—even when this action puts him and his family into jeopardy.

OCCUPATION

The WARRIOR follows a career path that requires him to decide right from wrong.

FBI AGENT

Chasing and catching the bad guys gives this man intense gratification. His entire job fits into exactly what his goal in life is—to bring justice to the world. He is often frustrated by the rules and regulations, because sometimes they tie his hands when he is about to punish the wicked. But, all in all, this job makes him feel vindicated and valued.

The WARRIOR is loyal, meticulous and willing to give his life for the job. He spends long hours searching for clues to a killer and derives great satisfaction when the arrest is made.

ENVIRONMENTAL ACTIVIST

He is totally dedicated. He believes that other people are evil if they disagree with his conclusions. Working with him is difficult. But saving the planet is a calling that this man cannot turn away from.

He will go anywhere if he believes the cause is right. The WARRIOR works longer hours than anyone else and finds the answers that are needed to save the forest, the river or the spotted owl. He loves what he does and is passionate in the defense of his convictions.

CAVALIER

This man fights only if he believes in the crusade. Not a mercenary, killing for nothing but gold and glory is not something that appeals to him. He must be a true believer to join the war. Once committed, he is unfazed by the horrors of combat.

This man often rises in the ranks to stand right beside the king. When he gives his oath, he stands true. Whether fighting for his queen or conquering a new land, if the WARRIOR believes in the cause, he never quits.

Atticus Finch in *To Kill a Mockingbird* by Harper Lee

WARRIORs
• have a strict moral code of behavior
• are trustworthy
• are intensely focused and
• have a strong work ethic

Other occupations WARRIORs might have:
• musketeer
• spy
• bomb specialist
• Navy SEAL
• judge
• firefighter
• missionary
• prosecutor
• detective
• vigilante

SECTION II
THE HEROINE ARCHETYPES

One might think that because women make up approximately half of the world's population, heroines would figure in approximately half of the world's fiction. Well, not exactly. In fact, in earliest fiction, the role of women was more typically as a prop to the hero. Women were usually relegated to being the object of the hero's love. In the course of the story she might even offer some small piece of aid to him such as Ariadne holding the end of the thread for Theseus, so he could find his way back out of the labyrinth. More frequently, the object of the hero's affection was merely an endangered damsel, such as Eurydice, for whom Orpheus descended into the underworld.

Unlike its male counterpart, the word "heroine" has never been limited to those who performed marvelous exploits. Very rarely did women appear in traditional "heroic" form, performing great deeds of bravery. The story of Antigone's steadfast loyalty to her brother and to the will of the gods, even in the face of certain death, was the rare exception, rather than the rule for female protagonists.

Who are your favorite heroines? Why?

To an extent, early literary heroines were a reflection of the options available to women, or at least those options perceived by the authors. As in real life, a woman might attach herself to a single male, as loving daughter, wife, or mother. Or, she might choose a freer but less secure path, choosing her manner of life—and her men—for herself. That option, perhaps less welcome to the powers that be, was portrayed as more likely to result in tragedy. The practice of depicting women as either whore or madonna, with no shades of strength or morality between, remains a common enough trap for writers even today.

But even in those ancient times, hints of alternatives existed. Tales of fierce Amazon warrior tribes filtered through the stories of hapless victims in need of rescue. The clever means employed by Lysistrata and her fellow wives to gain peace demonstrated a recognition of the power of women even when viewed as the weaker sex.

Interestingly, heroine protagonists have actually predominated in fairy tales. Little is known of handsome Prince Charming, other than his propensity for seeking out and marrying an astonishing number of heroines. Instead, these sagas revolve around Cinderella, Sleeping Beauty, Snow White, and so on. The heroine still tended to require rescue, whether by lover's kiss or fairy godmother's magic, but the emphasis on her, rather than her hero, demonstrated the growing interest in and recognition of heroines.

As the role of women increased in society, so did the roles of heroines in literature. And as with the heroes, a pattern of eight distinctive heroine archetypes developed.

- The BOSS—a real go-getter, she climbs the ladder of success.
- The SEDUCTRESS—an enchantress, she charms to get her way.
- The SPUNKY KID—gutsy and true, she is loyal to the end.
- The FREE SPIRIT—an eternal optimist, she dances to unheard tunes.
- The LIBRARIAN—controlled and clever, she holds back.
- The WAIF—a distressed damsel, she bends, but does not break.
- The CRUSADER—a dedicated fighter, she meets commitments.
- The NURTURER—serene and capable, she nourishes the spirit.

At her heart, every well-defined heroine falls within one of these eight archetypes. Through the archetype, the writer understands how the heroine thinks and feels. Her motivations and her methods are clear and known. A writer who understands the essential nature of the character can, in turn, communicate this essence. The audience recognizes this timeless character because of her appeal to the collective unconscious.

Heroine protagonists dominate fairy tales

There are eight female archetypes that have been used throughout literary history

Again, the existence of these archetypes does not mean that writers simply churn the same tired eight heroines out of a mimeograph machine. Heroines in the same archetypal family are not mere reproductions of each other. Heroines within a single archetype share a similar personality make-up, but they are not and should not be thought of as slightly different models of the Stepford wives.

For example, Murphy Brown, from the television program of the same name, is a BOSS. She forges through life, never doubting her way is the only way. She climbed that ladder of success, and she is not interested in looking back. Bold and brash, she can shoot incisive questions at high and low alike.

Another BOSS is Queen Elizabeth I, from *Elizabeth*. Unlike Murphy, she was born the daughter of a king. Granted, her fate sometimes seemed uncertain, but she knew how to hold tightly to what was hers. She made hard decisions and took calculated risks to ensure both her and her kingdom's survival.

Similar though these characters may be, they are not interchangeable. Murphy Brown could not have taken a backwater kingdom and turned it into a world power. She did not have the diplomatic skills to last in the turmoil of English politics. In turn, Elizabeth as a journalist boggles the imagination. She would have dictated every interview.

In the pages that follow, we provide a basic structure for your use in crafting a dynamic, believable, recognizable heroine. Each heroine archetype is described in detail, beginning with the general deportment and ways of thinking of each archetype. This overview explains the more apparent characteristics of the archetype.

Next, we discuss the personal attributes, or Qualities, of each heroine. These are the common personality traits recurring within an archetype. The heroines are not perfect women, and thus have both flaws and virtues. The good traits explain why audiences empathize with her; the bad traits explain why she has a story.

Then, for each archetype, we discuss Background. Venus might have emerged fully formed from the sea, but such spontaneous creation is relatively rare. A heroine's character arises from her origins, and so the writer must understand the heroine's personal history. A spoiled and petted child grows into a different woman from the girl who suffered abuse. Was she forced to care for younger siblings? Was her nose always in a

> The heroine archetypes are a reflection of the role of women in literature

Use of the archetype will not produce a stereotypical character. Rather, they provide a framework from which to build a unique heroine

book? Was she the popular cheerleader or the shy wallflower? Characters within a single archetype do not have carbon copy histories, but parallel experiences will show up in their backgrounds.

Next, we explore the heroine's Style. As with the heroes, each heroine archetype manifests itself in two distinct ways. Consider Mary Richards, of *The Mary Tyler Moore Show*, and her best friend, Rhoda Morgenstern. Both are SPUNKY KIDs, but they have clear differences. While Mary's perky attitude and sunny disposition light up a room, Rhoda is a bit edgier, a tad more cynical. Even though they share many common traits, the two women have different types of behavior.

We conclude each heroine archetype by discussing the kind of Occupations which tend to draw members of that particular group. We also discuss how the archetypal qualities influence the character's likely success and choice of career. For example, a SEDUCTRESS might choose to be a spy in order to gain fame and glory, but a CRUSADER would join the cause to win the war against an evil enemy. Each archetype brings its own set of desires and traits to its chosen occupation. The writer's job is to use the occupation to highlight the character's personality.

Heroines today are no longer limited to the role of victim, although such stories still need to be told. We have grown up with fables of old and their damsels in distress, but a wealth of stories are still waiting to be heard about daring maidens seeking a prize or take-charge women willing to risk all for a chance at the golden ring.

THE BOSS

The BOSS takes charge of her circumstances and makes things happen before most people get off the couch. She is a strong, tough woman, who gets her way no matter what the obstacles. She remains unconcerned when she ruffles feathers and steps on toes. Her goals and priorities are far more important than hurt feelings. She is outspoken, resourceful and persuasive.

Winning is everything to the BOSS. To achieve her ends, she can be calculating. She will shade the truth in order to gain her objective and she is not above manipulating circumstances to make things go her way. She sees nothing wrong with this. Whatever helps her get across the finish line is all in a good day's work.

If someone tries to obstruct her path, she can be blunt and downright brash. She will mow people down on her way to her goal and beware to those who stand against her. When confronted, she can be ruthless. Because of these attributes, sometimes she looks around and wonders why she has so few friends. But this self-contemplation only lasts a few moments, and she is onto the next project before the dust settles.

Can this woman possibly slow down long enough to connect with others? Yes, if she realizes why this is important to her well-being. Once she decides to love, she is fierce and intense—capable of wrapping her loved ones in a strong, caring embrace. Whatever this woman decides to do, she does it with intensity and gusto. The BOSS knows how to focus and accomplish anything.

QUALITIES
The BOSS values getting ahead and winning the game, but when it comes to personal relationships, she is at a loss.

VIRTUES
- *Confident*—This is a woman who always knows where she is going. She comes up with a plan, organizes what needs to be done and makes it happen. The BOSS rarely feels any twinges of doubt, so she does not waste a lot of time analyzing her position. She knows she is right, and that is the end of that.
- *Dynamic*—The BOSS is the kind of woman who walks into a room and commands attention. Because of her self-assurance, she sparks emotions ranging from admiration to jealousy. Her

Think about...
Barbra Streisand as Dolly Levi in *Hello, Dolly!*

Jennifer Lopez as Karen Sisco in *Out of Sight*

The BOSS:
- is self-assured
- is highly organized and
- is an achiever

53

energetic and forceful presence invariably makes things happen.

- *Competitive*—This woman is so self-assured, she is positive she will always win. Anyone who challenges that position is in for a battle. The BOSS utilizes all her resources and talents to triumph, and she never stops until her opponent has been defeated.

FLAWS

But she
also can:
- be aloof
- be extremely intolerant and
- be short-tempered

- *Blunt*—Political correctness does not head her list of priorities; it might not even be on her list at all. The BOSS does not mince words; she thinks sugarcoating is a waste of time. Sometimes this causes her unnecessary grief, but she does not see the need to change her abrupt behavior. After all, she gets things done.
- *Workaholic*—The BOSS thrives in environments where she has clear-cut agendas and goals. On the job is the best place to be. Here she can be competitive and know when she wins; her work is her world. She compulsively stays away from addressing her emotionally barren life. Feelings get in the way of achievements.
- *Arrogant*—She is always right—just ask her. The BOSS finds it hard to acknowledge that others also have ideas worth exploring. Her haughty stare and overbearing manner turn a lot of people off. But that does not matter. Life is too short to worry about what other people think.

BACKGROUND

The BOSS ruled her surroundings

Lucy in the comic strip *Peanuts* by Charles Schultz

As a small child, the BOSS asserted her position and staked out her territory. From the crib, she tried to dictate what she wanted and when, and was surprised when her parents did not automatically agree with her in every area. Her siblings were easier troops to command and she willingly took over when the other kids were unsure about what to do next.

The BOSS's entrepreneurial spirit quickly became apparent

She had the first lemonade stand in the neighborhood and was ruthless in pricing the competition out of existence. She was stubborn and bull-headed, but also smart and determined. In school, she was successful in class—earning gold stars and climbing up the ladder of achievement—unless she was butting heads with her teacher.

Out on the playground, she dictated what games would be played and who would be on what team. Her classmates may have grumbled at her high-handedness, but they could not argue with the results. Her team invariably won.

This girl took high school by storm. She was the debate coach's dream, the basketball team's captain or the class president. The BOSS had her finger in every pie and, seemingly without effort, kept up with all her activities. She worked harder than anyone else to make success happen in every area of her life—and she was never surprised when it did.

The BOSS was an achiever

Higher education had to have a purpose in order to engage her attention. She looked at every activity as a means to an end. By now, she had developed strong opinions about every aspect of her life. She had little interest in the usual girlish pursuits. She saw painting her nails and gossiping about the boys as a waste of time. She was much more likely to spend her time trading on the stock market or building her web design business.

STYLES

The BOSS might be the PRINCESS . . .

This kind of Boss has grown accustomed to constant applause for her many accomplishments or immediate acquiescence to her every demand. Whatever she tackles, she comes out a winner. Whatever she sets her mind to, she achieves. Nothing is out of her reach or so she believes. Think of Barbara Whiteman in *Down and Out in Beverly Hills*. Confronted with a dirty and disagreeable bum, she decides to whip him into shape while convincing her doubting husband it is the correct thing to do. All the while, she controls her household with an iron hand, sure that her decisions are absolutely right.

The Princess always knows what to do

She is certain that she is the best and relishes every challenge, knowing she belongs in the winner's circle. She was born to the role and makes sure everyone knows it. No one who's met her ever forgets her. Remember Queen Elizabeth I in *Elizabeth?* Initially, she deferred to her wise (and male) advisors, but soon

Did she rebel against attempts to force her to be a "sweet" girl or did her parents urge her onto greater achievements? Did she have to fill in for an absent parent?

Bette Midler as Barbara Whiteman in *Down and Out in Beverly Hills*

Cate Blanchett as Queen Elizabeth in *Elizabeth*

55

took the reins of her kingdom and destroyed any and all resistance to her rule.

The Princess is confident in her opinion

Martha in *Who's Afraid of Virginia Woolf?* knows her husband's failure is due to his refusal to follow her advice over the years. And she has no intention of ever letting him forget it. She knows the best way to do everything; it is her way or the highway. Never one to pull her punches, she calls a spade a spade.

When the Princess joins the company, it is just a matter of time before she becomes the president. The world is hers to conquer and she does it with panache. Remember the legend of Boadicea, Queen of the Iceni? When the Romans landed on English shores and tried to take over the island, this Celtic woman took arms against them, leading her people in battle. Part history and part myth, Boadicea proved that women were more than just birthing machines and chattel to be traded between men.

STYLES

. . . or else she is the TRAILBLAZER

This kind of a BOSS had none of the advantages of the Princess. In fact, she was probably ridiculed for being assertive. In Shakespeare's *The Taming of the Shrew*, Katherine's family despairs of ever finding a husband for her. Her father cringes at her demands, her sister wonders what will become of her, and Kate reacts with anger. All she wants is to rule her destiny, but those around her tell her it is not "womanly" to want such a thing.

The Trailblazer wants to run her own life

At some point in her past, she developed a burning desire to achieve and to become the best. She worked her way up the ladder of success, and, in her struggle to succeed, she developed a strong confidence in herself and her abilities. Carolyn Burnham in *American Beauty* demands perfection in every area of her life. Her career is far more important than her husband's needs and desires. Her intense personality is focused on catching "the King," her competitor. And of course, she succeeds far beyond even her wildest dreams.

Martha in
Who's Afraid of Virginia Woolf?
by Edward Albee

The legend of Boadicea, Queen of Iceni

Katherine in *The Taming of the Shrew* by William Shakespeare

Annette Bening as Carolyn Burnham in *American Beauty*

Nothing intimidates the Trailblazer

She has no time for failures. She made it, everyone else should stop whining and do the same. She is a bit more savvy than the Princess because she has seen the seamier side of life. Driven and determined, this woman will never stay on the bottom rung for long. Think of Loretta Castorini in *Moonstruck*. She has no patience for the way Ronny insists upon dwelling on his difficulties. Her exasperated advice for him is "Snap out of it!"

Remember *Murphy Brown*? With a sharp tongue and an indomitable will, this woman rules her news program and her co-workers, making sure she gets the best assignments and perks. Her future is in her hands and that is just where she wants it. She is not interested in hitching her star to anyone else's wagon. When she is in the driver's seat, she knows she will end up at the head of the pack. And everyone else had better fall in line behind her.

OCCUPATION

The BOSS considers only those positions that allow her to be in complete control of her own destiny.

FIVE STAR CHEF

The BOSS likes the constant variety, the changing situations she must deal with every minute of every day in a professional kitchen. She spends a lot of time reviewing what others are doing in her field in order to make sure she is the best.

She fires anyone who does not learn quickly or whose skills do not live up to her exacting standards. She is a tough manager, and many people do not like working for her. She demands and expects excellence, and she gets it.

PROSECUTOR

Always adept at sizing up people, the BOSS is quick to make decisions about whether or not a person is guilty. Because she is usually right in her assessment, she begins to believe that she can never be wrong. Once she has decided on guilt, she is fierce in her desire to put the criminal in jail.

Defeat is not an option. She turns over every stone in search of a conviction. Hating to lose a case, she may bend some rules in order to make sure it never happens.

Cher as Loretta Castorini in *Moonstruck*

Candace Bergen as Murphy Brown in the TV series *Murphy Brown*

BOSSes:
• have the ability to make quick decisions
• are realists
• are efficient managers and
• are both demanding and challenging leaders

Other
occupations
BOSSes
might have:
• entrepreneur
• pilot
• mayor
• surgeon
• publisher
• queen
• editor
• bank manager
• attorney
  general
• president
• CEO

MADAM

Her entrepreneurial spirit puts her ahead of her time. The BOSS's need for control outweighs society's scorn and ridicule. There is freedom in being beyond society's dictates, and she enjoys it.

Her common sense makes her willing to implement new business practices. She is the first to check her girls for disease and turn away the rough customers. No one intimidates her. She is a strong supporter of her "soiled doves."

THE SEDUCTRESS

The SEDUCTRESS holds enormous power over others, hypnotizing them with her charm and desirability. She is mysterious, manipulative and bewitching. Taking no prisoners, she is not easily fooled by anyone and holds the upper hand in any relationship.

A natural temptress, she creates a fantasy world. Men feel more powerful and desirable in her company, because she deliberately sets up that illusion. She may have a specific purpose in bewitching her man, but she can turn on the charm whenever she wants, even if she is not interested in anything particular. Seduction comes as naturally to her as breathing.

The SEDUCTRESS carries some emotional baggage. She has a streak of distrust a mile wide and ten miles deep. Her true desires and motivations are carefully concealed behind a sensual smile. Knowledge is power, so she makes sure no one knows her. Not willing to leave herself unprotected, revelations of the SEDUCTRESS's true self are few and far between.

To her, any relationship, whether with man or woman, must serve a purpose. No man will get close to her heart, but her siren song makes many men try. Other women may call her friend, but will be disappointed if they ever try to rely on her. She is much more interested in what people can do for her than in what she can do for them. Self-focused, she takes more than she truly gives.

QUALITIES

The SEDUCTRESS has a bad reputation with the girls, but that never bothers the men.

VIRTUES

- *Assertive*—The SEDUCTRESS has learned that to be on the offensive is to her advantage. She is confident that if she stays one step ahead of everyone, her interests will be well-protected. She does not care about being in charge as long as she is in control of her own destiny.
- *Strong*—This woman is a survivor. The SEDUCTRESS does whatever is necessary to get what she needs. Enduring whatever she has to, she makes full use of her powerful attractions and mental acuity. When the smoke clears, she is still standing.

Think about...
Sharon Stone
as Catherine
Tramell in
Basic Instinct

Jane Fonda as
Bree Daniel in
Klute

The
SEDUCTRESS:
- is independent
  and smart
- is able to size
  up people
  quickly and
  accurately
- is cool and
  calculating and
- is very, very
  savvy

59

- *Clever*—When things go wrong, the SEDUCTRESS always has a Plan B. Not easily flustered when a situation goes awry, she assesses the damage and is smart enough to cover her tracks and wipe away any fingerprints.

FLAWS

But she also can:
- use people
- be unable to say "I'm sorry"
- be cold-hearted and
- be a chameleon

- *Cynical*—The SEDUCTRESS is jaded. Scornful of others, she trusts only her own judgment. She is suspicious of everybody, especially men. In her experience, everyone is in it for themselves, and she is determined not to be stuck with the check when the party ends.
- *Driven*—Because she perceives herself as all alone and only able to depend on herself, the SEDUCTRESS spends most of her time striving for security. For most of these women, that means money and power. She spends the majority of her days and nights planning how to get it, then hoarding it when it comes her way.
- *Manipulative*—She has learned that honey catches more flies than vinegar. Because she is no dummy, she has perfected her honey-making skills, and the SEDUCTRESS sees nothing wrong with fooling people to get her way.

BACKGROUND

The SEDUCTRESS came of age early

Dominique Swan as Lolita in *Lolita*

The SEDUCTRESS developed her cynical attitudes very quickly. As a young girl, she discovered the effectiveness of using her charms to get her way. A smile of promise or a gleam of understanding in her big eyes got her what she wanted— whether from Daddy or the boy next door. Chances are, the adults around her let her know that her appearance was far more important than character or intelligence. Looking pretty, perhaps even precociously sexual, earned her far more attention and approval than kind words or good grades. Presenting an eagerness to please, whether or not heartfelt, also yielded benefits. She learned how shallow people can be, and how best to play on that superficiality.

The SEDUCTRESS valued friends for what they could bring her

In her family, men got all the good stuff, and women only got things by convincing the men to hand it over. Or maybe the women got nothing at all. As a consequence, she took any rivalry with other girls very personally. She felt the need to excel in all things feminine—the most polished make-up, the latest fashions, the most desirable boyfriends. But she likely had female friends as well—tame acolytes who followed her lead in fashion and social behavior. She learned to cloak her true feelings, and to instead offer whatever the crowd wanted. The perfect chameleon, she changed her persona as easily as other girls changed hair ribbons.

The SEDUCTRESS learned to use her charm to control others

If she wanted, she led the in-crowd, determining who was in favor and who was out. She instinctively understood other kids' fear of rejection, and so built a childhood empire. She probably dated the whole football team at one time or another and gained a reputation; but that reputation did not lessen her power. She was still the Prom Queen, and maybe the Homecoming Queen, too. She flirted with the male teachers to ensure her As and "wiled" her way through school, relishing every moment.

STYLES

The SEDUCTRESS might be the DARK LADY . . .

On the surface, this anti-heroine seems almost villainous. She manipulates to get her way and has no shame for the pain and anger she causes. But this SEDUCTRESS is not deceiving and conniving because she wants to be. No, this woman is a survivor, using the skills she has to get what she needs. Think of Delilah from *Samson and Delilah*. Given a task, she uses all her wiles to ensnare this man of God. She succeeds and wins her reward, trying not to spend much time or effort in feeling guilty.

The Dark Lady is a survivor

Absent the intervention of the Civil War, *Gone with the Wind*'s Scarlett O'Hara would have remained a petted and spoiled Southern belle. Perhaps she would not ever have been a truly nice woman, but she would have had no cause to employ the ruthless conduct for which she became known. But when the war years brought fear, deprivation, and humiliation, she uses every ounce of her skill to save Tara, and never go hungry again.

Did she see her mother suffer at the hands of men? Did she learn early that a smile and a wiggle gain the prize?

Hedy Lamarr as Delilah in *Samson and Delilah*

Vivian Leigh as Scarlett O'Hara in *Gone with the Wind*

The Dark Lady has an agenda

She is angry, bitter and, many times, out for what she can get. Consider Rebecca Sharp from William Makepeace Thackeray's *Vanity Fair.* She hides all her emotions behind a veil of charming deceit and ruthless sensuality. She uses her beauty like a weapon. It protects her from any emotional entanglements, and it keeps everyone at a safe distance. This lady has a heart, but it has been buried beneath layer after layer of calculation.

The Dark Lady uses others as tools

This woman makes no bones about using her sexuality to ensnare men. Matty Walker in *Body Heat* sizes up her prey and lures him into her web of murder and betrayal. He is in thrall to her powerful allure. She is able to predict and plan for his every move, even his discovery of her double-cross.

STYLES
. . . or else she is the SIREN

Maybe she is without a deep dark secret, but somewhere along the way, this SEDUCTRESS learned it is better to keep her emotions hidden than to trust the people around her.

The Siren plays a role

Her personal allure is so astounding it seems natural to rely on it to get ahead in this world. Consider Wanda in *A Fish Called Wanda.* She moves from man to man and back to the first in her pursuit of the jewels, ever ready to play one man against another. Because the use of her sexuality is instinctive, this woman cannot operate in any other way and she does not see any reason to change.

The Siren is savvy

This woman is nobody's fool. She is street smart and on the ball.

Many discount her intelligence and sharp mind. Her alluring looks and ability to fascinate enable others to write her off as merely cheesecake. Remember Sugar Kane in *Some Like it Hot*? Her sexy walk and wispy voice enchant both Joe and Jerry. But behind the glamour lies a girl yearning for love and affection.

She is valued for her surface charms only, but she is not above using that underestimation to her advantage. As *Evita* showed quite well, Eva Peron had a tremendous amount of political acumen. Her husband's enemies do not appreciate her abilities until she helps bring her mate to power.

A certain cynical bemusement at her fate gives this woman a world-weary air. She thinks all men are fools for seeing only skin deep and for not realizing that beneath her looks lie intelligence and spirit. Cleopatra, the tragic heroine of *Antony and Cleopatra,* is a queen in every sense of the word, but the Romans cannot see past her mysterious beauty to the powerful woman who managed to evade the enemies within her own country.

OCCUPATION

When she works, the SEDUCTRESS pursues only those occupations that let her exploit her charms.

SPY

She enjoys the intrigue and the matching wits with enemy agents. The best in the business, she is most effective at charming information out of the enemy and using her chameleon-like talents to ferret out a country's secrets.

Anyone lucky enough to employ the SEDUCTRESS will be well-served—that is, if she stays loyal. She has no problem becoming a turncoat if she senses that she is being misused, and as an enemy, she is deadly.

MODEL

She grew up as the prettiest baby, constantly applauded for her looks. This woman is not at all dumb, and it seems natural to make as much money as she can using her obvious assets. A shrewd woman, she puts the money away or invests it in her own company.

The SEDUCTRESS makes sure she gets the best jobs with the best designers and photographers. Her career is her security, and for as long as it lasts, she is determined to squeeze every drop of money and power out of it that she can.

MISTRESS

This occupation has reinforced the SEDUCTRESS' belief that men are meant to be used. After all, the only thing they see when they look at her is her body. Her admirers shower wealth and attention on her and she does not even have to iron their shirts.

Cleopatra in
*Antony and
Cleopatra*
by William
Shakespeare

The
SEDUCTRESS:
• is decisive
• has the
  ability to
  determine a
  person's
  potential
• is pragmatic
  and
• has a carefully
  hidden
  intelligence

Other occupations the SEDUCTRESS might have:
• saleswoman
• singer
• stewardess
• actress
• aerobic
  instructor
• cosmetologist
• junior
  executive
• trophy wife
• cocktail
  waitress

Men flock to her because she knows how to make them feel like a king. She portrays herself as the perfect woman, hiding her true feelings. Being able to lie through her teeth comes in handy.

THE SPUNKY KID

The SPUNKY KID has moxie. She sometimes hides behind her sarcastic wit, and her lack of confidence may make her play down her best attributes, but she is spirited, cheerful and the most loyal of friends. Quick with a wide grin and a good word, she knows and likes everyone, and the world likes her right back.

She is the heroine underdog. People empathize with her; they see every woman in her. The chips may be stacked against her, but she is not one to give in or give up. Everyone who knows her, loves her—they just can't help themselves. Audiences root for her happy ending.

The SPUNKY KID does not care about being top dog, but she does carve out her own niche. She is creative and willing to explore new ideas, but playing prima donna is not her style. Being part of the team makes her happy. She will always put the group ahead of herself.

She can dress to the nines, but feminine frivolity is just playing dress-up for her. Jeans and sneakers are her more usual garb. To her chagrin, her last pair of tights always seems to have a run.

Romantic relationships are an area where the SPUNKY KID always has a rough time. Men think of her as a pal or worse, a sister. Fortunately, this eternal bridesmaid keeps her sense of humor. She just might make it after all.

QUALITIES

A cheerleader in the truest sense of the word, she urges everyone she knows on to victory.

VIRTUES

• *Sense of Humor*—The SPUNKY KID's most endearing quality is her dry sense of humor. Witty and clever, she is able to laugh at any situation and anybody, including herself. No matter what predicament she finds herself in, laughter is sure to be a part of it.

• *Reliable*—In every facet of her life she is dependable. When she makes a commitment, she keeps it—even to her own detriment. An enthusiastic go-getter, the SPUNKY KID can be counted on to get the job done. Trust in her word, because she never lets a person down.

Think about...
Meg Ryan as Annie Reed in *Sleepless in Seattle*

Margot Kidder as Lois Lane in *Superman*

The SPUNKY KID:
• is wholesome and refreshing
• is cooperative and
• is a team player

65

- *Supportive*—The best of friends, she is always there with a comforting hug or a sympathetic ear whenever she is needed. Integrity and honor are values she strongly believes in, and if the SPUNKY KID is told a secret, she never betrays the confidence.

But she
can also:
- be unaware that she undermines herself
- slide into the martyr role and
- be unassertive in her love life

FLAWS

- *Sarcastic*—Combine her sharp wit with her sense of humor and the result can be a lethal weapon. Though the SPUNKY KID usually uses humor only against herself, if she is angry, watch out for the snappy comeback, usually muttered in caustic undertones.
- *Unassuming*—She never sees her own worthy attributes. She always downplays her beauty, dismisses her intelligence and never claims credit. She tends to work in the background, and her actions are usually selfless to the point of exhaustion. The SPUNKY KID has a problem using the word "no."
- *Skeptical*—When love or good fortune arrives, the SPUNKY KID is astonished and sure there must be some mistake. She never expected this to happen and waits for the other shoe to drop.

BACKGROUND
Everyone loved the SPUNKY KID

Little Orphan
Annie by
Harold Gray

Odds are, no childhood trauma wrecked her life. The SPUNKY KID was probably the apple of her parents' eyes. Adored and wanted, her family offered strong support and approval without reservation. They loved her for whoever she was.

She probably did not get a lot of pushes to excel, because her family was so happy with her. Other children starred in the school plays, other children shoplifted. The SPUNKY KID never gave her parents any grief, but never reached for the stars either. Perfectly content, she walked the middle of the road.

The SPUNKY KID was a neighborhood favorite
She shared her toys and played well with others. She never lacked for friends among her schoolmates. Playing dolls with the girls and tossing a baseball with the boys held equal appeal. She might have been the neighborhood tomboy, but what she liked best was spending time with her friends. Her friendship was genuine, and relationships mattered to her. She never put on a

show for the sake of what she could gain. Willing to be friends with all the kids, even the ones who were on the fringes of the social scene, she reveled in being part of the gang.

The SPUNKY KID had plenty of team spirit

She was a cheerleader or member of the band—one of the group, but never the leader. She participated in many after-school activities. Teachers liked her and depended on her to keep the peace among her schoolmates. But she was no goody-two-shoes—just a nice, normal teenager.

The boys saw her as a pal, not a girlfriend; so she always had a problem attracting their romantic attention. She was more likely to end up pitching baseballs in the backyard instead of swirling around the prom dance floor, and she yearned to change her predicament.

STYLES

The SPUNKY KID might be the GIRL NEXT DOOR . . .

A sunny optimist, this SPUNKY KID is perky, upbeat and fun to be around. She is the efficient co-worker, the right-hand gal or the manager of the coffee shop on the corner. Up and coming in her career, she is capable of contributing to any project needing a moderating voice and enthusiasm. First and foremost, she is a team player.

In the *Mary Tyler Moore Show*, Mary Richards can be counted on to brighten the room and see the silver lining. She acts as voice of reason, peacemaker and general source of good cheer. Despite the frequent insanity around her, she never gives up her role as healer of disagreements.

The Girl Next Door always has a good word

She never lets bad luck get her down. Think of Mary Ann from *Gilligan's Island*. She might not get the admiring glances that followed Ginger's every move, but her fresh faced optimism is always welcome. The genuine affection the other castaways feel for her is never in doubt.

The Girl Next Door is willing to lend a hand

In *While You Were Sleeping*, Lucy Moderatz gets caught up in a tissue of lies, all stemming from the purest of motives. She has nothing to gain from the situation she finds herself in. She claims to be the mugging victim's fiancée only so the hospital

---

Margin notes:

Is she the son her father never had? Or was she overshadowed by a glamorous older sister? Did her mother place little importance on looks and instead emphasized getting along with everyone?

Mary Tyler Moore as Mary Richards in the TV series *The Mary Tyler Moore*

Dawn Wells as Mary Ann Summers in the TV series *Gilligan's Island*

Sandra Bullock as Lucy Moderatz in *While You Were Sleeping*

Whoopi Goldberg as Deloris Van Cartier in *Sister Act*

will permit her to see him, Lucy is lost in a maze of misunderstandings that arouse her guilty conscience. But her subsequent inability to tell his family the truth arises from concern for them, not herself.

In *Sister Act*, Deloris Van Cartier has plenty of reason to feel overwhelmed and sorry for herself. But she has no time for self pity. Aside from avoiding the bad guys, there is a convent that needs just the kind of good spirited help she can offer.

STYLES
. . . or else she is the WORKING GIRL

Not quite as cheerful as the Girl Next Door, this SPUNKY KID has a tad more cynicism. Of course, she thinks of it as realism. No rose colored glasses cover her eyes, and she does not think the world owes her a living. Prepared to pay her dues for her successes, she never looks for anyone to give her a handout.

Melanie Griffith as Tess McGill in *Working Girl*

In *Working Girl*, Tess McGill was enrolled in night school while working days in the financial district as a secretary. Her abilities are overlooked by the prep school types, but she believes in herself and watches for her chance. But when her talents earn her a secretary of her own, she is almost incredulous—she was going to get the coffee herself.

The Working Girl has game

She jumps at opportunities, or makes her own. Never one to hold back in her efforts, she throws herself into her work, determined to make lemonade with the lemons life hands her.

Stephanie Plum in the Janet Evanovich mystery series

Stephanie Plum, the plucky heroine of Janet Evanovich's mystery series, seizes the day, and always comes through in the end. Who would think a lingerie buyer could become a primo bounty hunter? Gutsy perseverance makes up for lack of experience.

The Working Girl maintains her sense of humor

Cathy in the comic strip *Cathy* by Cathy Guisewite

Cathy in Cathy Guisewite's comic strip, lives the life of the single woman in the big city. She never lets go of her optimism, but never quite has her head in the clouds either. She faces career pitfalls, blind dates, smothering parents and a clicking biological clock—all with a rueful smile and a sassy remark.

Valerie Harper as Rhoda Morgenstern in the TV series *The Mary Tyler Moore Show*

Remember Rhoda Morgenstern from *The Mary Tyler Moore Show*? Unlucky in love, she keeps trying, always ready with a sarcastic quip. More often than not, she is her own target of her good humor. The Working Girl is not trying to get a laugh at someone else's expense. She just knows that the world laughs with—not at—the one who can laugh at herself.

OCCUPATION

Continuous interaction with people must be a part of any job for the SPUNKY KID.

DISC JOCKEY

The warmth and banter of a radio station is one of the things the SPUNKY KID loves about her job. Her job performance has nothing to do with her looks but, instead, depends on her quick repartee and biting humor.

Her low-key humor and sarcastic asides win her fans galore, and she loves meeting them in person. She is the first to volunteer for the station's publicity gigs and enjoys meeting her adoring public.

REPORTER

This woman enjoys the fast pace and contact with a variety of people. Identifying with the disadvantaged, she goes the extra mile to nail a bad guy or to figure out who is cheating the public. She is always the first one to grasp the perfect angle the story should take.

She is not afraid to dive in and take chances if she thinks a story is important. She is generous with the glory, too, and her co-workers uniformly like and respect her. The SPUNKY KID keeps her word and her sources know they can trust her with inside information.

GOVERNESS

The children adore her. She is serious about the daily lessons but not averse to taking time out to climb the nearest apple tree. Although she will punish a wayward child, she is also quick to give warm hugs and praise when praise is due.

Not too keen about all the restrictions and rules, she is determined to find ways around them so she and her charges can have fun while learning. The SPUNKY KID is not one for pomp and circumstance. She often hides a biting wit behind her downcast gaze.

SPUNKY KIDs
• are friendly with everyone
• can mediate problems with compassion and fairness
• are good at finding practical solutions and
• believe in the innate good-ness of people

Other occupations SPUNKY KIDs might have:
• wedding planner
• high school teacher
• police dispatcher
• hotel manager
• physical therapist
• pet shopowner
• human resource manager

THE FREE SPIRIT

Skipping through life, the FREE SPIRIT is genuine, fun-loving and energetic. She may be a handful for anyone who has to deal with her, but she makes the experience worthwhile in her zany, high-spirited way. Impossible to be mad at for any length of time, she charms the socks off everybody who gets sucked into her orbit.

Because she is impulsive, she often finds herself in jams and needs help getting out of them. Luckily for her, there is usually someone around to pick up the pieces. Or else, her crazy logic will save the day. Either way, she lands on her feet, ready for the next adventure.

The FREE SPIRIT makes decisions with her emotions. She depends on her instincts to direct her path. To others, her decision making process may seem wacky at best, but to her, it only makes sense to follow her inner voice. To the surprise of her family and friends, she often comes out of situations a winner. But she never had any doubts.

Planning is not in her vocabulary. She is sometimes overwhelmed by all the promises she has made to numerous friends—and those are just the promises she remembers! And she can be a compulsive talker, monopolizing the conversation, spinning endless tales of delight. Her friends are thankful that her anecdotes are always amusing, but not so thankful when she interferes in their lives—with only the best intentions, of course.

QUALITIES

She is ready to lend a hand to any project, but when the going gets tough, she is often out to lunch.

VIRTUES

- *Sincere*—The FREE SPIRIT always lets people know right where she stands. She is not conniving because it is so much easier to be honest and truthful. Being a genuine person is her natural instinct, and this is a woman who always follows her instincts.
- *Upbeat*—Life inevitably seems to work out for this woman. Her sunny disposition makes it easy for her to see the bright side of every situation. The FREE SPIRIT has nine lives, and she believes in the possibilities of tomorrow. She knows there

---

Sidebar:

Think about...
Lucille Ball as
Lucy Ricardo in
the TV series
I Love Lucy

Calista Flockhart
as Ally in the
TV series
Ally McBeal

The
FREE SPIRIT:
- is a woman
  who lives in
  the present
- is an "original"
- is a trendsetter
  and
- is slightly
  eccentric

is a solution to every problem, she merely has to figure out who to call.

- *Imaginative*—Many people watch this woman in action and write her off as a ditz. Untrue. The FREE SPIRIT is amazingly resourceful and ingenious when she needs to be. She might stumble along the way, but she accomplishes the task set before her.

FLAWS

- *Impulsive*—Oh, if only this woman would think just a little before she goes out the door in the morning. The FREE SPIRIT sometimes (unintentionally, of course), hurts people because she speaks before she thinks and acts before she plans.
- *Meddling*—A long rocky road, paved with good intentions, stretches behind this woman. The FREE SPIRIT has a finger in everybody's pie and loves to stir her friends' pots. She is uncontrollably drawn to interfere, regardless of the wishes of her victims.
- *Undisciplined*—Jill of all trades but master of none, the FREE SPIRIT rarely sticks with anything for long. Erratic, she never writes things down and constantly forgets her commitments. She flies by the seat of her pants, which makes fulfilling promises impossible.

But she also can:
- be a bit klutzy
- be an excessive talker
- be inclined to exaggerate and
- be easily distracted

BACKGROUND

The FREE SPIRIT had a strong sense of individuality

As soon as she popped her head over the edge of the crib, her wide-eyed enthusiasm enchanted all those around her. This child never did anything predictable, but she had such winning ways, no one objected to her methods. The FREE SPIRIT was loved by all. Happy, content and cheerful, she captured the adults' attention and inspired the children's mischief. Since kids are supposed to be spontaneous and carefree, no one worried about her tendency to leap before she looked.

Alice in *Alice in Wonderland* by Lewis Carroll

The FREE SPIRIT jumped from one prank to another

She was a favorite of her classmates, willing to try anything once . . . and often twice. The other boys and girls wanted some of her star dust to rub off on them. Being around this girl meant a good time, with a little spice thrown in. The combination was irresistible.

As she grew into her teenage years, her family and friends might have worried about her flighty behavior, but excused it. How could anyone stay angry at such an entertaining child?

The FREE SPIRIT followed her own path

This was the girl who had a different hair color each week and followed her own goofy fashion drum. Unconcerned about the impression she left, this young woman was certain that no matter what she wore to the prom, it would be the best outfit there. Within a few minutes of entering the ballroom, she had everyone convinced she was right.

Pursuing her education meant an entirely different thing to the FREE SPIRIT than what her family and tradition dictated. She was apt to pick up and move to New York to experience the big city, or start her own business, selling homemade soap from the back of her van. Just when disaster seemed imminent, she always pulled the rabbit from the hat and giggled when all were astonished at her luck.

STYLES

The FREE SPIRIT might be the COMEDIAN . . .

Her crazy sense of humor and buoyant personality are good defense mechanisms in which to hide her fear of belittlement. This FREE SPIRIT bowls everyone over with her enthusiasm, concealing any troubled thoughts. Think of Muriel Pritchett in *The Accidental Tourist*. Quirky and opinionated, this gal bemuses her man and pushes him into seeing life in a whole new way.

The Comedian is always good for a laugh

Simultaneously, this woman dazzles with her smile and confuses with her scatterbrained logic. She is a little frenzied, a little brassy, but she can also step back and laugh at herself if the opportunity arises. Remember *Auntie Mame*? Patrick Dennis' hilarious tale of his upbringing tells of his dear aunt, Mame, and her crazy schemes. As an orphaned nephew, his life is turned upside down when he comes to live with this woman. One wild escapade after another ensues and he can barely catch his breath to express any kind of opinion on what is happening to him.

Were her parents hippies or conservatives? Did she have a strong support system or none at all?

Geena Davis as Muriel Pritchett in *The Accidental Tourist*

Mame in *Auntie Mame* by Patrick Dennis

The Comedian is hard to pin down

This woman won't sit still long enough for anyone to get a handle on her. Playful, creative and young at heart, she is loved by children and basks in the easy acceptance they offer. Grown men fall all over themselves to get near, and even other women are enthralled with her charisma. Gloria Mundy in *Foul Play* can do no wrong. Hopping from one near disaster to another, she comes out smelling like a rose.

Goldie Hawn as Gloria Mundy in *Foul Play*

She has hidden hurts and a desperate need to be accepted. Adults sometimes discount her because of her zany behavior and ideas. She finds herself caught in a vicious cycle, unable to show her serious and intelligent side without being ridiculed. So, she often slides back into the role that everyone expects of her. Think of Phoebe Buffay from the TV show *Friends*. Even her closest companions often sweep aside her suggestions, discounting her intuition until too late.

Lisa Kudrow as Phoebe Buffay in the TV series *Friends*

STYLES

. . . or else she is the DARLING

This FREE SPIRIT grew up loved and adored by everyone around her. Unlike her sister, the Comedian, she is too self-assured and overly optimistic. A classic example of this woman is Jane Austen's *Emma*. Sure of every opinion, Emma charges into her friends' love lives trying to be the ultimate matchmaker. Positive she knows best, she spends little time contemplating her own problems. Not until her disasters are brought forcefully to her attention, does she curb her spirits.

Emma in *Emma* by Jane Austen

The Darling believes in what she is doing

An extrovert, she lives for the next party or event. And she starts planning one right away if there is an open space on her calendar. She gets restless without a challenge to keep her occupied. Think of Ariel from *The Little Mermaid*. Warned by her father about the evils of the outside world, she ignores the advice and soon finds herself in hot water.

Ariel in Walt Disney's *The Little Mermaid*

The Darling is the world's greatest promoter

Remember Hazel Flagg in *Nothing Sacred*? This small town girl pretends to be dying from radium poisoning in order to win a trip to New York City. She has no idea of the repercussions of her actions.

Carole Lombard as Hazel Flagg in *Nothing Sacred*

She does not think things through. Since someone is always around to clean up her messes, the Darling rarely has to face the consequences of her actions. Somehow, it always seems to work out.

Dharma from the show *Dharma and Greg* has a plan for every occasion and effortlessly tugs her bemused husband along for the ride. With a bright smile and friendly manner, she wins over a reluctant set of in-laws and takes the starch out of them in the process. Never mind that they hold their breath when she walks into the room. Whether revamping a friend's wardrobe or setting up love matches, this woman is confident she can make a difference for the better. She might be a tad spoiled, but she has a heart of gold. She will do anything for her thousands of friends. Even disrupt their lives.

Jenna Elfman as Dharma in the TV series *Dharma and Greg*

OCCUPATION

The FREE SPIRIT gravitates to careers that allow her to express herself and her unconventional views.

FREE SPIRITs:
• charm others to work and volunteer for any job
• are innovative
• make emotional decisions that are unreasonable and illogical and
• waste a lot of time talking

BEAUTICIAN

She tries to answer all the phones and greet all the customers. Captivating and hospitable, she treats the salon as her home and all her clients as family. She has to make time for her friends, and the boss really should be more understanding about it.

Enthusiasm is this woman's middle name. While she may not always remember just exactly how the client wanted her hair cut, the FREE SPIRIT easily convinces her the punk hairdo is perfect for her.

KINDERGARTEN TEACHER

This woman loves children. She still has so much of the juvenile in herself that she immediate relates to every student in her room. The FREE SPIRIT enjoys helping children learn and seeing them blossom. Everyone's favorite teacher, she is loved by the kids.

While she does not much care for all the paperwork and considers the teachers' meetings deadly dull, she can quickly scamper back to her little charges and dive into the fun again. For her, there is nothing like a game of Candyland to brighten up the day.

SHOWGIRL

Entertainment is her life. The FREE SPIRIT naturally is drawn to anything with bright lights and applause. Tinsel on the outside, she is pure gold on the inside. She gives her last dollar to the down-on-his-luck cowboy because she never gives a minute's thought to where her next meal is coming from. Something will turn up!

She forgets her shoes and her fan, but her boss keeps her because once she gets on stage, she lights up the dance hall with her dazzling smile, sweet voice and colorful dancing.

Other occupations FREE SPIRITs might have:
• actress
• fashion designer
• travel agent
• receptionist
• florist
• retail store buyer
• manicurist
• jazz singer

THE WAIF

The WAIF projects a child-like innocence, a soul-stirring susceptibility. She is naïve, enigmatic, yet resilient. Everyone she meets wants to save her, but she can surprise people with her incredible inner strength and fortitude. She touches the vulnerable place deep inside all of us with her soft touch and wistful glance.

Think about...
Ingrid Bergman
as Ilsa Laszlo in
Casablanca

This woman has an ethereal quality, even though it may be hidden beneath layers of makeup, spandex and hair spray. Her delicate fragility makes her an easy target. She always seems to find herself between a rock and a hard place. But do not underestimate her. She adapts to any situation she falls into without complaint. The WAIF does not fight back; instead, she endures untold hardships until she is rescued.

Demi Moore as
Molly Jensen in
Ghost

Drifting through life, this woman desperately seeks a home base. She dreams of warm hugs, happy families and a sweet life, but she never seems to find herself in this happy picture. The WAIF draws the attention of the wolves of this world and she has no clue about how to get rid of them.

With the advent of feminism, this heroine has come under considerable attack. But she still exists and her power as an appealing woman cannot be denied. There is something refreshing about a heroine who does not talk back or fight every battle, but rather, allows a man to be a man and believes that if left well enough alone, situations will resolve themselves.

QUALITIES

The WAIF is the two faces of every man's fantasy. She is both Madonna and whore.

The WAIF:
• is sensitive
  and gracious
• is patient and
• is gentle

VIRTUES

- *Pure*—She might have come through terrible traumas, but there is still something about the WAIF that is genuine and unspoiled. Inside she remains uncorrupted by the mean, cruel world. The taint of rage and suspicion never seems to touch her.
- *Trusting*—The WAIF greets the world with an open response, a fresh enthusiasm. A child at heart, she is willing to risk everything for a chance at happiness. Her natural inclination is to commit herself into someone else's care.

• *Kind*—Generous and warm-hearted, the WAIF extends her aid to anyone in need. She goes out of her way to make sure everyone is helped and to offer a sympathetic hand. Since she often needs to be saved herself, it is understandable that she is so attuned to others' distress.

FLAWS

• *Impressionable*—She is easily influenced by those around her. The same trusting nature that endears her to all allows others to take advantage of the WAIF. Pliable and naive, she submits to any strong opinion, trusting the judgment of others over her own.

But she also can:
• be long-suffering
• be easy prey and
• be off in another world

• *Passive*—It is easier for the WAIF to give in rather than to fight for herself. She goes along to get along. Her submissiveness can attract men who demand all of the control, and her fear can overwhelm any desire to escape.
• *Insecure*—The WAIF is ruled by her vulnerability, and she often finds herself in trouble because of it. She wants so badly to be loved that she rushes into relationships, hoping and praying that they will work. She is not sure her opinion is important. In fact, she wonders if maybe *she* is unimportant.

BACKGROUND

The WAIF was molded by her sense of isolation

Sweet and unsure, this baby girl searched every adult face looking for the love she so desperately desired, but never found the answer in anyone's gaze. She was an orphan, whether literally or simply because her family failed to give her the love and attention she craved. She never found a support system—which was the one thing she truly needed.

Judy Garland as Dorothy in *The Wizard of Oz*

She was easily intimidated by the playground bully, but her pretty face and gentle manner inevitably drew many a rescuer to her side, much to her relief. This child never initiated contact with the other kids; but if someone sought her out, she was a loyal and true friend. But she usually was disappointed in the end. She never anticipated the betrayals or power games common in childhood.

The WAIF escaped one disaster after another

This girl never had one person's attention, never found her rightful place. Looking for love, she drifted from her father to

Was this girl the pampered daughter of the richest man in town who was never around? Or did she grow up dirt poor? What if her mother continually belittled her? Or was she a street kid quietly struggling for her existence?

her mother, from teacher to coach, from boyfriend to boyfriend, trying to find comfort from the storm.

She was easily convinced to try out for the school play, or be a cheerleader, or run for homecoming queen: whatever her boyfriend, or mother, or teacher wanted for her—she agreed. But none of these activities seemed to touch her inner core. She still searched for that unreachable solace.

The WAIF accepted everyone and everything

Homework and good grades were never a priority for this girl. Higher education probably was not in her future. Unless, of course, she felt it was expected of her. Then she willingly went to her parents' alma mater and pledged the same sorority her mother, aunt and sisters had. She never criticized or complained about plans that were made for her and easily forgave any transgression against her.

STYLES
The WAIF might be the INNOCENT . . .

Juliet in *Romeo and Juliet* by William Shakespeare

Cloistered and sheltered, she has been given everything on a silver platter, but this child-woman lacks experience and street smarts. Think of Shakespeare's Juliet from *Romeo and Juliet*. Drawn into an illicit love affair with a mortal enemy of her family, she is unable to extract herself from the coming tragedy. When she thinks her true love has died, she seeks her own death instead of revenge.

The Innocent always falls for the wrong man

Amanda in *The Glass Menagerie* by Tennessee Williams

The trophy wife of a rich man or the daughter of a protective father, this WAIF is a butterfly trying to escape her suffocating cocoon. But her compliant and obedient nature makes it seemingly impossible for her to break free. Remember Amanda from *The Glass Menagerie*? This lovely girl wistfully dreams of breaking out of her small world, but instead, finds herself entertaining "gentlemen callers" at her mother's command.

The Innocent is smarter than she looks

Robin Wright as Princess Buttercup in *The Princess Bride*

Think of Princess Buttercup from *The Princess Bride*. At first, she believes she has lost her love, and thus submits to a betrothal made in hell. But once she realizes her mistake, nothing can persuade her to go through with the ceremony. Appearances can be deceiving. She may not be worldly, but the Innocent has a sharp mind. Somehow she finds the right path to take and she can be stubborn once she decides which way to go. When backed into a corner, she will strike back with any weapon she can find.

Always standing apart, she is an observer, not a participant in life. Because of this, she sees things others miss. Her artless awe of the world brings a fresh take to the cynical people trying to influence her decisions. Princess Aurora in *Sleeping Beauty* waits for her prince and awakens to a world filled with wonder and excitement. Her delight in a newfound love and the experience of being awakened touch many a hardened heart.

Princess Aurora in Walt Disney's *Sleeping Beauty*

STYLES
. . . or else she is the ORPHAN
This is the woman with a painful past, the parent-less child thrown out of her home or the tortured outcast from society. The story of Cinderella has been passed down for centuries and has tugged the heartstrings of countless boys and girls. Abused by her wicked stepmother and tormented by her hateful step-sisters, she accepts her lot and merely wishes for a better life.

The classic fairy tale *Cinderella*

The Orphan may have a hardened veneer, but it is only a brittle glass façade. Her spirit has been buffeted to the breaking point by the blows she has suffered, making her as fragile inside as the Innocent is on the outside. Roslyn Taber in *The Misfits* finds herself without a husband and without resources. But instead of ranting and raving at her fate, she stoically soldiers on. Her docile acceptance of this awful news draws many a savior's eye.

Marilyn Monroe as Roslyn Taber in *The Misfits*

The Orphan needs a knight in shining armor
Think of Thelma from *Thelma and Louise*. Verbally abused and dismissed by her husband, she is pushed into a weekend trip by her nagging friend. Unknowingly, this one step will set her free—inside and out. Louise rescues Thelma from her mundane and stifling existence. Thelma starts to take chances and live a little. But she still falls into situations where her kindness and pure heart are used against her.

Geena Davis as Thelma Dickinson in *Thelma and Louise*

The Orphan defends herself only out of desperation
Battered and bruised, she struggles on with the dim hope of salvation. This Rapunzel must wait for her prince to come and rescue her from her self-imposed ivory tower because she can-

Peta Wilson as
Nikita in the
TV series *La
Femme Nikita*

not do it herself. She takes action in her own defense, only after all hope of rescue is lost.

Nikita in *La Femme Nikita* is forced into the role of assassin and can never summon the energy or the heart to break free of her predicament. She tries to brace herself against any more hurt, striving to insulate her emotions from a world that has mercilessly abused her.

OCCUPATION

WAIFs
• are underesti-
 mated
• work best
 when they
 have a boss
 they want
 to please
• tend to
 procrastinate
 and
• never feel
 work is a
 priority

The WAIF never seeks out a position, she falls into one. Work is only a sideline, never a career.

WAITRESS

Juggling tables and soothing cranky customers is not what the WAIF really likes to do. But she has to pay the bills, so she is forced to continue in this dead-end job. She cannot seem to work fast enough or smile long enough to earn bigger tips, and her dreamy manner drives her boss up the wall.

She never loses her temper with obnoxious patrons, and in the end, everyone gets what they ordered. But this woman is just biding her time, hoping something better will come along.

ACTRESS

Other
occupations
WAIFs
might have:
• teacher's aide
• maid
• bus driver
• file clerk
• bank teller
• photographer's
 assistant
• cashier
• gardener
• cleaning lady

She has no problem with the long hours and the grueling press coverage. At least she has a job where she is told exactly what to do. She is allowed to hide behind the image, protecting her heart and soul from further agony.

The WAIF allows people to project onto her what they want to see, and because of this, she might well be one of the most famous actresses in Hollywood. She is compliant and easy to work with, but frequently is manipulated by those around her. Sometimes she becomes lost in what everyone else thinks she is, and needs help finding the way back to her true self.

INDENTURED SERVANT

Circumstances cast her adrift in the New World. The WAIF did not choose to leave the old ways behind, but she buckles down and endures this hardship as she has always done.

As a servant, she is neither the best nor the worst. Wanting to please, this woman often gets distracted by the footman's toothache or the cook's need for fresh parsley. Much to her master's annoyance.

THE LIBRARIAN

Everything in its place, and a place for everything. Even if the LIBRARIAN fails to actually achieve this sense of order, she does strive for it. Bright, conscientious and orderly, she values the intellectual world over the physical. Her attempts to classify and categorize help her maintain a view of life as a mental challenge

Dressed to repress, the LIBRARIAN does not lead with her sexuality. She lives in her head. She tends to think that only she has the answers. More often than not, she is right, but she can be a bit stubborn about considering other opinions. After reviewing her options, she chooses a path that suits her best. Once on course, she does well.

Still waters run deep. The LIBRARIAN might not be the Playboy centerfold, but when she lets her hair down, she reveals the passionate woman inside. After all, she actually read the *Kama Sutra*, instead of just looking at the pictures. Her capacity for excitement may be untapped, but it is there, just waiting to be released.

She is not the kind of woman to inspire a helping hand in others. Her straitlaced presence and keen mind discourage any encouraging words. Used to getting things done on her own, self reliance is her middle name. And she likes it that way. Other people's opinions can be messy and are often useless. She knows what she needs to do and she is not one to shirk her duty. After making all her decisions for so long, the thought of asking for assistance appalls her.

QUALITIES

The LIBRARIAN knows the location of every book—except the book of love.

VIRTUES

- *Efficient*—The LIBRARIAN gets things done. She does not procrastinate, she does not dither, she does not make excuses. She looks a matter over, decides how best to accomplish the task, and then she does it. Making it look easy is one of her specialties.
- *Serious*—She is not one to fool around. Life is work, not a walk in the park. The LIBRARIAN is earnest about things she cares about—whether her job or her friends or her love

Think about...
Kathleen Turner as Joan Wilder in *Romancing the Stone*

Katharine Hepburn as Rose Sayer in *The African Queen*

The LIBRARIAN:
• is solitary
• is analytical and
• is detail-oriented

life, if she ever gets one. She does have a sense of humor—but do not look for her to laugh off important issues.

- *Dependable*—Count on this woman. She never leaves anyone in the lurch. Her careful precision insures that the project is done exactly the right way with no mistakes. Once given a job, the LIBRARIAN sticks with it until certain it is completed and correct.

FLAWS

But she
also can:
- be introverted and uptight
- be socially insecure and
- be defensive about maintaining the status quo

- *Rigid*—The concept that "rules were made to be broken" is foreign to the LIBRARIAN. Change is not something she appreciates, especially if she is the one in charge. This lady has a stubborn streak, and if pushed too hard, she turns into a formidable obstacle.

- *Repressed*—Feelings are not subject to the same sort of analysis that facts are, and that makes feelings frightening. The LIBRARIAN hides behind her intelligence, creating her own safe world. She wonders what the outside world is like, but is too scared to jump in.

- *Perfectionist*—If a thing is worth doing, it is worth doing well. And if it is not done right the first time, try, try again. And again. Unless she is sure she can do it flawlessly, it might be best not to try at all. Or so the LIBRARIAN thinks.

BACKGROUND

The LIBRARIAN's family was probably bewildered by her early displays of bright inquiry. If her family valued beauty over brains, she suffered, but if born into an intellectual family, she was in her element. Shying away from girlish pursuits like doing her nails and chasing the boys, this girl learned to keep her nose in a book if she wanted to be safe and secure.

Daria in the animated series on Comedy Central

The LIBRARIAN's gifts set her apart

Her exceptional talents separated her from other children. She never really fit into the mainstream; something set her apart. She might have been brighter than other children her age, or perhaps she was a prodigy of some kind. She may have reveled in her loner status, or wistfully wished she could be like everyone else. Either way, her identity is entirely structured by a sense of not really belonging.

This was the girl who knew every answer on the science quiz. Inwardly directed, she had few, if any, dates in high school. To hide her dismay, she spent all her time in the library, researching her next history project. She was the class valedictorian, but every now and then, she secretly yearned to be the Prom Queen.

The LIBRARIAN never felt pretty. A plain mud hen surrounded by beautiful swans, this girl never learned to used her feminine wiles to succeed. Instead, she made her way using what was above her neck, not below. Since she found success with her methods, she lifted her nose at her peers who used other means. She might envy the social success of the other girls, but she would never have traded her intelligence for their beauty. Or so she tells herself.

The LIBRARIAN thirsted for knowledge

Books were her closest friends, and she never abandoned them. Her education, formal or self pursued, never ends. Her attempts to fit into society occur less and less as she immersed herself in whatever career she had chosen. She might not ever achieve glamour and excitement, but she is determined to make a difference in her own way.

STYLES

The LIBRARIAN might be the KNOW-IT-ALL . . .

Bright and confident, this LIBRARIAN has lots of facts at her fingertips. And she is happy to share them with anyone who is in need. She has no problem demonstrating her superior intelligence, and is not afraid to show her disdain for those who fail to measure up.

In *Cheers*, Diane Chambers has no doubt that she is head and shoulders above the rest of the habitués of the neighborhood bar in education, culture and intelligence. She would like nothing better than to raise the tone of the conversation, and keeps trying to do so, no matter how frequently she is rebuffed.

The Know-It-All has hidden passions

Unless the situation calls for a show of knowledge, this woman is not the life of the party. Unable to imagine herself using any skill other than her brain, she stuffs her emotions deep down inside. But beneath her cool exterior beats a passionate heart. In *The Big Easy*, Anne Osborne wears her prim attire like a suit of armor. She has no doubt that she will show the local police force how to clean up the corrupt city. But as the mystery heats

What happened during her childhood that caused her to be so reserved? Why is the intellectual life so important to her?

Shelley Long as Diane Chambers in *Cheers*

Ellen Barkin as Annie Osborne in *The Big Easy*

83

up, so does she. The sultry New Orleans atmosphere seeps beneath her icy exterior, and causes a meltdown.

The Know-It-All holds her own in any argument

Her measure of success is not snaring a husband or social position. She prefers the pleasures of the mind to outward shows. She uses her facility with language to present her views, however unpopular they may be. In *The Music Man*, Marian does not worry about her lack of popularity. She is fully satisfied that she has her priorities straight in preferring Balzac to balderdash.

Or, think of Rosalind in *As You Like It*. She displays her exceptional mental gifts in the brilliant flow of her conversation. Capable of conversing with all types, from fool to genius, this woman is sure of her position and delighted to engage in conversation in order to prove it.

STYLES
. . . or else she is the BOOKWORM

Like her more outspoken sister, this LIBRARIAN has a lot of book learning and a sparkling intelligence. She has a strong sense of humor, which she often exercises at the expense of others. Frequently, the victims of her sarcasm are oblivious, because her quips fly right over their heads. But this woman is used to laughing alone.

The Bookworm takes note of the details

Introverted, she is not distracted by outward appearances. She is able to take in fine points overlooked by more outgoing types. Agatha Christie's Miss Marple tends to be underestimated— what use is an old woman? But her powers of observation inevitably lead to discovery of the evil doer. Her command of logic and deductive reasoning, combined with her knowledge of human nature, make her one of the top amateur detectives in all of literature.

In Shakespeare's *The Merchant of Venice*, Portia cleverly discovers the loophole that saves Antonio's life. She points out the flaw in the contract—Shylock might have his pound of flesh, but only if he can procure it without spilling blood. Her clever reasoning turns a tragedy into a comedy.

The Bookworm carefully reviews all the angles of a situation. In *The X-Files*, Dana Scully's understated investigations lead the agents to the right solution. She takes her time, never jumps off

Shirley Jones as
Marian Paroo in
The Music Man

Rosalind in
As You Like It
by William
Shakespeare

Miss Marple in
*The Mirror
Crack'd* by
Agatha Christie

Portia in
*Merchant of
Venice* by
William
Shakespeare

half-cocked like her more emotional partner and considers all the evidence before coming to a conclusion.

The Bookworm is uncertain of her physical charms

Confident though she may be with her intellectual prowess, this woman does not think highly of her outward appearance. Abby Barnes, the witty and capable veterinarian of *The Truth About Cat & Dogs*, has much to offer. But she is convinced that her Plain Jane appearance cannot compete with a showier, but far less witty, woman.

OCCUPATION

The LIBRARIAN favors jobs that keep her in the background and allow her to deal more closely with information, rather than people.

RESEARCH SCIENTIST

She appreciates being judged and accepted for her mind, not her body. Since "just the facts, ma'am" is any lab's mantra, she fits right in. The LIBRARIAN feels good about helping society and is happy to do whatever it takes to make the breakthrough.

Her work is meticulous. When she comes to a conclusion, nobody has any doubt that she has the data to back up her claim.

ACCOUNTANT

She finds it enormously satisfying when the long column of statistics totals up just the way it should. Numbers are easy to work with and never get their feelings hurt. Not like people. No, sir. Numbers are terrific. Numbers are predictable. Numbers are her friends.

The LIBRARIAN is more comfortable in her tiny cubicle than she is going out and recruiting new clients. And do not expect her to be the life of the office Christmas party. But in this job, her assets definitely exceed her deficits.

SCHOOLMARM

Educating the children of the poor backwoods farmer is a worthwhile goal, and the seclusion of the frontier town gives her plenty of time alone with her books and papers. She enjoys keeping track of all the children's scores and making sure they all know the three R's.

Other occupations LIBRARIANs might have:
• musician
• professor
• astronaut
• loan processor
• chemist
• computer analyst
• IRS agent
• supreme court justice

Teaching requires more than "book learnin'." The LIBRAR-IAN actually has to deal with recalcitrant students and parents who pull their kids out of school at harvest time. But this lady never gives up. She is stubborn and determined to make a difference in her students' lives.

THE CRUSADER

Ready for action, the CRUSADER marches in. This is a heroine in the truest sense—deeds of valor are right up her alley. She is confident, tenacious and headstrong against opposition. Lines of battle have been drawn, and she never backs down from a contest. The world has veered off its course, and she is just the one to set it straight again. From her perspective, if she does not do it, it will probably not get done. Or at least, not done correctly.

The CRUSADER is a fighter, through and through. Do not try and calm her down or attempt to divert her into having a picnic. She just brushes right past, intent on her cause. If she meets up with a brick wall, she goes over, under or around, but quitting is never an option.

The task in front of her is all-important and everyone should realize that. She walks right past those who disagree. Anyone not part of the solution is part of the problem. Her compassion is for those she champions, not the people she tramples over to succeed in her mission.

She has no faith in the intrinsic merit of human nature; no belief that all will end well if left alone. The CRUSADER knows that action is necessary, and she is the one to get the job done. Fully prepared to stand alone against the enemy, she views those who fall short of her rigid standards with scorn. If necessary, she can become a one woman army.

QUALITIES
The CRUSADER believes in commitment, but is much more committed to a cause than to her loved ones.

VIRTUES
- *Courageous*—This woman risks everything in pursuit of her mission. The CRUSADER faces danger, of any kind, without flinching. Brave in the face of opposition and bolder than many a man, she is fiercely resolved to win every encounter.
- *Resolute*—The CRUSADER's determination is absolutely unyielding. She has decided which side is right and will not be swayed from her path. Her intense focus on every mission makes her an extremely formidable opponent.
- *Persuasive*—The belief in her cause shines in her eyes and gives her the words to convince almost everyone of the righteous-

Think about…
Helen Hunt
as Jo Harding
in *Twister*

Julia Roberts as
Erin Brockovich
in *Erin Brockovich*

The
CRUSADER:
- is determined
- is dynamic and
- is not easily
  discouraged

87

ness of her position. If the CRUSADER needs help, she uses reason or even emotion, whichever works, to gain supporters.

FLAWS

But she
also can:
• be stubborn
• be quick-
tempered and
• be so
engrossed in
her work that
she neglects
those closest
to her

• *Obstinate*—The CRUSADER is not easily diverted from her mindset or her goal—no matter how misguided her ideas, actions or presumptions are. And do not make the mistake of thinking she will be pleased to have any errors in her reasoning pointed out. Actually, this may cause her to dig her heels in even deeper.

• *Rash*—Stopping to think is never high on her list. She rushes in regardless of the fears of those around her. Personal safety is not a priority for the CRUSADER. Her cause is more important. Her reckless attitude might win the battle, but it can also lose the war.

• *Opinionated*—She has no trouble saying what she really thinks, regardless of the wisdom of speaking up at a particular moment. Issues regarding the CRUSADER's mission are non-negotiable in her mind. Her strident statement of her position can easily raise hackles in others.

BACKGROUND

The CRUSADER has always fought for her cause

The CRUSADER's personality developed from her reaction to injustice. She never turned her face to the wall. Whether she personally experienced the wrong or merely witnessed it, this defining moment molded her into an avenging angel.

Mulan in
Walt Disney's
Mulan

Her parents may have been amazed by her tireless energy and capacity to feel the pain of others. Or maybe they were the source of the injustice she fought. Was her childhood one traumatic event after another, requiring her to develop the skills to face life's battles? Or did she learn about the harsh realities from the safety of her living room? Whatever happened in her past, she is not capable of letting go or forgetting.

The CRUSADER made a difference

She did her best to drag the other kids into her campaigns. Charity races, walk-a-thons, or just standing up to a bully, she roused her playmates to the cause. She championed the most unpopular victims, because it was the right thing to do.

Intense and directed, she was involved only in high school activities with importance far beyond those hallowed halls. She saved the whales, ran the food drive or, while serving as school newspaper editor, butted heads with the principal over student rights. She also devoted some time to her studies, but only if education fit into her long term plan of action.

The CRUSADER never eased up

Too busy for a social life, she never had a date unless it was for a protest march. A boyfriend would have demanded way too much of her precious time. She assumed there would be time enough for romance when the struggle was over. Whatever the battle, she was certain that if she did not do the job, no one else would. Or, at least, no one would do it as well as she could. In her experience, if events were left to themselves, the world fell apart. She neither gave nor accepted excuses.

Does she feel responsible for the wrong she is trying to right? Or does she feel a need to give back because she has been so fortunate?

STYLES

The CRUSADER might be the ZEALOT . . .

This CRUSADER moves unswervingly towards her goal, and heaven help anyone who gets in the way. She is a true believer in the absolute necessity for the completion of her task. This Superheroine pulls off the impossible task, while making it look all in a day's work.

The Zealot has a mission

She has to save the world. It is her duty, her mission, her purpose in life. *Buffy, The Vampire Slayer* was destined from birth for her demon-fighting role. She is totally committed to the literal protection of the world from evil. Her persistence in the drive to overcome obstacles standing in front of her is unwavering.

Sarah Michelle Gellar as Buffy in the TV series *Buffy, The Vampire Slayer*

In Damon Runyon's *Guys and Dolls*, Sister Sarah answers her calling to save souls from the vices that tempt them. She is fervent in her belief, and certain of the righteousness of her cause. In the face of temptation, it is she who entices the sinner to the moral path.

Sister Sarah Brown in *Guys and Dolls* by Damon Runyon

The Zealot does not let personal matters interfere with her goals

When she is in the heat of battle, she has no time or interest for anything else. She is able to direct her focus with single-minded determination. Think of Joan from *Messenger: The Story of Joan of Arc.* This young girl believes her mission is a task given to her by God and no one can persuade her otherwise. Fervent

Milla Jovovich as Joan of Arc in *Messenger: The Story of Joan of Arc*

89

and devout, her passionate views transform her into a mighty force that changes the political landscape. She may lose the battle, but she does win the war.

The burning desire to change the world pervades her life. The Zealot brooks no interference and takes no prisoners. *Xena, Warrior Princess* gives up any pretense of a "normal" life without blinking an eye, if it means that she is one step closer to her objective. Her strength of will and indomitable spirit make it impossible for this woman to understand why other people give up in the face of adversity. She believes that fear is usually the strongest enemy, and she shows how to put that enemy to rout. She never gives up and never gives in. Never.

Lucy Lawless as Xena in the TV series Xena, Warrior Princess

STYLES
. . . or else she is the RESCUER

This CRUSADER is not out to save the whole universe—just the piece of it that belongs to her. All is not right with her world. She steps up to the plate when a pinch hitter is needed.

The Rescuer rights wrongs

She knows she has the right and obligation to go after what she wants. *Norma Rae* has to fight and fight hard for fair wages and treatment, but she keeps going even the face of the jeers and taunts of her fellow workers. This woman is not just going to make things right, she is going to make them better than right.

Sally Field as Norma Rae in Norma Rae

Sophocles' tale of *Antigone*, one of the first heroines in literature, shows a woman who will not be swayed even by the threat of death from following the path she knows is right. The gods demand certain funeral rites. It is her duty to see that her brother is able to go to the underworld. She will face execution rather than allow the body of her brother to go unburied. She wars against the male power structure, and shows far greater bravery than any of the men who scorn her.

Antigone in Antigone by Sophocles

The Rescuer pushes back

The Rescuer has a specific target, and is determined to wage war until she has won. She fights back when wronged. She bides her time, watching for her chance to gain the upper hand. In *Jane Eyre*, Charlotte Brönte presents a heroine, unique for her time, who gives as good as she gets when faced with injustice and mistreatment.

Jane Eyre in Jane Eyre by Charlotte Brönte

90

In *Alien*, space trucker Ellen Ripley is not the captain, but when terror strikes, she takes control. Her primary goal is to get out alive. She uses every weapon at her disposal to defeat the savage alien. Utterly ruthless in battle, she is unclouded by conscience, remorse or delusions of morality. When it becomes clear that survival will cost the ship, she does not hesitate. Winning against this evil enemy is everything.

Sigourney Weaver as Ellen Ripley in Alien

OCCUPATION

The CRUSADER seeks out jobs that let her make an impact and change lives.

CRUSADERs
• move quickly to action
• excel in emergencies and
• command and inspire others

PARK RANGER

She is on the frontline in the battle to save the earth. All her energy goes into protecting the animals and the environment from those evil, marauding humans.

Her brisk manner does not always make her the easiest ranger to follow down the forest path. The CRUSADER knows her job, and she shares her breadth of knowledge with an enthusiastic idealism, but litterbugs had better not expect much compassion.

Other occupations CRUSADERs might have:
• social worker
• union organizer
• environmental activist
• adult education teacher
• feminist
• revolutionary
• cancer specialist

FIREFIGHTER

She is one of the few women on the force and she takes this responsibility seriously. Firmly believing in her right to be there, she is oblivious to the negative comments of her fellow firefighters. Rescuing babies from flaming buildings and resuscitating heart attack victims give her satisfaction. The CRUSADER *is* making a difference.

Her captain has one worry about her: she has a tendency to rush into burning homes before assessing the risk. But he has a hard time convincing her that she should think before she saves.

MISSIONARY

Whatever her cause, be it saving good men from the evils of demon liquor or working the deep jungles of Africa winning souls for her God, she has never been happier. Heat, sickness and danger scarcely penetrate this woman's consciousness.

No one could ask for a person with more stamina and determination, but the CRUSADER can be quite abrupt with anyone who disagrees with her. This woman is not a diplomat and she has no desire to become one.

THE NURTURER

The NURTURER takes care of everyone around her. She makes sure that all her loved ones are happy and content before taking a break or thinking of herself. Common sense and a steady hand make her an ideal mother, companion or friend. Her serene, capable and patient manner invariably soothes troubled souls or hurting hearts.

She is a wonderful listener, even if someone has told her the same story ten times. In an age where everyone is too busy to slow down and smell the roses, this woman knows how important it is to spend time on the things that really matter. Not distracted by the minutiae in life, she focuses on what truly counts.

Pleasant and enjoyable to have around, she can mediate any problem. People depend on her competence and steadiness in moments of crisis. She is the glue that holds everyone and every situation together. And she likes it that way. She has a need to be central and indispensable in the lives of those she loves.

The one problem this woman has is her inability to say "no." The NURTURER has a terrible time disappointing anyone. Instead, she finds herself working late into the night in order to satisfy all the demands of her family and friends. While quite good at dispensing sound advice, she sometimes has a difficult time following it herself.

Think about...
Barbara Billingsley as June Cleaver in *Leave It to Beaver*

Michelle Pfeiffer as Isabeau in *Ladyhawke*

QUALITIES

No sacrifice is too great for the NURTURER, and she never lets anyone forget it.

The NURTURER:
• is a mentor
• is calm, cool and collected
• is easy to get along with and
• has a will of iron

VIRTUES

• *Altruistic*—The NURTURER instinctively puts the needs of others before her own. She believes that she can make a difference in someone's life. She willing sacrifices her own interests to make sure that the person gets the help she thinks is needed.

• *Optimistic*—She sees people and their dreams through her rose-colored glasses. The NURTURER feels her job is to cheer others on and encourage them to achieve. "Everything works out for the best" is this woman's motto. If someone believes long enough in something, it is sure to happen.

• *Capable*—This woman is a rock in a crisis. The NURTURER is great under pressure and keeps her head when those around her are losing theirs. Competent and composed, she is unflappable when the storm hits and unshakable when the rebuilding begins.

FLAWS

- *Idealistic*—She wistfully dreams of a utopian existence where everyone gets along, but often is disappointed when those around her argue and cause pain. The NURTURER spends her life trying to make everyone happy, but can never entirely succeed.
- *Self-sacrificing*—Why does she always end up doing everything? Maybe because she cannot say no, but when she is tired, the NURTURER feels put upon and blames others for all the work she does. Martyrdom lurks right around the corner.
- *Compromising*—The NURTURER never wants to hurt anyone's feelings. She struggles until the bitter end trying to find a solution that makes everyone happy. She compromises her very soul in order to stop a disagreement.

But she also can:
- be long-suffering
- hold a grudge and
- resent being pushed around

BACKGROUND

The NURTURER needed to be needed

From an early age, the NURTURER found satisfaction in taking care of other people. She was the little girl who made sure all the kids were included in the games or the kid who sat up with her sick grandma, bringing the patient everything that was needed. By trying to guarantee everyone around her was happy, she gained a sense of fulfillment. After awhile, she came to crave this feeling of satisfaction on a continual basis.

Hayley Mills as Pollyanna in *Pollyanna*

The NURTURER reveled in the experience of caring for others

She loved cuddling the babies and kissing the toddlers. Every mother in the neighborhood vied to get this girl as their babysitter. The mundane tasks of bathing, feeding and caring for children was a pleasure for this girl. It gave meaning to her life. She might have been the eldest sister whose mother depended on her to keep her siblings safe and the house well-kept.

Though some of the kids labeled her a goody-two-shoes, she was universally liked in high school. She was president of the Future Homemakers of America or the Volunteer of the Year for a local service organization. A friend to all, her relaxed personality and good listening skills meant she was often the one who spotted trouble before it happened. And she made sure the

Was her need to love and be loved fulfilled in her childhood, or is she still searching for it? Did she care for her younger siblings after a parent's death? Was she an only child who yearned for a big family?

issue was resolved before she walked away. Because of this, the teachers grew to depend on her as the peacemaker.

The NURTURER loved to be with people

Warm and congenial, this young woman often found herself married early, with a baby on the way. And she was perfectly content with this outcome. But she also could find herself pursuing a higher education if she felt it would help her help more people. She could become very determined if the bottom line meant something to others. Never ruffling feathers, she still found a way to make her dreams come true.

STYLES

The NURTURER might be the CAREGIVER . . .

Emma Thompson as Elinor Dashwood in *Sense and Sensibility*

This kind of a NURTURER is confident in her role. She grew up with nurturing role models, and her impulse to care for others was encouraged and rewarded. Because of this, she is laid-back and secure. Think of Elinor Dashwood from Jane Austen's *Sense and Sensibility*. Warm and accepting, she tends to her sister's future, cares for sick neighbors, but yearns for a husband and home of her own in the privacy of her thoughts.

The Caregiver always creates a home wherever she is

Michael Learned as Ma Walton in the TV series *The Waltons*

This woman is happiest tending to her household or holding a friend's hand through a crisis. Never one to fret, she has a beaming smile and a plate of cookies ready for her welcome guests. Ma Walton from *The Waltons* is a perfect example of this kind of woman. Happy to create a loving home for her big family, she makes sure everyone has a full belly and a contented smile on their face.

Isabella in *Measure for Measure* by William Shakespeare

With a garden of flowers on her apartment's front stoop, a pot of homemade soup on the stove and a half-woven scarf on her loom, the Caregiver's peaceful and agreeable personality makes everyone happy to be around her. Shakespeare's Isabella from *Measure for Measure* is drawn out of her path toward the nunnery in order to save her brother's life. Her lovely presence turns the tables on the villain and she finds true love because of her loyalty to her family.

The Caregiver is happiest at home

Content with herself, she does not spend a lot of time worrying about getting ahead at work. She would much rather be at home tending the hearth and her family's needs. Dorothy Boyd in *Jerry Maguire* believes in her boss' principles—even when he does not. She is willing to go with him to build a new business; her strength and encouragement—and acceptance of his foibles—are the real reasons behind his success. But her heart is with her young son and she dreams of a happy home life instead of money and power.

Renée Zellweger as Dorothy Boyd in *Jerry Maguire*

STYLES

. . . or she is the WISE WOMAN

Bound by duty and love, this NURTURER cares for her family and friends with a steely determination. She is the woman who has seen it all and knows just what advice to dispense. And she is sure to make all those around her aware of her sage guidance. Think of Claire Huxtable in *The Cosby Show*. While her husband cracks jokes and her children squabble between themselves, this woman's steady hand makes sure that all will be well.

Phylicia Rashad as Claire Huxtable in the TV series *The Cosby Show*

The Wise Woman has "been there, done that"

Though she may not always relish the job of mother and housewife, or resident keeper, she is willing to dig into the work to make sure things are done correctly. She takes excellent care of each person in her orbit. Nothing gets past this woman. She has eyes in the back of her head, and kids, husbands and co-workers know not to try and pull any tricks with her around. Remember *Mary Poppins*? This governess descends on her family and soon has the household running like clockwork. No one can imagine what they did without her.

Julie Andrews as Mary Poppins in *Mary Poppins*

The Wise Woman is efficient and in control

She might nag a bit, but only because she knows what is best for all around her, and she wants to make sure everyone is content and happy. Her sound advice is invariably correct and she shakes her head when others fail to follow her suggestions. Deanna Troi, the ship counselor from *Star Trek: The Next Generation*, knows when her crewmates are troubled, and her job is to help them through it. She never fails.

Marina Sirtis as Counselor Deanna Troi in the TV series *Star Trek: The Next Generation*

Many times, her own needs are lost in the constant whirlwind of taking care of all the people she feels tied to. But the Wise Woman always finds a way to get everything done. She is determined that those she loves will never go wanting. Think of Ruth from the Old Testament. A widow, she takes her moth-

Ruth in the Old Testament

er-in-law, Naomi, under her wing and manages to survive against all odds. This enduring love story between two women is a testament to true kindness.

OCCUPATION

The NURTURER is happiest with occupations that allow her to serve and care for others.

PARAMEDIC

Her hours are filled with saving people, and she finds enormous satisfaction in that. She likes holding the hand of the kid who broke his leg. She finds it gratifying to console the woman who lost her husband.

The NURTURER is best at working with people—both those she works beside and those she helps. Her skills are exceptional when a crisis hits. She never loses her cool. In an emergency, she knows who needs her help and gives it gladly.

SOCIAL WORKER

The NURTURER knows that all her hard work is worthwhile when a child lights up because he is being placed in a loving home, when a couple completes the adoption process, or when a man stops taking drugs. She is totally committed to the families she is trying to help.

This woman is often commended for her hard work. She steers through the rapids of office politics to give aid to those who need it. Her calm demeanor and pleasant attitude hide a heart that weeps for those she is unable to help.

LADY of the MANOR

Happy and content as the wife of the local nobleman, she enjoys her children, and supports and encourages her husband. Taking care of her tenants with healing herbs gives her endless satisfaction. She revels in all her tasks.

Her eternal optimism in life's possibilities prods her family to go on, even through the obstacles. She is there to hug and kiss her children when they fall or to console her husband when the crops fail. The NURTURER is the foundation on which her family is built.

NURTURERs
• are good mediators
• are skilled at drawing out people
• handle crises well and
• find ways to make everyone happy

Other occupations NURTURERs might have:
• homemaker
• pediatric doctor
• defense lawyer
• nanny
• special education teacher
• nun
• nursery school owner

SECTION III
USING THE ARCHETYPES TO CREATE CHARACTERS

As more than one writer has noted, character is plot. The events occurring in a story cannot be separated from the characters involved in those events. Instead, the action in a story, from the inciting incident to the epilogue, must be inevitable in light of the personalities of the characters. Accordingly, fiction writers must aspire to create living, breathing, feeling characters to inhabit their stories.

So how is it done? Why do some characters seem to leap off the page and dance around the armchair where the reader sits, devouring page after page? Or, on the other hand, why do some heroes and heroines never manage to connect with the reader, leaving them to fade into obscurity?

The sixteen archetypes described in the previous pages comprise the basis for the population of all good fiction. To create dynamic characters instead of forgettable ones, writers must begin with the universal elements of character that the audience is predisposed to recognize, accept and enjoy. Any memorable character created by a fiction writer has its roots in these frameworks. This basis gives a firm foundation to any writer—beginning or advanced.

But only the basis. A writer cannot simply lift the archetypes from these pages and paste them into a new work. This would only create wooden heroes and one dimensional heroines. Instead, the writer must mix in his own view of life, using his own experiences to shed new light on these ancient forms. The

Archetypes provide the universal elements upon which to base characters

breath of life for these characters comes from the writer, not the archetypal system.

Think of a budding character as a lump of raw clay that can be molded into any shape the writer envisions. The archetype is the clay. As the writer works the clay, certain features appear as various decisions are made. What kind of background does this character have? Who were his parents? Does she have sisters? What was his childhood like? Happy? Frightening? A mix of joy and sadness? These decisions regarding the final sculpture must be consistent with the chosen archetype, but are otherwise wholly within the writer's discretion.

The writer must answer other questions. What qualities will be emphasized, which others downplayed? What style is this hero or heroine? What occupation will this character have? And, most of important at all, how do these decisions affect the plot and the conflicts in the story?

The process by which the personality is sculpted varies from writer to writer. Some writers might fill these details in as they write, adding the bits and pieces of clay as needed. Others feel more comfortable exploring their characters, mapping out every aspect of the final piece of work before a single word is committed to a computer screen file. Neither method is better than the other. Only the writer can decide the method that works best for a particular story.

There is one more decision a writer must make as she creates her characters. The archetypal system is not rigid in its use. There are a variety of ways that it can be utilized. In the following section, we discuss the three ways the archetypes may be used in creating a hero or a heroine.

There is not only one way to create a hero or heroine

CORE ARCHETYPES

First, a writer may choose to create a core archetype. A core archetype fits wholly within the frame of a single archetypal description, and remains consistent in nature throughout the course of the story. A core archetype may experience his journey, grow and even change somewhat over the course of the tale, but when the story ends, will still fall within the same archetypal pattern.

EVOLVING ARCHETYPES

A writer may decide to create an evolving archetype. A character who is an evolving archetype begins the story as a member of one archetypal family, but is so changed during the course of the story that she is no longer a member of the original archetypal family, but has shifted into another.

LAYERED ARCHETYPES

Or, a writer may instead choose to create a layered archetype. A layered archetype combines attributes of two archetypal descriptions. One archetypal pattern is likely to be rather dominant within the character, but features of the secondary archetype shine through to reveal internal contradictions. Dominance of the archetypal family may shift during the story, but a layered archetype character concludes the story still defined by the same two archetypes.

Remember, no method of archetypal use is better than another and each of these methods can be found throughout centuries of literature. Each method has produced generations of well-rounded, fascinating heroes and heroines. The writer is free to chose the elements needed in order to create the characters wanted.

Specific characters demand certain stories. Certain stories demand specific characters. Whether a writer uses core, evolving or layered archetypes, the key is to breathe life into the hero and heroine by using the archetype as a starting point, not the end of creativity.

There are THREE ways to create great characters:
• Core Archetypes
• Evolving Archetypes
• Layered Archetypes

CORE ARCHETYPES

Some characters are so clearly drawn that the audience knows, truly and completely knows, that character. Think of Mr. Spock, of *Star Trek* fame. "Fascinating," he says, and the audience immediately comprehends what he is thinking. His character is so well understood that a single word is sufficient to convey his thoughts. How can this man convey the essence of himself using so little?

And what about *Wonder Woman* strutting across the screen or comic strip page, bringing order and justice to a world gone awry? Can anyone doubt she will find the most expedient means to foil the villains, all without mussing a hair? Is there any question at all regarding her actions?

Why? Why are some characters so dynamic that they evoke loyalty and applause year after year? Why do they become cultural icons, known across generations, class lines and territorial borders?

Because audiences enjoy characters who deliver as promised.

When one of the sixteen archetypes described in Sections I and II is used in its pure form, it is a core archetype. A core archetype does not deviate from the essence of the archetypal characteristics. His motivations stay true to type; her goals are wholly consistent with her manner. Do not make the mistake of scorning such clear-cut characters. Writers who employ core archetypes are not using stereotypes. Every example given from literature, film and television in Sections I and II is a core archetype, yet all are complex, living, breathing plausible people.

Using one core archetype creates powerful heroes and heroines. Audiences may love to hate these characters, or they may hate to leave at the end of the story. But audience reaction is never neutral. The essence of the collective unconscious touched by these archetypal souls invariably invokes strong response.

Use of a core archetype does not limit the writer's choices. There are an infinite number of potential variations in each of the heroes and heroines outlined in the previous pages. The unique combination of chosen traits and backgrounds provides a writer endless possibilities in populating his stories with fascinating characters.

Consider again Mr. Spock. He is a core PROFESSOR through and through. His internal conflicts derive from his

Leonard Nimoy as Mr. Spock in the TV series *Star Trek*

Lynda Carter as Diana Prince in the TV series *Wonder Woman* commitment to logic and his unwillingness to accept and embrace the emotional aspects of his personality. Many episodes of *Star Trek* are devoted to exploring the inherent conflicts that exist within this core archetype. Decades after the TV program ended, and years after Leonard Nimoy last appeared in a *Star Trek* film, this hero is still as clear in people's minds as any ever created.

But this Professor is very different from Seth Brundle, the core PROFESSOR presented in *The Fly*. Seth was devoted to his research in the development of teleportation. His commitment to the expansion of knowledge extended to risking his life to test his prototype, resulting in tragedy. Even as he was faced with horrific changes, he pursued his research, causing viewers to be very afraid.

Jeff Goldblum as Seth Brundle in The Fly

Sherlock Holmes is still another example of a core PROFESSOR, yet very different from his brothers Spock and Brundle. Like Spock, he is a devotee of logic. Like Brundle, he is willing to risk his life to reach a solution. But he has no wish to reject his human heritage, and no audience was ever afraid of Holmes' fanaticism. Even though all three of these characters are wholly confined to a single archetype, there is no mistaking one for the other. They are not interchangeable. Indeed, writers in the *Star Trek* universe have even poked fun at the very notion that archetypal characters are mere reproductions of each other by having yet another core PROFESSOR, Lieutenant Commander Data, act out his fantasy of being Sherlock Holmes. The result was always most un–Holmes-like and proved the point that each of these PROFESSORs are unique.

Sir Arthur Conan Doyle's Sherlock Holmes

The number of possibilities are similarly limitless within each archetypal family. Consider the CRUSADER archetype. Super heroine Wonder Woman fits the bill perfectly. But so does Ripley from *Alien*, who battled relentlessly against the murderous foe without benefit of super powers. And both of these women are very different from *Jane Eyre* who championed other, less brave, souls. All are core CRUSADERS but each is a very different woman.

Sigourney Weaver as Ellen Ripley in Alien

Jane Eyre in Jane Eyre by Charlotte Brönte

A writer has much to gain by employing a core archetype:
- Core Archetypes are instantly recognizable. Unambiguous characters, they find their way into our cultural legacy. Everyone knows their names and knows what they believe.

Hamlet's anguish echoes through the ages. No one who has ever heard his story can forget this man's anger and pain at a parent's betrayal. A true LOST SOUL. His tragedy can never be forgotten.

Norma Rae's mission to change the workplace forced her into the role of a CRUSADER. Her personality highlighted and complimented the calling she had chosen. Her beliefs became her audience's.

- Core Archetypes live up to expectations. Whether good or bad, the reader is able to relax and enjoy the story instead of worrying about what will happen next. These characters are not confusing or contradictory.

A viewer watching Lucy Ricardo in *I Love Lucy* knows that ditsy Lucy will get in trouble. Every episode reinforces Lucy's core archetype, the FREE SPIRIT.

Indiana Jones, a SWASHBUCKLER, guarantees a wild ride. A film featuring this exciting character will not offer two hours of intellectual discourse. The audience is guaranteed an adventure, and they know it.

- Exaggerated core archetypes become "larger than life" heroes and heroines. The writer can embellish and embroider the personality without losing the character in a maze of varying motivations and goals.

Watching the Lone Ranger, a WARRIOR, ride across the plains, the loyal fans of this hero knew that he would catch the bad guy and save the day.

Scarlett O'Hara, from *Gone with the Wind*, flounces into the room and immediately draws attention. Throughout the book and subsequent movie, there is never a question who this woman is. After sixty years, this SEDUCTRESS still dominates the imagination.

At times, an author may choose to disguise a character with an alter ego. Many superheroes, such as Wonder Woman or Superman, use their mild mannered personas to hide their genuine selves. Usually, this alter ego is a deliberate ploy on the part of the character to conceal his or her identity. Characters such as Zorro and the Scarlet Pimpernel assume a personality entirely different from their real selves in order to mislead the villains.

Most often, the attributes of the assumed identity are those of an archetype different from those of the character's actual core. However, despite this deception, the character does remain true to the core archetype. The other attributes are assumed in order to further the goals and motivations that stem from the core archetype, not the assumed identity.

Other alter ego characters:
- Batman
- Spiderman

Core archetypes stand out. They are some of the most unforgettable heroes and heroines. Never assume that using core archetypes will stifle creativity or a character's growth.

EVOLVING ARCHETYPES

Heroes and heroines may make their first appearance in a story as CORE ARCHETYPES. There are times, however, when a writer needs to push his character in a new direction. A plot twist may dictate that a hero develop new qualities in order to survive or an emotional upheaval may force a heroine to change her views of life. In these cases, dramatic growth and evolution within the character's personality are required.

There are other reasons a writer may chose to have a hero change. At first, a character may not even fit the definition of a true hero. Perhaps the negative attributes of an archetype have been emphasized, more than the positive qualities. As the story progresses the audience may start to lose sympathy for the chosen hero or heroine.

As the writer takes his hero through his emotional journey, negative traits must be softened, or perhaps even eliminated, new lessons about life must be learned, and the hero must undergo change in order to tell the tale in a successful way. When the audience begins to turn against a character, the writer can regain their sympathy for the hero by having him overcome these negative qualities, or inner conflicts, in the plot of the story. When this growth process occurs, the character may emerge as a wholly different archetype. Of course, the same hold true for the writer's heroines.

This is an EVOLVING ARCHETYPE.

Look at Kate in the movie *French Kiss*. In the opening scene of the film, she is trying to overcome her fear of flying, but she cannot push herself to accomplish the task. She would rather stay on the ground, safe and sheltered, not taking any chances. Rigid and fearful, this woman is showing a few of the negative qualities inherent in the LIBRARIAN archetype. But when her fiancé flies to Europe without her, and falls in love with another woman, Kate finds the strength and courage to overcome her fear and break out of her comfort zone. She is unwilling to let go of her well-laid plans without a fight. She boards a plane, intent on winning back her man.

On the plane, she meets Luc, who challenges her uptight attitude. As Kate progresses through her story, experiencing the joys of Paris, the love of Luc's family, and the realization that her fiancé is not the man for her, she begins to enjoy life and revel in the unexpected. Her uptight rigid attitude and resent-

An Evolving Archetype starts out as one core archetype and ends up a totally different core archetype by the end of the story

Meg Ryan as Kate in French Kiss

ment of Luc subside. She begins to develop a sunnier disposition and a willingness to explore new ways of living. By the middle of the movie, she has become a SPUNKY KID.

At a key turning point in the movie, Kate must decide whether or not to keep her savings so she can buy the home she has planned for all her life, or give the money to Luc so he can achieve his dream of owning a vineyard. The LIBRARIAN had carefully saved every penny, but the SPUNKY KID gives freely and without regret to help her love achieve his dream.

Another example can be found in the film *Trading Places*. Billy Ray Valentine starts the story as a down-and-out CHARMER; a street bum, this man tries to scam every person walking by him, hoping for some easy money. He may be down on his luck, but he continues to smile and laugh at life, teasing every passerby and trying to pacify the police with his charisma. This man is showing some of the negative qualities inherent in the CHARMER archetype. Manipulative and irresponsible, he is going nowhere and—without change—the audience will not stick around for the ride.

Eddie Murphy as Billy Ray Valentine in *Trading Places*

As luck would have it, he is hand-picked by two elderly gentlemen for an "experiment." With nothing left to lose, Billy Ray agrees to the plan and finds himself in another world—one he rapidly begins to adapt to and appreciate. His innate intelligence and cunning mind are put to good use figuring out the stock market. He learns to apply himself and begins taking control of his destiny. When he learns of the nasty scheme behind his changed circumstances, his cool analysis of the situation calms his comrade. He takes charge and plans a surprise takeover. This man has shed his negative CHARMER personality and evolved into a decisive and capable CHIEF.

In one of the most telling scenes in the movie, Billy Ray invites all of his old gang to his new, beautiful home. As the party escalates, and expensive items begin to disappear or are destroyed, Billy Ray realizes he is no longer interested in the free and easy life of a CHARMER. This CHIEF promptly kicks his "friends" out.

When working with EVOLVING ARCHETYPES, the writer must create enough motivation for the character to justify the profound changes that occur. Using backstory, plot and other characters, the writer must force his hero or heroine into growth and change in order to survive and overcome the obstacle placed before them. Growth is painful and characters who change for no apparent reason are not believable. Just as in real life, heroes will only change their behavior when there is no other choice. The writer must find a plausible way to eliminate all other options.

In *French Kiss*, each obstacle placed in Kate's path provided a believable catalyst for the next step in her emotional growth and the evolution of her character. In *Trading Places*, the villains unwittingly offer an opportunity to a man willing to transform himself in order to change his circumstances. All Billy Ray needed was the chance to shine.

There are several benefits to be gained by using an evolving archetype in a story:

- A character who must change substantially in order to succeed adds tension and suspense to any plot. Will the hero change his ways and win the day? Or will he resist growth and end his story in tragedy?

  Think of Will Hunting, in *Good Will Hunting*. Throughout the story, the audience wonders whether this BAD BOY will find a way past his demons to embrace the woman who loves him and a bright future. Not until the end of the movie do we know that this man will become the PROFESSOR he is meant to be.

  Or, remember Beast from *Beauty and the Beast*. The challenge for this hero is to open up his LOST SOUL heart and allow Belle to soothe him and change him back into a CHIEF. Taking a risk on love is scary for a man who has isolated himself. But to break the curse put upon him, Beast must stop sulking and take decisive action.

- A writer can explore a multitude of attributes when using two different archetypes in one evolving character. Will a CRUSADER lay down her sword and develop skills that encourage people, becoming a NURTURER in the process? Can a BEST FRIEND stand up to his family and dare to experience adventure, changing into the SWASHBUCKLER he has always wanted to be? By changing the hero or heroine during the course of the story, a writer can explore a wide range of qualities through the experiences that lead to the evolution of the character.

  Think of Sara Connor in *The Terminator*. At first, this shy, unassuming waitress is bemused and panicked over her changing circumstances. She refuses to believe that she is the chosen mother of a savior and wants desperately to escape her

Matt Damon as Will Hunting in *Good Will Hunting*

Beast in Walt Disney's *Beauty and the Beast*

future. This WAIF has no desire to fight the good fight. But, as she realizes what is at stake and falls in love with a man committed to the cause, this woman evolves and grows into a fierce CRUSADER, intent on protecting her child and saving the world.

Another example is Moses in *The Ten Commandments*. This young prince is confident in his role as Pharaoh's adopted son. Beloved and adored, he commands armies of men in his building program, relishing the competition to be the best. This CHIEF is sure of what tomorrow will bring. But when he finds out his true past and his real roots, the resulting emotional turmoil throws this man into deep despair. Exiled to the desert, he becomes a LOST SOUL. But his wandering ends when God plucks him out of his exile and sends him back to confront his past and the demons that lurk in the shadows. Moses ends up being a WARRIOR for his people and for his God.

- This technique helps to develop a story's theme. As the character grows and changes, the audience learns the lesson the writer is conveying by experiencing the hero's journey.

Rick in *Casablanca* is a fine example. This LOST SOUL has retreated from the world, scarred and angry at the betrayals he has had to endure. But when his lost love comes into his life, he is slowly drawn back into the family of mankind and realizes the crisis that looms in front of humanity. At the end of the movie, he sacrifices his own happiness for the sake of the better good and transforms himself into a noble WARRIOR.

A second example would be Judy Benjamin in *Private Benjamin*. This dizzy socialite signs up with the army on a whim, only to find herself in a real mess. In typical FREE SPIRIT fashion, she leapt without looking and is now stuck in a situation she (for once), cannot escape. This forces her to change, and she learns to accept the discipline she needs and shed her spoiled tendencies. Through the tough love of her commander, she changes into a SPUNKY KID—a woman who is part of the team and loyal to the cause.

A writer needs to be careful with the choice of which archetype evolves into which. It would take a tremendous reordering of a heroine's personality to turn her from a WAIF into a BOSS. This is not to say that it cannot be done, only that the distance between certain archetypes should be taken into account when evolving characters. Also, do not make the

Linda Hamilton as Sara Conner in *The Terminator*

Charleton Heston as Moses in *The Ten Commandments*

Humphrey Bogart as Rick in *Casablanca*

Goldie Hawn as Judy Benjamin in *Private Benjamin*

107

assumption that a character *must* change from one archetype to another in order to show growth. Each core archetype has enough variations to give the writer plenty of latitude in creating heroes and heroines. But evolving archetypes are an important element in a writer's toolbox. Used effectively, they can add tremendous depth and dimension to heroes and heroines and to the story itself.

To review, an evolving archetype is one that moves from one core archetype to another thorough the course of the story. The character is forced through interactions with other characters, a moment of crisis or the need for survival, to change and grow in order to meet his destiny. The writer must be sure to provide enough motivation for the characters' change to insure that the reader understands and accepts this evolution.

There are three benefits in using evolving archetypes. First, tension and suspense are added to any plot that includes an evolving character. The audience will stay tuned to see if the hero will make the necessary changes to overcome the obstacles before him. Second, a writer has the ability to explore a wider range of emotions and qualities within their protagonist using evolving archetypes. And third, using the heroine's journey from one archetype to another can highlight a story's theme.

Evolving archetypes are a unique way for a writer to build characters. It is certainly not the only tool in the writer's arsenal, but it offers an opportunity to explore new ways of creating heroes and heroines.

Two detailed examples of EVOLVING ARCHETYPES follow.

Evolving characters
1. Add tension and suspense
2. Add a wider range of qualities and
3. Highlight the story theme

MALE EXAMPLE
OF AN EVOLVING ARCHETYPE

Character—Edward Lewis (Richard Gere) in *Pretty Woman*

An updated Cinderella fairy tale that quickly became a romance classic, *Pretty Woman* warmed the hearts of audiences worldwide and remains a favorite today.

When the movie opens, Edward Lewis is a merciless opponent in business. Buying distressed companies, he guts them, getting whatever profits he can while caring little for what happens in the aftermath. As Vivian says at one point, it is sort of like stealing cars and selling them for parts.

Driven, decisive, eyes always on the goal, this CHIEF has little time to spare for love.

The reason for his ruthless business conduct is revealed as the tale of his relationship with his father unfolds. A wealthy businessman himself, Edward's father abandoned his wife and child for another woman. Edward grew up without the presence, let alone the favor, of his father.

Edward's need to earn that approval became a need to compete with his father. We learn that the elder Lewis also had a reputation of being a pitiless business shark. But as our hero grimly tells Vivian, the third company he pillaged was one that belonged to dear old Dad. Though his father died months ago, Edward still cannot shake the habits of a lifetime.

During the week in which this movie takes place, Edward has targeted the failing company of an elderly businessman. This man, and his grandson, have values that Edward believes are old-fashioned. They care about their employees more than they care about what they can earn by selling out.

This CHIEF is mildly contemptuous of an attitude he can only consider impractical. But Lewis has the benefit of Vivian's company, and she is a down-to-earth hooker with a heart of gold.

Vivian's ability to cut through to the heart of matters strikes a chord in Edward. She does not sugarcoat her opinion of him or his business dealings. He tells himself that he did not hire her for her opinions and does not care what she thinks. But, when she threatens to leave, he humbles himself to get her to stay.

Richard Gere as Edward Lewis in *Pretty Woman*

Julia Roberts as Vivian in *Pretty Woman*

109

This CHIEF's evolution or growth into a less driven man does not come without a struggle, but we see it happen step by step.

Review these qualities as they apply to this character:

CHIEF
• decisive
• unsympathetic
• inflexible

BEST FRIEND
• supportive
• tolerant
• self-
 sacrificing

- The CHIEF in him uses Vivian's companionship to further his business agenda, but the emerging BEST FRIEND accepts her unwillingness to help.
- It is only as a BEST FRIEND that Edward finds his attorney's greed and arrogance overwhelming.
- It is the BEST FRIEND who acknowledges his own admiration for the older man whose business he is trying to steal and feels the elder businessman's disapproval as strongly as he does Vivian's.
- The BEST FRIEND overcomes the CHIEF's need to conquer—and accomplishes more than the CHIEF ever dreamed possible. He finds a way to save the elder businessman's company.

RESOLUTION

This man's reward comes when the elder businessman, a far better person than Edward's own father, tells Edward he is proud of him. Edward has finally earned the paternal approval that had eluded him. By the time he gives "the fairy tale" to Vivian, he has been transformed. He is now caring and compassionate, and seeks solutions that are win–win situations for all.

The CHIEF *evolved* into a BEST FRIEND

FEMALE EXAMPLE
OF AN EVOLVING ARCHETYPE

Character—Rose DeWitt Bukater (Kate Winslet) in *Titanic*

Kate Winslet as Rose DeWitt Bukater in *Titanic*

Leonardo DiCaprio as Jack Dawson in *Titanic*

In a film that captured the imagination of romantics everywhere, one character's evolution stands out over the course of the film.

As the story begins, we find Rose on the verge of sacrificing herself on a literal altar. She is to marry a cold and cruel man so her family's reversal of fortune will not come to light. Desperately unhappy, this WAIF can find no solution to her dilemma beyond throwing herself into the sea. Saved from suicide by Jack, she finds the strength to carry on.

In the few days that follow, Rose begins to develop a more hopeful, less resigned outlook. Buoyed by Jack's optimism, and learning from his faith in his own abilities, she defies her mother and fiancé.

She begins to show some spirit!

She risks discovery when she poses nude for Jack. She runs away from her bullying fiancé and makes love in a car with her new beau. Spitting in her fiancé's face, she learns that the conventions and restrictions she had so passively accepted are not the only way to live life. With Jack's help, she begins to recognize the strength and determination that have been inside her all along.

She is no longer dependent upon the men in her life to rescue her. Indeed, it is she who saves the handcuffed Jack from drowning in the hold. When Rose finds the courage to strike the ax against those cuffs—knowing that if she misses, she will likely take off Jack's hand—she demonstrates that she has the internal fortitude to make her own way in the world. A WAIF could never have swung that ax.

By the time the ship is sinking, Rose has wholly forsworn her former WAIF-like self and has emerged as a SPUNKY KID.

- It takes a SPUNKY KID to rebuff all attempts to put her in a lifeboat and instead chose to be with Jack.
- It takes a SPUNKY KID to courageously stand at the top of the boat as it sinks, without succumbing to hysteria or despair.
- It takes a SPUNKY KID to plunge into the water and retrieve the whistle that led the rescuers to her.

111

Review these
qualities as they
apply to this
character:

WAIF
• kind
• passive
• insecure

SPUNKY KID
• sense of
  humor
• brave
• skeptical

• Finally, it takes a SPUNKY KID to start a new life for herself as Rose Dawson, completely alone, except for her memories

Would the audience have responded to Rose if she never changed? Would they have admired her if she had not saved Jack or spit in her fiancé's eye? It would have been a very different story if Rose had stayed a WAIF instead of evolving into a SPUNKY KID. The audience might not have taken this woman to their hearts. They may have become angry at Rose's inability to take a stand. With no empathy from the audience for the main character, the movie would have sunk at the box office.

RESOLUTION

The true joy of *Titanic* was seeing the character of Rose, decades later, still showing the spunk she discovered within herself on that doomed ship. Bent with age, she still showed a snappy sense of humor and a zest for life that she had not had when she first stepped aboard the luxury liner.

Despite her tremendous losses, we know she succeeded in leading a productive happy life.

The WAIF *evolved* into a SPUNKY KID

LAYERED ARCHETYPES

As a writer develops her story, she might struggle to keep a character within a single archetype. She may find herself wanting to explore a wider variation of qualities within her hero or create more inner torment by including competing instincts in her protagonist.

Using one core archetype should never be viewed as a straitjacket for the writer. Rather, it should be viewed as a starting point. Many complex and interesting heroes can be created using only one core archetype, but if the writer feels the need to go beyond the framework of an archetype and examine other characteristics, he or she should feel free to do so.

As the writer breathes life into his heroine, he may find that one core archetype is not going to satisfy the needs of his story. When he begins to choose the qualities and backstory of his heroine, he finds he needs more options to create the woman who will carry the story forward. Or he may realize as he creates his plot that his heroine will need other attributes in order to survive her journey and win her prize.

In order to expand the possibilities of plot and interactions among characters, the writer may wish to consider layering some strengths or flaws of another archetype onto those of the character's core archetype.

This is a LAYERED ARCHETYPE.

Imagine a writer has a hero who is a WARRIOR. As a core archetype, this man is a defender of the downtrodden and oppressed. He cannot permit any injustice to go unchallenged. However, because of a plot point, the writer decides this defender of truth, justice and the American way must abhor violence. This hero would never dream of carrying a gun on his righteous path.

So, the writer adds a layer of PROFESSOR, making intelligence and ingenuity this hero's weapons of choice.

Sound familiar? It should. *MacGyver* was a popular television program for years. MacGyver's WARRIOR instincts dominate his personality. One of his strongest convictions is that violence achieves nothing. Normally, this principle would be a severe drawback for someone working for a secret law enforcement agency. Fortunately, MacGyver's layering of PROFESSOR traits allow him to do his job. He sees the possibilities in every

> A Layered Archetype uses a Core Archetype as its base... but due to plot or other considerations, qualities from another archetype are layered on top of the core

> Richard Dean Anderson as Mangus MacGyver in the TV series *MacGyver*

situation, and his ingenuity gets him out of the most dangerous predicaments.

Unlike an evolving character, the LAYERED character does not change from one core archetype to another. A layered character has qualities from two or more archetypes at the same time. From the moment we meet him, MacGyver had PROFESSOR attributes layered on his WARRIOR core. Throughout the series, he maintained both of these personality traits.

In another film, *My Fair Lady*, we meet a woman yearning for a better life. As a poor flower girl she has limited options and no real hope of finding a way out of her predicament. This WAIF seems stuck in her place forever.

Audrey Hepburn as Eliza Doolittle in *My Fair Lady*

But to Eliza Doolittle's surprise, a man appears in her life and gives her a dream and an idea of how to achieve it. Now that she has been given a glimmer of hope, she is unwilling to settle for what she has. Taking a chance, she visits Henry Higgins, and demands to be taken seriously, bravely defying his sarcastic wit. Finally, he agrees to her proposal and she becomes his student, paving the way for a dramatic change in her circumstances.

No WAIF would take this action. But a SPUNKY KID certainly would.

Throughout the story, these two archetypes surface in this woman. Her determination to overcome her obstacles and learn a new way of speaking proves her SPUNKY KID credentials. But the WAIF aspect of her personality gives her the resiliency to endure Henry's verbal attacks. The combination of these traits allows this woman to bravely step forward, but without losing herself in the process. If Eliza were only a SPUNKY KID, she may have told Henry off on the first day, losing her chance. But if she were only a WAIF, she would never have stepped forward and grabbed at the brass ring. This woman's victory was made possible by the blending of both archetypes.

While working with LAYERED ARCHETYPES, the writer must skillfully weave the attributes of both archetypes into the character. The writer must make sure that neither the core of her hero nor the layered archetype disappear, but that both instincts continue to show themselves in the character.

In *MacGyver*, the WARRIOR hero never loses his concern for making things right, but the PROFESSOR in him would invariably find a unique way to fix the problem. Both archetypes provide this hero with important attributes—attributes that allow him to not only survive, but flourish.

In *My Fair Lady*, Eliza always had a feisty comeback, showing her SPUNKY KID side, but at the end of the day, she still brought Henry his slippers, proving she was a WAIF at heart. The WAIF in her personality endeared her to the audience, while the SPUNKY KID elements made us cheer for her. Both archetypes combine to give us a unique and sympathetic heroine.

There are several benefits to be gained by using a layered archetype in a story:

- The conflict between the two competing archetypes can result in warring instincts within the character. This creates more internal conflict that the hero or heroine must resolve.

  Think of Rocky Balboa from the *Rocky* series. This sweet, loving man would like nothing more than to take care of his Adrian and find a peaceful existence. His BEST FRIEND core is happiest when with his friends and his wife. But the call to arms is never left unanswered. When his honor or courage are questioned, his WARRIOR layer pushes him in the ring again and again.

  Sylvester Stallone as Rocky Balboa in *Rocky*

  Or remember Celie in *The Color Purple*. At her heart, this woman is a NURTURER. Forced by her father to give up her two children, she yearns to reunite with them. But a layer of WAIF makes it impossible for her to defy her father and later her abusive husband. For years, she languishes in despair, finding happiness only in the care of her home. But with the help of a new friend, she learns to appreciate her talents as a warm, caring woman and finally is reunited with her two grown children.

  Whoopi Goldberg as Celie in *The Color Purple*

- Layered characters give the writer more choices of qualities to emphasize or de-emphasize. This gives the writer more options to explore and create characters who are complex and multifaceted.

  Think of James Bond. This man is essentially a WARRIOR. He lives and breathes for his country, taking chances no sane man would contemplate. His core archetype gives him intensity and a certainty about what needs to be done. Bond never questions if he is on the right side of an argument. Even his signature, "Bond. James Bond." gives away his unshakable confidence in himself, and his mission. But his CHARMER layer gives this character a debonair air, even

  Sean Connery as James Bond in *Goldfinger*

115

when bullets are flying past his head. "Martini. Shaken, not stirred" is said by a man who knows his pleasures well.

Another example is Sally Bowles in *Cabaret*. This FREE SPIRIT spends every night on the stage, weaving a spell over those who watch her and portraying a brash, confident woman ready for anything. But behind the curtain, this woman is terribly fragile. Her vulnerability pushes her into relationships that are going nowhere. Her layer of WAIF makes her susceptible to any suggestion.

- Layered archetypes provide characters with the inner qualities to survive the obstacles put before them. The attributes of the layered archetype can provide the source of the strengths that will overcome the flaws of the core archetype.

Remember Rhett Butler in *Gone with the Wind*? This CHIEF relentlessly pursues the woman he loves, intent on winning her affection. Through war and pillage, marriage and death, he never loses sight of his ultimate goal. But the BAD BOY layering of cynicism and street smarts allow this man to see his love as she really is. Eventually, this persuades his CHIEF side to turn away from a prize he will never win—saving him from emotional bankruptcy.

Or, think of Clarice Starling in *Silence of the Lambs*. This CRUSADER is intent on finding the ruthless killer who stalks the unprotected. She has the courage to face the evil of Dr. Hannibal Lecter in order to make her mission a success. But the layer of LIBRARIAN in her slows down the CRUSADER's tendency to charge ahead without planning. This woman methodically solves the crime without ever losing sight of her goal.

When layering, care should be taken to be sure that the overlay does not result in the cancellation of the archetype's core traits. At her heart, a NURTURER is concerned with family the friends. Her driving force is to take care of others. But if a writer layers a BOSS' trait of isolation from the emotional elements of her life onto this core, the writer will have created a muddied character with no central personality to tug at the readers' heartstrings.

A writer must also be careful to use the layering technique in conjunction with the hero's journey. For example, if a CHIEF must learn to take time to assess situations before jumping into the fray, then layering the CHIEF with a PROFESSOR's analytical skills would be counterproductive. However, if the

Liza Minnelli as Sally Bowles in *Cabaret*

Clark Gable as Rhett Butler in *Gone with the Wind*

Jodie Foster as Clarice Starling in *The Silence of the Lambs*

CHIEF must learn that professional success alone is not enough when emotional needs are ignored, then layering a bit of a PROFESSOR's cool, logical approach will actually aid in creating an internal roadblock for the hero to overcome.

To review, a layered archetype is one in which the core archetype has a layer of one or more other archetype's qualities. The character produced from this blending is one who holds to the basic dimensions of the core, but who also shows elements of the layered archetype(s) throughout the story. The archetypes chosen will be represented within the character from the beginning of the story until the end.

There are three main benefits in using layered archetypes. First, warring instincts can cause conflict within a layered character. The two archetypes may give the hero or heroine competing impulses and the resolution of this conflict will intrigue the audience. Second, there are more qualities to chose from when dealing with a layered character. This allows the writer to create characters who are multifaceted. And third, a layer of another archetype may provide the hero or heroine with the capability of overcoming a core trait that is destructive.

Layered archetypes are just one more tool in the writer's hand that allow her to create the characters who inhabit her story and allows her to place her own unique stamp on them.

Two detailed examples of LAYERED ARCHETYPES follow.

> Layered characters
> 1. can cause more conflict within the character personality
> 2. can add more qualities and
> 3. offer the possibility of overcoming a flaw in the character

MALE EXAMPLE
OF A LAYERED ARCHETYPE

Character—John Rambo (Sylvester Stallone) in *First Blood*

First Blood, the movie that introduced John Rambo as an action hero, is the story of a Vietnam veteran, home from the war and at odds with a small-town sheriff. This action/adventure story became a classic and the two sequels did nothing to diminish the power of this man or his pain.

The opening shot of this movie tells the viewer immediately that Rambo is a loner. His silhouette is framed by pale sunlight. Remote and detached, he walks down a dirt road, pack in hand, a brooding look on his face.

All classic characteristics of a LOST SOUL.

When Rambo finds out that his last remaining war buddy has succumbed to Agent Orange poisoning, the pain and isolation on his face immediately pull the audience into his anguish. Tormented and an outcast, this man has no plans, no friends and seemingly, no future.

The sheriff picks him up, insults him and drops him off at the edge of town. The look of awareness Rambo gives him, before stepping out of the car, is a clue. Rambo has been pushed too far and now the unforgiving nature of a LOST SOUL takes precedence. He may be fatalistic about his chances, but his survival is at stake.

Peculiar and introverted, this LOST SOUL cannot fit himself into this small town's ways. He will not play the game with the sheriff and makes himself a dangerous enemy. His monosyllabic responses, his passive resistance, his deep, bitter anger at his treatment by the police, all of these traits reveal that Rambo is fundamentally a LOST SOUL.

But Rambo is more than a LOST SOUL.

He has a hefty layering of WARRIOR in him.

A pivotal moment in the movie is when Rambo turns and watches the sheriff drive off. Dropped at the edge of town and warned not to return, a LOST SOUL would shrug his shoulders and move on. But the WARRIOR in Rambo rebels at the injustice of what has happened. He goes back.

Chased into the Northwest mountains, Rambo shows his resiliency. He is tenacious about surviving. He kills a corrupt

cop and feels justified. He has no remorse. All traits of a WAR-
RIOR.

Once pushed, he relentlessly exacts his revenge and systematically destroys everything in his path. Breaking the law is irrelevant to Rambo. Righting the wrong done to him is para-
mount

Review these
qualities as they
apply to this
character:

- It is the WARRIOR in Rambo who fights back.
- It is the LOST SOUL in Rambo who cries out in pain to his
  commander, mourning the loss of his friends in Vietnam.
- It is the WARRIOR in Rambo who uses his cunning and
  brute strength to battle an army of opponents.
- It is the LOST SOUL in Rambo who discerns the plans and
  motivations behind his enemies.

LOST SOUL
- a man of few
  words
- discerning
- unforgiving

WARRIOR
- tenacious
- principled
- obstinate

Without his WARRIOR layer, Rambo would never have
involved himself in this small town fight and without his LOST
SOUL core, this character would not have been nearly as
poignant and unforgettable.

RESOLUTION

Rambo continued to capture audiences in two sequels. In all
three movies, he never strayed from his LOST SOUL/WAR-
RIOR mix. At the start of each movie, he is alone and prefers
it that way. But inexorably, he is drawn into fights against evil
and injustice.

John Rambo is a LOST SOUL layered with WARRIOR.

FEMALE EXAMPLE
OF A LAYERED ARCHETYPE

Character—Princess Leia (Carrie Fisher) in *Star Wars*

Carrie Fisher as
Princess Leia in
Star Wars

Star Wars, the epic tale of a rag tag collection of rebels fighting a tyrannical empire, is rich in its assortment of strong, well-developed characters. The heroine of the piece is no exception.

Proud, imperious, accustomed to command, Princess Leia is a BOSS.

She is, literally, a princess, and despite her apparent youth, has shown herself to be a leader. She is an ambassador for her planet, and of course, a leader of the rebellion.

She recognizes no superior—Darth Vader may have her in his clutches, but that does not mean that he has one iota of power over her spirit. His power over her life or death does not stop her from insulting him, nor is she ever shaken from her belief in her own infallibility.

And it is not just the toes of enemies she is willing to step on. When Luke and Han save her from imminent termination, her response is to make cutting remarks about their abilities. That is, until she actually takes charge of the rescue.

When Leia blasts through the wall of the space station and jumps into the garbage receptacle, she is displaying a classic BOSS trait.

That quick decisiveness—the shoot first, ask questions later attitude distinguishes all BOSSes.

But, Leia is more than a BOSS.

She also has a hefty layering of CRUSADER thrown into her character.

Princess Leia coolly works towards the Rebels' goal of the destruction of the Empire. In the midst of a space battle, she calmly programs R2D2 to alert Obi Wan Kenobi. She helps plan the destruction of the Death Star. Her commitment to her cause is always evident.

- It is the decisiveness of the BOSS in Leia that allows her to stay two steps ahead of a virtually omniscient enemy. Despite the overwhelming odds, she trusts her own instincts.
- It is the CRUSADER in Leia who allows her to lie about the location of the rebel base, even in the face of the destruction of her home planet. Her commitment to her cause is unwavering.

- It is the confidence of a BOSS that allows Leia to stand fearless before powerful men who hold her life in their hands, and calculate the best tactic to turn the day.
- It is the CRUSADER in her who gives her strength to carry on when her world becomes the Death Star's target. Even through her pain, she recognizes the need to keep on fighting the good fight.
- It is the BOSS in Leia who criticizes every aspect of the efforts made to rescue her, all the while assuming her orders will be followed without question.
- It is the CRUSADER in Leia who showers Han with contempt when she tells him, *"If money is all you love, then that is all you will receive."*

RESOLUTION

The qualities of both the BOSS and the CRUSADER archetypes are crucial to Leia's character. It was the BOSS in Leia that made her worthy, in Han's eyes, of rescue, but it was the CRUSADER in her that finally won his heart.

Princess Leia is a BOSS layered with CRUSADER.

Review these qualities as they apply to this character:

BOSS
- highly organized
- self-assured
- short-tempered

CRUSADER
- courageous
- dynamic
- stubborn

REMEMBER . . .

A character may be created in three ways.

- CORE ARCHETYPE
  —remains the same
  A hero or heroine is a CORE archetype when the character thinks and acts consistently with the characteristics of a single archetype and remains consistent in nature to that core throughout the course of the story.

- EVOLVING ARCHETYPE
  —changes
  A hero or heroine commences the story as a member of one archetype, but as he or she passes through the journey unfolded in the story, he or she EVOLVES or changes into another archetype so that the character is no longer a member of the original archetype—but is a completely new archetype.

But as always...
in the final
process...
it is up to the
writer to be
creative and
imaginative
with characters

- LAYERED ARCHETYPE
  —has more than one archetype's characteristics
  A hero or heroine may be LAYERED with multiple attributes. The character has a single archetype as its emotional base, but also has the qualities of one or more other archetypes. The basic "core" of a layered archetype always stays the same, no matter what other strengths or flaws are added or removed.

All these ways of using the archetypes are good. One way is not necessarily "better" or "more complex" than the other ways.

Each method of using the archetype has value. The choice of core, evolving or layered archetype should depend only upon the writer's vision of the character's story.

ARCHETYPE INTERACTIONS

Perfection is not only unattainable; it makes for a boring story—and boring characters. During the course of a story, heroes and heroines not only encounter external obstacles, they have to deal with an internal conflict. On their journey, they must overcome some aspect of their personalities in order to survive and win the day.

During the discussion of the archetypes, it was noted that each one, male and female, had its own inherent flaws. By keeping these inherent flaws in mind while creating new characters, a writer can more easily produce meaningful and appropriate emotional hurdles for the heroes and heroines to overcome. Whether the writer uses a core archetype, an evolving archetype or a layered one, the intrinsic failings of each archetype are the basic building blocks of plot.

However, a story does not always focus on the growth of a single protagonist. Instead, a story may revolve around the relationship of two or more archetypes, each one very much a "protagonist."

When one heroic archetype is matched with another, even one of the same type, certain characteristics in each are likely to be highlighted. Because of the intrinsic differences between the archetypes, natural sympathy and antagonism will automatically spring up between any two archetypes. The particular match-up dictates which virtues and flaws are highlighted, and the light in which these strengths and weaknesses are seen.

Flaws create
conflict

For example, CHIEFs are known for their decisiveness. A BOSS might see the man as just plain wrong when his decision disagrees with hers, but would not care even a tiny bit how he reached his decision. However, a PROFESSOR will think that the man is foolish for not waiting to gather all of the information before acting. The PROFESSOR will be much less concerned with the exact nature of the CHIEF's decision, than he is with the manner it was reached.

Similarly, FREE SPIRITs are known for dancing to the beat of another drummer. A LIBRARIAN might find her seemingly illogical thinking to be a maddening distraction, but not bother to judge her actions. A LOST SOUL, however, probably appreciates the FREE SPIRIT's unconventional thinking, but finds her actions distracting, and wishes she would focus her attention on someone else.

This interplay between characters is frequently at the very heart of a story. Stories that focus on the interaction between archetypes fall into two major categories. There are *pairings* and *ensembles*.

Pairings
• two archetypes

Ensembles
• three or more archetypes

In pairings, two archetypes, of either the same or opposite gender, are matched up.

And in ensembles, more than two archetypes, of either mixed or single gender, are brought together in a story.

In both types, no single person is the protagonist—the story revolves around the relationships and character interplay, rather than a single heroic journey. Ensembles have been very successful in all forms of literature, from Chaucer's *Canterbury Tales* to today's television dramas and situation comedies. For example, despite its repeated changes in the characters and actors, the television program *Law & Order*, with its host of archetypal CHIEFs, BOSSes, WARRIORs and CRUSADERs, continues to maintain its position high in the ratings. Knowing the archetypes and how they interact will help a writer to create effective, and entertaining, groups of characters. In the pages that follow, we set forth examples of the type of interaction that is likely to occur between the archetypes. First we consider selected examples of ever-popular same gender buddy pairings. Then we review each possible combination of male/female pairings. As you will see from our examples, an opposing gender pairing need not involve a romance with the requisite happily ever after ending. In fact, sometimes a romance would actually spoil the relationship.

For each of the pairings, we describe how these characters:
- *Clash*—what are the conflicts inherent between these personalities?
- *Mesh*—what are the qualities that naturally bring these two together?
- *Change*—what are the ways that these two help each other through life's lessons?

In addition, we provide a few suggestions about the initial reaction the separate archetypes would have to each other after a first meeting. First impressions are important in character development.

For each pairing, we provide one example of how the two archetypes have been matched in a story. These examples have been chosen from movies and television, old and new, and are some of the best examples of how these two archetypes interact. Note that in some of our examples the characters do not *clash* and then *mesh* and then *change*. Each story's needs are different and each hero and heroine unique. The writer must decide which interactions fit the tale and characters being created.

Following these pairings, we discuss ensemble casts. In an ensemble cast, the possibility for both clashing and meshing is substantially increased—so much so that generalities are not possible. The interaction is dependent upon the exact mix. A grouping of a CHARMER, a SPUNKY KID, a PROFESSOR, and a LIBRARIAN creates one set of interactions. Replace the LIBRARIAN with a BOSS, and the mix changes considerably.

Remember the difference between *Cheers* with Diane Chambers and *Cheers* with Rebecca Howe? Sam, Carla, and Frasier remained true to type with the advent of Rebecca, but she pushed different buttons. The dynamics among the characters shifted with the addition of the new archetype.

We have provided several descriptions of films and television programs that contain all-male, all-female and mixed gender archetypal ensembles. The writer should use these examples showing the possibilities for conflict and resolution with a multitude of archetypal protagonists to develop dynamic ensemble casts of their own.

Our examples of the conflict, attraction and journey that each hero and heroine experience are just that—examples. These are no more than suggestions to spark a writer's imagination. The

There are three possible ways archetypes can interact...
- clash
- mesh
- change

In ensembles, each archetype influences the interaction between the characters.

attributes emphasized in a writer's pairings and ensembles will depend upon both the archetypes chosen, and the backstories given the characters. The writer must be the final judge of the conflict/attraction between the characters.

Keep in mind that our suggestions speak to the internal goals, motivations and conflicts of the archetypes. We make no suggestions for external goals, motivations and conflicts. Those issues should arise from the characters' personalities, but are truly limitless in scope. Remember only that the external plot components should push the hero and heroine toward an emotional obstacle they must overcome to succeed. External plot points are there only to reveal and define a character. The audience remembers the characters, not the plot.

THE BEST FRIEND AND THE LOST SOUL

They *clash* . . .

The LOST SOUL says the BEST FRIEND:
• is too conventional
• ignores reality and
• is a steadfast ally

The BEST FRIEND and the LOST SOUL view the world from opposite extremes. The BEST FRIEND believes that good inevitably prevails over evil; the LOST SOUL knows that evil wins unless good is very, very careful. The LOST SOUL struggles to come up with reasons for living through another day. The BEST FRIEND plans on living for a long, long time, and is unenthusiastic about his buddy's willingness to put those plans at risk. The LOST SOUL finds his friend impossibly optimistic and is concerned by the BEST FRIEND's trust and friendship with others—he is bound to be hurt. The BEST FRIEND gets tired of the brooding looks and angry asides he confronts every day.

The BEST FRIEND says the LOST SOUL:
• has a death wish
• is psychotic and
• comes through in a pinch

They *mesh* . . .

Remember
*Lethal
Weapon*…
Mel Gibson as
Martin Riggs
LOST SOUL

Danny Glover as
Roger Murtaugh
BEST FRIEND

They clash and
mesh, but only
Riggs changes

The BEST FRIEND and the LOST SOUL both have a strongly developed sense of morality. While the LOST SOUL expects bad things and the BEST FRIEND is surprised by them, both feel outrage when confronted with evil. Neither turns his back on the innocent or helpless. Each is incapable of walking away from pain and suffering.

They *change* . . .

The BEST FRIEND is dismayed at the foolhardiness of his buddy, but he has to admit that risk-taking has its advantages. Never has he so fully experienced the life with which he thought he was happy. He gives up his complacency and occasionally takes a chance.

The LOST SOUL teeters on the edge of self-destruction, but his friend's optimism gives him the strength to pull himself back. The respect given by an undeniably good man enables him to see the value and worth of his own life. He opens his eyes to the positive aspects of the world he inhabits.

THE SPUNKY KID AND THE NURTURER
They *clash* . . .
The SPUNKY KID believes in going for the gusto in life. She helps her friends, but does not stop living for their sake, especially those who are undeserving. The NURTURER sacrifices everything to care for those to whom she owes her duty. The SPUNKY KID cannot appreciate the NURTURER's serenity; the NURTURER wonders why the SPUNKY KID cannot seem to settle down.

They *mesh* . . .
The SPUNKY KID and the NURTURER share a strong belief in loyalty, friendship and family. Both will fight to defend their loved ones, even if their rules of engagement differ. Neither would dream of letting down a friend or loved one. The NURTURER will calmly hold fast to her convictions, while the SPUNKY KID jumps in shouting, but both fight the good fight. Their friends can count on them to get tough when necessary.

They *change* . . .
The SPUNKY KID cannot help but be drawn to the tranquillity issuing from this woman. Quiet strength has its uses, and she discovers the true power of love. Her friend's unconditional acceptance of her, flaws and all, provides her with a recognition of her own worth.

The NURTURER recognizes her willingness to sacrifice herself can all too easily prove a wasted or worthless effort. Her friend's easy acceptance of teamwork allows her to see that she need not take on the cares of the world. She is able to grasp happiness for herself for a change, and discovers taking care of herself only increases her ability to care for others.

The SPUNKY KID says the NURTURER:
• gives too much
• doesn't take care of herself and
• is solid as a rock.

The NURTURER says the SPUNKY KID:
• has too sharp a tongue
• needs anchoring and
• is there when needed.

Remember *Fried Green Tomatoes...* Mary Stuart Masterson as Idgie Threadgoode SPUNKY KID

Mary-Louise Parker as Ruth NURTURER

They clash, mesh and both change

The WARRIOR
says the
CHARMER:
• is worthless
• has no morals
and
• is braver than
he looks

The CHARMER
says the
WARRIOR:
• needs to find
a sense of
humor
• is way too
aggressive and
• can be
depended
upon

Remember
48 Hours...
Nick Nolte as
Jack Cates
WARRIOR

Eddie Murphy
as Reggie
Hammond
CHARMER

They clash and
mesh

THE WARRIOR AND THE CHARMER

They *clash* . . .

The WARRIOR sees things as black and white and immediately detests the CHARMER's loose use of facts. The CHARMER finds the WARRIOR's dogged dedication to duty and honor a big pain in the neck. While the WARRIOR spends his time hunting down evil, the CHARMER hunts only for things for himself. Neither of them are willing to change their views of the world and their views are at opposite extremes.

They *mesh* . . .

The CHARMER and the WARRIOR are both good on their feet and use whatever opportunities come their way to advance their individual causes. Both are adept at sizing people up and using them for their benefit. If they fit into each other's plans, they will find some way to work together. The CHARMER will pour oil over any trouble, and the WARRIOR will grudgingly protect his companion.

They *change* . . .

The WARRIOR believes in truth and justice, but after hanging around the CHARMER he also realizes that a laugh and a joke along the way will not necessarily keep him from getting his man. He is impressed with his buddy's ability to adapt himself to changing circumstances, and begins to wonder if his strong-arm tactics are always the best way to get things done. He learns to lighten up and enjoy the ride.

The CHARMER protects only his interests, but being with the WARRIOR opens his eyes to the needs of others and the value of fighting evil. He learns to be more serious about his goals and finds himself stepping forward to defend the innocent, instead of using them for his benefit.

THE CRUSADER AND THE WAIF

They *clash* . . .

The CRUSADER finds the WAIF's endless dithering an annoyance and pushes her to make decisions. She cannot understand why the WAIF puts up with all the horrible men in her life. The WAIF tries to please the CRUSADER, but finds it impossible to satisfy her friend's demands that she buck up and get some courage. So, the WAIF retreats into herself, causing the CRUSADER to wonder why she even makes the effort.

They *mesh* . . .

Both the CRUSADER and the WAIF are pure of heart and always try to do the right thing. They recognize in each other a friend who will always be there for them in a pinch. If pushed into a corner, both of them come out swinging. The CRUSADER's instinct to protect is satisfied by her friend's neediness and the WAIF's need to be coddled is addressed by her buddy's instinct to defend her.

They *change* . . .

The CRUSADER is surprised at her friend's tenacity in the face of disaster, while at the same time keeping her gentle nature intact. Maybe hammering her will into her friend is really not the way to go. Handling the WAIF makes her become more patient and gentle so she can get the results she needs. She learns to trust in her friend always being there for her.

The WAIF gains courage being around the CRUSADER. Watching her friend struggle against the odds pushes her to stand up and lend a hand. She learns to fight back against evil and is less trusting of strangers who drift into her life. Her lack of direction is turned into a more focused outlook on her future.

THE PROFESSOR AND THE SWASHBUCKLER
They *clash* . . .

The PROFESSOR and the SWASHBUCKLER are like night and day. The PROFESSOR lives for knowledge, logic and rationality; the SWASHBUCKLER's heart beats for next thrill, the next tumultuous emotion. The SWASHBUCKLER wants to experience everything life has to offer, and damn the consequences. The PROFESSOR would much prefer to study the world from a safe distance. The PROFESSOR finds his buddy much too impetuous, while the SWASHBUCKLER wonders why his friend needs to know all the details before acting and is so plodding and dull.

They *mesh* . . .

The PROFESSOR and the SWASHBUCKLER are both intrigued by anything new. While the SWASHBUCKLER

The CRUSADER says the WAIF:
• Is too trusting
• lacks sense and
• is a sweet friend

The WAIF says the CRUSADER
• is too demanding
• is never satisfied and
• is always in her corner

Remember *Thelma and Louise...*
Geena Davis as Thelma Dickinson
WAIF

Susan Sarandon as Louise Sawyer
CRUSADER

They clash, mesh and change

The SWASHBUCKLER says the PROFESSOR:
• thinks too much
• comments on the obvious and
• knows his stuff

The PROFESSOR says the SWASHBUCKLER:
• looks before he leaps
• takes foolish chances and
• offers quite the adrenaline burst

129

Remember
*Independence
Day*...

Jeff Goldblum
as David
Levinson
PROFESSOR

Will Smith as
Steven Hiller
SWASHBUCK-
LER

They clash and
mesh

wants to give it a try and the PROFESSOR wants to take it apart, both see possibilities beyond the ordinary and are willing to explore and experiment until they figure it out. Both think outside the box.

They *change* . . .

The PROFESSOR cannot approve of his friend's rash behavior, but he also cannot argue with his success. Sometimes, a man has to just do it. The PROFESSOR begins to take risks he never dreamed would come his way, and discovers he likes the feeling.

The SWASHBUCKLER is uninterested in anything that does not involve action and lots of it. But his friend has taught him a trick or two—most of all, that a little advance planning can be useful in a pinch. Since the SWASHBUCKLER is willing to try anything at least once, he learns to follow his buddy's advice and do some research before taking off on his next trip.

The BOSS
says the
SEDUCTRESS:
• is conniving
• is a liar and
• is willing to do
  what it takes
  to win

The
SEDUCTRESS
says the BOSS:
• is too "in your
  face"
• will not let
  things go and
• wins every
  battle.

Remember *The
Turning Point*...

Shirley
MacLaine as
Deedee Rodgers
BOSS

Anne Bancroft
as Emma Jacklin
SEDUCTRESS

They clash and
mesh

THE BOSS AND THE SEDUCTRESS

They *clash* . . .

The BOSS is up front about what she wants. The SEDUCTRESS hides behind smoke and mirrors, and manipulates the people around her. The BOSS is offended by her friend's subterfuge and confronts her at every turn. The SEDUCTRESS tries to avoid conflict, not wanting to show her hand. Both women are determined to get what they want and will run over anyone who stands in their way. Including each other. The SEDUCTRESS hates to be pinned down. Something her buddy does well. The BOSS hates it when someone dissembles, and this friend is a master at it.

They *mesh* . . .

Smart and savvy, both the BOSS and the SEDUCTRESS are strong and admire this trait in others. A grudging respect flourishes between these women when they realize that neither can be pushed around. The BOSS finds the SEDUCTRESS hard to control, but admires her willingness to do anything to get ahead. The SEDUCTRESS finds the BOSS's blunt ways too obvious, but appreciates her strength of purpose.

They *change* . . .

The BOSS learns from her friend that subterfuge and intrigue can often gain the prize without an out and out war. She finds out that a smooth touch and a winning smile will turn people's hearts before a brutal confrontation will. Being a realist, she grudgingly tries her hand at new skills.

The SEDUCTRESS is willing to learn new tricks and finds that her friend's take charge manner and blunt confrontation are sometimes needed to get a point across. The BOSS will not allow her hide behind her mask, and the SEDUCTRESS finds it refreshing to be honest without worrying about what people will think.

THE CHIEF AND THE BAD BOY

They *clash* . . .

The CHIEF views the BAD BOY as a potential liability. He takes precautions to make sure the BAD BOY cannot derail him from the pursuit of his goal. The BAD BOY hates authority and since the CHIEF is the authority, he pushes the envelope, searching for any weakness. The CHIEF resents this questioning and tries to demand respect. The BAD BOY does not like to be pushed around and fights back, unwilling to cede control.

They *mesh* . . .

Both the CHIEF and the BAD BOY are determined and cool under fire. They enjoy taking on the odds and winning. The CHIEF soon learns that he can use the BAD BOY's street smart skills to his benefit. The BAD BOY finds that having the CHIEF in his corner can work to *his* benefit. Neither man is one to let an opportunity pass by, and when they work together, much can be accomplished. Both are willing to bend the rules in order to win.

They *change* . . .

The CHIEF usually plays by the rules, but hanging around the BAD BOY, he learns that breaking rules can often mean he reaches his goals in a quick fashion. This man is focused on achieving and not above applying others' means to get ahead. He is used to making quick decisions about people, but realizes his buddy has hidden depths and talents. Maybe judging a book by its cover is not such a good idea.

The CHIEF says the BAD BOY:
• only brings trouble
• acts before he thinks and
• is good in a street fight

The BAD BOY says the CHIEF
• is tough
• is a know-it-all and
• knows the ropes

Remember *The Sting...*

Paul Newman as Henry Gondorff CHIEF

Robert Redford as Johnny Hooker BAD BOY

They clash and mesh, but only Johnny changes

131

The BAD BOY learns that working within the system can make the system work for him. He studies the CHIEF's way of doing business and decides he might pick up a few good tricks that will help him get ahead. This boy is no fool. He sticks around, planning on enjoying some of the riches that are sure to come.

THE FREE SPIRIT AND THE LIBRARIAN

They *clash* . . .

It is a wonder the FREE SPIRIT and the LIBRARIAN manage to stay in a room together. In fact, the disorderly FREE SPIRIT does tend to get on the nerves of the neat and tidy LIBRARIAN.

The FREE SPIRIT wants to up and at 'em; the LIBRARIAN wants to sit back and examine all the ins and outs before acting. The LIBRARIAN throws out objections to every great plan her friend offers and frustrates the FREE SPIRIT. The FREE SPIRIT thinks the LIBRARIAN is a stick-in-the-mud and tells her so.

They *mesh* . . .

The FREE SPIRIT and the LIBRARIAN can both see more than what is in front of them. Together, they have what it takes to make a plan come together. The LIBRARIAN keeps matters practical, while the FREE SPIRIT reaches for the highest stars. The logic of one tempers the wilder schemes of the other. The resulting compromise tends to be just right.

They *change* . . .

The FREE SPIRIT may not really like having an anchor, but in her heart of hearts, she knows she needs one. Her constantly tilting world is placed back on its axis by the rationality of her friend. Her madness develops a method; she is able to see below the clouds through which she tends to fly.

The LIBRARIAN would spend her days wrapped in her thoughts if not for her friend's outgoing personality. Her friend certainly has strange ideas, yet somehow the schemes have a way of working out. She comes to appreciate the value of bypassing logic now and again.

Sidebar:

The FREE SPIRIT says the LIBRARIAN:
• is prissy
• worries too much and
• helps her out of scrapes

The LIBRARIAN says the FREE SPIRIT:
• never thinks before she acts
• is too wild and
• provides amazing insight

Remember *Laverne and Shirley*...

Penny Marshall as Laverne De Fazio FREE SPIRIT

Cindy Williams as Shirley Feeney LIBRARIAN

They clash, mesh and both change

THE CHIEF AND THE BOSS
They *clash* . . .

The CHIEF and the BOSS thrive on being in control. This relationship is fraught with a constant struggle to see who will win. When he realizes that this woman is as powerful and confident as he is, the knowledge challenges him to conquer her. He must prove to himself that he is the ultimate victor. For her, this relationship threatens all her gains. She must pick up the gauntlet in order to prove her significance.

They *mesh* . . .

Mirror images, the CHIEF and the BOSS both move as fast, make decisions as decisively and tell the truth as bluntly as the other. Finally finding someone who is just like them is wonderful. Respect and mutual satisfaction soon follow. Each understands what makes the other tick, and their synchronicity makes every hour count.

They *change* . . .

The CHIEF is amazed when he finds this woman. She is as smart and determined as he is, and she is unwilling to cede any ground without a hard-fought battle. She challenges his ideas and provokes him at every turn, but he soon realizes she is the perfect woman for him. He learns how to listen and how to yield gracefully.

The BOSS discovers that, unlike everyone else, this man simply will not budge. He refuses to bend to her will. She realizes that he is a match for her in every area, and she learns to appreciate his iron will. She discovers that trusting another to make some decisions does not diminish her power.

THE CHIEF AND THE SEDUCTRESS
They *clash* . . .

The CHIEF and the SEDUCTRESS are both accustomed to dictating terms in any relationship. When they are together, he tries to yank the reins away from her, while she tries to seduce him into giving them back. Strong and stubborn, neither is happy with this constant struggle for power. She thinks he is bossy, interfering and impossible to deal with. He gets tired of her constant attempts to put one over on him. Doesn't she realize he invariably wins?

The CHIEF says the BOSS:
• is pushy
• too competitive and
• a prize worth pursuing

The BOSS says the CHIEF:
• is domineering
• too sure of himself and
• a worthy opponent

Remember *Adam's Rib*...

Katharine Hepburn as Amanda Bonner BOSS

Spencer Tracy as Adam Bonner CHIEF

They clash, mesh and both change

The CHIEF says the SEDUCTRESS:
• is manipulative
• a gold digger and
• way too attractive

The SEDUCTRESS says the CHIEF:
• is frustrating
• rude and
• a powerful ally

133

Remember
*Gone with the
Wind...*

Clark Gable as
Rhett Butler
CHIEF

Vivian Leigh as
Scarlett O'Hara
SEDUCTRESS

They clash and
mesh.

They *mesh* . . .

The CHIEF and the SEDUCTRESS admire each other for being so focused. Emotion rarely clouds their thinking and they value someone who will not crumble in a crisis. Both of them are fighters, willing to do anything to achieve the end result. Each understands the other and neither has unrealistic expectations. Both are willing to negotiate to get what they want.

They *change*. . .

The CHIEF is astonished to find out that his usual, lightning assessment of someone is not correct. This woman has hidden layers and interesting facets. She surprises him and shocks him into realizing he needs to take his time in evaluating her. He learns that he can be wrong and still be powerful.

The SEDUCTRESS has finally met a man who sees her for who she truly is and does not judge her. Instead, he accepts her and even relishes her cunning intelligence. She is free to be herself without fear of abandonment. By learning to accept herself and trust another's unconditional love, she becomes trustworthy.

THE CHIEF AND THE SPUNKY KID

The CHIEF
says the
SPUNKY KID:
• is a pushover
• a joker and
• a genuine
   friend

The SPUNKY
KID says the
CHIEF:
• is a control
   freak
• egotistical and
• rock solid

They *clash* . . .

The CHIEF believes that work and goals are what matter. The SPUNKY KID thinks all of that is fine and good, but friends and family are far more significant in a person's life. When he announces she must follow Plan A, she is certain that Plan B looks much better. He cannot understand why she wastes her time on frivolous people who will never be able to help her get ahead. She does not understand why he is unwilling to find the game as enjoyable as the finish line.

They *mesh* . . .

When the chips are down, the CHIEF and the SPUNKY KID are there. When other people turn flaky and disappear, these two come through. They believe in duty and responsibility. He realizes she is someone he can depend on. She finds out that the man follows through. A grudging respect develops. His commitment to the goal, and hers to the team, unite them for a winning combination.

They *change* . . .

The CHIEF learns that this woman cannot be bullied into doing anything she does not feel is right, but when she signs onto his team, he can count on her. Her humor brings laughter into his life, and her integrity reminds him that the right way is often the best way. He learns how to make and keep friends.

The SPUNKY KID blossoms under his attention and desire. She realizes that she has judged him too harshly, jumping to conclusions in an attempt to protect her loved ones from his steely resolve. She recognizes that she has been taken advantage of on occasion and resolves to be smarter when lending her help.

THE CHIEF AND THE FREE SPIRIT

They *clash* . . .

The CHIEF thinks logically, while the FREE SPIRIT bases her decisions on emotion. He finds it impossible to understand her reasoning, and she wonders why he gets so angry and intense. He is all about the big picture; she is quite sure the picture should be hung on the other wall. He struggles for control, but cannot even pin her down long enough to read her the riot act.

They *mesh* . . .

The CHIEF and the FREE SPIRIT are hard to ignore. While she spends her time meddling and he spends his building his business, both make an impact on whatever task they attempt. They make their decisions quickly and emphatically. He appreciates her knack for getting what she wants and she enjoys his dynamic presence. Neither is bored with the other.

They *change* . . .

The CHIEF finally grasps that ideas from left field can be good and that traditional ways are not always the best. He has to loosen up just to keep up with her. He needs to share his emotions and understand hers. He learns not to take life so seriously.

The FREE SPIRIT becomes more focused and fact-oriented when she is faced with a decision. He gives her direction and stability, often yanking her back from the edge of the cliff. She realizes that looking before leaping is not as bad an experience as she thought it would be. Until the next time.

Remember *Pride and Prejudice*...

Colin Firth as Darcy
CHIEF

Jennifer Ehle as Lizzie
SPUNKY KID

They clash, mesh and both change

The CHIEF says the FREE SPIRIT:
• is a scatter-brain
• unconvention-al and
• everything he has been missing

The FREE SPIRIT says the CHIEF:
• is too serious
• pompous and
• a firm anchor

Remember *I Love Lucy*...

Desi Arnaz as Ricky Ricardo
CHIEF

Lucille Ball as Lucy Ricardo
FREE SPIRIT

They clash and mesh

THE CHIEF AND THE WAIF

They *clash* . . .

The CHIEF invariably knows what to do in any situation. The WAIF is never sure what to do. He has strong opinions about everything and makes sure they are heard. When she fails to state her views immediately, he bowls her over, intimidating her and pushing her around. Instead of fighting back, she distances herself. He finds it frustrating that he cannot reach her.

They *mesh* . . .

The CHIEF is in constant motion, moving forward, pushing obstacles out of his way. He has no fear of change; he is sure he will be able to control the outcome of his actions. The WAIF might be afraid of changing circumstances, but long ago she found a way to ride the tide. While she floats to safety, he boldly swims to shore. Both land on their feet.

They *change* . . .

The CHIEF enjoys being with her because she never pressures him or questions his abilities. Responding to her calming influence, he speaks more softly, grows more patient and listens more closely. He learns to value his own opposite.

The WAIF is bolstered by this man's strong beliefs and steady guidance. She gains self-esteem and confidence. She still bends, but no longer breaks. Instead of backing down from confrontation, she learns to stand up for herself.

THE CHIEF AND THE LIBRARIAN

They *clash* . . .

The CHIEF is focused on the goal. The LIBRARIAN is focused on the process. Both are incredibly stubborn and sure that they are right. Her attention to details drives him crazy. He is only interested in the bottom line; she cannot believe he makes decisions without knowing and analyzing every option. Neither of them backs down from their tenacious views on how to do things.

They *mesh* . . .

Both the CHIEF and the LIBRARIAN base their decisions on logical thinking. Serious, efficient and focused, these two will tackle any task with single-minded determination. When questioned, both defend themselves in a logical and precise manner. They approach their personal lives in the same way. He respects her dedication and intelligent answers. She respects his drive and commitment.

They *change* . . .

The CHIEF has to slow down and take a deep breath. There is no way this woman is going to make a decision until she is good and ready. He realizes that she leaves nothing to chance. He finds out that looking at the fine points of a situation can save him a lot of grief.

The LIBRARIAN becomes more open and receptive to ways outside her own narrow experience. He draws her away from sitting on the sidelines and pulls her right into the middle of the action. She learns that her way is not the only way and that there is more than one path for life's journey.

THE CHIEF AND THE CRUSADER
They *clash* . . .

The CHIEF is focused on himself—his obligations, his goals, his achievements. The CRUSADER is focused on her utopian dreams, her mission, her cause. She thinks he is selfish, in it only for himself; he thinks she is too idealistic, especially if his work clashes with her objective. Both of them are driven, stubborn and positive they are right. Neither backs down from a fight.

They *mesh* . . .

Both the CHIEF and the CRUSADER are always on the go. It is better to do something—anything—than just sit around and think about a better way of doing things. They admire each other's energy and commitment. Decisive and persistent, both of them play to win. Though they are both obstinate and opinionated, respect for the other's tenacity and stamina develops.

They *change* . . .

The CHIEF's focus broadens to encompass other peoples' goals. She teaches him to see another point of view and to realize that her objectives are as important as his. His respect for her makes him respect her cause. He learns to value another person's agenda.

The CRUSADER finds out that self-interest is not a dirty word. Sometimes she can do more for the people she is trying to help by being practical about what she can accomplish.

Remember
The King and I...

Yul Brynner as King Mongkut of Siam
CHIEF

Deborah Kerr as Anna Leonowens
LIBRARIAN

They clash and mesh and both change

The CHIEF says the CRUSADER:
• is a do-gooder
• starry-eyed and
• a faithful partner

The CRUSADER says the CHIEF:
• is selfish
• a male chauvinist and
• able to get her where she wants to go

Remember
The American President...

Michael Douglas as President Andrew Shepherd
CHIEF

Annette Bening as Sydney Wade
CRUSADER

They clash, mesh and both change

137

Taking a deep breath, she learns not to major in the minors anymore. She stops letting herself get bogged down in lost causes and hopeless battles.

THE CHIEF AND THE NURTURER

They *clash* **. . .**

Work and achievement are what matter to the CHIEF. Why can't she see that nothing significant gets done if a person fails to concentrate on his goals? The NURTURER cannot understand why he will not slow down and pay attention to his family. Why is he working so hard? Both of them feel the other spends far too much time on things that do not really matter.

They *mesh* **. . .**

Both the CHIEF and the NURTURER are calm, cool and collected when a crisis hits. Neither is easily flustered and they value this in the other. While she makes commitments out of love, he makes them out of duty. Both of them feel strongly about responsibilities and obligations. If they make a commitment, they keep it.

They *change* **. . .**

The CHIEF is soothed by her patient warmth. Following her example, he becomes more sympathetic. She softens his rough edges and provides him with a safe retreat from his hectic world. This allows him to relax and take things easy for a change. He learns to sit back and put his feet up.

The NURTURER finds that compromising to keep the peace is not always the best road to take. It is okay to take care of herself instead of always taking care of everybody else. He protects her from being taken advantage of. She realizes that focusing on a few loved ones is better than spreading herself too thin.

THE BAD BOY AND THE BOSS

They *clash* **. . .**

The BAD BOY never follows the rules. The BOSS believes rules insure success. She is a natural authoritarian and he hates authority. Since both of them are stubborn, they inevitably butt heads. He finds her devotion to the establishment irritating and boring. She finds his need to tear down the establishment childish.

The CHIEF says the NURTURER:
• is a martyr
• too forgiving and
• the picture of a warm hearth and home

The NURTURER says the CHIEF:
• is predatory
• much too controlling and
• there when he is needed

Remember *The Sound of Music...*

Christopher Plummer as Captain von Trapp CHIEF

Julie Andrews as Maria NURTURER

They clash and mesh, but only he changes

The BAD BOY says the BOSS:
• is stuck-up
• overbearing and
• a blue ribbon

They *mesh* . . .

The BAD BOY and the BOSS are filled with energy. While his can be destructive and hers is always directed, both of them fill a room with charisma and verve. They are both risk takers, willing to take chances to accomplish what is before them. There is a flash of lightning when these two meet. She finds his devil-may-care attitude hard to resist. He finds her sophistication a challenge.

They *change* . . .

The BAD BOY hangs around her and realizes that playing by the rules sometimes works. He has been beating his head against the wall for so long that it surprises him to find that a key opens doors more quickly than a sledgehammer. He realizes that working within the system can be rewarding.

The BOSS is intrigued by his methods and comes to understand that occasionally breaking the rules works. She realizes that she cannot always judge a book by its cover. Learning to break out of the mold, she is now willing to try new things.

THE BAD BOY AND THE SEDUCTRESS

They *clash* . . .

The SEDUCTRESS wants a ticket out, and is determined to find the man to help her do it. She quickly assesses the BAD BOY and realizes this is not the guy for the job. He sneers at her fixation on money and power. Neither of them trusts anyone, and certainly they are not about to trust each other. He is bitter and antagonistic about everything she strives for; she is convinced he has no ambition at all.

They *mesh* . . .

The BAD BOY and the SEDUCTRESS are both street smart and cynical. Their attitudes toward people and situations are the same. Both are independent and unwilling to yield any personal power to another. Since neither can fool or manipulate the other, they tolerate each other's presence. An alliance of mutual goals and survival occurs.

They *change* . . .

The BAD BOY realizes she understands him—his bitterness and his anger. Unlike other women, she never judges him. He

---

The BOSS says the BAD BOY:
• is a rule breaker
• a cocky wiseguy and
• a walk on the wild side

Remember *Terms of Endearment*...

Jack Nicholson as Garrett Breedlove BAD BOY

Shirley MacLaine as Aurora Greenway BOSS

They clash and mesh, but only she changes

The BAD BOY says the SEDUCTRESS:
• is a tramp
• a money-grubber and
• a beautiful babe

The SEDUC-TRESS says the BAD BOY:
• is beneath her notice
• going nowhere and
• a savvy stud

Remember *The Postman Always Rings Twice*...

John Garfield as Frank Chambers BAD BOY

Lana Turner as Cora Smith SEDUCTRESS

They clash and mesh

learns to let go of insults and trust her opinion. He finds out that standing in a corner snarling is not the best way to get ahead.

The SEDUCTRESS sees a shadow of herself in this man. He teaches her that money and power are not always worth what she has to sacrifice. She learns to trust his advice and be satisfied with what she has. She realizes that pride in one's self is more valuable than any material gain.

THE BAD BOY AND THE SPUNKY KID

They *clash* . . .

The BAD BOY never buys anyone's story until he proves it to himself. The SPUNKY KID believes that most people tend to tell the truth. She is a team player, willing to help when needed; he cannot abide any rules except those of his own making. She cannot stand his cocky attitude. She tries to be his friend, but he makes fun of her. He thinks she is about to take a fall and hates her need to belong.

They *mesh* . . .

Though it takes the BAD BOY a long time to trust someone, once he does, he never betrays a friend. The SPUNKY KID is nothing if not loyal. She stands by the commitments she makes. Since both value this trait beyond all others, they immediately spot it in each other. He appreciates her wit and she likes his quick rebuttal. Admiration follows. But their mutual sense of honor is what draws them together.

They *change* . . .

The BAD BOY trusts this woman's faithful support. He knows how rare real loyalty is and is unwilling to let it go when he finds it. With her help, he puts down the heavy chip on his shoulder and tones down his cocky attitude. Because he learns to trust her implicitly, he is willing to take the chance and be part of the team.

The SPUNKY KID finds that listening to the beat of a different drum leads to new and exciting experiences. She has always toed the line, but with this guy, she realizes it can be refreshing to go off the beaten trail. She learns to let loose and live a little.

The BAD BOY says the SPUNKY KID:
• is too perky
• wears rose-colored glasses and
• is willing to stick by him

The SPUNKY KID says the BAD BOY:
• is dangerous
• moody and
• worth redeeming

Remember *Grease...*

John Travolta as Danny Zuko BAD BOY

Olivia Newton-John as Sandy Olsen SPUNKY KID

They clash and mesh, and both change

THE BAD BOY AND THE FREE SPIRIT

They *clash* . . .

The BAD BOY is vitally aware of what a big, bad world it is out there. The FREE SPIRIT sees life as a fun adventure and cannot understand his sullen view. She spends a lot of time trying to rope him into her next escapade, but he is determined to stay apart in order to protect himself. He thinks she is a scatter-brained lunatic. People take advantage of her. Doesn't she see all the pitfalls before her?

They *mesh* . . .

The BAD BOY and the FREE SPIRIT share a joy of breaking the rules. Though she does it with a grin and a wave, and he sneers from his position of independence, both feel the need to spread their wings and push the envelope. Their mutual wildness causes them to be impulsive and undisciplined. This willingness to experience life to the fullest draws them together. He likes how quickly she jumps on his bike, ready for any thrill. She likes his fast moves and street-smart confidence.

They *change* . . .

The BAD BOY cannot hang around this lady for long and not change his attitude. She is far too cheerful and upbeat to ignore. With her help, he becomes more open with his emotions and some of his anger drains away. He starts to enjoy life.

The FREE SPIRIT listens to his lessons about what could befall her if she trusts too easily. She becomes a little more savvy. His quick assessment of people is often more accurate than hers, and she finds it prudent to trust his opinion. She learns to be more discerning.

THE BAD BOY AND THE WAIF

They *clash* . . .

The BAD BOY struts through life, pretending he is right where he wants to be. The WAIF, on the other hand, hates any kind of confrontation and goes out of her way to avoid it. He thinks she is a wimp and takes delight in goading her into new experiences. She hates taking chances and detests him for pushing her around. She is easy prey and he is definitely on the prowl.

The BAD BOY says the FREE SPIRIT:
• is a ditz
• a social animal and
• a ray of sunshine

The FREE SPIRIT says the BAD BOY:
• is cold-hearted
• too negative and
• a fun ride

Remember *Pulp Fiction*...

John Travolta as Vincent Vega BAD BOY

Uma Thurman as Mia Wallace FREE SPIRIT

They clash and mesh

The BAD BOY says the WAIF:
• is a baby
• playing with fire and
• a pure light

The WAIF says the BAD BOY:
• is scary
• condescending and
• a window to a new world

Remember *Dirty Dancing...*

Patrick Swayze as Johnny Castle BAD BOY

Jennifer Grey as Frances "Baby" Houseman WAIF

They clash, mesh and both change

They *mesh* . . .

The BAD BOY and the WAIF are both afraid to come in out of the storm. Rejection is a deadly kiss for them. She withdraws emotionally and drifts through life. He withdraws physically and hides behind a sneer. The two misfits often find each other on the outside looking in. He sees the pain she is carrying inside and identifies with it. She notices the loneliness he is trying to hide and consoles him.

They *change* . . .

The BAD BOY finds that he desperately wants to live up to her innocent trust. Through her example, he finds that a kind touch and a patient response cause him less trouble in the long run. He learns to give other people a chance.

The WAIF expands her horizons with this man. His wild streak forces her out of her safe and solitary box. He teaches her to be wary of people until they prove themselves. She is grateful for his loyal presence and savvy when she confronts her demons. She becomes more confident and self-assured.

The BAD BOY says the LIBRARIAN:
• is repressed
• a know-it-all and
• a challenge

The LIBRARIAN says the BAD BOY:
• is a delinquent
• crass and
• able to bring out her wild side

Remember *9 1/2 Weeks...*

Mickey Rourke as John BAD BOY

Kim Basinger as Elizabeth LIBRARIAN

They clash and mesh, but only she changes

THE BAD BOY AND THE LIBRARIAN

They *clash* . . .

Neither the BAD BOY nor the LIBRARIAN values the kind of knowledge the other has. She is bound to tradition and convention. Her learning has come from studying and working within the system. He is drawn to the unconventional and bound by nothing. His knowledge comes strictly from the streets. She finds him boorish and illiterate; he sees only her petty rules and stifling regulations.

They *mesh* . . .

The people around them often discount the BAD BOY and the LIBRARIAN. While he responds in anger, and she slips back into her safe world, they are both hurt by this disregard. Both live apart from society. The mainstream has passed them by. They respond to each other's isolation and sympathize with the pain it causes. Stuck in the roles society has cast them in, they see in the other a fellow casualty.

They *change* . . .

The BAD BOY realizes this woman's keen intelligence can teach him some important things. She opens his eyes to other possibilities and avenues. She is responsible and dependable, and he finds he can trust her with his heart. He learns to see himself in a different light.

The LIBRARIAN lets her hair down. He loosens her up and pushes her into new and exciting experiences. Unlike most men, he recognizes her femininity and revels in it. He relates to her as a female, not simply a cool professional. She discovers the wild, sexy woman hidden within her.

THE BAD BOY AND THE CRUSADER

They *clash* . . .

The CRUSADER is on a mission. The BAD BOY's only mission is himself and he likes it that way. She is resolute about her cause. He fritters away his time, causing trouble. Idealistic, she thinks his is a wasted life. Cynical, he wishes she would stop nagging him to get involved. They are both stubborn and proud. When they clash, sparks fly, as neither admits defeat.

They *mesh* . . .

The BAD BOY and the CRUSADER fight the world. Hers is a war to save others from pain. His is a war against the social rules that try to keep him in his place. Both rail against the unfairness done to the underdogs. Though she works within the system and he often fights against it, they respect each other's tenacity and courage.

They *change* . . .

The BAD BOY is swiftly drawn into her way of life. Her persuasive talents are hard to resist and he finds himself knee deep in her cause before he knows it. As a team, they learn how to work and fight together, and he finds in her a worthy mate. He learns to be more positive and less pessimistic.

The CRUSADER has her eyes opened wide to the other side of life. Her idealism is tempered by reality, and he teaches her how and where to fight her battles for maximum effect. He is able to draw her away occasionally from her fervent war against the world. She starts to relax and finds the courage to accept the things she cannot change.

The BAD BOY says the CRUSADER:
• is cold
• obsessed and
• someone who will protect his back

The CRUSADER says the BAD BOY:
• is good for nothing
• part of the problem and
• the solution she has been looking for

Remember *Guys and Dolls...*

Marlon Brando as Sky Masterson BAD BOY

Jean Simmons as Sister Sarah Brown CRUSADER

They clash, mesh and both change

The BAD BOY
says the
NURTURER:
• is a goody-
  two-shoes
• smothering
  and
• a warm retreat
  from pain

The NURTURER
says the
BAD BOY:
• is a bad
  example
• a malcontent
  and
• in need of
  rescue

Remember
*As Good As
It Gets...*

Jack Nicholson
as Melvin Udall
BAD BOY

Helen Hunt as
Carol Connelly
NURTURER

They clash and
mesh, but only
he changes

The BEST
FRIEND says
the BOSS:
• is rude
• a tyrant and
• a capitvating
  dictator

The BOSS
says the
BEST FRIEND:
• is small
  potatoes
• weak and
• true blue

THE BAD BOY AND THE NURTURER

They *clash* . . .

The BAD BOY hates the world, while the NURTURER wants to make it a better place. She is sure that if we all could get along, everything would work out perfectly; he is sure the world will stay bad no matter what anyone does. She is the quintessential good girl, spending all her time making sure everyone is happy. He is her opposite and is out to make everyone as miserable as he is.

They *mesh* . . .

The BAD BOY and the NURTURER address each other's deepest desires. He desperately needs to be taken care of, and she wants to be needed in the most desperate way. In a crisis, both handle the trouble with aplomb. While she is optimistic about the outcome and he is pessimistic about their chances, each is impressed with the other's resourcefulness and cool manner.

They *change* . . .

The BAD BOY responds to her kindness. She is safe and comforting. Slowly, he allows her to draw him into society and he finds that not all people are out to destroy him. Becoming less of a loner, he learns that happiness is possible.

The NURTURER loses some of her unrealistic idealism. The world is a tough place. With his guidance, she comes to understand that not everyone can be helped or needs her help. She finds that she is not irreplaceable in other people's lives. She learns to say "no" to others and "yes" to herself.

THE BEST FRIEND AND THE BOSS

They *clash* . . .

Getting ahead is all the BOSS lives for; getting by is good enough for the BEST FRIEND. She cannot believe his complacent attitude. Doesn't he realize that there are worlds out there to conquer? He is bemused by the effort she is willing to put into her search for fame and fortune. He would rather spend time with his friends. Doesn't she know that people count more than success?

They *mesh* . . .

Each is everything the other is not. The BOSS has the drive to push to the head of every endeavor, but she is not one to give pats on the back as she advances. The BEST FRIEND has the affability to make friends everywhere he goes, but he is not among the town's movers and shakers. She admires the ease with which he adds to his wide circle of buddies. He respects her golden touch. They are Yin and Yang.

They *change* . . .

The BEST FRIEND observes this woman's drives and determination, and realizes he has been stuck in a rut. He risks breaking out of his self-imposed existence and begins to assert himself. He learns to focus on a goal and achieve it.

The BOSS sees the genuine affection that he gives to and receives from his friends, and it opens her eyes to what she has been missing. Taking the time to lend a helping hand does not necessarily hold one back; if anything, it is a power boost. She realizes that friendship is not another word for weakness.

THE BEST FRIEND AND THE SEDUCTRESS
They *clash* . . .

The SEDUCTRESS' low expectations of people allow her to justify using them for getting what she wants. Her tactics make it hard for the BEST FRIEND to see any good in her. He sees virtue in almost everyone, but she is a tough case. Doesn't she know that friendship is the most precious commodity? She wonders what color the sky is in his universe. Doesn't he understand that this is a dog-eat-dog world?

They *mesh* . . .

The BEST FRIEND is accustomed to being all things to all people—everyone can count on him to pitch in whenever it is necessary. The SEDUCTRESS has learned the value of molding herself into whatever woman she has to be at a particular moment. He becomes what others need while she becomes what others want, but their responsiveness to the needs and desires of others strikes a chord in each other.

They *change* . . .

The BEST FRIEND is a trusting soul. As a result, he has misjudged folks once or twice. She shows him that putting a bit of

Remember
American Beauty...

Kevin Spacey as Lester Burnham
BEST FRIEND

Annette Bening as Carolyn Burnham
BOSS

They only clash

The BEST FRIEND says the SEDUCTRESS:
• is manipulative
• a bother and
• beguiling

The SEDUC-TRESS says the BEST FRIEND:
• is not worth her time
• naïve and
• a trustworthy man

Remember
Risky Business...

Tom Cruise as Joel Goodson
BEST FRIEND

Rebecca De Mornay as Lana
SEDUCTRESS

They clash and mesh, but only he changes

145

distance between himself and others is good common sense. He learns to stop giving people the benefit of the doubt and not to take everyone at face value.

The SEDUCTRESS has been distrusting for so long, it is hard for her to recognize a real-life nice guy. When she does see him for what he is worth, her entire view of the world shifts. There really are good people inhabiting this planet. She starts to trust others and becomes more open-minded.

THE BEST FRIEND AND THE SPUNKY KID

They *clash* . . .

These two have a natural affinity for each other, but they often cannot see beyond the friendship. As far as they are concerned, friends should not become lovers. Why mess up a good relationship? Both the BEST FRIEND and the SPUNKY KID go off looking for greener pastures, purposefully ignoring the lush colors in their own backyard.

They *mesh* . . .

The BEST FRIEND and the SPUNKY KID are both people lovers. They find their happiness in friends and family, and appreciate that the other enjoys the same thing. Neither one is the sort to get ahead in the world by climbing over the backs of co-workers or talking trash about their enemies. Both appreciate the other's loyalty and commitment.

They *change* . . .

The BEST FRIEND is a little too laid back and content with his lot. She has faith in him and helps him find his own direction. He no longer has to run in place; he can move out of his rut. He focuses on his own hopes and dreams instead of those of others.

The SPUNKY KID is a bit lacking in confidence, especially when it comes to men. But she is completely comfortable with him. His unconditional acceptance of her opens her eyes to her own abilities. She sees that her lack of confidence is only that, not a reflection of a lack of abilities. She learns to have faith in herself.

The BEST FRIEND says the SPUNKY KID:
• is caustic
• a clown and
• his best buddy

The SPUNKY KID says the BEST FRIEND:
• mocks her
• is self-satisfied and
• her closest pal

Remember *While You Were Sleeping...*

Bill Pullman as Jack Callaghan BEST FRIEND

Sandra Bullock as Lucy Moderatz SPUNKY KID

They clash and mesh, but only he changes

THE BEST FRIEND AND THE FREE SPIRIT

They *clash* . . .

The BEST FRIEND worries about this woman. She always leaps without looking, and then he has to pick up the pieces. Why can't she exercise a little caution? The FREE SPIRIT worries about him, too. She doesn't understand his need to consider only the risks, and never the benefits. He is stuck in the mud, while she flies. Why can't he just let loose now and then?

They *mesh* . . .

The BEST FRIEND and the FREE SPIRIT both know exactly what is best for everyone around them. They have advice for everyone—for their friends' own good, of course. These two understand each other's need to put the lives of their friends and neighbors back on track. They may disagree on what has to be done to fix other people's problems but never on whether something should be done.

They *change* . . .

The BEST FRIEND has his two feet solidly on the ground. But seeing her fly, he feels stuck in cement. There is safety in being part of the ground crew, but he wonders what the view is like from up above. He discovers that taking risks brings satisfying rewards.

The FREE SPIRIT soars through the upper atmosphere, but after awhile, she finds that airline food stinks. She starts to wonder how a home-cooked meal tastes and hankers after a house of her own to go with it. His stability is comforting, and not at all boring. She learns to become more grounded, and less of a frequent flyer.

THE BEST FRIEND AND THE WAIF

They *clash* . . .

The BEST FRIEND sees the best in others—if there is anything good to see. But he is not interested in wasting his time with folks who are bad news, and cannot understand the WAIF's continual involvement with those types. Why can't she see people for what they are? She sees people as she hopes they are, and so she cannot understand why he is so critical of her friends. Why can't he see what people can be?

The BEST FRIEND says the FREE SPIRIT:
• is impractical
• irresponsible and
• a delight

The FREE SPIRIT says the BEST FRIEND:
• is boring
• predictable and
• a steadfast companion

Remember *Clueless*...

Alicia Silverstone as Cher Horowitz FREE SPIRIT

Paul Rudd as Josh BEST FRIEND

They clash and mesh

The BEST FRIEND says the WAIF:
• is a whiner
• wishy-washy and
• needs him

The WAIF says the BEST FRIEND:
• is powerless
• unassertive and
• safe

Remember
The Wedding Singer...

Adam Sandler
as Robbie Hart
BEST FRIEND

Drew Barrymore
as Julia Sullivan
WAIF

They clash,
mesh and both
change

They *mesh* . . .

The BEST FRIEND does not put up with the truly wicked, but neither does he demand perfection. He happily accepts foibles and flaws in his friends. The WAIF would never think of trying to change someone. She likes everyone the way they are. The acceptance these two offer each other is a pleasant change from the criticism offered by the rest of the world.

They *change* . . .

The BEST FRIEND is not usually one to play the superhero, but she brings out all of his protective instincts. Although he tends to avoid confrontation, he becomes more assertive because she needs his help. He learns that aggression is sometimes necessary.

The WAIF has never known someone who is so accepting of her. He is not interested in changing her or making her into something she is not. Basking in the glow of his unconditional love, she gains the confidence to stand up for herself. She discovers that she has more strengths and abilities than she suspected.

THE BEST FRIEND AND THE LIBRARIAN

The BEST
FRIEND says the
LIBRARIAN:
• is
  condescending
• brittle and
• a scholar of
  love

The LIBRARIAN
says the
BEST FRIEND:
• is obtuse
• unimaginative
  and
• turns her
  pages

They *clash* . . .

The LIBRARIAN is a "just-the-facts" kind of gal, while the BEST FRIEND is interested in the people who are the subject of those facts. She is irked by his inability to understand that one must be emotionally uninvolved in order to be effective. He cannot fathom her failure to consider the impact of situations on people. Her focus on details maddens him; his preoccupation with emotions drives her up the wall.

They *mesh* . . .

The BEST FRIEND and the LIBRARIAN are not the sort to make false promises. They follow through on commitments every time. If they say they will do something, that something gets done. Each values the trustworthiness of the other, particularly in a world filled with people who think nothing of saying one thing and doing another. Finding someone who walks the walk is a revelation.

They *change* . . .

The BEST FRIEND is more interested in people than in information. However, her example shows him that having the facts at hand can create advantages. He learns to let go of other people's burdens and focus on what he can actually achieve.

The LIBRARIAN sees the satisfaction he gets from his relationships with people. Books can be good company, but she begins to realize that a person has many more fascinating facets than even the most interesting tome. She learns to value people and what they bring to her life.

THE BEST FRIEND AND THE CRUSADER

They *clash* . . .

The BEST FRIEND is not a judgmental person and he accepts others as they are. The CRUSADER expects all to conform to her exacting standards. He is bewildered by her insistence upon faultless virtue. Doesn't she realize that no one is perfect? She is amazed at his ability to tolerate the failings in others. Can't he understand that by not being part of the solution, he is part of the problem?

They *mesh* . . .

The BEST FRIEND and the CRUSADER are both helpers. He wants to make things better for his friends. She wants to make the world better for everyone. While their efforts have a different direction, they both appreciate someone who cares about others. Add in the fact that each is willing to actually do something to make things happen and viola, a happy couple.

They *change* . . .

The BEST FRIEND always focuses on the people in his life, but she opens his eyes to the major issues around him. She inspires him to take action. He becomes more dedicated in his efforts to make things right and less complacent about the way things are.

The CRUSADER finally stops to take a breath, thanks to his influence. She begins to see people as more than just victims who need her protection. She sees them as individuals, not statistics. Individuals who have hopes, aspirations and agendas of their own. She discovers the people behind her crusades.

Remember
The Truth About Cats & Dogs...

Janeane Garofalo as Abby Barnes
LIBRARIAN

Ben Chaplin as Brian
BEST FRIEND

They clash and mesh, but only she changes

The BEST FRIEND says the CRUSADER:
• is a fanatic
• too wound up and
• a passionate partner

The CRUSADER says the BEST FRIEND:
• is too laid-back
• a lightweight and
• a man she can trust

Remember
Dave...

Kevin Kline as Dave Kovic/Bill Mitchell
BEST FRIEND

Sigourney Weaver as Ellen Mitchell
CRUSADER

They clash, mesh and both change

The BEST
FRIEND says
the NURTURER:
• is smothering
• interfering and
• his soulmate

The NURTURER
says the
BEST FRIEND:
• is a pushover
• a buttinski and
• a man who
cares

Remember
*Sense and
Sensibility*...

Hugh Grant as
Edward Ferrars
BEST FRIEND

Emma
Thompson
as Elinor
Dashwood
NURTURER

They only mesh

THE BEST FRIEND AND THE NURTURER

They *clash* . . .

The BEST FRIEND and the NURTURER both act to help the people they love. But they never agree on what needs to be done. She is a mother bear with cubs—charging in to protect them. He is likely to solve the problem by removing those cubs to a place of safety. Her habit of going out of her way to confront other maddens him; she cannot even imagine why he lets a threat continue to exist.

They *mesh* . . .

The BEST FRIEND and the NURTURER both love people. They genuinely enjoy spending time with others, listening to their hopes, dreams and fears, and helping to solve their problems. An evening spent planning the improvement of all their family members will be followed up the next morning with them sorting out the lives of their friends. These two are soulmates.

They *change* . . .

The BEST FRIEND sees her martyrdom. This makes him realize his own. In struggling to prevent her from taking over the lives of others, he discovers his own tendency to live through others. He becomes more involved in his own life and less in that of his friends.

The NURTURER thinks he needs fixing. But he is so comfortable in his own skin that she has to stop and take another look. Realizing that trying to change him would be a mistake, she acknowledges she might have made similar mistakes in the past. She learns to be more accepting of people as they are.

The CHARMER
says the BOSS:
• is a shrew
• humorless and
• a door worth
opening

The BOSS says
the CHARMER:
• is conceited
• all form, no
substance and
• dangerously
irresistible

THE CHARMER AND THE BOSS

They *clash* . . .

The CHARMER is all play, the BOSS is all work. He looks at life as a game; she is serious and determined about everything. He gets frustrated with her inability to lighten up and have some fun. She cannot fathom why he refuses to knuckle down and get to work. For her, the job is what matters and commitments cannot be taken lightly. He hates responsibility and sees a job only as a means to pay the rent.

They *mesh* . . .

When these two people walk into a room, they cannot be ignored. Dynamic and stimulating, both the CHARMER and the BOSS want to win. He charms his way to the top, she works her way up the ladder. They see in each other a powerful competitor and a lively intelligence. They represent a challenge to each other's skill. Both of them enjoy the even match.

They *change* . . .

The CHARMER finds out that life is not always a game. Some things are worth hard work. This woman is not the usual pushover for his charm that most women are. To win her, he has to become more determined and decisive. He learns that charm only goes so far and there really is no substitute for genuine effort.

The BOSS realizes that stopping to smell the roses actually refreshes her, and she can accomplish more when she gets back to work. His appreciation for the finer things in life helps her relax. She comes to realize that laughter and joy are the best part of life.

THE CHARMER AND THE SEDUCTRESS

They *clash* . . .

The CHARMER and the SEDUCTRESS battle over the same prizes: money and power. He plays the game for challenge, she plays simply to survive. Neither lets their defenses down in order to connect emotionally. Since they both look out for number one, no one agrees to be number two. With this man and woman, life is an endless game of masquerade.

They *mesh* . . .

The CHARMER and the SEDUCTRESS appreciate the skill of the other, respecting the talent that goes into producing the illusion. Both are risk takers and think that winning is worth the gamble. Survival and winning are the goals, so they never disagree about what is important. They both share a keen perception of people. Protecting their own interests, this couple amuses each other.

They *change* . . .

The CHARMER looks at her and sees his twin. The shock of being treated cavalierly teaches him that his past deceptions have

---

Remember *The Taming of the Shrew*...

Richard Burton as Petruchio
CHARMER

Elizabeth Taylor as Katherina
BOSS

They clash, mesh and both change

The CHARMER says the SEDUCTRESS:
• is a quick roll in the hay
• a black widow and
• the only woman who understands him

The SEDUC-TRESS says the CHARMER:
• is a boy toy
• too perceptive and
• the only man who understands her

Remember
*North by
Northwest...*

Cary Grant as
Roger Thornhill
CHARMER

Eva Marie Saint
as Eve Kendall
SEDUCTRESS

They clash,
mesh and both
change

caused pain. Understanding her motivations gives him a keen sense of how he himself operates. He learns to sympathize and treat others with more care.

The SEDUCTRESS is surprised to find herself warming to this laughing, teasing man. He is her kindred spirit, a man who understands her games. When he looks at her, she sees no condemnation. She starts to let down her guard and trust another.

THE CHARMER AND THE SPUNKY KID

They *clash* . . .

The CHARMER
says the
SPUNKY KID:
• is irritating
• too honest
  and
• tried and true

The SPUNKY
KID says the
CHARMER:
• is out of her
  league
• slick and
• a dreamboat

She believes in family and commitments. He wants a good time with a variety of people. The CHARMER and the SPUNKY KID are diametrically opposed in the relationship area. She tells all her secrets to her friends, the thought of which gives him the chills. Appearances are important to him, while she values actions. Honesty and integrity are her core; he changes his core values to fit his circumstances.

They *mesh* . . .

The CHARMER and the SPUNKY KID will always be laughing—at each other and at the world. Humor draws them together, and teasing is a constant source of entertainment and a way to show how much they care without risking too much. Both enjoy people and make friends easily. Fun to be around, they find in each other a natural playmate. When together, neither worries about being bored.

Remember
*An Affair to
Remember...*

Cary Grant as
Nickie Ferrante
CHARMER

Deborah Kerr as
Terry McKay
SPUNKY KID

They clash and
mesh, but only
he changes

They *change* . . .

The CHARMER finds that he cannot fool this woman. She sees through his mask of jokes and bravado to the true man beneath. And she accepts him. He finds solace in her loyalty and love. He learns to value being with only one woman.

The SPUNKY KID is amazed that this captivating, sought-after man loves her! This knowledge brings a new confidence. She realizes she can be a sexy, vibrant woman. He appreciates her humor, but does not discount her as just a funny sidekick. She begins to value her sensual side.

THE CHARMER AND THE FREE SPIRIT

They *clash* . . .

The FREE SPIRIT is genuinely warm. The CHARMER is purposefully warm to get his way. Good-hearted, she assumes everyone is her best friend. He has never had a best friend—only acquaintances who find him delightful to have around. He thinks she is crazy to be so open and sweet. Her constant well-meaning interference annoys him, while she sees his dishonesty and nonchalance as being sad.

They *mesh* . . .

Both the CHARMER and the FREE SPIRIT light up a party. Gregarious and good with people, together they knock the socks off of everyone who meets them. They are both "originals." Both think money is to be used *now* when they have it. Life is to be enjoyed to the fullest. After all something will always turn up to keep the creditors at bay. They are irresistibly drawn to one another's sparkling personality.

They *change* . . .

The CHARMER realizes that he has more fun with this woman than any other. Her enchanting smile and open heart are enough for him. Watching her operate, he realizes he can charm someone and love them at the same time. He learns to stop using people.

The FREE SPIRIT becomes more skeptical about the people around her. He teaches her to stand back a bit and let people prove they are trustworthy before giving them her last dollar. She finds out that not everyone needs or wants her helping hand and that the world will not end if she focuses on her own life.

THE CHARMER AND THE WAIF
They *clash* . . .

The CHARMER glides through life, enjoying the sunshine and forgetting about his obligations. The WAIF dreams of security and finds his tall tales depressing. Why can't he level with her? Her interest is dampened when she finds him untrustworthy. He finds her focus on his faults irritating. Why can't she live a little?

They *mesh* . . .

Both the CHARMER and the WAIF are dreamers. They live in a fantasy world all their own and are sure that is where they would rather stay. Both understand the need to escape once in awhile and wonder if maybe escaping together might not be

The CHARMER says the FREE SPIRIT:
• is interfering
• klutzy and
• up for anything

The FREE SPIRIT says the CHARMER:
• is a fibber
• a user and
• loads of fun

Remember *Shakespeare in Love*...

Joseph Fiennes as Will Shakespeare CHARMER

Gywneth Paltrow as Viola De Lesseps FREE SPIRIT

They clash and mesh

The CHARMER says the WAIF:
• is meek
• subdued and
• oh-so-intriguing

The WAIF says the CHARMER:
• is unreliable
• too sure of himself and
• oh-so-tempting

153

Remember
Oklahoma!...

Gordon MacRae
as Curly
CHARMER

Shirley Jones as
Laurey Williams
WAIF

They clash,
mesh and both
change

more fun. In each other, they find a partner who is willing to believe in the impossible.

They *change* . . .

The CHARMER spends a lot of time wooing this woman. She is an enigma he is determined to figure out. When he realizes he has hurt her fragile heart with his games, he decides to stop. For the first time, he thinks about how his actions have harmed others and moves to correct the wrongs.

The WAIF becomes a little wiser about judging people and their motives. Trusting by nature and habit, she finds out that not everyone will protect her. With him, she feels secure because he understands and supports her. She learns to be more outgoing without losing her protective shield.

THE CHARMER AND THE LIBRARIAN

The CHARMER
says the
LIBRARIAN:
• is uptight
• snide and
• longing to let
  down her hair

The LIBRARIAN
says the
CHARMER:
• is flamboyant
• able to push
  the envelope
  and
• the star in her
  fantasies

They *clash* . . .

The LIBRARIAN plans ahead and keeps lists. The CHARMER lives for the moment and plays it by ear. She has not gone out on a date in years and would never dream of starting with him. He thinks she is too uptight and is annoyed with her nagging attention to the rules. This is the classic story of the ant and the grasshopper—one trying to cover every detail, the other living for the moment.

They *mesh* . . .

Both the CHARMER and the LIBRARIAN are incomplete paintings. They hide part of themselves from the outside world. Holding themselves back from real interaction, they realize how alike they are in their fear of showing their true selves. She secludes herself behind endless details and monotonous duties. He lives behind a curtain of smiles and wit. Each identifies with the other.

Remember
The Big Easy...

Dennis Quaid as
Remy McSwain
CHARMER

Ellen Barkin as
Annie Osborne
LIBRARIAN

They clash,
mesh and both
change

They *change* . . .

The CHARMER is amused by her sly humor and struck by her keen intelligence. For a man who skims along the surface, he is surprised when he finds such a treasure buried beneath her straight-laced suit. He learns to appreciate the layered depths of this woman.

The LIBRARIAN is yanked out of her safe cocoon by this man. His playful teasing brings a smile to her lips, and she lightens up and learns to go with the flow. His sharp questions and intelligent objections challenge her rigid views. She finds out that there are other ways to view the world.

THE CHARMER AND THE CRUSADER
They *clash* . . .
The CRUSADER is selfless to a fault, entirely devoted to her mission. The CHARMER's only mission is himself. Serious and steadfast, she keeps any pledge she makes. Promises and duty are anathema to this man. She is appalled by him—all that flash and glamour with no heart for anything important. He thinks she is a dead bore constantly prattling on about her cause.

They *mesh* . . .
Both the CHARMER and the CRUSADER are confident. She is confident she is right, he is confident in his sweet-talking talents. He admires her ability to move people, not with smiles and charisma, but with determination and drive. She is awed by his ability to manipulate situations and people. They both seek the limelight—she is sure it will help win supporters, he is happy to be the center of attention.

They *change* . . .
The CHARMER is struck by her fervent belief in the cause. He becomes aware that his smiles and handshakes can help suffering people or influence important outcomes. He enjoys guiding people into helping her instead of just helping himself. He learns that it feels good to help others and becomes less selfish.

The CRUSADER finds out that life is about more than winning the objective. He persuades her to relax and slow down. She realizes that a quick grin wins converts more easily than her grim gaze. She begins to charm the opposition and becomes less single-minded.

THE CHARMER AND THE NURTURER
They *clash* . . .
The CHARMER focuses solely on his own needs, while the NURTURER spends all of her time meeting other people's needs. He is cool, cynical and hides behind his artful grin; she is warm, kind and guileless behind her gracious smile. For a while, she tries to reform him. But she has spent most of her life

The CHARMER says the CRUSADER:
• is a fanatic
• has a one-track mind and
• lights his fire

The CRUSADER says the CHARMER:
• is uncaring
• fickle and
• an escape from problems

Remember *The Way We Were*...

Barbra Streisand as Katie Morosky CRUSADER

Robert Redford as Hubbell Gardner CHARMER

They clash and mesh

The CHARMER says the NURTURER:
• is stifling
• a homebody and
• a safe harbor

The NURTURER
says the
CHARMER:
• is undepend-
able
• a smooth
operator and
• her cup of tea

Remember
*Groundhog
Day...*

Bill Murray as
Phil Conners
CHARMER

Andie
MacDowell as
Rita
NURTURER

They clash and
mesh, but only
he changes

around people, and it does not take her long to identify him as
a con man.

They *mesh* . . .

Both the CHARMER and the NURTURER are easy to be
around and instinctive people pleasers. Both are at home in the
midst of a crowd. He spins mesmerizing tales to get his way,
while she cocoons her loved ones in a warm embrace. She
enjoys his charming manner, and he is intrigued by her patient
kindness.

They *change* . . .

The CHARMER is jarred by her care and concern for others
into realizing that helping out is not a crime. He becomes more
truthful in order to gain her confidence. Giving of himself earns
her approval and he is willing to go the extra mile for her. He
finds that actions speak more loudly than sweet nothings.

The NURTURER loves having this enchanting and irresistible man around to entertain her, instead of constantly being
the one doing the pleasing. He encourages her to spend more
time on herself and forces her to narrow her focus. She learns
to take care of herself and to say "no" once in awhile to others.

THE LOST SOUL AND THE BOSS

The LOST SOUL
says the BOSS:
• is too blunt
• unsympathetic
and
• a strong ally

The BOSS says
the LOST SOUL:
• is moody
• uncooperative
and
• fascinating

They *clash* . . .

The LOST SOUL feels every lash of her tongue and withdraws
into a dark, brooding silence. The BOSS cannot understand
why the man takes everything so personally. He spends much of
his time analyzing himself—his faults, his injuries, his pain. Busy
pursuing her goals, she has no time for angst. He is put off by
her pushy manner and angered by her brusqueness.

They *mesh* . . .

Both the LOST SOUL and the BOSS are proud. Almost too
proud. They come off as cold and harsh, and consistently drive
people away. This puts them outside the warmth of acceptance
and friendship. They both understand isolating it is to have no
friends. His mystery intrigues her and she appreciates his opinions. He sees through her bluster and sympathizes with her isolation.

They *change* . . .

The LOST SOUL finds her self-assured manner a breath of fresh air. He realizes her strength and courage serve her well, and she encourages him to find the confidence to change his life and re-enter society. He learns not to take every word to heart.

The BOSS is shaken when he easily discerns what makes her tick. He sees through her and identifies her hidden loneliness. He sometimes knows her better than she knows herself. She finds out that taking a moment to enjoy the subtle pleasures of life is refreshing. She starts to watch her words and not cause pain.

THE LOST SOUL AND THE SEDUCTRESS

They *clash* . . .

The LOST SOUL has been wounded and just does not have the strength to climb out of his pit of hell. The SEDUCTRESS has pulled herself up by the pointy heels of her stiletto pumps and has no intention of being be pushed down again. She finds him weak; he finds her brittle. His dreams are gone and he mourns their loss. She has been cynical most of her life and likes it that way.

They *mesh* . . .

Both the LOST SOUL and the SEDUCTRESS are realists. Both have been savaged by the world around them and neither is willing to give anyone the benefit of the doubt. His illusions were shattered, while she has no memory of ever having any. He wears his resignation as a statement. She shadows hers with a web of lies and smiles. They are attracted to the vulnerability they see in each other.

They *change* . . .

The LOST SOUL finds himself drawn into the spotlight with this woman. He can no longer lurk in the shadows and ignore the world around him. She teaches him to be tougher and less emotional. He stops looking back and begins to look forward.

The SEDUCTRESS finds that every word she speaks to this man is taken to heart. She must be careful not to hurt his already deeply wounded soul. With this man, she realizes she has to become more sensitive and caring. She learns to offer solace rather than just seduction.

Remember *Moonstruck*...

Cher as Loretta Castorini
BOSS

Nicolas Cage as Ronny Cammareri
LOST SOUL

They clash, mesh and both change

The LOST SOUL says the SEDUCTRESS:
• is heartless
• a manipulative and
• holds him spellbound

The SEDUC-TRESS says the LOST SOUL:
• is a whiner
• too critical and
• a touch of splendor

Remember *Bull Durham*...

Kevin Costner as Crash Davis
LOST SOUL

Susan Sarandon as Annie Savoy
SEDUCTRESS

They clash, mesh and both change

The LOST SOUL
says the
SPUNKY KID:
• is heading for
a fall
• sassy and
• a breath of
fresh air

The SPUNKY
KID says the
LOST SOUL:
• is introverted
• self-righteous
and
• an underdog
who needs her
friendship

Remember
Educating Rita...

Michael Caine
as Frank Bryant
LOST SOUL

Julie Walters
as Rita
SPUNKY KID

They clash,
mesh and both
change

THE LOST SOUL AND THE SPUNKY KID
They *clash* . . .

The LOST SOUL is pensive and solemn. He finds little to be happy about. Her smiles and optimism remind him of everything he thinks is lacking in his life. The SPUNKY KID is disturbed that he is unwilling to share in her humor or laugh with her. He is way too depressed for her taste. She enjoys being with people and has a wide circle of friends to entertain; he wants nothing to do with anyone and wishes she would leave him alone.

They *mesh* . . .

Both the LOST SOUL and the SPUNKY KID are devoted, loyal companions. If they give their heart or their word, they never let down a friend or lover. Integrity and honor are important to them and when they find these qualities in another, they hold onto that relationship. He is surprised at her steadfastness; she is relieved to find out he is more than just gloom and doom.

They *change* . . .

The LOST SOUL lightens up with this woman. Her sparkling humor and refreshing outlook on life drive the cobwebs out of his deep, dark prison. He can laugh and feel secure in her friendship. With her help, he learns to be less critical of others failures and more accepting of his own faults.

The SPUNKY KID wants to interact with people—to be a part of the team. She needs to be loved, and feels she must earn that right. He teaches her that being alone once in awhile is refreshing. She learns to discern the motivations of other people and protect herself.

The LOST SOUL
says the
FREE SPIRIT:
• is a chatterbox
• flighty and
• an intriguing
provocation

The FREE SPIRIT
says the
LOST SOUL:
• is a downer
• a critic and
• a challenge to
her outlook
on life

THE LOST SOUL AND THE FREE SPIRIT
They *clash* . . .

The LOST SOUL and the FREE SPIRIT are dark vs. light. She is filled with gaiety and loves bright lights and crowds of people. He searches for refuge away from the teeming masses. His world is somber and his outlook matches his lifestyle. Her upbeat manner and constant meddling drive him deeper into his cave. She finds him stubborn. Working with him is impossible.

They *mesh* . . .

Both the LOST SOUL and the FREE SPIRIT are eccentric and are viewed by others as out of the ordinary. They share the sense of separation that comes with the knowledge of being different from the mainstream. They spot in each other the same sincerity and appreciation for the small pleasures of life.

They *change* . . .

The LOST SOUL is unable to hide from this woman. Her bubbly chatter fills his dark life with sunshine. With her support, he realizes that life is there to explore, and he doesn't have to hide anymore. He learns to go along with her plans and enjoy the ride.

The FREE SPIRIT flits from subject to subject, but with this man's intense personality, she curbs this tendency. She finds out that she needs to look carefully before she leaps and reconsider before she interferes. He soothes her frantic impulses and grounds her. She starts to appreciate serenity.

THE LOST SOUL AND THE WAIF
They *clash* . . .
The LOST SOUL broods over every slight. The WAIF kindly overlooks all insults. Where he is highly critical of everyone, friend or foe, she passively accepts whatever comes her way. His sensitivity revolves around his pain and his injuries. She spends far more time feeling everyone else's pain rather than her own. He finds her irritatingly patient. She finds him deliberately unforgiving.

They *mesh* . . .
Both the LOST SOUL and the WAIF are isolated from others. He hides himself away, while she withdraws to a place inside herself. Neither wishes to interact or join the team. They are both lost, and finding a way out without help is beyond their capabilities. Their sensitivity and isolation bring them together. Each understands the other's need for self protection through withdrawal from the world.

They *change* . . .
The LOST SOUL finds her loyalty to be a revelation. His idealism will never fully recover, but he discovers that strength has many faces. Her need to be protected forces him out of his

Remember
*The Accidental
Tourist...*

William Hurt
as Macon
LOST SOUL

Geena Davis
as Muriel
FREE SPIRIT

They clash and
mesh, but only
he changes

The LOST SOUL
says the WAIF:
• is too trusting
• too open and
• too alluring

The WAIF says
the LOST SOUL:
• is too harsh
• too secretive
and
• too intriguing

Remember
Casablanca...

Humphrey
Bogart as
Rick Blaine
LOST SOUL

Ingrid Bergman
as Ilsa Laszlo
WAIF

They clash and
mesh, but only
he changes

159

retreat. For her sake, he will move mountains. He becomes stronger and more willing to fight back.

The WAIF finds in this man someone as in need of rescue as she is. To win him and heal him she must become braver and more courageous. He teaches her to be less trusting of others. She learns that being in tune with another is a comforting refuge.

THE LOST SOUL AND THE LIBRARIAN

They *clash* . . .

The LOST SOUL and the LIBRARIAN are both sure they are right. Each trusts only their own opinion. She finds his sulky, angry manner irritating and a waste of time. He finds her persnickety attention to detail all right—until she doesn't do it his way. Both are rigid, stubborn and highly critical, and neither is willing to take the first step to cross the wide divide between them.

They *mesh* . . .

The LOST SOUL has always wanted the world to be perfect, and has always been disappointed. The LIBRARIAN also believes in perfection. While he yearns for ultimate perfection, she tries to impact her own environment, content with what she can accomplished. Both find in each other a serious seeker of truth and a dedicated perfectionist.

They *change* . . .

The LOST SOUL finds that this woman is dependable and he can trust her to accomplish any task set before her with a painstaking attention to detail he can only envy. Her logical outlook rebukes his sulks and pushes him to change. He learns to let go of some of his pain.

The LIBRARIAN finds that trusting his judgment often saves her hours of analyzing a problem. His creativity brings her a new outlook on life—it is more than just books and charts. She discovers the world is multi-faceted and achingly beautiful.

THE LOST SOUL AND THE CRUSADER

They *clash* . . .

The CRUSADER is out to make a difference and will rope others into her cause when possible. The LOST SOUL has retreated from any involvement with the outside world. She

---

The LOST SOUL says the LIBRARIAN:
• is bossy
• soulless and
• another lover of perfection

The LIBRARIAN says the LOST SOUL:
• is stuck in the past
• obstinate and
• a mystery waiting to be solved

Remember *The X-Files*...

David Duchovny as Fox Mulder LOST SOUL

Gillian Anderson as Dana Scully LIBRARIAN

They clash and mesh

---

thinks he is selfish and depressing. He finds it painful to watch her—he has seen it before and knows how horrible it can be when a person has to give up. Her first instinct is to do something. His is to sit back and observe.

They *mesh* . . .

The LOST SOUL and the CRUSADER both need to control their environment. He has to withdraw from society in order to achieve this goal. She is still fighting the good fight, trying to change the world for the better. They are both very quick to judge, and can be unforgiving and uncompromising. But they admire what they call their decisiveness and they share an honorable stoicism.

They *change* . . .

The LOST SOUL sees the big picture with this woman. She will not allow him to hide in his own little world. Her passionate conviction that she can make a difference revives his idealism. He begins to believe again. He learns there are still battles worth fighting.

The CRUSADER realizes this man has his heart in the right place. He may be a man of few words, but those he chooses are often gold. She learns that not everything can be conquered and that it is better to choose her battles well. She begins to give in a little and accepts that some things cannot be changed.

THE LOST SOUL AND THE NURTURER

They *clash* . . .

The LOST SOUL wants to be left alone. He has retreated, either physically or mentally, and puts up barriers and obstacles so he can't be touched. People disappoint and anger him. The NURTURER wants to be surrounded with loved ones. She spends her whole life dealing with people and making them happy. She cannot understand his abrupt and harsh manner. He cannot understand why she refuses to leave him alone.

They *mesh* . . .

The LOST SOUL and the NURTURER compliment each other. He needs help and she loves to be needed. She is self-sacrificing to a fault and will not stop until he is healed. Once they love, they are both devoted and committed. Her warm acceptance makes coming out of his hideout worthwhile. She finds his

The LOST SOUL says the CRUSADER:
• is too idealistic
• heading for disappointment and
• a courageous companion

The CRUSADER says the LOST SOUL:
• is bitter
• egocentric and
• a devoted mate

Remember *Buffy, the Vampire Slayer...*

Sarah Michelle Gellar as Buffy Summers CRUSADER

David Boreanaz as Angel/Angelus LOST SOUL

They clash and mesh, but only he changes

The LOST SOUL says the NURTURER:
• is a nag
• sentimental and
• a woman who can help him

The NURTURER says the LOST SOUL:
• is a grouch
• unforgiving and
• a man in need

Remember
*Beauty and
the Beast...*

Beast
LOST SOUL

Belle
NURTURER

They clash and
mesh, but only
he changes

sensitivity and need a powerful draw. Neither will allow the other to get away.

They *change* . . .

The LOST SOUL is brought into the family of man. Her calm patience soothes his weary soul. He feels accepted and loved. This security lends him some stability. This woman will never hurt him, even to her own detriment. He learns to trust in love.

The NURTURER becomes less of a martyr. This man demands attention and is jealous of the time she spends away from him. Their relationship becomes number one with her and she revels in the freedom of taking care of only him. She starts to prioritize and stops compromising.

THE PROFESSOR AND THE BOSS

The PROFESSOR
says the BOSS:
• is pushy
• rash and
• a dynamic
  mate

The BOSS
says the
PROFESSOR:
• is anal
  retentive
• plodding and
• a brilliant
  companion

They *clash* . . .

The PROFESSOR is accustomed to considering every option, every scrap of information before making a decision. The BOSS prefers to charge in and get the job done. She is impatient with his insistence upon details. He is appalled by her inability to wait until all the facts are in. He wonders how she can be so successful. She is stymied that such a bright guy cannot seem to make up his mind.

They *mesh* . . .

Remember *The
Philadelphia
Story...*

Katharine
Hepburn as
Tracy Lord
BOSS

Cary Grant as
C. K. Dexter
Haven
PROFESSOR

They clash and
mesh

The PROFESSOR and the BOSS never give up. He is a firm believer in slow and steady winning the race, while she tramples over angels in her haste to rush in. But, regardless of their methods, both stay on course until the finish line is reached. He admires her determination, and she approves of his ability to stay focused.

They *change* . . .

The PROFESSOR discovers that the world outside his book strewn study does not always wait for the facts to come in. Having all the information may be nice, but sometimes action has to be taken now. He learns that a quick assessment can still be accurate.

The BOSS learns there is merit in looking carefully before she leaps. Not every situation is clear at first glance. She discovers the benefits of a little introspection and she discovers that some things are worth taking time over. She realizes that sometimes there is great value in the journey, not just in reaching the destination.

THE PROFESSOR AND THE SEDUCTRESS

They *clash* . . .

The PROFESSOR is not exactly opposed to the physical world, but he is baffled by anyone who emphasizes it. He dismisses people who do not consider the brain the most important organ. But the SEDUCTRESS is equally baffled by his preoccupation with her mind. What is wrong with this guy? Can't he see what she has to offer below the neck?

They *mesh* . . .

Both the PROFESSOR and the SEDUCTRESS are accustomed to being alone with their thoughts, even in crowded rooms. Each appreciates the other's ability to withhold action until every angle has been reviewed and every possibility weighed. He admires her ability to calculate the odds, and she understands his need to consider all eventualities. These two do never act without taking a hard look at their options.

They *change* . . .

The PROFESSOR ruefully acknowledges that the cover is not the best means for judging a book—or a woman. Reading is all well and good but sometimes, a little hands on experience is the only way to truly learn. He learns to relish the physical joys of life.

The SEDUCTRESS discovers she has a bit more to offer than her charms. Someone really can appreciate her for her mind. Sex does not have to be a commodity offered in trade, and conversation is not just a tool to be used to fascinate a man. She starts to turn down the volume of her sex appeal and let her mind be appreciated.

THE PROFESSOR AND THE SPUNKY KID

They *clash* . . .

The PROFESSOR has never seen see the point of cultivating a lot of friends. People tend to interfere with his intellectual pursuits. The SPUNKY KID wonders how someone with an I.Q. off the charts can have no concept of emotional intelligence. If he just got involved in something outside the lab, she

---

The PROFESSOR says the SEDUCTRESS:
• is wasting her talents
• too obvious and
• mesmerizing

The SEDUC-TRESS says the PROFESSOR:
• is condescending
• infuriating and
• the ultimate challenge

Remember *Bell, Book and Candle...*

James Stewart as Sheperd Henderson PROFESSOR

Kim Novak as Gillian Holroyd SEDUCTRESS

They mesh, but only she changes

The PROFESSOR says the SPUNKY KID:
• is a lightweight
• a pest and
• the only one for him

The SPUNKY KID says the PROFESSOR:
• is unfriendly
• unfeeling and
• smarter than the average bear

163

Remember
*Time After
Time...*

Malcolm
McDowell as
H. G. Wells
PROFESSOR

Mary
Steenburgen as
Amy Robbins
SPUNKY KID

They clash,
mesh and both
change

knows that he would realize interaction with people has its value, too.

They *mesh* . . .

The PROFESSOR and the SPUNKY KID are good people. They have no ulterior motives—"what you see is what you get." He will go out of his way to lend a helping hand only when he contributed to the problem, but he is not going to stab anyone in the back. She appreciates his honesty. He admires her dependability. These two stick to their word and both know the rarity of that quality.

They *change* . . .

The PROFESSOR hates to admit it—but she might actually be right! There is a big world outside his study. And all those peo- ple—they really are more interesting than he had ever suspect- ed. He finds out that he can learn a thing or two from other people.

The SPUNKY KID has never considered herself the sharpest knife in the drawer, but maybe it is time for a shift in her self- concept. There are many different forms of intelligence, and she discovers she is better equipped than she thought. She gains in self-confidence and discovers her new possibilities.

The PROFESSOR
says the
FREE SPIRIT:
• is irrational
• irresponsible
 and
• irresistible

The FREE SPIRIT
says the
PROFESSOR:
• is fussy
• stuffy and
• a straight
 arrow

THE PROFESSOR AND THE FREE SPIRIT
They *clash* . . .
The PROFESSOR cannot understand this puzzling, frustrating woman whose actions are unpredictable. He wonders how she manages to exist, flitting from one topic to the next, never stop- ping to analyze the world. The FREE SPIRIT is baffled by his need to understand. She enjoys being in the moment, while he wants to study it.

They *mesh* . . .
The PROFESSOR and the FREE SPIRIT perceive possibili- ties where others find only problems. He knows a clever solu- tion, while she just makes one up. They both think outside the box. There is a bit of flakiness in every genius, and a bit of genius in every flake. He appreciates her ability to look beyond the obvious, while she discovers that his vast store of knowledge can come in handy.

They *change* . . .

The PROFESSOR realizes that life is more than a logical progression from Point A to Point B. He learns to appreciate the scenery a bit more—and not just determine its chemical make-up. Her spontaneity brings fresh air to his musty existence; he find himself breathing deeply. He learns that having fun is not necessarily a crime.

The FREE SPIRIT has always enjoyed the merry-go-round called life, but taking time to examine the world up close can be rewarding. Having two feet on the ground makes it a bit easier for her to stay balanced when she reaches for the stars. She realizes that stopping to think before acting will not hurt her.

THE PROFESSOR AND THE WAIF

They *clash* . . .

The PROFESSOR is not known for his aggressive tendencies, but even he finds it hard to understand the WAIF's unwillingness to stand up for herself. Why is she such a pushover? Has she never heard of rational self interest? She is bothered by his need to harp on her lack of a backbone. How can he not realize that fighting is scary?

They *mesh* . . .

The PROFESSOR and the WAIF both tend to withdraw from other people and complex social situations. Parties and the night life are not a part of their expectations. It is a relief to meet someone who shares this discomfort with socializing. He admires her ability to sustain long periods of solitude without complaint. She welcomes his desire to keep his distance.

They *change* . . .

The PROFESSOR discovers that offering protection is not as antiquated a notion as he thought. In fact, feeling needed is a pretty good thing to feel. He discovers the action he-man underneath the passive lab coat. He learns that strength does not interfere with his intelligence.

The WAIF realizes she can rely on his gentle power to carry her through the storm. But even as she relishes the shelter he offers, she acknowledges his urgings for her to stand on her own two feet. She realizes that other people do not always know the best thing for her. She begins to question the judgment of others.

Sidebar

Remember *Annie Hall...*

Woody Allen as Alvy Singer PROFESSOR

Diane Keaton as Annie Hall FREE SPIRIT

They clash and mesh

The PROFESSOR says the WAIF:
• is whiny
• wimpy and
• wonderful

The WAIF says the PROFESSOR:
• is complex
• cold and
• a constant companion

Remember *The Fly...*

Jeff Goldblum as Seth Brundle PROFESSOR

Geena Davis as Ronnie Quaife WAIF

They clash and mesh, but only he changes

The PROFESSOR
says the
LIBRARIAN:
• is a pseudo-
intellectual
• out of her
league and
• a pearl beyond
price

The LIBRARIAN
says the
PROFESSOR:
• is an intellec-
tual fraud
• a know-it-all
and
• her match

Remember
Jurassic Park...

Sam Neill as
Alan Grant
PROFESSOR

Laura Dern as
Ellie Sattler
LIBRARIAN

They only mesh

THE PROFESSOR AND THE LIBRARIAN

They *clash* . . .

The PROFESSOR and the LIBRARIAN are both accustomed to others coming to them for information. A rival in the know-how department—even when fully worthy—is simply unwelcome. Each is too accustomed to being the "smartest kid on the block" and neither takes kindly to being questioned, regardless of who is doing the questioning.

They *mesh* . . .

Life can be a little lonely at the top of the intellectual heap. Telling a joke no fun when no one gets the punch line. The PROFESSOR and the LIBRARIAN recognize each other as kindred spirits. They are intrigued to discover someone of the opposite sex whose intellectual ability is equal to their own.

They *change* . . .

The PROFESSOR discovers that it really is possible to have an intelligent conversation with a woman. She might not agree with every word he says, but when she disagrees, she has a reason. His world view takes a radical shift. He realizes that he is not required to shut down his brain in order to enjoy the physical world.

The LIBRARIAN is amazed. There is an intelligent man in the universe. She gains confidence in her own charms when he makes it clear that he is delighted by her mind—*and* her body. Sure in the knowledge that he takes her seriously, she comes to accept and revel in her feminine side.

The PROFESSOR
says the
CRUSADER:
• is tiring
• zealous and
• a passionate
partner

The CRUSADER
says the
PROFESSOR:
• is selfish
• unfeeling and
• a knowledge-
able ally

THE PROFESSOR AND THE CRUSADER

They *clash* . . .

The CRUSADER is a bundle of enthusiastic commitments. The PROFESSOR only gets excited about his own work. She is amazed that he can be so selfish. Doesn't he care about injustice in the world? He is amazed she spends so much energy on worldly issues. Doesn't she have more productive ways to spend her time?

They *mesh* . . .

The PROFESSOR and the CRUSADER never let anyone get away with anything less than the whole truth. She appreciates his ability to cut through the smoke screens and get to the heart of the matter. He admires her unwillingness to bend facts to fit her point of view. Each greatly admires the other's unswerving and sincere devotion to the unvarnished truth.

They *change* . . .
The PROFESSOR has always sought knowledge for its own sake. But he finds that other purposes are as valid, if not more so. Her zeal brings him out of his self-absorbed existence and into the world of passion and commitment. He discovers that caring about others does not have to interfere with his pursuit of knowledge.

The CRUSADER fights the good and noble fight without end. But his analytical example shows her that there is more than one kind of truth, more than one kind of justice and more than one way to fight. She finds that all of life is not a battle.

THE PROFESSOR AND THE NURTURER
They *clash* . . .
The NURTURER feels strongly for those she loves. The PROFESSOR is quite happy to analyze feelings, but certainly never allows himself to actually feel them. She cannot understand how his self-imposed isolation from the world. How can he not know that people need people? He cannot understand why she is so enmeshed in the doing for other people. Observing them is fine, and even commenting on their foibles, but really getting involved will only lead to trouble.

They *mesh* . . .
The NURTURER and the PROFESSOR are both calm, cool and collected. It takes a lot to ruffle their feathers. He admires her ability to keep her head amid chaos. She respects his genius for calculated action. She leaps to the defense of her cubs, while he pursues a measured plan, but when the going gets tough, these two stand firm.

They *change* . . .
The PROFESSOR thought he was happy with his solitary existence, but his emotions have been thawed by her warmth and caring love. She brings him into her family, introduces him to the shelter of kith and kin. He realizes that opening himself to another does not diminish him.

Remember
Short Circuit...

Ally Sheedy as
Stephanie Speck
CRUSADER

Steve
Guttenberg as
Newton Crosby
PROFESSOR

They clash and
mesh, but only
he changes

The PROFESSOR
says the
NURTURER:
• is simple
• overly
  protective and
• a quiet
  confidant

The NURTURER
says the
PROFESSOR:
• is intimidating
• critical and
• knows the
  solution

Remember
Frasier...

David Hyde
Pierce as
Niles Crane
PROFESSOR

Jane Leeves as
Daphne Moon
NURTURER

They clash and
mesh

167

The NURTURER has always thought with her heart, not with her head. But his example of rational decision-making shows her that it is possible to do the right thing even if a person needs to put some thought into it. She discovers that to take care of others, she must take care of herself first.

THE SWASHBUCKLER AND THE BOSS
They *clash* . . .

The SWASH-
BUCKLER says
the BOSS:
• is inflexible
• a party pooper
and
• worth the
trouble

The BOSS says
the SWASH-
BUCKLER:
• is reckless
• undisciplined
and
• an adrenaline
rush

The BOSS has her whole life planned down to the last second. She has no time to spend on adventure—there are companies to run, worlds to conquer. The SWASHBUCKLER rarely plans so much as a meal ahead of time—there are too many mountains to climb, universes to explore. She wonders how he can make such a game out of life. He wonders how she can make life such a chore.

They *mesh* . . .

The SWASHBUCKLER may not do things the way the BOSS likes, but he does get things done. She reluctantly admits that he is as effective as she is. These two thrive on competition. Even if the job is not as adventurous as he would like or prestigious enough to appeal to her, they will achieve their purpose. Both of them enjoy challenges and see in the other a worthy comrade.

Remember
Star Wars...

Harrison Ford
as Han Solo
SWASHBUCKLER

Carrie Fisher as
Princess Leia
Organa
BOSS

They clash and
mesh

They *change* . . .

The SWASHBUCKLER has leapt off a lot of cliffs, and not always with the benefit of a parachute. A few glances before that leap would not really do any harm and might save him some bruises. He learns to become more stable and less eager to take foolhardy chances.

The BOSS has always moved from one task to the next, without ever stopping to admire the fern growing in that decorator planter on her desk. A glimpse at his exciting life leaves her yearning for a few risky enterprises. She no longer needs to devote every waking moment to getting ahead. She discovers that life can be an adventure instead of a job.

THE SWASHBUCKLER AND THE SEDUCTRESS
They *clash* . . .

She is not amused by the SWASHBUCKLER's wild antics. The SEDUCTRESS considers his constant foolhardiness to be the height of stupidity. He knows why he risks life and limb—for the fun. What he has a harder time grasping is why she takes the risks *she* does—chancing bruised hearts and broken homes to get her way. She could be having a good time instead of just making it look like a good time.

They *mesh* . . .

The SWASHBUCKLER and the SEDUCTRESS know the pleasure of the flesh. Temptation beckons and each answers the call. She tells herself he is only a temporary diversion, while he convinces himself that he is just out for a good time. But they are fooling themselves. When they get together, the reaction is explosive. Both find it impossible to break away from the sexual spell.

They *change* . . .

The SWASHBUCKLER sees that a little bit of forethought can be advantageous. He still watches for opportunities more than he makes them, but he begins anticipating them as well. He learns to think before he acts.

The SEDUCTRESS plans her life down to the smallest detail to make sure she gets the best goodies. But she often fails to make allowances for the unexpected. His ability to react quickly to surprises teaches her the advantages of spontaneity. She discovers that winning is not always everything. Enjoying the game is what matters most.

THE SWASHBUCKLER AND THE SPUNKY KID
They *clash* . . .

The SPUNKY KID is a team player and is bewildered by anyone who is not. Doesn't he know that more gets done when everyone works together? The SWASHBUCKLER is used to being on his own, and is content to keep things that way. He is frustrated by her need to be part of the gang. Doesn't she realize that people just slow you down in the race for the prize?

They *mesh* . . .

The SPUNKY KID is feisty and brave, and the SWASHBUCKLER likes that in a woman. No wilting flower, she is knee deep in the trenches with him when danger comes. As for him, he steps up to the plate when she needs a pinch hitter and she values his ability to fit in where she needs him. And both

The SWASH-
BUCKLER
says the
SEDUCTRESS:
• is a schemer
• a floozy and
• captivating

The SEDUC-
TRESS says the
SWASHBUCK-
LER:
• is a good-for-
nothing
• foolish and
• sensational

Remember
*Indiana Jones
and the Last
Crusade...*

Harrison Ford as
Indiana Jones
SWASHBUCKLER

Alison Doody as
Elsa Schneider
SEDUCTRESS

They clash and
mesh

The SWASH-
BUCKLER
says the
SPUNKY KID:
• is aggravating
• too independ-
ent and
• his partner

The SPUNKY
KID says the
SWASHBUCK-
LER:
• is unreliable
• not a team
player and
• a challenge

Remember
*Raiders of the
Lost Ark*...

Harrison Ford as
Indiana Jones
SWASHBUCKLER

Karen Allen
as Marion
Ravenwood
SPUNKY KID

They clash,
mesh, and both
change

will be cracking jokes the whole time. These two meet jeopardy bravely, with smiles on their faces.

They *change* . . .

The SWASHBUCKLER may have enjoyed his solitary travels, but he discovers that partnership has its advantages. He can rely on her, and he finds he likes being able to count on someone else for a change. She watches his back. He learns to accept companionship.

The SPUNKY KID sees the world though new eyes, thanks to him. She sees more possibilities, both in herself and in her environment. He pulls her out of her rut, and she finds that she likes life a bit better out of the mainstream. She becomes more self-confident and more comfortable with who she is.

THE SWASHBUCKLER AND THE FREE SPIRIT

The SWASH-
BUCKLER says
the FREE SPIRIT:
• is annoying
• a nut and
• nonstop
    entertainment

The FREE SPIRIT
says the
SWASHBUCK-
LER:
• is brusque
• bossy but
• oh, what a
    man!

They *clash* . . .

The SWASHBUCKLER is a jack of all trades—give him a little wire and a twig, and he can make a ladder. He is able to turn his hand to any task and is frustrated by the FREE SPIRIT's utter lack of practicality, especially when she starts to meddle in his plans. She, on the other hand, is baffled by the importance he places on mere skill. She has imagination, and as far as she is concerned, that should be enough.

They *mesh* . . .

The SWASHBUCKLER and the FREE SPIRIT are footloose, fancy free and quite happy about it, thank you. These two know that life is a wonderful adventure—a ride to be savored. She loves the fact that it would never occur to him to try to curb her spirits. He is thrilled to meet a woman who has no intention of asking him to slow down. They have nothing to lose and they both like it that way.

Remember
*Indiana Jones
and the Temple
of Doom*...

Harrison Ford as
Indiana Jones
SWASHBUCKLER

Kate Capshaw
as Willie Scott
FREE SPIRIT

They clash and
mesh

They *change* . . .

The SWASHBUCKLER starts to see her as a worthy partner. Because she is willing to let him be free, he is able to acknowledge his feelings for her. He becomes more caring and less selfish when he discovers that love does not have to hold him back.

The FREE SPIRIT's tendency to interfere in this man's life has actually dragged her into his adventures. She enjoys the danger—of course, she does—really!—but she is uneasily aware that she brought on a lot of this trouble. She learns to hold back a bit and not meddle quite so much.

THE SWASHBUCKLER AND THE WAIF
They *clash* . . .
The SWASHBUCKLER finds his way through the world's dark alleys without any help and he has little time for those who do not even make the effort. He has no patience with someone who is unwilling to take the slightest risk. The WAIF thinks she has been getting by fairly well without causing any problems. She cannot comprehend his need for adrenaline. That stuff is poison as far as she is concerned.

They *mesh* . . .
The SWASHBUCKLER invariably manages to land on his feet. No matter how trying the circumstances, he pulls through. The WAIF floats through adversity, finding a way to accommodate others so she can fit into the situation with the least amount of controversy and effort. These two are at opposite poles, but both have the ability to adapt to changing circumstances. This talent is what generates the repeat between them.

They *change* . . .
The SWASHBUCKLER surfs through life alone. Friends might accompany him, but he has no permanent ties. But she needs him, truly needs him. He discovers that being needed is an exciting thrill. He learns to be there for someone.

The WAIF tiptoes through life, watchful for any danger. But seeing how he manages to get himself out of all those scrapes makes her realize that risk need not be fatal. She recognizes that the same old same old really is not so safe anyway—it was just a much better known quantity. She starts to step out more and to take a few chances.

THE SWASHBUCKLER AND THE LIBRARIAN
They *clash* . . .
The LIBRARIAN prefers to analyze a situation, sizing up the possibilities and probabilities. The SWASHBUCKLER prefers to roll up his sleeves and dive in. She finds his tendency to leap into a situation exasperating. How can he not see that a little forethought will save trouble? He considers her agonizing over

The SWASH-BUCKLER says the WAIF:
• is a drag
• pathetic and
• she needs him

The WAIF says the SWASH-BUCKLER:
• is brash
• a bully and
• the one who can save her

Remember *The Princess Bride*...

Cary Elwes as Westley SWASHBUCKLER

Robin Wright Penn as Buttercup WAIF

They clash, mesh and both change

the details a waste of time. Can't she understand that it is action, not thought, that gets the job done?

They *mesh* . . .

Neither the SWASHBUCKLER nor the LIBRARIAN has any difficulty completing the tasks they undertake. Each displays seemingly effortless capability. What's more, they do not necessarily follow the directions—each is imaginative enough to see a solution that the higher ups might not have envisioned. She briskly nods at the ease with which he finishes; he grins his approval of her accomplishments.

They *change* . . .

The SWASHBUCKLER enjoys his free lifestyle, but her example shows him that thinking ahead can be useful. Having someone along for this grand adventure called life is more fun than he would have thought. He becomes more open to commitment.

The LIBRARIAN is on the ride of her life and she has no desire to get off. This man shows her the world, and she is not going back to the library—unless it is to plan her next trip. Oh, yes, she will still plan ahead, but now there will be a few risks along the way! She learns to be more open to adventure and willing to take a chance.

THE SWASHBUCKLER AND THE CRUSADER

They *clash* . . .

These two have so much in common—but motivation is not one of them. The CRUSADER's every thought, every action is devoted to furthering her mission in life. The SWASHBUCKLER thinks and acts for the sheer fun of the moment, the rush of the excitement, the thrill of the game. He is perplexed by her zealous devotion to duty. She is astonished that he could veer off course for the sake of his own purposes. Why doesn't he realize this is life or death?

They *mesh* . . .

Fear does not appear in the vocabulary of either the CRUSADER or the SWASHBUCKLER. They forge the wildest rivers, climb the most treacherous mountains, and stroll down the darkest valleys with nary a glance behind them. They are invulnerable, or so they believe. Besides, when striving for a

---

Sidebar:

The SWASH-BUCKLER says the LIBRARIAN:
• is preachy
• annoying and
• a hidden treasure

The LIBRARIAN says the SWASHBUCK-LER:
• is irresponsible
• irrepressible and
• the best time she has ever had

Remember *Romancing the Stone*...

Michael Douglas as Jack Colton SWASHBUCKLER

Kathleen Turner as Joan Wilder LIBRARIAN

They clash, mesh and both change

The SWASH-BUCKLER says the CRUSADER:
• is dreary
• a fanatic and
• the most passionate woman he has ever met

The CRUSADER says the SWASHBUCK-LER:
• is selfish
• frivolous and
• good, clean fun

cause or enjoying the thrill of a lifetime, there is no time for worrying or hand-wringing.

They *change* . . .

The SWASHBUCKLER has had a long time to follow his love of the adventurous life without a thought to any serious issues. But her dedication brings him up short and makes him question his purpose in life. He learns to use his courage and skills for the sake of another.

The CRUSADER's commitment to her cause has been all consuming—and she suddenly realizes the price of her zealotry. His frank enjoyment of his capers opens her eyes to the pleasures that life has to offer. All work and no play has made her a bit dull, and she discovers that boring is—well, *boring*. She begins to be less driven.

THE SWASHBUCKLER AND THE NURTURER
They *clash* . . .

When the going gets too permanent, the SWASHBUCKLER is gone. That is his problem—he never stays in one place for any length of time. The NURTURER is confused by his need to constantly seek out new worlds and civilizations. How can he not want the warmth of hearth and home? He cannot understand her need to stay in one place. How can she not want to see everything there is to see?

They *mesh* . . .

The SWASHBUCKLER meets adversity with a cool head and a smile. The NURTURER wastes no time fretting, but patiently strives to overcome her problems. He admires her ability to forgo hand-wringing and fretting and just take care of a problem. She is pleased by his matter-of-fact handling of situations. Both accept that problems happen and each is certain that these too shall pass.

They *change* . . .

The SWASHBUCKLER has traveled far and wide, and home was wherever he hung his hat. But she shows him that having a place to come back to is a good feeling—and makes coming back very desirable. He learns to stay close to what matters to him.

Remember *Twister...*

Helen Hunt as Jo Harding CRUSADER

Bill Paxton as Bill Harding SWASHBUCKLER

They clash and mesh, but only he changes

The SWASHBUCKLER says the NURTURER:
• is constraining
• controlling and
• a place of comfort

The NURTURER says the SWASHBUCKLER:
• is rowdy
• thoughtless and
• in need of roots

Remember *Crocodile Dundee...*

Paul Hogan as Michael J. "Crocodile" Dundee SWASHBUCKLER

Linda Kozlowski as Sue Charlton NURTURER

They clash, mesh and both change

The NURTURER has never strayed too far from home. After all, she might be needed. But this man has taken her away from those who vie for her attention, and she discovers that taking a little time for herself is okay. She begins to find a way to tame her need to sacrifice for others, and instead indulges herself now and then.

THE WARRIOR AND THE BOSS

They *clash* . . .

The WARRIOR and the BOSS are two very stubborn people. Both of them are totally committed to their own agendas. He is interested in making things right; she is interested in getting her way. Opinionated and focused, if their goals conflict, they are constantly at loggerheads. If she irritates him enough, he holds a grudge. If he opposes her for long, she loses her temper.

They *mesh* . . .

Though the WARRIOR is focused on a particular job or mission, and the BOSS wants control in every area of her life, both are ambitious and driven. She never gives up. He responds to this trait, since it is one he shares. She admires his tenacity and his commitment to his cause. She can respect this man. She does not stand in the way of his goals, and he does not object to her reaching some of her own.

They *change* . . .

The WARRIOR realizes that he must choose his battles more carefully. This woman shows him that he should take care of his business before saving the world. She teaches him that a healthy self-interest can work to his advantage. He learns to let go of minor problems.

The BOSS discovers that this is a man she cannot push around. In order to co-exist with him, she must realize that there are other ways to do things that are just as effective as her ways. His integrity reminds her of what she has given up to get ahead. She discovers that the end does not always justify the means.

THE WARRIOR AND THE SEDUCTRESS

They *clash* . . .

The WARRIOR lives by a code of honor that he is not capable of functioning without. To him, the SEDUCTRESS imme-

---

The WARRIOR says the BOSS:
- is an obstacle
- a dictator and
- a bold partner

The BOSS says the WARRIOR:
- is obsessed
- too noble and
- a strong hero

Remember *Rio Grande...*

John Wayne as Lieutenant Colonel Kirby Yorke WARRIOR

Maureen O'Hara as Kathleen Yorke BOSS

They clash, mesh and both change

diately strikes him as a woman with no honor and little honesty. He judges her selfish ways with a merciless eye and an unforgiving heart. On the other hand, she finds his constant lectures annoying and unjustified. How dare he judge her lack of principles? She has her own code, but he is just too blind to see it.

They *mesh* . . .

Both the WARRIOR and the SEDUCTRESS endure. Neither lets someone victimize them and get away with it. Both have suffered and survived. In fact, not only have they prevailed over adversity, they have grown stronger because of it. They both believe the end justifies the means if that end fits into their own particular code of ethics. When they look into each other's eyes, they see a survivor.

They *change* . . .

The WARRIOR finally understands that she has her own morality which is different from his. His stern judgment has hurt her and he needs to make amends. He realizes he should not judge the book by its cover.

The SEDUCTRESS slowly realizes that this man's word is his bond. This builds trust in her heart and she finds herself willing to take a chance on other people as well. His devotion to his cause opens her eyes. She learns to care about others.

THE WARRIOR AND THE SPUNKY KID
They *clash* . . .

The WARRIOR is used to handling problems alone. He needs no help to accomplish his mission. The SPUNKY KID is sure that if everyone works together, the task will be accomplished. He is a loner, she is a team player. He cannot understand why she insists on including everyone and his brother in her plans. She finds his stubborn refusal of help incomprehensible.

They *mesh* . . .

Both the WARRIOR and the SPUNKY KID are two people who live by their word. Ethical and moral, they relate to the underdogs of the world. If they make a commitment, they follow through, even to the detriment of their own well being. Since both feel that their integrity is important, they respect the principle in the other. Though they look at things differently, their core values are the same.

The WARRIOR says the SEDUCTRESS:
• is dishonest
• dishonorable and
• a tempting treat

The SEDUCTRESS says the WARRIOR:
• is inflexible
• puritanical and
• a straight shooter

Remember *The Maltese Falcon...*

Humphrey Bogart as Sam Spade WARRIOR

Mary Astor as Brigid O'Shaughnessy SEDUCTRESS

They clash and mesh

The WARRIOR says the SPUNKY KID:
• is impertinent
• too outgoing and
• a steadfast heart

The SPUNKY KID says the WARRIOR:
• is humorless
• unforgiving and
• in need of a friend

Remember
Superman...

Margot Kidder
as Lois Lane
SPUNKY KID

Christopher
Reeve as Clark
Kent/Superman
WARRIOR

They clash and
mesh

They *change* . . .

The WARRIOR softens under her guidance. He has always been a loner pursuing his cause, but he finds that in her company, she eases the way with others. He starts to connect with people and finds out it is nice to lighten up on occasion. He learns to enjoy humor, people and life.

The SPUNKY KID has always lacked faith in the relationship area. When this man focuses, he is hard to resist and now he is concentrating all his attention on her. She flourishes under his undivided attention. He encourages her to focus and succeed in every area of her life. She becomes more confident and self-assured.

THE WARRIOR AND THE FREE SPIRIT

The WARRIOR
says the
FREE SPIRIT:
• is kooky
• a babbler and
• a ray of hope

The FREE SPIRIT
says the
WARRIOR:
• is no fun
• gruff and
• a solid
  defender

They *clash* . . .

The WARRIOR is boggled by the FREE SPIRIT. She talks a mile a minute, flits from goal to goal and has a thousand friends. She finds him far too serious for her taste. He seems filled with only anger and responsibility. She cannot understand why he will not let himself relax. He is sure that if she just had a little order in her life, she would be much better off. Her lack of control bothers him. Everything about him bothers her, especially his grim gaze.

Remember
Under Siege...

Steven Seagal
as Casey Ryback
WARRIOR

Erika Eleniak as
Jordan Tate
FREE SPIRIT

They clash and
mesh, but only
she changes

They *mesh* . . .

The WARRIOR and the FREE SPIRIT both care deeply, they just react in different ways. While she spends most of her time bringing joy to her friends and neighbors, he's trying desperately to protect and serve. She is enamored with his deep sense of responsibility and honor, while he finds her loving heart hard to resist. Though they are light and dark, they find a common ground to share.

They *change* . . .

The WARRIOR is a loner by nature, but this woman will not allow him to hide behind his cause. She forces him to identify and express his feelings. Spontaneity and joy become a normal, everyday occurrence and he finds he likes the variety. He learns to relent and unbend.

The FREE SPIRIT becomes more grounded and not so flighty. He shows her that with a little discipline, her scattered life can become manageable, and she can still maintain all her friendships. He teaches her that promises are important to keep. She starts to follow through on her word.

THE WARRIOR AND THE WAIF
They *clash* . . .
The WARRIOR is a fighter. The WAIF never fights, even if her life depends on it. This unresisting response to any kind of threat makes him furious. How can she not stand up for herself? She finds his constant attacks painful. Why won't he let her drift away from this scene of conflict? Where his responses are rough and harsh, hers are invariably soft and kind. He never trusts. She always does.

They *mesh* . . .
Their story is as old as time. The WARRIOR needs to protect. The WAIF needs protection. He is the quintessential rescuer and this woman wants to be rescued. They compliment each other's strengths and weaknesses. Each of them stands back and observes the world around them, unwilling to dive in unless pushed. Both are outsiders. This driving need to be saved and to save draws them together.

They *change* . . .
The WARRIOR finds out he does not always have to fight a battle to win. Her patience teaches him that sometimes doing nothing wins the day. He finds that a soft word instead of a harsh rebuke sways people to his cause. He learns to pick his battles.

The WAIF finds herself growing in self-confidence with this man. He teaches her that being a doormat is making her unhappy and that occasionally fighting for what she believes in is a satisfying experience. His love for her gives her the courage to speak up for herself. She begins to stand firm in her beliefs.

THE WARRIOR AND THE LIBRARIAN
They *clash* . . .
The WARRIOR solves his problems by taking action. The LIBRARIAN analyzes every angle before deciding what to do. His physical, intense presence throws her into a dither. Her methodical, thorough response to any issue drives him to distraction. Both of them are stubborn enough to think their way

The WARRIOR says the WAIF:
• is passive
• a weakling and
• a damsel in distress

The WAIF says the WARRIOR:
• is difficult
• unyielding and
• her knight in shining armor

Remember
Blade Runner...

Harrison Ford as Rick Deckard WARRIOR

Daryl Hannah as Pris WAIF

They clash, mesh and both change

177

is the only way, and neither is able to convince the other of that fact.

They *mesh* . . .

The WARRIOR and the LIBRARIAN are both loners. Neither of them minds a solitary existence. They often feel more comfortable alone than in a chattering crowd of people. Both of them are fundamentally serious and focused. They want things to be perfect—whether final justice or the card catalog. Their demand for perfection drives people away from them, but drives them closer to each other.

They *change* . . .

The WARRIOR realizes that he might be too quick in some of his decisions. Her methodical analysis of every fact draws his attention to details he might have missed. He begins to see the value of taking his time and seeing the other side. He learns to withhold judgment.

The LIBRARIAN finds herself the focus of this intense man's attention, and she revels in the unfamiliar experience. She becomes less conservative, more willing to take a few chances. His quick decisions teach her that not every detail needs to be reviewed before reaching a conclusion. She begins to take action.

THE WARRIOR AND THE CRUSADER

They *clash* . . .

If the WARRIOR and the CRUSADER are on different teams, a royal battle results. Both are stubborn and opinionated. Neither is likely to see the other side of an argument. They believe strongly that they are right and everyone else is wrong. Backing down is not an option. Since both are determined and obstinate, the battle is long, drawn out and fierce.

They *mesh* . . .

Brave and resolute, the WARRIOR and the CRUSADER are well-matched. Even if they are fighting against each other. Each grows to respect the other's commitment and dedication. Where others might question their sense of duty to their mission, these two immediately discern what drives the other. At last, they have each found a partner who believes as strongly as they do in what they are striving to attain.

The WARRIOR says the LIBRARIAN:
• is headstrong
• a critic and
• a true lady

The LIBRARIAN says the WARRIOR:
• is obstinate
• dogmatic and
• a courageous champion

Remember *True Lies*...

Arnold Schwarzenegger as Harry Tasker WARRIOR

Jamie Lee Curtis as Helen Tasker LIBRARIAN

They clash, mesh and both change

The WARRIOR says the CRUSADER:
• is obstinate
• unladylike and
• a partner against injustice

The CRUSADER says the WARRIOR:
• is bull-headed
• a tyrant and
• a partner against injustice

They *change* . . .

The WARRIOR is amazed to find someone else as committed and courageous as he is. He is no longer alone anymore in his drive to accomplish his task. Helping each other makes him realize that her goals are as important as his. He learns to see someone else's side.

The CRUSADER is amazed to find a man who understands her desire to sacrifice all for the cause. Unlike other men, he never nags her about staying home or cooking dinner. He supports her need to move mountains. She realizes that having a partner can smooth the path in front of her and lighten her load.

THE WARRIOR AND THE NURTURER

They *clash* . . .

The WARRIOR approaches life with intensity and conviction. The NURTURER is easy-going and calm in her daily tasks. She is quite stable and finds his dark, forbidding outlook a little too edgy for her taste. He finds her low-key diplomacy a cop-out. Though she tries to warm to him and figure him out, she eventually loses patience. Since both have a will of iron, when they fight, neither backs down.

They *mesh* . . .

The WARRIOR and the NURTURER are both protectors at heart. Both care about the needs of others. She spends most of her time helping the people closest to her, while he fights for the greater good. They relate to each other's need to help. They are capable and cool in a crisis. Wanting to make the world a better place, they realize that each has skills the other can use.

They *change* . . .

The WARRIOR starts to look beyond his narrow focus. Her warm encouragement gives him the opportunity to relax. She does not quibble about minor things, and he realizes that a long-term relationship with her is possible. He learns to win friends through diplomacy.

The NURTURER finds that it can be nice to be protected rather than always being the protector. He teaches her that some principles cannot be sacrificed just to achieve peace. Sometimes it is worth raising her hackles if she believes strongly in something. She starts to take time for herself.

Remember
High Noon...

Gary Cooper as
Bill Kane
WARRIOR

Grace Kelly as
Amy Kane
CRUSADER

They clash,
mesh and both
change

The WARRIOR
says the
NURTURER:
• is too
compromising
• a pollyanna
and
• a soothing
touch

The NURTURER
says the
WARRIOR:
• is rude
• hard to work
with and
• a good
protector

Remember
Ladyhawke...

Rutger Hauer as
Etienne Navarre
WARRIOR

Michelle Pfeiffer
as Isabeau
NURTURER

They clash and
mesh

The SEDUC-
TRESS is...
Goldie Hawn
as Elise Eliot
Atchinson

The SPUNKY
KID is...
Bette Midler as
Brenda Morelli
Cushman

The NURTURER
is...
Diane Keaton
as Annie
MacDuggan
Paradis

THE FIRST WIVES CLUB

This fun movie tells the tale of three college friends, all of whom have been dumped by their husbands for younger trophy models. When a suicide brings them together, they unite to get even against the men who done them wrong.

SEDUCTRESS Elise Elliot is an Oscar®-winning actress who surrounds herself with her own youthful image, and joyously accepts the homage of an adoring public as her due. But she fights a constant battle against age. Elise is so desperate to keep the years at bay, the only thing she lifts more often than her drink—is her face.

SPUNKY KID Brenda Morelli still carries a torch for her ex-husband, even though he lavishes expensive gifts on his new lady friend. Her sense of humor allows her to keep on keeping on, even making sure her son maintains a good relationship with his dad. But Brenda feels the pain of his rejection deeply.

NURTURER Annie MacDuggan believes her egotistical husband will come back to her, if only she gets her therapy right. Annie does her best to perform the juggling act necessary to please everyone in her family.

When these three get together, NURTURER Annie again tries to be the peacemaker between the more forceful Elise and Brenda. But it is the SPUNKY KID's ability to bring a team together that allows their revenge to be turned into a force that will help all women victimized by men. As they pull their plan together, and grow closer themselves, transformations occur.

SEDUCTRESS Elise realizes her talent, not her beauty, defines her career. She starts making smart and sober decisions, winning a standing ovation on Broadway. She evolves into a confident BOSS. NURTURER Annie realizes that she is worth some of her own attention, and tells her cheating husband to take a hike. And loyal SPUNKY KID Brenda gets the man she never stopped loving to open his eyes to her inner beauty.

These three women end the movie dancing and singing their song of independence.

GHOSTBUSTERS

Losing their funding at the university, three unemployed parapychology scientists strike out on their own. They are just in time to save New York from certain disaster at the hands of an evil god. But along the way, they find themselves in predicaments that defy the imagination.

Dr. Peter Venkman, the consummate CHARMER, is the first to propose setting up shop on their own. His idea to start a ghost removal service is not immediately accepted by his skeptical friends, but his smooth talk and sunny optimism soon win them over. Peter is in charge of "handling" their newest, and only, customer. And he is sure that taking her to dinner at a fancy restaurant will ensure they keep her business.

Convinced by Peter to take a third mortgage out on his childhood home, Raymond Stantz finds it hard to say no to anyone—including the ghost in his bed. Happy to be part of the team, he is chagrined when he is the cause of apparent defeat. But the StayPuff Man, with its smiling face and warm memories, could only be conjured up by a BEST FRIEND. Only this man could dream of being killed by a marshmallow.

Dr. Egon Spengler is the brains behind the operation. This PROFESSOR spends little time thinking about how many customers they have. He is far too intrigued with what is going on in the city and is determined to figure it out before it is too late. Egon spends most of his time inventing new contraptions and gadgets with which to trap and capture the ghosts.

Another PROFESSOR, Louis Tully, spends his time tallying his client's accounts and wistfully dreaming of the girl next door. He is sucked into an evil he has no defense for, but as soon as the spell is broken, he is eagerly discussing the finances of his rescuers.

An instant hit, this comedy lives long in the memory, not for the ghosts and goblins, but because of the funny and endearing characters starring next to the special effects.

WAITING TO EXHALE

Based on Terry McMillan's popular novel, this movie follows four African American women through the trials and tribulations of their love lives.

Savannah dreams of finding Prince Charming but finds herself involved with men who have girlfriends or wives. Her wry amusement at her predicament and her steady support toward her friends shows her to be a SPUNKY KID. At the end of this movie, she is still looking for a man to love and still waiting to exhale.

The CHARMER is...
Bill Murray as Dr. Peter Venkman

The BEST FRIEND is...
Dan Aykroyd as Dr. Raymond Stantz

The PROFESSORs are...
Harold Ramis as Dr.Egon Spengler and Rick Moranis as Louis Tully

181

The SPUNKY
KID is...
Whitney
Houston as
Savannah
Jackson

The BOSS is...
Angela Bassett
as Bernadine
Harris

The NURTURER
is...
Loretta Devine
as Gloria
Johnson

The FREE SPIRIT
is...
Lela Rochon as
Robin Stokes

Bernadine's outrage at her husband's betrayal is turned into a burning need for victory over the odds stacked against her. This BOSS takes no prisoners when battling for her dignity and her livelihood. In a memorable moment, she packs all of her husband's belongings into his car and douses it with gasoline. She slowly smokes a cigarette, and with a flip of her wrist, turns the car into an inferno. No regrets for this woman. The man is a fool who deserves what he gets.

A good friend and patient mother, Loretta is the glue who holds all her pals together. This NURTURER greets a new neighbor with the offer of a home-cooked meal, worries about her friend, Bernadine, when things look bad, and loves and forgives her son for almost anything. Of all the women in the movie, she is the one who ends up with a man—and a good man at that.

FREE SPIRIT Robin bounces from man to man, dreaming of a happy home, but never finding the gold at the end of the rainbow. She fiercely denounces the men who cheat on her friends, but never looks at her own woeful record in the love department. By the end of the movie, her emotional decisions have left her pregnant and unwed, but Robin looks on it as a new adventure.

The blending of these different women hit a chord in the public. Each of these unique personalities fit well with each other, showing how strong women can be when they stick together.

THE DIRTY DOZEN

This film tells the story of an officer's mission to turn twelve convicts into a crack commando team capable of pulling off a bold strike against Nazi Germany. Early in the movie, as the "dirty dozen" is introduced to their new commander, we receive glimpses of the archetypes represented. The initial promise of the personalities is repaid in full.

The CHIEF is...
Lee Marvin as
Major John
Reisman

The BEST
FRIEND is...
Donald
Sutherland as
Vernon Pinkley

The BAD BOY
is...
John Cassavetes
as Victor Franko

All business, CHIEF Major John Reisman wastes no time in beginning his task. As the major inspects the line of convicts, BEST FRIEND Vernon Pinkley is the only who offers a smile to his new commander, while BAD BOY Victor Franko cannot resist offering a challenge. The Major quickly tosses the rebel to the ground, earning the respect of his new troop. Meanwhile, LOST SOUL Archer Maggott displays his disconnection at every opportunity, his body always physically turned away from the group.

Reisman has two WARRIOR allies within the dozen. John Wladislaw was imprisoned for killing a medic in the field—an act he committed because the man was fleeing the battle with a pack containing medical supplies. Robert Jefferson killed in defending himself from a racist attack. But these two show no bitterness for the injustice of their convictions, and quickly move to aid their leader in his mission. When the BAD BOY tries to escape, endangering all of the convicts, they are the ones who prevent his flight.

The men go through the motions, building their quarters and learning the tasks for their mission. But it is BAD BOY Franco's continued cocky defiance that finally turns them into a team— the dozen are united in their refusal to wash without hot water. The disdain of the "regular" army pulls them together and devotes them to their cause. Their mission is nearly destroyed by LOST SOUL Maggott's tortured madness, but BAD BOY Franco has no compunction in shooting him.

Working together, this group manages to pull off a tremendous victory against the common enemy.

LITTLE WOMEN

A children's story that has never lost its luster, this earnest tale of four sisters growing up in the North during the era of America's Civil War still holds all its charm.

Eldest sister, Meg, is the calm center to the frantic activities of her sisters. Following in her mother's footsteps, this NURTURER is the first to scold and the first to hug. Once she has found the man she loves, she happily settles down to a life of babies and making a home. She has no yearning for the big lights or the fancy streets of Europe, but welcomes her sisters home when they arrive for weddings or funerals.

Questioning and challenging, Jo is constantly writing down her stories and dreaming of travel to exotic locations. A LIBRARIAN, her active mind is not at all content with the status quo. Her aunt is sure Jo will turn into an old spinster and deeds her house to her so she will have somewhere to live. Rather than being offended, Jo immediately sets about turning it into a school, intent on passing on her knowledge. When she does fall in love, it is with a man who loves her brain as well as her heart.

The two WARRIORs are...
Jim Brown as Robert Jefferson and Charles Bronson as Joseph Wladislaw

And the LOST SOUL is...
Telly Savalas as Archer Maggott

The NURTURER is...
Trini Alvarado as Meg March

The LIBRARIAN is...
Winona Ryder as Jo March

The WAIF is... Claire Danes as Beth March

The BOSS is... Samantha Mathis and Kirsten Dunst as Amy March

Dear, sweet Beth drifts around the fringes of the family, wanting only for them all to be together. This WAIF is always supportive, but never gets the energy to break out on her own. Her weak constitution causes the family to constantly worry about her, cosseting and cooing over Beth's every move. When she finally succumbs to her sickness, the sisters grieve for the loss of this tender spirit.

Amy barrels through life, demanding attention and wanting to always be included. This young BOSS is sure of where she is headed—her goal is marriage to a rich man. Her steel will cannot be bent, even when she falls in love. If Laurie fails to measure up, then she will not marry him.

Little Women shows the love and strength that a group of sisters can give each other. No argument can tear the bonds apart. They will always be close.

SAVING PRIVATE RYAN

Steven Spielberg's classic war movie depicts a unit of men sent to fetch the last remaining brother of three soldiers who have been killed in battle.

Captain John Miller is head of the unit commanded to find this needle in the haystack. This BEST FRIEND clearly finds the job irksome, but does not fight the order or question the assignment. With a quiet confidence, he leads his band of griping men across the battle-torn French countryside. With a joke and a smile, he quiets anger and with a steady and kind voice, he comforts the dying and wounded.

Sergeant Michael Horvath is second in command and keeps the troops in line. While the Captain stays above the fray, the Sergeant has no trouble whipping orders out and demanding obedience. A CHIEF, he is loyal to Miller and is the rock upon which the Captain can depend.

BAD BOY Private Reiben constantly questions and mutters about the orders they have been given. Angry and defiant, at one point, he states his intention of turning back. His confrontation with the Sergeant is a classic CHIEF/BAD BOY exchange. Only the calm voice of the Captain turns them into comrades once again.

Corporal Timothy Upham was happily content to be an interpreter, far away from the front lines. But this PROFESSOR is plucked out of his cocoon and by the end of the movie,

The BEST FRIEND is... Tom Hanks as Captain John Miller

The CHIEF is... Tom Sizemore as Sergeant Michael Horvath

The BAD BOY is... Edward Burns as Private Reiben

The PROFESSOR is... Jeremy Davies as Corporal Timothy Upham

and the WARRIOR is... Matt Damon as Private James Ryan

has learned some hard lessons about the real world and is no longer able to stay in his ivory tower.

And finally, the man the movie revolves around—Private James Ryan. This WARRIOR takes the news of his brothers' death with stoic calm. When informed of his release from duty, he nobly insists on staying with his unit. The battle for the bridge is too important to the cause, and they need every man. His determination wins grudging approval from the men sent to save him.

Saving Private Ryan shows all the brutality of war with an unflinching eye, but it also shines a bright light on the bravery of the men of the greatest generation.

STEEL MAGNOLIAS

In a small Louisiana town, six women share their lives and their strength.

NURTURER M'Lynn wants nothing more than for her beloved daughter, WAIF Shelby, to live. She is prepared to make any sacrifice for her child, even give a kidney. Shelby, however, endures her lot. Determined to give her husband the child she wants, she drifts into greater illness. M'Lynn cannot understand Shelby's refusal to do what is best for herself, but when her worst fears are realized, she calmly redirects her devotion to her grandson.

SPUNKY KID Truvy Jones smoothes over the rough spots among her friends. Her cheerful salon is the focal point for this disparate group of women. Under her dryers, all women are equal. She warmly opens her arms to FREE SPIRIT Annelle Desoto, never blinking an eye when Annelle travels from one passion to another. Truvy's practicality causes her to urge Annelle to ease up on her religious fervor with the same enthusiasm she urged her to give up her party girl habits.

Matronly Clairee Belcher is the sort of gracious BOSS only a Southern woman could be. She buys a radio station, then regally conducts a locker room interview of the local football team, asking the coach about the new uniforms, assuming all are interested in her interests. But she has only to raise a brow, or speak a few well-chosen words in her soft drawl to command instant obedience. Her contemporary, FREE SPIRIT Ouiser Boudreaux, parades through life, each outfit more outrageously mismatched than the last, and always being tugged about by her unruly dog.

The NURTURER is... Sally Field as M'Lynn Eatenton

The SPUNKY KID is... Dolly Parton as Truvy Jones

The FREE SPIRIT is... Shirley MacLaine as Ouiser Boudreaux

Another FREE SPIRIT is... Daryl Hannah as Annelle Dupuy Desoto

The BOSS is... Olympia Dukakis as Clairee Belcher

The WAIF is... Julia Roberts as Shelby Eatenton Latcherie

185

When Annelle's labor begins at the Easter picnic, the women's roles are clear. M'Lynn and Truvy rush to support Annelle, propping her up on both sides. Ouiser begins shouting for a doctor, nearly losing her dog in the process, while Clairee efficiently directs a car to drive up to take the pregnant woman away.

Together, these women show the steel beneath every woman's flowery façade.

ARMAGEDDON

With an asteroid speeding toward Earth, the fate of humanity lies in the hands of a group of irreverent oil drillers.

The two CHIEFs are... Bruce Willis as Harry S. Stamper and Billy Bob Thornton as Dan Truman

Two CHIEFs are in this mix. Harry S. Stamper takes charge, whether in his own oil company or in the middle of space. Dan Truman holds the reins at NASA's Houston Control. They both understand and respect the sense of responsibility that drives the other.

The SWASH-BUCKLER is... Ben Affleck as A.J. Frost

What CHIEF Harry does not understand is SWASHBUCK-LER A.J. Frost's unconventional style. A.J.'s reckless exploits consistently raise the hackles of his boss, especially when he sleeps with Harry's daughter. True love is no excuse for what a CHIEF can only view as a challenge to his authority. It is left to BEST FRIEND "Bear" Kurleenbear to cast oil on troubled waters. Strong, capable, and ready with a smile and a laugh, he helps keep a lid on the tension among the others.

The BEST FRIEND is... Michael Clarke Duncan as Jayotis "Bear" Kurleenbear

The WARRIOR is... William Fichtner as Colonel William Sharp

The stern sense of duty shown by WARRIOR Colonel William Sharp keeps him appalled at the depths to which NASA sank to find its heroes. He and Harry clash over the control of the mission. But the CHIEF's ability to inspire trust wins over even this honorable hero, and command of the space task passes from the astronaut to the oil driller.

And the CHARMER layered with LOST SOUL is... Steve Buscemi as Rockhound

A layered character, CHARMER/LOST SOUL Rockhound loves to live the high life. He came along for the prospect of reward, but easily loses hope when the chips are down. His fatalism endangers their success, but he just cannot help himself. He has to be physically restrained to prevent him from causing further damage, and when a volunteer for destruction is needed, he cannot be trusted with the task.

SWASHBUCKLER A.J. draws the short straw that means certain death, but Harry knows his daughter's happiness depends on A.J.'s return. He does not sacrifice to save the world, as a WARRIOR would, but he will lay down his life for his family. The men who know this CHIEF, know he will not fail.

GILLIGAN'S ISLAND

Their three hour tour turned into years of exile, but the ever popular castaways always managed to blow their chance at rescue. Despite the silly antics and wildly improbable events, audiences tuned in for another zany episode time after time.

BEST FRIEND Gilligan cheerfully helps out his fellow castaways, never objecting to his workman status. He continually exasperates CHIEF Skipper, but no one can stay mad at a BEST FRIEND for long. His optimistic outlook earns him forgiveness though the latest botched chance of rescue is usually his fault.

The lives of the castaways are made bearable by the know-how of the PROFESSOR who gave his "name" to his archetype. The others look to him to have the answer to any question. His encyclopedic store of knowledge enables them to use every resource available to make their island as comfortable as possible.

CHARMER Thurston Howell III cheerfully buys every comfort, and what money cannot purchase, his charismatic personality will. Of course, neither he, nor his lovely wife Lovey, a queenly BOSS, ever lift a finger for themselves. Their consistent air of entitlement get them whatever they want. Somehow the others just give in to their commands.

SPUNKY KID Mary Ann's perky enthusiasm keeps smiles bright no matter how hopeless the chances of rescue are, but the castaways count on SEDUCTRESS Ginger whenever some hapless male needs to be seduced into something he does not want to do. They always let her entertain them.

Each of the characters brought an essential ingredient to the mix. They had the right assortment of leaders and followers, planners and doers, to survive on Gilligan's isle.

L.A. CONFIDENTIAL

This film noir garnered awards and applause by showing a slice of early 1950s Hollywood. A gritty tale of sex and corruption, it stole the hearts of many a reviewer and fan. One of reasons was the wonderful characters populating the story.

Jack Vincennes is a police officer who knows how to play the game. This CHARMER loves the spotlight and makes sure his friend, the tabloid writer, is always around to take pictures of his

The BEST FRIEND is... Bob Denver as Gilligan

The CHIEF is... Alan Hale Jr. as Skipper Jonas Grumby

The PROFESSOR is... Russell Johnson as The Professor

The CHARMER is... Jim Backus as Thurston Howell III

While Natalie Schafer played Lovey, his wife, the "queenly" BOSS

The SPUNKY KID is... Dawn Wells as Mary Ann Summers

And the SEDUCTRESS is... Tina Louise as Ginger Grant

187

The CHARMER
is...
Kevin Spacey as
Jack Vincennes

The WARRIOR
is...
Russell Crowe
as Bud White

The CHIEF is...
Guy Pearce as
Ed Exley

And the WAIF
is...
Kim Basinger as
Lynn Bracken

latest catch. He sees no problem with taking a payback or two—all part of the job as far as he is concerned. His clear view of people and their motives keeps him one step ahead of everyone else. Almost.

WARRIOR Bud White grew up with an abusive father and watched his mother be beaten to death. Now, his mission is to save women and avenge the pain men have caused them. He feels righteous in bending the law in order to achieve his purpose. After all, abusive men deserve to die. His brute force hides a kind heart and a quick intellect that not many people appreciate.

Ed Exley plans to get ahead. He has figured out just how to do it and has no qualms about stepping over people to get it done. This CHIEF wants to do things by the book, but when all is said and done, he will do what it takes to get the glory, the awards . . . and the promotion. His skillful interrogation of a set of criminals, playing one off against the other, shows how powerful an opponent this man can be.

Though a whore, Lynn Bracken's presence permeates the movie. This WAIF drifts into every man's head, inspiring dreams and desires they cannot seem to control. She dreams of another life, but cannot shake herself out of the rut she has fallen into. She loves Bud with all her heart, but finds herself having sex with his supposed enemy. When he becomes enraged and hits her, she, of course, forgives him.

L.A. Confidential brought the film noir style back into vogue. Its complicated plot, beautiful scenery and fascinating characters live in the imagination long after the film is over.

THE BIG CHILL

The BEST
FRIEND is...
Kevin Kline
as Harold

The NURTURER
is...
Glenn Close
as Sarah

The CHARMER
is...
Tom Berenger
as Sam Weber

Seven college buddies come together to mourn the suicide of one of their old gang of radicals. The funeral and reception lead to an extended weekend of reminiscing and regrets.

BEST FRIEND Harold and NURTURER Sarah are, of course, the hosts of this reunion. Harry has become a responsible businessman and father, with no interest in confronting authority or making waves. Dr. Sarah bandages physical wounds and listens patiently to everyone's woes, hiding her own pain most of the time. Neither contemplate turning away any friend from their doorstep.

Sam Weber has become a big Hollywood star and relishes his celebrity. But this CHARMER has doubts about some of the selfish decisions he made in the past. PROFESSOR Michael has no real doubts about what he is doing, though he does like to spend endless hours analyzing his behavior, as well as all the others.

Nick arrives late to the funeral, and throughout the weekend ruffles feathers and questions everyone's placid lives. This BAD BOY has a run in with the police, and is angry when BEST FRIEND Harry smoothes the trouble over. He still wants to fight the system. Meg, on the other hand, totally bought into the "dress for success" establishment. A successful lawyer, this BOSS now yearns for something else—a baby. And she is hoping to negotiate a deal with one of the guys to get one.

SPUNKY KID Karen did the right thing and married a nice man, settling down in the suburbs with him and their children. But she dreams of finally consummating her secret passion for CHARMER Sam. And standing apart from all of them is Chloe. A WAIF, this younger woman watches all of them with a wry smile, sprinkling her amazing insights into the mix.

The Big Chill is a wonderful look at eight people with different agendas, wondering if where they are going is where they want to be and hoping their friends will have the answers.

STAR TREK: VOYAGER

Transported to a far quadrant of the galaxy, a Federation crew joins with a rebel force to find their way home.

BOSS Captain Janeway never wavers from her responsibility to lead her crew back to the Alpha quadrant. She listens to all opinions, but in the end, the decision for action will always be hers. She feels responsibility for her crew intensely, and every decision is made with their safety in mind. WARRIOR Chakotay recognizes that his duty toward his own crew required him to yield the reins of command to Captain Janeway. To that end, he forged an alliance with her. A friendship based wholly on mutual respect was the by-product of his devotion to duty.

SWASHBUCKLER Doctor revels in every new experience. He lives his life to the fullest degree, constantly adding to his understanding of human experiences. In contrast, LIBRARIAN Seven of Nine also devotes herself to discovering what it means to be an individual, but with considerably less relish. She is not unconscious of her sensual side; she simply considers it irrelevant. Order and logical explanations calm her.

The PROFESSOR is...
Jeff Goldblum as Michael

The BAD BOY is...
William Hurt as Nick

The BOSS is...
Mary Kay Place as Meg

The SPUNKY KID is...
JoBeth Williams as Karen

And the WAIF is...
Meg Tilly as Chloe

The BOSS is...
Kate Mulgrew as Captain Kathryn Janeway

The WARRIOR is...
Robert Beltran as Chakotay

The SWASH-BUCKLER is...
Robert Picardo as The Doctor

The BAD BOY is...
Robert McNeill as Thomas Paris

The LIBRARIAN is...
Jeri Lynn Ryan as Seven of Nine

The BEST
FRIEND is...
Garrett Wang as
Harry Kim

A PROFESSOR
layered with
WARRIOR is...
Tim Russ as
Tuvok

BAD BOY Tom Paris's defiant attitude has earned him more than a few trips to the brig, but his hotshot unconventionality and penchant for hunches have saved crew and ship from many an alien threat. Meanwhile, BEST FRIEND Harry Kim's calm dependability proves equally effective in pulling victory from the jaws of defeat. A natural peacemaker, he keeps Tom's quick temper out of trouble.

Tuvok, as any Vulcan must, has a PROFESSOR core. He represses his emotions and chooses the logical path at every turn. But like Chakotay, he also has the WARRIOR's rigid devotion to duty. His combination of the WARRIOR's protective instincts and the PROFESSOR's analytical prowess result in the perfect Chief of Security.

As the crew of the Voyager meets fresh obstacles each week in their journey home, the advantages offered by differing archetypes are illustrated.

FINAL THOUGHTS

We hope you have enjoyed this book, and we especially hope that it has generated many new and exciting ideas for stories you would like to write.

Please remember, this book is not a "written in stone" formula. None of the ideas or suggestions in this book are meant to confine you to any one concept.

This book is meant to be a starting place—a jumping off point. Use it to generate intriguing new characters.

AND FINALLY . . .

We wish you the best of luck with your story, whether it be short story, a novel or a screen play. We hope this book has been helpful.

Please e-mail any one of us and let us know your thoughts, ideas and comments.

Tami Cowden—tamidcowden@aol.com

Caro LaFever—CaroLaFever@aol.com

Sue Viders—viders@worldnet.att.net

APPENDIX: FILMS

Accidental Tourist, The—1988
The LOST SOUL—Macon Leary (Willian Hurt)
The FREE SPIRIT—Muriel Pritchett (Geena Davis)

Adam's Rib—1949
The CHIEF—Adam Bonner (Spencer Tracy)
The BOSS—Amanda Bonner (Katharine Hepburn)

Adventures of Robin Hood, The—1938
The SWASHBUCKLER—Sir Robin of Locksley
(Errol Flynn)

A Fish Called Wanda—1988
The SEDUCTRESS—Wanda (Jamie Lee Curtis)

African Queen, The—1951
The LOST SOUL—Charlie Allnut
(Humphrey Bogart)
The LIBRARIAN—Rose Sayer
(Katharine Hepburn)

Alien—1986
The CRUSADER—Ellen Ripley
(Sigourney Weaver)

American Beauty—1999
The BEST FRIEND—Lester Burnham
(Kevin Spacey)
The BOSS—Carolyn Burnham (Annette Bening)

American President, The—1995
The CHIEF—President Andrew Shepherd
(Michael Douglas)
The CRUSADER—Sydney Ellen Wade
(Annette Bening)

An Affair to Remember—1957
The CHARMER—Nickie Ferrante (Cary Grant)
The SPUNKY KID—Terry McKay (Deborah Kerr)

Annie Hall—1977
The PROFESSOR—Alvy Singer (Woody Allen)
The FREE SPIRIT—Annie Hall (Diane Keaton)

Armageddon—1998
The CHIEF—Harry S. Stamper (Bruce Willis)
The CHIEF—Dan Truman (Billy Bob Thornton)
The SWASHBUCKLER—A. J. Frost (Ben Affleck)
The BEST FRIEND—Jayotis "Bear" Kurleenbear
(Michael Clarke Duncan)
The CHARMER and LOST SOUL—Rockhound
(Steve Buscemi)
The WARRIOR—Colonel William Sharp
(William Fichtner)

As Good As It Gets—1997
The BAD BOY—Melvin Udall (Jack Nicholson)
The NURTURER—Carol Connelly (Helen Hunt)

**Austin Powers: International Man of
Mystery**—1997
The SWASHBUCKLER—Austin Powers
(Mike Myers)

Basic Instinct—1992
The SEDUCTRESS—Catherine Tramell
(Sharon Stone)

Beauty and the Beast—1991
The LOST SOUL—Beast
The NURTURER—Belle

Bell, Book and Candle—1958
The PROFESSOR—Shepherd Henderson
(James Stewart)
The SEDUCTRESS—Gillian Holroyd (Kim Novak)

Beverly Hills Cop—1984
The CHARMER—Axel Foley (Eddie Murphy)

Big Chill, The—1983
The CHARMER—Sam Weber (Tom Berenger)
The NURTURER—Sarah (Glenn Close)
The PROFESSOR—Michael (Jeff Goldblum)
The BAD BOY—Nick (William Hurt)
The BEST FRIEND—Harold (Kevin Kline)
The SPUNKY KID—Karen (JoBeth Williams)
The WAIF—Chloe—(Meg Tilly)

Big Easy, The—1987
The CHARMER—Remy McSwain (Dennis Quaid)
The LIBRARIAN—as Annie Osborne
(Ellen Barkin)

Blade Runner—1982
The WARRIOR—Rick Deckard (Harrison Ford)
The WAIF—Pris (Daryl Hannah)

Body Heat—1981
The SEDUCTRESS—Matty Walker
(Kathleen Turner)

Braveheart—1995
The WARRIOR—William Wallace (Mel Gibson)

Bull Durham—1988
The LOST SOUL—Crash Davis (Kevin Costner)
The SEDUCTRESS— as Annie Savoy
(Susan Sarandon)

Cabaret—1972
The FREE SPIRIT and a WAIF—Sally Bowles
(Liza Minnelli)

Casablanca—1942
The LOST SOUL—Richard "Rick" Blaine
(Humphrey Bogart)
The WAIF—Ilsa Lund Laszlo (Ingrid Bergman)

Clueless—1995
The BEST FRIEND—Josh (Paul Rudd)
The FREE SPIRIT—Cher Horowitz
(Alicia Silverstone)

Color Purple, The—1985
The WAIF layered with NURTURER—Celie
(Whoopi Goldberg)

Crocodile Dundee—1986
The SWASHBUCKLER—Michael J. Dundee
(Paul Hogan)
The NURTURER—Sue Charlton (Linda
Kozlowski)

Dave—1993
The BEST FRIEND—Dave Kovic/Bill Mitchell
(Kevin Kline)
The CRUSADER—Ellen Mitchell
(Sigourney Weaver)

Die Hard—1988
The WARRIOR—John McClane (Bruce Willis)

Dirty Dancing—1987
The BAD BOY—Johnny Castle (Patrick Swayze)
The WAIF—Frances 'Baby' Houseman
(Jennifer Grey)

Dirty Dozen, The—1967
The CHIEF—Major John Reisman (Lee Marvin)
The WARRIOR—Joseph Wladislaw
(Charles Bronson)
The WARRIOR—Robert Jefferson (Jim Brown)
The LOST SOUL—Archer Maggott (Telly Savalas)
The BAD BOY—Victor Franko (John Cassavetes)
The BEST FRIEND—Vernon Pinkley
(Donald Sutherland)

Dirty Harry—1971
The WARRIOR—Harry Callahan (Clint Eastwood)

Down and Out in Beverly Hills—1986
The BOSS—Barbara Whiteman (Bette Midler)

Educating Rita—1983
The LOST SOUL—Dr. Frank Bryant
(Michael Caine)
The SPUNKY KID—Rita (Julie Walters)

Elizabeth—1998
The BOSS—Queen Elizabeth (Cate Blanchett)

Erin Brockovich—2000
The CRUSADER—Erin Brockovich (Julia Roberts)

Escape from New York—1981
The BAD BOY—Snake Plissken (Kurt Russell)

Evita—1996
The SEDUCTRESS—Eva Peron (Madonna)

Ferris Bueller's Day Off—1986
The CHARMER—Ferris Bueller
(Matthew Broderick)

First Blood—1982
The LOST SOUL layered with WARRIOR—John
Rambo (Sylvester Stallone)

First Wives Club, The—1996
The NURTURER—Annie MacDuggan Paradis
(Diane Keaton)
The SPUNKY KID—Brenda Morelli Cushman
(Bette Midler)
The SEDUCTRESS—Elise Eliot Atchinson
(Goldie Hawn)

Five Easy Pieces—1970
The BAD BOY—Robert Dupea (Jack Nicholson)

Flubber—1997
The PROFESSOR—The Professor (Robin Williams)

Fly, The—1986
The PROFESSOR—Seth Brundle (Jeff Goldblum)
The WAIF—Ronnie Quaife (Geena Davis)

Foul Play—1978
The FREE SPIRIT—Gloria Mundy (Goldie Hawn)
The BEST FRIEND—Tony Carlson (Clevy Chase)

48 Hours—1982
The WARRIOR—Jack Cates (Nick Nolte)
The CHARMER—Reggie Hammond
(Eddie Murphy)

Fried Green Tomatoes—1991
The SPUNKY KID—Idgie Threadgoode
(Mary Stuart Masterson)
The NURTURER—Ruth (Mary-Louise Parker)

French Kiss—1995
The CHARMER—Luc Teyssier (Kevin Kline)
The SPUNKY KID—Kate (Meg Ryan)

Ghost—1990
The WAIF—Molly Jensen (Demi Moore)

Ghostbusters—1984
The CHARMER—Dr. Peter Venkman (Bill Murray)
The BEST FRIEND—Dr. Raymond Stantz
(Dan Aykroyd)
The PROFESSOR—Dr. Egon Spengler
(Harold Ramis)
The PROFESSOR—Louis Tully (Rick Moranis)

Godfather—1972
The CHIEF—Don Vito Corleone (Marion Brando)

Godfather II, The—1990
The CHIEF—Don Michael Corleone (Al Pacino)

Goldfinger—1964
The WARRIOR and a CHARMER—James Bond
(Sean Connery)

Good Will Hunting—1997
The BAD BOY—Will Hunting (Matt Damon)

Gone with the Wind—1939
The CHIEF and a BAD BOY— Rhett Butler
(Clark Gable)
The SEDUCTRESS—Scarlett O'Hara (Vivien Leigh)

Grease—1978
The BAD BOY—Danny Zuko (John Travolta)
The SPUNKY KID—Sandy Olsen
(Olivia Newton-John)

Groundhog Day —1993
The CHARMER—Phil Conners(Bill Murray)
The NURTURER—Rita (Andie MacDowell)

Guys and Dolls—1955
The BAD BOY—Sky Masterson (Marlon Brando)
The CRUSADER—Sister Sarah Brown
(Jean Simmons)

Hello, Dolly!—1969
The BOSS—Dolly Levi (Barbra Streisand)

High Noon—1952
The WARRIOR—Will Kane (Cary Cooper)
The CRUSADER—Amy Kane (Grace Kelly)

Home Alone—1990
The BAD BOY—Kevin McCallister
(Macaulay Culkin)

Honey, I Shrunk the Kids—1989
The PROFESSOR—Wayne Szalinski (Rick Moranis)

Hud—1963
The BAD BOY—Hud Bannon (Paul Newman)

Independence Day—1996
The PROFESSOR—David Levinson (Jeff Goldblum)
The SWASHBUCKLER—Steven Hiller (Will Smith)

Indiana Jones and the Last Crusade—1989
The SWASHBUCKLER—Indiana Jones
(Harrison Ford)
The SEDUCTRESS—Dr. Elsa Schneider
(Alison Doody)

Indiana Jones and the Temple of Doom—
1984
The SWASHBUCKLER—Indiana Jones
(Harrison Ford)
The FREE SPIRIT—Willie Scott (Kate Capshaw)

It's a Wonderful Life—1946
The BEST FRIEND—George Bailey
(Jimmy Stewart)

Jailhouse Rock—1959
The BAD BOY—Vince Everett (Elvis Presley)

Jerry Maguire—1996
The CHIEF—Jerry Maguire (Tom Cruise)
The NURTURER—Dorothy Boyd
(Renée Zellweger)

Jurassic Park—1993
The PROFESSOR—Alan Grant (Sam Neill)
The LIBRARIAN—Ellie Sattler (Laura Dern)

King and I, The—1956
The CHIEF—King Mongkut of Siam (Yul Brynner)
The LIBRARIAN—Anna Leonowens (Deborah Kerr)

Klute—1971
The SEDUCTRESS—Bree Daniel (Jane Fonda)

L.A. Confidential—1997
The CHARMER—Jack Vincennes (Kevin Spacey)
The WAIF—Lynn Bracken (Kim Basinger)
The CHIEF—Ed Exley (Guy Pearce)
The WARRIOR—Bud White (Russell Crowe)

Ladyhawke—1985
The WARRIOR—Etienne Navarre (Rutger Hauer)
The NURTURER—Isabeau (Michelle Pfeiffer)

Lethal Weapon—1987
The LOST SOUL—Martin Riggs (Mel Gibson)
The BEST FRIEND—Roger Murtaugh
(Danny Glover)

Little Women—1994
The NUTURER—Meg March (Trini Alvarado)
The LIBRARIAN—Jo March (Winona Ryder)
The WAIF—Beth March (Claire Danes)
The BOSS—Amy March (Kirsten Dunst/
Samantha Mathis)

Lolita—1997
The SEDUCTRESS—Lolita (Dominique Swain)

Maltese Falcon, The—1941
The WARRIOR—Sam Spade (Humphrey Bogart)
The SEDUCTRESS—Brigid O'Shaughnessy
(Mary Astor)

Mary Poppins—1964
The NURTURER—Mary Poppins (Julie Andrews)

Mask of Zorro—1998
The SWASHBUCKLER—Zorro (Antonio Banderas)

Men in Black—1997
The SWASHBUCKER—Agent Jay (Will Smith)
The LOST SOUL—Agent Kay (Tommy Lee Jones)

Messenger: The Story of Joan of Arc—1999
The CRUSADER—Joan of Arc (Milla Jovovich)

Misfits, The—1961
The WAIF—Roslyn Tabor (Marilyn Monroe)

Moonstruck—1987
The LOST SOUL—Ronny Cammareri
(Nicolas Cage)
The BOSS—Loretta Castorini (Cher)

Mulan—1998—Animated
The CRUSADER—Mulan

Music Man, The—1962
The LIBRARIAN—Marian Paroo (Shirley Jones)

My Fair Lady—1964
The CHIEF—Henry Higgins (Rex Harrison)
The WAIF layered with a SPUNKY KID—Eliza
Doolittle (Audrey Hepburn)

9 1/2 Weeks—1982
The BAD BOY—John (Mickey Rourke)
The LIBRARIAN—Elizabeth (Kim Basinger)

Norma Rae—1979
The CRUSADER—Norma Rae (Sally Field)

North by Northwest—1959
The CHARMER—Roger Thornhill (Cary Grant)
The SEDUCTRESS—Eve Kendall (Eva Marie Saint)

Nothing Sacred—1937
The FREE SPIRIT—Hazel Flagg (Carole Lombard)

Notting Hill—1999
The BEST FRIEND—William Thacker
(Hugh Grant)

Officer and a Gentleman, An—1982
The BAD BOY—Jack Mayo (Richard Gere)

Oklahoma!—1955
The CHARMER—Curly (Gordon MacRae)
The WAIF—Laurey Williams (Shirley Jones)

Out of Sight—1998
The BOSS—Karen Sisco (Jennifer Lopez)

Patton—1970
The CHIEF—General George S. Patton
(George C. Scott)

Philadelphia Story, The—1940
The PROFESSOR—C. K. Dexter Haven (Cary
Grant)
The BOSS—Tracy Lord (Katharine Hepburn)

Pollyanna—1960
The NURTURER—Pollyanna (Hayley Mills)

Postman Always Rings Twice, The—1946
The BAD BOY—Frank Chambers (John Garfield)
The SEDUCTRESS—Cora Smith (Lana Turner)

Pretty Woman—1990
The CHIEF who evolves into a BEST FRIEND—
Edward Lewis (Richard Gere)
The WAIF—Vivian Ward (Julia Roberts)

Princess Bride, The—1987
The SWASHBUCKLER—Westley (Cary Elwes)
The WAIF—Buttercup (Robin Wright Penn)

Private Benjamin—1980
The WAIF who evolves into a SPUNKY KID—Judy
Benjamin (Goldie Hawn)

Pulp Fiction—1994
The BAD BOY—Vincent Vega (John Travolta)
The FREE SPIRIT—Mia Wallace (Uma Thurman)

Raiders of the Lost Ark—1981
The SWASHBUCKLER—Indiana Jones
(Harrison Ford)
The SPUNKY KID—Marion Ravenwood
(Karen Allen)

Rebel Without a Cause—1955
The BAD BOY—Jim Stark (James Dean)

195

Return of the Dragon—1972
The WARRIOR—Tang Lung (Bruce Lee)

Rio Grande—1950
The WARRIOR—Lieutenant Colonel Kirby Yorke
(John Wayne)
The BOSS—Mrs. Kathleen Yorke (Maureen O'Hara)

Risky Business—1983
The BEST FRIEND—Joel Goodson (Tom Cruise)
The SEDUCTRESS—Lana (Rebecca de Mornay)

Rocky—1976
The BEST FRIEND layered with a WARRIOR—
Rocky Balboa (Sylvester Stallone)

Romancing the Stone—1984
The SWASHBUCKLER—Jack Colton
(Michael Douglas)
The LIBRARIAN—Joan Wilder (Kathleen Turner)

Royal Wedding—1951
The CHARMER—Tom Bowen (Fred Astaire)

Sabrina—1995
The CHIEF—Linus Larrabee (Harrison Ford)
The WAIF—Sabrina Fairchild (Julia Ormond)

Samson and Delilah—1949
The SEDUCTRESS—Delilah (Hedy Lamarr)

Saving Private Ryan—1998
The BEST FRIEND—Captain John Miller
(Tom Hanks)
The CHIEF -Sergeant Michael Horvath
(Tom Sizemore)
The BAD BOY- Private Reiben (Edward Burns)
The PROFESSOR—Corporal Timothy Upham
(Jeremy Davies)
The WARRIOR—Private James Ryan (Matt
Damon)

Sense and Sensibility—1995
The BEST FRIEND -Edward Ferrars (Hugh Grant)
The NURTURER -Elinor Dashwood
(Emma Thompson)

Shakespeare in Love—1998
The CHARMER—Will Shakespeare
(Joseph Fiennes)
The FREE SPIRIT—Viola De Lesseps
(Gwyneth Paltrow)

Short Circuit—1986
The PROFESSOR—Newton Crosby
(Steve Guttenberg)
The CRUSADER—Stephanie Speck (Ally Sheedy)

Silence of the Lambs—1991
The CRUSADER layered with a LIBRARIAN—
Clarice Starling (Jodie Foster)

Sister Act—1992
The SPUNKY KID—Deloris Van Cartier
(Whoopi Goldberg)

Sleeping Beauty—1959, Animated
The WAIF—Princess Aurora

Sleepless in Seattle—1993
The SPUNKY KID—Annie Reed (Meg Ryan)

Some Like It Hot—1959
The SEDUCTRESS—Sugar Kane (Marilyn Monroe)

Sound of Music, The—1965
The NURTURER—Maria (Julie Andrews)
The CHIEF—Captain von Trapp
(Christopher Plummer)

Star Wars—1977
The SWASHBUCKLER—Han Solo (Harrison Ford)
The BOSS layered with a CRUSADER—Princess
Leia Organa (Carrie Fisher)

*Star Wars: Episode One - The Phantom
Menace*—1999
The WARRIOR—Anakin Skywalker (Jake Lloyd)

Steel Magnolias—1989
The NURTURER—M'Lynn Eatenton (Sally Field)
The SPUNKY KID -Truvy Jones (Dolly Parton)
The FREE SPIRIT—Ouiser Boudreaux
(Shirley MacLaine)
The FREE SPIRIT—Annelle Desoto (Daryl Hannah)
The BOSS—Clairee Belcher (Olympia Dukakis)
The WAIF—Shelby Latcherie (Julia Roberts)

Sting, The—1973
The CHIEF—Henry Gondorff (Paul Newman)
The BAD BOY—Johnny Hooker (Robert Redford)

Superman—1978
The WARRIOR -Clark Kent (Christopher Reeve)
The SPUNKY KID—Lois Lane (Margot Kidder)

Taming of the Shrew, The [aka *Bisbetica
Domanta, La*]—1967
The CHARMER—Petruchio (Richard Burton)
The BOSS—Katharina (Elizabeth Taylor)

Ten Commandments, The—1956
The CHIEF who evolves into a LOST SOUL
who evolves into a WARRIOR—Moses
(Charlton Heston)

Terms of Endearment—1983
The BAD BOY—Garrett Breedlove (Jack Nicholson)
The BOSS—Aurora Greenway (Shirley MacLaine)

Thelma and Louise—1991
The CRUSADER—Louise Sawyer (Geena Davis)
The WAIF—Thelma Dickinson (Susan Sarandon)

Time after Time—1979
The PROFESSOR—H.G. Wells (Malcom
McDowell)
The SPUNKY KID—Amy Robbins
(Mary Steenburgen)

Titanic—1997
The CHARMER—Jack Dawson (Leonardo
DiCaprio)
The WAIF who evolves into a SPUNKY KID—Rose
De Witt Bukater (Kate Winslet)

To Catch a Thief—1955
The CHARMER—John Robie (Cary Grant)

Top Gun—1986
The SWASHBUCKLER—Lieutenant Pete Mitchell
(Tom Cruise)

Trading Places—1983
The CHARMER who evolves into a CHIEF—Billy
Ray Valentine (Eddie Murphy)

True Lies—1994
The WARRIOR—Harry Tasker
(Arnold Schwarzenegger)
The LIBRARIAN—Helen Tasker (Jamie Lee Curtis)

196

Truth About Cats & Dogs, The—1996
The LIBRARIAN—Abby Barnes (Janeane Garofalo)
The BEST FRIEND—Brian (Ben Chaplin)

Turning Point, The—1977
The BOSS—Deedee Rodgers (Shirley MacLane)
The SEDUCTRESS—Emma Jacklin (Ann Bancroft)

Twister—1996
The SWASHBUCKLER—Bill Harding (Bill Paxton)
The CRUSADER—Jo Harding (Helen Hunt)

Under Siege—1992
The WARRIOR—Casey Ryback (Steven Seagal)
The FREE SPIRIT—Jordan Tate (Erika Eleniak)

Waiting to Exhale—1995
The SPUNKY KID -Savannah Jackson
(Whitney Houston)
The BOSS—Bernadine Harris (Angela Bassett)
The NURTURER—Gloria Johnson
(Loretta Devine)
The FREE SPIRIT -Robin Stokes (Lela Rochon)

Way We Were, The—1973
The CHARMER—Hubbell Gardner
(Robert Redford)
The CRUSADER—Katie Morosky
(Barbra Streisand)

Wedding Singer, The—1998
The BEST FRIEND—Robbie Hart (Adam Sandler)
The WAIF—Julia Sullivan (Drew Barrymore)

When Harry Met Sally—1989
The BEST FRIEND—Harry Burns (Billy Crystal)
The LIBRARIAN—Sally Albright (Meg Ryan)

While You Were Sleeping—1995
A BEST FRIEND—Jack Callaghan (Bill Pullman)
A SPUNKY KID—Lucy Moderatz (Sandra Bullock)

Wizard of Oz, The—1939
The WAIF—Dorothy Gale (July Garland)

Working Girl—1988
The SPUNKY KID—Tess McGill (Melanie Griffith)

Young Frankenstein—1974
The PROFESSOR—Dr. Frederick Frankenstein
(Gene Wilder)

You've Got Mail—1998
The BEST FRIEND—Joe Fox (Tom Hanks)

TELEVISION PROGRAMS

Ally McBeal
The FREE SPIRIT—Ally (Calista Flockhart)

Andy Griffith Show, The
The BEST FRIEND—Sheriff Andy Taylor
(Andy Griffith)

Buffy, the Vampire Slayer
The LOST SOUL—Angel (David Boreanaz)
The CRUSADER—Buffy (Sarah Michelle Gellar)

Columbo
The PROFESSOR—Lieutenant Columbo
(Peter Falk)

Cosby Show, The
The NURTURER—Claire Huxtable
(Phylicia Rashad)

Daria
The LIBRARIAN—Daria—animated

Dharma and Greg
The FREE SPIRIT—Dharma (Jenna Elfman)

Family Ties
The CHIEF—Alex P. Keaton (Michael J. Fox)

Frasier
The PROFESSOR—Dr. Niles Crane
(David Hyde Pierce)
The NURTURER—Daphne Moon (Jane Leeves)

Friends
The FREE SPIRIT—Phoebe Buffay (Lisa Kudrow)

Gilligan's Island
The SPUNKY KID—Mary Ann Summers
(Dawn Wells)
The PROFESSOR—The Professor
(Russell Johnson)
The CHIEF—Skipper Jonas Grumby (Alan Hale Jr)
The SEDUCTRESS—Ginger Grant (Tina Louise)
The BOSS—Lovey (Natalie Schafer)
The CHARMER—Thurston Howell III
(Jim Backus)
The BEST FRIEND—Gilligan (Bob Denver)

I Love Lucy
The CHIEF—Ricky Ricardo (Desi Arnaz)
The FREE SPIRIT—Lucy Ricardo (Lucille Ball)

La Femme Nikita
The WAIF—Nikita (Peta Wilson)

Laverne and Shirley
The FREE SPIRIT—Laverne De Fazio
(Penny Marshall)
The LIBRARIAN—Shirley Feeney
(Cindy Williams)

Lone Ranger, The
The WARRIOR—The Ranger (Clayton Moore)

MacGyver
The WARRIOR layered with the PROFESSOR—
MacGyver (Richard Dean Anderson)

Magnum P.I.
The CHARMER—Thomas Magnum (Tom Selleck)

Mary Tyler Moore Show, The
The SPUNKY KID—Mary Richards
(Mary Tyler Moore)
The SPUNKY KID—Rhoda Morgenstern
(Valerie Harper)

Maverick
The SWASHBUCKLER—Bret Maverick
(James Garner)

Murphy Brown
The BOSS—Murphy Brown (Candace Bergen)

Remington Steele
The CHARMER—Remington Steele
(Pierce Brosnan)

Star Trek
The CHIEF—Captain James T. Kirk
(William Shatner)
The PROFESSOR—Mr.Spock (Leonard Nimoy)

Star Trek: The Next Generation
The NURTURER—Deanna Troi (Marina Sirtis)

Star Trek: Voyager
The BOSS—Captain Kathryn Janeway
(Kate Mulgrew)
The BAD BOY- Tom Paris (Robert McNeil)
The SWASHBUCKLER—The Doctor
(Robert Phillips)
The WARRIOR—Chakotay (Robert Beltran)
The LIBRARIAN—Seven of Nine (Jeri Lynn Ryan)
The BEST FRIEND—Harry Kim (Garrett Wang)
The PROFESSOR—Tuvok (Tim Russ)

Waltons, The
The NURTURER—Ma Walton (Michael Learned)

Wonder Woman
The CRUSADER—Diana Prince (Lynda Carter)

Xena: Warrior Princess
The CRUSADER—Xena (Lucy Lawless)

X-Files, The
The LOST SOUL—Fox Mulder (David Duchovny)
The LIBRARIAN—Dana Scully (Gillian Anderson)

LITERATURE BY TITLE

Adventures of Huckleberry Finn by Mark Twain
The BAD BOY—Huck Finn

Alice in Wonderland by Lewis Carroll
The FREE SPIRIT—Alice

Anna Karenina by Leo Tolstoy
The CHARMER—Count Alexey Kinilich Vronsky

Antigone by Sophocles
The CRUSADER—Antigone

Antony and Cleopatra by William Shakespeare
The CHIEF—Marc Antony
The SEDUCTRESS—Cleopatra

As You Like It by William Shakespeare
The LIBRARIAN—Rosalind

Auntie Mame by Patrick Dennis
The FREE SPIRIT—Auntie Mame

Catcher in the Rye, The by J. D. Salinger
The BAD BOY—Holden Caulfield

Cathy by Cathy Guisewite
The SPUNKY KID—Cathy

Cinderella, a fairy tale
The WAIF—Cinderella

Count of Monte Cristo, The by Alexandre Dumas
The WARRIOR—Edmond Dantas

Ellery Queen (The series) by Ellery Queen
The PROFESSOR—Ellery Queen

Emma by Jane Austen
The BEST FRIEND—Mr. Knightly
The FREE SPIRIT—Emma

Glass Menagerie, The by Tennessee Williams
The WAIF—Amanda

Harry Potter by J.K. Rowling
The PROFESSOR—Harry Potter

Jane Eyre by Charlotte Brönte
The CRUSADER—Jane Eyre

Jason and the Argonauts—a myth
The SWASHBUCKLER—Jason

Little Orphan Annie by Harold Gray
The SPUNKY KID—Annie

Measure for Measure by William Shakespeare
The NURTURER—Isabella

Old Testament
Book of Genesis
The LOST SOUL—Cain
Book of Ruth
The NURTURER—Ruth

One for the Money by Janet Evanovich—a series
The SPUNKY KID—Stephanie Plum

Peanuts by Charles Schultz
The LOST SOUL—Charlie Brown
The BOSS—Lucy

Peter Pan by James M. Barrie
The SWASHBUCKLER—Peter

Pride and Prejudice by Jane Austen
The CHIEF—Fitzwilliam Darcy
The SPUNKY KID—Elizabeth

Romeo and Juliet by William Shakespeare
The WAIF—Juliet

Scarlet Pimpernel by Baroness Emmuska Orczy
The WARRIOR—Sir Percy Blakeley

Seven Voyages of Sinbad the Sailor, The by John Yeoman
The SWASHBUCKLER—Sinbad

Sherlock Holmes, (The series) by Sir Arthur Conan Doyle
The PROFESSOR—Sherlock Holmes

To Kill a Mockingbird by Harper Lee
The WARRIOR—Atticus Finch

Vanity Fair by William Makepeace Thackeray
The SEDUCTRESS—Rebecca Sharp

Who's Afraid of Virginia Woolf? by Edward Albee
The BOSS—Martha

Winnie the Pooh by A.A. Milne
The BEST FRIEND—Christopher Robin

Wuthering Heights by Emily Brönte
The LOST SOUL—Heathcliff

LITERATURE BY AUTHOR

Albee, Edward
Who's Afraid of Virginia Woolf?
The BOSS—Martha

Austen, Jane
Emma
The BEST FRIEND—Mr. Knightly
Pride and Prejudice
The CHIEF—Fitzwilliam Darcy

Barrie, James M.
Peter Pan
The SWASHBUCKLER—Peter

Brönte, Charlotte
Jane Eyre
The CRUSADER—Jane

Brönte, Emily
Wuthering Heights
The LOST SOUL—Heathcliff

Carroll, Lewis
Alice in Wonderland
The FREE SPIRIT—Alice

Dennis, Patrick
Auntie Mame
The FREE SPIRIT—Mame

Doyle, Sir Arthur Conan Doyle
The Sherlock Holmes series
The PROFESSOR—Sherlock Holmes

Dumas, Alexandre
The Count of Monte Cristo
The WARRIOR—Edmond Dantas

Evanovich, Janet
The Stephanie Plum series
The SPUNKY KID—Stephanie Plum

Fairy Tale
Cinderella
The WAIF—Cinderella

Gray, Harold
Little Orphan Annie
The SPUNKY KID—Annie

Guisewite, Cathy
Cathy
The SPUNKY KID—Cathy

Lee, Harper
To Kill a Mockingbird
The WARRIOR—Atticus Finch

Milne, A.A.
Winnie the Pooh
The BEST FRIEND—Christopher Robin

Old Testament, The
Book of Genesis
The LOST SOUL—Cain
Book of Ruth
The NURTURER—Ruth

Orczy, Baroness Emmuska
The Scarlet Pimpernel
The WARRIOR—Sir Percy Blakeley

Queen, Ellery
The Ellery Queen series
The PROFESSOR—Ellery Queen

Myths
Jason and the Argonauts
The SWASHBUCKLER—Jason
Sinbad the Sailor
The SWASHBUCKLER—Sinbad

Rowling, J.K.
Harry Potter
The PROFESSOR—Harry

Salinger, J. D.
The Catcher in the Rye
The BAD BOY—Holden Caulfield

Schultz, Charles
Peanuts
The LOST SOUL—Charlie Brown
The BOSS—Lucy

Shakespeare, William
Antony and Cleopatra
The CHIEF—Marc Antony
The SEDUCTRESS—Cleopatra
As You Like It
The LIBRARIAN—Rosalind
Measure for Measure
The NURTURER—Isabella
Romeo and Juliet
The WAIF—Juliet

Sophocles
Antigone
The CRUSADER—Antigone

Thackeray, William Makepeace
Vanity Fair
The SEDUCTRESS—Rebecca Sharp

Tolstoy, Leo
Anna Karenina
The CHARMER—Count Alexey Kinilich
Vronsky

Twain, Mark
The Adventures of Huckleberry Finn
The BAD BOY—Huck Finn

Williams, Tennessee
The Glass Menagerie
The WAIF—Amanda

MORE SCREENWRITING BOOKS FROM
LONE EAGLE PUBLISHING

*Stage & Screen
Book Club Selection*

HOW *NOT* TO WRITE A SCREENPLAY
101 Common Mistakes Most Screenwriters Make
by Denny Martin Flinn

Finally, what may be the last screenwriting book a writer will ever need to buy! Written by Hollywood screenwriter Denny Martin Flinn, HOW *NOT* TO WRITE A SCREENPLAY carefully identifies and examines the 101 common mistakes screenwriters invariably make when writing a screenplay. Having read tons of screenplays as an executive, Flinn has come to understand that while all good screenplays are unique, all bad screenplays are the same. Flinn's book will teach the reader how to avoid the pitfalls of bad screenwriting, and arrive at one's own destination intact. Every example used originates from a legitimate screenplay. Flinn's advice is a no-nonsense analysis of the latest techniques for crafting first-rate screenplays that sell. Includes script excerpts.

Denny Martin Flinn is a produced screenwriter and has authored the books *What They Did For Love* and *Musical! A Grand Tour*. He has also written two mystery novels for Bantam. Mr. Flinn lives in Los Angeles.

$16.95 ISBN 1-58065-015-5, original trade paper, 6 x 9, 240 pp.

LOS ANGELES TIMES BEST SELLER...
ELEMENTS OF STYLE FOR SCREENWRITERS
The Essential Manual for Writers of Screenplays
by Paul Argentini

In the grand tradition of Strunk and White's *Elements of Style*, Paul Argentini presents an essential reference masterpiece in the art of clear and concise principles of screenplay formatting, structure and style for screenwriters. Argentini explains how to design and format manuscripts to impress any film school professor, story editor, agent, producer or studio executive. The ultimate quick reference guide to formatting a screenplay—no book in shorter space, with fewer words, will help screenwriters more than this concise volume. Includes a playwrite chapter for structure and format and an updated list of literary agent contacts.

Paul Argentini is a screenwriter, playwright and novelist.

$11.95 ISBN 1-58065-003-1, original trade paper, 5.5 x 8.5, 176 pp

FADE IN MAGAZINE presents
SECRETS OF THE SCREEN TRADE
by Allen B. Ury

Finally, a practical, no-nonsense look at the real secrets of creating, developing, and maintaining a career in the unforgiving celluloid jungle. From concept to sale and beyond, it's the four-one-one on how to write to impress the people who've seen it all before — Hollywood's agents, producers, and studio executives. Whether you are a seasoned pro or a novice, SECRETS OF THE SCREEN TRADE will help you improve your writing. You'll learn how to create truly unforgettable characters, develop better structure for all movie genres, and get the inside track to selling your screenplay to Hollywood.

Allen B. Ury is a staff writer for *Fade In* magazine. He has more than fifteen books to his credit as well as scores of magazine articles. As a screenwriter, he has sold several projects to major film studios, including Disney and New Line Cinema. He has analyzed and written coverage for well over 500 screenplays.

$18.95 ISBN 1-58065-060-0, original trade paper, 6 x 9, 176 pp.

To order, call 800.451.1741 or go to www.watsonguptill.com

MORE SCREENWRITING BOOKS FROM
LONE EAGLE PUBLISHING

"I LIKED IT, DIDN'T LOVE IT"
Screenplay Development From the Inside Out
by Rona Edwards & Monika Skerbelis

The most commonly used rejection line spewed by studio executive honchos when they do not buy a script is, "I liked it, didn't love it." What happens to your screenplay or novel when it leaves your hands and is submitted to a studio or production company? What happens to it after it's optioned or sold? What does "in development" really mean? Rona Edwards and Monika Skerbelis shed light on all those questions for both those who are new to the business, and those already journeying through the "storied" halls at a film studio, television network, or production company. Edwards and Skerbelis tackle how to find new ideas, what it takes to be a development executive or a story analyst, how to work with producers and writers, and tips for pitching. They present exercises created to assist the reader in developing their writing skills.

Rona Edwards and Monika Skerbelis have lived the life of a studio and development executive, having developed and sold screenplays for the past 15 years. They have taught feature film development classes at UCLA for the past seven years. Both authors live in Los Angeles.

$18.95, ISBN 1-58065-062-7

SECRETS OF SCREENPLAY STRUCTURE
How to Recognize and Emulate the Structural Frameworks of Great Films
by Linda J. Cowgill

Linda Cowgill articulates the concepts of successful screenplay structure in a clear language, based on the study of great films from the thirties to present day. SECRETS OF SCREENPLAY STRUCTURE helps writers understand how and why great films work, as well as how great form and function can combine to bring a story alive. Cowgill includes many helpful anecdotes, insider strategies, as well as "do's" and "don'ts" which will help readers make their writing more professional, and therefore more marketable.

Linda J. Cowgill received her Masters in Screenwriting from UCLA, after winning several screenwriting awards and fellowships. She has taught screenwriting seminars at the Boston Film Institute, the American Film Institute, and the prestigious Kennedy Center in Washington, D.C. Currently Ms. Cowgill teaches screenwriting at Loyola Marymount University in Los Angeles. Ms. Cowgill has written more than 12 features and teleplays.

*Stage & Screen
Book Club Selection*

$16.95 ISBN 1-58065-004-X, original trade paper, 6 x 9, 224 pp.

WRITING SHORT FILMS
Structure and Content for Screenwriters
by Linda J. Cowgill

Contrasting and comparing the differences and similarities between feature films and short films, WRITING SHORT FILMS offers readers the essential requirements necessary to make their writing crisp, sharp and compelling. Emphasizing characters, structure, dialogue and story, WRITING SHORT FILMS dispels the "magic formula" concept that screenplays can be constructed by anyone with a word processor and a script formatting program. Writing a good screenplay, short or long, is a difficult job. Citing numerous examples from short films as well as feature films, Cowgill teaches strategies to keep a short film on track and writer's block at bay. Chapter headings include The Three Part Nature of Film Structure, Proper Screenplay Format, and Dialogue—The Search for the Perfect Line.

*Stage & Screen
Book Club Selection*

Linda J. Cowgill is the author of *Secrets of Screenplay Structure.*

$19.95 ISBN 0-943728-80-0, original trade paper, 6 x 9, 250 pp.

Tax planning for you and your family

2021

Editors-in-Chief

Nancy Belo Gomes, CPA, CA, MBA
Toronto

Marlene Cepparo, FCPA, FCA
Toronto

Paul Corupe, BA
Toronto

Contributing KPMG Editors

Line Arsenault, MTax,
Ottawa

Steven Carreiro, CPA, CA
Burnaby

Carla Figliomeni, LLM. (Tax), TEP
Toronto

Ryan Gill, CPA, CA, CPA (New Hampshire)
Vancouver

Priyanka Kumar, CPA, CA, LLM Fisc.
Montreal

Anouk Leclair, LL.L., LL.M. Fisc.
Montreal

Paul Lynch, CPA, CA
Toronto

David Magdalinski,, CPA, CMA
Edmonton

Ruth C. L. March, CPA, CA, TEP
Halifax

Colin Miller, CPA, CA
Lethbridge

Megan Ni,CPA, CA
Calgary

Justin R. Park, MTax, CPA, CMA,
CFP   Toronto

John Tang, MAcc, CPA, CA
Toronto

Prepared by:

42728970

ISSN 1207-5957
ISBN 978-0-7798-9701-8 (2021 edition)

A cataloguing record for this publication is available from Library and Archives Canada.

Printed in the United States.

THOMSON REUTERS®

THOMSON REUTERS CANADA, A DIVISION OF THOMSON REUTERS CANADA LIMITED

One Corporate Plaza	Customer Support
2075 Kennedy Road	1-416-609-3800 (Toronto & International)
Toronto, Ontario	1-800-387-5164 (Toll Free Canada & U.S.)
M1T 3V4	Fax 1-416-298-5082 (Toronto)
	Fax 1-877-750-9041 (Toll Free Canada Only)
	E-mail CustomerSupport.LegalTaxCanada@tr.com

Contents

Foreword

Many Canadians do not give much thought to how they can reduce their taxes until it's time to file their tax returns each spring. By then, many tax saving opportunities for the year may be lost. Filing your tax return is essentially a once-a-year accounting to the government to settle up your taxes owing or refund due for the previous year — it is the tax planning steps that you take throughout each year that can save the most money at tax time.

In this book our tax professionals set out common rules and tax planning opportunities that may be available to individuals. A few hours invested in reading this book may pay off substantially in tax savings and in the organization of your financial affairs.

This book cannot replace your tax adviser

The income tax system is constantly changing. If you thought you knew the rules even a couple of years ago, you will discover they may have since been modified. We also cannot predict what changes are in store for the future.

Information in this book is current to June 30, 2020 and reflects the law and publicly announced proposals for changes as of that date. Note that, due to the COVID-19 pandemic, the government did not deliver a 2020 federal budget before this book went to press. In addition, this book only provides a brief overview of selected tax measures that were introduced as a result of COVID-19, as these measures generally expire by the end of 2020. However, we do provide information on certain benefits and subsidies that may have to be reflected on you or your company's 2020 tax return. Contact a tax professional for an update on the status of these and other tax measures. Your tax adviser can also help you determine how your tax obligations may be affected by any other COVID-19 support payments that you received in 2020.

This book deals only in general terms. The Canadian tax system is extremely complex, far more than the book makes it appear. The details fill volumes, not a single book. If you carry on your own business, or manage a corporation, you may benefit from personalized tax advice. Even if your affairs seem relatively simple, consulting a qualified tax professional (not just a tax return preparer) may result in savings that far outweigh the fees.

Chapter 1

Tips for achieving your financial goals

- Create a financial plan and stick to it (1.1.1)

- Define your short-, medium- and long-term goals (1.1.1)

- Track your net worth and cash flow, and set an annual growth target (1.1.2 and 1.1.3)

- Save systematically by "paying yourself first" (1.1.3)

- Build an investment strategy that suits your unique circumstances and needs (1.1.4)

- Set benchmarks for measuring the performance of your investment portfolio and your investment manager (1.1.4)

- Contribute up to $2,500 annually to an RESP and earn a 20% government grant (1.2.1)

- Encourage your children to invest the money they earn (1.2.2)

- Think about using RRSP funds for a down payment on your first home under the Home Buyers' Plan (1.2.3)

- Increase the frequency of your mortgage payments to reduce your mortgage interest (1.2.3)

- Plan to minimize capital gains tax on dispositions of vacation homes (1.2.4)

- Set up an emergency fund or line of credit (1.3.1)

- Make sure you have adequate insurance and a current will (1.3.2 and 1.3.3)

- Consider a power of attorney (1.3.4)

- Shop around when choosing your financial and investment advisers (1.4)

In this chapter, we offer a primer on financial planning with emphasis on the impact of taxes on your ability to meet your family's financial goals. We also point out tax planning ideas in this book that may help you to achieve these goals. Given the importance of financial planning for your retirement, this area is discussed separately in Chapter 20.

1.1 Developing your financial plan

For many Canadians, the very idea of financial planning is mystifying. It shouldn't be. Saving for retirement, financing your child's education or buying a house are within the reach of most of us—the purpose of financial planning is to clarify your objectives, set a realistic timetable for achieving them and marshal your financial resources to support your plan. Of course, the process may require some financial discipline by changing your expectations, paring down your current lifestyle or simply prioritizing expenses and making choices. Having a sound financial plan will likely ease your financial anxiety by giving you a realistic picture of your family's finances and lay out a clear path for achieving your goals.

Create a financial plan and stick to it.

Tax planning to manage your family's overall tax obligations should be an integral part of your family's financial plan. The balance of this book is full of ideas about how to save taxes; the rest of this chapter is an overview of the financial planning framework in which your tax planning should take place.

1.1.1 Define your financial and lifestyle goals

Putting your dreams on paper is the first step toward realizing them. Start by writing out what you want and when you want it. If you have a spouse or common-law partner, compile your list together, compromising where necessary to make sure that you are both committed to the same objectives. You might also include your children and have them develop their own plan as a teaching exercise to build or enhance their own financial literacy.

Define your short-, medium- and long-term goals.

While your list should take into account your family's well-being and future financial security, be sure to include any desired lifestyle items like a vacation home, major renovations, a luxury car or a swimming pool. If you want to take a sabbatical from work to, for example, eventually start your own business, write it down. As part of this exercise, consider the discussion of building your investment strategy in 1.1.4, common financial goals in 1.2 and important financial safeguards in 1.3.

When you have completed your list, divide it into short-, medium- and long-term goals and rank them in order of priority within each section. Set a timeframe for meeting each goal. Then do a bit of research and estimate the cost of achieving your goals, making sure to account for inflation. You may want to engage a financial planner or accountant to help you with the numbers. Don't let the amounts overwhelm you—over time the effects of compound growth can provide significant returns on your investments.

Nevertheless, you may need to revise your list by allowing more time to achieve a certain goal or by dropping items that are beyond your means.

As time goes by, your list will serve as a guide for directing your savings and investments and as an indicator of your progress. Since your personal and financial circumstances and goals are bound to change, it is important to revisit your list once or twice a year and revise it to reflect new priorities and achievements.

1.1.2 Track your net worth

Now that you have a better idea of where you want to go, the next step is to take a snapshot of where you are financially today—your net worth. Calculating your net worth is simply a matter of adding up your total assets (what you own) and then subtracting your total liabilities (what you owe) from your total assets. The resulting figure is the springboard for most aspects of financial management and planning.

It's also a good idea to separate your assets by ownership—whether they are owned by you, your spouse or jointly can help in determining potential strategies for income splitting (see Chapter 5) and estate planning (see Chapter 21).

A close look at your assets will show you whether most of your assets are personal items, such as your home or your car, or investment assets, such as savings accounts, shares and mutual funds. This review should also indicate how liquid your assets are and help you determine whether your investments are sufficiently diversified to balance expected rates of return with the degree of risk you are prepared to take (see 1.1.4).

Similarly, a close look at your liabilities may indicate whether your insurance coverage is adequate (see 1.3.2) and how your debts are affecting your bottom line. As we'll see in 7.2.3, interest incurred for personal reasons on credit cards, consumer loans and mortgages is not deductible for tax purposes, while interest on loans taken out to purchase income-generating investments or earn business income may be deductible. As a result, the interest on your consumer debts may cost you more than the return on your investments. Where possible, you should try to pay down your consumer debts first, giving priority to those with the highest interest rates, and try to make sure that all loans you take out in the future are for a tax-deductible purpose.

Updating your net worth calculation once or twice a year is a good way to track your financial health and progress toward achieving your financial goals. For example, if you can increase your net worth by 8% each year, your net worth will double every nine years. Ways to increase your net worth include:

> Track your net worth and cash flow, and set an annual growth target.

- improving the rate of return on your investments
- investing more of your income by spending less on discretionary items and minimizing taxes
- reducing your debt by paying off your consumer and other high-rate loans and accelerating your mortgage and other debt payments.

1.1.3 Cash management and budgeting—the cornerstone of financial planning

The formula for accumulating the necessary funds to achieve your financial goals is no secret. Unless you expect to inherit money or win a lottery, the way to start building wealth is to save and regularly invest a portion of your income. Through the mathematical "miracle" of compounding, your investment assets can grow exponentially over time. The more savings you have to invest and the longer they are invested, the greater your net worth will be.

One way to increase your net worth is to gain better control over your savings and expenses with a personal or family budget. List the amounts of money you expect to receive through your work or other sources and the amounts you pay out monthly for living expenses, such as rent or mortgage payments, groceries and entertainment. This will allow you to realistically assess your cash flow and help you prioritize your spending.

Considering this information and any non-recurring expenses, set your budget for the next month or the remainder of the year. Once your budget is set, review it regularly for reasonableness and compare your actual spending against it.

Without making lifestyle changes, there is usually little you can do about your rent or mortgage payments, car payments and other fixed expenses. However, the exercise of preparing—and sticking to—a budget will probably reveal many opportunities to easily reduce your discretionary expenses such as travel, entertainment and gifts. For example, changing where and how you shop can reduce your expenditures. Though not required, there are plenty of excellent software packages available that can help you create and monitor your family budget.

Save systematically by "paying yourself first". When preparing your budget, do not simply plan to save the amount left over at the end of each month—chances are there won't be as much left as you intended. Instead, get into the practice of saving a fixed amount of at least 10% of your income at the beginning of each month (or some other period) and using the balance for your expenses. Commonly known as the "pay yourself first" plan, this technique helps you to save systematically and to be less prone to making impulsive or needlessly expensive purchases. Although it may take you a few months to get used to having less cash readily available, you will probably be surprised at how quickly you will adjust. Consider having your financial institution automatically transfer your savings amount to a separate account, registered retirement savings plan (RRSP) (see Chapter 3) or Tax-Free Savings Account (TFSA) (see 4.1) on a monthly or other regular basis.

Once the maximum CPP/QPP and Employment Insurance premiums have been deducted from your employment income for the year, consider directing the extra cash then available toward your savings or paying down debt (especially debt with non-tax deductible interest). Your take-home pay will stay the same, and you will be better off. Similarly, if you pay off a car loan, you could direct the amount of your payments to your savings.

1.1.4 Develop an appropriate investment strategy

Build an investment strategy that suits your unique circumstances and needs. Today's economic realities are forcing Canadians to take care of their own financial health. Even with professional advisers, most investors should take an active interest in their investment activities.

Modern investment wisdom suggests that it's not what you select but from where you select it. Known as "asset allocation", this process works as well for $10,000 as it does for $1 million. Simply put, asset allocation is the process of deciding how to invest a pool of resources among a broad array of assets. The process also helps you stick to your financial plan and avoid making rash decisions as rates of return go up or down. It is typically considered the single most important part of managing a portfolio.

Asset allocation involves three decisions. The first decision entails selecting between asset classes: cash, fixed income and equities.

The second decision includes determining market exposure—in many cases, you may consider diversifying your investments geographically. Canada represents only a small portion of the world's capitalization, and substantial investment opportunities are considered to exist beyond our borders. Today, global investments are available through a variety of mutual funds and low-cost exchange-traded funds.

The last asset allocation decision is currency exposure. For example, if you held U.S. funds while the U.S. currency was depreciating against the Canadian dollar, you may have realized a loss if you converted to Canadian funds at a higher rate than you purchased the U.S. funds. Investing in U.S. currency may be advantageous for Canadians with recurring U.S.-denominated expenses for travel or vacation properties located in the United States.

"Hedging" is an investment strategy through which an investor attempts to manage the various risks in a portfolio by holding different currencies in markets that are expected to move in opposite directions. Since hedging transactions require sophisticated knowledge of global markets, many investors ignore this strategy. Many investors instead choose to achieve additional diversification by investing in a hedge fund.

Along with these three decisions, asset allocation comes in two forms: strategic and tactical. Strategic asset allocation takes a long-term view and divides a portfolio among several asset classes according to the inherent risks and rewards of each asset. Tactical allocation consists of short-term market predictions that could last an hour or a day. This type of allocation often proves difficult because variables used in selecting the asset mix continually change and the portfolio must be adjusted to keep up with market movements. Other disadvantages may include higher fees, lack of liquidity in esoteric markets like precious metals, and the potential to misread economic signals.

While there is no perfect asset allocation for any one person, there are definitely inappropriate allocations. The following are some tips for getting the right mix.

Determine your objectives and risk tolerance—Before you make any investment decisions, determine your objectives and risk tolerance and decide your asset allocation. Risk tolerance is influenced by factors such as your age, your family situation and investor personality. For example, a 55-year-old with two dependent teenage children may have a dramatically different risk tolerance than an empty-nester or single person of the same age. Also, if you have a defined benefit pension plan, the amount of risk you will accept with your RRSP may differ from that of someone whose RRSP is their only retirement savings vehicle.

Risk tolerance should also reflect your ability to replace losses. A person with a high net worth may be able to weather a loss of $50,000 in the market. But for a retiree with a fixed pension, such a loss could be devastating. Asset allocation has to be a function of your investor profile and risk tolerance. If it's right, you should sleep well in any market environment.

For a discussion of revising your investment strategy as you approach retirement, see 20.2.2.

Consider your total portfolio—Many investors make a classic mistake at the outset by separating their registered from non-registered investments. However, in an asset allocation decision, it is irrelevant whether investments are in an RRSP or other registered plan. Your total investment portfolio should be considered holistically so that the right proportion of your total assets can be allocated according to your allocation model. Once you have completed your asset allocation, then you can decide, from a tax perspective, which investments are more effective to hold inside your RRSP (see 3.1.6) or TFSA (see 4.1).

Plan for a long horizon and stay on course—Once you have determined your asset allocation, plan to let your investments grow for at least five to seven years, long enough to go through an average full market cycle. Many investors often make the mistake of buying what's hot because they think it's a great time to be in the market, then panic and sell as soon as the investment loses value. A disciplined approach to long-term asset allocation will probably give you higher returns in the long run.

Pay attention to fees—Be aware of management fees and commissions. A saving in fees of 1% per annum on a $100,000 investment earning a 6% annual return for 10 years could save you well over $15,000. You can't control the market, but you can control the fees and commissions you pay. If you do not know the amount of your fees, do not be afraid to ask your investment adviser or financial institution holding your investments. You may want to benchmark those fees against others to ensure you are not overpaying and inherently reducing your overall rate of return. Over the long term, the compounding effect of excessive fees can have an adverse effect on achieving your goals on schedule.

Inflation is a risk—Inflation is another factor you cannot control, though you can plan for it. Depending on the rate of inflation, it can be a costly mistake to think of money in nominal terms instead of its real value. If your money isn't growing, you're losing it. Consider a $1,000 investment earning an average rate of return of 6% per year. After 10 years, the investment will be worth $1,790, but inflation will have eroded its real value. Assuming an annual inflation rate of 3%, this erosion will amount to $450 by the end of the 10th year, bringing the investment's real value down at that time to $1,340.

Rebalance annually—One of the most important steps in managing your investments is to regularly rebalance your portfolio according to your asset allocation. With discipline, this allows you to manage your investments for profit, by selling high and buying low.

For example, you may have decided originally that an investment mix of 40% in stocks and 60% in bonds met your objectives. However, due to a prosperous period in the economy, you find that the stock component of your portfolio grows to 55% while bonds now represent only 45% by value. In this case, the discipline of strategic asset allocation would have you take profits and rebalance your original mix so that when the economy reverses—as it always does—you will be positioned to take advantage of the change.

Choose the right investment firm and monitor your investments' performance—Select an investment firm or adviser that fits your circumstances and needs and has consistently shown strong performance over the long term, compared to its competitors. Your written investment policy should establish appropriate benchmarks that relate to your particular asset mix, such as market indices, to judge the performance of your investment portfolio and your investment manager. See 1.4 for general advice on choosing your professional advisers.

> Set benchmarks for measuring the performance of your investment portfolio and your investment manager.

Don't try to outsmart the market—Focus your attention on getting the asset allocation right and then, within each asset class, try to keep your costs at a minimum. Make sure you are well diversified. Be consistent in your investment style and stick to your plan. Don't think that what happened in the past will happen in the future. In the financial market, history rarely repeats.

1.2 Some common financial goals

1.2.1 Planning for your children's education

Having a college diploma or university degree can greatly expand your children's range of occupational opportunities and will probably enhance their future earning power. But with government support falling and tuition fees rising over the last decade, putting a child through college or university is becoming costlier. If your child decides to move away from home to study or attend an institution outside Canada, the cost would increase significantly. Most of us would be hard-pressed to finance these costs out of current income, so planning is crucial.

Like any financial planning endeavour, decisions about funding your child's education should be made with an eye toward the effects of taxation. Below are a few common options for reducing your family's overall tax burden so that more funds will be available to finance your child's education.

Registered Education Savings Plans (RESPs) can be effective education savings vehicles, especially due to the availability of Canada Education Savings Grants (CESGs). Under this program, the government will provide a grant of 20% on the first $2,500 of annual contributions made in a year to an RESP. As such, the grant may be worth up to

> Contribute up to $2,500 annually to an RESP and earn a 20% government grant.

$500 each year for each beneficiary, giving you an easy extra 20% return on your first $2,500 of contributions each year per beneficiary. For low- and middle-income families, the CESG grant may be even higher. The maximum lifetime grant is $7,200 per beneficiary. The RESP rules are discussed at greater length in Chapter 4.

As an alternative or in addition to an RESP, you could invest in tax-efficient growth mutual funds in your child's name. Any income from these funds is normally taxed under the preferential rules for capital gains (see Chapter 6) or dividends (see Chapter 7). Any capital gains distributed by the fund or realized on the sale of the fund will be taxable in your child's hands at your child's lower tax rate (or not taxed at all if his or her income is low enough). Until your child turns 18, the dividends and interest will be taxed in your hands due to the attribution rules discussed in 5.2.3; however, assuming you have selected a tax-efficient mutual fund, this will usually amount to a small proportion of the fund's overall return. Choosing a non-registered mutual fund provides some investment control and flexibility—there are no restrictions on the use of the funds and there is no limit on the amount that can be deposited.

If your child has a disability, you may be allowed to establish a Registered Disability Savings Plan to provide for his or her future financial needs, including education (see 4.6).

If you receive the Canada Child Benefit (see 2.3.2) for 2020, consider depositing the payments to an account in your child's name. As with RESP funds, these deposits may add up to a significant investment over time and, since the rules that prevent income splitting discussed in Chapter 5 don't apply, any investment income will be taxed in your child's hands, if at all. You may wish to withdraw the balance from the account annually and purchase higher-yielding investments on your child's behalf (see 5.3.12).

Another strategy to consider if interest rates are rising is to split income by entering into a family loan with your child via a family trust (see 5.3.4 and 21.5.4).

1.2.2 Encouraging your child to invest

If you have a child who works part-time (e.g., summer employment) with an income below the federal basic personal tax credit amount ($13,229 for 2020—see 2.2) and the Canada Employment Credit amount ($1,245 for 2020) that can be earned tax-free, consider filing a personal income tax return for him or her. By reporting this earned income, your child will build up RRSP contribution room that may be useful in a later year when he or she becomes taxable (see 3.1.3). This can be especially helpful when your child is in the teenage years and can expect to earn much more income in the future, since any unused RRSP deduction room is carried forward indefinitely. If your child has cash available (and your financial institution can set up a plan), he or she may contribute now to start enjoying tax-free investment growth but delay claiming the related tax deduction until a later year when your child has enough income to be taxable. Alternatively, if your child is over 17 and has a social insurance number, he or she could consider putting savings into a TFSA (see 4.1).

Instead of giving your child money that is easily spent, consider having him or her start an RRSP. The amount you can contribute may seem minimal—only 18% of the child's earned income from a summer or

Encourage your children to invest the money they earn.

part-time job, plus the $2,000 lifetime overcontribution if the child turned 18 in the prior year (see 3.3.4). But the funds in the RRSP will enjoy tax-free compounding, which will accumulate significantly over time. For example, assuming a 6% cumulative rate of return, $1,000 a year invested in an RRSP each year beginning at age 16 will grow to $13,972 by the beginning of the year in which the child turns 26; at age 30, the RRSP will grow to $24,673, and if the annual contribution is made until the child retires at 65, the RRSP will be about $273,000. Because the same principals discussed in 1.1.4 apply, ensure that you have an appropriate investment strategy in place for your child and their RRSP. You can even encourage them to get involved in the process to build their financial literacy.

Chapter 5 discusses options for splitting income with children. These strategies can significantly lower your family's overall tax burden and help your child become financially independent.

1.2.3 Buying a home

If you are renting your home, instead of buying, you may be missing out on a potential investment opportunity. A home can be a reliable hedge against inflation, a great retirement savings vehicle and an effective tax savings strategy—as we'll see in 6.5.2. If you own a home and sell it for a gain, the gain is usually tax-free as long as it has been your principal residence for income tax purposes and the disposition is properly reported.

So if you can afford to buy a home, you should generally not rent. If you are renting while you are saving for a home, consider moving to less expensive rental accommodations and saving more toward your down payment. The sooner you start putting your money toward a mortgage the better off you will be. Below are a few tax planning and other issues for prospective home buyers to consider.

If you are buying your first home, you may qualify for a 15% tax credit on up to $5,000 of your costs (see 2.7.3).

Think about using RRSP funds for a down payment on your first home under the Home Buyers' Plan.

If you qualify, the Home Buyers' Plan can be a possible source of cash for financing your down payment. If you are saving to buy your first home, think about using your RRSP as your savings vehicle; if you qualify under the Home Buyers' Plan discussed at 3.3.6, you can generally withdraw up to $35,000 as a loan from your RRSP to buy or build a home, without counting the withdrawal as income for tax purposes (for withdrawals made on or before March 19, 2019, you can only withdraw up to $25,000). You must then repay the loan, without interest, over 15 years starting in the second year following the year of withdrawal.

If you do plan to withdraw RRSP funds under the Home Buyers' Plan, consider making your RRSP contribution for the year at least 90 days before you make the withdrawal to preserve your ability to deduct the contribution amount. If you are depending on your RRSP for retirement income, you should forecast the decline in income that would result from the loss of the tax-free compounding when you withdraw a large chunk of RRSP funds now and pay it back over 15 years. See 3.3.6 for a more detailed discussion of the Home Buyers' Plan.

Once you have a mortgage, consider accelerating your mortgage payment schedule to reduce the amount of interest you'll pay over the life of your mortgage.

Increase the frequency of your mortgage payments to reduce your mortgage interest.

Accelerating your payment schedule doesn't necessarily mean that you will be shelling out any more cash than you do now. Here's the trick: figure out how much you can or want to pay each month and multiply that amount by 12. This is your annual payment. Then divide this number by 52 to determine the amount to pay weekly. Over the course of a year, your total mortgage payments will be identical, but more frequent payments will reduce your principal more quickly and reduce your overall interest cost.

Another way to save on mortgage interest is to maintain your original payment level when your mortgage comes up for renewal, even if interest rates have fallen. Also, each time you renew, consider increasing your payment by whatever you can commit—even an extra $50 or $100 will save you money in the long run.

1.2.4 Vacation properties

Buying a cottage, ski chalet or condo can provide years of enjoyment for your family. For a variety of reasons, a recreation property may also be a sound investment. You may save on your family's vacation costs. You may even find it easy to make up some of the property's costs by renting it out when your family is not using it. As long as market demand for desirable vacation properties remains steady, the value of your vacation home could rise significantly during the time you own it.

Whether you plan to keep the property in the family or sell it for future gain, bear in mind that capital gains tax (see 6.2.1) may apply on the difference between the property's cost when you bought it, plus capital improvements made, and its fair market value when you sell it or at the time of your death (or your spouse's death). The longer you own your cottage, the bigger the gain is likely to be.

Plan to minimize capital gains tax on dispositions of vacation homes.

To avoid leaving your survivors with a tax bill, which they may have to fund by selling the property, consider purchasing enough life insurance to fund the taxes that will arise on your death. You may be able to shelter some of the gain on the property's sale on your death (or your spouse's) through the principal residence exemption (see 6.5.2). You may be able to protect future gains from tax by transferring the property to one of your children or to a family trust (see 6.5.2 and 21.5.4). Consider also our more general discussion of estate planning in Chapter 21.

If your vacation property is situated in the U.S. and you are a Canadian resident, the double hit of U.S. estate tax and Canadian income tax arising on death can carry a potentially high tax burden. The Canada-U.S. tax treaty may ease the potential for double taxation, but, as discussed in 19.4, some rather complex tax planning may be required and you should seek professional tax advice.

Whether your vacation property is in Canada or the U.S., it's important to keep track of the property's adjusted cost base and capital improvements for tax purposes (see 6.2.1).

1.3 Preserving your family's financial security

The achievement of your financial goals can be delayed or derailed by unexpected changes of circumstance. Your family's financial plan should include measures to address risk and protect your family's financial security.

1.3.1 Do you have a line of credit and/or an emergency fund?

In today's business environment, you cannot count on having a job for life. In addition to cash flow, job loss can affect your company-funded benefits and pension plan. Generally speaking, you should have an

> Set up an emergency fund or line of credit.

emergency fund large enough to handle the loss of a job for six months to one year. Canada Savings Bonds, money market or T-bill funds and cashable guaranteed investment certificates are good places to park emergency reserves.

Another way to provide an emergency fund is to establish a line of credit with your financial institution. Be careful to only use it when necessary, because the interest you'll incur will be non-deductible for income tax purposes and you will have to repay it according to the line of credit's terms.

1.3.2 Do you have enough insurance?

Review your insurance needs with your financial advisers to determine the appropriate amount and form of your insurance coverage in various areas, including property loss, death, disability, sickness, personal liability and liquidity crisis.

A review of your financial plan should consider your need for life insurance. In the event of your death, life insurance may be critical for providing replacement income for your dependants and for funding your

> Make sure you have adequate insurance and a current will.

estate's tax and other liabilities. Life insurance plays many other important roles in estate planning. Some tax planning and other issues involving life insurance are discussed in 21.7.

One of your most valuable assets is your ability to earn income through employment or self-employment. Review your need for disability or critical illness insurance—if you become disabled, the financial consequences can be devastating. Most disability insurance policies do not provide a level of income over and above what you need for basic ongoing living expenses. In the long term, this could leave you without enough funds set aside for your retirement since disability income usually stops at age 65.

Make sure you have sufficient insurance to protect you from significant financial loss due to damage or destruction to your home, automobile or other personal assets. Without adequate coverage, the emotional trauma of such losses could be compounded by irreversible damage to your family's finances. Depending on your occupation or circumstances, you should also assess your need for other forms of insurance such as health and professional or director's liability coverage.

1.3.3 Is your will up-to-date?

Have you and your family members reviewed your wills within the past two years, or has there been a change in your family circumstances? Are your wills structured in a tax-efficient manner? Remember that if you die intestate (without a will) your assets will be distributed according to provincial law, possibly differently from what you would have wished. Be sure to seek advice of a lawyer (or a notary in Quebec) to ensure your will is legally valid and accurately reflects your wishes. You should also consult a tax adviser for assistance in reducing your estate's tax liability, including probate fees and U.S. estate tax.

For a more detailed discussion of the role of your will in planning for the orderly distribution of your estate and the minimization of taxes on death, see 21.2.

1.3.4 Do you have a power of attorney?

A power of attorney for property allows you to designate a person who will take control of your financial affairs if you become incapacitated due to illness or injury. If this happens and you do not have a power of attorney, control may yield to a provincial public trustee, which can restrict your family's ability to access your financial resources.

A power of attorney for personal care is someone you designate to make decisions about your health care, housing and other areas of your personal life if you become mentally incapable of making those decisions for yourself.

Powers of attorney are usually limited to decisions regarding your health care, property and finances. In some provinces (including Ontario and Quebec), you can empower different people to make decisions about your property and about your health care and medical treatment.

Like your will, your powers of attorney should be prepared with professional advice—consider having both drawn up at the same time.

Consider a power of attorney.

Note that a power of attorney operates only while you are alive. Once you die your will takes over, and your executor will manage your estate's affairs.

Changes in your personal circumstances could necessitate changes to your powers of attorney—it's a good idea to review them periodically.

In some cases, a trust can be an effective alternative to a power of attorney (see 21.5.4).

1.4 Selecting your professional advisers

Financial planning is broad in scope, and you may need advice from professionals with expertise in different areas. For some financial decisions, it will be worth the expense to invest in professional advice, whether from an accountant, lawyer, tax adviser, insurance broker, investment counsellor or a personal financial adviser. And in some financial planning endeavours, such as estate planning, professional legal and tax advice is a must.

Given what's at stake—your family's finances—you should take the time to shop around for advisers who are knowledgeable and experienced in their fields and with whom you feel comfortable. When interviewing prospective advisers of any profession, be sure to cover the following topics:

> Shop around when choosing your financial and investment advisers.

- Ask for client references, preferably from three or four people in circumstances similar to your own.
- Inquire into the professional's educational background, qualifications and level of experience.
- Ask whether the adviser belongs to any professional networks and associations to determine what sorts of resources are available to him or her.
- Make sure that you understand the fee arrangement and how the adviser is compensated.
- Be cautious of advisers whose objective may be to sell you investments, tax shelters, insurance or anything other than independent advice.

The level of your need for advisers depends primarily on the complexity of your affairs and your own knowledge of financial matters. You will get better value for the fees you pay to your advisers if you spend some time up front educating yourself. After all, it's your money and you must ultimately take responsibility for its handling and performance.

If you have a spouse, be sure that he or she is acquainted with your advisers, since your spouse will need to deal with them in the event of your death or disability. It is also a good idea to keep an up-to-date list of your advisers' names and phone numbers in one place, perhaps in the same place as your will and list of assets.

Chapter 2

Tips for claiming tax deductions and credits

- If you're unmarried and support a family member, don't miss out on the eligible dependant credit (2.2.1)

- Working parents and students—claim your child care expenses (2.3.1)

- Claim the tax credit for adoption expenses if you adopt a child in Canada or from another country (2.3.3)

- Take advantage of the tax credit for interest paid on student loans (2.4.4)

- If you're separating, co-operate to minimize your joint tax bill (2.6)

- Combine your family's medical expenses on one return (2.7.1)

- Choose your own 12-month period for medical expense claims (2.7.1)

- Plan for the timing of your family's medical expense payments (2.7.1)

- Take advantage of Canada's tax break for political contributions (2.7.2)

- If you are buying your first home, claim the tax credit on up to $5,000 of the purchase price (2.7.3)

In this chapter, we describe how your tax bill is calculated and highlight some commonly available and sometimes overlooked deductions and credits that can be claimed on your income tax return, depending on your family status and personal circumstances.

2.1 Taxes, credits and deductions

2.1.1 Calculating your tax balance due or refund owing

To understand how deductions and credits work, you need to understand the basic tax calculation. We describe it briefly here. (For Quebec residents, the provincial tax calculation is completely separate and not as described below. See Chapter 17.)

You start by adding up your various kinds of income—employment, business, interest, grossed-up dividends, taxable capital gains, and so on. This gives you **total income**. From this figure you subtract certain deductions, some of which we'll look at in this chapter—to reach **net income**, a figure used for certain purposes later. Then some additional deductions are allowed, primarily losses carried forward from previous years, giving you **taxable income**.

You then calculate your **federal tax**, applying the federal **tax rates** and **brackets** to your taxable income using the formula shown on Schedule 1 of your tax return. Then you subtract various **non-refundable tax credits** (see 2.1.2), and certain others such as the dividend tax credit (see 7.1.1). This gives you **net federal tax**.

Your next step is to add your **provincial tax**. You compute your provincial tax in essentially the same way as your federal tax, using taxable income calculated for federal tax purposes but applying your province's tax brackets, rates and credits to your taxable income. Depending on the province, you may also have to add a provincial surtax and/or health care levy. Federal and provincial tax rates and brackets for 2020 are set out in Appendix I. Federal and provincial non-refundable tax credits for 2020 are set out in Appendix II.

If you are self-employed, you may also be required to add your Canada Pension Plan (CPP) contribution and Employment Insurance premiums payable on your self-employment income at this point.

Finally, you record all source deductions of tax (withheld by your employer, for example) and instalments paid, both of which are credited to your account. Along with these are the **refundable credits**—including the employee or partner GST/HST rebate (see 2.9.4)—which are given the same treatment so that they can effectively be refunded to you even if you pay no tax for the year. (Some provinces also provide refundable tax credits.) The bottom line is your **balance owing** or **refund claimed**, and that will be the amount you remit by April 30 or receive when your return is assessed.

2.1.2 Deductions versus credits—what's the difference?

Before we get into the specific deductions and credits available, you need to understand the different effects of a deduction and a credit. You can refer back to the discussion in 2.1.1 as we go through this.

A **deduction** (or "write-off") reduces your taxable income, on which your federal tax is calculated. Bearing in mind that provincial tax rates and brackets vary, the combined effect of the federal and provincial taxes and provincial surtaxes means that, as long as you are still paying some tax, a deduction is worth about 23% where your taxable income is under $49,000; about 34% where it is from $49,000 to $97,000; about 42% where it is from $97,000 to $150,000; about 47% where it is from $150,000 to $214,000; and about 51% where it is over $214,000.

In other words, a $100 write-off (of, say, deductible moving or child care expenses) is worth about $23 to $51 in tax savings, depending on your tax bracket.

A **credit**, on the other hand, is a direct reduction in tax; $100 of a credit such as the credit for political contributions (see 2.7.2) is worth exactly $100 to you.

There is a twist, however. Under the federal-provincial tax collection agreement, provinces can top up the federal amounts or add their own credits if they wish, but at minimum they must offer the same basic credits as those available federally. As a result, the credits will be worth more, once you factor in the equivalent provincial credit. For example, for 2020, the maximum value of the basic personal credit (see 2.2) is $1,984 (if your income is less than $150,000) for federal purposes, but, if you live in Ontario, the value of the credit to you is actually $2,528 once the federal and provincial basic personal credit values are combined.

Finally, note the distinction between refundable and non-refundable credits. Because they are treated as having been paid by you, just like source withholdings and instalments, refundable credits are always worth what they say they are. Non-refundable credits, like deductions, become worthless once you reach the point of paying no tax at all for the year.

2.1.3 Transferring credits between spouses

Some of the non-refundable credits outlined below, such as charitable donations (see 8.1), can be transferred between spouses if not otherwise usable (see Schedule 2 of your tax return).

Where you have a choice as to which spouse will claim certain credits, credits are worth slightly more to very high-income individuals in some provinces. That is because some provinces (i.e., Ontario and PEI) impose additional surtaxes on individuals with high basic provincial tax.

If you are paying a surtax and your spouse is not, it is better for you to claim most of the credits that can be allocated between the two of you.

2.2 Personal, spousal and dependant credits

Every individual gets a basic federal credit, which allows you to receive a basic amount of income tax-free. In 2020, the maximum basic federal credit is $1,948, which offsets the federal tax on your first $13,299 of income, assuming your income for the year is less than $150,000. (On your income tax return, you claim a "basic personal amount" of $13,299, which you later multiply by 15%.)

2.2.1 Spousal/partner and eligible dependant credits

If you are married, you can claim a further federal credit of up to $1,984 for 2020 if your spouse's net income is under the credit amount of $13,299.

If you are single, widowed, divorced or separated, and you support another family member (such as a parent or child) in your home, you can claim the eligible dependant credit for that person. This will allow you the same claim as if that person were your spouse.

A caregiver credit is available if you provide care for an infirm relative age 18 or over or if the person for whom you are claiming the spousal/partner and eligible dependant credit is infirm (see. 2.5.4).

Common-law spouses, including unmarried same-sex couples, who meet certain criteria (below) are treated identically to legally married couples for all purposes relating to income tax. This means that the spousal credit can be claimed for a dependent common-law opposite-sex or same-sex spouse. It also means that a taxpayer who has a common-law spouse cannot claim the eligible dependant credit for a child.

> If you're unmarried and support a family member, don't miss out on the eligible dependant credit.

Common-law spouses are treated as spouses if they are two people who "cohabit in a conjugal relationship", where either they have had a child together, or they have cohabited for at least 12 continuous months at the time the determination is made. Separation is considered to terminate this "cohabiting" if the couple separates for at least 90 days because of a breakdown in their relationship.

2.3 Children

2.3.1 Child care expenses

A special set of tax rules allows you to deduct child care expenses, within limits, if they have been incurred to allow you or your spouse to work, carry on business, attend school or carry on grant-funded research.

Working parents and students—claim your child care expenses.

You can claim child care expenses for your child or your spouse's child. You can also claim them for a child who was dependent on you or your spouse and whose net income in 2020 is less than or equal to the basic personal amount of $12,298 to $13,229. The child must be under 16 at some time in the year, unless he or she is mentally or physically infirm.

Eligible child care expenses include caregivers, daycare services, day camps, boarding schools and overnight camps. The deduction is based on when the services are provided rather than when the amounts are paid, so prepaying in December does not give you the deduction a year earlier.

For two-parent families, child care expenses usually must be deducted by the spouse with the lower income. Single parents can deduct child care expenses from their own income. Common-law couples who meet certain criteria are treated the same as spouses for purposes of calculating child care expenses (as well as for all other tax purposes—see 2.2.1).

The amount of child care expenses you can claim is subject to various limits, depending on the age of the child and whether the child has a disability. In addition to the limit for each child, your expenses are subject to an overall limit of two-thirds of the "earned income" (basically salary and wages) of the lower-income spouse or single parent.

The various limits on child care expense deductions are as follows:

	Annual Limit Per Child
Child under age seven	$8,000
Child age seven to 16	$5,000
Child over age 16 and infirm but not eligible for disability tax credit (see 2.5.1)	$5,000
Child any age eligible for disability tax credit	$11,000
Additional limitation	2/3 of lower-income spouse's "earned income"

> **Example**
>
> Mary and Adam are married and have two children under age seven. Mary earns $120,000 and Adam earns $28,000. They pay $12,000 in 2020 to a nanny to take care of their children while they are working.
>
> Adam must be the one to claim the expenses, since he is the lower-income spouse. His deduction is the least of: (a) the amount paid—$12,000; (b) $8,000 per child—$16,000; and (c) two-thirds of his earned income—$18,667. He can therefore claim $12,000 as a deduction against his $28,000 of employment income. This will reduce his tax bill by about $2,760.
>
> If Mary were a single parent, she could claim the same amount as a deduction against her own income of $120,000 and reduce her tax bill by about $5,040.

Different limits apply where one or both parents are attending school full-time or part-time (see 2.4.5).

Payments to a boarding school or overnight camp are subject to limits for each week that the child attends the school or camp. The weekly limit is $200 per child under age seven, $125 per child aged seven to 16 or over age 16 and infirm but not eligible for the disability tax credit, and $275 per child eligible for the disability tax credit (see 2.5.1).

There are special circumstances where the lower-income spouse is not expected to care for the children. These are: where the spouse is disabled, in prison or hospital, or confined to bed or a wheelchair, for at least two weeks; attending full-time high school or post-secondary school; or where the spouses have separated for at least 90 days. In such cases, the higher-income spouse can claim the deduction up to the weekly limits noted above for each week that the condition continues.

The tax treatment of child care expenses for Quebec purposes is discussed at 17.3.2.

2.3.2 Canada Child Benefit

The Canada Child Benefit provides non-taxable monthly payments to eligible families. The maximum annual benefit is $6,765 per child under the age of 6 and $5,708 per child aged 6 through 17.

To qualify for the benefit, you must be a resident of Canada, you must live with your child and be the parent who primarily cares for your child, or have shared custody of the child.

Entitlement to the Canada Child Benefit for the July 2020 to June 2021 benefit year is based on adjusted family net income for the 2019 taxation year. Benefit payments are recalculated each July based on information from your income tax return from the previous year.

If your family has less than $31,711 in net income, you will receive the maximum benefit. If your adjusted family net income is between $31,711 and $68,708 the benefit will begin to be phased out at a rate of 7% for a one-child family, 13.5% for a two-child family, 19% for a three-child family and 23% for a family of four or more children.

If your adjusted family net income exceeds $68,708, benefits will be further reduced and will be phased out at rates of 3.2% for a one-child family, 5.7% for a two-child family, 8% for a three-child family and 9.5% for a family with more than three children, on the portion of income above $68,708.

> *Example*
>
> Mary and Adam from our example in 2.3.1 have a family income of $148,000 for 2019. One of their children is two years old and the other is four. Their Canada Child Benefit amount for the July 2020 to June 2021 benefit year will be calculated as follows.
>
> The maximum benefit amount for two children under age six is $13,530. The benefit will be reduced by 13.5% of Mary and Adam's income between $31,711 and $68,708, which equals $4,995. The benefit will be further reduced by 5.7% of their income between $68,708 and $148,000, which equals $4,520, for a total reduction of $9,515. As such, their annual benefit will amount to $4,015 ($13,530 – $9,515 reduction). Their monthly payments will be about $335.

If you have a child who is eligible for the disability tax credit (see 2.5.1), your Canada Child Benefit payments may include an additional amount of up to $2,886 per year. The phase-out of this amount generally aligns with the phase-out of Canada Child Benefit payments.

Amounts received under the Canada Child Benefit are not taxable and do not reduce benefits paid under the Goods and Services Tax credit (see 2.9.3). These amounts are also not included in income for the purposes of federal income-tested programs delivered outside of the income tax system, such as the Canada Education Savings Grant (see 4.4) and the Canada Disability Savings Grant (see 4.6).

2.3.3 Adoption expense tax credit

Claim the tax credit for adoption expenses if you adopt a child in Canada or from another country.

If you adopt a child under 18, a 15% non-refundable credit is available. For 2020, the maximum eligible expenses claimable are $16,563 per adoption. Eligible expenses include fees paid to licensed adoption agencies, court and legal expenses, reasonable travel and living expenses for the child and adoptive parents, translation fees and mandatory fees paid to a foreign institution. You can only claim the credit for the year in which the adoption is finalized, but at that time you can claim your adoption-related expenses incurred in previous years.

Quebec provides a refundable credit for adoption expenses (see 17.3.4).

2.4 Students

2.4.1 Tuition fees tax credit

Tuition fees paid for an individual for a year qualify for a non-refundable 15% federal credit for 2020. You may be able to claim certain tuition fees paid for your child or another person under the transfer rules discussed below.

To be eligible for a credit, the fees must be paid to a Canadian university, college or other post-secondary educational institution, or to an institution certified by Human Resources and Skills Development Canada. Occupational skills courses that are not at the post-secondary level may also be eligible for the credit, as well as fees paid to institutions in other countries. Generally, any fees you claim must total more than $100 per institution.

Along with admission fees, eligible tuition fees include library and lab charges, examination fees, application fees, mandatory computer service fees, charges for certificates, diplomas and degrees, and the cost of books included in the fees for a correspondence course. Also eligible are mandatory ancillary fees for health services, athletics and various other services (but not student association fees or fees covering goods of value that you retain such as a computer or a cooking student's utensils).

Fees paid to an educational institution, professional association, provincial ministry or similar institution for an examination required to obtain professional status recognized by federal or provincial statute, or to be licensed to practise a profession or trade in Canada, are eligible for this credit.

Fees paid to private schools for grade-school or high-school education will not entitle you to a federal tax credit. Certain schools offering the equivalent of university courses (Advanced Placement) can qualify for tuition credits. Religious private schools may be able to provide a tax receipt for some of your tuition fees, treating that amount as a charitable donation (see 8.1) made toward the school's religious instruction.

A 15% refundable Canada Training Credit can be claimed for the first time in 2020. You can begin to accumulate $250 each year in a notional account to cover eligible tuition and training costs, starting in 2019. To qualify for the 2020 credit, you must be at least 25 years old and less than 65 at the end of 2019, be a Canadian resident throughout the year, and have 2019 earnings of at least $10,000 but not over $147,667. If you meet the conditions, you may claim in 2020, the tax credit that is equal to the lessor of half of the eligible tuition and fees paid for the year and your notional account balance for the year (to a maximum amount of $5,000 over your lifetime). The portion of the tuition fees refunded through the Canadian Training Credit will not be eligible under the Tuition Tax Credit. Additionally, unlike the Tuition Tax Credit, education institutions outside of Canada will not be eligible for the purposes of the Canada Training Credit.

2.4.2 Transfer and carry forward of unused student credits

If you are not able to use your tuition credit in 2020 (because you have no tax to pay), up to $5,000 (worth up to $750) may normally be transferred to your spouse or to a parent or grandparent. You can carry forward any unused and untransferred tuition credit amounts and claim them against your taxable income in any later year. Note, however, that such amounts carried forward cannot be transferred—only the student can claim them in a later year.

If you carried forward unused amounts from the education and textbook tax credits, which were repealed starting in 2017, you can still claim the amounts you carried forward for taxation years after 2016.

2.4.3 Tax exemption for scholarships and bursaries

Scholarship, fellowship or bursary income is tax-free if the income is connected to a qualifying educational program that you were enrolled in as a full-time student in the immediately preceding or current taxation year, or if the income is connected to a specified education program (with not less than 12 hours in the month spent on courses in the program). Scholarships and bursaries provided to attend elementary and secondary schools are also tax-exempt. Amounts received for post-secondary programs up to and including doctoral degrees are exempt but post-doctoral fellowships do not qualify for this exemption.

Such income is only exempt to the extent the award was intended to support your enrolment in the program.

If you receive a scholarship, fellowship or bursary in connection with a part-time program, the exemption is limited to the cost of tuition and course materials (unless you qualify for the disability tax credit or cannot attend full-time due to a mental or physical impairment).

2.4.4 Tax credit for interest on student loans

Take advantage of the tax credit for interest paid on student loans.

Students and former students can claim a 15% non-refundable federal tax credit in 2020 on their interest paid on student loans under the *Canada Student Loans Act*, the *Canada Student Financial Assistance Act*, the *Apprentice Loans Act* or equivalent provincial programs. The credit is available for interest paid in the year or any of the five preceding years. Although the credit is not transferable, it can be carried forward for up to five years.

2.4.5 Other considerations for students

Single parents who are students and two-parent families where both parents attend school full-time may be able to deduct additional child care expenses, above the usual limits for child care expense deductions described in 2.3.1. For single students or two-parent student families, child care expense claims above the general limits are limited to two-thirds of your actual net income (instead of earned income). For each week that the single parent or both parents attend school full-time, the weekly limit is $200 per child under age seven, $125 per child aged seven to 16 or over 16 and infirm but not eligible for the disability tax credit, and $275 per child eligible for the disability tax credit.

For part-time students, the child care expense deduction is subject to these limits for each month (rather than week) for which the part-time education credentials are met.

For students claiming the child care expense deduction, "full-time" attendance at school means that you must attend a designated educational institution or a secondary school and be enrolled in a program of the institution or school that is at least three consecutive weeks long and requires you to spend at least 10 hours per week on course work. You are attending school "part-time" if the program lasts at least three consecutive weeks and involves at least 12 hours per month on course work.

Some students may have qualified for government assistance as a result of the COVID-19 pandemic. If you received assistance under the Canada Emergency Student Benefit (CESB), you should be prepared to report these payments and pay tax on them, just like regular income. In particular, you must report these taxable benefits on your 2020 income tax return. The government has said it will provide a T4A tax slip to students to report these payments.

In certain cases, students may also be able to deduct their moving expenses (see 13.1.2).

Students can also withdraw funds from their RRSPs (within limits) to help finance their education (see 3.3.7).

If you are a student who lives in Quebec, see 17.4.1.

2.5 People with disabilities

2.5.1 Disability tax credit

If you suffer from a severe and prolonged impairment in physical or mental functions, you can get an additional non-refundable federal tax credit of $8,576 (worth $1,286) for 2020. Depending on the nature of the impairment, your status must be certified by a medical doctor, nurse practitioner, optometrist, audiologist, speech-language pathologist, occupational therapist, psychologist or physiotherapist.

To qualify as having a severe and prolonged impairment, your ability to perform a "basic activity of daily living" must be "markedly restricted", and the impairment must have lasted or be expected to last for at least a year. Further, your impairment must be present all or substantially all the time (i.e., at least 90% of the time). People who must undergo therapy (e.g., dialysis) at least three times a week for an average of 14 or more hours of therapy in order to sustain their vital functions are also eligible for the credit.

The *Income Tax Act* has specific definitions to determine whether you qualify. The rules can be found on the Canada Revenue Agency's (CRA) Disability Tax Credit Certificate, Form T2201. If you have a disability and reside in Quebec, see also 17.9.

It is often difficult to determine whether a person qualifies or not, and the Tax Court of Canada has issued numerous decisions interpreting these rules. In some cases, the court has found the CRA's view to be incorrect. Therefore, if you believe you fit within the *Income Tax Act*'s definition of disabled, you could consider pursuing your claim further if the CRA denies it.

You may also be able to claim a portion of your medical expenses for the medical expense credit (see 2.7.1).

If you have a dependent relative who qualifies for the disability tax credit but does not earn enough income to be able to use all of it, the dependant's unused credit can be transferred to your return. For this purpose, eligible dependants include your spouse, child, grandchild, parent, grandparent, sibling, aunt, uncle, niece or nephew.

If you support a dependent child age 18 or over who has a disability, you can also claim the Canada caregiver credit (see 2.5.4).

Additional assistance is available for children under 18 at the end of the year with severe disabilities in the form of a supplementary credit of $5,003 (worth up to $750) for 2020. The supplement amount is reduced by certain amounts claimed such as child care expenses (see 2.3.1), the disability supports deduction (see 2.5.2) and the medical expense tax credit (see 2.7.1).

2.5.2 Disability supports deduction

If you have a disability, you can deduct some or all of the costs of disability supports needed to allow you to earn employment or business income, carry on grant-funded research, or pursue your education, unless the costs have been reimbursed by a non-taxable payment (such as an insurance payment).

The disability supports deduction is limited to your "earned income" (which includes salary and business income), plus, if you attend school, the lesser of the difference between your net income and your earned income and $375 per week of school attendance (to a maximum of $15,000).

Eligible disability supports expenses include, among other things, amounts paid for sign-language interpretation services, job coaching services, real-time captioning services, teletypewriters that allow deaf or mute people to use telephones, and speech synthesizers, equipment and software that allows blind people to use computers or read print, note-taking services, tutoring services, talking textbooks and attendant care services provided in Canada. Most of these expenses are eligible for the deduction, but only if a medical practitioner certifies the need for the items or services.

As an alternative, disability supports expenses can generally be claimed for purposes of the medical expense credit (see 2.7.1), whether or not you are earning income or attending school. In some cases, it may be more beneficial to claim these costs as medical expenses on your own or your spouse's tax return. To determine which option generates greater tax savings, calculate and compare the net tax results of claiming these costs through the disability supports deduction versus the medical expense credit.

2.5.3 RRSP withdrawals under the Home Buyers' Plan

Under the Home Buyers' Plan (see 3.3.6) you can withdraw up to $35,000 as a loan from your RRSP to buy or build a home and not pay tax on the amount as long as you repay it over 15 years beginning in the second year following the year of withdrawal. This is an increase from the previous limit, which was $25,000 for withdrawals before March 20, 2019.

Since the Home Buyers' Plan was originally intended to help first-time home buyers, you are generally ineligible if you or your spouse owned a home that you lived in as your principal place of residence in any of the five calendar years up to and including the current calendar year.

However, for withdrawals made after 2019, you can still participate in the Home Buyers' Plan following the breakdown of your marriage or common-law partnership, provided that you live separate and apart from your spouse or common-law partner for at least 90 days.

The five-year qualifying period under the Home Buyers' Plan does not apply to persons with disabilities and their relatives if the new home is more accessible to or better suited to the personal needs and care of a person with a disability who will reside there.

See 3.3.6 for a more detailed discussion of the pros and cons of participating in the Home Buyers' Plan.

2.5.4 Canada caregiver credit

If your spouse or common-law partner, minor child or eligible relative is dependent on you because of a mental or physical infirmity at any time in the year, you can claim the non-refundable Canada caregiver credit. You can also claim the credit if you provide care for infirm dependants of your spouse or common-law partner.

The dependant does not have to live with you for you to claim the credit. However, the federal credit is no longer available for non-infirm parents over 65 years of age who live with you.

The Canada caregiver credit is based on two maximum amounts: a high maximum amount and a low maximum amount. The maximum Canada caregiver credit that can be claimed depends on the age and relationship of the infirm dependent. For eligible infirm dependants age 18 or older, the high maximum amount is $7,276 in 2020 (worth up to $1,091, unless the low maximum amount applies).

The second, low maximum amount of $2,273 can be claimed for:

- an infirm dependent spouse or common-law partner for whom you claim the spouse or common-law partner amount (see 2.2.1)
- an infirm dependant for whom you claim the eligible dependant credit (see 2.2.1)
- an infirm child who is under the age of 18 years at the end of the tax year (see 2.5.1).

This credit amount is reduced dollar-for-dollar by the dependant's net income above $17,085 and is completely phased out at an income of $22,088 or at $24,361, depending on whether the low or high amount is used.

If claiming the second, lower amount produces less tax relief than you would receive by claiming the higher maximum (i.e., $7,276 for 2020), you may be eligible for a top-up to offset the difference. No top-up is allowed for amounts claimed for an eligible dependant who is age 18 or younger at the end of the year.

Example

Line earns $80,000 annually and cares for her infirm spouse, Max, who has no income in 2020. Line's caregiver and spousal credits are calculated as follows:

Line's maximum regular spousal amount is $13,229, plus the maximum $2,273 caregiver amount, for a total spousal amount for an infirm dependent spouse of $15,502 (A). Because Max has no income in 2020 and is older than 18, Line is entitled to the full maximum caregiver amount of $7,276 (B). Because Line's spousal amount (A), exceeds the maximum caregiver amount (B), she receives no caregiver top-up or caregiver credit, but she is entitled to a spousal credit of $2,325 (15% of A).

As the following table shows, if Max earns $13,000, Line's 2020 spousal credit is $375 (15% of A) and her caregiver credit is $716 (15% of C), for combined credits of $1,091. As the table also shows, if Max earns $18,000, Line cannot claim a spousal credit (because her spousal amount (A) is nil), but she is entitled to a Canada caregiver credit of $954.

Line's spouse income	$13,000	$18,000
Spousal amount		
Base amount + low maximum ($13,229 + 2,273)	15,502	15,502
Less spouse's income	(13,000)	(18,000)
Amount (A)	2,502	—
Canada caregiver amount		
Base amount + high maximum ($17,085 + 7,276)	24,361	24,361
Less spouse's income	(13,000)	(18,000)
	11,361	6,361
Amount (B)	claim max. of 7,276	
Canada caregiver top-up amount		
Amount B	7,276	6,361
Less amount A	(2,502)	(0.00)
Amount (C)	4,774	6,361
Canada caregiver credit		
15% of Amount (C)	716	954
Spousal credit		
15% of Amount (A)	$375	—

2.5.5 Home accessibility tax credit

If you are 65 or older or you are eligible for the Disability Tax Credit and you renovate your home to make it safer, more accessible or more functional for you, you may be able to claim a non-refundable tax credit for up to $10,000 of eligible expenses per year (worth up to $1,500). Eligible expenses include wheelchair ramps, walk-in bathtubs and grab bars, among others.

2.6   Marital breakdown—Child and spousal support payments

While marriage breakdown may give rise to bitter disputes, you and your spouse (through your lawyers, if necessary) should co-operate to minimize your joint tax bill and share the resulting savings.

> If you're separating, co-operate to minimize your joint tax bill.

Child support is not taxed as income to the recipient or deducted from income by the paying parent.

Spousal support payments are deductible to the payer and taxable to the recipient if they meet some well-defined and strict criteria.

To be deductible, the spousal support payment must be an *allowance*, which has been established in advance as a recurring payment. The amounts payable must be predetermined. (Amounts that are required to be adjusted for inflation can still be considered predetermined.)

Additionally, the allowance must be:

- paid under a written agreement or under a decree, order or judgment of a competent tribunal
- payable on a periodic basis for the maintenance of the recipient (your spouse or ex-spouse)
- paid at a time when you are living apart from your spouse or ex-spouse because of the breakdown of your marriage.

Payments to former common-law spouses may be deducted on the same basis, where the recipient is an individual who cohabited with you "in a conjugal relationship" or you are the legal parent of that person's child.

Note that the "periodic basis" requirement excludes one-time payments and transfers of property in settlement of rights of the marriage.

Payments made directly to third parties, rather than to your spouse or ex-spouse, are allowed in limited circumstances. Such payments can include medical bills, tuition fees and mortgage payments for your spouse or ex-spouse's home. Among other requirements, the court order or written separation agreement must specifically provide for the payments and must specifically provide that the relevant tax rules will apply, to make the payments deductible to you and taxable to your spouse or ex-spouse.

In general, you may deduct payments made before obtaining a court order or signing a written separation agreement, provided the order or agreement is signed by the end of the year following the year in which the payment is made, and the order or agreement specifically provides that the amounts paid earlier are to be considered as paid and received pursuant to the agreement.

If you are the support payer, you cannot deduct legal costs to establish, negotiate or contest the amount of support payments. However, if you are the recipient, you can deduct legal costs to obtain an order for child support, establish the amount for spousal support, enforce existing rights or have the support amounts increased.

Spousal or child support paid to a non-resident of Canada is deductible if the above criteria are met.

If you receive a lump-sum spousal support payment over $3,000 relating to prior years, you may ask the CRA to determine whether it is more advantageous to you to recalculate the tax on that income as if you received it in those prior years. This measure is intended to relieve the higher tax liability that may result if the entire lump-sum is taxed in the year of receipt, rather than year by year as the right to receive the payments arose.

Child support paid under arrangements concluded before May 1997 is treated the same way as spousal support payments.

2.7   Other commonly available credits

2.7.1   Medical expenses

Medical expenses over a certain threshold entitle you to a non-refundable tax credit. The threshold is 3% of your net income, or, if your net income exceeds $79,900 in 2020, a flat $2,397. All qualifying medical expenses above this amount give rise to a 15% federal credit (if you live in Quebec, see also 17.8).

> **Example**
>
> Alison's net income is $50,000. She spends $2,500 on qualifying medical expenses in 2020. Given that 3% of Alison's net income is $1,500, the remaining $1,000 qualifies for the medical expense credit. The federal credit is 15% of that, or $150.

Medical expense claims made on behalf of dependent minor children are pooled with those of you and your spouse for purposes of the medical expense threshold of 3% of your net income and $2,397, whichever is less.

For amounts paid on behalf of any other close relative dependent on you for support, you can claim medical expenses that exceed the lesser of 3% of the dependant's net income for the year and $2,397. The list of qualifying medical expenses is very long, and you should refer to the CRA's Income Tax Folio S1-F1-C1 "Medical Expense Tax Credit" (see 2.10) if you need specific details. The list includes:

- payments to medical practitioners, dentists and registered nurses, hospital fees not covered by public health insurance and diagnostic procedures
- prescription drugs
- institutional care (e.g., nursing home)
- the care and supervision of persons with severe and prolonged disabilities living in a group home
- guide dogs (both purchase cost and upkeep cost)
- eyeglasses, hearing aids and dentures

- costs of moving to accessible housing, home renovations and driveway alterations required for someone with a mobility impairment
- sign language interpreter fees
- medical intervention to help conceive a child
- cost for an animal specially trained to perform tasks for a patient with a severe mental impairment to assist them in coping with their impairment
- cost of disability supports not claimed for purposes of the disability supports deduction (see 2.5.2)
- a long list of specific devices, ranging from crutches to insulin needles, wheelchair lifts, speech synthesizers, visual fire alarm indicators and TDD devices for the deaf.

Expenses for purely cosmetic medical procedures that are aimed solely at improving your appearance, such as liposuction, hair replacement and teeth whitening, are not eligible for the medical expense credit.

Since self-employed individuals are allowed to deduct premiums to a drug or dental plan (see 11.2.11), these premiums are not eligible for the medical expense credit for those individuals.

Because of the threshold of 3% of net income, you should combine all of the family's medical expenses on one return. It is normally better for the lower-income spouse to make the claim, provided that spouse has enough tax to pay to use up the credit, since the 3% threshold will be smaller. On the other hand, the credit might be slightly more valuable to a high-income spouse because it will reduce the application of high-income provincial surtaxes levied in some provinces (see 2.1.3).

> Combine your family's medical expenses on one return.

When claiming medical expenses, you can pick any 12-month period ending in the year. If, for example, you made no claim for 2019, and you have large medical expense bills in February 2019, January 2020, and November 2020, you might be better off to use January 2019 as the end of your 12-month period, claim the February 2019 and January 2020 expenses for 2020, and leave the November 2020 expenses to be claimed on your 2021 return.

> Choose your own 12-month period for medical expense claims.

You can also plan for the timing of medical expenses, since they are based on when they are paid. If you are using a December end for the 12-month period, and you have pending expenses (perhaps for medical equipment purchases or large dental bills) that are due early in the new year, consider prepaying them so that you can claim them one year earlier.

> Plan for the timing of your family's medical expense payments.

2.7.2 Political contributions

Contributions to federal political parties and to candidates in federal election campaigns entitle you to a non-refundable federal tax credit. A donation of $400 will cost you only $100.

Take advantage of Canada's tax break for political contributions.

To encourage small political donations by many people, the federal credit is most generous at the lowest levels. The credit is 75% for the first $400 of political donations (worth $300); 50% for the next $350 (worth $175); and 33.33% for the next $525 (worth $175). There is no additional credit for donations beyond $1,275. As such, the maximum credit allowed is $650.

> **Example**
>
> Jacquelin contributes $500 to a federal political party in 2020. Jacquelin's political contribution credit for 2020 will be 75% on the first $400 ($300) plus 50% on the next $100 ($50), for a total of $350. There is no reduction in provincial tax resulting from this credit.

In addition, many of the provinces have their own credits for contributions to provincial parties and candidates. The Quebec credit for political donations is discussed at 17.7.2.

2.7.3 First-time home buyers

If you are buying your first home, claim the tax credit on up to $5,000 of the purchase price.

If you are acquiring your first home, you may qualify for a non-refundable tax credit for first-time home buyers on up to $5,000 of the home's cost (worth up to $750).

The credit can be claimed by you or your spouse or common-law partner. To qualify, neither of you can have owned another home or lived in another home owned by your spouse or common-law partner in the year of purchase or in any of the four preceding years. A qualifying home is one that is currently eligible for the Home Buyers' Plan (see 3.3.6) that you or your spouse or common-law partner intend to occupy as your principal place of residence within one year of acquiring it.

You can also claim the credit for certain home purchases by or for the benefit of a disabled family member who is eligible for the disability tax credit (see 2.5.1).

2.7.4 Other credits

There are a number of other non-refundable credits available when computing "basic federal tax" (and provincial equivalents reducing provincial taxes and surtaxes, as discussed in 2.1.2). These include the credit for donations to registered charities (see 8.1), the pension income credit (see 20.3.5), age credit (see 20.3.4), the dividend tax credit (see 7.1.2), and the credit for work-related expenses of employees (see 10.7.1).

Other federal-only credits include the investment tax credit, which is an incentive for those carrying on business to invest in particular regions or sectors of the economy (see 11.2.14) and the foreign tax credit (also available in Quebec), which offsets the impact of foreign tax paid on income from a foreign source, to reduce double taxation (see 18.2.2).

2.8 Other commonly available deductions

2.8.1 Legal fees

Whether you can deduct legal fees you have paid depends on why you paid them.

Legal fees are generally deductible if they are paid for the purpose of earning income from business or property. Legal fees to acquire or preserve a capital asset are normally not deductible, though there are exceptions.

Legal fees associated with an objection or appeal of your income tax assessment (see 9.5) are deductible. This includes the costs of negotiations with CRA officials prior to filing a formal Notice of Objection. The fees are also deductible if you are appealing a Quebec income tax assessment or an income tax assessment of a foreign government, or an Employment Insurance or Canada/Quebec Pension Plan decision.

Legal fees to collect unpaid salary or wages owed to you by your employer or former employer are deductible.

Legal fees generally can be deducted where they are incurred to obtain a "retiring allowance" (including severance pay) or a pension benefit (see 10.8.5), but generally only up to a limit of your income from those sources (in the current year or past years).

Finally, you may deduct legal costs to establish or enforce a right to child support. (See 2.6; see also 17.13.1 if you live in Quebec.)

2.8.2 Northern residents

If you live in northern Canada for not less than six consecutive months beginning or ending in a year, a special deduction is available to help offset the higher costs of living and the hardship and isolation relative to the more populated parts of the country. The deduction is limited to the lesser of 20% of your net income and, if you live in the "prescribed northern zone", up to $22 per day ($8,030 per year). If you live somewhat further south, in the "prescribed intermediate zone", you can only claim half as much. As well, if your employer pays the cost of travel for you and your family (e.g., an annual trip to southern Canada), a deduction is available to offset part or all of the taxable benefit that is thereby included in your income (see 10.8.9). A similar deduction is available for Quebec tax purposes if you live in northern Quebec.

2.8.3 Other deductions

Some other common deductions are covered in other chapters. See, for example, 3.1.3 (contributions to RRSPs), 6.2.3 (allowable business investment losses), 6.4 (capital gains deduction), 7.2.3 (interest paid), 10.8 (deductions available to employees) and 13.1 (moving expenses). Some of the deductions relating to self-employment (carrying on business) are discussed in Chapter 11.

2.9 Canada/Quebec Pension Plan Contributions, Employment Insurance and GST

2.9.1 CPP/QPP contributions and EI premiums

A federal credit of 15% of all Canada (or Quebec) Pension Plan (CPP/QPP) contributions and EI premiums is available, effectively giving you back about 23% of these amounts when the equivalent provincial credit is factored in. If you are employed, these amounts are normally taken off your pay at source by your employer.

If you are self-employed, you will normally have to calculate and remit both the employer and employee portions of CPP/QPP (but not EI) contributions on your net self-employment income. Self-employed individuals may deduct the employer's portion (see 11.2.3).

2.9.2 EI clawback

If you receive Employment Insurance benefits and your net income exceeds a certain threshold, a portion of your benefits received during the year will be taxed back through a special tax, commonly called a "clawback", paid through your income tax return.

The clawback applies if your net income for 2020 exceeds $67,750. You must repay $30 for each $100 of net income over your threshold, up to a maximum of 100% of the benefits received. Benefits that are not clawed back are taxed as regular income.

The clawback does not apply if you are receiving EI benefits for the first time in the last 10 years or if you are receiving only maternity, parental, sickness or compassionate care benefits.

2.9.3 GST/HST credit

The Goods and Services Tax/Harmonized Sales Tax (GST/HST) credit is aimed at low-income individuals and families. It is designed to offset the GST/HST paid by consumers on most goods and services. For 2020, the annual credit is $296 per eligible adult and $155 per child under 19 in the family, reduced by 5 cents for each dollar that family net income exceeds $38,507. The credit is tax-free and is generally paid in quarterly instalments to qualifying families, based on their previous year's income. If your GST credit is less than $50 quarterly, you should receive it in one lump-sum payment in July.

An extra GST credit supplement of up to $155 is available if you are single, separated, widowed or divorced and have no children. The GST credit supplement is the lesser of $155 or 2% of net income over $9,590. The total of the GST credit and the supplement are reduced by 5 cents for each dollar of income over $38,507.

Many provinces also have sales tax credits for low-income taxpayers. For the Quebec credit, which parallels the GST credit, see 17.13.4.

2.9.4 GST/HST rebate

In addition to the GST/HST credit described in 2.9.3, certain employees and members of partnerships can claim a GST/HST rebate on their income tax returns. The rebate is generally available to employees who claim income tax deductions relating to their employment expenses, and partners who claim deductions on expenses they incur outside the partnership to earn partnership income. (See 10.9, 11.3.7 and 12.3.2 for more details.)

2.10 References

The following publications and more information, including forms and brochures, can be obtained on the CRA's website at *www.canada.ca/en/revenue-agency.html* or by telephone request at 1-800-959-8281 for individual income tax and trust-related enquiries or 1-800-959-5525 for business and self-employed individual enquiries.

Booklet T4114, "Canada Child Benefit"

Income Tax Folio S1-F1-C1, "Medical Expense Tax Credit"

Income Tax Folio S1-F1-C2, "Disability Tax Credit"

Income Tax Folio S1-F1-C3, "Disability Supports Deduction"

Income Tax Folio S1-F2-C1, "Qualifying Student and the Education and Textbook Tax Credits"

Income Tax Folio S1-F2-C2, "Tuition Tax Credit"

Income Tax Folio S1-F2-C3, "Scholarships, Research Grants and Other Education Assistance"

Income Tax Folio S1-F3-C1, "Child Care Expense Deduction"

Income Tax Folio S1-F3-C3, "Support Payments"

Income Tax Folio S1-F4-C2, "Basic Personal and Dependant Tax Credits"

Information Circular 75-2R9, "Contributions to a registered party, a registered association or to a candidate at a federal election"

Pamphlet P102, "Support Payments"

Pamphlet P105, "Students and Income Tax"

Chapter 3

RRSPs and other tax-assisted retirement plans

- Consider a self-directed Registered Retirement Savings Plan (RRSP) for greater flexibility (3.1.6)

- Think about transferring shares that you already own to your self-directed RRSP (3.1.6)

- Think about using your RRSP to shelter future gains on high-growth private company shares (3.1.6)

- Think about boosting your self-directed RRSP's foreign content (3.1.7)

- Contribute as much as you can to an RRSP (3.1.9)

- Contribute early in the year instead of the following February (3.1.9)

- Think twice before borrowing funds to contribute to your RRSP (3.1.9)

- Withdraw funds from your RRSP in low-income years (3.2.1)

- Contribute to your spouse's (or common-law spouse's) RRSP if your spouse's projected income on retirement will be lower (3.3.1)

- Make spousal RRSP contributions in December instead of the following February (3.3.1)

- Transfer pension commuted value, retiring allowances or severance pay to your RRSP (3.3.2)

- Top up your RRSP with a non-deductible $2,000 overcontribution (3.3.4)

- Consider shares of a labour-sponsored venture capital corporation for your RRSP (3.3.5)

- Consider Home Buyers' Plan withdrawals to buy or build your first home (but be sure to weigh the loss of RRSP growth) (3.3.6)

- Consider withdrawing RRSP funds under the Lifelong Learning Plan to help pay for training or post-secondary education programs (3.3.7)

- Consider contributing to your RRSP instead of a money-purchase RPP (3.5.1)

- Find out about the vesting of your pension benefits, especially before making a career change (3.5.1)

- Weigh the advantages of establishing an "individual pension plan" (3.5.2)

Deferred income plans, particularly RRSPs and registered pension plans, are the most widely used tax shelters in Canada. Put simply, almost everyone should have one.

The concept of deferred income plans is simple, although the particular rules can be complex. In this chapter, we'll take you through the basic rules, so you understand the system in general. We also discuss the options you have and steps you can take for tax planning.

The rules are essentially the same for Quebec tax purposes.

3.1 Registered Retirement Savings Plans—RRSPs

3.1.1 What is an RRSP?

Although RRSP stands for "registered retirement savings plan", these plans do not necessarily have anything to do with retirement. They can be used for a variety of purposes, such as financing your first home or training or post-secondary education, or simply as a tool for tax deferral.

The concept behind an RRSP is simple. If you agree to put some of your salary or self-employment income away and not have immediate access to it, the tax system will tax that income—along with all the interest and other income it earns—when it is *received* rather than when it is *earned.*

Example

If you earn $60,000, you pay tax on $60,000.

Suppose you earn $60,000 but you put $2,000 of that into an RRSP. You will be taxed on only $58,000—the amount you have received.

If, some years later, the $2,000 you put away has grown (in a tax-free environment) to $3,000, you can take the $3,000 out of your RRSP, and it will be taxed (added to your income) at that point.

Again, the original $2,000, now grown to $3,000, is being taxed in the year it is received rather than when it was earned.

The rules governing RRSPs are more complex than the above example indicates, of course. The amount you can contribute to an RRSP is limited in various ways.

3.1.2 How do you set up an RRSP?

An RRSP can be set up easily at almost any bank or trust company or through an investment adviser, life insurance agent, mutual fund company or mutual fund distributor. Basically, you just fill out a form and contribute money to the plan. Some institutions will give you your official tax receipt immediately; others will send it to you later, in time for you to file it with your tax return.

3.1.3 How much can you contribute?

Contributions to an RRSP are deductible for any given year if they are contributed in *the year or within 60 days after the end of the year.* So if you contribute by March 1, 2021, you can get a deduction for your 2020 tax return (and any resulting refund will come sometime in the spring of 2021 after you have filed your 2020 return).

Three factors limit the amount you can contribute to an RRSP: a dollar limit; a percentage of the previous year's "earned income"; and your "pension adjustment". We'll look at each of these in turn.

Dollar limit

The RRSP contribution limit rose to $27,230 in 2020 (from $26,500). For 2021 the limit will be $27,830.

Percentage of previous year's earned income

The annual deduction (subject to the $27,230 limit and pension adjustment) is limited to 18% of the *previous* year's earned income. That is, 18% of your 2019 earned income is used to determine your 2020 contribution (to be made by March 1, 2021).

"Earned income" for most employees is the same as "salary"—the gross amount of salary, before deductions for income tax, EI, CPP, etc., which are withheld at source. "Earned income" includes net business income, if you are self-employed or are an active partner in a business (see 16.2.4). It also includes:

- research grants, net of deductible related expenses
- royalties from works or inventions that you wrote or invented
- taxable spousal and child support received (see 2.6)
- net rental income from real estate
- disability pension income received under the CPP/QPP.

Earned income is *reduced* by:

- deductible maintenance and child support you pay
- most deductible employment-related expenses, such as union dues and travelling expenses (but not pension plan contributions)
- net business losses
- rental losses from real estate.

Earned income does not include most investment income, such as interest or dividends, or capital gains. Nor does it include pension benefits, retiring allowances, severance pay, death benefits or amounts received from an RRSP, RRIF or deferred profit-sharing plan.

If your 2019 earned income was more than $151,278 your 2020 contribution is limited to $27,230 (minus the pension adjustment as discussed below). Otherwise, you are limited by the 18% factor.

Pension adjustment

Once you have calculated your maximum contribution limit as 18% of your previous year's earned income, subject to the dollar limits discussed above, you must subtract your pension adjustment for the previous year, if any. This figure represents the deemed value of your pension earned for the previous year. In other words, the more that has been put aside (by you and your employer combined) towards your retirement pension, the less you can contribute to an RRSP.

If you are *not* a member of an employer's pension plan or deferred profit-sharing plan, your pension adjustment is zero, and you can contribute the full 18% of your previous year's earned income (subject to the annual $27,230 limit).

Otherwise, your pension adjustment for 2019 should have appeared on your 2019 T4 slip, as well as on your Notice of Assessment received in 2020 following the filing of your 2019 return.

For "money-purchase" pension plans (see 3.5.1), the pension adjustment is the total contributions made to your pension by you and your employer combined. The same applies to deferred profit-sharing plans (see 3.6), except that the contributions are made only by your employer. For "defined benefit" pension plans, the pension adjustment is based on a calculation that takes into account the benefit you may receive on retirement based on your past year's employment.

> **Example**
>
> Melanie is a chemical engineer who belongs to her employer's pension plan. Her 2019 earned income was $60,000. Her pension adjustment for 2019, as reported on her 2019 T4 slip and her 2019 assessment received from the CRA in mid-2020, is $3,200.
>
> Before accounting for her pension adjustment, Melanie's contribution limit for 2020 is 18% of her 2019 earned income, to a maximum of $27,230. For 2019, 18% of her earned income is $10,800. From this amount she must deduct her pension adjustment for 2019 of $3,200. Melanie may therefore contribute up to $7,600 to an RRSP by March 1, 2021 for a deduction on her 2020 tax return.

In some situations, the calculation of your RRSP limit may also be reduced by a past service pension adjustment (PSPA). In general terms, a PSPA can arise when your pension benefits under a defined benefit pension plan are improved on a retroactive basis.

If you terminate your employment before retirement, you may be entitled to a pension adjustment reversal (PAR). The PAR is designed to give you back some of the RRSP contribution room lost due to pension adjustments (PA) while you were a member of a company pension plan.

If you were a member of a defined contribution plan or deferred profit-sharing plan, your PAR will be the total of all PAs reported by your employer since 1990 that have not yet "vested" (see 3.5.1). If you were a member of a defined benefit plan and you have not reported any PSPAs, your PAR will be equal to your total PAs since 1990 less the post-1989 portion of any lump sums paid to you or transferred to an RRSP or money-purchase pension plan (if you have reported any PSPAs, your PAR calculation will be more complex but, whatever your plan, your employer's pension plan administrator will figure it out for you). You will not be entitled to a PAR if you maintain any entitlement to periodic pension payments from the plan. The PAR is only available to you if you transfer the commuted value of your defined benefit plan to a locked-in RRSP, also known as a locked-in retirement account.

PARs increase RRSP room for the year of termination. If you have ended or will be ending company pension plan membership in 2020, you may want to encourage your employer to report your PAR shortly after your termination so you can make use of the related extra RRSP room as soon as possible. Your employer must report your PAR for your year of termination within 60 days of the end of the quarter in which termination occurred (or by January 31 of the following year if termination occurs in the fourth quarter).

Carry forward of unused deduction room and undeducted contributions

If you contribute less than the maximum to an RRSP in any year, you can "carry forward" the extra deduction room and contribute that much more in any following year. You can also carry forward unused RRSP room created by a PAR. If you contribute an amount for a year but choose not to deduct the amount for that year, you can claim the deduction in any later year (provided you still have contribution room).

> **Example**
>
> Melanie, from the previous example, has $7,600 of contribution room for 2020. She chooses to contribute only $5,000 to an RRSP for the year.
>
> Melanie has unused RRSP contribution room of $2,600 to carry forward. As a result, she may increase her contribution by that amount in any following year. If Melanie's contribution limit for 2021 is again $7,600, she can contribute up to $10,200 for deduction in 2021.

You should carefully review your assessment notice from the CRA to make sure the contribution limit reported is correct, before relying on it. An incorrect statement from the CRA does not entitle you to deduct a contribution you would not otherwise be entitled to.

In some cases you might contribute more than you can actually deduct. We discuss overcontributions in 3.3.4.

3.1.4 What's your contribution worth?

What is your contribution worth in tax savings? It depends on your marginal tax rate. Tax rates and brackets vary among the provinces (see Appendix I), but for 2019 they are approximately:

- 23% on income from $13,000 to $49,000
- 34% on income from $49,000 to $97,000
- 42% on income from $97,000 to $150,000
- 47% on income from $150,000 to $214,000
- 51% on income over $214,000.

In the example above, if Melanie's taxable income (after other deductions) is between $49,000 and $97,000, her contribution of $5,000 to an RRSP would save her about 34% of that amount, or $1,700, in tax for 2020. For someone whose taxable income stays over $214,000 even after making the RRSP contribution, the same $5,000 contribution would be worth about $2,550. Clearly, RRSPs are more tax-effective for those with higher incomes.

You should keep the value of your deduction in mind and try to take maximum advantage of the carryforward mechanism in claiming your RRSP deductions. In a low-income year, for example, it may be advantageous to make your maximum RRSP *contribution*, but to defer claiming the *deduction* until a later year when your income is taxed at a higher marginal rate.

3.1.5 What happens to the funds in the RRSP?

While your funds are in the RRSP, they are not subject to tax at all. No matter what amounts of interest, dividends, capital gains—or losses—result, there will be no tax effect until you withdraw the funds. (As we shall see in 20.4, you must close out the RRSP by the end of the year in which you turn 71, but even then, the tax effects can be partially deferred.)

The effects of having income compound without tax are quite dramatic. Compare the following two situations: Scenario 1, where you invest $5,000 of your salary in an RRSP for 10 or 20 years at 6%, and Scenario 2, where you earn the same 6% but it is subject to tax. (The example assumes a 51% marginal tax rate.)

	Amount invested 2020	After 10 years 2030	After 20 years 2040
Scenario 1:			
Invest $5,000 before tax in an RRSP	$5,000	$8,954	$16,036
Tax on withdrawal		(4,567)	(8,178)
After-tax amount following withdrawal (A)		4,387	7,858
Scenario 2:			
Invest $5,000 less current tax of $2,500 outside an RRSP (B)	2,500	3,360*	4,515*
Additional after-tax return from investing in RRSP (A – B)		$1,027	$3,343
*Net of annual tax on investment income earned.			

In Scenario 1, you pay 51% in tax when you withdraw the funds, but they have grown substantially in the meantime. After 20 years, your $5,000 is worth $7,858 *after* tax. In Scenario 2, since the annual 6% interest is taxed, you have only about 3% to reinvest for compounding purposes. The fact that you can use the $4,515 (after 20 years) directly in Scenario 2, without having to pay 51% tax on it as in

Scenario 1, doesn't come close to making up for the tax-free compounding of interest.

Of course, if you are paying non-deductible interest such as mortgage interest, that interest also effectively compounds on a pre-tax basis, and you might be better off to pay down your mortgage rather than contribute to an RRSP. In such a case, you can generally use all your unused RRSP contribution room by making and deducting a "catch-up" RRSP contribution in a later year, when you have the funds to contribute.

As we mentioned earlier, your RRSP can be invested in many different forms. The simplest, and usually lowest-paying, is a deposit account that pays interest monthly or twice a year. Many people invest instead in longer-term Guaranteed Investment Certificates (GICs) and term deposits. Equity mutual funds are popular as a method of indirectly investing RRSP funds in a range of different equity investments, but they can entail a higher level of risk and management fees. See 1.1.4 for tips on choosing investments and advice on developing an appropriate investment strategy.

3.1.6 Self-directed RRSPs

If you're a do-it-yourselfer who would like a wider range of investment choices and you're willing to take a little more risk with your funds, you can set up a self-directed RRSP and gain hands-on control over the investment of funds in your RRSP. This is normally done through a financial consultant with a brokerage firm or financial services institution, and is typically subject to an annual fee in the $100 to $250 range (plus normal commissions on any stock trades or mutual funds, where applicable). Some financial institutions offer a low- or no-fee self-directed plan—it pays to shop around to find the plan that's right for you. With a self-directed plan, you decide what to invest in within your RRSP. There are restrictions—the system tries to ensure that your money, while not necessarily "safe", is at least invested in reasonable places. "Qualified investments" for an RRSP include:

> Consider a self-directed RRSP for greater flexibility.

- cash
- government, Crown corporation or municipal bonds
- GICs, term deposits and treasury bills (T-bills)
- certain government-insured mortgages
- shares or bonds of corporations listed on Canadian stock exchanges
- RRSP-eligible mutual funds and segregated funds
- shares listed on certain foreign stock exchanges, bonds of certain foreign governments and mutual funds and segregated funds invested in foreign markets (see 3.1.7)
- certain small business shares
- gold and silver bullion (under certain conditions)
- a debt obligation that has an investment grade rating and is part of a minimum $25 million issuance
- any security (other than a futures contract) that is listed on a designated stock exchange.

The rules governing the details (e.g., which mortgages and small business shares are qualified investments) are extremely complex, and you should consult a professional adviser if you wish to do more with your self-directed RRSP than simply buy, say, government-backed T-bills and government bonds (which are generally regarded as good, safe investments). If you have the time to give it the attention it needs, a self-directed RRSP can prove to be much more rewarding in the long run. The control you will gain over investment decisions can diversify your risk and give you the flexibility to pursue a different range of investment opportunities—including some that are generally only possible through self-directed RRSPs, like strip bonds, mortgage-backed securities, index funds and other less common RRSP investments. If you only plan to invest in mutual funds and GICs, a self-directed RRSP may not be required; in this case, you may be better off using a regular plan to save on annual administration fees.

The broader range of investment options you may acquire with a self-directed RRSP comes with a higher level of risk. The financial markets are volatile, but they tend not to move in step with each other, so you may be able to minimize the level of overall risk in your portfolio through diversification—holding a mix of different types of investments (i.e., cash, fixed income and equities) and ensuring that at least a portion of them have fixed rates of return, such as GICs or strip bonds.

Your investment mix or asset allocation should also be a function of your age, family situation and risk tolerance. When determining your investment mix and allocating your assets, be sure to consider your total portfolio, and not just those investments inside your RRSP. See 1.1.4 for details on developing an appropriate investment strategy.

Think about transferring shares that you already own to your self-directed RRSP.

Consider contributing shares (or interest-bearing investments) that you already own to your self-directed RRSP in lieu of cash contributions. Shares in small businesses can be contributed in limited circumstances (for example, you, your spouse and other related persons, either individually or collectively, cannot own 10% or more of the corporation's shares). Also, most shares of Canadian public corporations are fair game, as long as you don't own 10% or more of the company's shares. In both cases, an investment is also prohibited if you do not deal at arm's length with the corporation. If you have shares that you intend to hold for a long time, you can contribute them to your RRSP and get a tax deduction without any cash outlay.

A transfer of investments to your RRSP can trigger a capital gain (see 6.2.1), since the transfer is deemed to take place at fair market value. However, you are prohibited from claiming a capital loss (see 6.2.2) on the transfer of investments to your RRSP. Professional advice should be obtained before entering this type of transaction.

If you have shares that have declined in value, you cannot transfer the shares to your RRSP to trigger a capital loss to use to offset any capital gains you may have realized—the tax law won't let you claim a capital loss on the transfer of investments to your RRSP.

However, you can sell the shares on the open market, contribute the proceeds in cash to your RRSP and, after 30 days, have your RRSP acquire a similar position. This strategy will permit you to trigger the capital loss on the shares, which you can apply against other taxable capital gains, while effectively transferring ownership of the shares to your RRSP so that any future growth will be tax-sheltered.

Previously, you could swap investments owned outside your RRSP with assets inside your plan. Under the RRSP anti-avoidance rules (see 3.4), these swaps are no longer allowed, except in limited circumstances.

Note that capital gains and dividends are effectively fully taxed when withdrawn from an RRSP, since you're taxed on the total amount withdrawn. So if you contribute shares (or buy shares inside your RRSP), any capital gains and dividends will eventually be taxed at a higher rate than if you earned them directly (see 6.2.1 and 7.1.2). However, if you leave the funds in the RRSP for long enough, the deferral of tax and tax-free compounding of interest may more than make up for the tax rate differential. Nonetheless, consider holding fixed income investments inside your RRSP and equities outside your RRSP as part of your overall asset mix.

When considering investments within your RRSP, bear in mind the one major drawback of long-term investments such as five-year GICs. If you decide to withdraw the funds sooner for tax purposes, or to use the Home Buyers' Plan (see 3.3.6) or Lifelong Learning Plan (see 3.3.7), you may find that you cannot get access to your investment due to GIC restrictions, or a significant interest penalty may arise.

If you are a shareholder of a start-up company or a company that has high growth potential, you may want to consider owning part or all of the shares through your RRSP or transferring such shares to your RRSP early in the company's life cycle when the

> Think about using your RRSP to shelter future gains on high-growth private company shares.

shares have relatively low value. Future gains on the shares will then be sheltered from tax inside the RRSP and you will be able to diversify your investment base by having your RRSP sell the shares and acquire a broader range of investments. (Bear in mind our comments above on capital gains and dividends. Also, note that the shares will not qualify as an RRSP investment if you own more than 10% of the company at any time.)

It is even possible for you to arrange for your RRSP to hold your own mortgage—in other words, you put funds into your RRSP, receive a tax deduction, and lend the funds to yourself. This is not easy to do, however; the mortgage must be federally insured, and various other restrictions apply.

Investing in your own mortgage may make you feel good, but does not always make sense financially. Since the investment must be at the market rate, you may be no better off depending on the size of the mortgage, once all fees (legal, insurance, appraisal, etc.) are taken into account. As a rule of thumb, to be a worthwhile investment, the mortgage's principal should be in the $50,000 to

$100,000 range with a term of at least five years. Alternatively if you don't have that much cash in your RRSP, some financial institutions offer a program through which the mortgage is "shared" between your RRSP and your institution. You should also consider whether holding a mortgage in your RRSP is consistent with your overall investment strategy.

3.1.7 Self-directed RRSP investments in foreign properties

Think about boosting your self-directed RRSP's foreign content.

There is no limit to the amount of property held by your RRSP that is invested in foreign property, allowing you more scope to diversify your self-directed RRSP's holdings in foreign content, such as shares listed on certain foreign stock exchanges, certain foreign government bonds and other foreign properties.

Don't let periodic downturns in foreign markets scare you away from increasing your RRSP's foreign holdings. As long as you plan to invest for the long term, your RRSP's foreign content will increase the diversity of your investment mix and thus reduce your overall investment risk. See 1.1.4 for details on the importance of diversifying your investments geographically as part of your overall investment strategy.

3.1.8 RRSP fees

Administration, trustee and investment management and counselling fees related to your RRSP are not deductible. However, you can use funds already deposited in your RRSP without having to pay tax on the amount as you would if you withdrew the money for another purpose. Alternatively, you can pay these fees from funds outside your RRSP and the amount will not count as part of your contribution for the year.

If you have not used all of your available contribution room and you do not foresee doing so in the future, consider contributing the amount of the fees and paying them with funds inside the plan so you get a regular RRSP deduction for that amount. On the other hand, if you have or will be maximizing your RRSP contributions, you are better off paying the fees with other funds so you do not erode the amount of RRSP funds available to grow tax-free.

3.1.9 How to make the most of your RRSP

Contribute as much as you can to an RRSP.

If you have cash in the bank earning interest, even if you are young and not yet concerned about retirement, you should contribute as much as possible to an RRSP. The example we saw in 3.1.5 shows how valuable it is to have your funds earning tax-free income.

Contribute early in the year instead of the following February.

If possible, you should contribute early, rather than waiting until the deadline. Your 2020 contribution, for example, may be made any time before March 1, 2021 if you intend to deduct it on your 2020 tax return. If you contribute at the beginning of 2020, all of the income earned for that extra year will accumulate tax-free. The effect of early contributions over several years will be dramatic. Do ensure, however, that you have enough contribution room before you commit your contribution for the year, and remember that each year's contribution will be limited to 18% of your previous year's earned income (less your pension adjustment).

You can store up any unused RRSP contribution room if you can't afford to make a contribution now, and make your contribution and claim the deduction in later years.

If you're behind on your RRSP contributions, you might be thinking about taking out an RRSP loan. Generally, this strategy only makes sense if you can repay the borrowed funds within about a year, or if

> Think twice before borrowing funds to contribute to your RRSP.

your income for the current year falls into a higher tax bracket than usual. Otherwise, the non-deductible interest that you will pay on the loan may negate the tax benefits of your contribution. Instead, consider making regular catch-up payments later when you have the funds to contribute.

If you have the cash and the contribution room, but do not want to claim a deduction in the current year because you are already in a low tax bracket, make the contribution but delay the deduction. As discussed in 3.1.3, you can claim the deduction in any later year. If you are confident of being in a higher tax bracket within the next year or so, this strategy can maximize the tax-free growth of funds while also maximizing your tax savings.

For cash-flow purposes, you may wish to set up a monthly transfer of a few hundred dollars from your regular bank account to your RRSP account. That will ensure steady contributions to the RRSP over the course of the year.

3.2 How do you get money out of an RRSP?

At any time, you may withdraw cash from your RRSP. The amount will be included in your income for that year and taxed as ordinary income, just as if it were salary, even if some of the value of the RRSP represents capital gains (which outside an RRSP are normally only partially taxed and, in some cases, could be entirely exempt).

A percentage to cover tax will be withheld at source by the financial institution and remitted to the CRA (and Revenu Québec if appropriate) on your behalf. For federal purposes, a withdrawal of up to $5,000 is subject to 10% withholding; over $5,000 and up to $15,000, 20%; and over $15,000, 30%. In Quebec, a single RRSP withdrawal is subject to one-half of the federal withholding plus a 15% Quebec withholding, regardless of the amount of withdrawal. You will then report the income and amount of tax withheld on your annual income tax return and either receive a refund or, if not enough tax was withheld, pay the difference. Keep in mind that an administration fee may also apply to the withdrawal.

The government allows you to make tax-free RRSP withdrawals (within limits) if you use the funds for certain purposes, such as buying a new home (see 3.3.6) or financing training or post-secondary education for you or your spouse (see 3.3.7). Generally, you must repay the amount withdrawn under these plans over a certain amount of time or it will become taxable.

You must wind up your RRSP by the end of the year in which you turn 71. At any time before then, you can transfer your RRSP funds tax-free to an annuity, a registered retirement income fund or a life income fund (for locked-in retirement accounts only).

Starting January 1, 2020, you can also transfer your RRSP funds tax-free to an Advanced Life Deferred Annuity (ALDA), a new type of a life annuity where the commencement may be deferred until the end of the year in which you turn 85. To qualify as an ALDA, the annuity contract must satisfy certain requirements, including that this contract:

- provides periodic payments which are generally equal
- provides that, following the death of the annuitant, a lump-sum death benefit provided to a beneficiary does not exceed the premium paid for the annuity less the sum of all payments received by the annuitant
- permits a refund to the annuitant of any portion of the premium paid for the contract to the extent that the premium paid for the contract exceeded the annuitant's ALDA limit, and
- provides no other payments, such as commutation or cash surrender payments, or payments under a guarantee period.

The lifetime dollar limit of an ALDA is $150,000, indexed to inflation after 2020.

Your various options for maturing your RRSP are discussed in 20.4.

3.2.1 Early withdrawals—your RRSP as a tax averaging tool

As discussed in 3.1.5, the funds in your RRSP are not taxed until the year in which you withdraw the funds. As a result, RRSPs can be used as a tax averaging tool rather than just a mechanism for retirement saving. If you are still fairly young and not too worried about retirement income, you can withdraw funds from your RRSP whenever there is a tax benefit to doing so.

Withdraw funds from your RRSP in low-income years.

Suppose you plan to take some time off to care for your young children, for example, or to go on an extended vacation or take up some other activity. During such years, where your employment income will be low, you can withdraw funds from your RRSP and perhaps pay tax at the low tax rate of about 23% (depending on your province) instead of the middle or high rates. The advantage of low-rate taxation will have to be balanced against the advantage of tax-free growth available by leaving the funds in the RRSP.

In an anticipated low-income year following a high-income year, you can even consider contributing in February, claiming a deduction (say at the higher rate of about 34%) for the previous year, and withdrawing the funds later in the current year, to be taxed at the low (23%) rate for the current year.

You will need to plan around the withholding tax on RRSP withdrawals discussed in 3.2, however. You may be able to arrange withdrawals so that they incur the least possible withholding tax, leaving you with the use of the funds until you file your tax return the following April. Bear in mind, however, that you may have a tax liability to settle in the following April to the extent that your tax rate on all sources of income exceeds the withholding tax rate.

3.3 Special RRSP rules

A number of rules deal with special situations relating to RRSPs. We will refer to them only briefly; you should consult your professional adviser if you are in these situations.

3.3.1 Spousal plans

The RRSP rules allow you to contribute to an RRSP for your spouse, and claim the deduction yourself. Your total contributions (to your own and your spouse's plans) are still subject to your normal limits (18% of your previous year's earned income or $27,300 for 2020, minus any pension adjustment). The

> Contribute to your spouse's (or common-law spouse's) RRSP if your spouse's projected income on retirement will be lower.

advantage is that your spouse will be the one who ultimately reports the income for tax purposes, when the funds are withdrawn on retirement or otherwise. If your spouse has less income than you, either on retirement or at some earlier time (including, for example, due to expected parental leave), this can result in significantly less tax on the income.

Spouses can split certain pension income, which may reduce the need for spousal RRSPs to accomplish retirement income splitting (see 20.3.6).

If you are over 71 (the age at which you must mature your RRSP; see 20.4) and have "earned income" in the previous year, this will create new RRSP room for you in the current year. As long as your spouse is 71 or younger, you can still claim a deduction for a spousal RRSP contribution.

To prevent spousal RRSPs from being used for "income splitting" (see Chapter 5), the amount you contribute will be taxed back to you (rather than your spouse) to the extent any amount is withdrawn by your spouse in the year in which you contribute or in the next two calendar years (see 5.3.9).

> Make spousal RRSP contributions in December instead of the following February.

This rule does not apply if the spouses are separated or divorced. We explore this rule in more detail at 5.3.9, in the chapter on income splitting.

> **Example**
>
> Jon and Nancy are married. Jon contributes $5,000 to Nancy's RRSP in February 2021, and claims the deduction on his 2020 tax return.
>
> If Nancy withdraws the funds at any time up to the end of 2023, $5,000 of the amount withdrawn will be treated as Jon's income, not Nancy's. (If, however, Jon's contribution had been made in December 2020, this would only be the case until the end of 2022.)

In general, there will be little effect on the real ownership of the funds under provincial law if you and your spouse separate or divorce. The rule in most provinces is that such funds will be pooled and shared between the spouses. There are rules in place to allow a tax-free division of RRSP funds in such situations.

3.3.2 Transfers to and from RRSPs

Transfer pension commuted value, retiring allowances or severance pay to your RRSP.

RRSPs can generally be transferred, with no tax consequences, to other RRSPs, registered retirement income funds (RRIF) or annuities.

Starting January 1, 2020, you can also transfer an RRSP to an Advanced Life Deferred Annuity with no tax consequences. The commencement of this new type of life annuity may be deferred until the end of the year in which the annuitant turns 85.

Under pension legislation you may be prevented from immediately withdrawing pension benefits (known as the "commuted value") from your employer's plan on your departure from the company. This legislation is commonly referred to as "locking-in" legislation. Pension benefits subject to these rules may be transferred to a locked-in RRSP, also known as a "locked-in retirement account" (LIRA).

Locked-in RRSPs are essentially subject to the same restrictions on withdrawal of funds as the original pension plan. For example, depending on the applicable pension legislation, you cannot usually access the locked-in plan funds until you are within 10 years of the retirement date set out in the plan documents. Even then, you can only use the plan funds to purchase an annuity or a special RRIF that will provide a lifetime income, called a "life income fund" (LIF) or, in some provinces, a "life retirement income fund" (LRIF) (see 20.4.5). With a LIF or an LRIF, you have more flexibility in deciding how to invest the funds.

Where the pension legislation permits a transfer from a registered pension plan to a locked-in RRSP, LIF or LRIF, there are generally no tax consequences to such transfers, though the tax rules may restrict the amounts that can be transferred from a "defined-benefit" pension plan.

You may be able to "unlock" funds in a locked-in RRSP or LIRA under certain circumstances. The rules are different in each province—consult your professional adviser for more information on unlocking.

Employees with years of service before 1996 may be able to transfer a "retiring allowance" to an RPP or RRSP. In particular, special rules allow a retiring allowance (which, for tax purposes, includes severance pay, termination pay, and amounts received for wrongful dismissal as well as unused sick leave credits) to be transferred tax-free to an RRSP, rather than taxed as income when received. The amount that can be transferred is normally limited to $2,000 for each calendar year (or part year) of employment before 1996, plus $1,500 for years of employment before 1989 for which employer pension contributions or deferred profit sharing plan contributions have not vested.

3.3.3 Death

On death, a taxpayer is normally taxed on the entire amount of any RRSPs or RRIFs, except where the funds are left to the taxpayer's spouse or financially dependent child, in which case they are included in the spouse's or child's income. See 22.4.1 for details.

3.3.4 Overcontributions

The RRSP contribution limits are discussed in 3.1.3. What happens if you contribute more than the maximum?

First, bear in mind that your financial institution will not prevent you from overcontributing. Your financial institution is not obliged to tell you how much you can or cannot contribute.

Second, any contributions over the maximum are non-deductible. However, once the funds are in your RRSP, they are taxable when withdrawn (whether on retirement or earlier), just like the funds that were deductible when you contributed them. Therefore, there is double taxation—once when you earn the income (and receive no deduction despite putting the funds into the RRSP), and again when you withdraw the funds from the RRSP.

If you are facing double taxation because of an overcontribution, you may be able to correct the problem if you act quickly to file a prescribed form and withdraw the overcontribution.

Third, in certain rare circumstances (subject to penalties noted below), overcontributing might be valuable despite the double taxation, because of the beneficial effect of tax-free compounding (as illustrated in the table in 3.1.5). Also, you can often deduct an overcontribution in a later year as new contribution room is created.

There is a rule preventing excessive overcontributions. At any one time, up to $2,000 can be overcontributed without penalty. Above the $2,000 level, the excess is subject to a penalty tax of 1% per month until the excess is withdrawn. If you are not generating new contribution room from year to year (e.g., because you have no earned income in the prior year), your overcontributions should be withdrawn in the year of making the contribution or the next year to avoid tax on the withdrawal.

The $2,000 figure is designed to catch those cases where you might have miscalculated your pension adjustment (see 3.1.3) and contributed a little too much. However, as long as you are certain about your pension adjustment, you can use the $2,000 if you wish. So if you are already contributing your maximum for 2020, consider making an additional contribution of up to $2,000 to further benefit from the compounding of tax-free growth.

> Top up your RRSP with a non-deductible $2,000 overcontribution.

3.3.5 Labour-sponsored venture capital corporation shares

In some provinces, a combined federal/provincial credit of 30% to 35% (depending on the province) may be available for an investment of up to $5,000 per year in shares of a "labour-sponsored venture capital corporation", or LSVCC.

The federal LSVCC credit is 15% for purchases of provincially registered LSVCCs. The federal tax credit for federally registered LSVCCs was eliminated for 2017 and later years.

Consider shares of a labour-sponsored venture capital corporation for your RRSP.

You can buy shares in a labour-sponsored venture capital corporation and contribute them to your RRSP. You can also generally have the shares bought directly by your self-directed RRSP (see 3.1.6), provided the RRSP uses "new" or previous contribution funds (but not earnings). Either way, you claim the credit on your personal income tax return.

When combined with the deduction for the RRSP contribution, a $5,000 investment in a provincially registered LSVCC may cost you as little as $950 after tax (assuming a 15% provincial credit along with the 15% federal credit). Particularly if you are not otherwise making the maximum possible RRSP contribution, an investment in an LSVCC for your RRSP may be worth considering. Before taking the plunge and investing in an LSVCC, make sure you evaluate the relative merits from an investment perspective, as they are generally a higher risk and possibly illiquid investment.

3.3.6 The Home Buyers' Plan

Under the Home Buyers' Plan, if you qualify, you are allowed to withdraw up to $35,000 (increased from $25,000) in respect of withdrawals made after March 19, 2019 a loan from your RRSP to buy or build a home, without counting the withdrawal as income. You must then repay the loan, without interest, over 15 years starting in the second year after the year of the withdrawal.

Who may use the Home Buyers' Plan?

The Plan may only be used by what the government calls a "first-time buyer". You are not a "first-time buyer" if you have owned and lived in a home as a principal place of residence at any time during the five calendar years up to and including the current year. (For the current year, you can use the Plan up to 30 days after you acquire a home.) If your spouse has owned and lived in a home during that period, and you have inhabited that home during the marriage, you also do not qualify. (Remember that "spouse" includes a common-law spouse as outlined in 2.2.1.)

Past participation does not prevent you from participating in the Plan again, as long as you have fully repaid to your RRSP the amounts previously withdrawn and you have not owned a home in the past five calendar years (including the current year).

As noted in 2.5.3, the five-year qualification test is waived for disabled persons and their relatives for purchases of new homes that are more accessible or better suited to the personal needs and care of a disabled person who will reside there. The five-year qualification test is also waived following the breakdown of a marriage or common-law partnership, in certain circumstances.

How does the Plan work?

You can borrow (withdraw) up to $35,000 from your RRSP under the Plan. If you and your spouse each have RRSPs, you can borrow up to $70,000 between the two of you if you are taking joint ownership in the property. A qualifying home must be acquired before October 1 of the year following the year of the withdrawal. You must also begin or intend to use the home as a principal place of residence no later than one year after its acquisition. No tax will apply to the withdrawal.

When you withdraw the funds, you fill out Form T1036 certifying that you have entered into a written agreement to purchase a home and stating its address. Once you have done this, the financial institution will not withhold tax when it pays the funds to you.

Note that the Plan does not give you any right to withdraw funds from your RRSP if you didn't already have that right. If your RRSP funds are invested in term deposits or other long-term obligations, you will still need to negotiate with the financial institution to have the funds released as cash. Similarly, if your RRSP funds are in your employer's group RRSP or a LIRA ("locked-in RRSP"), you may not be able to get them out.

Once you borrow the funds, you must normally complete the purchase by September 30 of the *following* year. (A one-year extension may be available if the deal falls through and you buy a replacement property.) If you withdraw less than the $35,000 maximum, you can in many cases withdraw a further amount up to the following January 31 and treat the total as one withdrawal.

The requirement to repay the funds begins in the second year following the withdrawal. You can opt to make any year's repayment up to 60 days after the end of the year.

Example

Olivia has $30,000 in her RRSP. She signs an agreement in September 2020 to purchase a new home. In November 2020 she completes Form T1036 and withdraws $15,000 from her RRSP. The purchase closes in January 2021.

No tax will be withheld from the $15,000 that Olivia withdraws, so she can use the full amount towards the home purchase. Since she withdrew the funds in 2020, Olivia must repay $1,000 (1/15 of the total) to her RRSP during 2022 or by March 1, 2023. If she chooses to repay only $600, she will have to include $400 in income for 2022 and pay tax on that amount.

If Olivia repays no more than $1,000 in 2022 (or by March 1, 2023), she would be required to repay 1/14 of the balance, another $1,000, in 2023 (or by March 1, 2024). Suppose she repays $8,000 in 2022, leaving a balance owing of $7,000. For 2023, she would still be required to repay 1/14 of the balance, or $500. The fact she has prepaid more than required reduces but does not eliminate her obligation to continue paying the balance in later years.

If you do not make repayments as required, you must include the shortfall in income for tax purposes, like Olivia in the example above when she repays only $600. In effect, the shortfall is treated as a permanent withdrawal from your RRSP and you're taxed on it.

Contributions in the year you use the Plan

If you contribute to an RRSP and withdraw the same funds within 90 days under the Plan, you cannot deduct your contribution. For purposes of this rule, any balance that was already in your RRSP can be considered as withdrawn first. Thus, it is only to the extent the amount of your new contribution is needed for the withdrawal (within the 90-day period) that a deduction will be disallowed.

Some special situations

Consider Home Buyers' Plan withdrawals to buy or build your first home (but be sure to weigh the loss of RRSP growth).

The Plan may be used for building a new home on an existing lot that you own. Instead of an agreement to purchase the home, you must have an agreement in place to construct it.

If you withdraw the funds but your home purchase does not close, you can generally cancel your participation in the Plan and return the funds to your RRSP with no adverse tax consequences. Alternatively, if you buy another qualifying home as a replacement, you can remain in the Plan.

If you have contributed to a spousal RRSP, your spouse must normally wait two to three years before withdrawing the funds or they will be taxed back to you (see 3.3.1). However, with the Home Buyers' Plan, your spouse can borrow the funds to purchase a qualifying home, and to the extent they are not repaid over the 15-year repayment period, it is your spouse that must include the difference in income, not you. If your spouse withdraws the funds and does not purchase a qualifying home, so that the full amount withdrawn is taxed in the current year, the attribution rule *will* apply and you, not your spouse, will be taxed on the withdrawal.

If you become a non-resident of Canada, you must repay the entire outstanding balance to the RRSP within 60 days of leaving Canada. Otherwise, the balance will be included in your income for the year that you became non-resident.

If you should die while you have an outstanding balance to repay, that balance will be included in your income for the year of death and tax will be payable by your estate (see 22.2.1). However, if you leave a surviving spouse, your executor and your spouse may make a special election to have your spouse take over the obligation to repay the funds over the remainder of the repayment period, and the balance will not be included in your income for the year of death.

Should you use the Home Buyers' Plan?

At first glance, the Plan seems attractive, since it gives you ready access to a potentially large amount of cash. However, there are three costs to consider.

First, you lose the tax-free compounding in your RRSP (see the example in 3.1.5). Balanced against this cost is the fact that you have probably reduced the mortgage interest expense you would otherwise have to pay out of after-tax dollars. Even still, the value of the RRSP may be much less at your retirement than it would be otherwise. If you are depending on your RRSP for your retirement income, you will want to forecast the reduction in income that will result from withdrawing a large amount of the funds now and repaying it to the RRSP over 15 years starting in the second year after the year of withdrawal.

Second, you have to be able to sustain the cash flow to repay the RRSP; if you cannot, you will end up being taxed on the funds you have withdrawn. When determining the cash you need to handle your mortgage and property tax payments, don't forget the 1/15 minimum repayment to the RRSP in each year beginning with the second year after the withdrawal (due by 60 days after the end of the year). Of course, since you are simply repaying borrowed funds and not contributing new money to the RRSP, no deduction is available for the amounts you repay.

Third, you may not be able to claim a deduction for your RRSP contribution for the current year if you make your contribution and withdraw it for the Home Buyers' Plan within 90 days. This will depend on the balance in your RRSP. If your withdrawal does not exceed the value you had in the RRSP 90 days before the withdrawal, you have no problem.

Nevertheless, if you need the funds to help you purchase your first home, the Home Buyers' Plan may be a significant help.

Planning for the Home Buyers' Plan

If you're thinking about tapping your RRSP to purchase your first home but your RRSP is not yet at $35,000 and you intend to use the Home Buyers' Plan to its fullest, make your contribution early enough so that it can sit in the RRSP for 90 days before you withdraw the funds. Then the amount you contributed can be withdrawn as well without affecting your deduction for the contribution.

If you are planning to buy a new home and you are close to the four-year cutoff that will re-qualify you as a "first-time buyer", consider waiting and making your purchase at a time when you can use the Home Buyers' Plan. For example, if you sold your last home in 2016, you can use the Plan as of January 1, 2021.

If you are about to be married and your future spouse owns a home that you will be living in, consider borrowing funds under the Home Buyers' Plan before your wedding. Once you are married, you will not be able to use the Plan. However, you are not restricted by a previous home owned by your spouse, as long as you do not live in it while married. Therefore, if you plan on buying a new home after your wedding, you should not (romantic considerations aside) move into your spouse's current home until you have made your withdrawal under the Plan.

The same applies if you have been living in a common-law relationship (and have not had a child together) for less than 12 months. Once you reach 12 months of living together, you are considered "married" for income tax purposes (see 2.2.1). If your partner owns your present home, but you plan on moving up to a larger home, consider withdrawing funds under the Home Buyers' Plan before you have lived together for 12 months. However, you will have to take ownership (or at least part ownership) of the new home in your own name.

3.3.7 The Lifelong Learning Plan—RRSP withdrawals for education

Consider withdrawing RRSP funds under the Lifelong Learning Plan to help pay for training or post-secondary education programs.

You can tap your RRSP to help finance your own or your spouse's education. Under the Lifelong Learning Plan, students in full-time training or post-secondary education and their spouses can withdraw up to $10,000 per year from their RRSPs over a four-year period, as long as the total amount does not exceed $20,000.

Withdrawn amounts must be repaid to an RRSP in equal instalments over 10 years, or they will be included in the income of the person who made the withdrawal. The first repayment will be due 60 days after the fifth year following the first withdrawal at the latest (or earlier in certain circumstances such as failure to complete courses).

There is no limit on the number of times you can participate in the Lifelong Learning Plan over your lifetime. Starting the year after you repay all of the withdrawn amount, you can participate in the Lifelong Learning Plan again and withdraw up to $20,000 over a new qualifying period.

If you die or emigrate from Canada, outstanding amounts will be included in your income in the year of death or emigration. In the case of emigration, you can avoid the income inclusion by repaying the outstanding amount within 60 days of emigration. In the case of death, your surviving spouse and your executor can make a special election to take over the obligation to make the repayments over the remainder of the 10-year period and the balance will not be included in your income in the year of death.

3.4 Anti-avoidance rules

As we saw in 3.1.6, you can hold only certain types of qualifying investments in your RRSP. Special anti-avoidance rules prevent individuals from holding prohibited investments in their RRSPs and from using these accounts in tax planning arrangements that the government considers unacceptable.

If the anti-avoidance rules apply you'll be subject to harsh penalties, so it's important to ensure that your RRSP investments comply with the rules.

Under these rules, some investments that previously qualified for RRSPs became prohibited as of March 23, 2011 and are not "grandfathered". As a result, you may have investments in your RRSP, such as certain private company shares, that were qualified investments when your RRSP acquired them but are now prohibited investments under the anti-avoidance rules. If you made a special election by March 1, 2013, you do not have to remove these investments from your RRSP but you will have to withdraw any income or capital gains from these investments from your RRSP within 90 days after the end of the year in which the income or capital gains are earned or realized. You will then pay tax on the income or gains at your regular rate for this RRSP withdrawal.

3.5 Registered pension plans—RPPs

3.5.1 Ordinary RPPs

A registered pension plan (RPP) is set up by an employer for its employees. Large companies, and many smaller ones, have such plans. These are quite different from the Canada Pension Plan (or, in Quebec, the Quebec Pension Plan), to which all employed and self-employed taxpayers must contribute.

The employer contributes (and deducts for tax purposes) an annual amount on behalf of each employee. Unlike most other employment benefits, these amounts are not taxed as benefits from employment in the year they are contributed. Instead, employees are taxed on the income from the pension when they *receive* it, which is normally after retirement.

In some cases, employees may be required or permitted to make additional contributions to the plan, which they can deduct for tax purposes in the year contributed.

There are two general kinds of pension plans: money-purchase and defined benefit. Money-purchase plans are analogous to RRSPs, in the sense that the amount of the pension payments is determined by the contributions and the investment income they earn.

Contributions to a money-purchase plan are generally limited to the lesser of 18% of your pensionable earnings for the year or $27,830 for 2020.

Many large and public employers provide defined benefit plans. With such plans, you know from the beginning how much your pension will be, usually based on a percentage of your actual salary over a specified number of years. It is up to the employer to contribute enough, and to the pension fund management to invest wisely, to make sure that the plan remains sufficiently funded to make those payments.

Once an employee retires and starts receiving pension income, the pension income is taxed as regular income as it is received. Up to $2,000 per year may be eligible for the pension income tax credit (see 20.3.5).

If you receive a lump-sum pension payment relating to prior years, you may ask the CRA to determine whether it is more advantageous to you to recalculate the tax on that income as if you received it in those prior years. This measure is intended to relieve the higher tax liability that may result if the entire lump-sum is taxed in the year of receipt, rather than year by year as your right to receive the income arose. Eligible payments must total at least $3,000 in the year and include superannuation or pension benefits (other than non-periodic benefits), wrongful dismissal and other employment-related payments arising from a court order or similar judgment, and certain other amounts.

If you have terminated your employment but are not yet eligible to receive pension income, you can transfer lump-sum amounts from the RPP to a locked-in retirement account or a locked-in RRIF (see 20.4.5). Generally, locked-in funds cannot be withdrawn in a lump sum; they must be used to provide a lifetime income. (In some provinces, if the amount of pension is below a certain threshold, it may be paid as a taxable lump sum. Other circumstances such as shortened life expectancy or financial hardship can also give rise to commutation of a pension.)

The amount you can transfer from a defined benefit RPP to an RRSP or RRIF is limited to the amount of annual pension given up under the RPP multiplied by a factor based on your age at the date of the transfer. The factor is 9.0 if you are under 50, gradually rising to 12.4 at ages 64 and 65. Generally, any amount over this limit must be paid to you in cash and is taxed as income in the year received.

If you are a member of a money purchase RPP, the plan may allow payouts in the form of the same income stream currently permitted under a RRIF. If the relevant pension legislation and the plan allow it, you would have to withdraw from your money purchase account a minimum amount each year (corresponding to the existing RRIF rules—see 20.4.4), beginning no later than the year in which you turn 72. Note that, due to COVID-19, the Canadian government lowered the minimum amount that must be withdrawn from a RRIF in 2020 by 25%.

This rule allows members of money purchase RPPs to benefit from the same advantages as RRIF-holders without taking on greater investment management responsibilities or higher investment management fees. If you are a former member of a money purchase RPP who previously transferred your money purchase account to an RRSP or RRIF, you can transfer the funds back into the RPP if you wish. Contact your RPP's administrator to determine whether your plan accommodates this option.

Starting January 1, 2020, members of money purchase RPPs may also transfer their RPP funds tax-free to an Advanced Life Deferred Annuity, a new type of life annuity where the commencement may be deferred until the end of the year in which the annuitant turns 85.

Also starting January 1, 2020, money purchase RPP administrators are permitted to establish a separate annuities fund under the plan to receive transfers of amounts from members' accounts to provide a Variable Payment Life Annuity to members directly from the plan.

Consider contributing to your RRSP instead of a money purchase RPP. If you've been making voluntary contributions to your registered pension plan under a money-purchase provision, consider contributing to an RRSP instead. Though the amount you can contribute is normally the same and your administration and investment management fees may be higher, the RRSP may give you much greater flexibility in terms of your investment choices.

Find out about the vesting of your pension benefits, especially before making a career change. If you are a member of a company pension plan, find out how long it takes for your employer contributions to "vest". Once they are vested, the pension you have earned becomes yours and, if you change jobs, many plans will permit the transfer of your pension benefit to your new employer's plan. If they are not vested, you get your own contributions back with interest when you leave—but no pension down the road. The vesting of your pension benefits can be a major factor in career change decisions.

You may have the option to receive pension benefits from a defined benefit RPP while still working part-time or full-time, with certain restrictions—see 20.2.6.

3.5.2 Individual pension plans—IPPs

An individual pension plan (IPP) is exactly what the name implies—a defined benefit registered pension plan designed and structured for one individual member. Sometimes a spouse or other family member can also be a member of the IPP. Some owner-managers may also qualify to have this type of pension plan registered with the CRA.

As a defined benefit pension plan, the benefit payable at retirement is specified and IPP contributions are made accordingly. The amount needed to provide a defined benefit rises at ages closer to retirement since less time is available to accrue investment income in the plan.

An IPP may be worth considering if you are already in your employer's group RPP but the benefits from that RPP are less generous than you would like.

In contrast to RRSPs, which can be cashed in any time, contributions made to the IPP will be locked in under applicable pension benefits legislation until retirement, when they must be used to provide retirement benefits (usually in the form of a life annuity or life income fund). Annual minimum withdrawals from an IPP are required once the plan member reaches age 72 (see 20.4.4). An RRSP, on the other hand, provides a variety of options on termination or retirement (see 20.4).

In the past, the main advantage of the IPP was that you and your employer would usually be allowed to make higher annual contributions than you would otherwise be entitled to under the RRSP route.

> Weigh the advantages of establishing an "individual pension plan".

Keep in mind that past service contributions made after March 22, 2011 must be funded first out of a plan member's existing RRSP assets or by reducing the individual's available RRSP contribution room before new deductible contributions for the past service can be made.

IPPs can no longer provide retirement benefits for past years of employment that were pensionable service credited on or after March 19, 2019 under a defined benefit plan of an employer, other than the IPPs' participating employer (or its predecessor employer). As a result, you'll have to include any assets transferred from a former employer's defined benefit plan to an IPP that relate to benefits provided in respect of prohibited service in your income for income tax purposes.

Your employer will be required to top up the funds in the IPP if investment performance is poor and there will be insufficient funds (as determined by an actuary) to pay you the defined benefit pension promised under the plan (which could be a point of concern to your employer). A further advantage is that an IPP is generally creditor-proof, while many RRSPs are not.

In addition, start-up and ongoing costs of administration of an IPP are higher than those of your RRSP. This is due to the complex regulatory environment governing pension plans. For example, an actuarial valuation is required at start-up and for the next three years and certain forms must be filed annually.

The rules regarding IPPs are complex. Consult your professional tax adviser for more information.

3.6 Deferred profit-sharing plans—DPSPs

Deferred profit-sharing plans (DPSPs) are less common than registered pension plans. They operate the same way in that contributions are made by the employer and are only taxed in the employee's hands when received, normally on retirement.

Employer contributions to DPSPs are based on current or accrued profits but may have a defined minimum contribution. Such plans may be used, for example, by smaller companies that are not sure of profits and do not wish to commit themselves to large pension contributions, especially if they end up losing money for the year.

Employer contributions to DPSPs are generally limited to the lesser of 18% of your earnings for the year or $13,915 for 2020. Employee contributions to a DPSP are not permitted. Contributions to a DPSP are reported as a pension adjustment on your T4 slip and so they reduce the amount you can contribute to an RRSP in the following year (see 3.1.3). Employer contributions vest in an employee after 24 months of plan membership.

DPSPs cannot be set up for employees who are also major shareholders (over 10% of any class of shares) in the employer corporation, or for members of their families. They therefore cannot be used for owner-managers of small businesses.

Starting January 1, 2020, DPSPs can be transferred, with no tax consequences, to an Advanced Life Deferred Annuity, a new type of life annuity where the commencement may be deferred until the end of the year in which the annuitant turns 85.

3.7 References

The following publications and more information, including forms and brochures, can be obtained on the CRA's website at *www.canada.ca/en/revenue-agency.html* or by telephone request at 1-800-959-8281 for individual income tax and trust-related enquiries or 1-800-959-5525 for business and self-employed individual enquiries.

Guide T4040, "RRSPs and Other Registered Plans for Retirement"
Guide RC4112, "Lifelong Learning Plan (LLP)"
Income Tax Folio S3-F10-C1, "Qualified Investments – RRSPs, RESPs, RRIFs, RDSPs and TFSAs"
Income Tax Folio S3-F10-C2, "Prohibited Investments – RRSPs, RESPs, RRIFs, RDSPs and TFSAs"
Income Tax Folio S3-F10-C3, "Advantages – RRSPs, RESPs, RRIFs, RDSPs and TFSAs"
Information Circular 72-22R9, "Registered retirement savings plans"

Information Circular 77-1R5, "Deferred profit sharing plans"
Information Circular 78-18R6, "Registered retirement income funds"

Also, see the following selected topics on the CRA's website:

"What is the Home Buyers' Plan?"
"Contributing to your spouse's or common-law partner's RRSPs"
"Withdrawing from spousal or common-law partner RRSPs"

Chapter 4

TFSAs and other tax-assisted savings plans

- Contribute up to $6,000 annually to your Tax-Free Savings Account (TFSA) to enjoy tax-sheltered growth (4.1)

- Consider the potential family income splitting benefits of a TFSA (4.1.1)

- Determine your best tax strategy for dividing your investments among TFSAs, RRSPs and RESPs (4.2)

- Consider a Registered Education Savings Plan (RESP) for education cost planning, tax deferral and income splitting with the plan's beneficiary (4.3)

- Consider making large lump-sum payments to an RESP to take full advantage of tax-sheltered growth within the plan (4.3.1)

- Think about establishing a self-directed RESP to increase your investment options (4.3.2)

- Determine which type of RESP best suits your needs—individual, family or group (4.3.2)

- Contribute up to $2,500 annually to an RESP and earn a 20% government grant (4.4)

- If your child does not pursue higher education, consider transferring up to $50,000 to your own or your spouse's RRSP (4.5.2)

- If you have a child with a disability, consider setting up a Registered Disability Savings Plan (RDSP) to provide for his or her future financial security (4.6)

TFSAs, RESPs and RDSPs are tax-assisted savings vehicles similar to RRSPs discussed in Chapter 3 but their purposes are quite different. TFSAs can earn tax-sheltered investment income you can withdraw at any time, RESPs are education investment vehicles, and RDSPs can help you save for a disabled family member's long-term financial security.

In this chapter, we discuss the rules governing contributions to and payments from these plans and compare their benefits to help you decide where you should invest your savings.

4.1 Tax-Free Savings Accounts—TFSAs

Contribute up to $6,000 annually to your Tax-Free Savings Account to enjoy tax-sheltered growth.

Tax-Free Savings Accounts (TFSAs) are a tax-assisted savings plan introduced in 2009. TFSA contributions are not tax-deductible, however you can withdraw the income earned in the TFSA and your contributions to it at any time tax-free.

4.1.1 How much can you contribute?

You can contribute up to $6,000 per year to a TFSA as long as you are 18 or older and resident in Canada. If you have made no contributions to date and you are 29 or older in 2020, you can contribute a total of $69,500. You can carry forward unused contribution room indefinitely. You can hold more than one TFSA, subject to your contribution limit.

Years	TFSA contribution limit	Total
2009–2012	$5,000 per year	$20,000
2013–2014	$5,500 per year	$11,000
2015	$10,000 per year	$10,000
2016–2018	$5,500 per year	$16,500
2019–2020	$6,000 per year	$12,000
		$69,500

Unlike the $2,000 overcontribution allowed for RRSPs, there is no cushion for excess contributions to a TFSA and the penalty for overcontributions is harsh. If you have an excess TFSA amount at any time in a calendar month, you are liable for a penalty tax of 1% of that month's highest excess amount. Because the test applies at any time in a calendar month, withdrawing the excess amount will only stop the penalty from applying in the month after the withdrawal.

Like an RRSP, interest on funds borrowed and fees incurred to invest in a TFSA are not tax-deductible. Unlike an RRSP, however, you may be able to use your TFSA as collateral for a loan.

Income splitting benefit for families

Consider the potential family income splitting benefits of a TFSA.

TFSAs may offer an opportunity for income splitting for families in which one spouse has more income than the other. You can give funds to your spouse to contribute to his or her own TFSA, as long as your spouse has available contribution room, and the normal income attribution rules that would tax the investment income in your hands will not apply (see 5.2.2).

4.1.2 Withdrawing funds

You can make a tax-free withdrawal from a TFSA at any time. The amount withdrawn is added to your contribution room, but not until the next year. You can re-contribute the amount you withdrew in the next year or later.

> **Example**
>
> Scott contributed $63,500 to his TFSA before the end of 2019. In January 2020, he contributes $6,000 so that he has contributed the maximum amount of $69,500. He decides to withdraw $5,000 in June 2020 so that only $64,500 of his contributions remains in his TFSA. In this case, he cannot re-contribute the $5,000 he withdrew until 2021. At that time, he can re-contribute the $5,000 withdrawal along with his new contribution limit for 2021 (assumed to be $6,000), for a total of $11,000.
>
> Investment income earned in Scott's TFSA is treated the same way. If Scott's $6,000 investment in 2020 earns $300 and he withdraws the $6,300 in December 2020, he can re-contribute the entire $6,300 in 2021 along with his new $6,000 contribution limit for that year, or $12,300 in total.

Similarly, if you invest some of the funds in your TFSA in the stock market and your share investment appreciates rapidly, say from $20,000 to $30,000, you could sell the shares and realize the $10,000 tax-free capital gain in the TFSA, withdraw the $30,000 cash proceeds and still be able to re-contribute the full $30,000 amount to the TFSA along with any other unused TFSA contribution room in the following year or later.

As a result, you could potentially contribute much more than the contribution limit annually, and therefore earn more tax-free investment income.

Consider contributing investments that are expected to increase significantly in value over a short time in a TFSA. You can withdraw the income and capital gains earned tax-free at any time, and any withdrawals you make will create additional contribution room.

When choosing your investments, keep in mind that capital losses realized in a TFSA cannot be claimed against capital gains realized outside the TFSA.

4.1.3 Which investments qualify?

TFSAs are generally allowed to hold the same qualified investments as RRSPs (see 3.1.6), such as cash, guaranteed investment certificates (GICs), term deposits, mutual funds, government and corporate bonds, publicly traded securities, and in certain cases, shares of small business corporations. A TFSA should not invest in a business as it is taxable on any income that it earns in a year from carrying on a business directly.

You can transfer investments you already own into your TFSA. The rules are similar to those for transferring investments into your RRSP (see 3.1.6).

Note that your TFSA cannot hold investments in "non-arm's-length entities", which are generally companies in which you, your spouse and other related persons, either individually or collectively, own 10% or more of the shares.

Special anti-avoidance rules apply harsh penalties to income from prohibited investments held in TFSAs and from deliberate over-contributions, so it's important to ensure your TFSA investments comply with the rules.

Note that, starting in 2019, new rules extended the joint and several liability shared by your TFSA and its trustee to you, as holder of your TFSA, for any tax owing on income from carrying on a business in your TFSA.

4.1.4 Special situations

Various rules apply to special situations, including the death of a TFSA holder and ceasing Canadian residency. Some violations of the TFSA rules may trigger penalties.

Death—Generally, investment income earned in the TFSA after the account holder's death is no longer tax-exempt. Special rules apply if there is a surviving spouse (see 22.4.2).

Non-residents—If you become non-resident, you can maintain your existing TFSA and your investment income and withdrawals will remain exempt from Canadian tax. While you are non-resident, however, no new contribution room will accrue. You must also consider foreign tax implications of TFSA income and withdrawals, if they apply.

For example, earnings in a TFSA are tax-free for Canadian tax purposes, but they are taxable for U.S. tax purposes. U.S. citizens may still benefit from establishing a TFSA if they have enough foreign tax credits to offset the additional U.S. taxable income (see 18.3.3). However, don't overlook onerous reporting requirements in the U.S. because the TFSA may be considered a foreign trust (see 18.7.4).

Withholding tax does not apply to a non-resident's withdrawals from a TFSA but it may apply to payments to a non-resident beneficiary of income earned in a TFSA after the account holder's death.

4.2   Where should you invest your savings?

Determine your best tax strategy for dividing your investments among TFSAs, RRSPs and RESPs.

With all its advantages, you'll want to consider making a TFSA an important part of your tax and financial planning. Of course, you'll need to weigh these advantages against the benefits of other tax-assisted savings plans such as RRSPs (see Chapter 3) and RESPs (see 4.3) and other financial priorities such as paying down your mortgage.

Whether you should choose to save your money in an RRSP, TFSA or RESP depends on your circumstances. Generally, if you have enough resources, you should invest in all the relevant plans. Though TFSA savings are initially limited, as contribution room increases, a TFSA may become a much more significant supplement to your RRSP.

RRSPs versus TFSAs

A TFSA is like a mirror image of an RRSP: RRSP contributions are tax-deductible but the contributions and investment earnings are taxed when you withdraw them. TFSA contributions are not tax-deductible but withdrawals of contributions and investment income are tax-free.

As such, your best tax strategy for dividing your investments between TFSAs and RRSPs may depend on any differences between your current tax bracket and the one you expect to be in when you start withdrawing funds from your RRSP.

If you expect your future income to fall into the same tax bracket as your current income, the tax benefits of a TFSA and an RRSP will be similar. That is, the value of the tax deduction for an RRSP contribution will generally equal the value of withdrawing funds tax-free from a TFSA.

If you expect your future income to fall into a lower tax bracket than your current income, an RRSP investment can provide a tax advantage because the tax deduction you get today will be more than the tax you will pay when you withdraw the money from your RRSP.

If your income falls into a lower tax bracket now but you expect it to be higher in the future, a TFSA offers a greater tax benefit because you would pay a higher tax rate on RRSP withdrawals than you will pay today on the income you contribute to the TFSA.

TFSAs for seniors

Unlike an RRSP, which has to be wound up when you reach age 71, you can maintain your TFSA for your entire lifetime and so your TFSA should be integrated with your retirement income plan (see 20.4.7).

RESPs and TFSAs

If you're saving for your child's education, keep in mind that, unlike a TFSA, an RESP offers an annual guaranteed rate of return of $500 (20% on $2,500 annual contributions) via the federal government's Canada Education Savings Grant (see 4.4).

Once your children turn 18, you may want to consider giving them funds to invest in their own TFSAs to help finance their post-secondary education or other expenses.

TFSA versus mortgage paydown

If you're considering whether to invest in a TFSA or pay down your mortgage, once you've taken all the relevant factors into account, it probably makes sense in most cases to reduce your non-deductible mortgage interest as soon as possible.

Funds earning interest

Assuming you have TFSA contribution room, it almost always makes sense to invest in a TFSA if you have money sitting in a bank account earning taxable interest.

4.3 Registered Education Savings Plans—RESPs

Registered Education Savings Plans (RESPs) can help you build an education fund for your child or grandchild (or a relative's or friend's child) by allowing you to earn investment income in a tax-deferred environment. You can set up an individual plan with organizations such as life insurance companies, mutual fund companies and financial institutions or you can enroll in a group plan offered by a non-profit scholarship or education trust foundation. If the child goes to college or university, the RESP provides funds to help cover the child's expenses.

Consider an RESP for education cost planning, tax deferral and income splitting with the plan's beneficiary.

Unlike RRSPs, contributions to an RESP are *not* tax-deductible to the contributor. However, the income in the plan grows tax-free, so RESPs enjoy the effect of tax-free compounding of investment income, which we illustrated in 3.1.5. When the child withdraws the funds, the income portion will be taxable to the child. As a student, the beneficiary will probably not have much other income and will be eligible for the tuition tax credit (see 2.4), so he or she will likely pay little or no tax. The investment income payments from an RESP are all taxable as regular income, even if the investment income was earned as dividends or capital gains, which are normally taxed at a lower rate.

4.3.1 How much can you contribute to an RESP?

The overall lifetime limit for RESPs contributions is $50,000 per beneficiary. Overcontributions are taxed at a rate of 1% for each month that they remain in the plan.

Income generated in an RESP may be sheltered from tax for a maximum of 35 years (or 40 years if the beneficiary has a disability). You can make contributions to the plan for up to 31 years (35 years if the beneficiary has a disability). The plan can exist and earn tax-sheltered income for four more years, after which the plan must be wound up.

If an RESP contributor dies, his or her estate can continue to contribute to the plan.

Consider making large lump-sum payments to an RESP to take full advantage of tax-sheltered growth within the plan.

Since there is no annual contribution limit, you may want to consider making a large lump-sum payment to the RESP to take advantage of the tax-sheltered growth. This tax savings needs to be weighed against the Canada Education Savings Grant you may lose if you do not make annual contributions (see 4.4). The best approach is to start investing in an RESP in the first years after your child is born to maximize the benefit of government grants (see 4.4) and earn potentially higher returns from making earlier investments.

Determining how much your child's education will eventually cost can be daunting; software tools are available that can help you project how much you need to save today to meet your child's future education costs.

If you wish, you can withdraw your own contributions to an RESP without any tax consequences since you did not get a tax deduction when you contributed the funds. However, you cannot withdraw the income earned by the RESP tax-free. You may also be required to repay some or all of any Canada Education Savings Grants upon an RESP withdrawal for non-education purposes (see 4.4).

4.3.2 Choosing the right type of RESP—Group and individual plans

If you choose to set up an individual plan rather than enroll in a group plan, the investments can be self-directed and tailored to your circumstances. The types of investments that may be held in an RESP are the same as those that may be held by an RRSP (see 3.1.6).

Think about establishing a self-directed RESP to increase your investment options.

Keep in mind that your financial institution may charge additional fees for this flexibility.

You can choose between a single-beneficiary and a multi-beneficiary plan. Under a single-beneficiary plan, the beneficiary does not have to be related to you—he or she can be anyone you choose. You can also set up a single-beneficiary RESP for yourself if you're planning to pursue post-secondary education in the future.

If you are saving for the education of more than one person, you may want to consider a multi-beneficiary or family plan. The beneficiaries under a multi-beneficiary plan may only include your children, brothers, sisters, grandchildren or great-grandchildren.

Determine which type of RESP best suits your needs—individual, family or group.

You cannot contribute to the plan for a beneficiary after he or she reaches age 31. Although you can usually change the beneficiaries after you set up either a single or multi-beneficiary plan if you wish, certain plans may have conditions restricting the changing of beneficiaries. Understanding the terms of any plan contract you consider is critical.

If you have set up single-beneficiary plans for siblings, you can transfer assets among these plans without tax penalties and without triggering the repayment of Canada Education Savings Grants (see 4.4), as long as the beneficiaries of the plans receiving the transfers were under 21 when the plans were opened.

Group plans tend to be more restrictive in terms of required scheduled contributions and the contributor usually has no say in how the contributed funds are invested.

Group plans may require that children be enrolled in the plan before they reach a certain age. They generally allow only one beneficiary to be named and may not allow you to change the beneficiary after he or she reaches a certain age. Again, make sure you understand the terms of the plan before entering into an RESP contract.

4.4 Canada Education Savings Grant

Under the Canada Education Savings Grant (CESG) program, the federal government will provide a direct grant to an RESP of 20% of the first $2,500 of annual contributions made to the RESP in a year (with enhanced rates on the first $500 of contributions of lower and middle income families—see below). The grant will be worth up to $500 per year for each year the beneficiary is under 18, to a maximum of $7,200 per beneficiary. The grant amount will not be included in the annual and lifetime contribution limits for the beneficiary.

Contribute up to $2,500 annually to an RESP and earn a 20% government grant.

If the maximum contribution is not made in a year, entitlement to the grant can be carried forward to a later year (within restrictions). The total CESG per beneficiary per year is capped at $1,000 or 20% of the unused CESG room, whichever is less.

> **Example**
>
> Robin contributes $1,000 in 2019 to an RESP for her newborn son. This contribution earns a CESG of $200 (20% of $1,000), leaving $1,500 in CESG contribution room available for carryforward in future years.
>
> In 2020, Robin contributes $4,500 to the plan. In this year, the contribution for the CESG is limited to the $2,500 of new contribution room arising in the year, plus the $1,500 carried forward. Therefore, the CESG is only 20% of $4,000, or $800.

Note that only unused CESG contribution room can be carried forward; in our example, even though a CESG was earned on only $4,000 of Robin's $4,500 contribution, the extra $500 of contribution could not be carried forward and claimed for CESG purposes in later years. If you expect your annual contributions to vary, consider deferring your "excess" contributions to the next year to secure maximum grants.

CESG contribution room accumulates at the rate of $2,500 per year ($2,000 per year for 1998 to 2006), whether or not the child is currently an RESP beneficiary. So even if you do not start making CESG-eligible RESP contributions in your child's first year, you can make catch-up payments eligible for the grant in later years (subject to the lifetime limit of $7,200 per beneficiary and the annual limit per beneficiary of $1,000 or 20% of the unused CESG room).

The CESG rate on the first $500 of contributions is 40% for families with income under $48,535 in 2020 and 30% for families with income between $48,536 and $97,069. The maximum contribution eligible for the CESG remains at $2,500, while the $500 maximum CESG payable for a year is increased for low and middle income families to accommodate the enhanced CESG rates. For example, a lower income family that contributes $2,500 in a year could receive a CESG totalling $600—that is, 40% on the first $500 ($200) and 20% on the remaining $2,000 ($400). Unused access to the enhanced CESG rates cannot be carried forward to future years.

To qualify for the CESG, the RESP beneficiary must be a resident of Canada under age 18 and must have a Social Insurance Number (SIN) (see 4.8). You can apply for a SIN for your child by contacting Service Canada. Bear in mind that SIN processing may take several weeks.

If you have already set up an RESP, you should confirm that it qualifies for CESG purposes. If you want to receive a CESG for 2020 but you do not have a plan, you'll need to set one up and make a contribution before December 31, 2020. To qualify for the CESG, the contributions must be new—money cannot be withdrawn from existing RESPs and recontributed to a new plan to qualify for the grant. If you change the plan's beneficiary, the grant funds can stay in the RESP if both the old and new beneficiaries are under 21 years old and are related to you.

There are special rules for beneficiaries in the years they become 16 or 17. RESPs for beneficiaries aged 16 and 17 are eligible for CESGs only if:

- Contributions to all RESPs for the child totalled at least $2,000 before the end of the calendar year in which the child turned 15 and the contributions remain in the RESPs, or
- There were contributions for the child of at least $100 per year in any four years before the end of the calendar year in which the child turned 15 and the contributions remain in the RESP.

If your child chooses not to pursue post-secondary education, you will have to repay the CESG funds received but you will only have to pay back the principal amount of the grant. You do not have to pay back the income earned on the grant funds; however, the income will be taxed when it is withdrawn from the RESP (see 4.5.2).

4.5 Payments from an RESP

4.5.1 If the beneficiary pursues higher education

Your RESP can begin making educational assistance payments to the plan's beneficiary once he or she enrolls as a full-time student in a qualifying educational program at a qualifying post-secondary institution. Part-time students aged 16 and over are eligible to receive up to $2,500 of educational assistance payments for each 13-week semester. Students with disabilities can also receive educational assistance payments for part-time study.

Payments from the plan can be used to cover the student's living expenses and educational expenses such as tuition fees and books, although certain plans may restrict which expenses payments can cover. A beneficiary cannot receive more than $5,000 during the first 13 weeks of his or her post-secondary education unless pre-approved by Human Resources and Social Development Canada. After the first 13 weeks, there is no limit on the amount that can be paid, as long as the student continues to qualify. If there is a 12-month period in which the student is not enrolled in a qualifying education program for 13 consecutive weeks, the $5,000 maximum applies again.

You can decide whether to let the student use the principal amount contributed to the plan or only the income accumulated in the plan. You can also decide how much is paid out of the plan and when the payments are made, subject to what the plan you choose allows. You may want to spread the payments over the duration of the student's program to minimize taxes. If your RESP received CESGs, in most cases, a part of each income payment will be attributed to the CESG funds received by the plan. Bear in mind that managing these different income streams can be complex, especially where group RESPs are involved.

If you contributed to a group RESP, the principal you contributed to the plan will be the first year's payment to the student. The plan administrators will determine the student's share of the income from the pooled funds in the plan and start making those payments in the student's second year of post-secondary education.

For an educational program to qualify, generally it must be at least three weeks long, require at least 10 hours per week of instruction (or 12 hours per month for part-time students) and be at a designated educational institution. Correspondence courses and other distance education courses may also qualify, as well as universities outside Canada if the student is enrolled in a course of at least 13 weeks leading to a degree.

Some group RESP plans may have other restrictions, such as prohibiting the beneficiary from changing schools or requiring the beneficiary to meet a minimum academic standard.

Special rules apply if the beneficiary becomes a non-resident of Canada, for example, to attend an institution in another country (see 13.3.6).

4.5.2 If the beneficiary does not pursue further education

If your child does not pursue higher education, consider transferring up to $50,000 to your own or your spouse's RRSP.

What happens to the RESP funds if the intended beneficiaries decide not to enroll in college or university? In the past, if none of the intended beneficiaries went on to higher education, the family would only get back the original amounts contributed to the RESP, while the income earned over the years would be forfeited. However, these rules have been eased in cases where none of the RESP's intended beneficiaries are post-secondary students by age 21 and the plan has been running for at least 10 years. (If a beneficiary is mentally impaired, these conditions may be waived.) Under the current rules, you may transfer up to $50,000 of RESP income to your RRSP (or your spouse's) during your lifetime to the extent you have available RRSP contribution room. This allows the RRSP deduction to offset the inclusion of the RESP funds in your taxable income.

If you do not want to contribute the income to an RRSP or you do not have enough RRSP contribution room to do so, you will be subject to an extra tax of 20% of the excess RESP income, on top of your regular taxes on the amount (the extra tax is designed to make up for the taxes deferred while the funds were in the plan). You must wind up the RESP before March 1 of the year following the year in which you first withdrew income from the RESP if the beneficiary does not go to university or college.

Family plans are subject to the same contribution limits per beneficiary as single-beneficiary plans but, if one of your children decides against post-secondary school, the funds you have contributed for this child and the income earned on those contributions can be re-directed to benefit your other children who do pursue post-secondary education. If your plan received CESGs, the remaining beneficiaries can use up to $7,200 of CESGs funds each.

Group RESPs will return your contributions, but the income earned will remain in the plan to be distributed to the plan's beneficiaries who go on to post-secondary education.

4.6 Registered Disability Savings Plans—RDSPs

Registered Disability Savings Plans (RDSPs) can help you save for the long-term security of a child with a disability who is eligible for the disability tax credit (see 2.5.1). These plans are similar to RESPs in that contributions to RDSPs are not tax-deductible, but investment income can be earned in the plan tax-free.

If you have a child with a disability, consider setting up a Registered Disability Savings Plan to provide for his or her future financial security.

Investment income, but not contributions, will be taxable to the beneficiary when it is paid out of the RDSP.

Anyone can contribute to an RDSP and there is no annual limit on the amount you can contribute. Contributions on behalf of any one beneficiary are capped at a lifetime maximum of $200,000. Contributions can continue to be made until the end of the year the beneficiary turns 59.

RRSP funds can be transferred tax-free on death to the RDSP of the RRSP holder's financially dependent infirm child or grandchild, subject to the beneficiary's lifetime contribution limit.

If you saved in an RESP for your disabled child and he or she does not pursue post-secondary education, you may be able to transfer the investment income in the RESP tax-free to your child's RDSP.

The beneficiary must begin receiving payments from the plan by the end of the year he or she turns 60, subject to maximum annual limits based on life expectancy, the age of the beneficiary and the value of the plan's assets.

These plans qualify for Canada Disability Savings Grants (CDSGs), which are similar to Canada Education Savings Grants (see 4.4). Under this program, your RDSP contributions earn CDSGs at matching rates of 100%, 200% or 300%, depending on family net income and the amount contributed. An RDSP beneficiary can receive up to $3,500 of CDSGs in their RDSPs annually and up to $70,000 of CDSGs in their RDSP over their lifetime. CDSGs can be paid to an RDSP until the end of the year in which the beneficiary turns 49. Unused entitlements to CDSGs can be carried forward for up to 10 years.

Lower-income families may also be entitled to receive Canada Disability Savings Bonds (CDSBs) of up to $1,000 per year (to a maximum of $20,000 over the beneficiary's lifetime). CDSBs can be paid into an RDSP until the end of the year in which the beneficiary turns 49. Eligibility for CDSBs is linked to family net income, rather than amounts contributed. Like CDSGs, you can carry forward unused CDSB entitlements for up to 10 years.

Starting January 1, 2021, you will no longer need to close an RDSP after a beneficiary becomes ineligible for the disability tax credit. In addition, the beneficiary will no longer need to obtain medical certification that they are likely to become eligible for the disability tax credit in the future for the plan to remain open.

4.7 Anti-avoidance rules

As with RRSPs (see 3.4), you can hold only certain types of qualifying investments in your RESP or RDSP. Special anti-avoidance rules prevent you from holding prohibited investments in these accounts or using them in tax planning arrangements that the government considers unacceptable.

4.8 References

The following publications and more information, including forms and brochures, can be obtained on the CRA's website at *www.canada.ca/en/revenue-agency.html* or by telephone request at 1-800-959-8281 for individual income tax and trust-related enquiries or 1-800-959-5525 for business and self-employed individual enquiries.

Guide RC4092, "Registered Education Savings Plans (RESP)"
Guide RC4460, "Registered Disability Savings Plan"
Guide RC4466, "Tax-Free Savings Account (TFSA), Guide for Individuals"
Income Tax Folio S3-F10-C1, "Qualified Investments – RRSPs, RESPs, RRIFs, RDSPs and TFSAs"
Income Tax Folio S3-F10-C2, "Prohibited Investments – RRSPs, RESPs, RRIFs, RDSPs and TFSAs"
Income Tax Folio S3-F10-C3, "Advantages – RRSPs, RESPs, RRIFs, RDSPs and TFSAs"
Information Circular 93-3R2, "Registered Education Savings Plans"
Information Circular 99-1R1, "Registered Disability Savings Plans"

Information about how to apply for a Social Insurance Number is available on Service Canada's website at *https://www.canada.ca/en/employment-social-development/corporate/portfolio/service-canada.html.*

Chapter 5

Reducing your family's tax bill through income splitting

- Watch out for the income splitting tax on certain income received by minor children (5.2.4)

- Consider whether the new income splitting tax for adults affects your family business arrangements (5.2.5)

- Beware of the "general anti-avoidance rule" (5.2.7)

- The higher-income spouse should pay household expenses (5.3.1)

- Pay your spouse's tax bills with your own funds (5.3.1)

- Pay the interest on your spouse's third-party investment loans (5.3.1)

- Give your spouse up to $6,000 annually to invest in their Tax-Free Savings Account (5.3.1)

- Pay a salary or consulting fee to your spouse and/or children (5.3.2)

- Think about loaning business assets to your spouse or child (5.3.3)

- Consider making spousal investment loans when interest rates are rising (5.3.4)

- Have your spouse or child earn income on income from loaned or transferred funds (5.3.5)

- Shelter future gains by transferring property at fair market value (5.3.6)

- Shelter future gains by transferring capital assets to your children (5.3.7)

- Transfer shares that will pay capital dividends (5.3.8)

- Contribute to your spouse's RRSP (5.3.9)

- Make spousal RRSP contributions by December 31 (5.3.9)

- In the year your children turn 17, give them funds they can invest (5.3.10)

- Let your children invest their own earnings (5.3.11)

- Deposit Canada Child Benefit payments to your child's bank account (5.3.12)

- File a joint election to split pension income with your spouse (5.3.13)

- Claim baby-sitting wages paid to your adult children as child care expenses (5.3.14)

"Income splitting" is a term used to describe strategies to save taxes by shifting income from the hands of a family member in a higher tax bracket to the hands of a second family member in a lower tax bracket so that the same income is taxed at a lower rate of tax—or not at all if the second family member's income is

low enough. In this chapter, we discuss the tax rules that are in place to prevent many forms of income splitting and point out some of the income splitting opportunities that are available.

5.1 Why income splitting?

The Canadian tax system uses progressive tax rates, whereby the marginal rate of tax (tax on additional income) increases as taxable income increases.

Marginal rates of tax, tax brackets and surtaxes for 2020 vary widely from province to province, but are *approximately*:

- 23% on income from $13,000 to $49,000
- 34% on income from $49,000 to $97,000
- 42% on income from $97,000 to $150,000
- 47% on income from $150,000 to $214,000
- 51% on income over $214,000.

As you can see, the tax payable on two $75,000 incomes will be significantly less than that on one $150,000 income — about $12,600 less. Taxpayers, therefore, have an incentive to "split" income between, for example, a high-income earner and a non-working spouse or children.

The federal *Income Tax Act* contains measures to prevent the most obvious kinds of income splitting (similar rules apply for Quebec purposes). However, some opportunities are available. We review the rules here, so you understand the context in which to plan, and then discuss the planning opportunities that remain.

5.2 Rules that prevent income splitting

5.2.1 Indirect payments

The *Income Tax Act* provides that a payment or transfer made "pursuant to the direction of, or with the concurrence of" a taxpayer to some other person is to be included in the taxpayer's income to the extent it would have been if the payment was made to the taxpayer. So, for example, if you arrange for your employer to pay part of your salary to your spouse, the income will still be taxed in your hands and you will not have accomplished anything.

5.2.2 Attribution between spouses

Suppose you earn $150,000 per year and your spouse earns $25,000. Your marginal tax rate (tax on any additional income) is 47% and your spouse's is 23%. Assume you have $10,000 in bonds that generate $1,000 per year in interest and decide to give, or lend, the bonds to your spouse. As a result, your spouse hopes to pay only $230 tax on the income instead of the $470 that you would pay.

This is the kind of transaction that the attribution rules cover. These rules attribute income from property (in our example, the $1,000 of investment income each year) back to the person who transferred or loaned the property.

The attribution rules that apply to spouses provide that where property (including money) is *transferred or loaned, directly or indirectly* by you to your spouse (or a person who has since become your spouse), then all *income or loss from the property*, and any *capital gain or loss* on the disposition of the property will be *attributed back* to you. So, in our example, the $1,000 income on the $10,000 investment that you gave to your spouse must be reported on your tax return, not your spouse's—and so will be subject to tax of about $470 rather than about $230. This will be true year after year—as long as you and your spouse remain together, any income from the bonds will be taxed in your hands. If you transfer shares, for example, and your spouse sells the shares at some later time, any capital gain or capital loss relative *to your* original cost must be reported as your capital gain or loss, subject to the usual rules for capital gains (see Chapter 6).

Note that common-law couples who meet the criteria outlined in 2.2.1 are considered spouses for tax purposes, and are therefore subject to these attribution rules as well.

There is an exception to these attribution rules; an exception that also applies to the other attribution rules we will see later. If you transfer for fair market value consideration (for example, sell the bonds to your spouse for $10,000 cash) and report the resulting gain, the attribution rule will not apply. (If you realize a loss on the transfer, a special rule deems the loss to be zero. However, the denied loss can be added to your spouse's cost for tax purposes.)

If the consideration includes indebtedness (for example, you sell the bonds for a $10,000 promissory note), or if you simply lend funds or property to your spouse, then you must charge and report interest on the loan to avoid these attribution rules. The interest rate must be at least equal to the lesser of the CRA's prescribed interest rate at that time (see 9.3) and a commercial rate of interest. For this exception to apply, the interest must actually be *paid* in each year or by the following January 30. If the January 30 deadline ever passes without the interest being paid, that year's income and *all* future income from the loaned property will be attributed back to you as the lender.

Example

On January 1, 2020, you lend $10,000 cash to your spouse, who puts the money in an investment and earns $400 interest over the year.

If you do not charge interest, then the $400 will be attributed back to you and taxed in your hands. Suppose you do wish to charge interest. The minimum rate required to prevent the attribution rules from applying would have to be the lesser of:

- the rate that would apply between two arm's-length parties (assume 3% for this example); and

- the CRA's prescribed rate at the time the loan was granted (assume 2%—see 9.3).

If your spouse is required to pay interest on the anniversary date of the loan and actually pays you at least $200 in interest by January 30, 2021, then the $400 interest will not be attributed back to you in 2020. Your spouse can deduct the interest paid to you and the amount will be taxable to you as interest income.

Setting up a system for automatic payment, such as an automatic bank transfer between you and your spouse, can help ensure that the interest payments are not inadvertently missed.

The CRA's (and Revenu Québec's) prescribed rate is set quarterly (see 9.3).

5.2.3 Attribution between parents and children

Suppose you give $10,000 in bonds to your daughter, who is in high school and can earn $1,000 in interest without paying any tax at all.

Where property is transferred or loaned to a child, there will be attribution of income (or loss), but usually not of capital gains or losses. The attribution rules apply only for years in which the child is still under 18 *at the end* of the year (though the attribution rules discussed in 5.2.6 may apply once your child turns 18).

Not all children under 18 are caught by the rule. It depends on the child's relationship with the taxpayer who transfers or lends the property. Attribution applies where the taxpayer and the child "do not deal at arm's length", a phrase that is defined to include all persons who are "related" as defined in the *Income Tax Act*. Generally, this covers one's child (including adopted children), grandchild, great-grandchild (including one's spouse's child, one's child's spouse, etc., where "spouse" includes a common-law spouse as outlined in 2.2.1) or brother or sister (including brother-in-[common]-law and sister-in-[common]-law). This rule also specifically applies to nieces and nephews. For other relationships, it is a "question of fact" whether two taxpayers deal at arm's length.

Although the attribution rule for minors does not usually apply to capital gains and losses, the transfer of the property itself to the minor is generally deemed to take place at fair market value. Any capital gain or loss accruing up to the time of the transfer is triggered immediately in the transferor's hands, and it is only the gain or loss accruing *after* the transfer that, when realized, is taxed in the child's hands.

As a result of the attribution rules, the $1,000 of income transferred to your daughter in our example above would be taxable to you. You may also have to pay capital gains tax (if any) on the deemed disposition of the $10,000 in bonds transferred, though future capital gains or losses will accrue to your daughter.

The exceptions that we saw in 5.2.2, where the transferred property is acquired for fair market value or where interest is paid on any indebtedness or loan, also apply to this attribution rule.

5.2.4 Income splitting tax on certain income received by minor children

Some income splitting arrangements with minor children attract a special "income splitting tax" (previously called the "kiddie tax") in the minor child's hands. The tax neutralizes the benefits of certain arrangements, including some plans involving the use of family trusts (see 21.5.4), by subjecting certain types of dividend, interest, partnership or trust income received by, or used for the benefit of, minor children to tax at the top marginal tax rate, instead of the lower rate that would usually apply on income received by a minor child. Certain capital gains as described below are also subject to this tax.

The types of income subject to this tax are generally referred to as "split income" and include:

- taxable dividends and other shareholder benefits from private Canadian and foreign company shares (received directly by the individual or through a trust or partnership)
- income (e.g., interest) from debt of a private corporation, partnership or trust
- taxable capital gains realized by a minor child (and capital gains allocated to a minor child by a trust) from the disposition of a private corporation's shares to a person who does not deal at arm's length with the minor child or trust. These capital gains will be treated as dividends and thus will neither benefit from the capital gains inclusion rates (see 6.2.1) nor qualify for the capital gains exemption (see 6.4)
- taxable capital gains realized by a minor child or allocated through a trust from the disposition of debt, shares of a private corporation or a partnership or trust interest (other than property that is qualified small business corporation shares (see 6.4.1) or qualified farm and fishing property (see 15.4.1)) to the extent income from that property would have been subject to the tax on split income
- income that is directly or indirectly paid or allocated to a minor child from a trust or partnership where the income has been derived from a business or rental property and a person (i.e., a partnership, corporation, trust or individual) related to the minor child is actively involved in these activities or holds 10% or more of the fair market value of the shares of the corporation carrying on the business. These rules also apply if a person related to the minor child has an interest in the partnership, whether directly or indirectly, through another partnership.

Watch out for the income
splitting tax on certain
income received by
minor children.

Parents are jointly and severally liable for the tax on split income if they were active in the business or were a shareholder of the corporation from which the income was derived. The only credits allowed against income subject to this tax are the disability tax credit, the dividend tax credit and the foreign tax credit.

The tax does not apply to income earned by minor children from property acquired on the death of their parent or income earned by minor children who have no parent resident in Canada for tax purposes at any time in the year.

These rules have been expanded to also target, in certain more limited circumstances, income paid directly or distributed through a trust to your spouse or child who is 18 or older at the end of the year. Income splitting may still be accomplished by allocating the above types of income to older family members, provided the tax on split income for adults discussed in 5.2.5 and the attribution rules discussed in 5.2.2 and 5.2.7 do not apply.

5.2.5 Income splitting tax on certain income received by adult family members

Consider whether the
new income splitting tax
for adults affects your
family business
arrangements.

Income splitting arrangements with adult family members may also be subject to a tax on split income.

You may be subject to this tax when you receive amounts that are considered "split income" as described in 5.2.4 such as dividends, interest or certain capital gains from a private corporation if someone related to you is actively engaged in the corporation's business or owns directly or indirectly 10% or more of the fair market value of its shares, such as a family operating company. For this purpose, related people include spouses, siblings, parents, grandparents, children and grandchildren.

Income you receive directly from a related business or from partnerships or trusts that is derived from such a related business may also be subject to the tax on split income. These amounts will be taxed at the highest marginal rate.

The tax on split income does not apply to taxable capital gains from the disposition of qualified small business corporation shares (see 6.4.1) or qualified farm or fishing property (see 15.4.1).

This tax also does not apply to salary or wages you earn if you work for the business. The tax may not apply to other amounts you receive if you have made a significant contribution to, or investment in, the business.

These rules include several tests for determining whether you make a significant contribution to a related business. Some of the rules apply differently depending on the age of the adult. You may not be subject to the tax if:

• You're 18 or over and you have been engaged in the business's activities on a regular, continuous and substantial basis during the year or in any five previous years. These five years do not have to be consecutive. You can meet this test if you work an average of at least 20 hours per week in the business during the relevant years.

- You're 25 or over and you own 10% or more of the votes and fair market value of the corporation. This corporation must earn less than 90% of its income from providing services and cannot be a professional corporation such as one operated by an accountant, lawyer, doctor or dentist (see 16.1.2). Also, the corporation cannot derive more than 10% of its income from other related businesses.

Even if you cannot meet any of these tests, you may still not be subject to the tax on split income if you are 25 or over and the amount you receive can be considered a "reasonable return" on your contributions to the business. This "reasonableness" test considers your contributions to the business through any combination of:

- Labour contributions
- Property contributions (for example, capital or loans)
- Risks assumed
- Amounts received from the business in the past
- Any other relevant factors.

If you are 18–24 years old and you have contributed capital to the business, you will be allowed a prescribed rate of return on that capital. If the capital came from an inheritance, was earned from an unrelated business or was salary, you will be allowed a reasonable rate of return on this contribution. For these purposes the capital cannot be borrowed, even from arm's length sources.

Some relief from the tax on split income is also available in special circumstances such as:

- Income from property inherited by individuals under age 25
- Income from property transferred after a marriage breakdown
- Income received by an individual whose spouse is the business owner if the spouse is 65 or older and the income would not have been considered split income to the spouse (to align with the pension income splitting rules (see 20.3.6))
- Taxable capital gains from the deemed disposition of capital property on death (see 22.2.3)
- Income that would not have been subject to the tax on split income if it was earned by an individual's deceased spouse in their last taxation year.

Similar to the rules on split income for minor children in 5.2.4, the only credits allowed in the calculation of the tax on split income are the dividend tax credit, foreign tax credit and disability tax credit.

> Susan's business sells plumbing supplies. All the shares of this company are owned by a holding company. The shares of the holding company are owned by Susan and a family trust for the benefit of Susan's husband Brian, 49, and their children Alexandra, 23, and Taylor, 16.
>
> Brian works part-time in the business. Alexandra is a full-time university student and is away from home for most of the year. She has never worked for the plumbing supply company or contributed to its business. Taylor is a high school student.
>
> The plumbing supply company pays a dividend to the holding company in 2020, which then pays a dividend of the same amount to the family trust. The trust distributes half the amount to Brian and half to Alexandra. These amounts are included in their 2020 income for tax purposes.
>
> As long as Brian works at least 20 hours per week in the business in 2020, the amount he receives from the trust will not be subject to the tax on split income. However, the amount that Alexandra receives will be subject to the tax on split income and will be taxed at the highest marginal rate because Alexandra does not contribute to the business.
>
> If Taylor had received any of the distribution, it would be subject to the tax on split income that applies to minor children, as we saw in 5.2.4.

Example (margin label)

5.2.6 Attribution on loans to adult family members

One further rule applies to loans (but not transfers) of property to other persons with whom the taxpayer does not deal at arm's length—such as, for example, one's children who are over 18, or one's in-laws or grandparents. If one of the main reasons for the loan was to achieve income splitting and thereby reduce taxes, the income is attributed back to the lender. So, if you lend $20,000 to your adult son who is in university, and the purpose is to allow him to earn $600 interest and pay little or no tax on it (rather than, say, to allow him to use the $20,000 to pay for his tuition), the $600 of interest is attributed back to you. The exception where interest is charged and paid, as outlined in 5.2.2, applies in this case.

5.2.7 Special anti-avoidance rules

If you are creative, you may have thought of some possible ways around the attribution rules we have just described. Don't bother. The federal and Quebec tax laws contain special rules designed to thwart the loopholes that some taxpayers exploited in years past. We summarize them here only briefly; basically, anything you can think of has probably been thought of before.

Substituted property. If property is substituted for transferred or loaned property, the attribution rules apply to income or capital gains from the substituted property, and so on *ad infinitum* (to the extent that attribution would have applied to income from the original property). If you give $10,000 in bonds to your spouse, who then sells them and buys $10,000 in stocks, any dividends and capital gains on the stocks is attributed back to you.

Transfers to a trust or corporation. In general, transfers to a trust cause the attribution rules to apply in the same way as if the transfers were made directly to the beneficiaries of the trust. Transfers to a corporation that result in a benefit to a "designated person" (spouse or related minor children, using the same definition we saw in 5.2.3) are also caught in most cases. For example, if you and your spouse each own half the shares in a corporation, and you give $10,000 to the corporation so that your spouse will benefit, you are taxed as though you had received a specified amount of interest from the corporation. This attribution rule does not apply where the corporation is a "small business corporation" (see 6.2.3).

Back-to-back loans and transfers. If you lend or transfer property to a third party, who then lends or transfers it to a "designated person" (your spouse or related minor children), it is treated as though you had lent or transferred the property directly.

Guarantees. If you arrange for a third party (e.g., a bank) to lend funds to a "designated person" on the strength of your guarantee, it is treated as though you had lent the funds directly.

Repayment of existing loan. If you lend funds to a "designated person", and they use the funds to pay off another loan that they used to buy property, your loan will effectively be treated as if it had been used to buy that property. (This is the flip side of the "substituted property" case covered above.) For example, if your spouse borrows $10,000 from a bank to invest in bonds, and you then lend your spouse $10,000 that is used to pay off that bank loan, the interest from the bonds is attributed back to you.

Reverse attribution. The attribution rules can be ignored if you try to have them apply in a manner not intended by the tax rules.

General anti-avoidance rule. The *Income Tax Act* provides a general anti-avoidance rule (GAAR), applicable to all transactions. If you come up with a way of avoiding the attribution rules that is not caught by the existing rules but is a misuse or abuse of the *Income Tax Act*, it may be caught by GAAR.

> Beware of the "general anti-avoidance rule".

5.3 Income splitting opportunities

In this section, we discuss the planning opportunities available to achieve income splitting. For many of these to work, you need to keep careful documentation. Separate bank accounts for spouses will allow you to trace each one's funds properly. (Under provincial family law, this will not normally affect either spouse's rights to the family's funds on marriage breakdown.)

5.3.1 Increasing the lower-income spouse's investment base

The simplest technique is to make sure that daily living expenses (such as groceries, mortgage or rent payments, and credit card bills) are paid by the higher-income spouse. This allows the lower-income spouse to maintain a larger investment base for earning future income that is taxed at a lower rate.

> The higher-income spouse should pay household expenses.

Pay your spouse's tax bills with your own funds.

Another way to effectively transfer funds is for you to directly pay your spouse's income tax liability—both in April and any instalments that are due during the year (see 9.2.2). Simply make sure that the payment for your spouse's taxes is drawn on your own account. Since the amount you pay goes directly to the government and is not invested by your spouse, there is no property from which income can be attributed. The result is that any funds your spouse would otherwise use to pay income taxes can be invested without the income being attributed back to you.

Pay the interest on your spouse's third-party investment loans.

If your spouse has taken out an investment loan from a third party, consider providing him or her with the funds to pay the interest. There is no attribution provided you do not pay any principal on account of the spousal loan. (Since the amount you pay is not actually invested by your spouse, there is no property from which income can be attributed.) The interest payment will be deductible on your spouse's tax return. This technique preserves your spouse's assets and thereby increases his or her investment income.

Give your spouse up to $6,000 annually to invest in their Tax-Free Savings Account.

You can give your spouse up to $6,000 annually to invest in his or her own Tax-Free Savings Account (TFSA), provided he or she has available contribution room. Since the attribution rules do not apply to amounts transferred to a TFSA, any investment income earned within your spouse's TFSA is not attributed back to you. See 4.1 for details.

5.3.2 Employing your spouse and children

If you carry on a business, either personally or through a corporation, consider paying a salary to your spouse and/or children. The salary must be "reasonable" in light of the services they perform for the business. Such services might include bookkeeping, other administrative work, business development planning and acting as a director of the corporation (for adults). The CRA and Revenu Québec may consider the amount paid to be a "reasonable" salary, as long as services are genuinely being provided. To help you determine a reasonable amount, consider how much you would pay an arm's-length person for the same services.

Pay a salary or consulting fee to your spouse and/or children.

The cost of payroll taxes, Canada Pension Plan contributions, Employment Insurance premiums, worker's compensation and provincial health tax, if applicable, should be weighed against any potential tax savings.

Consider also whether your spouse can provide services on a contract (consulting) basis rather than as an employee. This would allow your spouse to earn self-employment income (see Chapter 11), including writing off certain expenses. This plan should only be implemented with appropriate professional advice.

Another possibility is to bring your spouse into partnership with you, but be careful of the tax on split income (see 5.2.5). Taxation of partnerships is discussed in 11.3 and 16.2.

5.3.3 Transfers of business assets

The attribution rules, as we have noted, apply to income from *property*—such as interest, dividends, rent and royalties. They do not, however, apply to income earned from a *business*. If you can transfer or

> Think about loaning business assets to your spouse or child.

lend business assets in such a way that your spouse or child carries on business on a regular and continuous basis to earn income from business rather than from property, there is no attribution. Such a step should only be undertaken with proper professional advice, to ensure that the legal steps required to effect the transfer are properly completed and minimize the possible application of the tax on split income rules or the general anti-avoidance rule.

Note that this generally cannot be done for a passive interest in a partnership (including an interest in a limited partnership). Income from the partnership's business is technically business income, but it is deemed to be property income for purposes of the attribution rules unless the taxpayer is actively engaged in the partnership's business or is carrying on a similar business.

5.3.4 Spousal loans

As we saw in 5.2.2, the attribution rules do not apply where property or funds are loaned and interest is charged at a minimum rate, provided the interest is actually paid. Where assets are expected to produce a

> Consider making spousal investment loans when interest rates are rising.

return that is well above the minimum rate (the lesser of a reasonable commercial rate and the CRA prescribed rate, see 9.3), it may make sense to lend the funds or assets and charge a rate of interest sufficient to avoid triggering the attribution rules. The excess yield from the assets over the amount of interest charged is then effectively transferred to the lower-income taxpayer and not attributed back to the lender.

If interest rates are rising, the current CRA prescribed rate may be relatively low, since there is a time lag before it is set each quarter. Where such an opportunity arises, consider making a loan to your spouse (or other family member) on which interest is charged, "locking in" at the low prescribed rate, and having your spouse use the funds to invest at current market rates.

5.3.5 Reinvesting attributed income

We have seen that attribution applies to the income from property that is transferred or loaned. But what about the income from that income (secondary income)? Suppose you give $20,000 to your spouse, who earns $600 in interest in the first year, and the $600 is attributed back to you. In the second year, your spouse invests the $600 as well as the $20,000, and the $600 generates a further $18 in interest.

This "secondary income" of $18 is not attributed back to you, as it is not income from the property that was transferred. It is thus taxed in your spouse's hands. Over time, a significant stream of such secondary

> Have your spouse or child earn income on income from loaned or transferred funds.

income can be built up. However, accurate records must be maintained. You may wish to have your spouse keep two bank accounts, one for the income that is attributed back to you and one into which all income from the first account is deposited. Only the income from the first account would be reported on your return.

5.3.6 Transfers for fair market value

Shelter future gains by transferring property at fair market value.

As we have seen, the attribution rules also do not apply where property is transferred in exchange for consideration equal to the property's fair market value. (Where the consideration includes indebtedness, such as a promissory note, interest must be charged as outlined above.) A transfer at fair market value may be beneficial where the assets are expected to produce a high yield or to increase in value in the future. (Bear in mind, however, that the transfer may trigger a capital gain or loss subject to the rules discussed in 5.2.2 and you should ensure that the tax on split income rules will not apply to the income earned on the property (see 5.2.5).)

5.3.7 Transferring capital property to children

Shelter future gains by transferring capital assets to your children.

As we saw in 5.2.3, the attribution rules for minor children do not usually apply to capital gains. If you have assets that are expected to increase substantially in value (such as shares of a corporation), consider transferring them to your children or to a trust for your children. Any dividends will be attributed back to you as long as your children are under 18 at the end of the year in which the dividend is paid, but capital gains on the sale of the assets will not be. You should also ensure that the capital gains will not be subject to the income splitting tax discussed in 5.2.4.

For example, suppose you own shares in a public corporation. You invested $10,000 originally, and they are now worth $20,000. You expect the corporation to do well over the coming years. If you give the shares to your children, you will be deemed to have disposed of them at $20,000 and will realize a $10,000 capital gain. If, a few years later, your children sell the shares for $100,000, the $80,000 capital gain will be taxed in their hands, not yours, and possibly taxed at a lower marginal rate.

Other assets that might be appropriate for transfer to children are those that normally generate capital gains but not income. Examples include jewellery and art.

Transfers to children should be done with proper professional advice. In some provinces, there is a question as to whether minors can legally own property such as shares. You may need to set up a trust for this purpose.

5.3.8 Payment of capital dividends

Normally, dividends that are paid on shares you transfer to your spouse or minor children are attributed back to you. However, the tax system provides for "capital dividends", which are always tax-free. Such dividends include a distribution of the untaxed half of a corporation's capital gains. (For an example, see 14.2.4.)

If you transfer shares of a private corporation, and the shares later pay capital dividends, there is no attribution of the income because it is not taxed in anyone's hands in the first place. As well, any income earned from reinvesting the capital dividends is not attributed.

Transfer shares that will pay capital dividends.

Keep in mind that if one of the main purposes of the share transfer is to pay a capital dividend to the new shareholder, the dividend may be subject to an anti-avoidance rule that would deny the capital dividend treatment and treat the dividend as a taxable dividend, resulting in attribution.

5.3.9 Spousal RRSP

A contribution to your spouse's RRSP, as we saw in 3.3.1, is specifically allowed for federal and Quebec tax purposes. When the funds are turned into an annuity or RRIF on retirement, no income is attributed back to you as long as your spouse withdraws no more than the minimum amount from the RRIF in the year of the RRSP contribution or the next two years.

Contributions to your spouse's RRSP, if withdrawn by your spouse, are taxed back in your hands to the extent you have made any spousal contributions in the year of withdrawal or in the two previous years. This

Contribute to your spouse's RRSP.

means that you can split income, provided you can wait 24 to 36 months and make no spousal contributions in the meantime. It also means foregoing the benefits of leaving the funds to grow tax-free in the RRSP (see 3.1.5).

Example

On December 31, 2020, you make a first-time contribution of $26,500 to an RRSP for your spouse.

This entitles you to a deduction of $26,500 for 2020 (assuming you have adequate contribution room—see 3.1.3—and have made no contributions to your own RRSP for 2020). Any withdrawals up to the limit of $26,500 from your spouse's RRSPs in 2021 or 2022 will be attributed back to you, but on January 1, 2023, your spouse can withdraw the full $26,500, which will be taxed in your spouse's hands provided you make no further spousal RRSP contributions in 2021, 2022 or 2023.

Of course, when you contribute to a spousal RRSP you use up your own RRSP contribution room, so the tax advantages of this technique are somewhat limited, but it does achieve income splitting over the long term.

Make spousal RRSP contributions by December 31.

You must also consider whether your spouse having a higher income at retirement will affect eligibility for the age credit (see 20.3.4) or trigger the Old Age Security clawback (see 20.3.2).

Note that in this example, if you contributed to the RRSP for 2020 on January 1, 2021 rather than December 31, 2020, your spouse would have to wait until January 1, 2024 to withdraw the funds without attribution back to you. Contributions to spousal plans should thus not be put off to January or February, as is often done with one's own contributions.

5.3.10 When your children turn 17

In the year your children turn 17, give them funds they can invest.

Consider giving your children funds that they can invest. If your child turns 17 in the year you make the gift, the funds can be invested in a one-year (or longer) term deposit or certificate, with the first interest payment being made in the year in which the child turns 18, and no attribution will result. (If the investment is for more than one year with compounding interest, the interest earned must still be reported annually—see 7.2.1.) Do not simply lend the funds without considering the special attribution rule discussed in 5.2.6.

You might also consider a gift of enough funds so that the income earned on the funds will cover the child's university tuition and residence over four (or more) years. Of course, you must be prepared to lose the funds, since they will legally belong to your child and not to you. Consider using a trust (with proper legal advice) if this is a concern.

5.3.11 Your adult children's employment income

Let your children invest their own earnings.

Consider lending your child, interest-free, an amount equal to what he or she earns over the summer and would otherwise spend. This will allow the child to earn investment income on his or her own earnings, and the investment income will not be attributed back to you.

Suppose you have a daughter who attends university and earns $20,000 over the summer, and your normal arrangement with her is that she uses her income to pay for her tuition and basic expenses. If you lend her $20,000 interest-free instead, she can use the funds you lend her to pay her tuition and living expenses, and invest her summer earnings. Since the $20,000 invested represents her own funds, the income earned on that amount will not be attributed back to you and will be taxed at her marginal rate (or not taxed at all if her income is low enough). You could then repeat this process through several years of university, and have your daughter pay back the entire amount of the loan when she graduates, using the funds she has invested from her own earnings. Alternatively, you could lend her less money each year, as she will have her investment income available as an additional source of funds.

5.3.12 Canada Child Benefit

Deposit Canada Child Benefit payments to your child's bank account.

The attribution rules do not apply to payments your family receives under the Canada Child Benefit (see 2.3.2).

As a result, you can direct these payments to an "in trust" bank account for your child so that the investment income earned on these amounts will be taxed in your child's hands. You may wish to withdraw the balance from the account annually and purchase higher-yielding investments on your child's behalf.

5.3.13 Splitting pension income and CPP/QPP benefit payments

If you earn income eligible for the pension income tax credit (see 20.3.5), you may be able to split this income with your lower-income spouse by filing a joint election with your personal income tax returns. See 20.3.6 for details.

You can also split income by directing that up to 50% of your Canada or Quebec Pension Plan (CPP/QPP) benefits be paid to your spouse, provided both of you are over 60. If you do this, a portion of your CPP/QPP

> File a joint election to split pension income with your spouse.

is assigned automatically to your spouse; if your spouse does this, a portion of their CPP/QPP is assigned automatically to you. In both cases, the attribution rules will not apply. See 20.3.1 for details.

5.3.14 Paying children over 18 for child care

The deduction for child care expenses was discussed in 2.3.1. No deduction is allowed for payments you make to a person related to you who is under 18. Once your older children turn 18, if you are the lower-income spouse you can claim amounts paid to them for child

> Claim baby-sitting wages paid to your adult children as child care expenses.

care or baby-sitting services that permit you to earn employment or business income. Your adult child will need to give you a receipt and report the income for tax purposes.

5.4 References

The following publications and more information, including forms and brochures, can be obtained on the CRA's website at *www.canada.ca/en/revenue-agency.html* or by telephone request at 1-800-959-8281 for individual income tax and trust-related enquiries or 1-800-959-5525 for business and self-employed individual enquiries.

Guide T4040, "RRSPs and Other Registered Plans for Retirement"

Income Tax Folio S3-F10-C1, "Qualified Investments - RRSPs, RESPs, RRIFs, RDSPs and TFSAs"

Income Tax Folio S3-F10-C2, "Prohibited Investments - RRSPs, RESPs, RRIFs, RDSPs and TFSAs"

Income Tax Folio S3-F10-C3, "Advantages - RRSPs, RESPs, RRIFs, RDSPs and TFSAs"

Also, see the following selected topics on the CRA's website:

"Contributing to your spouse's or common-law partner's RRSPs"

"Withdrawing from spousal or common-law partner RRSPs"

"Guidance on the application of the split income rules for adults"

"Tax on split - income excluded shares"

Chapter 6

Capital gains and losses

- Consider delaying the sale of all or part of an asset until after year-end to defer capital gains tax (6.2.1)

- If you have unused net capital losses, carry them back or forward to offset taxable capital gains (6.2.2)

- Carry over unused "allowable business investment losses" to reduce taxable income (6.2.3)

- Classify your gains as capital gains and your losses as business losses, where possible (6.3)

- Make the Canadian securities election to ensure capital treatment for gains on your stock market transactions (6.3)

- "Purify" your corporation to create qualified small business corporation shares eligible for the lifetime capital gains exemption (6.4.1)

- Plan around your CNIL balance when using the capital gains exemption (6.4.3)

- If you've sold an asset but not received all of the proceeds, claim a capital gains reserve (6.5.1)

- Consider changing principal residence ownership to shelter gains on recreation properties (6.5.2)

- Make the election to treat rented-out property as your principal residence (6.5.2)

- Look into the tax deferral benefits for capital gains on investments in eligible small businesses (6.5.3)

Capital gains and losses are given special treatment in the federal income tax system. Capital gains are effectively taxed at a lower rate than regular income; and individuals are entitled to an exemption for capital gains on certain kinds of property.

The rules are substantially the same for Quebec purposes. In this chapter, we'll describe the rules in general and take a look at some of the planning opportunities that are available.

6.1   What is capital?

Before we get into the rules that apply to capital gains and losses, it helps to understand what we mean by "capital". Capital property is property that, if sold, will lead to a capital gain (or capital loss). The alternative is property that, when sold, leads to full income inclusion of any gain as income from business. For example, if you speculate on real estate, and you buy and sell a number of properties, your gains on the sales will probably be business income rather than capital gains.

There are no clear rules defining capital property. The *Income Tax Act*'s only comment is to define a "business" as including "an adventure or concern in the nature of trade". The courts have developed guidelines over the years, from which a general picture emerges. If you buy property with the intention of reselling it, and particularly if you sell it quickly and engage in many such transactions, your profit is likely to be considered income from business. If you buy property with the intention of earning income (e.g., rent or dividends) from it, and particularly if this is an isolated transaction and you hold the property for a long time, any gain on a sale is likely to be a capital gain.

As we'll see in 6.2.1, most capital gains are only one-half taxed and gains on certain small business shares and farm or fishing property may be eligible for the lifetime capital gains exemption (see 6.4). So it is much better to have capital gains than regular income. On the other hand, capital losses are of limited use since they can only be used to offset capital gains (see 6.2.2), while business losses can be deducted against other sources of income.

6.2 Capital gains and losses

6.2.1 Ordinary capital gains

Capital gains occur only when property is sold (or is deemed to be disposed of under special rules, which we'll see in 6.5.4). If you own, say, a rental property that has increased in value tenfold, you do not pay any tax on the increase until you actually sell the property. The capital gain is taxed only in the year of the sale.

The basic calculation of a capital gain is easy to understand: proceeds of disposition (normally the sale price), minus any selling expenses (e.g., real estate commissions), minus the "adjusted cost base", equals the capital gain. In most cases the adjusted cost base is simply your cost of the property, but this figure is "adjusted" in various ways. (For the adjusted cost base of an interest in a partnership, see 11.3.5.) Where you have used an election to trigger part of your lifetime capital gains exemption (see 6.4), your adjusted cost base will be higher than the actual cost.

Capital gains are, in effect, taxed at a lower rate than regular income. This is done by including in income only the taxable portion of the capital gain, which is one-half of the capital gain.

Example

Addy paid $5,000 (including commission) for shares of the Capital Bank in 2010. On March 1, 2020, she sells the shares for $6,100, of which her broker keeps $100 as commission.

For 2020, Addy has a capital gain of $1,000. The taxable capital gain is one-half, or $500, and this amount is included in her income for tax purposes.

We have mentioned in earlier chapters the marginal tax rates on ordinary income. With one-half taxation of capital gains, the effective tax rates are approximately:

Income level	Salary income	Capital gains (1/2)
$13,000–$49,000	23%	11.5%
$49,000–$97,000	34%	17.0%
$97,000–$150,000	42%	21.0%
$150,000–$214,000	47%	23.5%
$214,000 and up	51%	25.5%

The exact tax rates and brackets vary by province (see Appendix I). Keep in mind that the tax on split income discussed in Chapter 5 could affect tax rates on certain capital gains (see 5.2.5).

If you have very large capital gains, minimum tax may apply (see 7.6).

> Consider delaying the sale of all or part of an asset until after year-end to defer capital gains tax.

If you sell an asset after the end of the year, any tax on the capital gain will be payable one year later, giving you the use of the funds for an extra year, except to the extent you are required to make quarterly tax instalments (see 9.2.2). A sale on December 31, 2020 will require tax to be paid by April 30, 2021; a sale on January 1, 2021 will require tax to be paid by April 30, 2022.

Note that most stock and bond market transactions normally settle two business days after the trade is entered. (This is standard practice in the brokerage industry and is recognized by the CRA.) Because weekends and public holidays may affect the determination of "business days", if you intend to do any last-minute 2020 trades, consider completing all trades before Christmas (i.e., before December 25) and be sure to check the settlement date with your broker to ensure the trade settles before December 31.

In some circumstances, you may wish to sell half of an asset at the end of December and the other half at the beginning of January. Doing this will split your capital gain across the two years. This can be beneficial for two reasons. First, you may be able to reduce the marginal rate that applies in both years by keeping your total taxable income below the high tax bracket threshold for each year (which is about $214,000 for 2020). Second, you may be able to avoid minimum tax, due to the $40,000 minimum tax exemption available for each year (see 7.6).

6.2.2 Ordinary capital losses

A capital loss occurs when the capital gain calculation produces a negative amount; that is, the adjusted cost base is greater than the proceeds of disposition minus the selling expenses. Just as capital gains are less heavily taxed than regular income, capital losses are less useful to you than regular (business) losses.

An allowable capital loss is *one-half* of a capital loss. This amount can only be offset against taxable capital gains. In normal circumstances, if you have no taxable capital gains, the loss *cannot* be used against other income.

Example

Nate earns an annual salary of $90,000. In October 2020, Nate sells some shares of a bank, which cost him $2,000 several years before, for $5,000 after commission. In November 2020, he sells some shares of an Internet-based company he bought in 2000 for $18,000, and receives only $9,000 since the price of the stock has come down.

Nate has a $3,000 capital gain on the bank shares, which is a $1,500 taxable capital gain. He also has a $9,000 capital loss on the Internet company shares, which is a $4,500 allowable capital loss. This allowable capital loss wipes out the taxable capital gain, but the extra $3,000 of allowable capital loss cannot be used to reduce his salary income of $90,000. This loss can only be used against taxable capital gains of other years, as outlined below.

If you have unused net capital losses, carry them back or forward to offset taxable capital gains.

Allowable capital losses that cannot be used in any given year, as in this example, can be carried back and applied against taxable capital gains of any of the previous three years, subject to whether the capital gains exemption was used in that prior year. They can also be carried forward indefinitely; this balance is known as "net capital losses" and can be used against taxable capital gains in any future year. The inclusion rate for loss carryovers (e.g., for losses occurring before October 20, 2000, when the inclusion rate was higher) is adjusted to match the inclusion rate of the taxation year in which they are used.

If you have any net capital losses that cannot be used in the current year, look into whether you can carry them back to any of your three prior years' returns. The CRA and Revenu Québec are required to reopen and reassess your return when you make such a claim. Make sure as well that you keep track of any such losses that you cannot carry back, and carry them forward to use in future years.

6.2.3 Allowable business investment losses

There is an exception to the general rule that allowable capital losses cannot be used against ordinary income. The exception applies to allowable business investment losses, which arise when there is a loss on shares of, or debt owing by, a small business corporation. The availability of an "allowable business investment loss" (ABIL) is an extra incentive to invest in private Canadian businesses.

The term "small business corporation" has a very specific meaning in the *Income Tax Act*. It need not, in fact, be small. The corporation must meet a number of tests, such that it be resident in Canada, a private corporation, not controlled in any manner by non-residents or public corporations, not listed on a Canadian or any of about 25 foreign stock exchanges, and, most importantly, that all or substantially all (taken by the CRA to mean 90% or more of the value) of its assets be used in an active business carried on primarily in Canada. Shares and debts in other small business corporations can qualify as such assets.

A capital loss on the shares or debt of a small business corporation (including, in some cases, simply determining that the debt has gone bad and will not be repaid) is called a "business investment loss". One-half of this amount is the ABIL, which can be deducted against any other income such as employment income or investment income. However, the amount of the ABIL that can be deducted against other income must be reduced by any capital gains exemption claimed in prior years. The amount of this reduction is treated as an allowable capital loss, which you can use to offset any taxable capital gains. In addition, if an ABIL is deducted against other income, you must realize an equal amount of taxable capital gains in later years before you can use the capital gains exemption again.

> **Example**
>
> Laura carries on business as the proprietor of a clothing store, from which she nets $120,000 per year in business income. In 2002, Laura invested $20,000 in shares in XYZ Jewellery Inc., a corporation run by her sister that meets the definition of "small business corporation". In December 2020, the corporation goes bankrupt and Laura's shares become worthless.
>
> Laura has a $20,000 business investment loss in 2020, resulting in a $10,000 allowable business investment loss. She can use this against her $120,000 business income, and so will be taxed in 2020 on the net amount of only $110,000.

Allowable business investment losses that cannot be fully used (because you have already wiped out all of your income) are treated similar to business losses (see 11.4.1). That is, they can be carried back and used to

Carry over unused ABILs to reduce taxable income.

offset income in any of the three previous years (even though you have already filed returns and paid tax for those years), or they can be carried forward and used to offset income in any of the next 10 years. Any unused balance remaining after the 10th year is reclassified as a net capital loss.

6.3 Capital gains vs. income

Depending on the nature of your activities, there may be some question about whether your gains or losses from disposing of property are capital in nature or instead are fully taxable as business income or deductible as business losses.

Normally it is advantageous to classify your gains as capital gains and your losses as business losses, to the extent possible within the law. Where your activities do not lend themselves to a clear distinction between income and capital, you may have some leeway to

Classify your gains as capital gains and your losses as business losses, where possible.

classify the transaction as either. Of course, you should be consistent; you could not take two essentially identical dispositions and call one a capital gain and the other a business loss.

If you are audited, the CRA could reassess you on your classifications of a property sale as income vs. capital. You would then have to decide whether to appeal the assessment via a Notice of Objection (see 9.5.1) or to accept it and pay the resulting tax liability, plus accrued interest. If you are unsure as to whether property you own is capital property or not, you should consult your professional adviser.

If you wish to ensure that your current and future trades on the stock market will always result in capital gains rather than business income, you may file an "Election on Disposition of Canadian Securities" (federal Form T123) with your tax return. This will prevent the CRA or Revenu Québec from claiming that you are buying securities for the purpose of selling them and therefore earning business income rather than capital gains.

> Make the Canadian securities election to ensure capital treatment for gains on your stock market transactions.

Once you do so, all "Canadian securities" you ever own will be considered capital property for the rest of your life. This includes, generally, shares in Canadian corporations, investments in mutual funds, and bonds, debentures or other debt issued by individuals or corporations resident in Canada (except a corporation related to you). Certain taxpayers, such as traders and dealers, are not allowed to make this election.

The downside of making the election is that you will never be able to claim losses on Canadian securities as business losses in the future. Since this position is generally difficult to establish for shares anyway, this may not be a significant drawback. You should consider your entire financial position and obtain professional advice to determine the likely effects of the election.

6.4 The lifetime capital gains exemption

Every individual (but not a trust or corporation) is entitled to a lifetime "capital gains exemption" of up to $883,384 for 2020 on certain small business shares. This exemption amount is indexed for inflation annually.

For certain farm and fishing property, the exemption is $1 million (see 6.4.2).

Technically, under the *Income Tax Act* and on the CRA's forms, the exemption is called the capital gains *deduction*. Where it applies, the taxable capital gain is still included in income for tax purposes (see 6.2.1), but an offsetting deduction from net income is allowed when computing "taxable income", the last step on the tax return before calculating tax and tax credits (see 2.1.1).

Note that your $883,384 (or $1 million exemption for farming and fishing property) is limited to the *total* gains on both small business shares and family farming and fishing businesses over your lifetime. If in 2020, for example, you have already claimed an exemption of $600,000 against a capital gain on qualifying small business corporation shares, the maximum remaining exemption available to you for other small business shares would be reduced to $283,384. For eligible farming and fishing property, the amount remaining would be $400,000.

6.4.1 Qualified small business corporation shares

As noted in 6.4, up to $883,384 of capital gains on "qualified small business corporation shares" can be sheltered from tax by the lifetime capital gains exemption.

The meaning of "small business corporation" was discussed in 6.2.3. The definition of "qualified small business corporation share" is very complex. In very general terms:

- all or substantially all (considered by the CRA to mean 90% or more of the value) of the business's assets must be used for carrying on an active business in Canada or be shares and debt in other small business corporations (or any combination thereof);
- nobody but you or a person "related" to you can have owned the shares for the two years before you sell them; and
- throughout the two-year period, more than 50% of the corporation's assets must have been used principally in an active business carried on in Canada or invested in other small business corporations (or any combination thereof).

Consult your tax adviser for details as to how these rules apply to any shares you own.

> **Example**
>
> Jacinta has not used any of her lifetime capital gains exemption in the past. She owns all the shares of a corporation. The shares, which are "qualified small business corporation shares", originally cost her $20,000. On March 1, 2020, Jacinta sells the shares for $200,000.
>
> Jacinta's capital gain is $180,000. One-half of the gain, or $90,000, is included in Jacinta's income for 2020, but an offsetting capital gains deduction of $90,000 is allowed in computing her "taxable income"—so she pays no extra tax, except possibly for minimum tax (see 7.6). Of her $883,384 lifetime exemption that is fully available in 2020, Jacinta still has $703,384 ($883,384 minus $180,000) of capital gains, or $351,692 of taxable capital gains, that can be exempt in the future.

As you can see from the example, it doesn't matter whether you think of the exemption as covering $883,384 (in the example, $180,000 plus $703,384) of capital gains, or $441,692 ($90,000 plus $351,692) of taxable capital gains. It comes to the same thing.

If you own shares in a small business, and are considering selling them or transferring them to a family member, you should investigate whether the corporation's shares qualify for the lifetime capital gains exemption. There may be steps you can take to "purify" the corporation so that it meets the criteria discussed above.

> "Purify" your corporation to create qualified small business corporation shares eligible for the lifetime capital gains exemption.

It is also possible to transfer the assets of a business that you carry on personally (as a proprietor) into a corporation on a tax-free basis in order to take advantage of the lifetime capital gains exemption. This procedure, known as a "section 85 rollover", requires professional advice, as do other mechanisms for "crystallizing", or locking in, the lifetime capital gains exemption (see 14.1).

There is also a special election that lets you take advantage of the exemption for qualified small business corporation shares if the corporation goes public, without having to actually sell the shares. (Once the corporation becomes a public corporation, the shares no longer qualify for the lifetime capital gains exemption.)

Because the exemption amount is indexed (resulting in annual increases), you may benefit by disposing of shares early in a year rather than later in the previous year if it makes sense from a business perspective.

6.4.2 Qualified farm and fishing property

The lifetime capital gains exemption generally applies to property used in a family farming or fishing business that meets certain conditions. In general terms, the property will qualify if you have owned the property for at least two years before you sell it, have used the property in the business of farming or fishing on a regular and continuous basis, and have earned more gross income from farming or fishing than from other sources. (If you acquired a farm property before June 18, 1987, it will be qualified farm property if it was used in the business of farming by you or a family member either in the year you sell it or in any five previous years.) Similar rules allow the exemption to be claimed for capital gains realized on the sale of shares of a family farm or fishing corporation or an interest in a family farm or fishing partnership.

If you own farm or fishing property that you are considering selling, you should obtain professional advice to determine whether you are eligible for the lifetime capital gains exemption.

6.4.3 Restrictions on use of the exemption

The *Income Tax Act* provides rules to prevent people from taking what is considered unfair advantage of the lifetime capital gains exemption. The exemption is supposed to exempt capital gains from being taxed. If, however, you are able to use the system of capital gains taxation to claim capital-related losses against other income, the rules prevent you from getting the exemption as well. We'll look at the details in this section.

Allowable business investment losses

If you have allowable business investment losses (see 6.2.3), your available capital gains exemption claim will be restricted to the extent that the ABILs are or can be written off against your ordinary income. The idea is that such losses should effectively be netted against your taxable capital gains first. In other words, you cannot both have a gain that is sheltered by the capital gains exemption and also use allowable business investment losses against your other income.

Cumulative net investment loss (CNIL)

As discussed in 7.2.3, interest paid on a loan is deductible if you use the loan to invest in shares. Even though your reason for buying the shares may be to obtain capital gains, the fact that the shares *could* pay dividends (which are income from property) is generally considered enough to make the interest on the loan deductible as interest on funds borrowed to earn income from property.

Tax policy-makers consider it unfair for people to be able to take out large loans, write off the interest, and use the funds to buy shares that would increase in value, giving them a capital gain that is tax-free due to the capital gains exemption. This kind of "double-dipping" is not allowed.

Your capital gains deduction (normally taken, as we have seen, when calculating your "taxable income") is therefore *reduced* by the amount of your cumulative net investment loss, or CNIL (pronounced "see-nile"). The basic idea is that if you borrow money, buy an investment and the investment goes up in value, you should not be able to get both the capital gains exemption and your interest expense write-off.

The actual calculation is rather more complicated. Your CNIL is the total of your investment expenses minus all your investment income, cumulative since January 1, 1988. "Investment expenses" include interest you have deducted, investment counsel fees, partnership losses (except where you are an active partner), losses from rental property, and most tax shelter write-offs. Investment income includes interest, dividends ("grossed-up" as explained in 7.1.2), rental income and income from a partnership where you are not an active partner.

Example

Ian has not used any of his lifetime capital gains exemption in the past, but has claimed a total of $10,000 in net investment expenses since 1995, so his CNIL balance is $10,000. He owns all the shares of a corporation. The shares, which are "qualified small business corporation shares", originally cost him $20,000. On March 1, 2020, Ian sells the shares for $200,000.

Ian's capital gain is $180,000. One-half of the gain, or $90,000, is included in Ian's income for 2020. Because of his $10,000 CNIL balance, the offsetting capital gains deduction is only $80,000, not $90,000.

In effect, Ian must "eat through" his CNIL balance and pay tax on the $10,000 before he can start to use his capital gains exemption.

Note that the CNIL limitation applies even though the investment expenses and the capital gain are unrelated. However, taxable capital gains that are actually taxed, because you cannot or do not offset them with your lifetime capital gains exemption, effectively reduce the impact of the CNIL balance.

Note also that the calculation of the exemption (and CNIL) is done at the end of the year. It is therefore possible to realize a capital gain that you think is exempt, but for which you cannot claim the exemption because you create a CNIL balance later on in the same year. So if you have a

> Plan around your CNIL balance when using the capital gains exemption.

CNIL balance, consider reducing or eliminating it before the end of the year. This can be done by increasing your investment income. For example, if you are the owner-manager of an incorporated business (see Chapter 14), you may be able to reduce your salary and increase your dividends from the corporation to use up your CNIL balance. There may also be situations where you can advance interest income receipts before the end of the year, or defer deductible interest payments until after December 31, to reduce your CNIL.

6.5 Special cases

6.5.1 Reserves

If you sell a property for a capital gain but do not receive all of the proceeds right away, you may be able to claim a reserve, to defer recognition of the gain for tax purposes.

If you've sold an asset but not received all of the proceeds, claim a capital gains reserve.

Suppose, for example, you sell a house you have been renting out. The house cost you $200,000 and you sell it for $400,000. But you take back a mortgage for $200,000. You can normally claim a reserve on the capital gain, reflecting the fraction of the sale price that you haven't yet received. In this case, since you haven't received half of the sale price, you would only have to recognize half of the gain in the year of sale.

However, under the reserve rules, you must recognize at least 1/5 of the gain each year (cumulatively), so that the entire capital gain must be accounted for by the fourth year after the year of sale. (A longer capital gains reserve period is allowed when you sell farming and fishing property to your child—see 15.4.3.)

Claiming a reserve might not be beneficial where you may be in a higher tax bracket in later years or if it will cause a clawback of your Old Age Security benefits for multiple years (see 20.3.2).

6.5.2 Principal residence

A gain on selling your home is normally completely exempt from taxation. The exemption is based on the definition of "principal residence". This term includes, among other things, a house, a condominium and a share in a co-operative housing corporation. It also includes the land around the house, but normally only up to 1/2 hectare (about 1.2 acres).

You, or your spouse or child, must have "ordinarily inhabited" the residence for it to qualify, so you can't use the exemption on property you rent out without ever having lived in it, or for vacant land. However, it need not have been your "principal" residence in a literal sense. It can be a cottage, for example.

If you sell your principal residence, you are required to report certain information on your income tax return. This information includes the address of the property, the date you acquired it, and the amount of the disposition proceeds. You must designate the property as your principal residence in your return. In addition to reporting the sale and designating it on your return, you must also complete a special designation form, Form T2091, "Designation of a Property as a Principal Residence by an Individual (Other Than a Personal Trust)".

Since 1982, each family unit is limited to one "principal residence" at a time. For this purpose, the family unit means you, your spouse (including a common-law spouse as outlined in 2.2.1) and any unmarried children under 18. So if you designate your house as your principal residence for a period of several years, your spouse cannot also designate your cottage as a principal residence over the same period.

Before 1982, each taxpayer was entitled to a principal residence exemption. So if you and your spouse or another member of your family unit have owned two residences (such as a regular home and a summer cottage) since before 1982, it may be possible to structure your holdings so that the pre-1982 portion of the capital gain on the second residence will be exempt. Consult a professional adviser on this matter.

Consider changing principal residence ownership to shelter gains on recreation properties.

If you have adult children, consider giving them the ownership of a second residence. If you own your house and your 19-year-old son owns the cottage, he can designate it as his principal residence when he sells it. However, at the time you transfer it to him, you generally will have to recognize any increase in value since you purchased it. You should also be sure you are satisfied with the legal effect of what you are doing—giving away your cottage—before you embark on such a transaction for tax purposes. Of course, you should also consider any other taxes that could apply, such as Land Transfer Tax.

An exemption is also available in some cases where you rent the property out, either before or after you use it as your own residence. If you move out of your home and rent it out, you can continue to designate it as your residence for up to four years (provided you do not claim any other property as your principal residence and you file a special election with your tax return for the year in which you begin to rent the property). If you move due to relocation of your or your spouse's employment, the four-year period can normally be extended indefinitely, provided you move back to the home upon leaving that employment. However, if you claim capital cost allowance (CCA, see 11.2.7) on the property, it rescinds the election to extend the period in which the principal residence exemption may be claimed.

Make the election to treat rented-out property as your principal residence.

If you acquire property and rent it out, and then move in at some later date, you can file a special election with your tax return for the year in which you move in to defer the capital gain that would normally apply when you change the property from income-earning to personal-use. If you do this, you may be able to get an exemption for four years during which you rented the property. This election may not be allowed if CCA has been claimed on the property when it was income-producing.

6.5.3 Capital gains rollover for investments in eligible small businesses

Look into the tax deferral benefits for capital gains on investments in eligible small businesses.

Under a tax incentive to encourage investments in small business corporations, individual investors may defer capital gains on a small business investment where the proceeds from the investment are used to make other small business investments. The deferred gain reduces the tax cost of the new investment, which may be subject to tax when it is disposed of later.

Example

On March 31, 2020, Will sells an eligible share investment in Bio Ventures Inc. for $100,000. Since Will had initially invested $40,000 in the company, he realizes a capital gain of $60,000. If only $90,000 of the total proceeds is reinvested in shares of the replacement investment, Agri Tek Inc., then 90% of the gain can be deferred, or $54,000. Will's capital gain, one-half of which will be subject to tax, is equal to the portion that cannot be deferred, or $6,000. The deferred gain of $54,000 reduces the adjusted cost base of the Agri Tek Inc. shares to $36,000, resulting in a potentially larger gain when the shares are sold in the future.

There are currently no limits on the total amount that can be reinvested. You do not have to deal at arm's length with the corporation you are investing in.

To qualify for the rollover treatment, an investment must be ordinary common shares issued from the treasury of an eligible "small business corporation" (see 6.2.3). At the time of the share issue, the total carrying value of the corporation's assets and the assets of any related corporations cannot exceed $50 million. Throughout the period the investor holds the shares, the issuing corporation must be an eligible "active business corporation" (that is, the company must essentially meet the tests for a small business corporation, except that it does not need to remain a private corporation).

Among other requirements, you must hold the eligible investment for six months before a gain can be deferred. You must acquire the replacement investment at any time in the year of the disposition or within 120 days after the end of that year. For example, if you sell an investment in 2020, you must acquire another by April 30, 2021 to qualify for the deferral.

6.5.4 Other rules

Death—When you die, you are generally deemed for tax purposes to have sold your capital property for its current fair market value, thus triggering a capital gain on all of the increase in value that has accrued since you purchased it. The treatment of capital gains on death is discussed in detail in 22.2.3.

Non-arm's-length transfers—When you give or sell property to a member of your family, you are normally deemed to have received fair market value for it, triggering recognition of any accrued capital gain (or loss) for tax purposes. However, if you transfer property to your spouse, it is normally deemed to have been sold at your cost unless you elect to realize a gain. This rule also applies to common-law spouses who meet the criteria outlined in 2.2.1.

Personal-use property—No capital loss is available on personal-use property, except for "listed personal property" (jewellery, works of art, stamps, coins and rare books) losses that can be used only against listed personal property gains.

As well, the adjusted cost base and proceeds of disposition of personal-use property are deemed to be $1,000, which essentially means that capital gains on personal-use property only apply to the extent the sale price exceeds $1,000. The $1,000 deemed adjusted cost base and deemed proceeds of disposition do not apply if the property is acquired as part of an arrangement in which the property is donated as a charitable gift.

If you change a property from personal use to income-earning use, you are normally deemed to have sold it at its fair market value, requiring you to recognize for tax purposes any accrued capital gain.

Options—Special rules apply to determine capital gains where you purchase or grant options (e.g., on the stock market).

Superficial loss—If you sell property (e.g., shares) to trigger a capital loss, and you or your spouse or a corporation controlled by either of you acquire identical property within 30 days before or after your sale, the capital loss will be a "superficial loss" and ignored for tax purposes. The denied loss will be added to the cost of the identical property.

Insurance or expropriation proceeds—If property of yours is lost or destroyed or expropriated, any insurance settlement or expropriation payment is considered proceeds of disposition for purposes of the capital gains calculation described in 6.2.1.

Charitable donations—If you donate certain capital property to a registered charity, you may not have to pay tax on any inherent capital gain but you can still get a tax credit for the full value of the donation (see 8.2.2).

Pre-1972 property—If you have property that you have owned since before 1972, when capital gains were not taxed at all, only the gain accruing after 1971 will be taxed. For publicly traded shares, valuation is easy; for real estate and shares in private businesses, valuation as of December 31, 1971 may be difficult to determine. When you report such a gain, you will need to estimate the value of the property on that date, and use that as the cost of the property (assuming it is higher than your actual cost).

6.6   References

The following publications and more information, including forms and brochures, can be obtained on the CRA's website at *www.canada.ca/en/revenue-agency.html* or by telephone request at 1-800-959-8281 for individual income tax and trust-related enquiries or 1-800-959-5525 for business and self-employed individual enquiries.

Guide T4037, "Capital Gains"
Income Tax Folio S1-F3-C2, "Principal Residence"
Income Tax Folio S4-F8-C1, "Business Investment Losses"
Income Tax Folio S3-F10-C1, "Qualified Investments - RRSPs, RESPs, RRIFs, RDSPs and TFSAs"

Chapter 7

Investments

- Consider acquiring preferred shares instead of debt to reduce the overall tax rate (7.1.2)

- If you're the higher-income spouse, consider electing to report your spouse's dividend income on your own return (7.1.6)

- Look into the potential benefits of investing in a dividend reinvestment plan (7.1.7)

- Defer tax by acquiring investments that mature shortly after year-end (7.2.1)

- Structure your investments to make interest deductible (7.2.3)

- Consider the merits of acquiring an exempt life insurance contract (7.3.2)

- If you're considering investing in tax shelters, don't let tax write-offs drive your decision (7.5)

- Before investing in a tax shelter, obtain its identification number (7.5.1)

- Be aware of the possible impact of minimum tax on otherwise tax-free capital gains (7.6.3)

In this chapter, we look at how investment income is taxed, how interest expense can be written off, and a few types of tax shelters, along with a number of tax planning ideas that you should keep in mind. We also discuss special tax rules that apply to foreign investments. The chapter concludes with a discussion of Canada's alternative minimum tax, which may apply depending on the nature of your investments. For advice on developing an appropriate investment strategy, see 1.1.4.

7.1 Dividends

7.1.1 What is a dividend?

A dividend is a distribution of after-tax profits to the shareholders (owners) of a corporation. A corporation may have many classes of shares. Preferred shares often have priority over common shares on the payment of dividends and also have priority over common shares on the winding-up of a corporation.

Preferred shares typically pay a fixed annual or quarterly dividend. In some ways, they are similar to bonds or other debt, since the return is a fixed percentage. However, in certain situations a corporation may not be *required* to pay dividends on its preferred shares as long as it does not pay dividends on its common shares. If the corporation suffers losses, its board of directors may well decide not to pay dividends on preferred shares.

From a tax point of view, for individuals, preferred shares are generally identical to common shares (which typically pay dividends that bear some relationship to the corporation's profits).

7.1.2 How is a dividend taxed?

Dividends received by individuals from Canadian corporations are taxed in a rather peculiar manner, designed to reflect the fact that the corporation paying the dividend has already paid tax on its profits. The amount included in the individual's income is "grossed-up" to notionally reflect the total amount of pre-tax income that the corporation is presumed to have earned. The individual then receives a credit to offset the tax the corporation is presumed to have paid. In no case, however, is the *actual* income earned or tax paid by the corporation taken into account.

"Eligible" Canadian dividends received by individuals from public corporations and Canadian-controlled private corporations (CCPCs) that have been paid out of business income taxed at the high corporate tax rate are grossed-up by 38% for 2020. That is, you add 38% to the amount received and show the total as income from dividends on your tax return. The offsetting federal dividend tax credit for 2020 is 15% of the grossed-up dividend (i.e., 20.7% of the actual dividend). Similar credits are available at the provincial level.

Dividends received from CCPCs that pay tax at the small business rate (see 14.1) are treated differently. These "non-eligible" dividends are grossed-up by 15% for 2020, and the federal dividend tax credit for 2020 is 9% of the grossed-up dividend (i.e., 10.4% of the actual dividend).

In 2020, assuming the highest marginal tax rate applies, eligible dividends are taxed at combined federal and provincial rates ranging from 29.64% to 42.62%. Non-eligible dividends are taxed at rates ranging from 40.37% to 48.89%, depending on your province of residence.

> **Example**
>
> Melissa earns $80,000 of employment income per year. She also owns shares in Canadian Inc., a public company, which pay her a dividend of $1,000 in 2020.
>
> Melissa's income for 2020 will be $80,000, plus the $1,000 dividend, plus a gross-up of 38% of the dividend, or $380. Her tax will be calculated on this income of $81,380. From the tax, she will deduct her regular credits (see Chapter 2) and a federal dividend tax credit of $207 (20.7% of the actual dividend). Melissa then calculates her provincial dividend tax credit in a similar fashion. The net result is that the dividend is taxed at a significantly lower rate than the marginal rate of about 34% that applies to her ordinary income.

(See 14.2.1 for more detail on the dividend tax credit from the perspective of the corporation.)

Remember that this information applies only to dividends from Canadian corporations. Dividends from foreign corporations are taxed as ordinary income.

Since preferred shares pay dividends rather than interest (which is taxed like regular income, as we'll see in 7.2), preferred shares may offer a better after-tax rate of return than many interest-earning investments while still coming close to a guaranteed yield. While the yield is never completely guaranteed, many major public companies will continue to meet preferred share dividend expectations even when they suffer losses.

> Consider acquiring preferred shares instead of debt to reduce the overall tax rate.

The yields on preferred shares usually reflect the fact that dividends are less heavily taxed than interest (as well as the fact that dividend payments are not deductible to the corporation). You or your investment adviser will have to monitor preferred share distributions and prices on the market to find the best yields.

7.1.3 Stock dividends

A corporation will sometimes pay a stock dividend by issuing new shares to pay the dividend rather than giving you cash. In such a case, the gross-up and dividend tax credit still apply, and you must pay tax on the stock dividend even though you have received no cash. The amount of the dividend on which the gross-up is calculated is the increase in the corporate paid-up capital resulting from the issue of new shares. If you sell the stock in order to produce cash to pay the tax, you may also have a capital gain or loss.

7.1.4 Capital dividends

You may also receive capital dividends from private corporations. They are completely tax-free (see 5.3.8). A capital dividend is generally a distribution of the untaxed one-half of capital gains realized by the corporation. As we saw in 6.2.1, that fraction of the capital gain is not taxed at all. The capital dividend mechanism is used to distribute the untaxed portion without any tax consequences to the shareholder. (For an example, see 14.2.4.)

7.1.5 Dividends received by a corporation

Intercorporate dividends are normally tax-free, subject to certain anti-avoidance rules that may apply to deem an otherwise tax-free amount to be a taxable capital gain. The common assumption is that once a corporation has paid tax on its income, its profits can be distributed through a chain of holding corporations with no further tax consequences until an individual receives a dividend at the end of the chain. However, a special refundable tax—"Part IV tax"—can apply to intercorporate dividends in some circumstances, including most dividends received on investments in public corporations. The Part IV tax rate for certain corporations is 38-1/3%. Since intercorporate dividends may be taxable in certain other circumstances, professional advice in this area is strongly recommended.

7.1.6 Election to transfer dividends from spouse

Since the dividend tax credit is a credit against tax owing, it is worthless if there is no tax to pay. If your spouse's income is very low, remember that any income your spouse earns in the year reduces the spousal credit amount dollar for dollar and that no spousal credit is available for 2020 once your spouse's income is approximately $13,229 or more. Thus any amount of the grossed-up dividend income reported on your spouse's return can reduce your spousal tax credit. At the same time, since your spouse does not pay any tax, the dividend tax credit is of no use.

If you're the higher-income spouse, consider electing to report your spouse's dividend income on your own return.

In such a case, you may elect to report all of your spouse's dividend income on your own tax return. While this may result in the income being taxed at a higher rate, it will avoid the erosion of the spousal tax credit. You will have to calculate tax both ways to see which is better. This election is done by including the dividends directly on Schedule 4 (Investment income) of your tax return, not Schedule 2 (Amounts transferred from spouse). If you live in Quebec, you do not need to make the similar election for Quebec tax purposes. Quebec taxpayers can claim the unused portion of their spouse's non-refundable tax credits, including the dividend tax credit (see 17.2).

7.1.7 Dividend reinvestment plan (DRIP)

Look into the potential benefits of investing in a dividend reinvestment plan.

Dividend reinvestment plans may offer a cost-effective way of building your investment portfolio. DRIPs give investors the opportunity to automatically reinvest their cash dividends by purchasing additional shares or fractional shares directly from the company on the dividend payment date. The additional shares are usually purchased at a discount from the current share price and without brokerage commissions.

Many of these plans allow you to periodically purchase more shares of the company with cash at a discount for nominal or no fees. (Depending on the nature of the plan, the discount may trigger a taxable shareholder benefit—check with your broker or the plan's administrator to avoid surprises.)

Bear in mind that you will still be liable for tax on the dividends in the current year. Because the dividend income is reinvested, you will have to pay the tax with other funds (or sell some of your investment). Amounts reinvested will also incrementally increase the cost base of your investment, which will affect the average cost of the shares for capital gains tax purposes when you sell them (see 6.2.1).

7.2 Interest income

Interest income is taxed at the same rates as employment or business income.

7.2.1 Accruing interest

Suppose you acquire a five-year GIC for $1,000 that will return $1,160 after five years (assuming a compound interest rate of 3%). When do you report the $160 in interest?

Each year you must declare the interest accrued to the anniversary date of when you acquired it. Your financial institution should issue you a T5 slip showing the interest accruing on all such long-term investments, regardless of whether you receive the cash.

Example

In 2015, Christine lent $10,000 to her cousin, Ben, who is attending university and needed the funds for tuition and residence. Ben agreed in writing to pay 6% annual interest (not compounded) on the loan, but that he will not pay back the loan or the interest until after he has graduated and secures a job.

Christine is required to report and pay tax on $600 of accrued interest income each year beginning in 2016. If, in 2020, Ben pays her $13,000 to cover the loan and all interest, she will only report $600 as income in 2020, since she will have already reported $2,400 over the previous four years (2016-2019).

The accrual rules apply to almost all kinds of investments, including strip bonds (see 7.2.2 below), Canada Savings Bonds, and mortgages or loans to third parties or to relatives on which interest is allowed to accrue.

> Defer tax by acquiring investments that mature shortly after year-end.

As a general tax deferral strategy, acquire investments that mature shortly after year-end rather than just before. For example, if you are investing in T-bills on July 15, 2020 and you can choose between maturity dates of December 29, 2020 and January 2, 2021, then you should choose January 2 if all else is equal. That way you will defer reporting and paying tax on the income by one year. Of course, tax considerations should not override normal investment considerations, such as the available rates of return and the question of when you will need access to the funds.

7.2.2 Strip bonds and clipped coupons

Strip bonds are long-term government or government-backed (e.g., provincial hydro) bonds that pay interest when their coupons are cashed in. A typical bond might have a 20-year term, have a face value of $100,000, and come with coupons paying $2,500 in interest, cashable every six months. At the end of the 20 years one simply redeems the bond for $100,000.

Brokerage firms often acquire such bonds and split up the bond and its coupons, selling them separately. The $100,000 bond maturing in 20 years, in our example, might be sold for $10,000, while the forty $2,500 coupons would be sold at prices reflecting the length of time until their maturity.

For tax purposes, the difference between the discounted price of the bond (or coupon) and the amount you receive when it is redeemed is considered interest. Because of the annual accrual rule, such bonds generally are unattractive to many taxpayers—you have to pay tax annually on interest that you will not receive for some time. However, they can be excellent investments for self-directed RRSPs and other tax-deferred plans (see Chapters 3 and 4).

Be cautious when acquiring strip bonds or clipped coupons—or, for that matter, any long-term bond. If you need to sell them before they mature, you will find that their value may fluctuate considerably due to trends in interest rates. If interest rates in general have gone up, the resale value of your bond or coupon will likely have gone down.

7.2.3 Deductibility of interest expense

As a general principle, interest is deductible for tax purposes as long as the loan was used for the purpose of earning income from a business or property. Such expenses are also called "carrying charges".

If you borrow money to buy common or preferred shares on the stock market, or to invest in a business, the interest you pay is generally deductible. Similarly, if you buy an investment with a fixed interest rate, you generally can deduct interest on your loan.

Interest is not deductible if the loan is taken out for some purpose other than to earn income subject to tax. Examples include:

- home mortgage, except to the extent you use a home office for business purposes (see 11.2.10)
- car loan, where the car is used solely for personal use
- credit cards, except to the extent the charges are for business expenses
- loan to contribute to an RRSP, TFSA or RESP
- interest on late income tax or instalment payments.

If you dispose of the property that you borrowed money to acquire, you can continue to deduct the interest in certain cases even though the underlying source of income has been lost. The rules in this area are complex, and professional advice may be required if you are in this situation.

For Quebec purposes, you may only deduct expenses paid to earn income from property from your investment income earned in the year (see 17.11.1).

Interest on a car loan, where the car is used for your employment or business purposes, is limited to the employment or business portion of $300 per month (see 12.3.1).

Structure your investments to make interest deductible.

Since interest on consumer loans and home mortgages is normally not deductible, while interest on loans taken out to purchase income-generating investments is generally deductible, you should try to ensure that all loans you take out are for a deductible purpose. For example, if you have funds that you could put towards either a home mortgage or investments and you plan to do both, you will probably be better off to use the funds towards the mortgage and take out a loan to purchase the investments.

The CRA often pays special attention to deductions for interest expense. It is wise to keep on file, along with your tax return, accurate records showing the amount of the loan, the purpose of the loan and the interest paid during the year, along with the relevant financial statements and possibly a confirming letter from your financial institution.

For minimum tax purposes, interest expense must be added back to your income if it relates to tax shelters or other "tainted" deductions (see 7.6.2.).

7.3 Other tax-effective investments

7.3.1 Mutual funds

Mutual funds are pools of assets that are invested by professional managers, either in general investments or in a particular sector (such as real estate or natural resources). Investors purchase units if the mutual fund is a trust or purchase shares if the fund is a corporation.

Mutual fund trusts are flow-through entities for tax purposes—taxable income earned inside the entity is treated as if you held the investments directly, instead of through the fund. As such, the income retains its character for tax purposes (e.g., as dividend income, capital gains or interest) when it is distributed to you during the time you own the units, and taxed accordingly. A management fee, also known as a management expense ratio, is paid from income earned by the fund to compensate the fund's professional managers. Although the fee is a cost of the fund itself, the amount of the fee will affect your rate of return.

When you redeem or sell the units or shares, you are taxed on the capital gain, if any, according to the regular treatment of capital gains discussed in 6.2.1.

7.3.2 Exempt life insurance contracts

The life insurance industry has developed attractive and highly sophisticated products that can help you meet two objectives at once: having insurance coverage and providing retirement income from tax-sheltered growth.

These policies allow you to pay insurance premiums and make deposits to a tax-sheltered investment account at the same time. You can choose between more conservative investments, such as GICs, or investments that involve more risk, such as equity indices. Unlike RRSP contributions, which are tax-deductible and thus are made with before-tax dollars, insurance premiums are not deductible. In both cases, the income earned is tax-sheltered until maturity of the plan or policy. Funds withdrawn from the policy during your lifetime are taxable to the extent the amount withdrawn exceeds its adjusted cost basis. On death, the entire amount (that is, the original insurance amount plus the accumulated cash value) is received tax-free as a death benefit. Alternatively, funds withdrawn may be treated as a loan against your policy that is repaid from the death benefit.

> Consider the merits of acquiring an exempt life insurance contract.

If you have maximized your TFSA and RRSP contributions, this type of life insurance policy may provide another opportunity for you to shelter your savings from tax.

Keep in mind that new rules reduce the maximum amount of tax-exempt savings allowed inside new insurance policies, starting January 1, 2017. These rules generally do not apply to existing policies.

There are many issues to look at when considering whether to acquire such a contract, such as the underlying mortality costs and administrative expenses, a guaranteed minimum rate of return compared to a similar return in a non-tax sheltered environment, your required life insurance coverage, your income objectives, investment management fees, the financial reserves and strength of the insurance company and so on. Professional advice is a must when assessing the merits of this type of "investment". Insurance policies are, however, a potential opportunity for those who cannot otherwise find alternative tax deferral arrangements.

Life insurance is discussed in more detail at 21.7.

7.4 Special rules for investments in foreign property

Over the past few years, tax rules and reporting requirements have been introduced to address the government's perception that many Canadians are avoiding Canadian tax by transferring their assets and income outside of the country. Some of these rules are discussed below.

The tax rules in this area are complex and penalties for non-compliance may be onerous. If you own investments outside of Canada, you should consult with a tax adviser to make sure your Canadian tax obligations are met.

If you own assets or other property in the U.S., see Chapter 19. If you contribute to or are a beneficiary of a trust resident outside of Canada, see 7.4.3.

7.4.1 Reporting rules for foreign investment property

You have to file an annual information return with the CRA if you own or have interests in foreign property where the aggregate cost is more than $100,000 at any time in the year. For these reporting purposes, foreign property includes:

- funds in foreign bank accounts
- rental property outside Canada
- Canadian securities held outside Canada
- investments in foreign corporations, trusts, partnerships or other foreign entities.

Excluded from these rules are interests in foreign affiliates (see below), property used in an active business, property held in RPPs, RRSPs, RRIFs and TSFAs, and personal-use property such as a vacation property.

Form T1135, "Foreign Income Verification Statement", is due at the same time as your personal tax return and can be filed electronically. To complete the form, you must:

- describe each foreign property

- provide the country location of the foreign property held
- disclose the maximum cost amount during the year
- disclose the cost amount at the end of the year
- identify whether any income (or loss) was earned from the property during the year
- identify whether any capital gain (or loss) arose on the property's disposition.

You are still required to report your foreign property even if you receive a T3 slip or a T5 slip for the property.

If you hold your foreign property in the account of a Canadian registered securities dealer or a Canadian trust company, you may be able to use a streamlined reporting option. Under this option, you can choose to report the total aggregate value of all such property on a country-by-country basis instead of reporting the details of each property separately.

If you have specified foreign property that is valued at more than $100,000 but less than $250,000 throughout the year, you may also be able to use a simplified method to report the property.

New immigrants to Canada do not have to file this information return in the year in which they become resident.

The CRA can extend the three-year reassessment period for your taxation year to six years if you failed to report income from a foreign property on your income tax return and did not file Form T1135, filed it late or reported incorrect information on the form.

Similar reporting rules apply if you own (together with related persons) 10% or more of a foreign corporation, if you transfer or lend property to a non-resident trust (or a corporation controlled by it), or if you receive distributions from, or are indebted to, a non-resident trust.

The information required is extensive and the penalties for non-compliance are severe. You should seek help from your tax adviser if you own or have an interest in such foreign property.

7.4.2 Taxation of foreign investment property

Canadian residents are subject to Canadian tax on income and capital gains from their foreign investments. Foreign income and capital gains are generally subject to the same tax as domestic income.

Capital gains from foreign sources are taxed in the same way as capital gains from Canadian sources—see Chapter 6 for details.

Foreign-source dividends, interest, royalties and rental income received by individuals are generally fully taxable. The tax credit that applies to dividends received by individuals from Canadian corporations (see 7.1.2) does not apply to dividends received from a foreign source.

If you have paid any tax to a foreign government on your foreign investment income, you may be able to claim a foreign tax credit to offset the Canadian tax on that income (see 18.2.2).

If you own U.S. investments, see Chapter 19 for details.

If you have any form of foreign investment, you should ask your tax adviser how the Canadian tax rules apply to you.

7.4.3 Trusts resident outside of Canada

If you are a Canadian resident contributor to a non-resident trust or a Canadian resident beneficiary of a non-resident trust, you may face a substantial tax liability as a result of tax rules regarding the taxation of income earned by non-resident trusts.

These rules generally apply to non-resident trusts that have a Canadian resident contributor, or a Canadian beneficiary and a contributor with a significant connection to Canada.

If the rules apply, the trust is deemed to be a resident of Canada and will be taxed in Canada on its income and capital gains that are connected with Canada.

If you have an interest in or are involved in any way with a non-resident trust, contact a tax adviser for help in determining the potential impact of these rules. (For a general discussion of the taxation of trusts, see 21.5.)

7.5   Tax shelters

Tax shelters are no longer as important to tax planning as they used to be. For a variety of reasons, there are now relatively few publicly offered vehicles for sheltering your ordinary income from tax.

If you're considering investing in tax shelters, don't let tax write-offs drive your decision.

You should only invest in a tax shelter if, after taking the tax benefits into account, there is a reasonable expectation of profit from the shelter. The CRA is extremely aggressive in challenging tax shelter-related deductions. The tax benefits alone should not control your investment decision.

Strict rules are in place that make many tax shelters unattractive. For example, "at-risk" rules prevent you from writing off more than the original cost of your investment (that is, in a limited partnership tax shelter—see 7.5.3). Other rules take aim at certain types of tax shelter investments that have rights to receive future income, such as limited partnership structures involving mutual fund limited partnerships, curtailing the tax benefits of such investments.

The federal government also wants to discourage taxpayers from participating in certain charitable donation tax shelters. If you participate in such a tax shelter, the CRA may disallow a deduction or tax credit you claim as a result of that participation and assess tax, interest or penalties. If you object to this reassessment, the CRA is allowed to collect up to 50% of the assessed income taxes, interest or penalties in dispute. Normally, the CRA cannot collect amounts in dispute if an objection or appeal is outstanding (see 9.5.4).

When investing in tax shelters, you must be aware of the possible application of the minimum tax (see 7.6). Finally, you must always be aware of the possible application of the general anti-avoidance rule discussed in 5.2.7.

7.5.1 Tax shelter identification number

Anyone selling an interest in a tax shelter must obtain an identification number from the CRA (and Revenu Québec, in some cases) and provide that number on all documents and financial statements relating to the shelter. If you do not have the identification number, or if any penalties relating to the identification number are payable by the promoter and have not been paid, you will not be able to claim the benefits of the shelter.

The identification number does not indicate approval by the CRA or Revenu Québec of the proposed benefits. It merely ensures that the shelter has been registered for administrative purposes, making audit and reassessment easier for the CRA and Revenu Québec if they eventually decide to disallow some or all of the tax benefits.

> Before investing in a tax shelter, obtain its identification number.

If the promoter of a tax shelter you invest in has not filed its required information return as part of the registration process, the CRA can extend the normal three-year reassessment period for your tax return until three years after the information return is filed.

7.5.2 Information reporting for aggressive tax planning

Along with the tax shelter registration rules described above, the federal government has requirements for reporting aggressive tax planning transactions. Under these rules, you may be required to report a transaction if it contains at least two of the following hallmarks:

- The promoter or tax adviser of the transaction is entitled to contingent remuneration.
- The promoter or tax adviser requires confidentiality protection for the transaction.
- You obtain contractual protection for the transaction.

If you are required to report a transaction, you will have to file the prescribed form RC312 by June 30 following the calendar year in which the transaction first became reportable.

Like the tax shelter rules, the CRA can extend the normal three-year reassessment period to three years after the form reporting an aggressive tax planning transaction has been filed.

A similar aggressive tax planning reporting regime applies in Quebec.

7.5.3 Tax shelters involving limited partnerships

Tax law changes over the years have curtailed the benefits of tax shelters involving the purchase of an interest in a limited partnership.

A limited partnership is a partnership, in that you share the profits of the business with the other partners, and report a percentage of the partnership's income (or loss) directly as your income—whether or not you have received any of the profits. This flow-through concept is in contrast to corporate profits, which are reported only when distributed as dividends, as we saw in 7.1.2. However, a limited partnership is similar to a corporation in that you have limited liability—you cannot be sued for the partnership's debts, provided you are a passive investor. In general, you can only lose your original investment.

Because you can report partnership losses directly on your own tax return, limited partnerships used to be an attractive investment where the partnership business was expected to have losses in its initial years (either real losses due to start-up costs, or tax-created losses due to high write-offs available on certain kinds of investments).

However, you may not write off more than the original cost of your investment. The "at-risk" rules in the *Income Tax Act* do not allow you to deduct more than the amount you have at risk in a limited partnership. Other rules severely restrict the use of limited partnerships to create losses where there is "non-recourse" debt (i.e., you are required to contribute amounts to the partnership, but cannot be forced to do so from your own funds, only from the profits from your partnership interest).

Losses from limited partnerships must be added back to income for minimum tax purposes (see 7.6.2).

7.6 Minimum tax

7.6.1 What is the minimum tax?

The minimum tax was enacted as a political solution to the perception that many high-income taxpayers were paying little tax through the use of tax shelters and other so-called tax preferences. It is relatively narrow in focus, concentrating on specific shelters and credits.

The minimum tax is an alternative tax calculation. You must calculate your tax both normally and under the minimum tax rules, and pay the higher of the two.

In simplest terms, you calculate minimum tax by taking your taxable income, adding back "tainted shelter" deductions (such as resource write-offs and tax shelters) and 60% of the untaxed one-half of capital gains, taking a $40,000 exemption and then calculating federal tax at 15% for 2020. Most personal credits, but not the dividend tax credit or investment tax credits, are then allowed as with regular tax.

A similar calculation is required at the provincial level, with provincial minimum tax rates (except Quebec) ranging from 33.7% to 57.5% of federal minimum tax (with possible adjustments for provincial credits and provincial surtax, depending on the province). The Quebec minimum tax generally mirrors the federal system but with its own rules and calculations. The Quebec minimum tax rate is 15%.

Minimum tax paid can be recovered in the next seven years to the extent your regular tax exceeds your minimum tax (see 7.6.2). Minimum tax does not apply to the year of death.

7.6.2 • Calculating the tax

Somewhat simplified, the calculation is as follows:

1. **Start with your taxable income** (after all deductions allowed for regular tax purposes).

2. **Add back the deductions** that you are not allowed to claim for minimum tax purposes:

   - losses from any investment that requires a tax shelter identification number (see 7.5.1)
   - losses from a partnership that is a tax shelter (see 7.5.3)
   - certain resource-related deductions
   - certain carrying charges, including interest expense relating to any of the above (see 7.2.3)
   - rental property capital cost allowance and interest expense in excess of income from the property
   - 60% of amounts claimed under the employee stock option deduction (see 10.4.1 and 10.4.2).

   These are sometimes called "tainted" deductions, since you cannot claim them for minimum tax purposes.

3. **Add 60% of the untaxed one-half of capital gains**, regardless of whether the rest of the gain was eligible for the capital gains exemption. (The exemption is still allowed for minimum tax purposes.)

4. **Deduct the gross-up on dividends** (see 7.1.2). Since the dividend tax credit is not allowed for minimum tax purposes, you are only taxed on the actual dividend received, rather than on the grossed-up amount.

5. **Deduct $40,000** as your basic minimum tax exemption.

6. **Calculate federal tax at 15% for 2020.**

7. **Deduct personal credits** (see Chapter 2), such as your basic credit, other dependants, old age, disability (for self or spouse only), CPP/QPP contributions, EI premiums, tuition, medical and charitable. Do not deduct investment tax credits (see 11.2.14), political contribution credits (see 2.7.2), pension tax credits (see 20.3.5), transfer of unused tax credits from spouse (see 2.1.3), tuition credits transferred from a child (see 2.4.2), dividend tax credits (see 7.1.2) or labour-sponsored venture capital credits (see 3.3.5).

8. If the resulting tax is higher than your federal tax calculated normally, you must **pay the minimum tax**.

Provincial minimum tax is then generally calculated by multiplying the federal minimum tax amount by the applicable provincial minimum tax rate.

If you find that you have to pay minimum tax in any given year, the excess of your minimum tax over your regular tax becomes a "minimum tax carryover", which can be used in any of the next seven years.

In a future year, you can use the carryover to the extent your regular tax exceeds your minimum tax.

> **Example**
>
> Riley's 2020 regular federal tax is $30,000. His 2020 minimum tax (federal) is $35,000.
>
> Riley must pay the $35,000 tax and provincial taxes (about, say, $53,000 in total). However, he has a $5,000 federal minimum tax carryover. If, in 2021, his regular federal tax is $32,000 and his minimum (federal) tax is $22,000, Riley can deduct the carryover from his regular federal tax and pay only $27,000 basic federal tax (before calculating provincial tax).

7.6.3 Tips for minimizing minimum tax

Exempt capital gains

Be aware of the possible impact of minimum tax on otherwise tax-free capital gains.

The minimum tax can have a serious impact on the taxation of capital gains, particularly where the lifetime capital gains exemption would otherwise eliminate your regular tax entirely.

> **Example**
>
> Max sells the shares of his small business corporation for a $480,000 capital gain, which is fully exempt under the lifetime capital gains exemption of $883,384 for 2020 (see 6.4.1). Max has no other income in 2020.
>
> Max will pay no regular tax. For minimum tax purposes, however, his adjusted taxable income will be about $144,000 (one-half of $480,000 × 60%), minus the basic $40,000 exemption. His federal minimum tax will therefore be 15% of $104,000, or $15,600. The federal minimum tax of $15,600 (net of personal credits) may be carried forward for seven years and applied against regular federal tax payable in those years.

Interest expense and business losses

Two important deductions are not affected by the minimum tax. The first is deductible interest paid (see 7.2.3) on loans not used for tax shelter purposes. The second is business losses and loss carryforwards (see 11.4) other than loss carryforwards that are attributable to "tainted" shelters (see 7.6.1). Where it otherwise makes sense from a business perspective, you can claim such deductions without triggering any minimum tax liability. Keep in mind, however, that high interest expense may give you a high cumulative net investment loss (see 6.4.3) and may make the capital gains exemption unavailable to you, to the extent you would otherwise want to use it (see 6.4.1 and 6.4.2).

Tax shelter deductions

Be aware of possible minimum tax implications when planning for large tax shelter claims, particularly on resource properties and flow-through shares. Resource expenses that exceed your total income from such funds (and are therefore claimed as losses) must be added back for minimum tax purposes.

To the extent you have loss carryforwards from previous years that are attributable to "tainted" shelters, they must also be added back to your taxable income for minimum tax purposes.

7.7 References

The following publications and more information, including forms and brochures, can be obtained on the CRA's website at *www.canada.ca/en/revenue-agency.html* or by telephone request at 1-800-959-8281 for individual income tax and trust-related enquiries or 1-800-959-5525 for business and self-employed individual enquiries.

Income Tax Folio S3-F2-C1, "Capital Dividends"
Income Tax Folio S3-F6-C1, "Interest Deductibility"

Also, see the following selected topics on the CRA's website:

"Tax shelters"
"Minimum tax"

Chapter 8

Charitable donations

- Combine two or more years of charitable donations into one year (8.1)
- If you have a spouse, combine your charitable donations and claim them on the higher-income spouse's return (8.1)
- Consider donating publicly traded securities or other assets to charity (8.1)
- Think about donating publicly traded securities instead of cash (8.2.3)
- Consider planned charitable gifts and bequests (8.3)

Canada's tax system provides special incentives to encourage Canadians to donate to charities. In this chapter, we provide an overview of these incentives and discuss ways of planning your gifts to make the most of the available tax benefits.

8.1 Tax credit for charitable donations

Charitable donations entitle you to a three-tier credit. The first $200 of donations for the year (total to all charities) gives you a 15% federal tax credit, worth about 23% when provincial tax is taken into account. Donations above that level give you a 29% federal tax credit, worth about 47% when provincial tax is factored in (see 17.7 if you live in Quebec). If your income is above about $214,000 in 2020, you will get a 33% federal tax credit, worth about 51% including the provincial credit, for the portion of your donation above $200 that equals your income over $214,000.

> **Example**
>
> Elizabeth's income for 2020 is $226,000 and she makes a charitable donation of $20,000. She will claim a 23% federal and provincial tax credit for the first $200, which equals $46. Elizabeth will be able to claim the top tax credit rate of 51% for $12,000 of her donation, which matches the amount of her income over $214,000. This credit equals $6,120. For the remaining $7,800 of her donation, she can claim a tax credit of 47%, which equals $3,666, for a total federal and provincial tax credit of $9,832.

The 33% federal donation tax credit applies for 2016 and future years. Donations carried forward from 2015 or earlier years are not eligible for this higher credit rate.

For federal purposes, charitable donations above $200 for the year are therefore given the same treatment as if they were deductible, if you are in the top two federal tax brackets. If you are in a lower bracket, the credit for large donations is worth far more than a deduction.

To claim charitable donations, you must have official receipts that show the recipient organization's charitable registration number. You may claim receipts made out in either your name or your spouse's.

The maximum amount of donations you can claim in a year is 75% of your net income, however this limit is effectively increased to 100% for certain kinds of donations (e.g., ecologically sensitive land). To the extent you have receipts for more than this amount, or if you choose not to claim a donation for any other reason, you can save the receipts and claim the credit in any of the following five years.

The annual limit for donations in the year of death and the year before (including bequests and legacies) is 100% of net income for the year (see 8.3 for more on making charitable bequests in your will).

Combine two or more years of charitable donations into one year. If you donate only small amounts over a year, consider combining two or more years of donations into one year to put yourself over the $200 threshold. A $100 donation above the $200 level for the year can save you about $47 in tax, depending on your tax bracket, instead of saving only about $23 below the $200 level.

Once you are over the $200 level, consider making extra contributions in December rather than early in the new year. Your tax saving through the donations credit will come one year earlier.

If you have a spouse, combine your charitable donations and claim them on the higher-income spouse's return. If you and your spouse donate separately, you should combine your receipts and claim them all on one return to avoid having to get the low-rate credit on $200 twice. If your spouse earns a higher income than you, he or she should claim all the donations.

Donations made by one spouse can also be split between the two spouses in whatever proportion they choose. Further, spouses are able to claim each other's unused charitable donation carryforwards from a prior year.

Consider donating publicly traded securities or other assets to charity. Instead of donating cash, you should also consider the potential benefits of donating property such as publicly traded securities, employee stock option shares, artwork or real estate. The tax treatment of donations of property—or "gifts in kind"—is more complex but may result in greater tax savings for you and may enhance the value of your gift to the charity. Gifts in kind are discussed in 8.2.2.

Note that the government discourages investments in certain charitable donation tax shelters. As a result, if you object to an assessment from the disallowance of a deduction or tax credit claimed for a tax shelter that involves a charitable donation, you may have to pay 50% of the disputed tax, interest or penalties to the CRA, pending the outcome of your objection (see 7.5).

8.1.1 Donations made by corporations

If you own a corporation, you may want to consider having the corporation make a donation. While individuals get tax credits, corporations can deduct donations made in determining taxable income, within specified limits. If your private corporation donates securities or other capital property, the corporation's capital dividend account will be increased by the non-taxable portion of the capital gain, and this amount can then be paid out to the corporation's shareholders tax-free. It's a good idea to compare the results of donating personally or through your corporation, as lower corporate tax rates may make it more beneficial to make the donation personally.

8.2 Types of charitable gifts

In this section, we look at some ways you can structure charitable gifts, both during your life and through your will, to further your philanthropic and estate planning goals and make the most of the available tax credits. The options are much broader than simply donating cash or leaving a sum of money to a charity in your will.

There are many ways to make gifts to charitable organizations—including gifts of property (such as securities, artwork, real estate), life insurance and annuities—with significant tax benefits. These benefits depend on the type of gift, the timing of the donation and the nature of the charitable organization.

A gift made today can provide a current tax saving and, in addition, a charitable insured annuity (see 8.2.7) will allow you the continued use of, or income from, the property itself.

8.2.1 Gifts to the Crown

The federal limit for claiming gifts to the federal or a provincial government ("Crown gifts") is 75% of net income, the same limit that applies to gifts made to other charities.

8.2.2 Gifts in kind

Both during your lifetime and on your death, you can donate property to a charity as an alternative to money. A gift of property is called a gift in kind. Examples include artwork, shares and real estate, as well as some more esoteric gifts we discuss below, such as life insurance. (You cannot "give" services, however—only property.)

A gift in kind is normally valued at its fair market value. For purposes of determining the tax credit for your donation, it will be the same as a gift of cash. Thus, the tax credit will generally be worth about 47% to 51% of the value of the property. However, at the time of the donation you are deemed to have disposed of the property at its fair market value—meaning that you must recognize any capital gain or income that would apply had you sold the property for that price.

If you have large capital gains in a year from other dispositions, gifts that trigger significant gains could result in a liability for alternative minimum tax (see 7.6). Before you make such a donation, run the numbers to determine whether minimum tax will result.

For purposes of the tax credit, the 75% net income limit is effectively increased to 100% of net income for:

- gifts of ecologically sensitive lands to municipalities and certain charities (with no income inclusion for resulting capital gains—see 8.2.5)
- gifts of "certified cultural property" (and capital gains on such property may not be taxable—see 8.2.5).

For donations of capital property resulting in taxable capital gains and donations of depreciable property that trigger recapture of capital cost allowance (see 11.2.7), a mechanism is in place to increase the 75% net income limit so that 100% of the taxable capital gain and recaptured CCA are included in the donation limit.

Individuals and corporations who donate securities listed on prescribed stock exchanges, mutual funds and segregated funds of life insurance companies to charities do not have to include any portion of the resulting capital gain in their income. (If you live in Quebec, see 17.7.)

These rules apply to donations of securities to private foundations as well as public charities, though private foundations are subject to some restrictions on the amount of stock they can hold in a corporation.

Similarly, if you exercise an employee stock option and donate the shares (or mutual fund units), you do not need to include any amount of the resulting employee benefit in your income. To be eligible for this treatment, the shares must qualify for the employee stock option deduction discussed in 10.4.1 and meet the criteria for donations of publicly listed securities noted above. The stock option shares must be donated in the year and within 30 days of the option being exercised. If the value of the stock option shares declines between when you exercise the option and when you donate the shares, the amount of your employee stock option deduction will be reduced accordingly.

If your corporation donates securities, its capital dividend account (see 14.2.4) will be increased by the non-taxable portion (or 100%) of the capital gain; this amount can then be paid to the corporation's shareholders tax-free (see 8.1.1).

Special rules apply to restrict the tax advantages on donations of publicly listed flow-through shares.

If you make a gift of capital property to a charity, you can file an election with your tax return to use a lower amount than the fair market value, for purposes of determining both your proceeds of disposition of the property and the value of your donation. You can elect any amount between the adjusted cost base (see 6.2.1) and the actual fair market value.

Whether the election is useful depends on a number of factors, including your tax bracket, your other sources of income and deductions, and your prospects for income in future years against which to use up the charitable donation carryforward.

This election can also be used by artists for gifts of work they have created (which is inventory rather than capital property).

8.2.3 Donating shares acquired through employee stock options

If you're an employee and you donate public company shares acquired under a stock option plan to a registered charity, you may be eligible for an additional deduction. This deduction effectively reduces the related income inclusion to nil, the same as would apply to a capital gain realized on the donation of other shares. One condition to qualify is that you must donate the shares to the charity within 30 days of the share acquisition (and in the same taxation year) under the stock option plan.

8.2.4 Shares vs. cash from sale of shares—which should you donate?

Say you want to make a $2,000 donation to a favourite charity and you have publicly traded securities that originally cost you $1,000 and that are now worth $2,000. Should you sell the securities and donate the proceeds, or should you simply donate the securities? Assuming your income is taxed at the top marginal rate of about 51% and you have already donated $200 in the year, the tax effects of both choices are as follows:

Think about donating publicly traded securities instead of cash.

- If you sell the shares and donate the pre-tax proceeds, a $1,000 capital gain will arise on the sale of the securities. You would then have to pay $255 in tax on the taxable portion of your gain (one-half of $1,000 × an assumed 51% tax rate). Your $2,000 donation will give you a tax credit of $1,020 (51% × $2,000). In the end, the donation will result in net tax savings of $765 ($1,020 tax credit – $255 capital gains tax).
- If instead you donate the shares directly, the charity will still get the full $2,000 value of the shares. The taxable portion of the $1,000 capital gain will be zero, and you will get the same tax credit for the donation, producing net tax savings of $1,020 (51% × $2,000).

As you can see, you will come out ahead if you donate the securities directly. You give up property of the same value but your tax savings are $255 more ($1,020 vs. $765) than they would be had you sold the securities and donated the proceeds.

8.2.5 Gifts of cultural property and ecologically sensitive land

Gifts of "cultural property" to certain public authorities or institutions (such as museums) also produce tax benefits. If the property being gifted is certified as cultural property, the donation will be equal to the property's fair market value for purposes of the credit but no taxable capital gain will arise. Any capital loss that may arise may be deductible in some circumstances.

The same treatment applies for gifts of ecologically sensitive lands to Canadian federal or provincial governments, municipalities or approved registered charities.

8.2.6 Gifts of life insurance

If you have a "permanent" life insurance policy (see 21.7), such as whole life or universal life, you can donate it to a charity by transferring the ownership of the policy to the charity and having the charity become the beneficiary of the policy. For tax purposes, the value of your donation will be the policy's fair market value, minus any policy loan outstanding. However, to the extent that value exceeds the tax cost of the policy to you, you must recognize the excess as income, as if you had cashed in the policy.

Once you have donated the policy to the charity, if you continue to pay the premiums on the policy, each such payment will be considered an additional charitable donation entitling you to a tax credit.

If you make the charity a beneficiary of a life insurance policy that you continue to own, the payment of the death benefit to the charity is considered a donation made by your estate. The donation can be claimed on your final tax return, on your return for the year prior to death or on the estate's tax returns as noted in 8.3.

8.2.7 Charitable insured annuity

Another option is to set up a "charitable insured annuity". You buy an annuity from a life insurance company and use part of the monthly payments to pay the premiums on a life insurance policy with a charity as the owner and beneficiary. Thus, you receive an income stream over your lifetime (from the annuity) and donation tax credits for the insurance premiums you pay. On your death, the charity receives the insurance proceeds.

8.3 Charitable bequests

Consider planned charitable gifts and bequests.

Charitable gifts can be made through your will. New rules for bequests made in 2016 or later years provide more flexibility than the previous rules for claiming tax credits related to donations made on death. A donation in your will may be allocated between your final tax return, your tax return for the year prior to death, the estate's tax return for the year the donation is made by the executors, and a previous tax return of the estate. The estate can also claim any unused donation tax credits in its tax returns for five years after the donation is made.

To be able to carry back donations to the deceased's tax returns or to a prior year of the estate, the estate must qualify as a "graduated rate estate" (see 22.2.2) and the donation must be made within 60 months of death.

The charitable donations limit in the year of death and the immediately preceding year is 100% of the deceased's "net income". If the donations are claimed in the estate's tax returns, the donations will be limited to 75% of the net income of the estate for federal tax purposes. Donations made in your will cannot be claimed by your spouse, unlike donations made during your lifetime.

If you name a charity as the beneficiary of your life insurance policy or a registered savings plan such as a TFSA, RRSP or RRIF, the death benefit or value of the registered plan at death can be claimed as a charitable donation in the same manner as donations made in a will as previously noted. Naming a charity as a beneficiary can also save probate fees (see 21.4) on the value of the policy, TFSA RRSP or RRIF if the proceeds would otherwise be paid to your estate.

It is possible that large bequests in your will (or large donations during your lifetime) may become unusable for tax purposes, if they far exceed the allowable threshold. You may therefore want to consider other options to maximize the tax credits and the funds available to your beneficiaries—both family members and charities.

Proper will planning can help ensure that your bequests will be made as you intend and provide significant tax savings for your estate.

Careful planning together with an informed adviser can ensure your philanthropic goals are met and the tax benefits are available when you need them most.

8.4 References

The following publications and more information, including forms and brochures, can be obtained on the CRA's website at *www.canada.ca/en/revenue-agency.html* or by telephone request at 1-800-959-8281 for individual income tax and trust-related enquiries or 1-800-959-5525 for business and self-employed individual enquiries.

Income Tax Folio S7-F1-C1, "Split-receipting and Deemed Fair Market Value"
Pamphlet P113, "Gifts and Income Tax"

Chapter 9

Dealing with the tax collectors

- File your return on time even if you can't pay your taxes owing (9.1.1)

- Pay your taxes owing by April 30 even if you're filing later (9.1.1)

- NETFILE or EFILE your return for a quicker refund (9.1.2)

- Consider prepaying instalments to reduce deficient instalment charges (9.2.2)

- Be aware of the CRA's interest rates and compounding of interest (9.3)

- If you know you owe interest on late or deficient instalments, think about paying an estimate with your final payment (9.3)

- Sign a waiver only if necessary (9.4.3)

- If you've neglected to file returns, report income and make tax payments, consider making a voluntary disclosure to reduce penalties and interest (9.4.5)

- File a Notice of Objection to preserve your rights to appeal (9.5.1)

- When your return is reopened on reassessment, consider requesting other adjustments (9.5.1)

- Be sure you understand the legal issues when appealing (9.5.2)

- Consider paying the amount owing even if you are filing an objection (9.5.4)

In this chapter, we deal with the administrative side of the tax system—how tax is collected, how your return is assessed and what you can do if you disagree with the Canada Revenue Agency or Revenu Québec as to the amount of tax you owe.

9.1 Tax returns

9.1.1 Filing your return

Most individuals are required to file their federal and Quebec tax returns by April 30 each year. When the due date falls on a Saturday, Sunday or public holiday recognized by the CRA, your payment is considered paid on time and your return to be filed on time if the CRA receives it or if it is postmarked on the next business day.

The deadline for individuals who have business income and their spouses (including common-law spouses—see 2.2.1) is June 15. Even though the return may not be due until June 15, any balance of tax owing for the year is due on April 30.

If you have no tax to pay for the year (as distinguished from no balance owing in April), no return is usually required unless you disposed of capital property (including your principal residence, see 6.5.2) or realized a capital gain in the year or unless the CRA or Revenu Québec requests one.

In all provinces except Quebec, you file a single return with the CRA to cover both federal and provincial tax. Quebec residents and taxpayers with business income from operations in Quebec must file a Quebec provincial tax return as well (see Chapter 17).

The return must be postmarked or transmitted electronically by the due date. If the return is late, an automatic penalty of 5% of any tax still owing applies. This penalty is increased by 1% of the unpaid tax for each full month that the return is late, to a maximum of 12 months. Repeated failures to file a return on time results in higher penalties.

File your return on time even if you can't pay your taxes owing.

To avoid the 5% penalty, you should file your return on time even if you are not able to pay your balance owing. Interest will accrue on the unpaid balance, but the penalty will not apply.

Pay your taxes owing by April 30 even if you're filing later.

Conversely, if you are unable to get your return completed (or your return is not due until June 15) but you have a rough idea of how much tax you owe, it is a good idea to pay that amount to the CRA or Revenu Québec by April 30. Make sure to have it credited to the correct taxation year (and not as an instalment for the subsequent year, for example).

When you're preparing your return or providing your information to a tax return preparer, check carefully to ensure you have all your information slips such as T4 slips from your employer or other slips reporting investment or trust income such as T3s and T5s. If you fail to report income of at least $500 more than once, you may face a penalty of up to 10% of the unreported income (note that an additional provincial penalty of 10% may also apply in some situations).

Using the CRA's "Auto-fill my return" service can reduce the likelihood of errors and the chance of missing information from T-slips. This service allows you and your representative to automatically fill in parts of a current-year income tax return. Otherwise, the CRA's "My Account" service also contains information on T-slips filed in their records which can also be checked for completeness.

If you have to file Form T1135 to report owning more than $100,000 in foreign property (see 7.4.1), remember that this form is due at the same time as your personal tax return. Even if you don't file your tax return on time, you should submit your T1135 form on time to avoid a penalty for late-filing it.

9.1.2 Electronic filing

The CRA offers two options for most taxpayers to file their returns in electronic form: NETFILE and EFILE. NETFILE (which is also offered by Revenu Québec) allows you to file returns prepared on your personal computer via the Internet. To use NETFILE, you will need CRA-approved tax preparation software and a web browser that meets the CRA's security standard.

Taxpayers who cannot use these electronic services due to CRA guidelines must file a paper return.

The EFILE system allows authorized tax return preparers or transmitters to file returns directly to the CRA using tax return preparation and transmission software. Most professional tax return preparers offer this service in addition to preparing the actual tax returns. If you prepare your own return, most EFILE preparers will charge a small fee to transmit it. The Quebec government also allows electronic filing for Quebec provincial tax returns.

The main benefit of these electronic filing options to taxpayers is the ability to have the return assessed and a refund paid in as little as two to three weeks, as opposed to a somewhat longer wait using the

> NETFILE or EFILE your return for a quicker refund.

conventional paper filing method. If you are expecting a refund, electronic filing should speed up the processing of your return and the delivery or electronic deposit of your refund.

Further, you do not need to file paper returns or receipts with the return. (You must keep your receipts and other supporting documentation for any later review by the CRA.) This reduces the paper burden on you and the tax authorities.

If you are concerned about a reassessment of your return down the road, electronic filing will normally get your return assessed sooner and start the three-year reassessment period (see 9.4) earlier.

If you have a balance due, you can use NETFILE or EFILE before the deadline but you will have until April 30 to mail in your payment. (You may also be able to pay your taxes electronically—see 9.2.3.)

9.2 Payment of tax

9.2.1 Source withholdings

Tax is withheld at source and remitted to the CRA and Revenu Québec by employers and others. Tax withheld from a payment to you is considered to have been paid by you to the tax authorities, even if your employer never remits it. It is also considered to have been paid to you in the sense that it forms part of your income.

Source withholding applies to the following kinds of payments, among others:

- employment income
- pension benefits
- Employment Insurance benefits
- withdrawals from an RRSP
- annuity payments
- Old Age Security benefits
- payments of passive income to non-residents (interest, dividends, rent, royalties, etc.)
- purchase of real estate from a non-resident (unless the non-resident has a certificate from the CRA and Revenu Québec, where applicable).

Note that there is no withholding of tax on interest, dividends, rent or royalties paid to Canadian residents. Self-employment income such as consulting fees (see 11.1) is also received without source deductions.

9.2.2 Instalments

You must pay instalments if the difference between your tax payable (including provincial tax except Quebec tax) and amounts withheld at source is more than $3,000 in both the current year and either of the two preceding years. For Quebec residents, since provincial tax is not collected by the CRA, the threshold is $1,800 of federal tax (see 17.1.3).

Quarterly instalments are due on the 15th of March, June, September and December.

There are four possible ways to determine your instalment obligations.

The first method is for your total instalments, paid in four equal payments, to equal the tax owing for the year on your sources of income from which tax is not withheld. In other words, your instalments should equal the balance owing at the end of the year.

The second method is for your quarterly instalments to equal the tax owing on your previous year's sources of income for which tax was not withheld. In other words, take the balance you had to pay last year after accounting for source withholdings, and pay that amount over the year in quarterly instalments.

The first method requires you to estimate your current year's income. If you guess low, you will end up not paying enough. The second method lets you use the previous year's income, but on March 15, when the first instalment is due, you might not yet have calculated your previous year's total tax. For this reason, the third method was introduced.

Under the third method, your March and June instalments are each one-quarter of the *total* tax owing on income from which tax was not withheld for two years ago. Your total instalments for the year must still equal the total amount for one year ago, as with the second method. Therefore, the September and December instalments must be enough to reach this total.

The fourth method is to simply pay the amount specified for the quarter on the instalment reminder statement mailed to you twice a year by the CRA and Revenu Québec.

Example

Alexander is self-employed as a consultant and has no tax withheld at source. His 2018 tax payable (combined federal/provincial) was $20,000. His 2019 tax payable was $24,000. He expects his total 2020 tax bill to be $27,000.

Alexander should pay quarterly instalments on March 15, June 15, September 15 and December 15, 2020, totalling $24,000, his tax payable for the previous year. If he wishes, he may pay four instalments of $6,000 each.

The CRA will advise Alexander in February 2020, however, that his March 15 and June 15 payments should be $5,000 each—one-quarter of his 2018 tax payable, since his 2019 figures are not yet available. If he makes these payments, and then pays $7,000 on each of September 15 and December 15, he will have paid the required $24,000 and met his instalment obligations under the "third method".

The $3,000 balance (assuming Alexander's estimate of income for 2020 turns out to be correct) will then be due on April 30, 2021. Because he is self-employed, however, his 2020 return need not be filed until June 15, 2021.

If instalments are made on time and in the correct amount as per any of the three methods or you follow the CRA reminder notices, no interest is payable. If instalments are not made when required or are deficient, interest is assessed at the CRA's and Revenu Québec's current high "prescribed rate" (see 9.3), compounded daily.

> Consider prepaying instalments to reduce deficient instalment charges.

You cannot *earn* interest by paying instalments early, but you can earn "contra-interest" at the same rate as applies to late payments, to offset interest that would otherwise be assessed on late instalments. If you've fallen behind in your instalments, consider making an extra or early payment to offset the (non-deductible) interest that will otherwise be assessed.

Alexander, from the above example, does not make any instalment payments for 2020 until June 15, 2020. On that day, he makes a single payment of $15,000. He then makes a $2,000 payment on September 15, 2020 and a $7,000 payment on December 15, 2020. At this time, he has paid his $24,000 tax instalment requirements equal to his 2019 tax payable.

Alexander should not owe much interest on instalments, assuming the prescribed interest rate stays constant through 2020. His June 15 payment can be thought of as three parts: $5,000 due in March, paid three months late; $5,000 paid on time; and $5,000 of the $7,000 not due until September, paid three months early. The payment that is early will generate "contra-interest" to offset the interest that Alexander would otherwise have to pay due to his being late with his March 2020 payment.

For federal purposes, if the interest owing on late instalments is greater than $1,000, you may be subject to an additional penalty of up to 50% of the interest.

9.2.3 Electronic tax payments and refunds

The federal government continues to promote the use of its "Direct Deposit" service whereby tax refunds, GST/HST credits and Canada Child Benefit payments will be deposited directly into your account at any financial institution in Canada.

To take advantage of the service, you can sign up online using the CRA's "My Account" service, by phone at 1-800-959-8281 or by mail by completing the "Canada's direct deposit enrolment form".

You may be able to pay your taxes electronically using the CRA's My Payment service and your financial institution's Internet banking services. Contact your financial institution for information about its electronic payment services.

You can use the CRA's My Account service to see your tax return and request changes to it (including making changes using CRA's online service ReFILE, if you had previously filed using NETFILE or EFILE (see 9.1.2)). You can also get information about your tax refund or balance owing, RRSP and TFSA contribution room, carryforward amounts such as capital and non-capital losses, and a summary of your instalment payments, among other things. You can authorize a representative such as a family member or a tax professional to access your information on My Account as well.

9.3 Interest

Interest that you owe on late payments of tax and instalments and on refunds is calculated at a prescribed rate, which varies quarterly based on the average yield of Government of Canada 90-day treasury bills. The CRA announces the new rate for each quarter in a news release about three weeks before the quarter begins.

Be aware of the CRA's interest rates and compounding of interest.

There are three different "prescribed" interest rates each quarter. The lowest rate, which is roughly the Bank of Canada rate for the previous quarter, applies for purposes of the attribution rules (see 5.2.2) and the employee and shareholder loan rules (see 10.3 and 14.2.6). The middle rate, which is two percentage points higher, applies to refunds paid by the CRA. The highest rate, which is a further two points higher, applies to late payments of tax and instalments owing by taxpayers.

Although the rate is expressed as an annual rate, it is in fact compounded daily, so the effective rate is somewhat higher than shown. A 5% interest rate, for example, is equivalent to a rate of about 5.13% in simple annual interest.

Interest that you owe on late payments runs from when the payment was due. Interest on refunds generally runs from 30 days after the due date for the return, or from the day on which you file your return, whichever is later. However, if you have a June 15 filing deadline because you have self-employment income (see 11.2.1), interest will not be paid until 30 days after April 30 or 30 days after the date that the return is actually filed, whichever is later.

Interest that you are required to pay to the CRA, such as on late payments of tax or instalments, is not tax-deductible.

Interest paid to you on a refund is taxable in the year in which you receive it. Thus, if you file your 2020 return when it is due in April 2021 and receive a refund in August 2021, you must report the interest from May 30, 2021 included in that payment on your 2021 return.

If you have tax owing at April 30 and you know interest will be charged because of late or deficient instalment payments, consider paying an estimate of the interest with your April 30 payment to stop any further interest from accruing.

If you know you owe interest on late or deficient instalments, think about paying an estimate with your final payment.

The federal prescribed interest rates are as follows for 2019 and the first two quarters of 2020.

CRA's Prescribed Interest Rates			
	Low Rate	Middle Rate	High Rate
2019			
January 1 – December 31, 2019	2%	4%	6%
2020			
January 1 – June 30, 2020	2%	4%	6%

As noted, the high rate applies to late tax and instalment payments and the middle rate to refunds. The low rate applies for the purposes of the attribution rules and shareholder and employee loans.

For Quebec purposes, the low rate is the same as the federal rate and the middle rate is lower (so less interest is paid to you on refunds). For late taxes, the Quebec high rate is higher than the federal rate, and 10% higher for late Quebec tax instalments.

9.4 Assessment, audit and reassessment

9.4.1 Initial assessment

When you file a conventional (paper) return, it is processed over a period of typically three to six weeks, after which you receive a "Notice of Assessment" and any refund owing to you. The processing includes a review of the numbers on your return to make sure they are consistent (for example, that the arithmetic is correct and that any numbers carried forward from prior years' tax returns are consistent with those in the CRA's systems).

Most EFILE and NETFILE users can expect their returns to be assessed in two to three weeks.

For a partnership, the tax authorities may issue a determination of the partnership's income or loss, which is effectively an assessment of each partner's portion of the income or loss (see 11.3.6).

9.4.2 Audit

Some time after the initial assessment, your return may be selected for audit. Most audits of individual taxpayers (as opposed to corporations) are "desk audits", in which the auditor will ask you to supply supporting material for claims you have made. Some audits are "field audits", in which the auditor will come to your place of business to look at your records. Increasingly, the CRA will review both your business records and personal records for certain audits.

If you file using one of the electronic options, you will not have to file any receipts with your return. However, the CRA or Revenu Québec may later "spot-check" your return to verify certain claims, such as donations, RRSP contributions or tuition fees. This is normally just a formality, designed to maintain the integrity of the electronic filing systems.

You should be aware of your rights on an audit. The auditor is not entitled to go on a "fishing expedition" through your books. He or she may request specific information, and you may ask why that information is needed. If you anticipate problems, you may want assistance from your professional advisers in dealing with the auditor.

If you and your family have a high net worth, the CRA may select your business and investment activities for audit as part of a project focusing on wealthy individuals. The CRA seems to be looking at individuals with complex affairs who may control or have broadly defined interests in a large number of entities such as corporations, trusts, partnerships and private foundations. If you are identified under this program, you may have a relatively short time to gather extensive information about your business and investment interests.

If you have a small or medium-sized business, the CRA may contact you as part of its Liaison Officer Initiative. Under this program, a Liaison Officer can visit taxpayers' businesses to provide general information and help them fulfill their tax obligations. The CRA says this service is not an audit but is designed to provide education and support.

9.4.3 Reassessment

If the audit (or an audit of another taxpayer) turns up an indication that your tax payable should be other than what was initially assessed, the CRA will issue a reassessment. If the reassessment results in more tax payable by you, this will not normally be done without you first being consulted and given an opportunity to explain your position.

A reassessment cannot normally be issued more than three years after the date of the original assessment. However, in cases of fraud, or misrepresentation attributable to "neglect, carelessness or wilful default", the reassessment may be issued at any time.

There are several other situations where the three-year limitation does not apply. The most important is where you have filed a waiver with the tax authorities. The waiver, which is usually directed to a specific issue

Sign a waiver only if necessary.

that is in dispute, will allow the CRA to reassess you on that issue at any time. You can revoke a waiver on six months' notice to the CRA. A common way to limit the CRA's additional time is to sign both a waiver and its revocation, and to staple the revocation to the waiver itself. The revocation will take effect after six months from the date of signing.

If you are asked by a CRA auditor to sign a waiver, consider the request carefully and obtain professional advice before agreeing.

First, consider the auditor's alternative if you do not sign the waiver. You are under no obligation to file a waiver simply to make the auditor's life easier.

Second, make sure that the waiver is very specific and waives the normal three-year period only in respect of the specific issues that are under investigation or dispute.

Similar rules apply for Quebec tax purposes.

9.4.4 Requests for Taxpayer Relief

What happens if you cannot pay your taxes or make a tax filing on time because of a natural or human-made disaster, serious illness, accident or another valid reason? The *Income Tax Act*'s Taxpayer Relief rules give the CRA the discretion to waive penalties and interest on overdue taxes if you were unable to pay on time because of circumstances beyond your control. (In the case of large natural disasters such as floods, the CRA may extend tax-related deadlines for everyone in the affected area.) Note that penalty and interest relief is only available for any taxation year that ended within the previous 10 years before the calendar year in which the taxpayer relief application is filed.

Under these rules, the CRA may also issue tax refunds even where the return is filed after the late-filing deadline (that is, generally three years from the original due date) and accept late-filed elections, or allow you to amend or revoke an election after the applicable deadline.

Aside from natural disaster or personal misfortune, the Taxpayer Relief rules can apply if you could not make a tax payment or file an election on time for more mundane reasons such as incorrect information provided in writing by the CRA or service disruptions such as strikes. But if you were simply negligent or unaware of the rules, you will still have to pay the usual penalties and interest on your overdue taxes.

In weighing your request, the CRA may consider your previous compliance record and your promptness in bringing the matter to the CRA's attention.

Note that several tax filing and payment deadlines were extended in 2020 due to COVID-19. For details, contact your tax adviser.

9.4.5 Voluntary disclosures

If you've neglected to file returns, report income and make tax payments, consider making a voluntary disclosure to reduce penalties and interest.

If you have neglected to report income, file an income tax return or file other information returns and you have an outstanding tax liability or you may be subject to a penalty, consider using the CRA's Voluntary Disclosures Program. Under this program, you may be able to make disclosures to correct inaccurate or incomplete information, or to disclose information not previously reported, and obtain some relief from interest and penalties.

The CRA has two programs for income tax voluntary disclosures as of March 1, 2018. The Limited Program applies to disclosures of intentional non-compliance. All other disclosures fall under the General Program.

If you make a voluntary disclosure under either the General or Limited Program, you will still have to pay any taxes owing and you will not be referred for criminal prosecution.

Under the General Program, you will not be charged any penalties and the interest charged can be reduced. Under the Limited Program, only gross negligence penalties will be waived and no interest relief is provided.

Under both Programs, penalty and interest relief is only available for any taxation year that ended within the previous 10 years before the calendar year in which the voluntary disclosure application is filed.

To qualify for this relief, your disclosure must be complete, it must include information that is at least one year past due, and it must involve a penalty (if no penalty is involved, the CRA will simply process the new information as it would any other request for adjustment). Additionally, you must come forward before the CRA has started an audit, investigation or other enforcement action. Payment of the estimated tax owing must be included with the voluntary disclosure application.

Voluntary disclosures may also be made regarding deficiencies in meeting other tax requirements, such as source deduction remittances and GST/HST reporting and payment obligations.

In most cases, you are entitled to use the Voluntary Disclosures Program only once.

To qualify for relief for Quebec tax purposes, you generally must meet the conditions for federal tax purposes.

You may want to contact your professional adviser to help you determine whether a voluntary disclosure makes sense in your circumstances.

9.5 Objections and appeals

9.5.1 Notice of Objection

If you cannot come to an understanding with the auditor and a reassessment is issued, or if you disagree with the original assessment, you may file a Notice of Objection. This is done by writing to the Chief of Appeals of your local district taxation office or tax centre, by using the My Account or My Business Account service, or by filing form T400A with the appropriate Appeals Intake Centre. This filing begins the formal administrative appeal process. The notice should set out the specific issue(s) that you are objecting to.

When you file a Notice of Objection, your objection is reviewed by an Appeals Officer within the CRA. The Appeals Officer is independent of the Audit Branch, and he or she should conduct the review impartially and objectively.

To be valid, a Notice of Objection must be filed either within 90 days of the date of the assessment or reassessment to which you are objecting, or within one year of the original due date for the return. For example, an objection to an assessment of your 2019 return would have to be filed by April 30, 2021 or 90 days after the (re)assessment you are objecting to, whichever is later if your tax return was due April 30, 2020. The same deadlines apply for Quebec purposes.

Filing your Notice of Objection before the deadline is vital—even if you are in the midst of discussions with the CRA authorities, and even if you have been assured that a reassessment in your favour will be issued. If you don't file a Notice of Objection, your legal right to appeal vanishes and any reassessment will be at the CRA's discretion.

File a Notice of Objection to preserve your right to appeal.

Even if the period for objecting has expired, you may request a reassessment of your return. In this case, you have no legal right to force a reassessment, but in many cases the reassessment will be issued anyway. The CRA will allow a reassessment of a return for any of the preceding 10 years, if the request meets the guidelines issued under the government's Taxpayer Relief rules (see 9.4.4).

In some cases, you can also apply to the CRA or the Tax Court of Canada for extension of the time for filing a Notice of Objection.

If the CRA issues you a routine reassessment for some reason after your own right to force a reconsideration of your return has expired, bear in mind that the reassessment reopens your return for 90 days. If this happens and there are other issues that you want to contest or change, you can raise them within the 90-day period and file a Notice of Objection to preserve your rights of appeal. However, you cannot do this if the return was reopened for any of a number of special reasons (such as a carryback of losses from a later year).

When your return is reopened on reassessment, consider requesting other adjustments.

If the CRA issues a reassessment, it will invalidate any Notice of Objection for that year and you will need to file another Notice of Objection to the new reassessment if your issue was not resolved.

Similar rules and deadlines apply for Quebec tax purposes.

You are not usually required to pay your tax assessment at the Notice of Objection stage but interest will continue to accumulate (see 9.5.4).

The rules for objections and appeals related to GST/HST or other indirect taxes are beyond the scope of this book.

9.5.2 Appeal to the Tax Court

The Appeals Officer is normally your last level of appeal within the CRA. A further appeal is available to the Tax Court of Canada (or the applicable provincial court if provincial taxes are in dispute).

Be sure you understand the legal issues when appealing.

You may have a choice between the Court's "informal" and "general" procedures for making an appeal.

The general procedure normally requires you to retain a lawyer. It is similar to higher court proceedings in provincial courts. If the amount of tax and penalties in dispute for any one taxation year is more than $25,000 of federal tax (about $40,000 including provincial tax other than Quebec tax), you must follow the general procedure. In certain "test cases", the CRA may also force a case below the threshold into the general procedure, in which case the CRA will be required to reimburse you for most or all of your legal fees.

The informal procedure, as its name suggests, is much less complicated. You may appear on your own, or have someone else (such as a lawyer, accountant, consultant or friend) there to assist you. No specific form needs to be filed to launch the appeal. The formal rules of evidence that normally apply to court proceedings will not necessarily apply. Under the informal procedure, your case will normally be heard more quickly than under the formal procedure, and a judgment given within a year of when you first file the appeal. The decision given is not binding as a precedent for future cases, whether yours or another taxpayer's.

If you are taking an appeal to the Tax Court of Canada, make sure you understand the legal issues involved. Even if you wish to represent yourself or be represented by a friend or relative, consult with a qualified tax professional before the appeal. Many issues in tax law have answers on which all the advisers (and the judge!) will agree, yet which will not be obvious to the non-expert.

9.5.3 Appeal beyond the Tax Court

A decision of the Tax Court of Canada under its informal procedure can be appealed to the Federal Court of Appeal but the grounds for such an appeal are restricted. A decision under the general procedure can be appealed directly to the Federal Court of Appeal. In either case, you would need a lawyer for such an appeal, which would typically take about two years from time of filing until judgment is given. Provincial decisions may be appealed to the applicable provincial appeal court.

Once a decision is given by the federal or provincial appeals courts, either you or the tax authority may seek "leave to appeal" from the Supreme Court of Canada. Only if the Supreme Court grants the application for leave to appeal can an appeal be made. The Supreme Court rarely grants leave to appeal in tax cases; typically only three or four tax cases a year reach the Supreme Court.

9.5.4 Amounts in dispute—should you pay up?

Suppose you are contesting an amount of $20,000 of tax, but you are not sure whether you will win or not. Although you have filed a Notice of Objection or perhaps an appeal, you are receiving notices from the CRA Collections asking you to pay even though the CRA cannot start collection action as long as you have an objection or appeal outstanding.

Nonetheless, it may be a good idea to pay the balance anyway. The interest rate charged on late payments (see 9.3) is likely higher than the rate you would otherwise earn with your money, or higher than the rate at which you must borrow from the bank. If you ultimately succeed in your appeal, you will recover all the funds you paid, plus interest (at the middle rate shown in 9.3).

> Consider paying the amount owing even if you are filing an objection.

Note also that when you receive a statement from the CRA, you normally have 20 days to pay without further interest charges applying. If you are going to have to pay anyway, you may as well take advantage of this "interest-free" period and pay the balance on the 20th day.

Taxpayers sometimes think they should not pay an amount in dispute because "that would be an admission of guilt", or because the CRA would then have no incentive to settle the case. Such reasoning is misplaced. You cannot prejudice your case by paying the tax. The determination as to your legal rights is not affected by whether or not the tax has been paid.

The only circumstance where you are better not to have paid your account is where you are applying for a waiver of interest and penalty, at the CRA's discretion, on the grounds of "inability to pay". Once you have paid, it will be difficult to argue that you cannot find the money to pay your tax bill and require a waiver of interest to be able to meet the requested payments.

9.6 References

The following publications and more information, including forms and brochures, can be obtained on the CRA's website at *www.canada.ca/en/revenue-agency.html* or by telephone request at 1-800-959-8281 for individual income tax and trust-related enquiries or 1-800-959-5525 for business and self-employed individual enquiries.

Information Circular 75-7R3, "Reassessment of a Return of Income"
Information Circular 00-1R6, "Voluntary Disclosures Program"
Information Circular 07-1R1, "Taxpayer Relief Provisions"
Pamphlet P148, "Resolving your dispute: Objection and appeal rights under the Income Tax Act"

Also, see the following selected topics on the CRA's website:

"Auto-fill my return"
"File your taxes online: Understand NETFILE"
"Voluntary Disclosures Program—Introduction"

Chapter 10

If you are employed

- Arrange to get non-taxable benefits (10.1.1)
- Ask to have your source withholdings reduced where possible (10.2)
- Pay interest owing on loans from employers by January 30 of the following year (10.3)
- Consider employees' profit-sharing plans for cash flow purposes (10.5.2)
- Transfer retiring allowances to an RRSP (10.6)
- Claim the employment tax credit to help cover your work-related expenses (10.7.1)
- Employed tradespeople—claim the deduction for the cost of new tools (10.8.8)
- Claim a rebate for GST/HST paid on expenses deductible from your employment income (10.9)

As a general principle, all income (including tips) and benefits from or related to your employment are taxed, except where the federal or Quebec rules specifically provide otherwise. Also as a general principle, you cannot claim any deductions against employment income, except for those that are specifically allowed by the tax system. There are, however, many special rules, and we examine some of them in this chapter.

10.1 Employment benefits

10.1.1 Non-taxable employment benefits

Certain employment benefits are not taxable, even though many of them are deductible expenses to the employer. The government is thus offering an incentive to employers to provide these benefits, since the after-tax returns are greater than simply providing additional salary. Non-taxable benefits include:

- Contributions to a registered pension plan (the pension is taxable when received—see 3.5.1)
- Contributions to a group sickness or accident insurance plan
- Contributions to a "private health services plan", such as those covering drugs, medical expenses and hospital charges not covered by public health insurance, and dental fees (except for Quebec purposes—see 17.10.2)
- All or a portion of the cost of free or subsidized school services for your children in certain circumstances (for example, if the services are provided in a remote area)
- Contributions to a supplementary unemployment benefit plan

- Contributions to a deferred profit-sharing plan
- Non-accountable moving allowance of up to $650 (see 13.1.3)
- Reimbursement of certain moving expenses on work-related relocation (see 13.1.3; however, any reimbursement or compensation to help finance the new residence is excluded—see 13.1.4)
- Payment of club dues (e.g., at golf courses) if your membership in the club is principally to benefit the employer's business (however, these dues are normally not deductible to the employer)
- Employee discounts, where such discounts are commonly available to other employees (but not below the employer's cost)
- Non-cash gifts to an unrelated employee of up to $500 annually (combined for all gifts) intended to mark holidays, birthdays and other special occasions (the total value in excess of $500 is taxable)
- A separate non-cash award to an unrelated employee of up to $500 annually intended to mark length of service or an employment anniversary
- The value of customer loyalty points on personal credit cards offered by third parties where the points were earned on employer-reimbursed business trips or other expenses of the employer, as long as the points are not converted to cash and the plan is not a form of remuneration or tax avoidance scheme
- Home computer, as long as it primarily benefits your employer and such computers are made available to all employees (or employees within the same class)
- Tuition fees for courses taken to maintain or improve your skills in an area related to your current or future employment responsibilities
- Costs of other business-related courses such as stress management, employment equity and language skills
- Scholarships provided to your children for elementary, secondary or post-secondary education (the amount is included in the student's income)
- Counselling services related to mental or physical health, employment termination or retirement
- Subsidized meals, where you are required to pay a reasonable charge covering the cost of the food
- Uniforms or special clothing you need for your job
- Transportation to the job in certain circumstances, if provided directly by the employer
- Board and lodging at, and transportation to, a "special work site" where you work temporarily or a "remote work site" that is remote from any established community
- Use of your employer's recreational facilities
- Transportation passes given to bus, rail and airline employees, except for airline employees travelling on a space-confirmed basis
- Transportation and parking costs, whether paid directly by the employer or reimbursed to you, if you are blind or are disabled due to a mobility impairment
- The cost of an attendant to assist you at work if you are disabled

- Items of nominal value, such as coffee, T-shirts with your employer's logo, mugs, plaques and trophies.

The CRA has said it will not tax employees on reimbursements of up to $500 that an employer paid to an employee for necessary personal computer equipment to perform work remotely because of the COVID-19 pandemic.

Note that where your employer deducts its contributions to a sickness or accident insurance plan, disability insurance plan or income maintenance insurance plan, any benefits you receive from the insurance will be taxable (but reduced by your own premium payments to the plan).

Ask your employer to make use of the non-taxable benefits outlined above as much as possible. If you have an employment benefit package where you and the employer share the costs, try to have the cost-sharing reallocated so your employer pays for all the non-taxable benefits and you pay for the benefits that are taxable if your employer pays them. In many cases, without changing the cost to your employer, you may be able to reduce your tax burden this way.

> Arrange to get non-taxable benefits.

One non-taxable benefit that is often overlooked is that of board and lodging at a "special work site". Unlike a "remote work location", a special work site need not be far from an established community; as long as the duties you perform at that location are of a temporary nature, and you maintain another residence, the food and lodging paid by your employer are a non-taxable benefit. This could apply, for example, if you spend several months in another city working on a project for your employer.

The CRA does not treat employer-provided overtime meals or reasonable allowances for overtime meals as a taxable benefit if:

- the value of a meal or meal allowance is no more than $17 (including GST/HST)
- the employee works two or more hours of overtime directly before or after his or her scheduled hours of work
- the overtime is infrequent and occasional (usually less than three times a week but sometimes more if the work is needed to meet out-of-the-ordinary demands such as major repairs or periodic financial reporting).

If the overtime occurs frequently, the CRA considers overtime meal allowances to be a taxable benefit because they are akin to extra remuneration.

10.1.2 Taxable employment benefits

In general, employment benefits other than those listed above are taxed as though you had received an equivalent amount of income. Examples include:

- Tips (gratuities) that you receive from customers or suppliers
- Board, lodging and rent-free or low-rent housing (with some exceptions for remote or special work sites)

- Travelling expenses for personal travel, including expenses for your spouse to travel on a business trip of yours, unless your spouse was engaged primarily in business activities on behalf of the employer during the trip
- Personal use of employer's automobile (see 12.2)
- Gifts, except for non-cash gifts with a combined cost under $500 per year as noted above
- Allowing you and/or your family to use a vacation property
- Holiday trips, prizes and incentive awards
- Cost of employer-paid courses for personal interest or technical skills not related to your employer's business
- Payment of provincial (public) health insurance premiums (no longer charged by most provinces)
- Life insurance premiums
- Reimbursement for the cost of tools used in employment duties
- Loans to employees (see 10.3)
- Tax equalization payments to relocated employees to offset higher taxes in their new work location
- Stock option plans (see 10.4.1)
- Income tax return preparation and financial counselling (but not retirement or re-employment counselling).

Where the employer pays sales tax on goods or services, and then provides those goods or services to you as a taxable benefit, the calculation of the taxable benefit will generally require an additional 5% to account for the GST. This policy applies, for example, to automobiles. If you live in an HST province, your province's HST rate applies (see 11.2.5); for Quebec, the benefit is increased by the GST and QST.

10.1.3 COVID-19 government assistance

If you received government assistance as a result of the COVID-19 pandemic, you should be prepared to report these payments and pay tax on them, just like regular income. In particular, if you stopped working because of the pandemic and received the Canada Emergency Response Benefit (CERB), you must report these taxable benefits on your 2020 income tax return. The government has said it will provide a T4A tax slip to individuals to report these payments.

You may have also received income from your employer through the Canada Emergency Wage Subsidy (CEWS). According to the government, your employer will provide you with information about this income on your T4 slip and you will be required to report and pay tax on these amounts just as you would your regular wages.

10.2 Reductions of source withholdings

Ask to have your source withholdings reduced where possible.

As we saw in 9.2.1, your employer and others are required to withhold tax at source and remit it to the CRA. The same rules generally apply for Quebec purposes.

In any situation where you expect to receive a refund after filing your return (e.g., due to personal tax credits, RRSP contributions, medical expenses or charitable donations, alimony and maintenance payments), you should review the TD1 form (and MR-19.V in Quebec) you file with your employer and seek to have source withholdings reduced. You can ask your local CRA district office to permit your employer to reduce your source withholdings for deductions not normally provided for on the TD1 form, such as RRSP contributions and alimony and maintenance.

However, if your employer withholds from your remuneration RRSP contributions (up to your available RRSP contribution room—see 3.1.3), union and professional dues and alimony and maintenance payments for direct remittance to the intended recipient, the employer can take these withholdings into account in calculating your tax withheld at source without requesting permission from the CRA.

Your employer must withhold Canada Pension Plan (CPP) contributions from your income if you are between 18 and 70 years old. However, if you are between 65 and 70 and receive pension benefits under the CPP or Quebec Pension Plan, you can opt out of making contributions to these plans (see 20.3.1).

If you have a loan from your employer on which imputed interest is assessed as a taxable benefit (see 10.3), your source deductions of income tax will reflect that taxable benefit. If, however, you are using the funds for a purpose that allows you an offsetting deduction, you may write to the CRA, setting out that fact, and request that your employer be permitted to reduce the source withholding. For example, where you use the loan proceeds for investment purposes or use the funds to acquire shares of your employer.

Many people look forward to receiving a tax refund, but it's not good tax planning to get one. If you get a refund, that means the CRA has been holding your money and not paying you interest on it for many months. Although fiscal responsibility is needed to make sure you can pay your tax when it is due, it is better to be required to make a payment to the CRA at filing time, since it means that you have had use of the funds (for investment or other purposes) in the meantime. However, as we saw in 9.2.2, you must pay instalments if the difference between your tax payable and amounts withheld at source in both the current year and either of the two preceding years is more than $3,000 or, if you live in Quebec, $1,800 (see 17.1.3).

Note that interest is not paid on refunds for the first 30 days of processing after the filing deadline—that is, until after May 30 for most employees. If you have a June 15 filing deadline because you have self-employment income (see 9.1.1), interest will not be paid until 30 days after April 30 or 30 days after the date that the return is actually filed, whichever is later (see 9.1.1 and 9.3).

10.3 Loans to employees

If you receive a low-interest or interest-free loan from your employer (or past or future employer), you are considered to have received a benefit from employment.

The benefit is set at the CRA's (and Revenu Québec's) current prescribed rate of interest, which varies quarterly, minus any interest you actually pay during the year or within 30 days after the end of the year. The prescribed rate is set out by the CRA on a quarterly basis, and the lowest rate applies to employee and shareholder loans (see 9.3). (There may be an offsetting deemed interest deduction, as we shall see.)

> **Example**
>
> Amélie receives a loan of $10,000 from her employer on January 1, 2020. She is required to pay it back one year later, without interest. Assume the prescribed rate throughout the entire year is 2%.
>
> Amélie is considered to have an employment benefit of $200, and will be required to include this amount in her employment income.
>
> But if, instead, the loan bore interest at 1%, and Amélie made an interest payment before January 30, 2021, her taxable benefit would be calculated as 1% (the prescribed rate of 2% minus her employer's 1% rate) of $10,000, or $100.

Pay interest owing on loans from employers by January 30 of the following year.

If you have received an interest-bearing loan from your employer, consider deferring the payment of interest on the loan until January 30 of the next calendar year. This will provide you with a cash flow advantage. Make sure you do pay the interest by that date, however.

Exceptions

A home purchase loan is taxed on the same basis as other employee loans, but the rate applied in calculating the imputed interest for the first five years of the loan will not be greater than the prescribed rate in effect at the time the loan was made. At the end of the five-year period, it is considered a new loan, and the prescribed rate at that time will be the maximum for the next five years.

> **Example**
>
> Alex receives an interest-free loan from his employer to help him buy a house. (He is not relocating, just moving from an apartment to a house.) At the time, the prescribed interest rate is 3%. Two years later, interest rates have gone up, and the prescribed rate increases to 6%.
>
> Alex will still pay tax on the interest benefit calculated at only 3% of the amount of the loan. If the prescribed rate had gone below 3%, he would, however, pay tax on imputed interest at the lower rate as long as it stayed below 3%.

Where you use funds borrowed from your employer to purchase investments or to purchase an automobile (or aircraft) to be used for your employment, you can obtain an offsetting deduction. The amount of imputed interest that you include in your income as a taxable benefit is deemed to have been *interest paid by you*. As a result, if such interest would otherwise have been deductible, you can deduct it. (As we saw in 7.2.3, interest paid on loans to acquire investments is deductible, and as we'll see in 12.3.1, interest paid on loans to acquire a car is deductible if the car is required by your terms of employment.) The effect is to eliminate the tax cost of the taxable benefit.

If you are a shareholder of the company as well as an employee, or if a member of your family is a shareholder, you must be especially cautious. It is possible that the *entire* amount of the loan, rather than the imputed interest, will be included in your income for tax purposes, unless stringent conditions are met. In general, you can avoid this rule if the loan is made for certain specific purposes and with arrangements for repayment within a reasonable time, provided the loan was made because of your employment relationship. Alternatively, the entire loan must be repaid within one year and not be part of a series of loans and repayments (see 14.2.6).

10.4 Stock option plans

10.4.1 Regular stock option plans

A stock option plan is an arrangement whereby a corporation gives an employee the right (an option) to invest in its shares at a given price. The price may or may not be less than the market price at the time the option is granted. For example, suppose you work for a corporation whose stock trades at $20. In 2020, you are given an option to buy up to 1,000 shares at $20, good until 2022. If, in 2021, the stock is trading at $30, you can exercise the option, buy 1,000 shares for $20,000, and then, if you wish, turn around and sell the shares on the market for $30,000.

The general rule is that you are considered to receive a benefit from employment, not when the option is granted (2020 in the above example) but when you exercise it (2021). The taxable benefit is the difference between the price you pay ($20,000) and the value of the shares when you exercise the option ($30,000). Your employer would, therefore, report a taxable benefit of $10,000 in your employment income for 2021. (The adjusted cost base of the shares you own will be $30,000, so you will not be double-taxed when you subsequently sell them.)

An offsetting partial deduction is available if certain requirements are met. The first requirement is that the shares be normal common shares (not preferred shares). Second, the exercise price must be no less than the fair market value of the shares at the time the option was granted. (Otherwise you could simply exercise the option the day you received it, so the benefit would be just like cash.) Third, you must deal at arm's length with the corporation (meaning essentially that you or members of your family do not control it). If these conditions are met, you can claim a deduction from income of one-half of the amount of the taxable benefit. The effect of this deduction is to tax the benefit at the same inclusion rate as a capital gain.

The government has proposed changes to these rules which have not yet been enacted. Under these changes, which were first announced in the 2019 federal budget, if you are an employee of what is considered a "large, long-established, mature firm", then you will be affected by changes to allow only the first $200,000 of employee stock option grants to benefit from the current tax treatment. This annual cap is based on the fair market value of the underlying shares at the time that the option is granted. This annual cap will not apply for employees of Canadian-controlled private corporations and "highly innovative, fast-growing companies". The government delayed the scheduled implementation date of January 1, 2020, and has not yet indicated how it intends to move forward with these rules or when they will apply.

For Quebec purposes, the deduction is generally limited to one-quarter of the amount of the benefit relating to a stock option. At the time of writing, Quebec has not yet indicated whether it intends to harmonize with the proposed federal changes to the stock option rules (see 17.10.3).

Stock options in Canadian-controlled private corporations receive preferential tax treatment (see 10.4.2).

You may wish to approach your employer about establishing a stock option plan as an employment benefit. It may cost your employer very little, and can even bring investment funds into the corporation. (The cost to your employer is the dilution of the existing shareholders' equity interests.)

10.4.2 Stock options in Canadian-controlled private corporations

If your employer is a Canadian-controlled private corporation (CCPC) with which you deal at arm's length, you report the taxable benefit related to stock options in your employer's company when you sell the shares, rather than when you exercise the option and acquire them. And, if you have held the shares for at least two years at the date of sale, you can claim a deduction when computing your taxable income for one-half of the benefit realized in the year the shares were sold, as long as you deal at arm's length with the corporation in your capacity as an employee. This exception is designed to stimulate employee participation in ownership of small businesses. It also recognizes that the valuation of shares in a private company at the time you exercise the option may be difficult.

Be cautious about relying on CCPC shares too much for your future retirement plans; shares in private corporations are generally not liquid, and they can drop in value should the corporation run into financial or business trouble.

If you receive shares in a CCPC through a stock option plan, consider contributing some of them to your RRSP or TFSA if the shares qualify for that purpose (see 3.1.6).

10.4.3 Stock option cash-out payments

The terms of some stock option plans may allow you to receive a cash payment equal to the value of the options instead of receiving shares. When you receive this form of payment, the same tax consequences may apply to the cash payment as would apply to the issuance of shares—the employment benefit is included in your income and the related one-half deduction is available if the required conditions are met. You can only claim the deduction of one-half of the employment benefit if your employer elects to forgo a deduction for the cash payment.

If your employer does not make this election, it will be entitled to a corporate tax deduction for the payment but you must pay tax on the full value of the employment benefit. This rule applies to all stock options that are cashed out regardless of when the options were issued.

If your employer decides to pay cash instead, the stock option rules would not apply and the cash payment would be taxable as regular employment income.

10.4.4 Stock purchase plans

A stock purchase plan is a possible alternative to a stock option plan. In a typical stock purchase plan arrangement, a defined group of employees (which could be all employees) may purchase a limited number of shares of the company at their fair market value or at a slight discount. The plan is usually administered by a trust. You contribute a portion of your salary to the trust and in many cases your employer will make matching contributions. The trustee then uses the funds to purchase the shares at their current fair market value.

Since you make your contribution from after-tax dollars, no additional tax arises. If your company does not contribute to the plan and your contributions are simply used to purchase the shares, there will be no tax consequences. However, if the shares are issued at a discount, you will be assessed a taxable benefit on the difference between the shares' purchase price and their fair market value.

If your company contributes to the plan, the tax consequences to you will depend on how the shares are purchased. If the shares are issued from treasury, the stock option rules will apply. If the shares are purchased on the open market, you will be assessed a taxable benefit equal to the value of the shares at the time they vest.

10.4.5 Stock bonus plans

Stock bonus plans reward employees with shares of the corporation instead of cash. In most cases, the same rules apply as those outlined in 10.4.1 for stock options.

10.4.6 Phantom stock plans

A phantom stock plan avoids the requirement that you acquire shares in the corporation, and thus may be more attractive to your employer's controlling shareholders. Under such a plan, you receive bonuses based on the increase in value of your employer's shares. Such bonuses are simply taxed as employment income when they are paid to you. If they are not paid to you on an ongoing basis, you will need to determine whether they constitute a salary deferral arrangement (see 10.5.1), in which case they will be taxed in your hands even if not received. This type of plan allows you to benefit from the potential appreciation in value of your company's shares without a cash outlay and with no risk of any loss in the value of the shares.

10.5 Deferred compensation

Various techniques have been tried over the years to defer paying tax on employment income by having some of it held back in one way or another. (In general, employment income is taxed when received.)

Registered pension plans and deferred profit-sharing plans were discussed in 3.5 and 3.6. They are accepted mechanisms for deferring employment income.

10.5.1 Salary deferral arrangements

The rules for salary deferral arrangements catch most arrangements for deferred compensation. For example, if you agree with your employer that your salary for 2020 will be $80,000, plus a further $20,000 to be paid in 2024, you will be taxed on the whole $100,000 in 2020. You will generally be subject to this taxation unless there is a substantial risk of forfeiting the future income.

The salary deferral arrangement rules allow certain exceptions. One is a self-funded leave of absence program, sometimes used by teachers, academics and others to fund sabbatical leaves. Provided you meet all of the conditions, you can arrange for your employer or a trustee to hold back a portion of your salary every year for up to six years, not recognize that portion as employment income each year, and receive it in the sabbatical year, paying tax on it then. Another exception is an arrangement whereby you have a right to receive a bonus to be paid within three years.

10.5.2 Employee profit-sharing plans

Consider employees' profit-sharing plans for cash flow purposes.

Employee profit-sharing plans do not defer the taxation of employment income. Rather, contributions are made by the employer, based on profits for the year. Although the contributions are paid to the plan, the amounts contributed are treated as income of the employees for tax purposes. Such plans can therefore operate as forced savings plans for bonuses. Income (such as interest income) earned within the plan must be allocated to specific employees, who pay tax on it as it is allocated (even if it is not paid to them).

Though these plans are not widely used, one of their tax advantages is that there is no source withholding on the amounts paid into the plan or on the amounts paid by the plan to you. Careful timing of the employer's contributions and the plan's disbursements can give you better cash flow than would a straight bonus payment.

If you receive payments from one of these plans and you or members of your family are significant shareholders in the company, you may be subject to a special tax if the company's contributions to the plan for you exceed 20% of your salary for the year.

10.5.3 Supplemental ("top-hat") retirement plans

Supplemental retirement plans are usually designed to provide retirement benefits similar to those offered under registered pension plans (see 3.5), but they are not subject to the same contribution limits. As a result, they are often used to enhance the retirement compensation packages of higher-income executives and employees (which is why they are also known as "top-hat plans"). Supplementary plans may be unfunded or funded. If they are funded, they will be treated as a retirement compensation arrangement (see 10.5.4).

Under the most common type of unfunded supplemental retirement plan, the employer simply makes a promise in a letter or more formal agreement to pay an additional amount to the employee on retirement. Because no funds are set aside, there is no immediate tax liability for either the employee or the employer. However, because the retirement benefits are not secured, their payment will ultimately depend on the employer's ability to pay on the employee's retirement.

If the payments from the supplementary retirement plan are arranged to qualify as retiring allowance payments (see 10.6), you may be able to transfer part or all the payments to your RRSP.

10.5.4 Retirement Compensation Arrangements

Retirement Compensation Arrangements (RCAs) are arrangements made outside the registered pension plan system, whereby a custodian will receive funds from an employer and make payments after the employee's retirement or termination. The employer receives a deduction for contributions to such plans, but a 50% refundable tax applies to the payments made to the custodian. The tax must be remitted to the CRA when the contribution is made and refunded when the payments are made to the employee. The employee does not report the income for tax purposes until he or she receives the payments from the custodian.

Restrictions may apply to RCA tax refunds when RCA property has lost value, effective for RCA tax on contributions made after March 28, 2012.

RCAs may also be funded through a letter of credit or through a life insurance policy. The letter of credit's terms usually allow it to be called upon if the employer does not fulfill its obligations under the RCA. The contribution to the RCA is equal to the amount charged by the financial institution for issuing the letter of credit. A letter of credit is often viewed as a compromise between an unsecured arrangement and a fully funded RCA.

There are also different methods for funding supplemental plans through exempt life insurance products (see 7.3.2).

If you're the beneficiary of an RCA and you or your family members own 10% or more of the company's shares, the RCA is not permitted to invest in your company or other related ones.

10.6 Retiring allowances, wrongful dismissal payments and severance pay

A "retiring allowance", as defined for tax purposes, includes what one would normally call severance pay or termination pay, as well as a court award or settlement for wrongful dismissal. It also includes, of course, a payment by an employer for long service on retirement.

A retiring allowance, like ordinary employment income, is included in your income in the year you receive it. If you receive your retiring allowance in a year after the year you terminated employment, you

Transfer retiring allowances to an RRSP.

151

may ask the CRA to determine whether it is more advantageous to you to recalculate the tax on that income as if you received it in the prior year to which the payment relates. This option relieves the higher tax liability that would otherwise result if the entire lump-sum is taxed in the year of receipt, rather than year by year as a right to receive the income arose. Eligible payments must total at least $3,000 in the year and include superannuation or pension benefits (other than non-periodic benefits), wrongful dismissal and other employment-related payments arising from a court order or similar judgment, and certain other amounts.

Though damages awarded for wrongful dismissal are usually taxable as a retiring allowance, the amounts may not be taxable if the settlement includes damages related to mental anguish, humiliation or loss of self-respect suffered on the job rather than as a result of losing the job. If you are suing for wrongful dismissal including damages for mental distress, ensure that any settlement contains a detailed breakdown of its components to show that it includes non-taxable general damages.

As we saw in 3.3.2, part or all of a retiring allowance can be transferred to an RRSP and thus sheltered from immediate tax. The amount that can be transferred is $2,000 for each calendar year (or part year) of service before 1996, plus $1,500 for each year (or part year) before 1989 for which employer contributions to your pension plan have not vested. (Vested pension rights are those that you can take with you on retirement or termination—see 3.5.1.)

Legal fees incurred in establishing your retiring allowance are deductible against the retiring allowance (see 10.8.5). Legal fees can be carried forward for up to seven years and deducted against the "retiring allowance" income. Note that you should probably not transfer the maximum amount to an RRSP if you have incurred legal fees in obtaining your award (even if the case was settled without going to court). If you transfer the entire retiring allowance into an RRSP, the legal fees will never become deductible. (When you take payments *out* of the RRSP, they are no longer considered a "retiring allowance".) However, if you intend to leave the funds to grow tax-free in the RRSP for many years, you may want to consider transferring the maximum anyway.

10.7 Tax credits for employees

10.7.1 Employment tax credit

Claim the employment tax credit to help cover your work-related expenses.

Employees can claim a 15% non-refundable tax credit to help cover their work-related expenses. The credit is based on your employment income for the year, to a maximum of $1,245 for 2020. A Canada Workers Benefit (previously the Working Income Tax Benefit tax credit) is also available for low-income employees.

For Quebec tax purposes, employees may claim up to $1,190 as a deduction for 2020.

10.7.2 Teachers' school supply tax credit

If you are a certified teacher or early childhood educator and you purchase school supplies for your classroom at your own expense, you may be able to claim a 15% refundable tax credit for up to $1,000 in eligible expenses per year (worth $150).

To qualify, you must certify that you purchased the supplies for the purpose of teaching or otherwise enhancing learning in a classroom or learning environment.

Eligible supplies include games, books, educational support software, items for science experiments, art supplies and stationery items.

10.7.3 Volunteer firefighters and search and rescue volunteers

If you are a volunteer firefighter, you may be able to claim a 15% tax credit based on an amount of $3,000 (worth $450). To be eligible, you must perform at least 200 hours of volunteer firefighting services in the year that consist primarily of responding to and being on call for firefighting and related emergency calls, and attending meetings and training.

If you are a ground, air or marine search and rescue volunteer, you may be able to claim a similar credit also based on an amount of $3,000 (worth $450). To claim the credit, you must perform at least 200 hours of service during the year.

If you perform at least 200 hours of combined eligible search and rescue and volunteer firefighting services in a year, you may claim either the credit for volunteer firefighters or search and rescue volunteers, but not both.

Alternatively, you may be eligible for a tax exemption of up to $1,000 if you received a payment from a government or municipality for carrying out your volunteer firefighter or search and rescue duties. If you choose to claim this exemption, you will not be eligible for the volunteer firefighters or search and rescue volunteers tax credit, so you should determine which is more beneficial.

10.8 Deductions from employment income

The only deductions allowed against employment income are those specifically provided for in the federal and Quebec tax rules. We look at some of them below.

10.8.1 Travelling expenses and allowances

If you are required by your employment to spend funds on employment-related travel, the amounts you pay will normally be deductible (provided it is not reimbursed by your employer). Examples might include parking, taxis and train fares. You cannot deduct the costs of travelling between your home to your workplace. If you use your own automobile for employment-related travel, see 12.3.

If you travel for a transportation company (e.g., as a bus or truck driver or a flight attendant), you can also deduct costs of meals and lodging to the extent you are not entitled to be reimbursed. The deduction for meals will be further restricted to 50% of your cost (see 11.2.9). For eligible long-haul truck drivers, the meals deduction limit is 80%.

10.8.2 Commission sales person's expenses

If you are employed as a sales person under a contract that requires you to pay your own expenses, and you earn commissions, you may be able to deduct the costs of your employment-related expenditures—the same kinds of costs you could claim if you were self-employed (see 11.2.2). To do so, you must be required by your contract of employment to pay your own expenses, and you must be ordinarily required to carry on your duties of employment away from your employer's place of business. The total expenses you claim this way cannot exceed your total commission income.

10.8.3 Supplies, assistant's salary and home office

If you are required by your contract of employment to pay for any supplies or to pay for an assistant or substitute, you can deduct the cost of the supplies or the assistant's salary.

You can also deduct expenses relating to a home office, in limited circumstances (see 17.10.6 if you live in Quebec). First, you must be required by your employment contract to maintain the office, and your employer must sign a certificate (federal Form T2200, which you must keep with your records and Quebec Form TP-64.3-V, which you must file with your Quebec tax return).

Second, either the home office must be the place where you "principally perform the duties of employment" or you must use it on a regular and continuous basis for meeting people (such as your employer's customers) in the ordinary course of your employment.

The second restriction is parallel to that which applies to self-employed individuals, as outlined in more detail in 11.2.10. You will normally only be able to claim it if you spend more of your time working at home than at your employer's premises.

You may also be able to deduct home office expenses where your employer asked you and other employees to work from home during the COVID-19 pandemic, as long as you are not directly reimbursed for these expenses.

There are some important clarifications still required from CRA to allow employees to fully understand which home office expenses they may be able to claim for the work from home period during this pandemic. Until the CRA releases additional guidance, you should ensure that you maintain accurate records of your work space expenses during the pandemic, as well as the cost of any eligible home office supplies (i.e., keep all of your receipts so that you can claim deductions for the 2020 tax year that the CRA will allow).

10.8.4 Union and professional dues

Union dues are deductible for federal tax purposes (see 17.10.4 if you live in Quebec). These are normally withheld at source and reported on the T4 and Quebec Relevé 1 you receive from your employer.

Dues required to maintain a legally recognized professional status are deductible, even if you do not need to maintain that status for your current job. Your status as a lawyer, engineer, accountant, physician, architect, nurse, dentist, etc., qualifies for this purpose. Dues to voluntary associations are not deductible, unless you are self-employed (see 11.2.2).

10.8.5 Legal fees

If you spend money on a lawyer to recover unpaid wages, you can deduct the legal fees.

Legal fees you incur to establish your right to a "retiring allowance" (which includes severance pay) or private pension plan benefits are deductible. You can only deduct the legal fees against the income from the retiring allowance or pension benefits in that year. To the extent you have not yet received that income, you can carry forward the expenses for up to seven years and claim them against such income in those later years. (See 10.6 if you transfer your retiring allowance to an RRSP.)

> **Example**
>
> Lewis was fired from his job in 2018. He retained a lawyer and sued for wrongful dismissal, spending $3,000 in 2018 and $5,000 in 2019 in legal fees. In 2020, the case is settled and his former employer pays him $50,000.
>
> Lewis can deduct his $8,000 in legal fees only in 2020 against his $50,000 "retiring allowance" income, thus recognizing only $42,000 as income in that year.
>
> Lewis could ask the CRA to recalculate his tax on the retiring allowance income as if it had been received in the year to which the payment relates (see 10.6).

See also 2.8.1 regarding the deductibility of legal fees that are not related to employment.

10.8.6 Musicians' instruments

If you are employed as a musician and required to supply your own instrument, you may deduct any maintenance, rental and insurance costs. If you have purchased the instrument, you may claim capital cost allowance (depreciation), at a rate of 10% for the first year and 20% of the remaining balance in each following year. All of these deductions can only be used to offset your income from employment as a musician, not against other income.

10.8.7 Artists' expenses

If you are employed as an artist (including a painter, sculptor, playwright, literary author, composer, actor, dancer, singer or musician), you may deduct up to $1,000 of your actual expenses incurred in order to earn income from such activities. This deduction is limited to 20% of your income from artistic employment, and the $1,000 limit is reduced by any amounts you claim as automobile expenses (see 12.3.1) and musical instrument costs (10.8.6). (No parallel deduction is allowed for Quebec tax purposes.)

Of course, if you earn income from your artistic activities that is not employment income, you are self-employed, in which case your business expenses are normally deductible (see 11.2.2).

10.8.8 Tradesperson's tools

Employed tradespeople—claim the deduction for the cost of new tools.

If you are an employed tradesperson and you must use your own tools on the job, you can deduct the portion of the cost of new tools that exceeds $1,245 for 2020, up to a maximum of $500.

You can also claim a rebate of the GST/HST (see 10.9) paid on the deductible portion of the purchase price of the new tools.

Your employer will have to certify that the tools you acquired are a condition of your employment. Computers, cell phones and other electronic communication devices and data processing equipment do not qualify for these purposes.

10.8.9 Northern employees

If your employer pays for you to take a vacation trip, with or without your family, the value of the taxable benefit is included in your income (see 10.1.2). If you live in northern Canada, a federal deduction is available to offset all or part of this benefit (a similar deduction is available for Quebec purposes). Provided you meet certain residency requirements, the deduction can eliminate the taxable benefit associated with up to two trips per year, based on the cost of airfare to the nearest large Canadian city. (There is no limit to the number of such trips if they are taken to obtain medical services not available locally.)

See also 2.8.2, regarding the special deduction for residents of northern Canada, and 10.1.1, regarding the non-taxability of benefits relating to a remote work site.

10.9 GST/HST rebate for employees

Claim a rebate for GST/HST paid on expenses deductible from your employment income.

Where you can deduct expenses from your employment income, such as those discussed in 10.8, you may generally be entitled to claim a rebate of GST or HST paid on those expenses, as long as your employer is a GST registrant and is not a financial institution. A QST rebate is available for Quebec taxpayers.

Documentation must be kept to support the claim for the rebate. The rebate claim is filed with your personal income tax return. That rebate will itself be considered income from employment in the year in which you receive it, except where it relates to capital cost allowance. If you drive your own car for employment-related travel, see 12.3.2.

10.10 References

The following publications and more information, including forms and brochures, can be obtained on the CRA's website at *www.canada.ca/en/revenue-agency.html* or by telephone request at 1-800-959-8281 for individual income tax and trust-related enquiries or 1-800-959-5525 for business and self-employed individual enquiries.

Guide T4041, "Retirement Compensation Arrangements"

Guide T4130, "Employers' Guide—Taxable Benefits and Allowances"

Income Tax Folio S1-F2-C3, "Scholarships, Research Grants and Other Education Assistance"

Income Tax Folio S2-F1-C1, "Health and Welfare Trusts"

Income Tax Folio S2-F3-C1, "Payments from Employer to Employee"

Income Tax Folio S2-F1-C2, "Retiring Allowances"

Income Tax Folio S2-F3-C2, "Benefits and Allowances Received from Employment"

Income Tax Folio S4-F2-C2, "Business Use of Home Expenses"

Information Circular 73-21R9, "Claims for meals and lodging expenses of transport employees"

Information Circular 77-1R5, "Deferred profit sharing plans"

Also, see the following selected topics on the CRA's website:

"Employee security options"

"Retiring allowances"

"Changes to your taxes when you retire or turn 65 years old"

Chapter 11

If you are self-employed

- Consider whether you are a consultant rather than an employee (11.1)
- Recover GST (or HST) that you've paid by claiming input tax credits for your business (11.2.4)
- If you're a residential landlord, consider the effect of not being able to claim input tax credits when setting rents (11.2.4)
- Be aware of your obligations for sales to customers in HST provinces (11.2.5)
- Simplify your paperwork by using the "Quick Method" for GST/HST and QST reporting (11.2.6)
- Acquire depreciable assets before year-end (11.2.7)
- Consider claiming less CCA than the maximum (11.2.7)
- Deduct public transit fares, taxis and other business travel costs (11.2.8)
- Document and claim your business meals and entertainment expenses (11.2.9)
- Write off your eligible home office expenses (11.2.10)
- If you're a partner, claim sales tax rebates on your unreimbursed partnership expenses (11.3.7)
- Use your loss carryovers to maximum advantage (11.4.1)
- Keep detailed documentation to support your write-offs for losses from rental properties (11.4.2)
- Consider the potential benefits of incorporating your business (11.5)

In this chapter, we highlight some of the major topics in the taxation of business income. If you are a professional, see Chapter 16 for additional information. If you are in a partnership, see also 16.2; if you are in Quebec, see also Chapter 17. Of course, anyone with a substantial amount of business income should obtain proper professional advice due to the many tax planning opportunities available.

11.1 Employee or independent contractor?

As you will see in this chapter, people who are self-employed, carrying on business for themselves, generally have a wider scope for tax planning than do employees.

Carrying on a business has nothing to do with setting up a corporation (see 11.5 and Chapter 14). Anyone can carry on business. If you set up a second-hand clothing-for-cash exchange in your basement, you are carrying on business. If you decide to put a name to your business (say, "XYZ Second-Hand Clothing"), that is just you carrying on business under that name. You have not created a new entity. You simply have a proprietorship, which means you are the proprietor of a business.

The distinction between employee and independent contractor (i.e., self-employed) is not always clear in cases where you receive most or all of your "work" income from one source. If you provide services to an organization, you can be an employee or an independent contractor, depending on the facts.

> **Example**
>
> Kathy is a technical writer. She develops software documentation under contract for ABC Corporation and is paid for each hour she works. She does a lot of her work at home, though she goes to ABC's offices for regular meetings.
>
> Is Kathy an employee of ABC, or an independent consultant who carries on business and whose major (or only) client is ABC?

In cases like this, one must look at all the facts to determine the person's status. There are no hard and fast rules. In general, you are more likely to be considered an employee if you:

- work a set number of hours per day
- have to account for your time to the company
- are told what to do each step of the way
- are a member of the company's group life, drug, dental and pension plans and receive other "benefits"
- use the company's computer equipment and supplies and have an office at the company.

By contrast, you would likely be considered an independent contractor carrying on your own business as a proprietor if you:

- agree to get the job done but don't make a commitment for any particular number of hours on any particular day
- work on your own with no supervision, and simply report back to the company periodically on progress
- issue invoices and receive payments (with no source deductions for income tax, EI or CPP/QPP) and receive no employee benefits
- use your own equipment and work at home, going to the company for planning meetings only
- provide services to more than one company.

These examples are fairly extreme. Between them is a large fuzzy area, where each case will depend on its facts. It doesn't matter very much what you and the company *call* your relationship; more specifically, calling it independent contracting doesn't make it independent contracting unless the facts support such a claim.

One case where the CRA has a clear administrative policy is that of real estate agents. You will be considered self-employed if you are entitled to the full amount of commissions, and either (a) you pay only a fixed amount to your broker for administrative operating costs, or (b) you pay a percentage of your gross commissions to your broker to cover such costs, and you set your own commission rate for sales on your listings.

If you are currently employed in a position where you maintain a fair amount of independence from your employer, investigate whether you can change your relationship so that you become an independent consultant rather than an employee. You will need to document the details of your relationship carefully, in case the CRA or Revenu Québec challenges you in the future.

Consider whether you are a consultant rather than an employee.

If you become independent, you will be able to use all of the planning tips throughout this chapter. You will lose certain advantages, however, including the right to Employment Insurance (EI) benefits, the employer's contribution to the Canada Pension Plan (CPP) for you (you will be required to pay both the employee and employer portions of the CPP—see 11.2.3), and possibly all of the employment benefits you now have (pension plan, drug plan, etc.). You may wish to negotiate to have your cash compensation increased in exchange for any employment benefits you are giving up.

The CRA has a questionnaire, Form CPT-1, through which your employer/client can supply the details of its relationship with you and ask for a ruling as to whether you are an employee or not for CPP or EI purposes (and, by extension, for income tax purposes). However, there is no requirement to apply for such a ruling, and you and your employer/client are not bound by the CRA's administrative decisions. If, after receiving professional advice, you believe that you are legally an independent contractor, then you are quite entitled to proceed on that basis.

11.2 Taxation of the business

In this section, we review how your business income is taxed. If you are a professional, see also Chapter 16.

11.2.1 Business year-end

Unlike corporations, all individuals, and all partnerships that have any individuals as members, generally have to use the calendar year for reporting their income.

11.2.2 Business income and expenses

As a general rule, business income for tax purposes is based on generally accepted accounting principles. (Among other things, this means operating on the accrual basis: you record your income when you have billed your clients, whether or not you have been paid.) However, there are many adjustments required for tax purposes. Some of them are discussed in the sections below.

When you earn business income, there is normally no withholding of tax at source. If you are providing services to a single organization and are able to classify your relationship as one of independent consultant rather than employee (see 11.1), you should submit invoices that will be paid in full, without tax (or EI premiums or CPP/QPP contributions) being taken off and remitted to the CRA. You may, however, be required to pay instalments of income tax. Instalments are discussed in 9.2.2.

In general, expenses are deductible if they are laid out to earn income from the business and are considered reasonable in the circumstances. There are certainly exceptions, as we shall see in the following sections. However, the underlying principle is the reverse of that for employees. Employees can only deduct expenses that are specifically permitted under the federal *Income Tax Act* and the *Quebec Taxation Act*. Someone carrying on business can deduct any expenses that are not specifically prohibited by these statutes, provided such expenses relate to the earning of business income and are reasonable in the circumstances.

11.2.3 EI, CPP and other payroll taxes

Employment insurance is available only to those who are employed. If you carry on business for yourself, you are neither required nor permitted to pay EI premiums. However, if your consulting contracts terminate and you are left without work, you cannot receive EI benefits.

Although you will not qualify for regular EI benefits, you can choose to voluntarily pay the employee's portion of EI premiums (up to $856 for 2020) to qualify for special EI benefits such as maternity, parental and adoptive, sickness and compassionate care benefits.

Canada and Quebec Pension Plan contributions are split equally between employees and their employers. If you are self-employed, you are required to pay the "employer's share" to make up what is not being paid for you, as well as your own share. Since you are not employed, no CPP/QPP contributions are withheld from your income. As a result, you will find yourself required to pay up to $5,796 for 2020 in mandatory CPP/QPP contributions when you file your personal tax return. You may then claim a deduction from taxable income for the portion of CPP/QPP contributions that represents the employer's share, up to $2,898 for 2020. You can also claim the non-refundable 15% federal tax credit for the employee's share of your CPP/QPP contributions (about $435, based on the credit amount of up to $2,898 for 2020—see 2.9.1). If it's any consolation, you'll be entitled to receive CPP/QPP retirement benefits after you turn 65, or optionally as early as age 60 at a reduced amount (see 20.3.1).

Starting in 2019, the CPP/QPP contribution rate increased. By 2023, the contribution rate will be 2% higher for self-employed individuals than it was in 2018. A new additional contribution rate of 8% for the self-employed will apply to earnings between the yearly maximum pensionable earnings and a new upper-earnings limit, starting in 2024. As a self-employed person, you will be able to deduct both the employer and employee share of these additional CPP contributions. When you retire, you may be entitled to a higher retirement benefit, depending on the amount of time you pay these increased contribution rates.

11.2.4 GST and claiming input tax credits

The Goods and Services Tax (GST) applies at a rate of 5% to taxable goods and services supplied in Canada. The Harmonized Sales Tax (HST), discussed in 11.2.5, is a blended federal/provincial sales tax that applies at different rates in Ontario, Nova Scotia, New Brunswick, Prince Edward Island and Newfoundland and Labrador. Generally, our comments on GST throughout this book apply equally to the HST, with some exceptions. Please note that this book only addresses certain selected GST/HST topics.

If you are self-employed, you can normally claim a refund ("input tax credit") of the GST paid on most expenses incurred in your business, including most capital assets, in your GST/HST return. Certain exceptions may apply.

To be eligible for input tax credits, you must register with the CRA. You are generally required to register if your total taxable revenues are more than $30,000 in the last four consecutive quarters or in a single quarter. If your revenues are below that threshold, you can still voluntarily register. Once you are registered, you must charge GST on all your taxable sales, even if your sales are less than $30,000.

While you can build the tax into your prices if you wish, you must advise your clients that the sale is subject to GST/HST (i.e., on invoices). You must generally provide your clients with documentation to support their own claims of input tax credits (see below). As is the case for income tax purposes, "personal or living expenses" are not eligible for input tax credits.

Make sure to keep accurate records so you can claim input tax credits where possible. Claims for input tax credits for GST paid must be supported by receipts or other documentation, not submitted with the GST return but held on file in case of audit. All documentation must show the vendor's name, the date (or, for a contract, the date the amounts are payable), and the total amount payable. Where the total (including all taxes) is $30 or over, the receipt must also show:

> Recover GST (or HST) that you've paid by claiming input tax credits for your business.

- the amount of GST, or a statement that the total includes GST, and a clear indication of which items are taxable, and
- the supplier's nine-digit GST registration number.

Where the total is $150 or over, the receipt must also show:

- the purchaser's name,
- the terms of payment, and
- a description sufficient to identify each item supplied.

Failure to have this documentation will normally lead to a reassessment of any input tax credit claim if the return is audited.

Input tax credits can only be claimed where the expenses were incurred in the course of providing "taxable supplies". A business engaged in providing supplies that are GST-exempt—such as a doctor, dentist, life insurance agent or financial institution—cannot claim input tax credits for GST paid on the costs of making those supplies.

If you rent out residential real estate (whether a house or an apartment building), the rent will generally be exempt from GST. As a result, you cannot claim input tax credits to recover any of the GST that you pay on utilities, property management fees and other costs. (Rent for commercial real estate is subject to GST.)

If you're a residential landlord, consider the effect of not being able to claim input tax credits when setting rents.

In Quebec, similar rules apply for Quebec Sales Tax (QST) purposes, with certain exceptions.

11.2.5 Harmonized Sales Tax

Be aware of your obligations for sales to customers in HST provinces.

No matter where in Canada your business is located, you should be aware of your obligations under the HST, the blended federal/provincial sales tax that applies in Ontario, Nova Scotia, New Brunswick, Prince Edward Island, and Newfoundland and Labrador.

The HST rates in these provinces are comprised of a 5% federal component and varying provincial components (see the table below). A major difference is that the HST applies on goods and services supplied in an HST province at the HST rate applicable in that province, instead of the 5% GST and any other applicable sales taxes (e.g., QST) that apply in other provinces. As noted, in 11.2.4, our comments about the GST throughout this book apply equally to the HST, though there are some exceptions such as the place of supply rules, which vary based on the nature of the supply.

All GST registrants must collect HST on taxable supplies made in the HST provinces. If you are registered for the GST, you are also registered for the HST. Collection, reporting and remittance of the HST is done through the CRA in the same way as the GST, with a few exceptions.

The HST could complicate your recordkeeping and sales tax reporting if you make taxable sales to customers both inside and outside the HST provinces. Depending on the province to which the goods or services are delivered, you will have to determine whether you should charge GST or HST, QST or provincial sales tax (PST) and at what rate. Special rules apply to determine whether goods or services are supplied (i.e., delivered) in one of these provinces.

The table below shows indirect tax rates that apply across Canada as at June 30, 2020.

Indirect Tax Rates in Effect as at June 30, 2020*		
	GST or HST Rate	**PST or QST Rate**
British Columbia	5% GST	7% PST
Alberta	5% GST	
Saskatchewan	5% GST	6% PST
Manitoba	5% GST	7% PST
Ontario	13% HST (5% federal and 8% provincial components)	
Quebec	5% GST	9.975% QST
New Brunswick	15% HST (5% federal and 10% provincial components)	
Nova Scotia	15% HST (5% federal and 10% provincial components)	
Prince Edward Island	15% HST (5% federal and 10% provincial components)	
Newfoundland and Labrador	15% HST (5% federal and 10% provincial components)	
* Other rates and other indirect taxes may apply.		

11.2.6 GST—the "Quick Method" and simplified accounting

Self-employed individuals and small businesses may elect to use the "Quick Method" to simplify recordkeeping for GST. Many businesses with annual sales (including tax) that do not exceed $400,000 (excluding financial services, real property, capital assets and certain other assets) can use this method. Annual sales include sales of associated businesses.

The Quick Method can be particularly useful for certain consultants. However, some businesses may not use this method, including businesses providing legal, accounting, actuarial, bookkeeping, financial consulting, tax consulting or tax return preparation services.

Under the Quick Method, your business must still charge and collect the tax at the normal rates. However, instead of remitting total GST collected minus total GST paid as it would under the usual method, the business remits to the CRA a flat

> Simplify your paperwork by using the "Quick Method" for GST/HST and QST reporting.

percentage of sales (including GST/HST). The percentages vary depending on whether your business operates exclusively outside of the HST provinces, exclusively in those provinces, or both in and out of those provinces. The rates also vary depending on whether your business primarily sells goods or services. Your business may have to use more than one rate, depending on its circumstances.

Certain input tax credits are still available, including those on real property and other capital assets purchased for use in taxable activities. You must still remit the full amount of tax collected on supplies that are not eligible for the Quick Method calculation, such as real property and capital assets.

For businesses operating exclusively outside the HST provinces, where sales are mostly services rather than goods, the flat percentage for GST is 3.6%. For qualifying suppliers of goods whose costs, including GST/HST, of taxable personal property (other than basic groceries and other goods for which no tax is paid) purchased for resale are at least 40% of taxable sales (including GST/HST but excluding basic groceries and certain other items), the flat percentage is 1.8%. Input tax credits can only be claimed for capital purchases.

For businesses operating exclusively in HST provinces, the rate differs depending on the province.

For businesses operating both inside and outside the HST provinces, the rules are more complex—advice from a qualified sales tax professional is recommended.

Under the Quick Method, a business can generally claim a 1% credit on the first $30,000 (including GST/HST) of eligible supplies on which GST or HST has been collected in each fiscal year.

Example

John is a computer consultant who works exclusively in Alberta. In May 2020, he bills his clients $50,000 plus $2,500 GST. Because he is able to use his clients' equipment and facilities, his cost of doing business is very low. He pays a total of $50 GST on $1,000 of business expenses during the year.

Normally, John would remit his GST collected minus his GST paid to the CRA for the year. This would be $2,500 minus $50, or $2,450.

By electing to use the Quick Method, however, John will be required to remit $1,890 (a flat 3.6% of his sales of $52,500), minus a credit of $300 (1% X $30,000). He thus remits $1,590 instead of $2,450.

John will effectively be subject to income tax on the $860 difference ($2,450 − $1,590).

As you can see, the Quick Method can be useful for eligible businesses that have few taxable expenses. If the business's taxable expenses are high, however, the loss of the ability to claim input tax credits may offset the benefit of the Quick Method's reduced remittance rate.

As an alternative to the Quick Method, the Simplified Method of accounting for input tax credits allows certain businesses to total up many of their GST-bearing purchases—including GST, provincial sales tax, late payment penalties and tips—and claim 5/105 of the total on purchases where 5% GST is paid for input tax credit purposes (different rebate rates apply to HST-bearing purchases).

Among other rules and conditions, your business's annual sales (including sales of associated businesses) generally must not exceed $1 million and taxable purchases must not exceed $4 million for you to use this method.

Not only does the Simplified Method make accounting for input tax credits simpler, it may also give you a slightly larger claim than you can make by totalling up individual amounts of GST paid.

For QST reporting in Quebec, there is a similar "Quick Method" and simplified accounting (however, the rates under the QST system are different).

11.2.7 Capital cost allowance

The treatment of capital expenses is one of the major differences between business income based on accounting principles and income calculated for income tax purposes. In both cases, you cannot simply write off the cost of purchasing major capital assets (furniture, buildings, computers, automobiles, etc.). You must spread the cost over several years.

For accounting (not tax) purposes, the business owners, with professional assistance, will decide on the appropriate depreciation to claim. Various methods of depreciation can be used.

For tax purposes, depreciation is subject to strict rules and limitations since it reduces your income (and thus the tax you pay). The income tax system of depreciation is called capital cost allowance (CCA); the rules are numerous and complex.

In general terms, your capital assets are grouped into classes, and capital cost allowance can be claimed annually against each class. The "declining balance" method is used for most classes; the maximum you can claim against each class is a fixed percentage of the "undepreciated capital cost". What you claim then reduces that balance for next year's claim.

Some common CCA rates	
Automobiles (class 10 or 10.1)	30%
Non-residential buildings:	4%
acquired after March 18, 2007 (class 1) (election required to use this rate and building must be put into a separate class)	6%
acquired after March 18, 2007 and used in manufacturing and processing (class 1) (election required to use this rate and building must be put into a separate class)	10%
Computer hardware (class 50)	55%
Most computer software (class 12)	100%
Furniture and fixtures (class 8)	20%
Eligible tools costing less than $500 (class 12)	100%

Acquire depreciable assets before year-end.

For most acquisitions, only one-half of the CCA you could otherwise claim for the asset will be allowed in the year of acquisition. As a result, acquiring an asset just before your year-end will accelerate the timing of your tax write-off, while acquiring the asset at the beginning of the year will delay your CCA claim. Assets are normally required to be available for use in the business and not simply "on the books" to be eligible for CCA, unless you have owned them for at least two years. (The term "available for use" has a specific and complex definition, and professional advice should be sought if you are unsure as to how it applies in your case.)

For capital property acquired after November 20, 2018 and available for use before 2028, such as equipment and buildings, you may be able to take a larger deduction in the year of acquisition of the property under the accelerated capital cost allowance rules. However, this larger first year deduction is ultimately offset by reductions to your capital cost allowance claims in future years. If you have acquired capital property after November 20, 2018, you should speak with your tax advisor to ensure you are taking advantage of these new rules.

Note that you are never required to claim the maximum CCA. You may in any year choose to claim less than the maximum, or nothing at all, for any given class of assets. The undepreciated capital cost for that class will remain intact, so you can make claims in later years based on that carried-forward balance.

Consider claiming less CCA than the maximum.

In some circumstances, you may wish to claim less CCA than you are entitled to. For example, if you have prior-year non-capital losses or investment tax credits that would otherwise expire, you are better off not to claim CCA, use up the losses or credits, and save your "undepreciated capital cost" balances for CCA claims in future years.

You might also choose not to claim CCA if you are in a low-income year and expect your income to be much higher (and thus taxed at higher marginal rates) in later years. Such a decision should only be made after careful analysis of the present value of the future tax savings, including the impact on your ability to make an RRSP contribution in the subsequent year.

11.2.8 Transportation expenses

If you rely on modes of travel other than an automobile for your business travel, you can generally deduct the related expenses. Keep records of all such business trips, and deduct the appropriate costs of public transit, taxis and so on. (If you use your own car, see 12.3.)

> Deduct public transit fares, taxis and other business travel costs.

You cannot consider transportation from your home to your own office as a business expense. However, if you have an office in your home and you travel from there to your client (who might happen to provide you with an office on its premises), you are engaging in business travel.

11.2.9 Meals and entertainment

If you treat a client or potential client (or a group of such people) to a meal, you can normally consider the cost of the meal as a business expense. The tax rules restrict the amount you can claim to 50% of the amount paid; the restriction is designed to deny a deduction for some of the personal benefit you receive (since you would need to eat anyway). The same 50% limitation applies to entertainment expenses, such as taking a client to a sports event. (If you pay Quebec tax, see 17.10.5.)

> Document and claim your business meals and entertainment expenses.

Similarly, if you are registered for GST purposes, you can generally only claim input tax credits for half of the GST paid on such expenses (see 11.2.4).

Make sure you claim all lunches and dinners that you can justifiably relate to your business. For audit purposes, you should make a notation on your receipt of the individual(s) entertained and the reason for the meeting.

11.2.10 Home office expenses

If you have an office in your home, you can claim a portion of your ongoing home expenses as business expenses, subject to the restrictions discussed below. The portion is normally based on the fraction of the home that is used for your office (you should usually exclude common areas, such as hallways, kitchen and washrooms, when making the calculation).

> Write off your eligible home office expenses.

> Mary is a software developer and works as a consultant to various companies. She works in her home, where her office is a room that is 200 square feet (18.5 square metres). The total area of the rooms in her house (bedrooms, living room, dining room and the office) is 2,000 square feet (186 square metres).
>
> Provided her home office qualifies (see below), Mary can claim 10% of her costs such as mortgage interest, property taxes, house insurance and utilities as expenses for tax purposes.

The expenses you can claim include:

- rent, if you are a tenant
- mortgage interest (but not the principal portion of blended mortgage payments)
- property taxes
- utilities, such as electricity, heat, water, gas
- telephone (if you have a separate business telephone which is fully deductible, consider whether you also use your personal phone for business calls)
- home insurance.

Also make sure to claim your business portion of some of the less obvious expenses, such as garden service, driveway snowplowing, and minor repairs. You will need to keep receipts on file; do not simply estimate your expenses.

You may also claim capital cost allowance on the appropriate fraction of your home, but this is often not advisable. If you claim CCA, the CRA will take the position that that fraction of your home is not part of your principal residence and disallow your claim for the principal residence exemption (see 6.5.2) for that portion of the home. Any CCA you claimed can also be "recaptured" into income when you sell your home. (If you bought your home at the top of the housing market and do not expect to recover your costs when you sell, claiming CCA may be a good idea, however.)

Home office expenses are subject to restrictions. First, you can only claim the expenses against your income from the business. You therefore cannot use home office expenses to produce an overall business loss that is applied against other income. However, losses disallowed because of this rule can be carried forward and used in any later year against income generated from the same business.

Second, the home office will only be allowed if:

- your home is your principal place of business—that is, you do not have an office elsewhere (if you have a client that provides you with an office on its premises, it is still the client's premises and it will not disentitle you to your claim for a home office), or
- the home office is used exclusively for your business and used "on a regular and continuous basis for meeting clients, customers or patients".

Les is an optometrist and has an office outside his home. He also has an office in his basement, where he does a lot of his business's paperwork and occasionally sees patients (usually neighbours who come over for treatment in the evening).

Les cannot claim any expenses for his home office unless he can show that he uses it "on a regular and continuous basis" to see patients.

Of course, supplies that relate exclusively to your home office are fully deductible and not subject to the above restrictions. Fully deductible expenses normally include a separate business phone, printer paper, printer ink, photocopier toner cartridges, computer repairs (assuming your computer is used only for your business) and so on.

If you pay Quebec tax, see also 17.10.6.

11.2.11 Health and dental premiums

Self-employed individuals whose primary source of income is business income may write-off premiums paid for supplementary health care coverage as a business expense. For the premiums to be deductible, your coverage must be no greater than the benefits provided to your arm's length employees. If you have no such employees, your deductible premiums are limited to $1,500 for yourself, $1,500 for your spouse and $750 for each child.

11.2.12 Convention expenses

The CRA allows you to deduct the costs of attending two conventions a year in connection with your business or profession. A portion of your expenses may be subject to the limitation on the deductibility of meals and entertainment expenses discussed at 11.2.9.

For the expenses to be deductible, the convention must be held at a location that can reasonably be considered to be within the scope of the host organization. For example, if the convention's sponsor is a business or professional body that is provincial in scope, the convention must be held in that province. Under the Canada-U.S. tax treaty, expenses to attend a Canadian-sponsored convention in the U.S. are deductible, but only if the Canadian organization is a national one. (The CRA does not allow you to deduct any costs for attending a convention held during an ocean cruise, no matter who sponsors it.)

11.2.13 Capital gains

Any capital gains that you realize are accounted for directly, through the capital gains system discussed in Chapter 6. Capital gains are calculated independent of the business's income.

11.2.14 Investment tax credits

Federal investment tax credits (ITCs) are available for investment in certain regions of the country (for example, parts of the Maritimes) and for investment in scientific research and experimental development.

ITCs are claimed in the return for the calendar year in which they are generated. Unused ITCs can be carried back three years or carried forward for up to 20 years.

11.3 Partnerships

If you join together to carry on business with one or more other people—which could include your spouse—you will be in partnership. You are still, for tax purposes, carrying on business. (As well as the discussion below, see 16.2, where we discuss some special rules applying to professional partnerships.)

11.3.1 How partnership income is taxed

Partnerships do not pay tax. Partnerships are required to file "information returns" with the CRA to report partnership income, but these are not tax returns. Some partnerships are exempt from this filing, based on a financial activity test and type of partnership.

The individual partners must each report their share of the partnership's income (or loss) as their own, *whether or not they have taken any of the profits out of the partnership*. The partnership is generally required to report income on a December 31 year-end basis. (Resource allowances and certain other resource-related expenses are claimed by the individual partner rather than at the partnership level.)

Note that a partnership cannot pay a "salary" to a partner. Even if you, as a partner, receive something called a "salary", it is really partnership drawings (withdrawal of profits or capital from the partnership). You are *not* taxed on your partnership drawings, but on your share of the partnership's income, which may be very different.

If the partnership suffers losses, you can normally claim your share of those losses against your other sources of income. (This may not be the case where the partnership is a limited partnership.)

11.3.2 Adjustment of partnership allocation

The allocation of partnership income (or losses) among the partners is normally left up to the partners to resolve. If you set up an unreasonable allocation for income-splitting purposes (see Chapter 5), however, the CRA may disallow your allocation and substitute a reasonable one.

For example, if you and your spouse are in partnership together and you supply all of the capital and do almost all of the work in your business, while your spouse does almost nothing, the CRA could disallow a 50/50 allocation of the business's income between the two of you. The tax on split income could also apply to your spouse's income (see 5.2.5).

11.3.3 Capital gains

Capital gains or losses realized by a partnership are allocated to the individual partners at the end of the partnership's taxation year.

11.3.4 Allocation of investment tax credits

Investment tax credits (see 11.2.14) earned by a partnership are allocated to the individual partners and claimed in the year in which the partnership's year ends.

11.3.5 Gain or loss on partnership interest

When you are a member of a partnership you own a "partnership interest", which has an adjusted cost base for capital gains calculation purposes (see 6.2.1). If you sell your interest in the partnership (or are deemed to dispose of it at fair market value on death or emigration—see 6.5.4 and 13.3.2), the adjusted cost base determines whether you have a capital gain or capital loss.

Your initial cost base of your partnership interest is the capital you put into the partnership. Each year, when you report your share of the partnership's income, that amount is added to your cost base (since you have already been taxed on it, it should not be taxed again if you sell your interest without withdrawing the profits). When you withdraw profits from the partnership (see 11.3.1), the amount you withdraw reduces your adjusted cost base. Thus, in simplified terms, your adjusted cost base of your partnership interest is your contributions, plus all partnership profits, minus all partnership losses and your withdrawals. (The details are much more complicated and there are many special rules, but that is the essence of it.)

11.3.6 Assessment of partnership

The CRA is able to issue a "determination" of a partnership's income or loss. This determination is much like an assessment of a taxpayer's tax (see 9.4.1), in that it is binding on the partners unless a Notice of Objection is filed. One partner would have to be designated by the partnership to file any such Notice of Objection, and the other partners would not be able to object directly to the determination.

11.3.7 Partners' sales tax rebates

Like employees, partners who are not registered themselves for GST purposes and who have unreimbursed expenses, such as automobile expenses that are deductible for income tax purposes, can generally claim a rebate for the GST, HST or QST paid on those expenses (see 12.3.2 for an example).

If you're a partner, claim sales tax rebates on your unreimbursed partnership expenses.

Make sure to keep records through the year and obtain invoices that indicate the amount of tax paid. The rebate is claimed with your individual income tax return.

11.4 Losses

11.4.1 Business losses

If your business expenses claimed for tax purposes exceed the revenues from the business, you have a loss. You also have a loss for tax purposes if you share in a portion of a partnership's loss.

You can only claim a business loss or loss arising from a partnership against other income if your business activity is clearly commercial and undertaken in pursuit of profit. If the activity has a personal element or has the aspect of a hobby, such as breeding race horses, the venture is considered to be in pursuit of profit if it is undertaken in a sufficiently commercial manner.

A business loss must first be used in the year in which it arises, to offset income from other businesses and other types of income, such as employment income, interest, (grossed-up) dividends and taxable capital gains. You do not have any choice in this matter; even if, for example, the tax on your dividend income could be offset by the dividend tax credit anyway, you must apply your business losses against any income you have in that year.

Use your loss carryovers to maximum advantage. Business losses not deductible in the year they arise can be applied to other years' income. These "non-capital losses" can be carried back for up to three years or carried forward for up to 20 years. They can be applied against any source of income in those years. All such claims are optional.

Example

Judy had no income in 2017 and she earned $40,000 in 2018 and $50,000 in 2019 as an employee. In 2020, she went into business for herself, and, for her 2020 business year, she suffered a loss for tax purposes of $100,000.

Judy can file a form requesting that her non-capital loss from 2020 be applied against any amount of her 2018 and 2019 income. She will then receive a refund for the tax she paid in those years. If she wipes out all of her 2018 and 2019 income, she will still have a $10,000 non-capital loss, which can be carried forward to future years..

Judy should not, however, use up $90,000 of her loss. She only needs to use enough to bring her 2018 and 2019 income so low that she pays no tax at all (about $11,809 for 2018 and $12,069 for 2019). If she wishes, she may choose to use even less, and leave some of the 2018 and 2019 income taxed at relatively low rates.

This example shows the need to use any non-capital losses carefully. When using non-capital losses against income for any given year, consider whether you want to keep some of the income taxed at a low rate. For example, if you have a loss in 2020 and are carrying it back to 2019, bear in mind that taxable income below $47,600 in 2019 was taxed at only about 24%. If you (confidently) expect to have a large income within the next few years, so that you can apply the loss against income that would otherwise be taxed at approximately 51%, you may be better off not bringing your 2019 taxable income below $47,600.

Of course, you should never use loss carryovers to reduce your taxable income below the level where no tax is payable anyway ($12,069 for 2019, or more depending on the credits you can claim—see Chapter 2).

11.4.2 Losses from rental properties

If you are a residential landlord, your losses from your rental property are deductible in the same way as other business losses as long as your rental business meets the general tax law requirements for business deductions. The CRA is quite aggressive in targeting rental loss deductions, so you should be sure to have adequate supporting documentation on hand to support your rental loss deductions.

The CRA is likely to question your rental losses if your ownership of the property has a personal-use element, for example, if you or one of your relatives live there rent-free or you plan to live there in the future. The CRA may ask for detailed documentation such as a floor plan of the building showing which areas you use, rent out and share with your tenants. You should also be prepared to show which of your expenses relate to the whole property as opposed to the rental portion only. If you rent to a relative, your losses may be disallowed if you charge a lower rent than you would charge an unrelated tenant.

> Keep detailed documentation to support your write-offs for losses from rental properties.

You should be prepared to prove the commercial nature of your rental activities. Where possible, keep complete records to show that you did thorough research on rental properties before you chose one to buy and complete records of the information that led you to believe your rental property would be a profitable investment. The tax courts have ruled that rental businesses may take several years—up to eight years in one case—to turn a profit. An explanation for your losses and description of steps taken to increase revenue or reduce expenses would also help support your case.

The Supreme Court has ruled that the tax system should not penalize taxpayers for lack of business acumen. Even if you do not have detailed profit projections and market research on hand, you should seek professional tax advice if the CRA seeks to deny your rental losses.

11.5 Should you incorporate your small business?

If you have an unincorporated business, you may be considering incorporation to save on taxes. But whether you and your business would gain a tax benefit from incorporation depends on your personal cash flow needs, the personal and corporate tax rates in your province and the status of your business. (If you are considering setting up a corporation for the sole purpose of holding your investments, see 14.6.)

If you rely on all of your business's profits to support your personal cash flow needs, incorporation may not be a good idea—the cost of setting up and maintaining the corporation could outweigh the tax benefits. But if you can leave some of your profits in the corporation to be reinvested in the business, incorporation could result in significant tax savings.

The taxation of corporations is discussed in 14.1. Generally, if you earn income through a corporation, the income is taxed at the corporation level and then again at the personal level when the corporation distributes its after-tax income to you as a shareholder in the form of a dividend. In theory, the total corporate and personal income tax incurred by using a corporation to earn income should be the same as the personal tax that would result if the income were earned directly by an individual who was taxable at the top marginal rate. In practice, this is not always the case. Before you incorporate your business, ask a professional tax adviser to help you compare the total amount of tax you would pay if you earn your business income directly or through a corporation. Some advantages of incorporating your business include the following:

Asset protection—Incorporation can limit your liability by keeping your personal and corporate assets separate. But since banks often ask small business owners for personal guarantees before they'll provide financing, incorporation may not protect you from all creditors.

Deferring expenses—You may be able to defer certain expenses if you incorporate. For example, if you report a bonus paid to an employee for tax purposes, you do not have to pay out the money until 179 days after the end of the corporation's fiscal year.

Fiscal year flexibility—As we saw in 11.2.1, an unincorporated business must use the calendar year to report income for tax purposes. An incorporated business can choose a non-calendar fiscal year, which may work better for your business cycle. If the fiscal year-end is in the later part of the calendar year, the payment of a bonus six months after the end of the year would put the payment into the next calendar year.

Access to the small business deduction—With a corporation, you may be able to take advantage of the special lower tax rates for the first $500,000 of active business income of small "Canadian-controlled private corporations" (see 14.1).

Income splitting—If your spouse and adult children are shareholders in the corporation, any dividends they receive will be taxed in their hands. However, dividends received by family members may be subject to the "tax on split income" (see 5.2.4 and 5.2.5). Your corporation can also employ your family members as long as the amount paid is reasonable for the work performed (see 5.3.2).

Capital gains exemption—If your corporation is a qualifying small business corporation, the lifetime capital gains exemption discussed in 6.4.1 may be available to shelter your gain and the gains of each of your family members that will arise when the shares of the corporation are sold or transferred through a will.

Group insurance and retirement benefits—Once you incorporate, you can create a registered pension plan and obtain tax-deductible group health and life insurance for yourself and your employees, which could include family members. (Unincorporated businesses can also deduct group health insurance premiums if certain conditions are met and within certain limits—see 11.2.11.)

Against these potential advantages, you need to weigh the legal and administrative costs of setting up and maintaining the corporation, keeping separate books and filing federal and provincial corporate tax returns. Also bear in mind that once you incorporate you can no longer deduct business and capital losses of the corporation against your other sources of income. Your decision about whether and when you should incorporate your business should be made with appropriate professional advice.

11.6 References

The following publications and more information, including forms and brochures, can be obtained on the CRA's website at *www.canada.ca/en/revenue-agency.html* or by telephone request at 1-800-959-8281 for individual income tax and trust-related enquiries or 1-800-959-5525 for business and self-employed individual enquiries.

Guide RC4022, "General Information for GST/HST Registrants"
Guide RC4058, "Quick Method of Accounting for GST/HST"
Guide RC4070, "Information for Canadian Small Businesses"
Guide RC4110, "Employee or Self-Employed?"
Guide T4002, "Self-Employed Business, Professional, Commission, Farming and Fishing Income"
Guide T4036, "Rental Income"
Income Tax Folio S2-F3-C2, "Benefits and Allowances Received from Employment"
Income Tax Folio S3-F4-C1, "General Discussion of Capital Cost Allowance"
Income Tax Folio S3-F6-C1, "Interest Deductibility"
Income Tax Folio S4-F2-C2, "Business Use of Home Expenses"
Income Tax Folio S4-F16-C1, "What is a Partnership?"

Chapter 12

If you use an automobile for business

- Keep track of—and maximize—business use of your car (12.1, 12.2.1, 12.3.1)
- Check to see if you qualify for a reduced standby charge benefit (12.2.1)
- Reduce the amount of time your company car is available for personal use (12.2.1)
- Avoid employer-owned vehicles costing over $30,000 (12.2.1)
- Take steps to reduce the taxable benefit from car operating costs (12.2.2)
- Claim a rebate for GST/HST paid on expenses deductible from your employment income (12.3.2)

If your employer provides you with an automobile, you may be assessed a taxable benefit for your personal use of the car. If you drive your own car in the course of your job or your business, you may be able to write off your work-related automobile costs against your employment or business income. In this chapter, we map out the complex rules that the CRA uses to arrive at your automobile-related taxable benefit or deduction. Along the way, we also point out some tax-saving opportunities.

12.1 Keeping a log

Whether you drive your employer's car or your own in the course of your work, keep careful track of the distance you drive for work-related purposes to verify your automobile-related tax claims with the CRA.

Keep track of—and maximize—business use of your car.

You may wish to keep a log book on the dashboard, or record your business driving in your daily appointment calendar. The log must show the total number of kilometres driven and total business kilometres for the year. It should also include the date, destination and distance driven for each business trip.

If you're a business owner, you may use a simplified log book for reporting your business travel to the CRA. After you have kept a full log book for one complete year to establish a base year, you can then choose to use a three-month sample log book to extrapolate business use for the entire year, as long as the results are within 10 percent of the use in the base year. You must be able to show that the vehicle's use in the base year remains representative of normal use.

Quebec employees using employer-provided automobiles are required to provide their employers with a copy of such a log book within 10 days of either the end of the year or the end of the period the automobile was available to them, or they will face a $200 penalty.

12.2 Using a company automobile

Special rules apply for determining the taxable benefit when your employer provides you with an automobile. (If you use your own car for employment purposes, see 12.3.1.)

There are two elements to the benefit that must be reported for tax purposes: a standby charge, and a benefit for operating costs. These will normally be reported together on your T4 slip (and Quebec Relevé 1) from your employer as a single amount, and included in your total "income from employment" for tax purposes.

12.2.1 Standby charge

The standby charge is, essentially, 2% of the original cost of the car for each month that it is available to you—that is, 24% per year. (For automobile sales persons, it can instead be 1.5% per month of the average cost of the dealer's cars acquired in the year.)

You can have your standby charge reduced if you can show both that:

- your business use of the car is more than 50% of the kilometres driven, and
- your personal use of the car is less than 1,667 km per month, or 20,000 km in total during the year.

Check to see if you qualify for a reduced standby charge benefit.

If you meet these conditions, your employer can reduce your reported standby charge to a percentage equal to the number of personal-use kilometres driven divided by 20,000 (assuming the car was available to you for a full 12 months). For example, if you drive an employer-owned car 25,000 km for business purposes and 15,000 km for personal purposes, your standby charge can be reduced to 75% (15,000 / 20,000) of the regular standby charge.

Note that driving between your home and your place of employment is normally *not* considered business use (unless you meet certain conditions—see 12.2.4). It can thus be very difficult to satisfy the above tests for a reduction in the standby charge.

When the car is leased, the standby charge is two-thirds of the monthly leasing cost instead of 2% of the purchase price. Up-front, lump-sum leasing charges (or "balloon" payments) are prorated over the term of the lease for purposes of the calculation.

The standby charge is based on the number of 30-day periods in the year that a company car is "made available" to you or a member of your family. However, the actual calculation is based on the number of *days* during which the car is available. This number is divided by 30 and rounded to the nearest whole number, and rounded down if it is exactly in the middle.

> Reduce the amount of time your company car is available for personal use.

If you can get the number of "available days" down to 345, which is 11.5 30-day periods, the standby charge will be reduced to only 11 times 2% of the automobile cost instead of 12 times 2%.

If you take three weeks or more of vacations or business trips during the year, leave the car at the company's premises during those times. If the car cost $30,000 new in 2020, you can thus reduce your taxable income for the year by $600 (and save about $300 in tax if you are in the highest tax bracket) by getting the number of "available days" down to 345. Note, however, that the CRA holds the view that the car is still made available to you during this time unless you are *required* to return the car and control over its use to your employer. You might wish to arrange for your employer to impose this requirement on you.

As we will see in 12.3.1, there is a ceiling on the capital cost of cars for capital cost allowance purposes that creates an element of double taxation. For example, if you drive a company car that was purchased in 2020

> Avoid employer-owned vehicles costing over $30,000.

and cost $50,000 (plus GST/HST and PST), your taxable standby charge benefit is 2% per month of the actual cost of the car. However, only $30,000 (plus GST/HST and PST) can be written off (over time) as capital cost allowance by your employer. In this situation, it may be more economical for you to purchase the car yourself and arrange for an appropriate increase in remuneration from your employer.

12.2.2 Operating cost benefit

Car operating costs include items such as gasoline and oil, maintenance, repairs, licences and insurance. Operating costs do not include interest, capital cost allowance for a car you own, lease costs for a leased car, parking costs, highway or bridge tolls.

The taxable benefit for operating costs is 28¢/km of personal use for 2020. If your employer pays any operating costs during the year for your personal use of an employer-provided car (and you don't fully reimburse your employer by the following February 14), the 28¢/km rate applies. If you are employed principally in selling or leasing automobiles, this rate is 25¢/km.

An alternative calculation is available for the operating expenses where your business use of the car exceeds 50%. If you notify your employer in writing *by December 31* that you wish this option, the operating costs benefit will be a flat 50% of the standby charge.

If you qualify for a standby charge reduction (see 12.2.1), you should look into whether you could also benefit from the alternative operating cost benefit calculation. A benefit of one-half of the standby charge will also be to your advantage where the cost of the car is relatively low (for a small car, or a car that was purchased used) and the number of personal kilometres is relatively high even though it is used for personal purposes less than 50% of the time.

Take steps to reduce the taxable benefit from car operating costs.

If your employer pays only part of the operating costs of an employer-owned car that you use, the taxable benefit from operating costs can cost you more than the amount the employer pays. Sometimes the employer pays only the insurance and the employee pays for all gas and repairs, or the employer does not pay most operating expenses but might cover an occasional major repair bill.

For example, suppose you put 20,000 km on your company car over the year, all of which is personal use (including driving to work and back). Your employer pays the insurance ($800 per year) and you pay the rest of the operating expenses. Your taxable benefit for operating costs will be 28¢ per personal-use kilometre, or $5,600, which will cost you about $2,800 in tax if you are in the top tax bracket. So having the employer pay for the insurance is very disadvantageous.

In such a case, you should repay the $800 to the employer *by February 14* of the following year, so that the "28¢ per kilometre" rule does not apply. Of course, your employer can pay you sufficient additional salary so that the after-tax amount will be enough to offset your repayment of the insurance costs.

12.2.3 Allowances and advances for automobile expenses

If you receive a reasonable allowance for automobile expenses, the allowance is not included in your income if it is based solely on the number of kilometres driven in performing your employment duties. If it is a flat amount not calculated in terms of your employment-related driving, it will be taxable (though you may be able to claim offsetting automobile expenses—see 12.3.1).

The CRA will agree to consider a flat periodic amount to be an accountable advance (rather than a taxable allowance) if you and your employer agree at the beginning of the year that you will receive a reasonable stated amount for each employment-related kilometre driven and you and your employer settle up at the end of the year regarding the difference between your actual business-related kilometres and the stated amount.

For 2020, the CRA and Revenu Québec accept as a "reasonable allowance" 59¢/km for the first 5,000 km and 53¢/km for each additional kilometre driven (4¢ more in the territories). In some cases, you may be able to justify a higher amount as "reasonable".

If you receive an allowance from your employer that is a combination of flat-rate and reasonable per-kilometre allowances that covers the same use for the vehicle, the total combined allowance is taxable as an employee benefit.

12.2.4 Employer-provided vehicles taken home at night

As noted, travel between home and work in a motor vehicle provided by an employer is generally considered personal use of the vehicle. However, in special cases, your employer may require you to take the vehicle home with you overnight, for example, if you are on-call to respond to emergencies or if there are security concerns over tools and equipment being left at a worksite or overnight at your employer's premises.

While the travel between work and home is still considered a taxable benefit in these cases, the benefit is reduced for employer-provided vehicles (except regular automobiles) that are specially designed or suited for the employer's business or trade and that are essential for carrying out the employee's duties. Examples include taxis, ambulances, hearses, and trucks and vans modified to carry or store tools, equipment or goods.

For these vehicles, the benefit is the operating benefit rate of 28¢/km for 2020 as long as the vehicle has not been used for any other personal use other than commuting between home and work and the employer has genuine business reasons for requiring the employee to take the motor vehicle home at night. In these cases, the benefit does not include a standby charge.

The use of these vehicles is considered business use if the employee drives directly from home to a point of call (e.g., an emergency scene) or vice versa.

12.3 Using your own automobile for business purposes

12.3.1 Automobile expense deductions for employees

If you are required by the terms of your employment to use your own automobile and are not receiving a (non-taxable) reasonable allowance based on the number of kilometres you drive for employment purposes (see 12.2.3), you can deduct a portion of your automobile expenses from your employment income. (Your employer must certify that you were required to use your own vehicle on federal Form T2200, which you must keep on file, and Quebec Form TP-64.3-V, which you must file with your Quebec tax return.)

You can deduct operating costs, such as gas, repairs and car washes, to the extent they relate to your employment. As noted in 12.1, you need to keep a detailed log of your driving to track your employment-related use as opposed to your personal use.

You can also deduct capital cost allowance (depreciation), or your monthly lease payments for the proportion of employment-related use. The allowable rate of capital cost allowance is 15% in the year of acquisition of the car, followed by 30% *on the remaining balance* in each subsequent year. However, there is a cap on the cost of the car for this purpose:

Car purchase year	Limit
2020*	$30,000**

* This amount has been the same since 2001.
**Plus GST/HST and PST on this amount.

Example

Michelle buys a new car in Ontario in July 2020 for $35,000 plus 13% HST. She is required to drive 10,000 km for employment-related purposes during the year. She also drives 10,000 km on personal trips.

Since half of her driving is employment-related, Michelle can claim half of the capital cost allowance normally allowed for a car. Although she spent $35,000, the cost is capped at $30,000, plus $3,900 HST (total of $33,900), for tax purposes. The maximum capital cost allowance for the year of acquisition is 15%. Fifteen percent of $33,900 is $5,085. Michelle can therefore claim half of this amount, or $2,543, as a deduction against her employment income for 2020.

Further, because she uses her car partly for business, Michelle can claim an HST rebate for 2020 from the CRA equal to 13/113 of her capital cost allowance claim—see 12.3.2.

If you're considering buying a new vehicle for work purposes this year, you could benefit from the enhanced capital cost allowance deduction for accelerated investment incentive property (AIIP), in the year of purchase. You could also benefit from the incentives for zero-emission vehicles, such as electric or hybrid cars. If you meet all the conditions, you may be able to deduct the full cost of the vehicle, up to $55,000 plus sales taxes, in the year of purchase.

You can also deduct interest on any loan you have taken out to purchase the car (including financing on the purchase itself, where you make monthly payments that combine interest and capital). Your monthly interest is limited to $300 for 2020.

Example

James bought a new car in January 2020 for $60,000, and pays $1,100 per month on his car loan. He paid $5,000 down and the loan interest rate is 7%. One-half of his driving relates to his employment.

Calculations show that James pays $320 per month in interest for the first month, and slightly less over the following months. His interest for tax purposes over the year is limited to $300 per month, or $3,600. Of this, he can deduct half, or $1,800, to reflect the proportion of his driving that was employment-related.

If you lease the car, your deduction for the lease payments is restricted to parallel the dollar limit on purchases:

Year lease entered into	Limit
2020*	$800**

* This amount has been the same since 2001.
**Plus GST/HST and PST on this amount.

Your maximum deductible monthly lease charge is the lesser of the maximum lease limit set out above and an amount determined through a complex formula that takes into account your leasing charges and cumulative payments, the manufacturer's suggested list price, the prescribed purchase limit for CCA purposes and refundable deposits.

If you lease the car and you make an up-front lump-sum payment (or "balloon" payment), the CRA normally considers the amount to be part of your normal lease charge in the year paid and your deduction may be restricted by the lease deduction limit. However, the full balloon payment amount may be deductible if the sum of:

- the amount of the balloon payment divided by the number of months in the term of the lease, plus
- your monthly lease payment

does not exceed your maximum monthly lease deduction limit.

If you are reimbursed by your employer for employment-related use of your automobile, the reimbursement payments are not taxed. Of course, you cannot deduct your own expenses to the extent you have been reimbursed for them.

Driving between home and work is normally considered personal use. If you travel from your home to a business call (to visit a client or supplier, for example), that will constitute business use. You can maximize your employment-related travel by making all of your business calls at the beginning and end of your day, before you go to work and after you leave work. You can thus make your entire trip from home to work count as travel for employment purposes.

12.3.2 GST/HST rebate for employees' auto expenses

Where you can deduct expenses from your employment income, you can also generally claim a rebate of GST or HST paid on those expenses, as long as your employer is a GST registrant and is not a financial institution (see 10.9). If you have auto expenses you're deducting from your employment income, you may be entitled to a GST or HST rebate, as the following example shows.

> Claim a rebate for GST/ HST paid on expenses deductible from your employment income.

Example

Continuing our first example in 12.3.1, Michelle is required to drive 10,000 km for employment-related purposes during the year. She also drives 10,000 km on personal trips. Over the year, she spends $2,260 (including 13% HST) on gas and repairs for her car and does not receive any reimbursement from her employer. All the expenses are paid in Ontario.

Since one-half of Michelle's expenses are required by her employment, she can claim $1,130 as a deduction from employment income. That figure, however, already includes $130 in HST that applied to the gas and repairs. Michelle can claim a rebate for the $130 on a form filed with her income tax return. The $130 rebate is taxable in the year she receives it.

Further, because she uses her car partly for business, Michelle can claim an HST rebate in 2020 from the CRA equal to 13/113 of her capital cost allowance claim. That is, Michelle can claim a refund of 13/113 of the $2,543 she can deduct as capital cost allowance, or $293. This $293 is deducted from the undepreciated capital cost of the car at the beginning of 2021.

In the above example, we assume that Michelle's employer is a GST registrant and not a financial institution. If she were employed by a financial institution or a non-GST registrant, she would not be entitled to the employee GST/HST rebate.

We have also assumed that Michelle did not receive a per kilometre allowance from her employer. If she had, she would not be able to claim a GST/HST rebate on any of her automobile expenses unless her employer certified on her Form GST370 that the allowance was "unreasonable" and that her employer would not be claiming a GST/HST input tax credit for her allowance. However, in the unlikely case that Michelle's employer certifies that her per kilometre allowance is unreasonable, the amount would be included in her income and her employer must withhold income tax and other source deductions on the amount.

A rebate is only available if GST/HST was paid on the purchase. Michelle cannot receive a rebate for the deductible portion of her car insurance, since insurance is not subject to GST/HST. Similarly, there would be no GST/HST rebate if Michelle purchased gas in the United States because no GST/HST would be included in its price.

Finally, note also that the 13/113 rebate rate is only used in Ontario because it imposes HST at a 13% rate. Had Michelle's expenses been incurred in a province with 5% GST only or in a province with a 15% HST rate, the rebate she generally would be entitled to claim for 2020 would be calculated using the rate imposed by that province. For example, if Michelle paid 5% GST on an expense incurred in Alberta or paid 15% HST on an expense in Nova Scotia, the rebate rate would be 5/105 of the GST-included price or 15/115 of the HST-included price, respectively. See 11.2.5 for GST/HST rates in each province. (GST or HST rebates are also available to members of partnerships—see 11.3.7.)

12.3.3 Automobile expense deductions for the self-employed

If you're self-employed, you can generally deduct the proportion of your automobile expenses that represents your business use of the vehicle, normally based on kilometres driven.

If half of your driving is done for your business (excluding driving from your home to your own place of business) and half is personal use, you can deduct one-half of the expenses of the car for that year. The expenses would include gas, car washes, repairs, insurance, interest on financing the vehicle, leasing costs if the car is leased and capital cost allowance if you own it.

However, there are limits to how expensive a vehicle you can write off. Your claims for CCA and leasing costs will be based on a maximum cost:

Car purchase year	Purchase limit	Lease limit
2020*	$30,000**	$800**

* These amounts have been the same since 2001.
**Plus GST/HST and PST on this amount (to the extent they are not recoverable).

If you have financed the purchase of a car, your monthly interest expense before determining the business portion will be limited to $300 for cars purchased in 2020.

The CRA counts lease termination payments as normal lease payments in the year paid, and their deductibility is also subject to your lease limit for the year. However, the CRA will make the adjustment at your request over the term of the lease (instead of just in the year of sale), provided none of the years to be adjusted are statute-barred.

The $30,000 purchase limit also applies for purposes of calculating GST/HST input tax credits (see 11.2.4) and QST input tax refunds.

See the planning tips suggested for employees in 12.3.1—the same techniques can help maximize your deductions for business-related use of your own car.

12.4 References

The following publications and more information, including forms and brochures, can be obtained on the CRA's website at *www.canada.ca/en/revenue-agency.html* or by telephone request at 1-800-959-8281 for individual income tax and trust-related enquiries or 1-800-959-5525 for business and self-employed individual enquiries.

Guide T4002, "Self-employed Business, Professional, Commission, Farming and Fishing Income"
Guide T4044, "Employment Expenses"
Guide T4130, "Employers' Guide—Taxable Benefits and Allowances"
Income Tax Folio S2-F3-C2, "Benefits and Allowances Received from Employment"
Income Tax Folio S3-F4-C1, "General Discussion of Capital Cost Allowance"

Chapter 13

If you are moving

- If you're planning to move, seek to meet the tests for deducting your moving expenses where practical (13.1.1)

- Plan to not have a taxable benefit on your employer-paid moving expenses where possible (13.1.3)

- Take steps to cease Canadian residency if you are moving abroad (13.3.1)

- Be aware of Canadian departure tax on emigration (13.3.2)

- If you rent your Canadian home after you emigrate, consider and plan for Canadian withholding tax on the rental income (13.3.5)

- Obtain a certificate of compliance from the CRA if you sell your Canadian home after you emigrate (13.3.5)

- If you wish to wind up your RRSP, consider waiting until after you become non-resident (13.3.6)

- Repay Home Buyers' Plan and Lifelong Learning Plan withdrawals within 60 days of becoming non-resident (13.3.6)

Moving expenses are often overlooked as a deduction. Depending on your circumstances, many of your expenses may be tax-deductible if you're moving within Canada to start a new job or business or attend school. If you're immigrating to or emigrating from Canada, there are complex tax rules that you'll need to consider before and after your move. In this chapter, we discuss the tax treatment of moving expenses and other tax rules related to moving, including some planning opportunities to help make your move as tax-efficient as possible.

13.1 Moving within Canada

13.1.1 Work-related moving expenses

If you start working at a new location of employment, or start a new business, and you move to a home that is 40 km closer to your new work location than your old home was, you can deduct moving expenses for tax purposes. The 40-km distance is measured by the shortest normal route of travel, including roads, bridges and ferries, rather than "as the crow flies".

Expenses incurred in moving from another country to Canada, or from Canada to another country, are not deductible for Canadian tax purposes unless you are either a student receiving scholarship or grant income (see 13.1.2), or a factual or deemed resident of Canada. If your employer reimburses you for expenses of moving to or from Canada, the benefit is not taxable as long as the reimbursed expenses are included in the list of moving expenses in 13.1.3.

Except to the extent you are reimbursed by your employer, you can deduct the following for moves within Canada:

- Reasonable travelling costs, including meals and lodging, to move you and the members of your household
- The moving costs for your household effects, including storage charges (such as packing, hauling, movers, in-transit storage and insurance)
- The cost of meals and lodging near the old and the new home for up to 1. days
- Lease cancellation costs
- The costs of revising legal documents to reflect your new address replacing driver's licences and automobile permits, and connecting and disconnecting utilities
- Selling costs for your old home, including real estate commissions
- Where you are selling your old home, the legal fees and land transfer tax payable when you buy a new home (but not GST/HST and QST)
- Mortgage interest, property taxes, insurance premiums and utility costs related to your old residence (provided it remains unoccupied), to a maximum of the actual costs during a period when reasonable efforts were made to sell the home, or $5,000, whichever is less.

If you're planning to move, seek to meet the tests for deducting your moving expenses where practical.

When considering a move, ensure if possible that your move coincides with a new employment location or a new place of business, and that your move meets the 40-km test.

As an alternative to providing detailed receipts for your actual moving costs for meals and vehicle expenses, you may use a simplified method of determining these moving costs. You can also use this option to calculate vehicle expenses if you used your own vehicle to transport household effects between your old and new residences. If you use the simplified method, supporting receipts are not required.

In the case of meals, you can claim, in Canadian or U.S. funds, a flat rate per meal under the simplified method of $17 per meal, to a maximum of $51 per day.

For vehicle expenses, you must keep a record of the number of kilometres driven during the move. The amount you can claim for vehicle expenses is determined by multiplying the number of kilometres travelled while moving by a flat per kilometre rate ranging from 48.0¢ to 64.5¢ per kilometre, depending on the province in which you begin travelling.

The 2020 rates per meal and per kilometre will be available on the CRA's website in 2021.

13.1.2 Students' moving expenses

If you are a student, you can claim moving expenses if you move when you begin a job (including a summer job) or start a business. If you are moving to attend full time post-secondary education (in Canada or abroad), you can deduct the expenses from the part of your scholarships, fellowships and research grants that are required to be included in your income.

13.1.3 Moving allowances and reimbursements paid by your employer

If your employer is paying your moving expenses, you may be assessed a taxable benefit for the payments, depending on how they are structured. Generally, if your employer pays you an allowance related to relocation expenses without asking you to account for the use of the money, the CRA considers it to be a taxable benefit. However, you may be able to deduct your actual qualifying expenses incurred (as listed in 13.1.1) if you move within Canada. If your employer reimburses you for your documented expenses or pays you an accountable advance, the payment is usually not considered a taxable benefit. Your employer can reimburse you for certain moving expenses for you and your family without conferring a taxable benefit, including:

- The cost of house-hunting trips to the new location, including child care and pet care expenses while you are away
- Travelling costs, including meals and lodging, while you and members of your household are moving from old to new homes
- The cost of transporting or storing your household effects and other personal property such as cars and boats while moving from old to new homes
- The costs of revising legal documents to reflect your new address, replacing driver's licences and automobile permits, and connecting and disconnecting utilities
- Selling costs of the old residence (advertising, legal fees, real estate commissions and mortgage prepayment or discharge fees)
- Where the old residence has been sold, legal fees to purchase the new residence and any taxes on the transfer or registration of title on the new residence
- Mortgage interest, property taxes, insurance premiums and utility costs related to the former residence (provided it remains unoccupied), to a maximum of the actual costs during a period when reasonable efforts were made to sell the home or $5,000, whichever is less.

If your employer pays a non-accountable moving expenses allowance of up to $650, it is not a taxable benefit as long as you certify in writing that you used the allowance for moving expenses. Any amount over $650 paid as a non-accountable moving allowance is considered a taxable benefit and you may be able to deduct your actual moving expenses.

Where possible, you should try to avoid being assessed a taxable benefit by arranging for your employer to reimburse you for your moving costs or pay you an accountable advance or a non-accountable moving allowance of up to $650, rather than paying you a non-accountable allowance over $650.

Plan to not have a taxable benefit on your employer-paid moving expenses where possible.

Moving allowances are treated differently for Quebec tax purposes. If you are relocated by your employer and receive a moving allowance, you do not have to include in your Quebec income an amount equal to two weeks' worth of your salary (based on your new salary after your relocation).

13.1.4 Other relocation payments

Your employer may make certain types of relocation payments to help you defray higher home financing costs in your new location. Most direct or indirect financing support payments are considered taxable benefits. These payments include:

- Mortgage interest differential payments made by your employer to compensate you where the interest rate on your new mortgage is higher than the interest rate on the old one
- Mortgage subsidy payments to offset the larger mortgage interest payments created by a higher mortgage principal amount due to higher housing prices in the new location for homes of the same size as your previous one
- One-half of the excess of reimbursements over $15,000 for a loss on the sale of a former residence, calculated as the difference between the employee's cost of the home and the selling price, or the difference between the selling price of the home and its fair market value as determined by an independent appraisal
- Tax equalization payments and cost-of-living payments made to compensate you for higher taxes and higher living costs in your new location.

13.2 Moving to Canada

When you immigrate to Canada, most property you own is deemed to be acquired by you at its fair market value as of your date of immigration (not including Canadian real estate, pension plans, stock options and certain other property). Thus, Canada will tax only the capital gain that accrues while you are resident in Canada.

If you are moving to Canada to settle permanently for the first time, you can bring your personal and household effects free of duties and taxes if you owned and used these goods before arriving in Canada. But if you sell or give the goods away within the first year, duty and tax will apply. If you are returning to Canada, you can bring your personal and household effects free of duties and taxes if you owned and used these goods abroad for at least six months before returning to Canada. The six-month stipulation is waived if you have resided outside Canada for five years or more. Leased goods are subject to duty and taxes because you do not own them.

If you are moving to Canada, you should obtain professional advice regarding ways to help minimize your tax burden. There may be steps you should take before you arrive in Canada.

13.3 Moving from Canada

13.3.1 Ceasing Canadian residence

Generally, Canada imposes tax on the worldwide income of its residents but only on the Canadian-source income of non-residents. So whether you are considered resident in Canada can make a significant difference to your potential Canadian tax liability after you move.

If you move to another country, you may still be considered a Canadian resident for tax purposes if you keep certain ties with Canada, such as maintaining a home, club memberships, credit cards or medical plan, or if your spouse or dependants remain in Canada. If you're moving to another country permanently or for an extended period, you may want to take steps to cease Canadian residency.

The *Income Tax Act* does not include rules for determining residency. The CRA assesses each situation on its own merits. Generally, you are considered a non-resident of Canada if your stay

> Take steps to cease Canadian residency if you are moving abroad.

abroad has a degree of permanence, you sever your residential ties to Canada and establish new ties elsewhere, you are considered a resident of another country, and your visits to Canada after your departure are occasional and sporadic.

Starting at the time of your departure, you should spend significantly less than 183 days in Canada per year. Days during any portion of which you are physically present in Canada count as full days.

Other steps that show you have ceased Canadian residency include:

- Selling your home in Canada or renting it to an arm's-length party on a long-term lease
- Selling your personal property such as furniture or cars or taking them with you to your new country
- Cancelling or suspending club memberships
- Cancelling your Canadian driver's licence and plate (you may want to obtain a driver's licence in your new country before giving up your Canadian licence)
- Closing your Canadian bank accounts or putting them on non-resident status
- Cancelling credit cards issued in Canada and having them re-issued in your new country
- Changing your mailing address for all correspondence
- Cancelling your Canadian medical plans and taking out new ones in your new country
- Situating your primary place of business outside Canada.

If you move to a country that has signed a tax treaty with Canada, the treaty may apply to resolve your residency in cases where the above items are not determinative.

As a non-resident of Canada, you are still subject to Canadian tax if at any time during a calendar year you:

- Are employed or perform services in Canada
- Carry on business in Canada
- Dispose of property not subject to Canadian departure tax (see 13.3.2), such as Canadian real estate
- Dispose of shares of private companies or interests in certain partnerships that derive their value from Canadian real estate
- Receive income from Canadian trusts
- Receive Canadian-source pension or dividend income, or
- Receive rental income from rental properties in Canada.

A tax treaty between Canada and your new country may reduce or eliminate your Canadian tax liability in many circumstances.

13.3.2 Canadian departure tax

If you leave Canada and become non-resident, you are deemed to have sold most of your assets at fair market value and have to recognize any resulting capital gains in the tax year that you depart. The range of assets treated as having been sold for fair market value on emigration includes *all* property, with certain exceptions such as:

- Canadian real estate
- Property that you already owned when you became resident in Canada or inherited while in Canada, if your residence in Canada totalled no more than 60 months out of the last 120-month period
- Pension entitlements, including RRSPs or RRIFs
- Property used in a business in Canada
- Certain stock options and other types of equity compensation
- Certain interests in Canadian trusts
- Tax-deferred accounts including RESPs, TFSAs, RDSPs and DPSPs.

Be aware of Canadian departure tax on emigration. For other property, the deemed disposition may result in an immediate tax liability on the resulting gains, although the CRA allows you to defer paying the tax on gains as long as you post acceptable security. Acceptable security could be a letter of credit, a mortgage or a bank guarantee. You do not have to post security for departure tax on the first $100,000 of capital gains. The tax is still due on gains for which you posted security or which qualified for the $100,000 exemption, but not until the assets are sold, gifted or on your death (whichever occurs first).

If you post the security, interest is not charged for the period up to the actual disposition of the property or death of the owner (whichever occurs first). If the security subsequently becomes deficient (e.g., due to a decline in value of the assets posted), you will have 90 days after you're notified by the CRA to make up the deficiency.

If you return to Canada at any time and you still own the assets for which you posted security, you can unwind the deemed disposition and treat it as though it did not occur. Thus, using the deemed security on $100,000 of capital gains can be beneficial if you plan to return to Canada before you sell the assets.

Gains accruing while you are non-resident on certain property known as "taxable Canadian property" continue to be taxable in Canada when you sell it. Taxable Canadian property includes, among others, shares of corporations not listed on a designated stock exchange, an interest in a partnership or an interest in certain trust that derive more than 50% of their value from Canadian real estate, Canadian resource property or timber resource property. If 50% or less of the value is derived from these types of property, keep in mind that these shares or interests may still be taxable Canadian property unless they meet this "equal to or less than 50% of their value" test for the 60-month period immediately before you sell them. Gains accruing while you are non-resident on shares that are considered taxable Canadian property may be exempt under the tax treaty between Canada and your new country.

Gains accruing while you are non-resident on certain other property, such as marketable securities, are not taxable in Canada, even if you return; however, you cannot claim losses accruing on such property while you are non-resident for Canadian tax purposes. When you return to Canada, the assets' cost base will be adjusted to ensure any pre-departure gain is captured later and any loss during the non-resident period is not available to offset the gain.

You must report all of your property subject to the deemed disposition on Form T1243, "Deemed Disposition of Property by an Emigrant of Canada" and file it with your tax return for the year you cease to be a resident of Canada. If you are an active or retired partner of a professional partnership and you are leaving Canada, see 16.2.5.

Security for private Canadian company shares

If you're a shareholder of a Canadian private company and you give up your Canadian residency status but retain your shares, the rules may create valuation and financing problems if your shares have significantly appreciated in value. For example, determining the fair market value of your shares generally requires professional assistance, resulting in valuation costs. If you don't have your shares valued, the CRA will fix the value. Financing your tax liability may also pose a problem if it is not advisable or possible to use the business's banking facilities and you do not have other liquid resources available to satisfy the debt.

In the past, the CRA has not normally accepted non-liquid assets, such as shares of private corporations, as security for future tax liabilities. The CRA prefers a letter of credit to other security; however, recognizing the dilemma many taxpayers will face, CRA officials say that they may accept such shares as security for the debt. The CRA will act as any other commercial lender and expect the normal representations, warranties and covenants to ensure that the shares retain their value. To satisfy the CRA, you may have to change existing collateral arrangements and shareholder agreements. You will also have to provide the CRA with details on the shares such as annual financial statements, corporate tax returns and organization charts.

If you plan on posting private corporation shares as security, your discussions with the CRA should begin well before the deadline for filing your departure-year tax return.

13.3.3 Capital gains exemption on emigration

Once you are non-resident, you cannot use the lifetime capital gains exemption discussed in 6.4. So if you still have some exemption room available and you own qualifying farm or fishing property (which includes Canadian real estate) or shares in a qualified small business corporation, you may wish to take steps to "crystallize" your gain before you emigrate. That way, you will trigger a gain that is absorbed by the exemption that would not otherwise be available after you have emigrated, and only the increase from the current fair market value will be taxed in Canada when you, as a non-resident, eventually dispose of the property.

Alternatively, if you realize gains on the deemed disposition of certain qualified farm or fishing property or shares in a qualified small business corporation, you would want to apply any of your remaining exemption against these gains.

13.3.4 Reporting rules for emigrants with property worth over $25,000

If you emigrate from Canada and you own property with a total value of $25,000 or more, you are required to file an information form (T1161) listing all your significant assets with your final Canadian tax return for the year of emigration. In determining whether your property exceeds the $25,000 reporting threshold, the following assets are not included:

- Cash, including bank deposits
- RRSPs, TFSAs, RESPs, RDSPs, private company pension plans (RPPs), RRIFs, retirement compensation arrangements (RCAs), employee benefit plans and deferred profit sharing plans (DPSPs)
- Items for personal use (such as household effects, clothing, cars, collectibles) whose fair market value is less than $10,000
- Property you owned at the time you last became a resident of Canada or property you inherited after you last became a resident of Canada if you were a resident of Canada for 60 months or less during the 10 years before you emigrated.

There are significant penalties for failure to file this form on time even if you are not otherwise required to file a tax return (e.g., if you keep your house in Canada and have no other assets).

13.3.5 If you rent or sell your Canadian home after emigration

Real property that you own in Canada is not subject to the deemed disposition rules discussed above when you emigrate. If you decide to rent your property, the tenant will generally have to withhold and remit to the CRA a 25% non-resident withholding tax on your gross rental income. If you will incur expenses to earn your rental income, you can file Form NR6 before your first non-resident tax payment is due and the withholding tax will be assessed on your net rental income. If you file the form, you will need to appoint a Canadian resident agent.

You must file Form NR4 and the related summary by the end of March each year to report rental income and taxes withheld, and you will have to file an annual rental income tax return by June 30 of each following year. Filing this income tax return late will result in assessment of the 25% withholding tax on gross rental income.

If you rent your Canadian home after you emigrate, plan for Canadian withholding tax on the rental income.

Generally, there is no Canadian income tax levied on the gain from selling a principal residence (see 6.5.2). If you sell your former principal residence while you are a non-resident of Canada, you must notify the CRA (and Revenu Québec if the property is in Quebec) of

Obtain a certificate of compliance from the CRA if you sell your Canadian home after you emigrate.

the disposition and request a certificate of compliance. If you don't obtain a certificate of compliance before the disposition, the purchaser must withhold and remit 25% of the gross proceeds to the CRA and a further 12.875% to Revenu Québec, where applicable. You should file the CRA's Form T2062 reporting the disposition before the closing date of the sale or within 10 days of the sale to obtain the certificate of compliance. (You must also file Revenu Québec Form TP-1097-V if the property is located in Quebec.)

If you sell your former principal residence after the end of the year following the year of your move, only a portion of the gain would be exempt under the principal residence exemption (see 6.5.2). The principal residence exemption calculation is based on the fraction of one plus the number of taxation years ending after 1971 for which the property was a principal residence and during which you are a resident of Canada over the total number of years (after 1971) it was owned by you. The "one plus" part of the calculation does not apply if you were not resident in Canada in the year the property was acquired. For each additional year that you do not sell your principal residence after you cease Canadian residency, the denominator increases while the numerator stays constant and a smaller portion of the gain is exempt from Canadian tax.

If you sell your principal residence, you are required to report certain basic information on Schedule 3 of your T1 income tax return. This information includes the address of the property, the date you acquired it, and the amount of the disposition proceeds. You must also complete a special designation form, Form T2091, "Designation of a Property as a Principal Residence by an Individual (Other Than a Personal Trust)".

If you plan to rent out your former principal residence, the property's use will change from personal to income-producing and will be subject to a deemed disposition at fair market value at that time. Any gain accruing up to the date of the change in use will be taxable but the principal residence exemption may reduce or eliminate the tax. Future increases in value will be taxable as capital gains since you can no longer shelter these gains from tax by claiming the principal residence exemption (see 6.5.2).

You may be able to make an election not to deem a change in use of the property. You cannot claim depreciation on the property while the election is in effect.

However, the election could be beneficial if you expect the property to increase significantly in value since you would be able to shelter some of the resulting capital gain with the principal residence exemption because of the proration calculation.

13.3.6 If you have RRSPs, TFSAs or RESPs

As noted in 13.3.2, your RRSPs are not subject to the deemed disposition rules when you leave Canada. For Canadian tax purposes, you can continue to make deductible contributions to your RRSP as long as you have contribution room available. Of course, if you have no income subject to Canadian tax, you would not realize any current tax savings from making contributions.

If you wish to wind up your RRSP, consider waiting until after you become non-resident.

If you need to collapse your RRSP, you may want to wait until you are a non-resident of Canada to do so. As a non-resident, you will be subject to a 25% withholding tax on the proceeds received from the plan. Many tax treaties reduce the Canadian withholding tax rate if the payments are periodic rather than lump-sum. If you collapse the plan while you're a resident of Canada, the proceeds will be taxed at your marginal tax rate, which will be about 51% if you are in the top tax bracket, depending on the province you live in.

Repay Home Buyers' Plan and Lifelong Learning Plan withdrawals within 60 days of becoming non-resident.

If you withdrew funds from your RRSP under the Home Buyers' Plan (see 3.3.6) or Lifelong Learning Plan (see 3.3.7) and you become a non-resident, you should repay the entire withdrawal within 60 days of becoming non-resident. To the extent you do not make the repayment within 60 days, the unpaid balance will be included in your income on your Canadian income tax return for the year of your departure.

If you have a TFSA when you become non-resident (see 4.1.4), you can maintain your existing TFSA and your investment income and withdrawals will remain exempt from Canadian tax. You should not contribute to your TFSA beginning with the date you become a non-resident because significant penalties apply to contributions made as a non-resident of Canada. No new contribution room will accrue for any year in which you are a non-resident for the entire year. You must also consider foreign tax implications of TFSA income and withdrawals, if they apply.

If you have RESPs (see 4.3), contributions may only be made for beneficiaries who are residents of Canada. The beneficiaries must have Social Insurance Numbers. Subscribers (i.e., contributors) do not need to be residents of Canada, but a subscriber must have a Social Insurance Number to open an RESP. Original contributions to the plan may be paid to the beneficiary without Canadian tax consequences. However, if the beneficiary is a non-resident of Canada when withdrawals are made from an RESP, any Canada Education Savings Grants (CESGs) paid to the plan must be repaid to the federal government. Investment income earned by the plan may be paid to a non-resident beneficiary if he or she attends a post-secondary institution, but non-resident withholding tax may apply to the payments.

13.4 References

The following publications and more information, including forms and brochures, can be obtained on the CRA's website at *www.canada.ca/en/revenue-agency.html* or by telephone request at 1-800-959-8281 for individual income tax and trust-related enquiries or 1-800-959-5525 for business and self-employed individual enquiries.

Guide T4058, "Non-Residents and Income Tax"
Guide T4130, "Taxable Benefits and Allowances"
Income Tax Folio S1-F3-C2, "Principal Residence"
Income Tax Folio S1-F3-C4, "Moving Expenses"
Income Tax Folio S5-F1-C1, "Determining an Individual's Residence Status"
Pamphlet T4055, "Newcomers to Canada"

Chapter 14

If you have your own corporation

- Keep the corporation a small business corporation at all times (14.1)
- Consider crystallizing your lifetime capital gains exemption (14.1)
- Multiply your access to the capital gains exemption (14.1)
- Defer income to the next calendar year by accruing bonuses (14.2.2)
- Maximize capital dividend payments (14.2.4)
- Consider a tax-free repayment of capital (14.2.5)
- Crunch the numbers to calculate your optimum salary/dividend mix (14.2.9)
- Consider the tax benefits of setting up a holding corporation (14.3)
- Look into the potential advantages of a corporate partnership (14.3.1)
- Weigh the potential advantages of incorporating your investments (14.6)
- Be cautious about having investment income in your corporation that carries on an active business (14.6)

In this chapter, we suggest some tax planning strategies that may be available if you are an owner/manager—that is, you carry on your business through a corporation. We do not discuss tax planning for the corporation itself, except in relation to how to most effectively get its profits into your hands. If you are thinking about setting up a corporation for running your business, see 11.5 for a discussion of some of the pros and cons. The tax rules in this area are substantially the same for both federal and Quebec tax purposes.

14.1 Taxation of the corporation

A corporation is a distinct legal entity, and if you have an incorporated business, the corporation's profits are not yours simply to take. You, as a director of the corporation (even if you are the sole director), act in a different capacity from yourself as a shareholder of the corporation. Legally, as a shareholder your only right is to elect the board of directors, who then cause the corporation to take specific actions.

To extract funds from the corporation you must follow one of the "correct" methods we discuss in 14.2. If you do not, the tax system will penalize you.

For tax purposes, the corporation's business and investment income will be calculated in much the same way as your own. (See 11.2 regarding the calculation of business income.) As with individuals, certain deductions (such as loss carryforwards) are available in computing taxable income. The corporation then pays federal and provincial tax on its taxable income.

For 2020, the federal general corporate tax rate is 15% for active business income and income from manufacturing and processing.

For small "Canadian-controlled private corporations", for 2020, the federal rate is 9% on the first $500,000 of active business income. (A Canadian-controlled private corporation is a corporation that is resident in Canada and is not controlled in any manner by any combination of non-residents or public corporations.) The general 15% corporate tax rate applies on active business income over the $500,000 threshold. For 2020, investment income of a Canadian-controlled private corporation (see 14.6) is taxed at a federal rate of 38.7%.

The federal small business rate is not available for large corporations. It begins to be phased out once the capital of the corporation and its associated group exceeds $10 million and is completely eliminated for associated groups with capital of $15 million.

A corporation's $500,000 small business limit may also be phased out if the corporation and any associated corporations earn income from passive investments.

A business can earn up to $50,000 in passive investment income per year without affecting its small business deduction. However, the small business limit will be reduced by $5 for every $1 of investment income above the $50,000 threshold. As such, the small business deduction will be totally eliminated if the corporation (or its associated corporate group) earns investment income of $150,000 or more.

For this purpose, a corporation's passive investment income includes dividends from non-connected corporations, certain investment income earned outside Canada, and income from savings in certain life insurance policies (see 21.7), but excludes taxable capital gains (and allowable capital losses) from the sale of active assets and investment income that is considered incidental to the business.

Whether your business's investment income is considered active or passive may depend on your specific circumstances—your tax adviser can help you make this determination.

These rules operate together with the phase-out of the small business limit for corporations with taxable capital over $10 million. A corporation's small business limit will be reduced by the greater of the reduction under the passive investment income rules and the reduction under the taxable capital rules.

The general provincial corporate tax rate ranges from 10% to 16%. For 2020, all provinces have reduced rates for the first $500,000 of "small business income". The combined federal and provincial tax burden ranges from about 9% to 14% of income under the small business income thresholds. The remainder is taxed at combined rates ranging from about 25% to 31%.

Keep the corporation a small business corporation at all times.
If possible, ensure that your corporation remains a "small business corporation" (see 6.2.3) and that your shares are

"qualified small business corporation shares" (see 6.4.1) at all times. This will preserve, respectively, your ability to claim allowable business investment losses in respect of any loss on the corporation's shares (see 6.2.3), and the lifetime capital gains exemption on any gain (see 6.4).

Note that you cannot always predict when the sale of the shares will be triggered for tax purposes. On the death of any shareholder, there will be a deemed disposition of that shareholder's shares at their fair market value unless the shares are transferred to a spouse or a qualifying "spousal trust" (see 21.5.2).

As an alternative, you may wish to "crystallize" your capital gains exemption. "Crystallizing" means triggering a capital gain on your shares of a qualified small business corporation, while continuing to own (or at least control) the corporation. This may permanently increase your adjusted cost base of the shares and possibly eliminate the need for the corporation to retain its qualified small business corporation status. Several possible alternatives (such as selling shares to a family member or exchanging existing shares for a new class of shares) can be used to crystallize an exemption; professional advice should be sought.

> Consider crystallizing your lifetime capital gains exemption.

To protect your assets, you could arrange to have a family trust hold the interest in the corporation rather than having your spouse and children own the shares of the corporation directly. The family trust may be set up so that you and your family members (or others) are the beneficiaries and you are a trustee (possibly with other trustees) (see 21.5). This structure allows you to maintain control of the shares held by the family trust while offering the flexibility of income splitting with your family members, subject to limitations arising from the tax on split income (see 5.2.5).

If you arrange for your spouse to invest in common shares of your corporation, you can possibly double the available exemption of $883,384 for 2020 by each claiming it. Your spouse's own funds must be used for the investment, to avoid the attribution rules discussed in 5.2.2. You may also be able to multiply the exemption if your adult children or a family trust own the shares. (The income splitting tax may apply if minor children are involved, see 5.2.4.)

> Multiply your access to the capital gains exemption.

On death, it is possible to double the available capital gains exemption by leaving shares to your spouse or to a trust for your spouse (see 22.2.3 and 21.5.2).

14.1.1 Employers

If you are an employer and received amounts from the Canada Emergency Wage Subsidy (CEWS) or the Temporary Wage Subsidy as a result of a loss of business during the COVID-19 pandemic, you should ensure that you are prepared to correctly report these amounts on your 2020 return and remit any required taxes. Any subsidy amounts that you received and paid to your employees are considered government assistance and taxable income. As a result, these amounts should be reported on your corporation's T2 Corporation Income Tax Return or form T2125, Statement of Business Activities if you have an unincorporated business (e.g., you are a sole proprietor or a partner). Note that you will also have to report the amount that you paid to each employee for each CEWS claim period on your employees' T4 slips, so that they can properly report these amounts as taxable income.

14.2 Ways of extracting funds from the corporation

Since the corporation is legally a separate "person", you must follow one of the methods described below to get your hands on the corporation's income.

14.2.1 Dividends

Dividends are the distribution of a corporation's profits to its shareholders. They are not deductible to the corporation.

Generally, the Canadian taxation of dividends is based on the theory of "integration": If a corporation earns income, pays tax on it and pays what is left to you as a dividend, the combined effect of the corporation's tax and your personal tax should be about the same as if you had earned the income directly.

To attain integration, dividend income is "grossed up" (increased). You then claim an offsetting federal dividend tax credit. Similar credits are available at the provincial level (see 7.1.2). As a result of this gross-up and credit system, in theory, you and the corporation should pay the same combined amount of tax that you would pay if you had earned the income directly.

There are two types of dividends, and they require different gross-up and dividend tax credit calculations. This difference is intended to recognize that some active business income may be taxed at the lower corporate rate due to the "small business deduction" while other active business income may be taxed at the higher general corporate tax rate (see 7.1.2).

At the corporate level, cumulative income taxed at the high general corporate tax rate is tracked in the "general rate income pool" (GRIP) account. Dividends paid from the GRIP account attract lower personal taxes because corporate income tax has already been paid on the underlying income at a higher rate. To benefit from the lower personal taxes on dividends paid from the GRIP account (called "eligible dividends"), the source of the dividend should be properly documented at the time the dividend is paid.

Emi owns all the shares of EMI Ltd., which is a Canadian controlled private corporation. All of the income of EMI Ltd. is eligible for the small business income tax rate. In 2020, EMI Ltd. earns $100,000 in small business income, which is taxed at a combined federal/provincial rate of 13%. EMI Ltd. then pays the remaining $87,000 as a dividend to Emi.

Emi will "gross up" the $87,000 dividend by 15%, or about $13,050, and will pay tax on about $100,050, which conceptually represents the corporation's original income. Emi will then in theory receive a combined federal/provincial dividend tax credit worth about $13,000, equal to the amount of tax the corporation paid. So Emi and EMI Ltd. will together be effectively taxed as if Emi had earned the $100,000 as salary income.

The above treatment applies to dividends paid by Canadian controlled private corporations from income eligible for the small business income tax rate. Dividends from public companies and Canadian controlled private corporations that have been paid out of income taxed at the high general corporate tax rate are treated differently—see 7.1.2 for details of the treatment of both types of dividends.

Due to ongoing changes in federal and provincial tax rates, the goal of integration is rarely achieved in full. As a result, the actual combined federal and provincial corporate and personal tax rates that apply to the income should be taken into account when determining how much income to extract from your corporation in the form of dividends (see 14.2.9).

14.2.2 Salary

When the corporation pays you a salary, the amount paid is deductible to the corporation and taxable to you as employment income. If the corporation pays all of its profits to you as salary, you are therefore in much the same position as you would be if you earned the income directly, without having a corporation.

Although your salary may become quite high in such situations, the CRA's general policy is not to consider it an unreasonable deduction (for the corporation) where you are the owner/manager of the corporation. It is usually acceptable to consider that the corporation's income is due to your efforts, and therefore a salary equal to that income is a reasonable one. Of course, you are paying tax on the salary anyway.

You may decide on a base salary followed by a bonus, to be paid to you after the corporation has calculated its income at the end of the year. In general, you are taxed on employment income only when you receive it, while the corporation can accrue salary or bonus, counting it as deductible in the year even though it is paid after its taxation year-end.

Defer income to the next calendar year by accruing bonuses.

However, any salary or bonus that is deducted by the corporation must actually be *paid* to you no later than 179 days after the end of the corporation's fiscal year. Otherwise, it is deductible by the corporation only in the taxation year in which it is actually paid.

If the corporation's year-end occurs after early July, it can declare a bonus to you as of its year-end but pay the bonus within 180 days, which will be after December 31. The corporation can thus get a deduction from its income, but you do not have to recognize the income personally for tax purposes until the next calendar year. Keep in mind that employee (and employer) source deductions are payable to the CRA as part of the corporation's payroll remittance requirements at the time the bonus is paid.

14.2.3 Payments on loans from shareholders

If you lend funds to the corporation (or if you did so when originally setting up the business), the corporation can repay any amount of the loan without tax consequences. Such a repayment is neither deductible to the corporation nor taxable to you.

You could arrange to have the corporation pay you interest on your loan. The interest paid would normally be taxable to you as investment income. The tax effect would be about the same as if the corporation paid you that amount in salary. However, if your loan to the corporation does not *require* that interest be paid or there is no formal loan document, there is a danger that the interest would not be deductible to the corporation since it has not been paid pursuant to a legal obligation to pay interest. (Conversely, if you arrange for documentation requiring that interest be paid, the annual interest accrual rule discussed in 7.2.1 may require you to include interest in your income even in years when it is not paid!)

14.2.4 Capital dividends

Maximize capital dividend payments.

We mentioned capital dividends in 5.3.8 and 7.1.4. As you will recall from Chapter 6, only one-half of capital gains are taxed. When a "private" (i.e., non-public) corporation realizes a capital gain, the untaxed portion is added to its "capital dividend account". Similarly, one-half of capital losses reduces the capital dividend account.

Any amount in the corporation's capital dividend account may be paid out entirely tax-free to its shareholders. This preserves the non-taxability of the appropriate fraction of the capital gain. So if the corporation has realized any capital gains (net of realized losses), you should consider paying out capital dividends as your first choice for extracting funds.

Example

Eve owns all the shares of Evecorp Inc. In March 2020, Evecorp Inc. sells some land for a capital gain of $120,000, one-half of which is brought into Evecorp's income and taxed as a taxable capital gain.

Evecorp can pay a tax-free dividend of up to $60,000 (one-half of the capital gain) to Eve in 2020 or any later year, provided she elects beforehand to make the dividend a "capital dividend" and provided Evecorp does not realize capital losses that would reduce the capital dividend account. The capital dividend will then be completely tax-free to Eve. (Of course, because it is a dividend, it is not deductible to Evecorp.)

For the dividend payment to qualify for tax-free distribution, the appropriate tax election forms and directors' resolutions must be filed with the CRA before the dividends are declared payable from the corporation. If you do not file the tax elections in advance, two types of penalties could apply:

- a penalty of 1% of the capital dividend amount if the election and directors' resolutions are filed late (up to a maximum penalty of $500)
- a penalty of 60% of the excess of the actual dividend paid over the capital dividend account balance.

The latter penalty can be avoided by electing to treat the excess dividend as a taxable dividend. In light of these potential penalties, you should seek professional advice before making capital dividend payments.

Note also that if you allow a capital dividend account to build up in the corporation without paying capital dividends, the account can be reduced or wiped out by future capital losses. Once you have paid out capital dividends, however, they are safely out of the corporation, and subsequent capital losses will have no effect on them.

14.2.5 Repayment of capital

Any amount that is less than the corporation's "paid-up capital" may be paid out to the shareholders as a repayment of capital, generally with no tax consequences, if the paid-up capital is reduced by that amount.

> Consider a tax-free repayment of capital.

Paid-up capital (PUC) is essentially the amount of capital contributed to the corporation in exchange for its shares. However, the figure can be adjusted in various ways for tax purposes, as a result of transactions involving the corporation. As such, the legal PUC can often differ from the tax PUC.

If the corporation was originally funded with a substantial amount of capital, consider extracting funds by a reduction of the paid-up capital of the corporation. Make sure the corporation remains sufficiently capitalized to satisfy any requirements of its creditors or bankers.

> **Example**
>
> ABC Corp., a Canadian corporation, was capitalized with $500,000, the amount that the original shareholders contributed when subscribing for 1,000 common shares.
>
> If the directors of ABC approve a reduction in paid-up capital to $200,000 and a simultaneous repayment of $300,000 in capital to the shareholders, there will be no adverse tax consequences for either ABC or its shareholders. The $300,000 simply comes out tax-free. ABC then has 1,000 common shares issued with a paid-up capital of $200,000 and an adjusted cost base to its shareholders of $200,000.

14.2.6 Loan to shareholder

All of the mechanisms we have looked at so far—dividend, salary, repayment of a shareholder loan, capital dividend and repayment of capital—are legitimate ways to get your hands on the corporation's income or funds. We now turn to some of the rules designed to prevent you from doing so without following the normal routes.

Suppose the corporation simply lends you its funds. If you do not fit within certain exceptions, the entire amount of the loan will simply be included in your income. This is a very serious penalty, because the corporation receives no deduction for the loan, and you do not benefit from the dividend tax credit. The same rule applies if you become indebted to the corporation in some other way (e.g., you buy property from it but pay for the property with a promissory note rather than cash). However, where a loan has been included in your income and you subsequently repay it, you are allowed a deduction from your income for the amount of the loan repaid.

To avoid the income inclusion, bona fide repayment arrangements must be made at the time the loan is made and the loan must fall into one of the following exceptions:

- a loan to an employee who (along with family members) does not own 10% or more of the shares of any class of the corporation, where the reason for the loan is the individual's employment rather than the shareholding
- a loan to an employee, where the reason for the loan is the individual's employment rather than the shareholding, to help the employee purchase a home, shares in the employer or a related corporation, or a car to be used in employment duties (the rules do not specify a threshold for the percentage interest owned in the corporation for purposes of determining the reason for the loan)
- a loan that is repaid within one year of the end of the corporation's taxation year in which the loan was made and that is not part of a series of loans and repayments.

If the loan falls into one of the above exceptions but is made at a low or no rate of interest, you would be considered to have received a taxable benefit from the corporation based on the difference between the CRA's current low prescribed rate of interest (see 9.3) and the rate you are paying. This rule is exactly the same as for loans to employees, which we saw in 10.3. As in the case of employees, you may be allowed an offsetting deduction as a notional interest expense (which affects your entitlement to the capital gains exemption—see 6.4.3) if such expense would otherwise meet the rules concerning the deductibility of interest.

14.2.7 Deemed dividends

Certain types of actions that involve changes to a corporation's capital structure deem you to have received a dividend from the corporation. Generally, this happens when the corporation takes actions that would otherwise allow you to extract profits as a repayment of capital.

For example, if the corporation redeems shares that you own, any amount paid by the corporation exceeding the paid-up capital of the shares is deemed to be a dividend (and not part of your proceeds of disposition for capital gains purposes). The return of the paid-up capital on the redemption is generally tax-free.

14.2.8 Shareholder appropriations

We have covered all of the accepted mechanisms for extracting funds from a corporation. Suppose you don't follow any of the legalities, and you simply take the corporation's funds or property and use them as your own. If you are the sole shareholder, there would be no one to object to you doing this.

In such cases, the *Income Tax Act* deems that any benefit the corporation confers on you is income for tax purposes. So, for example, if you simply take $10,000 out of the corporation's bank account without declaring a dividend, that $10,000 is added to your income (without you benefiting from the dividend tax credit).

Since the $10,000 is taxable in your hands and the corporation is unable to deduct this amount, the $10,000 is taxed at both the corporate and personal levels. Clearly, it is to your advantage to follow the proper mechanisms for extracting funds. In the next section, we explore some of the considerations that will affect your decision as to the appropriate mix between salary, dividend and other forms of remuneration for yourself.

14.2.9 Determining your salary/dividend mix

Careful analysis is needed to calculate the best mix of salary and dividends for your case. It depends on your cash flow needs, your income level, the corporation's income level, payroll taxes on the salary, the corporation's status for tax purposes, and many other factors. Software and planning tools are available to assist in this task. Due to significant changes to the taxation of dividends in recent years (see 7.1.2), you should also consider engaging a qualified tax professional to assist in your analysis.

Crunch the numbers to calculate your optimum salary/dividend mix.

You may want to pay yourself enough salary to allow the maximum possible contribution to an RRSP (see 3.1.3). The same goes for any family members you've employed (see 5.3.2). Salaries paid to family members must be reasonable for the CRA to allow the corporation to deduct the salary amounts. If the CRA determines the salary to be unreasonable, the deduction to the corporation will be disallowed but the individual will still be subject to tax and so double taxation will result. To avoid this result, be sure to keep documentation on hand to support the reasonableness of the salaries.

If you are in a business that can suffer a downturn, paying out a large salary can prevent you from carrying back a later year's loss. Suppose, for example, your business earns $1 million in 2020, and you pay out $500,000 to yourself as a salary, leaving $500,000 as the business's income. If the business loses $1 million in 2021, you would have no way of carrying back the loss against your personal income. If you had left the funds as business income and paid out dividends, you would be able to carry back the 2021 loss to 2020, retroactively wiping out the business's 2020 corporate tax, and obtain a refund of that tax from the CRA.

14.3 Effect of having a holding company

You may choose to interpose a holding company between yourself and your corporation for various reasons. One reason for doing this is to pay out dividends from the operating business to the holding company to help protect the funds from the risks associated with the operating business, while keeping the income subject to a lower level of corporate taxation than would apply if it were paid out to you personally.

Consider the tax benefits of setting up a holding corporation.

For example, you own 100% of the shares of ABC Holdings Ltd., which owns 100% of the shares of ABC Manufacturing Ltd. Dividends may be paid from the manufacturing company to the holding company without any tax effects, provided certain conditions are met. Consult your tax adviser whenever you're paying dividends from one corporation to another.

If your spouse, children and other family members do not have any ownership in the business, you can consider bringing them in as shareholders at the time you set up the holding corporation. (See the estate planning example in 21.6.2 for one way of bringing in children as shareholders.) Doing so may be desirable for several reasons, including planning for your succession. However, if your children are under 18 you must be particularly careful about the attribution rules (see 5.2.3) and the income splitting tax for minor children (see 5.2.4). Some of these attribution rules do not apply if the corporation is a "small business corporation" (see 6.2.3).

When you're considering share ownership in a holding company for family members who are 18 or over, keep in mind that the attribution rules discussed in Chapter 5 and the income splitting tax for adults (see 5.2.5) may apply. In such cases, you may want to consider having your family members own shares directly in your operating company.

If your business has shareholders who are not related to you and you have family members who are involved in your business on a regular, continuous and substantial basis, a holding company may be appropriate. If you and your family members own shares in the holding corporation and the holding corporation owns all of your family's interest in the operating company, your internal family arrangements will be kept private from the operating company's other shareholders.

14.3.1 Corporate partnerships

An alternative to the use of holding companies is a corporate partnership. This is a partnership between your corporation and one or more other corporations (owned by other people).

Look into the potential advantages of a corporate partnership.

Advantages to this form of corporate structure include increased flexibility to allocate income and expenses between the partners and the ability to flow through income and losses and other attributes to the partners.

Professional advice should be obtained to determine whether a corporate partnership structure is appropriate.

14.4 Shareholders' agreements

When you share the ownership of a private corporation, it is usually wise to have a shareholders' agreement. Such an agreement can set out rights and obligations of the shareholders that go beyond the basic ownership of shares.

Typically, a shareholders' agreement provides for the orderly termination of the relationship between the shareholders if there is a future disagreement, or death or disability of one of the shareholders.

> **Example**
>
> Vivian and Harper start a small manufacturing business together. Each owns 50% of the shares of the corporation. Over the years, the business becomes very successful, but Vivian and Harper cannot get along and decide that one of them must leave.
>
> Vivian and Harper signed a shareholders' agreement that contains a "shotgun" clause. Vivian now offers Harper $1 million for Harper's shares in the corporation. If Harper refuses to sell, the agreement provides that Harper must buy Vivian's shares for the price Vivian is offering ($1 million).

The "shotgun" clause is just one example of a provision that can resolve (or prevent) major disputes between key shareholders. Typical provisions in a shareholders' agreement deal with:

- desire of a shareholder to sell his or her shares
- dissension among shareholders
- death or disability of a shareholder
- agreement as to who the directors and/or officers of the corporation will be
- agreement to vote the shares in a particular way on certain issues
- what will happen if the corporation's shares are awarded to a key shareholder's spouse on separation or divorce.

Tax considerations play a major part of planning for shareholder agreements. The tax treatment of life insurance payments, the availability of the lifetime capital gains exemption, the valuation of shares, and many other issues must be considered. Clearly, shareholder agreements should always be drafted with professional advice to properly address legal, business and tax issues.

14.5 Pension plans for small business owners

Registered pension plans were discussed in 3.5.1. Both money-purchase and defined-benefit pension plans can be used to accrue benefits for major shareholders who are employees. As an alternative to saving for retirement exclusively through an RRSP, consider having your company establish an individual pension plan, which we discussed in 3.5.2. This is a complex area; professional advice is essential.

If you are a small business owner and you don't want the trouble of administering a pension plan, you may simply want to set up an RRSP for yourself and ensure that you have sufficient "earned income" (i.e., salary from the corporation) to be able to make adequate contributions (see 3.1.3).

14.6 Investment income earned in a corporation

The Canadian tax system is designed so that income earned in a corporation and distributed to a shareholder as a dividend should attract the same amount of net income tax, both corporate and personal, as if the income was earned directly by an individual. However, this regime, known as "integration", does not always work perfectly in every province. In general, a tax cost arises in all provinces for individuals who earn investment income in a corporation rather than holding the investments personally.

An important part of the integration system is a federal refundable tax of 10-2/3% that applies to interest and other investment income earned by a Canadian-controlled private corporation. Most dividends received by a private corporation from public companies are also subject to a 38-1/3% refundable tax (Part IV tax). These refundable taxes are paid back to the corporation only when it has paid out sufficient taxable dividends (resulting in tax being paid by the shareholders). Combined federal and provincial corporate tax rates for investment income range from 48.7% to 54.7%, depending on the province.

Changes to provincial personal tax rates can also affect the way integration works. In some provinces, you may get a modest tax deferral advantage or you may have to effectively prepay tax if you earn investment income in a corporation. The precise calculation depends on your province of residence, your level of personal income, the extent to which you extract the funds from the corporation, and how you extract those funds.

Weigh the potential advantages of incorporating your investments. Looking beyond the potential for tax deferral or prepayment, you may benefit in other ways from holding investments in a corporation. For example, incorporating your investments can help you shield your investments from creditors, reduce probate fees on your death (see 21.4) and protect your assets from U.S. estate tax (see 19.4).

Incorporation also gives you control over the timing of dividend payments and thus the timing of income receipts in your own hands, allowing you to:

- maximize Old Age Security (OAS) benefits (if your income from sources other than investments for 2020 is less than $79,054 (see 20.3.2)
- reduce your exposure to alternative minimum tax (see 7.6)
- manage the timing of dividend payments in order to manage your cumulative net investment loss (CNIL) account balance (see 6.4.3)
- increase your earned income and thus your RRSP contribution room (see 3.1.3) through the payment of directors' fees and/or salaries.

Against the potential benefits, you also need to weigh the incremental costs of forming and maintaining the corporation, including substantial startup and ongoing legal and administrative costs.

Be particularly wary of moving investments into a corporation carrying on an active business. You may jeopardize the eligibility of the corporation's shares for the lifetime capital gains exemption (see 6.4.1) and decrease the amount of the small business deduction that the corporation and all associated corporations may claim (i.e., earning passive income in a corporation may limit the corporation's ability to claim the small business deduction) (see 14.1). In addition, the creditors of the active business will have access to the investments.

> Be cautious about having investment income in your corporation that carries on an active business.

14.7 Selling the business

If you decide to sell your incorporated business, there are two general approaches that can be taken. One is for the corporation to sell the assets of the business. The other is for you to sell the shares of the corporation.

If your shares are "qualified small business corporation shares" (see 6.4.1), you may be able to claim an exemption from tax for up to $883,384 of your gain on the sale in 2020. No capital gains exemption is available to the corporation if it sells the assets. From your point of view, you may be better off selling the shares.

The buyer of your business, however, would likely prefer to purchase the assets. One reason is that this will normally allow the buyer to claim higher capital cost allowance on the cost of depreciable assets (see 11.2.7).

No GST or other sales tax applies on a sale of shares. On a sale of assets, GST/ HST (and QST if applicable) usually apply but may be recovered by the purchaser through an input tax credit (or input tax refund for QST purposes) if the purchaser meets certain conditions (see 11.2.4). Alternatively, in many cases on the sale of part or all of a business, an election can be made to have no GST/HST (or QST) apply to the sale. Keep in mind that many conditions and exceptions apply to this election, especially if the business makes exempt supplies. Provincial sales tax generally applies to the sale of tangible assets other than qualifying manufacturing equipment, but the rules vary depending on the province.

To help maximize the value of your business and reduce taxes on its sale, consider making a "change in ownership" plan at least two years before you anticipate any actual sale or transfer of the business.

Needless to say, any purchase and sale of a business must be done with detailed professional advice.

If your business goes public without you selling the shares, you can make a special election to "crystallize" part or all of your accrued capital gain and get the capital gains exemption as if you had sold the shares (see 6.4).

14.8 References

The following publications and more information, including forms and brochures, can be obtained on the CRA's website at *www.canada.ca/en/revenue-agency.html* or by telephone request at 1-800-959-8281 for individual income tax and trust-related enquiries or 1-800-959-5525 for business and self-employed individual enquiries.

Guide T4012, "T2 Corporation – Income Tax Guide"
Income Tax Folio S3-F2-C1, "Capital Dividends"
Income Tax Folio S4-F16-C1, "What is a Partnership?"
Interpretation Bulletin IT-119R4, Archived – "Debts of shareholders and certain persons connected with shareholders"
Interpretation Bulletin IT-432R2, Archived – "Benefits conferred on shareholders"

Chapter 15

Farming

- Establish that your farming business is undertaken solely in pursuit of profit (15.1)
- Classify farming as your chief source of income (15.1)
- Claim deductions available for the self-employed (15.2)
- Consider using the "cash method" of accounting to defer taxes (15.2.1)
- Make the most of the lifetime capital gains exemption for qualified farm or fishing property (15.4.1)
- Take advantage of the intergenerational transfer rules (15.4.2)

The income tax system has special rules to deal with farming. We outline some of them in this chapter.

15.1 Farming—a business or not?

No matter what kind of activity you undertake, you are only allowed to write off losses for tax purposes if you are engaged in a business that is clearly undertaken in pursuit of profit (see 11.4.1). This issue comes up repeatedly in the case of part-time farmers.

"Farming", for tax purposes, includes a number of activities ranging from growing crops to raising livestock, fur farming, fruit growing, keeping bees and training horses for racing. The *Income Tax Act* classifies individuals engaged in farming into three groups. The principal difference among the groups is the extent to which they can deduct expenses relating to their farming activities.

At one extreme are the full-time farmers, for whom farming is a chief source of income. These people are allowed to treat their farming business like any other business, and can therefore claim losses against other income for tax purposes if they suffer losses in any given year (see 15.3.1).

> Establish that your farming business is undertaken solely in pursuit of profit.

At the other extreme are people whose farming activity is a personal pursuit. These people are sometimes called "hobby farmers", as farming is considered to be their hobby rather than something they are doing in order to make money. Hobby farmers may not deduct any losses from their farming activity.

In the middle are the people who undertake farming activities in pursuit of profit, but whose "chief source of income is neither farming nor a combination of farming and some other source of income that is a subordinate source of income".

These people are allowed only "restricted farm losses", limited to certain dollar amounts (see 15.3.2).

> **Example**
>
> Darryl lives on his farm and raises dairy cattle. Almost all his income comes from selling the cows' milk. In 2020, Darryl's dairy business has a bad year and he loses $30,000.
>
> Darryl can deduct his $30,000 against any other income he has (such as investment income) and carry it forward or back to be used in other years (see 15.3.1). His farming loss is very much like a loss from any other kind of business, such as manufacturing or retailing.

> **Example**
>
> Alison is a dentist who lives and works in Toronto. She spends her weekends on her ranch, where she keeps a stable of racehorses. In past years, Alison's horses have won a fair amount of prize money. In 2020, Alison has a bad year and spends $50,000 on maintaining her horses without winning any prize money at all.
>
> Alison's loss is likely to be considered a "restricted farm loss", and only a portion of it (see 15.3.2) is deductible against her dental practice income. Although her horse-racing business (which for income tax purposes is considered farming) is clearly a commercial venture, it is not a chief source of income to her and therefore falls into the "restricted" category.

Classify farming as your chief source of income.

You need to keep records that establish on an objective basis that your farming business is carried on in a sufficiently commercial nature. If your activities never actually turn a profit over many years, a claim that your activity is clearly commercial may be hard to sustain in court.

Many court cases have considered the question of whether farming, or farming in combination with some other subordinate source of income, constitutes a taxpayer's "chief source of income".

You may wish to consult a tax professional to determine how to best establish a claim that will entitle you to a full deduction for farm losses, rather than the more limited deduction for "restricted farm losses".

15.2 Computing farming income

Claim deductions available for the self-employed.

If you are engaged in a farming business—whether or not your losses will be "restricted" as we saw in 15.1—you may take advantage of a number of special rules when calculating income for tax purposes.

In addition to the specific rules for farmers discussed in this chapter, see 11.2 for deductions that can be claimed by the self-employed. If you successfully establish that your farming business is a commercial venture, such deductions will be available to you.

15.2.1 The cash method

Businesses are generally required to follow the accrual method of accounting for income. That is, you take your sales for the year into income, even though you may not have been paid for some of those sales until after your business year-end. You claim expenses the same way (see 11.2.2).

> Consider using the "cash method" of accounting to defer taxes.

For a farming business, you may choose to use the "cash method" instead. In general, this means you count payments received, rather than your sales—and only deduct amounts that you have paid, and not unpaid expenses that you have incurred. This usually provides a certain amount of deferral of income, and may result in lower tax payable. Once you have chosen the cash method, you are normally required to continue to use that method for the farming business for all subsequent years.

When you are using the cash method, you may, if you wish, include in income any amount up to the fair market value of your inventories on hand at year-end (subject to the mandatory inventory adjustment discussed in 15.2.2). The amount you include is then deductible in the following year. You might wish to do this for 2020, for example, if you had very low income in 2020 and can see by the spring of 2021 (when you file your return) that your 2021 income would increase enough to put you into a higher tax bracket.

15.2.2 Purchases of inventory and prepaid expenses

If you are using the cash method of accounting, it is clearly possible to generate a loss for tax purposes by purchasing large amounts of inventory. Special rules have been introduced to deal with this possibility and to limit the loss you can claim.

> **Example**
>
> Darryl, from our example in 15.1, purchased dairy cows for $5,000 just before his year-end on December 31, 2020. This purchase was included as an expense in arriving at his farming loss of $30,000. He had no other purchased inventory on hand at the end of the year. For income tax purposes, he is required to include $5,000 as a mandatory inventory adjustment to his 2020 income, reducing his farm loss to $25,000. In 2021, this $5,000 mandatory inventory will be treated as a farm expense.

In general, you are denied the portion of a loss that is attributable to purchases of inventory. However, for horses and certain registered bovine animals, you can deduct a portion of the loss. Professional advice should be obtained when dealing with these complex rules.

Claims for prepaid expenses are also restricted if the expenses relate to a year that is two or more years after the year of payment.

15.2.3 Cost of improving land for farming

Normally, when calculating income from a business, the cost of work done to improve land is considered a capital expense and is not deductible. However, for a farming business, amounts paid for clearing land, levelling land or installing a land drainage system are deductible.

15.2.4 Sales of livestock in a drought region

If you are farming in a region designated for the year as a "drought region", special relief is available if you sold a significant portion of your breeding herd. This rule is designed to allow you to defer paying tax if you are forced to sell off part or all of your herd because of drought.

The rule only applies if, by the end of the year, you have sold off (and not replaced) at least 15% of your "breeding herd". When it applies, some or all of your sales of the breeding animals are not counted into your income, but are deferred until a later year when your area is no longer designated as a drought region.

15.2.5 Business risk management programs

The federal government provides a group of business risk management programs for the agriculture, agri-food and agri-based products industry. The programs include:

- AgriInvest, a savings account in which producers can deposit a percentage of annual net sales, which the government will match
- The AgriStability program, which provides benefits based on a decline in current-year program margins as compared to reference years
- AgriRecovery, a rapid response program for disasters
- AgriInsurance, a crop insurance program that has been expanded to include additional commodities.

15.3 Farming losses

15.3.1 Ordinary farm losses

As we saw in 15.1, if your chief source of income is farming, or your chief source of income is "a combination of farming and some other source of income that is a subordinate source of income", you may deduct your farm losses as though they were ordinary business losses.

The carryforward available for such losses is 20 years. Farm losses can also be carried back and used against income of the past three years.

15.3.2 Restricted farm losses

As noted in 15.1, a loss from farming cannot *all* be used if you do not meet the "chief source of income" test. In this case, the loss you claim is limited to the first $2,500, plus one-half of the next $30,000 (that is, up to an additional $15,000).

> **Example**
>
> Alison, the dentist, whom we met in 15.1, loses $50,000 on her racehorses in 2020.
>
> Alison's "restricted farm loss" is $2,500, plus one-half of the next $30,000. Since her total loss is more than $32,500, she reaches the maximum and she can only deduct $17,500 against the income from her dental practice for 2020.

Any amount of loss that cannot be used because of the "restricted farm loss" rules can be carried back for three years and forward for 20 years, but can be used only against farming income. So, in our example, Alison has $32,500 that can be used to offset income from her horse operations during the years 2017 to 2019 and 2021 to 2040.

15.4 Transfers of farming assets

A number of special rules, as outlined below, are available to alleviate the tax burden of selling or transferring a farm and the assets of a farming business.

15.4.1 The lifetime capital gains exemption

As discussed in 6.4.2, a $1 million lifetime exemption from capital gains is available on the disposition of qualified farm or fishing property. If you are disposing of farm or fishing property, investigate whether it qualifies for the exemption. In general terms, farm land and buildings, shares of farm corporations and interests in farming partnerships may qualify for the exemption if they meet certain tests; equipment, inventory and most other assets do not qualify.

> Make the most of the lifetime capital gains exemption for qualified farm or fishing property.

In some circumstances, you may be able to take action, such as delaying the sale, so you can gain time to reorganize your affairs to take advantage of the exemption. You also may be able to take steps to increase the cost base of your qualifying farm property to reduce the tax liability that will arise in the future on the property's sale. The tax rules in this area are complex so you should seek professional tax advice if you own farm or fishing property that qualifies for the exemption.

15.4.2 Transferring farm or fishing property to your children or grandchildren

Normally, if you sell or give property to members of your family other than your spouse, you are deemed to have sold the property for its "fair market value", and thus have to recognize as a capital gain or income the difference between your original cost and the property's current value.

If you transfer property used in a farming or fishing business to a child, grandchild or great-grandchild (including a spouse of your child, a child of your spouse, etc., where "spouse" includes a common-law spouse as outlined in 2.2.1), you may not be subject to this rule. If you simply give the property, it is deemed to be transferred at your cost (adjusted cost base [see 6.2.1] for capital property, or undepreciated capital cost [see 11.2.7] for depreciable property). Any gain on the property will thus be deferred.

> Take advantage of the intergenerational transfer rules.

For this "rollover" rule to apply, you or your spouse or one of your children must have used the property "principally" in a farming or fishing business in which you, your spouse, your parent or your children were actively engaged on a regular and continuous basis.

When the rollover applies, the recipients (your child, grandchild, etc.) are deemed to have acquired the farm or fishing property for the amount at which you are deemed to have sold it, so the gain will eventually be taxed when the child sells the property at some later time. If your child sells the property within three years after the date of transfer, the gain on the sale could be taxed in your hands.

> **Example**
>
> Florence operates a grain farm in Saskatchewan. In 2020, Florence decides to retire and gives the farm to her grandson Charlie. The farmland cost her $10,000 in 1980 and is now worth $950,000.
>
> Florence is deemed to receive $10,000 for the land, and so has no capital gain. Charlie is deemed to have acquired the land for $10,000; if he ever sells the land, the $10,000 figure would be used as his cost for capital gains calculation purposes. (Of course, if Charlie transfers the farm one day to his child, a further rollover would be available, assuming the rules have not changed.)

If you are transferring farm or fishing property to a child, grandchild, etc., you may wish to realize a partial capital gain in order to use up your $1 million capital gains exemption and give your child a higher cost base on the property. If you sell the property for something in between your cost and the current market value, that amount would be accepted for tax purposes. Where land is being transferred, do not forget to consider the possible cost of provincial land transfer tax. GST, HST or QST may apply, depending on the circumstances. The transfer could also trigger alternative minimum tax (see 7.6) or a clawback of Old Age Security benefits (see 20.3.2).

Note that the tax rules do not let you transfer farm inventory to a child on a tax-free basis. Gifting farm inventory results in the same income inclusion as a sale of farm inventory at fair market value.

15.4.3 Capital gains reserve on sale of farm or fishing business to your child

We discussed capital gains reserves briefly in 6.5.1. It was noted there that the capital gain must be recognized at a cumulative rate of one-fifth each year, so that no reserve can last for more than four years after the year of sale.

Where you sell property used in a farming or fishing business (including land) to your child, grandchild or great-grandchild, the allowable reserve is 10 years rather than five. As with the rules discussed in 15.4.2, a spouse of your child, grandchild or great-grandchild, and a child, grandchild or great-grandchild of your spouse also qualify. (For this purpose, "spouse" includes a common-law spouse as outlined in 2.2.1.)

15.4.4 Farming partnerships

A partnership structure is common in farming businesses. In certain situations, taxpayers (usually spouses) may decide to split income by converting to a partnership structure from a proprietorship. Without proper planning, a disposition of the farming assets at fair market value may occur, resulting in capital gains, income and recaptured depreciation. This outcome can be avoided by filing appropriate election forms to defer taxable income.

Farming as a family partnership also provides an opportunity to transfer the interest in the partnership to a corporation and use the lifetime capital gains exemption as described in 15.4.1.

15.5 References

The following publications and more information, including forms and brochures, can be obtained on the CRA's website at *www.canada.ca/en/revenue-agency.html* or by telephone request at 1-800-959-8281 for individual income tax and trust-related enquiries or 1-800-959-5525 for business and self-employed individual enquiries.

Guide T4002, "Self-employed Business, Professional, Commission, Farming, and Fishing Income"

Income Tax Folio S3-F4-C1, "General Discussion of Capital Cost Allowance"

Income Tax Folio S4-F8-C1, "Business Investment Losses"

Income Tax Folio S4-F11-C1, "Meaning of Farming and Farming Business"

Chapter 16

If you practise a profession

- Consider the implications of the tax on split income rules for your professional corporation (16.1.2)

- Maximize your deductible interest (16.2.1)

- Pay retiring partners income or capital as appropriate (16.2.2)

- Consider paying club dues at the partnership level (16.2.3)

Most of income tax planning for professionals is the same as that for other self-employed people (see Chapter 11) as self-employed professionals are carrying on business the same way as the other self-employed people. However, there are a number of special rules that apply to professionals that we consider in 16.1. Since many professionals carry on their practice in partnership, we also look at some rules that apply to partnerships in 16.2.

16.1 Specific rules for professionals

16.1.1 The modified accrual method of accounting for income

As we noted in 11.2.2 and 15.2.1, businesses other than farming businesses are generally required to report income on the accrual basis. That is, you take your sales into income even though you may not be paid until after your year-end.

Most businesses must also account for work in progress—work that has been done but not yet billed.

Previously, there was an exception for designated professionals including accountants, dentists, lawyers, medical doctors, veterinarians and chiropractors. As a designated professional, you could elect to exclude work in progress from your income.

This election is sometimes called the "modified accrual" method or "billed-basis accounting" method. On one hand, it was not the same as the cash method, since billed amount must be reported as income even if they haven't been paid yet. On the other hand, excluding work in progress was still a step away from the full accrual method. Making this election could result in a deferral of tax.

However, the federal government eliminated this election, effective for taxation years that begin after March 21, 2017.

Designated professionals are now required to include the lesser of the cost and the fair market value of the work in progress in computing their business income, like other taxpayers, for tax years that begin after March 21, 2017.

If you made a previous election for your last taxation year that began before March 22, 2017, transitional relief is available over five years, starting from the first taxation year that begins after March 21, 2017. In that year, you were required to include 20% of the lesser of the cost and the fair market value of the work in progress in your income. After that, you must gradually increase the inclusion percentage as follows:

- 40% in the second taxation year
- 60% in the third taxation year
- 80% in the fourth taxation year
- 100% in the fifth taxation year.

Example

Dianne is a lawyer who is in sole practice. She spends almost the entire month of December 2019 preparing for a major trial to defend her client Michael. The trial takes place in January 2020. She does not bill Michael until the conclusion of the trial, in January 2020.

If Dianne elected in 2017 to exclude work in progress from her income, she would have to recognize income from her work in progress starting from 2018. As such, she would have to recognize income in respect of her work in preparing for the trial in her business year ended December 31, 2019. For that year, she must include 40% of the lesser of the cost and the fair market value of her work in progress in income. For her business year ending December 31, 2020, Dianne must include 60% of the lesser of the cost and fair market value of her work in progress in income.

On retirement or withdrawal from the business, the remaining work in progress is brought into your income. Such income is normally considered to be "earned income" for RRSP contribution limit purposes (see 3.1.3).

16.1.2 Professional corporations

Most provinces allow certain professionals to incorporate their professional practices. Provincial law governs professional corporations and so the applicable rules can vary depending on the province. You should seek professional advice to determine the rules that apply in your province and the most appropriate corporate structure for your professional practice.

Income splitting opportunities were previously available in provinces that allow your family members to be shareholders of your professional corporation. However, these opportunities are now significantly limited by the tax on split income rules, effective January 1, 2018 (see 5.2.5). You should consult with your tax advisor to properly assess the implications of the tax on split income rules on your professional corporation.

Consider the implications of the tax on split income rules for your professional corporation.

For tax purposes, a professional corporation is generally treated like any other small business corporation (see Chapter 14). If you are considering incorporating your practice, see 11.5 for a discussion of some of the pros and cons.

Professional corporations that are members of partnerships must use a December 31 business year-end (see 11.2.1). Other professional corporations may use an off-calendar year-end.

16.2 Specific rules that apply to partnerships

In 11.3, we discussed the taxation of partnerships in general. In this section, we look at some rules for partnerships that are particularly relevant to professionals.

16.2.1 Deductibility of interest paid by the partnership

As we saw in 7.2.3, interest paid is normally deductible as long as the funds borrowed are used to earn income from business or property. Where a partnership borrows funds for working capital, the interest is therefore clearly deductible.

As a member of a partnership, consider whether you can accelerate your drawings or have the partnership repay a portion of your capital contributions. You could then use the funds to pay off non-interest-deductible debt (such as a home mortgage), while the partnership can borrow funds to replace the lost working capital. The interest expense on the partnership's new borrowing would then become deductible to the partnership. Alternatively, you could borrow funds to inject back into the partnership. However, the CRA could challenge such an arrangement under the general anti-avoidance rule (discussed in 5.2.7) if it considers this type of refinancing technique to be a misuse or abuse of the *Income Tax Act*.

Maximize your deductible interest.

If the partnership borrows funds in order to make a distribution of profits and/or capital to the partners, the interest paid on such borrowings is normally deductible but only up to the amount of interest on the partnership's "net equity" as determined under generally accepted accounting principles.

16.2.2 Income payments to retired partners

Normally, if you withdraw from a partnership and you receive a payment to compensate for your interest in the partnership, the payment is considered capital. That is, any excess over your adjusted cost base in the partnership is a capital gain and taxed as discussed in Chapter 6. (Your adjusted cost base is essentially the amount you contributed to the partnership, plus your share of the profits on which you have been taxed, minus your drawings—see 11.3.5.)

Another option is available, however. If your partners agree to pay you a share of the income from the partnership and treat it explicitly as an income payment, you would be considered as still being a partner for tax purposes. You would therefore be taxed on that income, but your former partners would effectively pay less tax, since part of their partnership income and the related tax liability would be allocated to you.

When you (or a partner of yours) decide to withdraw from a partnership, you need to calculate the best way of paying out the retiring partner's interest.

Pay retiring partners income or capital as appropriate.

To avoid confusion or dispute, ensure your partnership agreement specifically addresses the tax treatment of payments to retiring partners.

> Joel, an accountant, retires from his firm at the beginning of 2020. There are three other partners, who share equally in profits. The firm's income for 2020 is $600,000. The partners agree to pay Joel $120,000 on his retirement, and declare the $120,000 to be a share of the income from the partnership (rather than as a repayment of his capital interest).
>
> Joel will be required to report the $120,000 as income for 2020. However, each of the partners will effectively get a deduction of $40,000, since after Joel's allocation, there is only $480,000 left to be divided three ways. Each partner will thus report $160,000 in income instead of $200,000 for 2020.

16.2.3 Club dues

Most club dues are not allowed as business expenses. Many professional partnership agreements provide that such dues should be paid by the partners personally (since they are not deductible from the partnership's income anyway).

Consider paying club dues at the partnership level.

There may be an advantage of having the partnership pay these dues even though they are not deductible. The individual partners' adjusted cost bases in the partnership are not reduced by such disallowed expenses, even though the assets of the partnership are reduced by making the payments. (As noted above, your adjusted cost base is essentially the amount you contributed to the partnership, plus your share of the partnership's profits, minus your drawings—see 11.3.5.) As a result, having the partnership pay the club dues can effectively reduce the capital gain (or increase the capital loss) on an eventual sale of the partnership interest or the retirement from the partnership.

16.2.4 RRSP contribution limit

As discussed in 3.1.3, the amount you can contribute to an RRSP is generally limited to 18% of your "earned income" for the previous year or $27,230 for 2020, whichever is less (minus your pension adjustment, if any). Whether partnership income is considered earned income depends on whether the partner is active in the partnership during the year.

Partnership income of active partners is included in earned income for purposes of calculating their RRSP contribution limits.

Continuing income payments to retired partners are not included in earned income. Retiring partners are deemed to be active for the entire calendar year in which they withdraw from the partnership, but any allocation of partnership income in following years is not eligible for RRSP purposes.

For example, if you withdraw from a partnership in September 2020, your partnership income reported on your 2020 tax return is included in earned income for purposes of computing your 2021 RRSP contribution limit. However, partnership income reported in 2021 and later years will not create new RRSP contribution room.

16.2.5 Emigration of a partner

If you emigrate from Canada, as either an active or a retired partner, any income allocated to you from the partnership will continue to be taxable in Canada. If the income is also taxable in your new home country, you should be able to claim a foreign tax credit (see 18.2.2) for any taxes paid in Canada to fully or partially offset taxes paid on the same income in the foreign jurisdiction.

As we saw in 13.3.2, when you become a non-resident of Canada, you are deemed to have sold most of your assets at fair market value at the time of emigration. You then have to pay tax on any resulting income or capital gains, or post acceptable security for the tax with the CRA. If you are a retired partner and you retain a right to continue receiving partnership income, the right is not considered an asset for the purposes of the deemed disposition on emigration, and therefore does not result in any capital gains or losses. Instead, you will have a full income inclusion based on the present value of your future income entitlements.

If you hold your partnership interest through a professional corporation (see 16.1.2), the shares of the corporation will be deemed sold when you emigrate, and the value of the shares will have to be determined to compute your Canadian departure tax liability. If the shares are qualifying small business corporation shares, you can apply your lifetime capital gains exemption against the gain on the deemed sale of the shares (see 13.3.3). Note that if your professional corporation retains a right to continuing partnership income, the CRA takes the position that this right is not an active asset, and thus may deny your claim for the lifetime capital gains exemption on the shares.

If you are an active or retired partner emigrating from Canada, it is strongly recommended that you review your situation with a tax professional before you leave Canada, both to plan for the tax consequences of your departure and to determine the tax consequences to you in the foreign country.

16.2.6 Death of a partner

When an active or retired partner dies, the partner is subject to the tax rules that generally apply on death. As we will see in 22.2.3, capital assets, such as stocks and real estate, are deemed for tax purposes to have been sold at fair market value on the date of death. Any accrued gains or losses on the assets are realized at that time, unless the assets are left to the deceased's spouse or to a spousal trust. In these cases, the assets are transferred at your tax cost (unless you elect otherwise—see 22.2.3) and your spouse or the spousal trust inherits the accrued tax liability.

A deceased partner's capital interest in the partnership is a capital asset if the full amount of the partner's capital contribution has not been paid out to the partner before death. However, continuing income payments of retired partners and other income rights of partners are not capital assets, and therefore are not subject to the deemed disposition rules on death.

A deceased partner's share of partnership income can be included in the partner's terminal return or possibly in a second, separate tax return (also known as a "rights or things" return—see 22.2.4). The advantage of claiming this income in a separate tax return is that the income may be subject to lower marginal tax rates and some of the same personal tax credits can be claimed as on the deceased's terminal return.

Similarly, continuing income payments of retired partners can be reported on the deceased's terminal return or on a separate return, or alternatively, they can be included in the income of the partner's estate or estate beneficiaries as they receive these amounts.

In light of the various choices for reporting income entitlements of deceased partners, you should ensure your will gives your executors sufficient discretion to file whatever tax elections and separate returns as are necessary to take full advantage of any tax saving opportunities in settling your estate. (For a general discussion of tax-oriented will planning, see 21.2.3.)

16.3 References

The following publications and more information, including forms and brochures, can be obtained on the CRA's website at *www.canada.ca/en/revenue-agency.html* or by telephone request at 1-800-959-8281 for individual income tax and trust-related enquiries or 1-800-959-5525 for business and self-employed individual enquiries.

Guide T4002, "Self-employed Business, Professional, Commission, Farming and Fishing Income"
Income Tax Folio S4-F16-C1, "What is a Partnership?"

Chapter 17

If you live in Quebec

- Be aware of differences between the federal and Quebec tax systems (17.1.4)
- Ask Revenu Québec to pay your refundable child care expense credit in advance in monthly instalments (17.3.2)
- Claim the refundable tax credit for children's activities (17.3.3)
- Claim a refundable credit if you adopt a child or have infertility treatment (17.3.4)
- Claim the refundable tax credit for seniors' activities (17.5.2)
- Claim the refundable tax credit for caregivers (17.6)
- Boost your Quebec business entertainment expense deduction by subscribing to eligible Quebec cultural performances (17.10.5)
- Defray the cost of a new environment-friendly car through Quebec's green vehicle rebate program (17.13.2)
- Claim the temporary residential waste water treatment systems tax credit (17.13.3)
- Claim the non-refundable tax credit for first-time home buyers (17.13.5)

Unlike the other provinces, Quebec administers its own tax system and Quebec residents must file a separate provincial tax return. The Quebec Taxation Act (Loi sur les impôts) *is largely modelled on the federal* Income Tax Act, *but, as we will see in this chapter, there are a number of differences.*

17.1 Quebec income tax

17.1.1 Quebec tax rates

Quebec's 2020 provincial income tax rates are listed in Appendix I.

Quebec residents are allowed a refundable Quebec abatement on their federal tax return, which reduces their federal tax by 16.5% of basic federal tax. As a result, Quebec residents earn federal non-refundable tax credits at a rate of about 12.5%, instead of the 15% rate earned in the other provinces. Quebec non-refundable tax credits are usually earned at a 15% rate, so an amount that is eligible for federal and Quebec credits is generally worth about 27.5% of the related amount (see Appendix III).

17.1.2 Dividends

For Quebec tax purposes, "eligible" Canadian dividends from public companies and Canadian controlled private corporations that have been paid out of income taxed at the high corporate tax rate (see 7.1.2) are grossed up by 38% for 2020. The offsetting Quebec credit for 2020 is 11.7% of the grossed-up dividend. As a result, the top marginal tax rate (combined federal and Quebec) is 40.11% for eligible dividends in 2020.

"Non-eligible" Canadian dividends are grossed-up by 15% and the Quebec credit is 4.77% of the grossed-up dividend. As such, the top marginal tax rate (combined federal and Quebec) is 47.14% for non-eligible dividends in 2020. (See 7.1.2 for federal rates on dividends.)

17.1.3 Instalments

Quebec instalment requirements parallel those for federal tax described in 9.2.2, with some minor differences.

If the individual's payment is less than 75% of the amount owed, the penalty for late or insufficient instalments is an extra 10% in addition to the normal interest rate. This penalty is substantially higher than the federal penalty, so if you can only pay part of your instalments, you are better off to pay your Quebec instalments on time.

The determination of who has to pay instalments is the same as under the federal system, as outlined in 9.2.2. Quarterly instalments are required where your balance of Quebec tax owing at the end of the year exceeds $1,800 for both the current year and either of the previous two years.

For Quebec residents, quarterly *federal* tax instalments are payable if you have federal taxes owing of $1,800 in the current year and either of the previous two years. Since Quebec tax can be higher or lower than federal tax for any individual (depending on many factors including those outlined throughout this chapter), there can be cases where you must remit federal instalments but not Quebec instalments, or vice versa.

17.1.4 Differences from federal tax

In the following sections, we highlight the principal differences between Quebec and federal tax law that affect personal tax.

Be aware of differences between the federal and Quebec tax systems.

If you live in Quebec, you should review the differences between the federal and the Quebec income tax systems, as highlighted below.

17.2 Basic personal and family credits

The federal basic credit is discussed in 2.2. Quebec offers a 15% personal tax credit of $15,532 (see Appendix III). The value of this credit for 2020 is $2,332 (i.e., 15% of the credit amount of $15,532).

Instead of a spousal tax credit, Quebec allows for the transfer of the unused portion of non-refundable tax credits between spouses. Under this measure, you may only claim the deduction resulting from the transfer after deducting all other non-refundable credits from your Quebec tax otherwise payable. This transfer mechanism also applies on the main tax return for the year of death of one of the spouses.

Students enrolled in full-time studies in vocational training at the secondary level and full-time studies at the post-secondary level can transfer to either parent an amount, known as the recognized parental contribution, relating to the unused portion of the student's basic personal credit amount for the year.

Quebec allows a refundable tax credit for contributions to an RESP (see 4.3), known as the Quebec Education Savings Incentive (QESI). The credit is added to the plan rather than refunded to the contributor. Each year, an RESP may receive a credit of 10% of the net contributions paid during the year, up to $250. Up to $250 of any rights accumulated during previous years can be added to this basic amount. Lower income families can claim up to $50 more each year, depending on their family income. The cumulative amount of the credit cannot exceed $3,600 per beneficiary.

Instead of the eligible dependant credit offered at the federal level (see 2.2.1), Quebec allows a credit for "other dependants" who are related by blood, marriage or adoption. To claim the credit, the dependant must be age 18 or over during the year, dependent on you, and ordinarily live with you, and you must not have benefited from a transfer of the recognized parental contribution from this dependant. For 2020, the credit amount is $4,348, which is worth up to $652.

Quebec also allows a non-refundable tax credit worth $267 for a "person living alone". For 2020, you may qualify if you have lived by yourself for the entire calendar year in a self-contained home with no person other than a minor or an adult child enrolled in post-secondary studies who is eligible for the tax credit transfer mechanism (see above). You may be a parent, grandparent or great-grandparent of this child. If you are a parent and you live with an adult child, you may be able to add a non-refundable single-parent family tax credit worth $330 to your person-living-alone credit.

If you are separated but you support your spouse in your home, you cannot claim this credit; however, if you pay only spousal support payments that you deduct on your tax return, you and your spouse can both claim the credit. The credit is reduced by 18.75% of Quebec family net income over $35,205, so the credit is fully eliminated if your family net income is $44,398 or more in that year.

The family net income test is used to reduce the tax credit for persons living alone, the Quebec age credit and the Quebec pension income credit (see 17.5). For 2020, your amounts eligible for claiming all three of these credits are added together and then the sum of these three credits is reduced by 18.75% of your family net income over $35,205.

17.3 Children

17.3.1 Child assistance payments

Instead of tax credits for dependent minor children, Quebec provides a non-taxable child assistance payment, payable in quarterly instalments. For 2020, the maximum annual payments for each eligible dependent child under 18 is $2,515 per child (in 2019 it was 2,472 for the first child; $1,735 for the second and third children; and $1,852 for each additional child). An additional maximum annual payment of $882 is granted to single-parent families. The payments begin to be phased out for two-parent families with income over $49,842 ($36,256 for single-parent families). Families with a child with a disability receive an additional monthly allowance of $198. If the child requires exceptional care, a supplement of $995 per month is added to the allowance for a disabled child so that the direct assistance for such a child is $14,316 for 2020.

17.3.2 Child care expenses

The Quebec tax rules for child care expenses are quite different from the federal rules discussed in 2.3.1. Child care expenses give rise to a refundable credit in Quebec instead of a deduction. (See 2.1.2 for a discussion of refundable credits and the difference between a deduction and a credit.) The credit is on a sliding scale, worth 75% of the expenses of low-income families, reduced to 26% for families with Quebec family net income over $162,975. Thus, the Quebec credit for child care expenses is more valuable to lower-income families, such as where both parents are attending school full-time.

Ask Revenu Québec to pay your refundable child care expense credit in advance in monthly instalments.

You may ask Revenu Québec to pay you the refundable credit for child care expenses in advance, in monthly instalments, if your estimated tax credit for the year is over $1,000 or if you are entitled to a work premium of over $500 for the year. To receive advance payments, you must make a request every year by filing form TPZ-1029.8.F-V.

Unlike the federal child care expense deduction, child care expenses eligible for the Quebec credit are not limited by either parents' earned income. Eligible expenses include child care costs incurred during a period in which you or your spouse received Employment Insurance or Quebec Parental Insurance Plan benefits.

To be eligible, the child must be, at any time in the year, either:

- age 16 or under and your child or your spouse's child
- age 16 or under and dependent on you or your spouse, and have income of no more than $10,662, or
- infirm and dependent on you or your spouse, and have income of no more than $10,662.

For 2020, Quebec child care expense claims are capped at $9,825 per child under age seven; at $5,170 per child age seven to 16; and at $13,445 where a child, at any age, has a severe and prolonged mental or physical impairment for which the disability credit can be claimed (see 2.3.1).

Nicole and Daniel have two pre-school children. In 2020, Daniel earns $136,000, and Nicole earns $30,000 working part-time. They pay $5,500 in day care, required to enable them both to work.

For federal purposes, Nicole can claim the least of (a) the amount paid–$5,500; (b) $8,000 per child–$16,000; and (c) two-thirds of her earned income–$20,000. She can thus deduct $5,500 from income.

For Quebec purposes, Nicole's credit is based on the least of (a) the amount paid–$5,500; and (b) $9,825 per child–$19,650. Since Nicole and Daniel's Quebec family net income is more than $162,975, the credit is 26% of $5,500, or $1,430.

Child care expenses paid to a boarding school or camp are subject to weekly limits of $200 per child under age seven; $275 per child of any age suffering from an impairment; and $125 per child age seven to 16.

The contribution payable by parents of children attending the province's early childhood centres is not eligible for purposes of the Quebec child care expense credit.

17.3.3 Children's activities

If your child participates in fitness or arts activities, you may be able to claim the children's activities tax credit. This credit equals 20% of amounts up to $500 paid in 2020 (up to $1,000 if your child is disabled) for eligible programs.

You may be able to claim this credit if your child is at least five but not yet 16 years old at the beginning of 2020 (or not yet 18 if he or she is disabled) and your household income for 2020 does not exceed $140,910.

Claim the refundable tax credit for children's activities.

Eligible children's physical programs involve activities that contribute significantly to your child's strength, endurance, flexibility and balance.

Soccer, hockey and other programs involving significant physical activity, such as dance lessons, are eligible. These programs must last at least eight weeks with at least one session per week. Children's camps can also qualify if they last at least five consecutive days and devote more than 50% of the children's time to physical activity.

Eligible children's art programs involve activities that are artistic, cultural, recreational or developmental.

All these programs must last at least eight weeks with at least one session per week. Children's camps can also qualify if they last at least five consecutive days and devote more than 50% of the children's time to eligible activities.

17.3.4 Adoption and infertility treatment expenses

The federal credit for adoption expenses is discussed at 2.3.3. Quebec also offers a refundable credit for adoption expenses to help finance the expenses associated with adopting children from within Canada or overseas. The credit is 50% of up to

$20,000 in expenses paid by you, or by you and your spouse, to a maximum credit of $10,000 per child. Qualifying expenses include court fees, legal fees, travelling and translation expenses (for adoptions from other countries), and fees charged by approved agencies.

Claim a refundable credit if you adopt a child or have infertility treatment.

Since the credit is refundable, it is available even if you have no tax to pay for the year. You must keep records of your qualifying expenses to be able to claim them.

If you're being treated for infertility, you may be able to claim a refundable credit for the costs associated with *in vitro* fertilization paid by you or your spouse, provided these treatments are not covered by Quebec's health insurance plan and they meet certain conditions. The tax credit rate ranges from 20% to 80% of up to $20,000 in eligible expenses, depending on your family's income. As such, the maximum annual credit ranges from $4,000 to $16,000.

17.4 Students

17.4.1 Tuition fees

Tuition fees qualify for an 8% non-refundable credit for Quebec tax purposes. Quebec allows the transfer of undeducted tuition fees to one of the student's parents or grandparents. Students can carry forward unused tuition fees indefinitely and claim them as a credit in later years.

Quebec also offers a non-refundable 15% tax credit for children under 18 and engaged in full-time (part-time if infirm) professional training or post-secondary education. For 2020, the credit is based on an amount of $2,933 for each term completed, for up to two terms per year.

17.4.2 Interest on student loans

A non-refundable tax credit is available for 20% of interest paid in the year on a student loan that you received under a federal or Quebec student loan program. You can carry forward any unused portion of the credit to a later year. To claim the credit, you must include a receipt from your financial institution showing the amount of interest paid.

17.5 Seniors

Quebec offers a 15% non-refundable age tax credit similar to the federal credit for persons who are 65 and older (20.3.4) and a credit for pension income (see 20.3.5). For 2019, the Quebec age credit is worth up to $490 (i.e., 15% of $3,267 which is the amount with respect to age) and the Quebec pension credit is worth up to $435 (i.e., 15% of up to $2,902 of pension income).

The amounts available for claiming each of these credits and the credit for persons living alone are added together and then reduced by 18.75% of your Quebec family net income for 2020 over $33,205 (see 17.2).

17.5.1 Home support, rehabilitation and safety equipment for seniors

Quebec allows a refundable tax credit for home support of persons age 70 or older. For seniors who are not recognized as dependent, the tax credit is 35% of up to $19,500 of eligible expenses, for a maximum refundable credit of $6,825. For dependent seniors, the credit is 35% of up to $25,500 of eligible expenses, for a maximum refundable credit of $8,925. If you and your spouse are both eligible for the credit, only one of you can claim it. The credit is reduced by 3% of your family income over $59,385 for 2020.

You cannot claim the same expense for this credit and for the medical expense credit described in 17.8, so be sure to do the math to see which credit provides the most benefit.

Individuals aged 70 or older are also able to claim a refundable tax credit equal to 20% of costs incurred for a qualifying stay in a private or public rehabilitation centre, up to a maximum of 60 days.

A refundable tax credit is also available for the purchase or rental of qualifying equipment used in the principal residence of a person aged 70 or older to improve his or her safety and security. This credit is equal to 20% of the amount paid over $250.

17.5.2 Seniors' activities

If you are 70 or older in 2020, your income for the year is $42,940 or less and you participate in fitness or arts activities, you may be able to claim the seniors' activities tax credit.

Claim the refundable tax credit for seniors' activities

This refundable credit equals 20% of amounts up to $200 (worth up to $40) paid for eligible physical activities and artistic, cultural and recreational activities similar to those eligible for the Quebec refundable tax credit for children's activities (see 17.3.3).

17.5.3 Seniors' assistance program to partially offset a municipal tax increase

If you are 65 or older in 2020 and your 2019 family taxable income does not exceed $52,600, an assistance program permits you to partially offset a municipal tax increase. Generally, the amount of the potential grant will be shown on either your 2021 municipal tax bill or a document issued by your municipality. If you are a long-time homeowner (at least 15 consecutive years), you may receive a grant to partially offset the municipal taxes payable on your residence following an increase in its value, if the increase significantly exceeds the average increase for certain residential properties and certain other conditions are met.

17.6 Caregivers of related adults

You may be able to claim a refundable tax credit for caregivers. Starting in 2020, this credit replaced the tax credit for informal caregivers of persons of full age. This credit can be claimed where either:

Claim the new refundable tax credit for caregivers.

- you provide care to a person aged 18 or older who has a severe and prolonged impairment and needs assistance in carrying out a basic activity of daily living, or
- you support and co-reside with a relative aged 70 or older.

This credit provides a universal basic tax assistance of $1,250 if you are a caregiver that co-resides with an eligible care receiver. This part of the credit can be paid by advance payments, on a monthly basis, as of 2021.

If you provide care to a person aged 18 or older with a severe and prolonged impairment, who needs assistance in carrying out a basic activity of daily living, a reducible additional amount of up to $1,250 can be claimed regardless of whether you co-reside with the care receiver. This additional amount is reduced by 16% for each dollar of the eligible care receiver's income that exceeds the reduction threshold applicable for the year. For 2020, the reduction threshold is $22,180 and the credit is reduced to nil when the care receiver's income exceeds $29,992. The reducible amount of the credit cannot be paid in advance to the caregiver.

Care receivers can include most direct family members or any other direct ascendant of the individual or the individual's spouse.

Another refundable tax credit is available for caregivers equalling 30% of total expenses of up to $5,200 paid in the year for specialized respite services for the care and supervision of an eligible person. The maximum credit amount of $1,560 is reduced by 3% of the caregiver's family income over $59,385 for 2020. If you are claiming the expense for another credit (for example, the medical expenses credit), you cannot also claim the expense for this credit.

> **Example**
>
> Roger has a severe and prolonged impairment, and needs assistance in carrying out a basic activity of daily living. Roger co-resides with his son, Richard, who provides him the care his impairment requires. In 2020, if Roger's net income is $15,000, then Richard can claim the universal basic tax assistance of $1,250 and the full reducible assistance of $1,250 (since Roger's net income does not exceed the reduction threshold of $22,180 in 2020).
>
> If Richard does not co-reside with his father, Richard is not eligible for the universal basic tax assistance and can only claim the reducible assistance of $1,250.

17.7 Donations

17.7.1 Charitable donations

In addition to the federal credit for charitable donations discussed in 8.1, in 2020 you can claim a Quebec non-refundable credit of 20% for the first $200 of charitable donations, and of 24% for amounts over $200. To the extent your income exceeds $108,391, you can claim a 25.75% donation tax credit.

Example

Lionel earns $200,000 in 2020, and he donates $30,000 to a registered charity. His provincial tax credit for his donation is $7,714, which is the total of:

- $40, which is 20% on the first $200

- $7,674, which is 25.75% of the lesser of:

  - $29,800, the amount of the gift exceeding $200, or

  - $91,609, the amount by which his $200,000 income exceeds the highest income tax threshold of $108,391

- $0, which is 24% of the amount of the gift less the two credit amounts used above ($30,000 − $200 − $29,800 = $0).

Instead, suppose Lionel earns $100,000 in 2020 and donates the same $30,000 amount. Now Lionel's provincial tax credit is $7,192, which is the total of:

- $40, which is 20% on the first $200

- $0, which is 25.75% of the lesser of:

  - $29,800, the amount of the gift exceeding $200, or

  - $0, the amount by which his $100,000 income exceeds $108,391

- $7,152, which is 24% of the amount of the gift less the two credit amounts used above ($30,000 − $200 − $0 = $29,800).

There is no income-related limit for the purpose of calculating the tax credits for gifts.

Capital gains arising from your gifts of publicly traded securities and other appreciable property are not included in your income for tax purposes.

Quebec's rules include a special restriction on the credit for gifts of works of art. The valuation of the gift is limited to the price the charity receives when it sells the art plus 25% of that amount. You can only claim the credit if the charity sells the art within five years of accepting the donation. This rule does not apply to donations to certain museums and galleries, recognized artistic organizations, governments or municipalities.

17.7.2 Political contributions

As noted in 2.7.2, many provinces provide credits for contributions to provincial political parties, riding associations and election candidates. In Quebec, only municipal electoral contributions are eligible. You can claim a non-refundable credit for municipal contributions of up to $155.

17.8 Medical expenses

For Quebec purposes, the non-refundable tax credit for medical expenses is reduced by 3% of Quebec family income, which is the combined net income of both spouses. Unlike the 3% federal reduction, the Quebec reduction is not capped, so many Quebec residents are not entitled to this credit.

The list of allowable expenses is similar to the federal list. Expenses for services provided for cosmetic purposes (such as liposuction, facelifts, botox injections and teeth whitening) are not eligible for Quebec purposes. Also, the amount you can claim for eyeglass frames is limited to $200 each for you, your spouse and any other person for whom you or your spouse purchased frames.

Quebec also offers a 25% refundable tax credit for certain medical expenses. The maximum amount for 2020 is $1,226, reduced by 5% of family income exceeding $23,700.

Also, as noted in 17.10.2, the taxable benefit for employer-paid private health insurance premiums qualifies as a medical expense for Quebec purposes.

17.9 People with disabilities

Quebec offers a non-refundable tax credit for persons with severe and prolonged physical or mental impairment. The Quebec credit is similar to the federal credit discussed at 2.5.1 and you must meet essentially the same criteria to be eligible. The supplementary credit for a child with a disability is not available in Quebec.

To claim the Quebec credit for the first time, you must file Form TP-752.0.14-V with your Quebec tax return for that year. For 2020, the maximum amount available for the credit is $3,449, which means it may be worth up to $517 to you.

17.10 Employment and self-employment

17.10.1 Parental Insurance Plan premiums

The Quebec Parental Insurance Plan (QPIP) provides benefits to any eligible worker who takes a maternity, paternity, adoption or parental leave.

Employers, employees and self-employed workers have to pay mandatory annual premiums up to a maximum of $388 for employees, $543 per employee for employers and $689 for self-employed individuals for 2020.

An employee's premiums factor into the calculation of his or her non-refundable personal tax credit, along with QPP, employment insurance and Health Services Fund contributions. Employer premiums are deductible, while self-employed worker premiums are partially deductible.

Benefits paid under the plan are taxable in the year received, and are subject to source deductions.

17.10.2 Employer-paid private health insurance

As we saw in 10.1.1, employer contributions to a private health services plan are non-taxable employee benefits for federal purposes. These contributions are, however, taxable for Quebec tax purposes. Thus, if your employer pays for your group sickness, drug or dental plan, the value of the benefit is included in your employment income on your Relevé 1 and must be reported on your Quebec tax return, even though it does not appear on your T4 slip for federal income tax purposes.

As a result, employer health plan contributions will normally make your employment income for Quebec tax purposes higher than it is for federal purposes. You (or your spouse) can claim the taxable benefit as a medical expense on your Quebec tax return (see 17.8).

17.10.3 Employee stock options

Quebec's tax treatment of employee stock options is similar to the federal treatment (see 10.4), except that the amount you are allowed to deduct from your taxable benefit may be less for Quebec tax purposes.

As we saw in 10.4.1, you may be able to claim a deduction for federal purposes of 50% of the taxable benefit arising from exercising employee stock options or from selling stock option shares in a Canadian controlled private corporation (see 10.4.2). For Quebec purposes, your deduction is generally limited to 25% of the amount of the benefit.

If you received your stock options from a small or medium-sized business engaged in innovative activities in Quebec, you may be able to claim a deduction of 50% of your taxable benefit. To qualify, the corporation must carry on business in Quebec and have an establishment there, and its assets and those of associated corporations must be less than $50 million in the taxation year ending in the calendar year before the options were granted. Also, the corporation must have claimed a Quebec tax credit for scientific research and experimental development in the taxation year ending in the calendar year that the options were granted or in one of its three previous taxation years.

You may also be able to claim a 50% deduction on a stock option benefit for options granted after February 21, 2017 if the corporation is publicly traded and its payroll in Quebec is at least $10 million.

If you donate stock option shares to charity you may be able to claim a 50% deduction on a stock option benefit for Quebec tax purposes.

17.10.4 Union and professional dues

Union and professional dues (excluding professional insurance), which are deductible for federal tax purposes (see 10.8.4), are not deductible on your Quebec tax return. Instead, they entitle you to a 10% non-refundable tax credit. This rule applies to employees and self-employed individuals alike. The cost of professional insurance is deductible for Quebec tax purposes.

17.10.5 Meals and entertainment expenses

As under the federal rules (see 11.2.9), if you are self-employed and you take a client or business contact out for a meal or entertainment event, your deduction for your costs as a business expense is limited to 50% of the amount paid for Quebec tax purposes.

For Quebec purposes, entertainment expenses are further limited to:

- 2% of total sales, if your total sales are $32,500 or less
- $650, if your total sales are between $32,500 and $52,000
- 1.25% of total sales, if your total sales are $52,000 or more.

Relief from these limits is available for certain sectors, such as businesses requiring frequent travel and sales agencies.

Boost your Quebec business entertainment expense deduction by subscribing to eligible Quebec cultural performances.

Some business entertainment expenses for cultural events held in Quebec are 100% deductible for Quebec tax purposes. These include the cost of a subscription to a symphony orchestra, classical or jazz ensemble, and opera, dance, theatre and vocal performances. To qualify for this special deduction, the subscription must be for at least three performances in eligible artistic disciplines.

17.10.6 Home office expenses

The federal tax rules governing deductions for home office expenses are discussed in 10.8.3 and 11.2.10. For Quebec tax purposes, the deduction for self-employed individuals is limited to 50% if the expenditures relate to the cost of maintaining a residence (e.g., maintenance and repair costs, rent, mortgage interest, property and school taxes, insurance premiums and depreciation). The home office expense claims of employees are not subject to this restriction.

17.10.7 Self-employed QPP/CPP and QPIP deduction

Self-employed individuals are generally eligible to deduct 50% of their QPP/CPP contributions on pensionable self-employed earnings and a portion of their QPIP premiums in calculating their net income. The remainder of these contributions and premiums is eligible for a non-refundable pension tax credit. This deduction also applies when calculating the income used to determine the 1% contribution to the Health Services Fund (see 17.12.2).

17.10.8 Career extension tax credit

If you are 60 or older in 2020 you may be able to claim a tax credit for career extension applied at a 15% rate to your eligible work income that exceeds a $5,000 threshold. The credit for workers age 60 or older is reduced by 5% of eligible work income over $35,205. The maximum amount of work income eligible for the credit varies based on your age. For 2020, if you are aged 60 to 64, the credit applies to $10,000 in income that exceeds the threshold. For workers age 65 or older, the credit applies to $11,000 of eligible work income in excess of $5,000. Eligible work income includes salary and business income, but excludes taxable benefits received from a previous employment as well as amounts deducted in computing taxable income, such as the stock option deduction.

17.11 Investments

17.11.1 Limit on deductibility of investment expenses

For Quebec purposes, your ability to deduct expenses incurred to earn income from property is limited to your income from such investments earned in the year. Investment expenses that cannot be used in the current year can be carried back to offset investment income earned in the three preceding tax years and they can be carried forward indefinitely, as long as the investment income in that year exceeds the investment expenses.

17.11.2 Rental expenses—documentation

If you use a building located in Quebec to earn rental or business income and you claim any expenses for renovation, improvement, maintenance or repair of the property, you must include with your Quebec income tax return Form TP-1086.R.23.12-V. On this form, you must disclose the contractor's name, address, social insurance number (if an individual) and QST registration number (if available), as well as the amount paid for the work carried out. This measure is designed to combat tax evasion in the contracting and renovation sectors.

17.11.3 Cumulative net investment loss

As we saw in 6.4.3, investment expenses and tax shelter write-offs create a cumulative net investment loss (CNIL), which reduces your ability to claim the lifetime capital gains exemption.

For Quebec tax purposes, certain special Quebec investment incentives are not included in your CNIL calculation (e.g., some provincial resource deductions and deductions for certain films). That is, they do not affect your ability to claim the capital gains exemption on your Quebec tax return.

17.12 Health Services Fund contributions

17.12.1 Health Services Fund contribution

Your contribution to the Health Services Fund is based on income from all sources (other than employment income). The income taxed is generally the total shown on your income tax return, including business income, investment income, pension or retirement income and taxable capital gains but not employment income, Old Age Security or alimony.

Certain deductions are permitted to arrive at the base amount for the contribution, and a further $15,170 exemption is allowed for 2020. If your 2020 income is between $15,170 and $52,745, your Health Services Fund contribution is 1% of income over $15,170, to a maximum of $150. If your income is over $52,745, your contribution is $150 plus 1% of your income over $52,745, to a maximum of $1,000. Your contribution is then indirectly offset by the non-refundable personal tax credit of 15% (see 17.2).

If you are required to pay income tax instalments (see 17.1.3), you must also pay quarterly instalments on your Health Services Fund contribution.

17.13 Other Quebec credits and deductions

17.13.1 Legal fees for establishing support payments

Under the federal system, if you are the recipient of support payments, you may deduct legal costs to establish or enforce a right to child or spousal support or to obtain an increase in child or spousal support amounts (see 2.6). For Quebec purposes, fees paid due to a court application to increase the level of support are deductible.

You can also deduct judicial and extrajudicial expenses paid regarding an initial right to receive support payments or an obligation to pay an amount for support, as long as the expenses are not reimbursed and you did not deduct them from income in a previous year.

17.13.2 Rebate for purchase or lease of green vehicles

Defray the cost of a new environment-friendly car through Quebec's green vehicle rebate program.

You may be eligible for a rebate if you purchase or lease a green vehicle. The rebate program mainly focuses on hybrid vehicles, rechargeable hybrid electric vehicles and vehicles that are exclusively electric. The rebate ranges between $500 and $8,000 for 2020 and is based on battery capacity in kilowatt-hours.

This rebate is in addition to a new federal incentive for purchasing zero-emission vehicles, which may provide as much as $5,000 (see 12.3.3).

17.13.3 Residential waste water treatment systems tax credit

You can claim a temporary refundable tax credit for upgrading the residential waste water treatment systems of your principal residence or cottage. The credit applies to the costs of constructing, renovating, modifying or rebuilding a system for discharging, collecting and disposing of waste water, toilet effluents or grey water.

Claim the temporary residential waste water treatment systems tax credit.

To be eligible for the credit, the work must be carried out on a dwelling of which construction must have been completed before January 1, 2017, by a qualified contractor under a service agreement entered into after March 31, 2017 and before April 1, 2022.

If you wish to claim the credit for 2020, you must have paid the eligible expenses after December 31, 2019 and before January 1, 2021.

The tax credit you can claim is capped at $5,500 per eligible dwelling, and it is based on 20% of the portion, of qualified expenditures you paid in the year that exceed $2,500.

17.13.4 Solidarity tax credit

Quebec's solidarity tax credit is a refundable tax credit for low- and middle-income families. This credit has three components: a housing component, a

Quebec sales tax (QST) component and a component for people who live in northern villages. You may be entitled to the credit even if you are not eligible for all three components.

If you are eligible for this credit, it will be paid to you monthly. You must be registered for direct deposit to your bank account.

17.13.5 First-time home buyers

If you are acquiring your first home located in Quebec, you may qualify for a non-refundable tax credit for first-time home buyers of up to $5,000 (worth up to $750). Combined with the federal credit for first-time home buyers discussed at 2.7.3, the non-refundable credit could be worth up to $1,500.

> Claim the non-refundable tax credit for first-time home buyers.

You or your spouse or common-law partner can claim the credit. To qualify, neither of you can have owned another home nor lived in another home owned by your spouse or common-law partner in the year of purchase or in any of the four preceding years.

A qualifying home is one that is acquired after December 31, 2017 that you or your spouse or common-law partner intend to occupy as your principal place of residence within one year of acquiring it. A housing unit includes a house that is detached, semi-detached or a row house, a manufactured home or mobile home, a condominium and an apartment in a multiple-unit residential complex.

You can also claim the credit for certain homes purchased by or for the benefit of a disabled family member who is eligible for Quebec's tax credit for a person with a severe and prolonged impairment in mental or physical functions.

17.14 References

Revenu Québec produces a number of publications to assist taxpayers, the most notable of which is the *Guide to the Income Tax Return* that accompanies the provincial income tax return. Quebec tax forms and guides are also available in French and English from the Quebec government's website at *www.revenu.gouv.qc.ca*.

Chapter 18

If you are a U.S. citizen in Canada

- Consider claiming the foreign earned income exclusion (18.2.1)

- Claim the maximum foreign tax credit (18.2.2)

- Keep records of expenses deductible on your U.S. return (18.3.1)

- Be aware of differences between Canadian and U.S. rules governing retirement income (18.3.3)

- Defer U.S. taxation of income accruing in your RRSP and other Canadian retirement plans (18.3.3)

- Be aware of non-qualified deferred compensation plans (18.3.3)

- Watch out for ownership of Canadian corporations and funds earning passive income (18.3.5)

- Consider making a Section 962 election to mitigate or eliminate the U.S. tax impact of the Global Intangible Low-Taxed Income regime (18.3.5)

- Be cautious of using the Canadian lifetime capital gains exemption (18.4.3)

- Review income splitting arrangements to prevent double taxation (18.6.2)

- If you're married, file a joint U.S. return where appropriate (18.7.1)

- Consider using the annual US$15,000 U.S. gift tax exclusion to transfer wealth to children and grandchildren (18.8.2)

- Consider using the increased U.S. lifetime gift tax exclusion available from 2020 through 2025 (18.8.2)

- Be aware of U.S. gift, bequest and foreign trust reporting rules (18.8.4)

- Consider expatriating from the U.S. to protect your Canadian assets from U.S. tax and to simplify your tax filing and reporting obligations (18.9)

In this chapter, we address the difficult and complicated tax problems of the United States citizen who lives in Canada. We can only scratch the surface, due to the interaction of two highly complex tax systems that are both subject to continual change. You should seek professional advice if you are a U.S. citizen living in Canada.

18.1 Two systems of taxation

The income tax systems of the United States and Canada are similar in some general ways, but very different in their details. A U.S. citizen resident in Canada must deal with both systems.

The United States is one of the few countries in the world that taxes its citizens on their worldwide income, whether or not they are physically in the United States. Canada taxes only Canadian residents on their worldwide income; non-residents (including Canadian citizens) are taxed by Canada only on certain income from Canadian sources.

The result is that U.S. citizens living in Canada must file returns under both systems, and they often must pay tax to both governments. Safeguards exist to prevent double taxation: clearly, you could not afford to pay a large percentage of your income to each country. But the safeguards, which are outlined in 18.2 below, are not perfect. Much of this chapter deals with the taxation issues that arise due to differences between the two systems' ways of calculating income and tax.

As a U.S. citizen resident in Canada, you should also consider how you may be affected by significant changes to the U.S. tax regime for individuals that became law in December 2017. These new rules affect tax rates and brackets, the treatment of earnings from non-U.S. corporations, gift and estate taxes and certain deductions and credits, among other things. Many of these changes take effect for 2018 but are set to expire after 2025. (See 18.3.1, 18.3.5, 18.3.8, 18.3.9, 18.5, 18.6 and 18.8 for details.)

In general, you will find that U.S. taxation is lower than Canadian. U.S. federal tax currently reaches a maximum rate of 37%. Canadian federal tax reaches 33%, but as a resident of Canada you also have a provincial tax liability, which raises the top rate to approximately 50% or more, depending on your province of residence. As a U.S. citizen not resident or domiciled in any state, you have no liability for any U.S. state tax except, perhaps, to the extent you have income arising in a state.

The 2020 U.S. income tax rates for single persons with no dependants and for married couples filing joint returns (see 18.7.1) are as follows. Amounts are in U.S. dollars:

Single (see 18.7.1)	
Taxable income	Federal tax
$0–9,875	10%
$9,876–40,125	$987.50 + 12% of the amount over $9,875
$40,126–85,525	$4,617.50 + 22% of the amount over $40,125
85,526–163,300	$14,605.50 + 24% of the amount over $85,525
$163,301–207,350	$33,271.50 + 32% of the amount over $163,300
$207,351–518,400	$47,367.50 + 35% of the amount over $207,350
$518,401 and up	$156,235.00 + 37% of the amount over $518,400

Married filing joint income tax returns (see 18.7.1)	
Taxable income	Federal tax
$0–19,750	10%
$19,751–80,250	$1,975.00 + 12% of the amount over $19,750
$80,251–171,050	$9,235.00 + 22% of the amount over $80,250
$171,051–326,000	$29,211.00 + 24% of the amount over $171,050
$326,001–414,700	$66,543.00 + 32% of the amount over $326,600
$414,701–622,050	$94,735.00 + 35% of the amount over $414,700
$622,051 and up	$167,307.50 + 37% of the amount over $622,050

The rates for other types of taxpayers are different; see 18.7.1 for a discussion of the types of filers.

The highest effective federal marginal rate is 37%. The 37% marginal rate applies to taxable income over US$622,050 for married taxpayers filing jointly. Married individuals filing separately (see 18.7.1) become subject to the highest rate at taxable income exceeding US$311,025.

18.1.1 Net investment income tax

If you have investment income, you may be subject to a U.S. net investment income tax in addition to regular income tax. A tax rate of 3.8% is applied to the lower of two amounts: net investment income for the year or modified adjusted gross income over a threshold amount. Net investment income includes interest, dividends, capital gains, certain annuities, royalties, rents and passive income from partnerships and "S corporations".

The thresholds for modified adjusted gross income are US$250,000 for married individuals filing jointly, US$200,000 for single filers and US$125,000 for married individuals filing separately.

This tax should be creditable in Canada (subject to the regular limitations) if the investment income is U.S. source income. The U.S. does not allow the net investment income tax to be offset with foreign tax credits. As a result, many U.S. citizens with significant investment income will pay U.S. net investment income tax.

18.2 Basic mechanisms for avoiding double taxation

There are three mechanisms in place to help ensure you do not pay tax twice on the same income.

18.2.1 Foreign earned income exclusion (U.S. tax law)

The simplest way to avoid double taxation is the U.S. "foreign earned income exclusion". On your U.S. tax return, you may exclude from your income up to US$107,600 of "earned income" (employment or self-employment income) earned from services provided outside the United States.

> **Example**
>
> Cathy is a U.S. citizen who lives in Calgary. She works at a company as an accountant and earns Cdn$100,000 in 2020. (Assume the Canadian and U.S. dollars are trading at par throughout 2020.) She has no other income.
>
> On her U.S. tax return, Cathy reports her income of approximately US$100,000. She then elects to use the foreign earned income exclusion and deduct the same $100,000, for total income of $0. As a result, she pays no tax to the United States. Her Canadian tax return is not affected by her U.S. citizenship.

If you do not have any income other than your employment or self-employment income and your annual income is under US$107,600 for 2020, this exclusion means you won't be subject to U.S. tax. You must still file a U.S. return (see 18.7.2) and claim the exclusion.

If you file as "married filing jointly" (see 18.7.1), you and your spouse can each claim up to US$107,600 for purposes of the exclusion against your respective earned incomes. This can be done even if your spouse is not a U.S. citizen.

The foreign earned income exclusion is first deducted and then added back to taxable income to calculate a tentative tax liability. Tax is then calculated on the amount of the foreign earned income exclusion as though it was the only taxable income for the year. The excess of the first amount over the second amount is the amount of tax payable. As a result of this calculation, tax is paid at higher graduated rates on the amount of taxable income that exceeds the foreign earned income exclusion amount.

Consider claiming the foreign earned income exclusion.

The regulations make it possible to elect the foreign earned income exclusion on late-filed returns in a number of cases. If you are eligible for the foreign earned income exclusion, you should normally claim it. However, in some circumstances (mostly involving carryovers of foreign tax credits—see 18.2.2), claiming a foreign tax credit can be more beneficial than claiming the exclusion. If you claim the exclusion and then, in a later year, elect not to claim it, you cannot normally claim it again for five years.

18.2.2 Foreign tax credit (both U.S. and Canadian law)

The foreign tax credit is a unilateral mechanism provided by many countries to prevent double taxation. Both the U.S. and Canada provide foreign tax credits. While the details differ, the concept is basically the same for both.

Claim the maximum foreign tax credit.

Consider the U.S. foreign tax credit as an example. If you are subject to U.S. taxation (because you are a citizen) but you have paid tax to Canada on Canadian-source income, you can, in general, claim a foreign tax credit to offset your U.S. tax on that income. Your credit cannot be greater than the Canadian tax you paid.

Dave is a U.S. citizen who lives and works in Toronto. He earns Cdn$1,000 (equivalent to US$1,000) in interest on his Toronto bank account in 2020. He also receives a salary in Canada and income from investments in the United States. Assume the Canadian and U.S. dollars are trading at par throughout 2020.

Dave is required to include the US$1,000 in his income for U.S. tax purposes. (Because it is investment income and not earned income, it is not eligible for the foreign earned income exclusion.) Assume that he is in the 35% U.S. bracket (i.e., his taxable income is less than US$518,401 and he is single), so his additional U.S. tax is US$350. If he is in a 51% tax bracket in Canada, so that he has paid the equivalent of US$510 to Canada (and Ontario) on the income, he can receive a foreign tax credit for the full US$350 on his U.S. return. By contrast, if his Canadian tax rate were lower and he paid only US$250 to Canada (and Ontario), he could only claim US$250 as his foreign tax credit.

The above example is highly simplified, but it demonstrates the basic effect of the credit. When you total up the tax to both countries (including provincial and state tax) and the foreign tax credits of each, you should end up paying an amount that is equal to the higher of the two countries' rates of tax.

The Canadian foreign tax credit follows essentially the same principles. Since Canada taxes Canadian residents on their worldwide income, Dave, in our example has to report his U.S.-source investment income on his Canadian tax return. He is then eligible for a foreign tax credit for U.S. taxes paid on his U.S.-source investment income to offset the Canadian tax that applies but only up to the amount of U.S. tax he would have paid if he was not a U.S. citizen. Canada only allows foreign tax credits for the amount of U.S. tax that would have been payable by non-U.S. citizens.

The U.S. then allows an additional credit under the Canada-U.S. tax treaty (see 18.2.3), which many taxpayers neglect to claim. (Note that each country's foreign tax credit generally applies only to foreign taxes on income from sources outside that country.)

The details of the foreign tax credit rules are very complicated. If you receive income for personal services performed in both the U.S. and Canada, it is a good idea to keep a diary to record U.S. and Canadian work days.

For U.S. foreign tax credit purposes, excess (non-creditable) foreign tax can be carried back one year and forward 10 years. For Canadian foreign tax credit purposes, certain excess foreign tax can be deducted from income in the current year. If the excess foreign tax relates to business income, the excess generally can be carried back three years and forward 10 years. Foreign taxes on investment income and employment income that are not used as a credit or deduction in the year can't be carried back or forward in Canada.

If you have various sources of income and need to claim a foreign tax credit under one or both systems, you should consult a professional adviser.

18.2.3 Canada-U.S. tax treaty

The third safeguard against double taxation is the Canada-U.S. tax treaty (also known as a tax convention). Both Canada and the U.S. have such treaties with many countries. The purpose of a tax treaty is twofold: to prevent double taxation and to reduce tax evasion by allowing exchange of taxpayer information between the two governments.

The Canada-U.S. treaty, for the most part, does not apply to limit the U.S. tax liability of U.S. citizens resident in Canada except in specific circumstances.

For example, the treaty allows a U.S. citizen resident in Canada to defer U.S. taxation of income in RRSPs and other pension plans, which are not qualifying deferral plans under U.S. rules. Absent this provision, U.S. tax could apply to the accruing funds, which are specifically exempt from Canadian tax (see 3.1.5 and 18.3.3).

If you are using the treaty to reduce your U.S. tax liability, you are generally required to disclose the specific details of the treaty benefits you are claiming on your U.S. tax return. If you do not, the treaty benefits can be denied. However, deferring RRSP income does not require disclosure with your U.S. tax return (see 18.3.3).

Under the treaty, if you are a Canadian resident and you receive U.S. social security benefits, you are not subject to U.S. tax on these amounts. However, 85% of the amount received is subject to tax in Canada.

18.3 Differences in calculating income

In theory, the foreign tax credit mechanism prevents you from paying tax twice on the same income. However, there are many differences between U.S. and Canadian calculations of income for tax purposes. These differences can lead to unexpected tax liabilities.

18.3.1 Deductions available in the U.S. but not in Canada

While you can normally deduct home mortgage interest and property taxes on your U.S. tax return, they are not deductible in Canada, except to the extent you can claim an office in your home (see 7.2.3 and 11.2.10).

As a result of the 2017 U.S. tax changes, the deduction for mortgage interest is limited to a mortgage balance of US$750,000 (or US$375,000 if married filing separately) for 2018 and later tax years. However, if the mortgage was taken out prior to December 16, 2017, it may be "grandfathered" and interest on a mortgage balance of up to US$1 million (US$500,000 if married filing separately) may still be deductible. For years after 2025, the mortgage balance limitation is scheduled to revert to US$1 million regardless of when the debt was incurred. In addition, the deduction for interest on US$100,000 of home equity debt is suspended for 2018 through 2025. The interest paid on home equity debt used to buy, build or substantially improve your main or second home is deductible. The home equity debt must be secured by the home that is being purchased, built or substantially improved. In addition, your mortgage and home equity debt balances are added together when considering the new US$750,000 limitation.

State taxes, which may be imposed to the extent you reside in or have income arising in a U.S. state, are generally deductible for U.S. income tax purposes, while provincial income taxes are not deductible in Canada. However, under the 2017 U.S. tax changes, the deductions that may be claimed for state and local taxes is capped at US$10,000 in aggregate (not indexed for inflation). This aggregate limitation includes state and local incomes taxes (or sales tax in lieu of income tax) and property taxes. The $10,000 limitation applies for 2018 through 2025. A deduction for foreign property taxes (e.g., Canadian property taxes) is no longer available for 2018 through 2025.

The treatment of certain other deductions has also changed. Before 2018, you could deduct certain expenses if their total exceeded 2% of your adjusted gross income. These expenses were called

> Keep records of expenses deductible on your U.S. return.

"miscellaneous itemized deductions" and included tax preparation fees, investment fees, employment-related expenses, safe deposit boxes fees, and others. All miscellaneous itemized deductions are suspended—meaning that these amounts will not be deductible—for 2018 through 2025.

Some other "itemized deductions" are still allowed. Before 2018, the sum of these itemized deductions were reduced by 3% of the amount by which your adjusted gross income exceeded a threshold amount (also referred to as the "Pease" limitation). This Pease limitation has been suspended until 2026. Therefore, the total amount of allowable itemized deductions should not be reduced for 2018 through 2025.

U.S. citizens can claim a qualified business income (QBI) deduction on their U.S. tax return, as of 2018. The deduction is up to 20% of your net QBI from a U.S. trade or business. QBI can include U.S. business income from partnerships, sole proprietorships, certain estates or trusts, and qualified REIT dividends. QBI can also include rental income from U.S. real estate in certain circumstances.

18.3.2 Deductions available in Canada but not in the U.S.

As we saw in 7.2.3, interest paid may be deducted for Canadian tax purposes where the funds were borrowed for the purpose of earning income from investments. The amount of interest expense that can be deducted is generally not limited by investment income.

For U.S. tax purposes, your investment interest expense deduction is limited to your investment income. You cannot write off interest expense against other income such as employment or business income. This principle extends, under a separate set of complex rules, beyond interest expenses to all deductions relating to "passive" activities, including limited partnerships and most rental losses. Amounts not allowed as deductions in one year can be carried forward and may be deducted in future years.

Other expenses and deductions that are permitted for Canadian purposes, such as RRSP contributions, one-half of the stock option benefit (see 10.4.2) and the lifetime capital gains exemption (see 6.4), are not allowed on your U.S. return.

18.3.3 Retirement and profit-sharing plans

RRSPs, TFSAs, RESPs, RPPs, RDSPs and DPSPs (see Chapters 3 and 4) can cause problems for U.S. citizens because they are not given any special status in the U.S. Internal Revenue Code.

Be aware of differences between Canadian and U.S. rules governing retirement income.

Employer contributions to a registered pension plan or a deferred profit-sharing plan are exempt from immediate Canadian tax (see 10.1.1). As we saw in 3.5.1, you are taxed on the funds only when you receive them (usually on retirement).

For U.S. tax purposes, there is no such exemption. The amount contributed by your employer is treated as an employment benefit and is taxed once the contributions have vested (that is, you are entitled to them even if you leave your employment). Furthermore, these amounts are explicitly excluded from the definition of "foreign earned income" under U.S. tax law, so you cannot make use of the foreign earned income exclusion (see 18.2.1). You may have to pay U.S. tax on these contributions, depending on the circumstances and the amount of your unused foreign tax credit carryover. When you later withdraw the funds, they should not be taxable in the U.S.

Your own contributions to an RRSP or RPP, which are deductible on your Canadian return, are not deductible for U.S. tax purposes unless the treaty specifically allows a deduction.

Defer U.S. taxation of income accruing in your RRSP and other Canadian retirement plans.

Income accruing in your RRSP, RRIF and other Canadian retirement plans (see Chapter 3) would normally be taxable in the U.S. As noted in 18.2.3, the Canada-U.S. tax treaty allows you to elect each year to defer the taxation of the accruing income until you actually receive the funds from the plan. This allows you to report the income in the same year for Canadian and U.S. purposes.

Previously, the election to defer income from an RRSP/RRIF was made on Form 8891. In 2014, the Internal Revenue Service announced that Form 8891 was no longer required as part of the income tax return and that the election to defer income from an RRSP/RRIF would be automatic.

Income earned in your TFSA and RESP is taxable in the U.S. because these plans have no special status in the U.S. Internal Revenue Code or the Canada-U.S. tax treaty. These plans are likely to be considered foreign trusts for U.S. purposes, which require additional annual reporting of contributions, distributions and earnings (see 18.7.4). U.S. citizens should consider the onerous filing requirements before deciding to invest in these plans. If you have existing plans with only modest amounts invested, you may want to consider collapsing the plans to avoid the additional annual filing requirements. The IRS has advised that the Form 3520 and 3520-A filing requirements may not apply to RESPs owned by U.S. citizens.

However, this IRS guidance does not exempt U.S. citizens with TFSAs from the additional filing requirements.

If you contribute to a regular IRA (U.S. Individual Retirement Account), your contributions are not deductible for Canadian tax purposes. Income accruing in an IRA is not taxed by Canada. When you withdraw funds from an IRA, Canada generally taxes the same amount that you would have had to include in your income under U.S. laws if you were a resident of the U.S. at the time of withdrawal. While you may be able to transfer lump sum payments received from an IRA into an RRSP free of Canadian tax, the amount transferred would be subject to U.S. tax. Foreign tax credits may alleviate double taxation.

Contributions to a U.S. deferred income plan by a U.S. employer may be taxable in Canada as an employment benefit or "retirement compensation arrangement" (see 10.5.4).

The Canada-U.S. tax treaty now allows deductions in one country for certain contributions to pension plans in the other country. These rules generally apply to cross-border commuters, employees on temporary assignment and U.S. citizens in Canada.

Employees temporarily transferred from Canada to the U.S. (for no more than 60 months in the 120 preceding months) can continue to contribute to their Canadian qualified plan and claim a deduction on their U.S. tax return, provided they were resident in Canada and participating in the Canadian plan before they began performing services in the U.S. Similar rules apply for U.S. residents who are temporarily transferred to Canada.

Cross-border commuters can contribute to a qualified plan in the country where they work and claim a deduction in the country where they are resident. U.S. citizens resident in Canada who work in Canada and contribute to a Canadian qualified plan can claim a deduction on their U.S. tax returns.

The use of non-qualified deferred compensation plans in the U.S. is discouraged by the related tax implications. Deferred compensation arises when an individual is entitled to receive an amount in a year that is not paid until a later year. These rules affect certain deferred stock unit plans, bonuses and other deferred compensation; stock option and stock appreciation rights plans that are not issued at a discount are exempt.

> Be aware of non-qualified deferred compensation plans.

Under these rules, only deferred compensation plans that meet specific distribution criteria allow recognition of income to be deferred for U.S. tax purposes. Additionally, the employee/director may need to make an election before the year in which the services are being performed if there is any employee discretion in the timing of the payments. If the plan does not meet the distribution requirements, the "deferred" compensation is fully taxable and a 20% U.S. penalty tax and interest charges apply.

If the amount is subject to substantial risk of forfeiture, it should not be included in current income for U.S. tax purposes until this substantial risk of forfeiture no longer exists (usually on the vesting date).

U.S. citizens with Canadian employers should tread with extra care in this area as their employers may not be designing their deferred compensation plans with the U.S. tax rules in mind.

18.3.4 Dividends

As we saw in 7.1.2, Canada taxes dividends from Canadian corporations using the "gross-up and credit" system, which results in less tax being levied than on other kinds of income. For U.S. purposes, most dividends are taxed at a lower rate (up to a maximum of 20% in 2020 plus, potentially, the 3.8% net investment income tax (see 18.1.1)). The actual amount that you receive, rather than the grossed-up amount, is included in income for U.S. purposes.

Capital dividends received from Canadian corporations are not taxable in Canada (see 7.1.4) but they are taxable for U.S. tax purposes.

18.3.5 Canadian corporations earning active or passive income

Owning an interest in a Canadian corporation that earns passive income can result in an unexpected U.S. tax liability. Under U.S. law, if you invest in a non-U.S. corporation that earns a substantial part of its income from investments (a "Passive Foreign Investment Company") and then sell the stock or receive an "excess" distribution, there may be a theoretical deferral of U.S. tax (which would have applied if you had earned the investment income directly). In such a case, an interest charge on this "deferred tax" may be imposed under U.S. tax law.

Watch out for ownership of Canadian corporations and funds earning passive income.

There is no minimum U.S. ownership required in a Canadian corporation to be subject to these rules. Capital gains would be treated as ordinary income for U.S. purposes, resulting in higher U.S. tax. Dividends from Passive Foreign Investment Companies are not eligible for the lower U.S. tax rate.

There are ways to not have the interest charge apply, however. One way is to elect to include your *pro rata* share of the corporation's earnings in your U.S. income on a current basis each year (which may result in a mismatch of income and foreign tax credits for Canadian and U.S. purposes).

Different rules apply if the investment income is earned in a foreign (e.g., Canadian) corporation of which more than 50% of the votes or value is owned by "U.S. shareholders" (a "Controlled Foreign Corporation" or "CFC"). Prior to 2018, to be considered a "U.S. shareholder" of a foreign corporation, you had to hold 10% or more of the votes of the corporation. However, the 2017 U.S. tax changes expanded the definition of a "U.S. shareholder" to include U.S. persons (e.g., U.S. citizens) who own 10% or more of the votes *or value* of a foreign corporation. In these cases, the Controlled Foreign Corporation rules require an annual income inclusion by the U.S. shareholders if the corporation earns passive income.

The 2017 U.S. tax changes imposed a one-time mandatory tax on all post-1986 accumulated foreign earnings of a Controlled Foreign Corporation (and certain other corporations). This is often referred to as the "mandatory repatriation tax". The accumulated earnings were required to be included in the income of an individual for the last taxable year of the corporation beginning before January 1, 2018. For most individuals, this meant the income was includible and the tax due with their 2017 tax U.S. tax returns (including extensions). Individuals had the option to elect to pay the tax in eight annual instalments. This election must have been made by the due date of the U.S. tax return for the year that the mandatory tax applied (including extensions); filing a late election is not permitted. Where an election is made to pay the tax in eight annual instalments, each annual instalment is generally due on April 15 for U.S. residents and on June 15 for U.S. citizens residing outside the U.S.

The 2017 U.S. tax changes also introduced a tax on "Global Intangible Low-Taxed Income" (GILTI), which may impact U.S. citizen shareholders of Controlled Foreign Corporations (e.g., controlled Canadian corporations). The GILTI applies for 2018 and later years. Generally, the GILTI brings into a U.S. citizen shareholder's income amounts earned by the corporation above a certain threshold. GILTI applies to nearly all types of income including active business income, thereby negating many of the benefits of using a corporation for tax deferral purposes. U.S. citizen shareholders of Controlled Foreign Corporations are required to include GILTI on their U.S. tax returns and are subject to U.S. tax on that income even if no amounts are distributed by the corporation to the individual.

However, U.S. citizen shareholders of a Controlled Foreign Corporation can make an election that may substantially reduce or eliminate the U.S. tax on GILTI (the "Section 962 Election"). If you are considering making this election, which is filed annually with an individual's U.S. tax return, you should first obtain professional tax advice.

> Consider making a Section 962 election to mitigate or eliminate the U.S. tax impact of the Global Intangible Low-Taxed Income regime.

The Passive Foreign Investment Company and the Controlled Foreign Corporation rules both impose onerous filing requirements on U.S. shareholders, and significant penalties may apply if you fail to file the forms on time. Annual planning is needed to avoid double taxation.

18.3.6 U.S. taxation of Canadian income fund investments

Most Canadian fund investments should be considered foreign corporations for U.S. purposes. The earnings distributed (including capital gains distributions) would be taxable as ordinary income for U.S. purposes. Capital distributions (i.e., return of capital) should not be taxable for U.S. purposes, provided all of the earnings have been distributed.

If you invest in Canadian funds, including mutual funds, unit trusts and exchange traded funds, consider the impact of the passive foreign investment company rules on your tax liability and filing requirements in the U.S., including annual reporting requirements for investments in foreign corporations.

18.3.7 Charitable donations

As discussed in 8.1, charitable donations of up to 75% of your net income entitle you to a credit for Canadian federal tax purposes (see 17.7.1 if you live in Quebec).

For Canadian tax purposes, charitable donations must normally be made to a Canadian charity to qualify (subject to certain specific exceptions). The Canada-U.S. tax treaty, however, provides that donations to U.S. charities will qualify, up to a limit of 75% of your U.S.-source net income. Note that, in order to claim donations made to U.S. charities, you must have U.S.-source net income. If you do not have any or enough U.S.-source net income, the donations may be carried forward for up to five years. You need to obtain receipts from the U.S. charities to support your claim.

Similarly, charitable donations are normally deductible in the U.S., subject to a limit of 60% of income for donations to public charities or 30% of income for donations to private foundations. However, donations to Canadian charities may only be deducted for U.S. tax purposes to the extent of 60% or 30% of your *Canadian-source* "adjusted gross income". For the 2020 tax year only, the 60% limitation has been increased to 100% for donations to public charities, but the 30% limitation for private foundations is unchanged.

As discussed in 18.6.1, U.S. citizens can either claim itemized deductions (which include donations) or a standard deduction (which doesn t include donations). After the standard deduction increase in 2018, most U.S. citizens now claim the standard deduction and very few claim itemized deductions and do not deduct donations on their U.S. tax returns. For the 2020 tax year only, U.S. citizens can deduct up to US$300 (US$600 if married filing jointly) of donations even if they claim the standard deduction.

18.3.8 Moving expenses

Moving expenses paid by your employer are not taxable benefits for Canadian purposes (see 13.1.3) and you can deduct certain work-related moving expenses (see 13.1.1).

For U.S. purposes, if your employer pays for the cost of moving your household goods and for transporting you and your family, the amounts may no longer be excluded from income and are considered a taxable benefit. In addition, a deduction for moving expenses is no longer permitted for U.S. purposes. These rules apply until 2026.

18.3.9 Child Tax Credit

The U.S. increased the income limit for the U.S. child tax credit as of 2018. The credit begins to phase out at US$400,000 of adjusted gross income for spouses filing jointly (US$200,000 for all others). The maximum amount of the credit is US$2,000 per qualifying child, of which US$1,400 is potentially refundable, even if no U.S. tax is owing. In order to claim the credit, the child must meet several requirements. Specifically, the child must be a U.S. citizen, national or resident, and have a Social Security Number.

If you cannot claim the child tax credit, you may be able to claim the credit for other dependants. This new credit applies for 2018 and beyond and may be claimed for dependant children who are age 17 or older, or for other dependant relatives that you support. The credit is limited to US$500 for each eligible dependant, is non-refundable, and is subject to a phase-out based on income earned.

18.4 Differences in taxation of capital gains

18.4.1 Basic calculation

The field of capital gains is where you find the most glaring differences between the Canadian and U.S. tax systems. Not only are many details different, but the basic scheme of taxation of capital gains is itself fundamentally different, which creates problems for U.S. citizens resident in Canada.

For Canadian tax purposes, only one-half of capital gains are taxed (see 6.2.1).

For U.S. tax purposes, short-term capital gains from property held for 12 months or less are normally taxed like other income, at your marginal rate (see table in 18.1). However, the rate for long-term capital gains (generally from property held more than 12 months) is limited to 20%, 15%, or even 0%, depending on your tax bracket. Certain gains and depreciation recapture are subject to a maximum rate of 25%. Keep in mind that the foreign exchange rate can significantly affect your total tax liability.

> **Example**
>
> Jeff purchases 100 shares of XYZ Corporation on the Toronto Stock Exchange when the Canadian dollar is at US70¢. He pays $20 per share including commission, or Cdn$2,000 (US$1,400). He sells the shares several years later, when the Canadian and U.S. dollars are at par, for $19 each (after commission), or Cdn$1,900 (US$1,900).
>
> For Canadian tax purposes, Jeff has a $100 capital loss, one-half of which can be deducted against taxable capital gains. For U.S. tax purposes, however, Jeff has a $500 capital gain, which is taxed. Since he does not pay any Canadian tax on the gain, no foreign tax credit is available to offset his U.S. tax (maximum 20%) on US$500.

18.4.2 Use of capital losses

For Canadian purposes, allowable capital losses (one-half of your capital losses) can only be used to offset taxable capital gains, though they can be carried back three years and forward indefinitely against such gains (see 6.2.2). An exception exists for allowable business investment losses (on shares or debt of small business corporations), which can be used against any income (see 6.2.3).

For U.S. purposes, capital losses can only be used against capital gains. In addition, single or married persons filing jointly can write off US$3,000 of capital losses against other income (US$1,500 for a married person filing separately). Unused capital losses can be carried forward (but not back) to be applied against capital gains or against US$3,000 (or US$1,500) per year of other income in any future year. Keep in mind that carrying back capital losses in Canada reduces the Canadian tax that is available as a foreign tax credit on the U.S. return for the carryback year.

18.4.3 The Canadian capital gains exemption

A lifetime capital gains exemption is available in Canada for certain small business shares, and farm and fishing property (see 6.4.1 and 6.4.2). No such exemption exists for U.S. tax purposes.

Be cautious of using the Canadian lifetime capital gains exemption.
If you sell small business corporation shares, farm or fishing property, the Canadian lifetime capital gains exemption won't protect you from U.S. tax on the gain, even if you are not subject to Canadian tax. Generally, you should steer clear of the options discussed in 14.1 to "crystallize" your gains and use up your exemption.

18.4.4 Foreign exchange gains or losses

When you sell Canadian property, you must calculate your gain for U.S. tax purposes using the U.S. dollar equivalent of your cost, as of the date you purchased the property. The proceeds are converted at the exchange rate in effect at the date of sale. This treatment can lead to a foreign exchange gain or loss that is independent of your (Canadian-dollar) gain or loss on the property.

Similarly, when you sell U.S. property, your gain for Canadian purposes must be calculated in Canadian dollars.

18.4.5 Pre-1972 holdings

As noted in 6.5.4, Canada taxes only capital gains accrued since 1972. The U.S. does not have any such rule. If you are a U.S. citizen and have owned property since before 1972, your gain for U.S. tax purposes could be substantially higher than your gain for Canadian tax purposes.

18.4.6 Principal residence

As we saw in 6.5.2, a gain on a "principal residence" is normally completely exempt from tax in Canada. The U.S. rules related to sales of a principal residence are very different from the Canadian rules and are more restrictive.

Under the U.S. rules, you may claim an exclusion of up to US$250,000 of gain on a principal residence. The exclusion is increased up to US$500,000 for spouses filing jointly.

Certain requirements must be met to claim the exclusion; for example, you and your spouse must have actually occupied the home for at least two of the past five years, and neither you nor your spouse must have claimed this exclusion in the past two years. Exceptions from the holding period requirement may apply in the event of a relocation for employment, health problems or unforeseen circumstances.

If you and your spouse file jointly but do not share a principal residence, the US$250,000 exclusion is available on the sale of one of the principal residences. Similarly, you can claim the US$250,000 exclusion if you marry someone who has used the exclusion in the past two years.

Be careful if you and your spouse sell more than one home during the two-year period. You would have to pay tax on the entire gain arising on one of the homes.

A further difference between Canadian and U.S. exemptions for a principal residence lies in the definition of the term. As we saw in 6.5.2, a vacation property such as a cottage generally qualifies for Canadian tax purposes, although you can only designate one principal residence for each year. For U.S. purposes, a home only qualifies if it is the place where you "regularly reside".

The U.S. rules provide that the gain will not be excluded if you put the property to a non-qualified use (e.g., you did not use it as a principal residence) after December 31, 2008, with certain exceptions for temporary absences.

18.4.7 Other capital gains differences

Canada and the U.S. have very different rules with respect to the transfer of capital property to corporations or partnerships, corporate reorganizations, estate freezes, mergers, windups, recapitalizations, debt forgiveness, and other matters. A transaction that is tax-deferred in Canada may not be tax-deferred in the United States, and vice versa. Investments in U.S. limited liability companies and "S corporations" also result in a mismatching of income recognition between Canada and the U.S., and higher effective tax rates. If you are involved in such transactions, professional advice is essential, especially since both systems continuously change.

18.5 Minimum tax

Canada's minimum tax was discussed in 7.6. The U.S. alternative minimum tax (AMT) has the same general structure, but there are some important differences.

First, the U.S. AMT exemption for 2020 is US$113,400 for married taxpayers filing jointly (or a surviving spouse) and US$72,900 for a single taxpayer. The U.S. exemption is phased out for those with adjusted minimum taxable income over US$1,036,800 if married filing jointly (US$518,400 if filing as a single taxpayer and married taxpayers filing separately). The exemption amounts and phase-out threshold are scheduled to expire after 2025, when they will revert to pre-2018 amounts.

Second, the U.S. AMT rate is calculated under a two-tier graduated rate schedule. A 26% rate applies to the first US$197,900 of alternative minimum taxable income over the AMT exemption amount, and a 28% rate applies to alternative minimum taxable income over US$197,900. The 28% rate comes into effect for alternative minimum taxable income over US$98,950 for married individuals filing separate returns. For long-term capital gains, the AMT rate is reduced to a maximum of 20%.

Third, the list of "AMT adjustments"—items added back to income for AMT purposes—is, of course, different between the two countries. For U.S. tax purposes, the list includes the standard deduction, itemized property and state taxes paid, oil and gas drilling costs, mining exploration and development costs, a portion of accelerated depreciation, certain stock option benefits and various other specific deductions.

Married U.S. citizens who file separately and have significant itemized deductions often owe AMT on their U.S. tax returns because the AMT calculation for married couples filing separately requires a "phantom" addition to AMT income if AMT income exceeds certain thresholds.

18.6 Income earned by children

18.6.1 Effects on dependant deduction

Before 2018, you could claim a deduction for a dependent child on your U.S. return. That child was then not able to claim the regular personal exemption on his or her own tax return. The effect was that any income the child earned was taxed.

The 2017 U.S. tax changes suspend personal exemptions until 2026, including the ability to claim one for your child. To account for this elimination, the standard deduction was increased beginning in 2018. This change applies for 2018 through 2025. For 2020, the standard deduction is US$24,800 for married couples filing jointly, US$18,650 for unmarried individuals with at least one qualifying child, and US$12,400 for unmarried individuals.

The increase in the standard deduction and the restrictions to itemized deductions (see 18.3.1) may result in more U.S. citizens claiming the standard deduction beginning in 2018.

18.6.2 Attribution rules

We discussed the Canadian attribution rules for minor children in 5.2.3. The basic rule is that if you give or lend funds to your child, the income from those funds (but not the capital gains) are taxed in your hands, rather than the child's, until the year your child turns 18.

Review income splitting arrangements to prevent double taxation.

The U.S. tax system accomplishes the same general anti-income-splitting objective in a very different way. Recent changes allow taxpayers to elect to tax the unearned income of a child at the parent's marginal tax rate or using the ordinary rates and capital gains rates applicable to trusts and estates. The top rate of 37% for trusts and estates (for 2020) applies at US$12,951 of taxable income and above. The option to elect is only available retroactively for the 2018 and 2019 tax years. For the 2020 tax year and beyond, the unearned income of a child will be taxed at the parent's marginal tax rate. This U.S. "income splitting tax" also applies to children aged 18 to 23 who are full-time students and whose earned income is less than half of their annual support.

Income splitting arrangements that are set up for Canadian income tax purposes can result in double taxation if you are not careful. For example, suppose you and your 13-year-old son are both U.S. citizens, your son has no income, and you lend funds to him with the intention of building up "secondary" income over time that will not be attributed back to you (see 5.3.5). The income on the funds you have lent would be taxed in your hands under Canadian law but in your son's hands under U.S. law. Because different taxpayers are paying the tax, no foreign tax credit would be available and you may end up being taxed twice on the same income.

Bear in mind that attribution problems may arise in certain cases if you and your spouse do not file a joint U.S. return (see 18.7.1). For example, if you give your spouse Cdn$100,000 to invest and the investment earns Cdn$5,000 in Canadian-source dividend income, you would pay Canadian tax on the income and your spouse will pay the U.S. tax. If you and your spouse file a joint U.S. return, all Canadian taxes would be combined for foreign tax credit purposes. But if you and your spouse do not file jointly, no foreign tax credit would be available because different taxpayers are taxable on the income.

In addition, if the income earned by your spouse is U.S.-source income, your spouse would be taxable on the income for U.S. purposes and you would be taxable on the income for Canadian purposes. Canada would not provide you with a foreign tax credit for U.S. tax paid by your spouse, resulting in double tax.

18.7 U.S. filing requirements

18.7.1 Joint return or not?

For Canadian federal tax purposes, every taxpayer is distinct and must file separately. Combining the income of two spouses is only considered for certain specific purposes, such as eligibility for the GST/HST credit (see 2.9.3).

For U.S. tax purposes, you have the option of filing a joint return with your spouse. If one spouse has little or no income, this usually results in less tax than if you file as "married filing separately".

For U.S. purposes, a joint return is mandatory (if you are married) if you wish to claim certain deductions and credits. The child and dependant care credit is one example. Another is the US$25,000 loss allowance for an owner who actively participates in rental real estate.

If you do not have a spouse, your filing status is "single", "head of household" or "surviving spouse", all of which have different implications for your U.S. tax return.

If you're married, file a joint U.S. return where appropriate.

If your spouse is a U.S. citizen, the decision as to whether to file jointly can be made annually. If your spouse is not a U.S. citizen, the decision to file jointly can only be made once.

If your spouse is not a U.S. citizen, has no U.S.-source income and thus is not subject to U.S. tax, consider filing a "married filing separate" return. As a "non-resident alien", your spouse's Canadian income is not relevant for U.S. tax purposes. By contrast, if your spouse has little income from any source but you are paying tax to the U.S., you may elect to include the spouse's income on your joint return. In this case, filing a joint return can be beneficial, as it gives you larger exclusions and wider tax brackets at the lower rates.

If you elect to file jointly with a non-resident alien spouse, you must always file jointly unless the election is revoked; however, once revoked, the decision can never be made again (unless you have a new spouse).

You should also keep in mind that the Canadian election to split pension income (see 20.3.6) is not relevant for U.S. tax purposes. The individual who earns the pension is required to report it for U.S. tax purposes.

18.7.2 Time requirements for filing

The requirements for filing Canadian tax returns are discussed in 9.1.

U.S. tax returns must normally be postmarked by April 15 each year.

If you are a U.S. citizen whose "tax home" (place of employment) and "abode" (place of residence) are *both* outside the U.S., your filing deadline is automatically extended to June 15 each year. You must attach a statement to your return identifying that you are eligible for this extension.

If you are unable to meet your U.S. filing deadline, you may file for an extension of the deadline to October 15. The extension will be granted automatically. U.S. citizens residing outside of the United States can request an additional two-month extension to December 15. This extension is not automatic, but is at the discretion of the IRS.

Even though you are permitted to file your return in June or October, you must pay your balance owing by April 15. Interest on any balance of taxes owing will accrue from April 15.

18.7.3 Estimated taxes

We discussed the Canadian tax instalment requirements in 9.2.2. The U.S. has parallel requirements, which are called payments of "estimated taxes".

Estimated tax payments are due quarterly, on April 15, June 15, September 15 and the following January 15. As with the Canadian system, you can generally choose either last year's tax or this year's tax as the basis for your quarterly estimated tax payments.

If you base your payments on the current year's tax, you need only pay 90% of the year's tax liability (regular tax or AMT) in estimated tax payments—22.5% each quarter. If you use last year's tax, you must normally pay 25% of that amount each quarter (or 27.5% each quarter if your prior-year adjusted gross income exceeded US$150,000). In order to use last year's tax, you must have filed a return in the previous year and the year must have been a 12-month period.

In either case, any balance still owing is due with your tax return or extension. No estimated tax payments are required if your total tax for the year is less than US$1,000.

If you do not make your estimated tax payments on time, non-deductible late payment penalties and interest will apply.

18.7.4 Disclosure requirements

As well as filing a tax return, you must disclose a substantial amount of financial information under U.S. law.

First, you must disclose holdings in any non-U.S. corporations that you and certain family members control directly or indirectly, or in which you have increased or decreased your interest. You must provide this information for each foreign corporation by filing a separate Form 5471, "Information Return of U.S. Persons with Respect to Certain Foreign Corporations". The IRS uses this information, among other things, to help determine your liability for tax on any undistributed income of closely held non-U.S. corporations that earn active or passive income.

Similar reporting rules apply to investments in foreign partnerships and foreign disregarded entities. This information is disclosed by filing Form 8865, "Return of U.S. Persons with Respect to Certain Foreign Partnerships", and Form 8858, "Information Return of U.S. Persons with Respect to Foreign Disregarded Entities". Form 8858 may be required if you own a rental property outside the United States or are self-employed outside of the United States.

In some cases, a Canadian corporation's reporting year must be the calendar year for U.S. reporting purposes.

Second, you are required to file a "Report of Foreign Bank and Financial Accounts" form annually with the U.S. Department of the Treasury if the total value of your foreign (non-U.S.) bank accounts, brokerage accounts, RRSPs, etc. exceeds US$10,000 at any time in the year. You must report:

- accounts where you have signing authority but no financial interests
- accounts of any entity in which you own, directly or indirectly, more than 50% of the voting power, equity, assets or profits
- accounts of trusts in which you have a greater than 50% beneficial interest in assets or income.

For tax years beginning on or after January 1, 2016, the due date for this form is automatically extended to October 15. This form must be filed electronically. A penalty of up to US$10,000 applies for non-willful violations of the disclosure rules. For willful violations, the penalty can be as high as US$100,000.

Third, if you hold foreign financial assets that exceed a specific dollar threshold, you are required to report certain information about these assets on Form 8938, "Statement of Foreign Financial Assets". The dollar threshold, which depends on your filing status and where you live, can be as low as US$50,000 of foreign financial assets. A higher threshold applies for taxpayers living outside the U.S.—US$200,000 for unmarried or married filing separately and US$400,000 for married filing jointly.

Specified foreign financial assets include bank accounts, investment accounts, RRSPs, RRIFs, registered pensions, equity compensation plans (for example, stock options), shares of private corporations, interests in partnerships, and certain non-U.S. life insurance policies.

If you meet the filing requirements for the "Statement of Foreign Financial Assets" and "Report of Foreign Bank and Financial Accounts", you have to file both even though some of the information may be the same.

Fourth, if you have interests in certain Canadian corporations that earn investment income and certain types of funds, you are required to file Form 8621, "Information Return by a Shareholder of a Passive Foreign Investment Company or Qualified Electing Fund" for each passive foreign investment company in which you have an interest. Canadian corporations that earn investment income and are not controlled by U.S. persons, as well as most Canadian mutual funds and exchange traded funds, are considered passive foreign investment companies.

Finally, as discussed in 18.8.4, reporting rules also apply for certain gifts and bequests over US$100,000 received in one year. Any transfers to and from foreign trusts (including loans) must also be reported by filing Form 3520, "Annual Return to Report Transactions with Foreign Trusts and Receipt of Certain Foreign Gifts". For U.S. citizens outside the U.S., Form 3520 is due on June 15.

If you are treated as the owner of a foreign grantor trust (such as an alter ego or joint partner trust), you must report annually on Form 3520-A, "Annual Information Return of Foreign Trust with a U.S. Owner". Form 3520-A is due on March 15 (i.e., before your U.S. personal tax return). An extension of the filing date for Form 3520-A is available, but you must file your application for the extension by March 15.

Canadian TFSAs and RESPs are generally considered foreign trusts for U.S. tax purposes. If you have a TFSA or have contributed to an RESP, you should file Form 3520 and Form 3520-A each year. As previously noted, the IRS has advised that the Form 3520 and 3520-A filing requirements may not apply to RESPs owned by U.S. citizens. However, this IRS guidance does not appear to exclude the Form 3520 and 3520-A filing requirement for TFSAs owned by U.S. citizens. In addition to the U.S. reporting requirements for foreign trusts, the income in your TFSA and RESP is taxable on your U.S. tax return each year (see 18.3.3).

Severe penalties apply under U.S. law for not complying with these reporting requirements.

18.8 U.S. gift and estate taxes

U.S. gift and estate taxes are part of a complex tax system for property transfers that has no equivalent in Canada. The transfer tax applies to transfers made during your lifetime (gift tax) and at death (estate tax).

In 2020, estate taxes are levied on a graduated scale based on the cumulative value of all gifts made during your lifetime and at death, ranging from 18% to 40%. The 40% rate applies to cumulative transfers over US$1 million.

In this section, we discuss how the gift and estate tax rules apply to U.S. citizens residing in Canada. If you are a non-U.S. citizen who owns U.S. property, see 19.4.

18.8.1 Lifetime gift and estate tax credit

U.S. citizens are permitted a lifetime estate tax exclusion to offset the transfer tax on US$11.58 million for 2020. This amount is indexed for inflation and is set to expire after 2025. At that time, the exclusion should revert to US$5.6 million (indexed for inflation), which was the amount available prior to the 2017 U.S. tax changes.

U.S. citizens are also permitted a lifetime gift tax exclusion, which is set at US$11.58 million for 2020. Similar to the lifetime estate tax exclusion, this amount is indexed for inflation and is set to expire after 2025. At that time, the exclusion should revert to US$5.6 million (indexed for inflation). Any exclusion amount used for gifts reduces the amount available on death.

18.8.2 Gift tax

Canada does not have a gift tax, although the giver of a gift (except to a spouse) is deemed to have sold the property at its current fair market value, possibly leading to income tax on a resulting taxable capital gain (see 6.5.4).

The U.S. does have a gift tax, which applies only to those who make very substantial gifts. The *giver* is liable for the tax. Where the giver and recipient are spouses who are both U.S. citizens, no gift tax applies at all. Otherwise, if only the giver is a U.S. citizen, gift tax may apply.

The gift tax generally does not apply to gifts to charities, U.S. political parties, and amounts given directly to institutions to pay for another person's tuition or medical expenses.

Up to US$15,000 may be given tax-free each year to any number of donees and up to US$157,000 to a spouse who is not a U.S. citizen.

A common estate planning strategy is to use the US$15,000 annual gift tax exclusion to transfer wealth to children and grandchildren. For the gift to be eligible for the exclusion, the recipient must have the right to use the gift without restriction. In these cases, steps should be taken to ensure that an adult retains control over the assets while the child remains a minor, such as opening a *Uniform Gift to Minors Act* account in the U.S. or establishing a formal trust (with certain powers for the child to ensure that the exclusion will apply).

> Consider using the annual US$15,000 U.S. gift tax exclusion to transfer wealth to children and grandchildren.

As previously noted, the lifetime gift tax exclusion is US$11.58 million for 2020 through 2025 (indexed for inflation). The exclusion is set to revert to US$5.6 million in 2026. As such, you may want to consider making taxable gifts during the years in which the higher gift tax exclusion is available. Using the increased lifetime gift tax exclusion available from 2020 through 2025 will not be retroactively eliminated if the giver using the increase survives beyond 2025, according to U.S. regulations. In other words, there will be no claw back of using the increased exclusion since it will revert to US$5.6 million in 2026.

Consider using the increased U.S. lifetime gift tax exclusion available from 2020 through 2025.

The Canadian tax (if any) that applies on a gift is an income tax, while the U.S. tax is not. As a result, no foreign tax credit applies in either system for taxes of the other system. Caution must therefore be exercised if you are making large gifts. A further problem with gifts is that, for U.S. purposes, your cost base of property (plus a portion of the gift tax paid) carries through to the recipient of a gift, whereas on death, any property left to your beneficiaries is treated as acquired by them at its fair market value. In Canada, the cost base to the recipient is increased to fair market value at the time of the gift or death (except for transfers to spouses).

You must also watch out for the Canadian attribution rules and the tax on split income, as outlined in Chapter 5.

The Canada-U.S. tax treaty does not provide any relief for U.S. gift tax, although you can elect to have a deemed disposition for U.S. purposes in order to match income recognition in the U.S. and Canada. Making this election would allow you to increase the property's cost base to its fair market value at the time the gift is made. However, making the election does not reduce any gift tax payable or allow you to claim foreign tax credits for income tax against gift tax or vice versa.

As discussed in 18.8.4, U.S. recipients of gifts from foreign individuals must also report gifts received if they exceed US$100,000 in a calendar year.

18.8.3 Estate tax

The U.S. imposes estate tax on death of U.S. citizens based on the fair market value of the deceased's gross estate, which includes all worldwide assets owned at death, regardless of whether the assets pass outside the will.

If the gross estate exceeds US$11.58 million in 2020, an estate tax return must be filed within nine months after the date of death, even if no estate tax is payable. Under the U.S. rules, the executor of the estate is personally liable for any taxes and penalties owed by the estate until official clearance is granted by the IRS.

The taxable estate is determined by deducting debts of the deceased (including the Canadian tax liability) and funeral and certain other death-related expenses from the value of the estate. The taxable estate is subject to graduated rates that reach 40% estate tax on amounts over US$1 million.

An unlimited marital deduction is provided for any amounts left to your spouse on death, if your spouse is a U.S. citizen. As a result, leaving all of your estate to your U.S. citizen spouse will result in no estate tax applying on your death.

The U.S. rules allow "portability" following the death of a U.S. citizen spouse. Any amount of the US$11.58 million exclusion amount not used by the first spouse to die is available to the surviving spouse. However, you should still consider taking steps so that the increase in value after the death of the first spouse to die is not subject to U.S. estate tax.

To use the portability provisions, a U.S. estate tax return must be filed for the first spouse to die in order to calculate the exemption amount available to the surviving spouse even if the estate value is less than US$11.58 million.

Generally, a marital deduction for a transfer to a U.S. citizen spouse is only permitted for property passing to the spouse outright with no restrictions on its use. But you may intend for the assets to be used by your spouse and pass to your children or others on your spouse's death, even if, for example, your spouse remarries. Such property may be treated as "qualified terminal interest property", which is eligible for the marital deduction if an election is made on the estate tax return and certain other requirements are met.

If you hold property jointly with a non-U.S. citizen spouse or other individual, the value of the property's inclusion in your gross estate would be based on the proportionate initial contribution to purchase the property. As such, it is important to save receipts or other documentation relating to property purchased jointly with others.

Life insurance proceeds are subject to U.S. estate tax if the proceeds are payable to the insured's estate or if the insured had any incidents of ownership, such as a right to change beneficiaries, borrow against the policy or cancel the policy. Certain options are available to minimize the estate tax burden on life insurance proceeds, including the use of life insurance trusts and gifting plans. To use these options, advice from an estate planning professional is essential.

Some items in an individual's estate are subject to both U.S. income and estate taxes. These items include accrued compensation or commissions for personal services received after death, investment income, instalment sales, employment survivor benefits and retirement plans such as IRAs. Planning options may be available to reduce the resulting double taxation. For example, you could gift income-producing assets to individuals or trusts during your lifetime or bequeath specific assets to charities. Professional advice on implementing these options is recommended.

18.8.4 U.S. reporting rules for gifts and foreign trusts

As a U.S. citizen, you must file an annual gift tax return if your gifts to one individual made in the calendar year exceed the annual US$15,000 exclusion (or US$155,000 to a non-U.S. citizen spouse), if you elect to split gifts with your U.S.-citizen spouse, or if any gifts are in trust. The return is due at the same time as your regular U.S. personal income tax return.

Be aware of U.S. gift, bequest and foreign trust reporting rules.

If you are a U.S. citizen and you transfer money or property to a non-U.S. trust or receive a distribution from one, you must report the transfer to the IRS. The penalty for not complying with these reporting rules is 35% of the gross value of the money or property transferred, and additional penalties for continued failure can run up to 100% of the transferred amount.

U.S. citizens must also report each gift or bequest received in a year if the total of all gifts and bequests received from any foreign person or foreign estate in that year is more than US$100,000. Penalties for non-compliance are substantial.

If you are treated as the owner of a foreign grantor trust (e.g., alter ego trust or TFSA), you must file Form 3520-A, "Annual Information Return for Foreign Trust with a U.S. Owner", each year by March 15 of the following year or apply for an extension by that date (see 18.7.4).

18.8.5 Generation-skipping transfer tax

The U.S. imposes a special tax to ensure gifts and bequests made to grandchildren do not skip a level of transfer taxation as a result of bypassing the intermediate generation. The generation-skipping transfer tax adds an additional tax on transfers from grandparents to their grandchildren or great-grandchildren that results in the same net gift that would have resulted had the gift passed from grandparent to parent to grandchild or great-grandchild.

A lifetime exclusion of US$11.58 million is available to offset the generation-skipping tax in 2020. This exclusion is separate from the lifetime exclusion for estate and gift taxes discussed in 18.8.1. Making the election to use this exclusion is extremely complex and should not be done without professional advice. Additionally, transfers to trusts having direct or contingent beneficiaries who are significantly younger than you should be made in consultation with a qualified tax adviser.

18.9 If you expatriate from the U.S.

Consider expatriating from the U.S. to protect your Canadian assets from U.S. tax and to simplify your tax filing and reporting.

If you are a U.S. citizen or green card holder living in Canada, you may wish to expatriate from the U.S. by renouncing your U.S. citizenship or surrendering your green card to protect your Canadian income from U.S. income tax and your Canadian assets from U.S. estate, gift and generation-skipping transfer taxes (see 18.8).

If you are considering expatriating, professional advice is recommended. You may be subject to tax consequences if:

- your average annual U.S. income tax liability exceeded US$168,000 in the five years before expatriation
- your net worth exceeds US$2 million at the time of expatriation, or
- you cannot certify that you have complied with all U.S. federal tax obligations for the five years preceding expatriation.

If you meet one of the above conditions, you are considered a "covered expatriate" and you might be treated as if you had sold all your property for its fair market value on the day before you expatriate and you would owe tax on any capital gain over US$725,000 for 2020. You can defer paying the tax until the property is sold but you will be charged interest on the deferred tax. You will not be able to claim a foreign tax credit to offset any foreign tax that may apply when you sell the property in a future year. Special income recognition rules apply in the year of expatriation to certain assets, including retirement plans (e.g., IRAs, RRSPs), tax-deferred accounts and interests in certain types of trusts. Before expatriating, planning should be undertaken to reduce the exposure to tax to the U.S. citizen at the time of expatriation and to U.S. citizen beneficiaries of estates or gifts.

If you are a covered expatriate, any U.S. citizen or resident (except for your spouse or a charity) who receives a gift or bequest from you at any time in the future may be required to pay tax on the transfer at the highest applicable rate of gift or estate tax (40% for 2020). This tax does not apply if you are subject to U.S. gift tax or estate tax (for example, if the property transferred is U.S. real estate). No credits would be allowed in Canada for gift or estate tax paid by the U.S. recipient.

If you were both a Canadian and U.S. citizen from the time of your birth, you have not resided in the U.S. for more than 10 of the 15 years before expatriation, and you reside in Canada at the time of expatriation, then you only need to meet the third test above (i.e., five years of tax compliance) in order to not be considered a "covered expatriate".

If you expatriated before June 17, 2008, different rules apply.

"Long-term" green card holders who surrender their green cards are subject to the same taxation rules as U.S. citizens. You are considered a long-term green card holder if you have held a green card in eight out of the last 15 years. Part of a year counts as a year for these purposes. For example, if you obtained a green card on December 28, 2012, you must count 2012 as one year and you would be considered a long-term green card holder starting on January 1, 2020.

Even if your green card is no longer valid for immigration purposes, you are considered a green card holder for tax purposes until you officially surrender your green card at a border crossing or U.S. consulate.

You should seek professional advice before renouncing your U.S. citizenship or surrendering your green card. You should also be aware that your green card can be taken from you if you are not residing in the U.S. and the expatriation rules above would apply at that time.

18.10 References

The following publications and more information, including forms and brochures, can be obtained on the CRA's website at *www.canada.ca/en/revenue-agency.html* or by telephone request at 1-800-959-8281 for individual income tax and trust-related enquiries or 1-800-959-5525 for business and self-employed individual enquiries.

Income Tax Folio S5-F1-C1, "Determining an Individual's Residence Status"
Income Tax Folio S5-F2-C1, "Foreign Tax Credit"

The following technical publications may be obtained from any office of the Internal Revenue Service, and are generally available at U.S. embassy and consular offices, or from the IRS's website at *www.irs.gov*.

Publication 17, "Your Federal Income Tax"
Publication 54, "Tax Guide for U.S. Citizens and Resident Aliens Abroad"
Publication 514, "Foreign Tax Credit for Individuals"
Publication 519, "U.S. Tax Guide for Aliens"
Publication 521, "Moving Expenses"
Publication 523, "Selling Your Home"
Publication 972, "Child Tax Credit"

Chapter 19

If you visit, work or own property in the U.S.

- Avoid becoming a U.S. resident while visiting the United States (19.1.1)

- If you own rental real estate in the U.S., elect the net rental income method (19.2.3)

- Beware of high effective tax rates when considering an investment in a U.S. limited liability company (19.2.5)

- Ensure a U.S. tax return is filed for every disposition of U.S. real property (19.3.1)

- Apply for a U.S. "withholding certificate" on the sale of U.S. real estate (19.3.1)

- Be cautious when acquiring shares in U.S. corporations due to potential U.S. estate tax exposure, even if held in your RRSP, alter ego trust or joint partner trust (19.4.1)

- Leave U.S. property to your spouse or a qualified trust (19.4.5)

- Mortgage property (non-recourse) to reduce the value of your U.S. real estate (19.4.5)

- Acquire property jointly with your spouse or another person (19.4.5)

- Split your worldwide assets with your spouse (19.4.5)

- Consider a split interest purchase with your child (19.4.5)

- Hold your U.S. property through a Canadian corporation (19.4.5)

- Hold your U.S. assets through a properly structured trust or a Canadian partnership that elects to be treated as a corporation in the U.S. (19.4.5)

- Sell U.S. property before death (19.4.5)

- Consider taking out life insurance to cover U.S. estate taxes (19.4.5)

- Be aware of drawbacks to gifting U.S. real estate (19.4.6)

In this chapter, we discuss the United States taxes that apply to Canadian residents who are not U.S. citizens and who work in the United States or acquire U.S. investments such as stocks and real estate. (Taxation of U.S. citizens resident in Canada is covered in Chapter 18.) Such investments are taxed in four ways: on the income they generate; on their sale; on gift; and on death of the owner. We also discuss the "snowbird" rules that can make you resident in the U.S. for tax purposes.

The interaction between the U.S. and Canadian tax systems can be highly complex. Cross-border transactions should be undertaken only with qualified professional tax advice.

19.1 U.S. residency rules for Canadians

As a Canadian, you can become resident in the U.S. for tax purposes if you spend a significant amount of time in the U.S. or if you hold a green card.

19.1.1 Snowbirds

If you spend a substantial portion of the year in the U.S., you may become a U.S. resident for tax purposes. If this happens you may be required to file tax returns and additional reporting forms in the U.S., even if you are deemed resident in Canada under the Canada-U.S. tax treaty's "tie-breaker" rules described below. If you become a U.S. resident for tax purposes, the cost of complying with filing requirements can be substantial.

Avoid becoming a U.S. resident while visiting the United States.

If you are physically present in the U.S. for a significant number of days (183 days or more in a three-year period, as calculated below), you may meet the substantial presence test, causing you to be deemed a U.S. resident for tax purposes. For this calculation, you must sum up the total number of days spent in the U.S. in the current year, 1/3 of the days in the preceding year, and 1/6 of the days in the second preceding year. Any part of a day spent in the U.S. counts as a full day unless you are travelling between two points outside the U.S. and you are in the U.S. for less than 24 hours. For example, if you arrive in the U.S. at 11:00 pm, that counts as a day. If you cross the border to go golfing or shopping for the day, that counts as a day. The U.S. immigration rules for counting days are not necessarily the same as the U.S. income tax rules. Also note that special rules for counting days apply for 2020 due to the COVID-19 pandemic. Seek professional advice if you exceeded 182 days in the U.S. in 2020 as a result of COVID-19.

Example

Simone spends the winter each year in Miami and the fall, spring and summer in Montreal. For 2018, 2019 and 2020, she is physically in the U.S. for 150, 90 and 140 days respectively.

For 2020, Simone's "physical presence" calculation is 140 + (1/3 $\times$ 90) + (1/6 $\times$ 150), or 195. Since this figure equals or exceeds 183, she is considered resident in the U.S. for 2020 (subject to the "closer connection" rule described below).

If you are deemed a U.S. resident under the substantial presence test but the number of days you spent in the U.S. in the *current* year is less than 183, you can be treated as a non-resident for U.S. tax purposes if you can establish that you have a "closer connection" to Canada than to the U.S. To make this determination, the IRS looks at factors such as where your family, automobile and personal belongings are located, where your driver's licence was issued, where you are registered to vote, where you derived the majority of your income for the year, and whether you are covered by provincial health insurance in Canada. This information is reported on Form 8840 "Closer Connection Exception Statement for Aliens", which is due by June 15 of the following year.

If your current year's days in the U.S. equal or exceed 183 days, you can gain a measure of protection from the Canada-U.S. tax treaty if you can establish that under the treaty you are resident in Canada and not the U.S. This protection is not as broad as being treated as a non-resident under the "closer connection" rule above.

For this purpose, you need to show that you have a permanent home in Canada and not in the U.S. If you have a permanent home available at all times in both countries, you must then prove that your personal and economic relations are closer to Canada. You have to file information with the IRS within certain time limits to be entitled to this treaty "tie-breaker" protection.

Although you may not be subject to U.S. income tax on your Canadian income, you are still required to follow the regular U.S. reporting rules, including reporting ownership of non-U.S. corporations and partnerships, reporting transfers to and distributions from non-U.S. trusts, and reporting receipts of foreign gifts and bequests. You must also file a Report of Foreign Bank and Financial Accounts (see 18.7.4).

If possible, plan to spend 182 days or fewer in the U.S. each year to minimize your U.S. filing obligations.

19.1.2 Green card holders

If you have a green card (also known as a permanent resident card), you are considered a U.S. resident for U.S. federal income tax purposes, regardless of where you live. You are required to file U.S. income tax returns annually to report your worldwide income, just like a U.S. citizen (see 18.7.1). You must also file the Report of Foreign Bank and Financial Accounts form annually (see 18.7.4).

Even if your green card has expired and is no longer valid for immigration purposes, you are still considered a U.S. resident for income tax purposes. If you have a commuter green card (which, unlike a regular green card, does not require that you live in the U.S.), you also have the status of a U.S. resident for income tax purposes.

As a green card holder, you cannot use the closer connection exception described above in 19.1.1 but it is possible to use the Canada-U.S. tax treaty to be considered resident in Canada for U.S. tax purposes, provided you have more ties to Canada than the U.S. and are a resident of Canada. This "tie-breaking" to Canada results in your worldwide income being taxable only in Canada and only your U.S. source income being taxable in the U.S. However, you are still required to file a U.S. tax return (as a non-resident) and all the U.S. reporting forms that a U.S. resident would otherwise be required to file, with some exceptions.

If you're considering tie-breaking to Canada, keep in mind that doing so could jeopardize your green card status because a green card holder is generally required to reside in the United States.

Green card holders also need to consider U.S. estate tax. Residing in the U.S. with a green card is generally an indication that you are domiciled in the U.S. and thus may be subject to U.S. estate tax on the value of your worldwide assets (see 18.8.3).

If you live in Canada with a green card, you may want to consider surrendering it to minimize your exposure to U.S. tax and U.S. filing requirements. Another reason for surrendering your green card if you live in Canada is that double tax may apply on certain income. This is because some of the benefits for U.S. citizens in the Canada-U.S. tax treaty are not available to green card holders.

To cease being considered a U.S. resident, you need to formally surrender your green card at a U.S. border crossing or U.S. consulate and complete Form I-407, "Abandonment of Lawful Permanent Residence". You may face U.S. tax consequences if you surrender your green card or have it revoked after holding it in eight or more of the preceding 15 years (see 18.9).

Before applying for or surrendering a green card, you should seek advice about your U.S. tax obligations. Careful planning can often help minimize adverse U.S. tax consequences.

19.2 Income from U.S. sources

Certain U.S.-source income is subject to U.S. income tax or U.S. tax withholding or disclosure requirements even if you are not resident in the U.S.

19.2.1 Obtaining a U.S. Individual Taxpayer Identification Number (ITIN)

If you invest in the U.S., you may be asked to provide an Individual Taxpayer Identification Number (ITIN) for tax reporting and withholding purposes. The IRS issues ITINs to individuals who are required to have a U.S. taxpayer identification number but who do not have a U.S. Social Security Number and are not eligible to obtain one.

You can obtain an ITIN by filing Form W-7 "Application for IRS Individual Taxpayer Identification Number". If you plan to invest in the U.S., consider seeking help from a professional tax adviser in navigating the ITIN application process.

Some taxpayers have been required to renew their ITINs, beginning in October 2016. ITINs that have not been used on a U.S. federal tax return at least once in the last three consecutive years may not be used on a tax return unless renewed by the taxpayer. ITINs issued prior to 2013 will expire based on a rolling renewal schedule published by the Internal Revenue Service. Further information on ITIN renewal and expiry is available on the IRS website.

If you have or are applying for a visa that entitles you to work in the U.S., then you should apply for a U.S. Social Security Number using Form SS-5. The quickest way to apply for a U.S. Social Security number is to apply in person at a U.S. Social Security Office in the U.S.

19.2.2 If you work in the U.S.

If you live and have a job in Canada and your employer sends you to work temporarily in the U.S., you will face U.S. federal and state tax and reporting requirements.

Canadians are generally subject to U.S. tax on their income from U.S. sources. Income from employment is considered to come from the location where the services were performed. If you physically work in the U.S., your income from the work is U.S.-source income and subject to U.S. tax under U.S. domestic law.

Your U.S.-source employment income is generally determined by allocating your total salary between your workdays in Canada and the U.S. in the year. Depending on the state you work in, you may also be liable for state income tax on your income earned in that state.

> **Example**
>
> Margot earns $100,000 in 2020 working as an analyst for a Canadian software company. She works a total of 240 days in 2020 and works 60 of these days in the company's U.S. location. The amount of Margot's U.S.-source income subject to U.S. federal tax for 2020 is 25% (60 ÷ 240) of $100,000, or $25,000. Note that the income subject to U.S. federal tax is reported in U.S. dollars.

The Canada-U.S. treaty offers some relief from U.S. tax on U.S.-source income, though this relief usually does not extend to U.S. state income tax (most states do not follow the treaty). As a Canadian resident employee, you are not subject to U.S. tax based on the Canada-U.S. treaty if:

- you earn less than US$10,000 of U.S.-source income in the year, or
- you spend less than 183 days in any 12-month period beginning or ending in the relevant fiscal year (including work and non-work days) in the U.S. *and* you are not paid directly or indirectly by a U.S. resident or "permanent establishment" in the U.S., which generally means a "fixed place of business".

The second exception generally should not apply if the U.S. entity reimburses your Canadian employer for your wages.

Thus, Margot in our example above would possibly not have U.S. federal tax on her U.S.-source income if she only spent 60 days in the U.S. and her Canadian employer paid her salary. However, the corporate tax implications for the Canadian employer should be considered.

If your U.S.-source employment income qualifies for relief from U.S. tax under the treaty, your employer must ask you to complete Form 8233 (and include your ITIN—see 19.2.1), after which your employer must certify it and file it with the IRS. If you do not qualify for the treaty exception, your employer may have to withhold U.S. federal tax from your wages and report the wages and related withholding to the IRS.

If you are self-employed, your U.S.-source income may be exempt from U.S. tax. Under a separate treaty provision, independent contractors are exempt from U.S. tax as long as they do not have a "permanent establishment" in the U.S.

Whether or not you qualify for an exemption under the treaty, you are required to file a U.S. income tax return (Form 1040NR) if you have U.S.-source income. You may also need to file a U.S. state return to report income earned in a state. Canada generally provides a foreign tax credit for any U.S. federal and state tax owing to offset Canadian tax on your U.S.-source income.

If you are a U.S. citizen or green card holder, you are subject to U.S. tax on your worldwide income (see 18.1) and certain treaty exemptions discussed above generally do not apply.

19.2.3 Rent from U.S. real estate

A withholding tax of 30% normally applies to the gross amount of any rent paid to a resident of Canada on real estate located in the United States. Unlike withholding taxes on interest and dividends, this tax is not reduced by the Canada-U.S. tax treaty.

> **Example**
>
> Leanne lives in Canada and owns a condominium in Arizona. She rents out the condominium for the entire year, receiving US$20,000 in rent. Her mortgage interest, maintenance costs, property taxes and depreciation total US$16,000.
>
> Over the year, 30% of the rent paid to Leanne, or US$6,000, should be withheld by her tenant and remitted to the IRS.
>
> At the end of the year, Leanne may elect to file a U.S. tax return and calculate U.S. tax on her net rental income, which would be only US$4,000 rather than US$20,000. She can then receive a refund for the withholding tax, to the extent it exceeds the tax payable on her U.S. return. However, note that state tax (and possibly an amount of city or county tax) may be payable on the rental income.

If you own rental real estate in the U.S., elect the net rental income method.

If you have any expenses related to your U.S. rental property (mortgage interest, maintenance, insurance, property management, property taxes, etc.), you would almost always want to elect the "net rental income" method. The amount subject to tax at your marginal rate would be substantially lower than the amount subject to 30% withholding.

Once you've elected to file on a net basis, the election is permanent and you will be taxed on the net basis in future years. If you make the election, it applies to all of your U.S. rental real estate. Make sure you take into account the fact that the election can only be revoked in limited circumstances. Beginning for the 2018 tax year, individuals must disclose in their U.S. federal non-resident income tax return (Form 1040NR) if this is the first year they are making the net rental income election or whether they have made the election in a previous year and it has not been revoked.

If you make the election, you can provide Form W-8ECI to your tenant or agent, and 30% of the gross rent would not need to be withheld.

Depreciation must be claimed for U.S. income tax purposes if the property is not solely for personal use. Unlike Canada's capital cost allowance system (see 11.2.7), depreciation is not a discretionary deduction in the U.S. Any allowable amount, regardless of whether you claim it, reduces the property's cost base and potentially increases the gain on its disposition.

19.2.4 Dividends and interest from U.S. corporations

Like rental payments, payments of dividends and interest by U.S. persons and corporations to residents of Canada are subject to U.S. withholding tax. The Canada-U.S. tax treaty limits the tax to 15% for dividends and nil for interest in most cases.

You do not file a U.S. income tax return in respect of dividend income on which the correct U.S. tax has been withheld or for interest that is exempt from U.S. income tax.

19.2.5 Income from U.S. limited liability companies

U.S. limited liability companies (LLCs) are created under state law. For U.S. tax purposes, LLCs are generally treated as disregarded entities (if they have only one member) or partnerships (if they have more than one member). As a result, the LLC's income flows through to the members and is taxable in their hands for U.S. tax purposes. The LLC itself does not pay tax in the U.S. unless it has elected to be treated as a corporation.

However, Canada treats the LLC as a corporation for Canadian tax purposes and taxes only distributions from the LLC.

The different tax treatments in Canada and the U.S. result in a combined Canadian and U.S. effective tax rate of 60% or more on income from U.S. LLCs, compared to a maximum tax rate of approximately 51% on income earned through a U.S. partnership. If you are considering an investment in a U.S. LLC, keep this high effective tax rate in mind.

> Be aware of high effective tax rates when considering an investment in a U.S. limited liability company.

19.3 Sale of U.S. properties

19.3.1 Withholding tax (FIRPTA) on sale of real estate

If you sell real estate located in the U.S., a federal withholding tax is normally payable on the proceeds under FIRPTA (the Foreign Investment in Real Property Tax Act of 1980). The required withholding is 15% of the sale price. Where proceeds are not more than US$300,000 and the buyer is an individual who will use the property as a residence, withholding may not be required.

The tax withheld can be offset against the U.S. income tax payable on any gain you realize on the sale, and refunded if it exceeds your U.S. tax liability when you file your U.S. tax return to report the disposition.

A U.S. tax return must be filed for each year in which you dispose of U.S. real property.

> Ensure a U.S. tax return is filed for every disposition of U.S. real property.

You may be able to reduce the FIRPTA withholding by applying to the IRS for a "withholding certificate" on the basis that your expected U.S. tax liability will be less than 15% of the sale price. You must make the application on or before the date the sale closes. The certificate will indicate the amount of U.S. tax that should be withheld by the purchaser. You must have or apply for an Individual Taxpayer Identification Number (see 19.2.1) to apply for a withholding certificate.

Apply for a U.S. "withholding certificate" on the sale of U.S. real estate.

Be sure to apply for a withholding certificate if you are making an instalment sale—otherwise, the 15% withholding is required on the entire sale price up front.

Some states such as California and Hawaii have state withholding tax provisions that parallel FIRPTA.

19.3.2 Income tax on the sale of U.S. real estate

For income tax purposes, you must file a U.S. tax return to report the disposition of U.S. real estate. You can offset any U.S. tax liability with the FIRPTA (and state) tax withheld. The maximum U.S. federal tax rate on capital gains for assets held for more than 12 months is 20% in 2020. Regular graduated U.S. rates apply for assets held for one year or less. The effective highest Canadian rate on capital gains depends on the province you live in and for 2020 ranges from 23.75% (Saskatchewan) to 27% (Nova Scotia). Canada only taxes one-half of the gain (see 6.2.1). However, 100% of the gain is taxed for U.S. purposes. State tax should also be considered. You will need an Individual Taxpayer Identification Number (see 19.2.1) to file your U.S. tax return.

The U.S.-Canadian exchange rate affects the amount of the gain taxable in Canada because the cost of the property is converted to Canadian dollars at the exchange rate at the time of purchase and the proceeds are converted at the exchange rate at the time of the sale. Any improvements added to the cost should be converted to Canadian dollars at the exchange rate at the time they were made.

If you have owned U.S. non-business real property and have been resident in Canada since before September 27, 1980, you can likely take advantage of the Canada-U.S. tax treaty (see 18.2.3) to reduce the amount of your gain that is taxable in the U.S. In this case, only your gain accruing since January 1, 1985 will be taxed.

Example

Roxanne bought a cottage in the U.S. for personal use in 1978 for US$10,000. On January 1, 1985, it was worth US$30,000. In 2020, Roxanne sold the cottage for US$60,000.

The U.S. taxes only US$30,000 of Roxanne's gain, which is the increase in value of the property since the beginning of 1985. State income tax may be based on a gain of either US$30,000 or US$50,000, depending on whether the state adheres to the Canada-U.S. tax treaty.

If you cannot establish a January 1, 1985 valuation, the gain accrued to that date is determined by assuming that the entire gain accrued equally over each month in the holding period.

To claim the benefit under the Canada-U.S. treaty, you need to make the claim on your U.S. return and include a statement containing certain specific information about the transaction.

U.S. tax on the sale of U.S. property generates foreign tax that can be used to reduce the Canadian tax on the sale. This applies to U.S. federal and state tax. (See 18.2.2 for an explanation of the operation of foreign tax credits.) If the property qualifies as your principal residence, as defined for Canadian tax purposes, you can shelter the amount of the gain taxed in Canada by claiming the Canadian principal residence exemption (see 6.5.2). However, using the principal residence exemption proportionately reduces the foreign tax credit available to you for Canadian tax purposes and may not be advisable if you have a home in Canada that would otherwise qualify as your principal residence.

19.3.3 Sales of U.S. stocks and bonds

If you are not a resident or citizen of the U.S., U.S. tax does not normally apply to sales of shares in U.S. corporations, whether public or private, regardless of where they are traded. The same applies to the sale of bonds.

However, if the majority of the corporation's assets are U.S. real estate, the corporation may be considered a "U.S. real property holding corporation" (unless it is a publicly traded company and you own less than 5% of the shares). In such a case, any gain on the sale of the shares of the corporation would be taxed by the U.S. in a manner similar to the sale of real property.

19.4 U.S. gift and estate taxes for Canadians

U.S. gift and estate taxes can impose a serious burden on the death of Canadians and other non-U.S. citizens who own U.S. stocks and real estate.

In this section, we discuss only federal gift and estate taxes. Some states impose gift and estate taxes that you should also consider.

The rules discussed here only apply in situations where both the deceased and the surviving spouse are Canadian citizens and residents. If either spouse is a U.S. citizen or resident, the planning alternatives outlined in this section may not be appropriate.

19.4.1 Property subject to estate tax

U.S. estate tax applies to the property of Canadians that is "situated within the United States". This includes:

- real property located in the U.S.
- certain tangible personal property located in the U.S.
- shares of U.S. corporations, regardless of the location of the share certificates and regardless of where the shares are traded
- debts of U.S. persons, including the U.S. government (with specific exceptions)
- U.S. pension plan and annuity amounts (including IRAs).

U.S. estate tax could apply to any of your personal assets that are located in the U.S. at the time of your death. U.S. case law has established that the assets must be located in the U.S. with a degree of permanence, so the tax probably would not apply to jewellery or other items you might take with you on vacation. However, furniture and artwork in your Florida condominium, for example, may be subject to U.S. estate tax.

For RRSPs, RRIFs, RESPs, RDSPs, TFSAs, alter-ego trusts, certain spousal trusts and joint-partner trusts, you consider the underlying property held in the account when considering which assets are subject to U.S. estate tax.

Be cautious when acquiring shares in U.S. corporations due to potential U.S. estate tax exposure, even if held in your RRSP, alter ego trust or joint partner trust.

Assets normally excluded from the definition of property situated within the U.S. include: shares of a foreign (non-U.S.) corporation, regardless of where the corporation's assets are situated; U.S. bank deposits that are not business related; certain U.S. corporate bonds that are publicly traded outside the U.S.; and certain debt obligations.

The "taxable estate" for estate tax purposes is the gross value of all of the deceased's property situated in the U.S., minus certain allowable deductions. The most significant deductions are:

- amounts left to the deceased's spouse if the spouse is a U.S. citizen
- amounts transferred to a "qualified domestic trust" (see 19.4.5)
- a deduction for a non-recourse mortgage (see 19.4.5) encumbering U.S. property
- a deduction for a share of the deceased's liabilities at time of death—including Canadian income taxes payable.

Once the "taxable estate" has been determined, U.S. federal estate tax applies on the cumulative value of all taxable gifts made during your lifetime and at death, at graduated rates ranging from 18% to 40% in 2020. An applicable credit amount then reduces this tax (see 19.4.2).

If you're considering whether to gift U.S. property to a beneficiary during your lifetime or leave the property to that individual in your will, keep in mind that the U.S. tax treatment of gifted property for beneficiaries is different from the treatment of bequests.

For property inherited on death, the beneficiary's cost base of property is adjusted to the fair market value on the date of death for U.S. tax purposes. For Canadian tax purposes, the cost base of property inherited on death is also adjusted to the fair market value on the date of death, except where the transfer is to a spouse and no election to recognize a gain has been made (see 22.2.3).

For U.S. purposes, transfers by gift result in the cost basis of the property being carried over from the gift giver to the gift recipient. The cost basis is not adjusted to fair market value on the date of the gift. When the recipient disposes of the property, he or she has to pay the tax on any capital gain that has accrued since the original acquisition of the property. In Canada, the treatment of a gift is the same as for a bequest—a gift to anyone other than a spouse results in an adjustment of the recipient's cost base to fair market value on the date of the gift.

Since the Canada-U.S. treaty provides relief for estate tax and not for gift tax (see 18.8.2 and 19.4.2) and since a beneficiary's cost base in a property is adjusted on death but not on a gift, it is rarely beneficial for tax purposes to gift property during life if that property would be subject to U.S. income or estate tax.

19.4.2 Lifetime estate tax credit

Under U.S. domestic law, non-residents of the U.S. who are not U.S. citizens can apply a credit amount of US$13,000 against the estate tax (for U.S. citizens, see 18.8.1). This credit amount effectively exempts US$60,000 of the estate from taxation.

The Canada-U.S. tax treaty increases the U.S. credit amount for residents and citizens of Canada from the US$13,000 allowed under U.S. law to US$4,577,800 in 2020, sheltering US$11.58 million of taxable estate. Note that the U.S. credit is set to decrease to US$2,185,800, adjusted for inflation, for individuals who die in 2026 and afterwards. This credit must be prorated by the value of the Canadian deceased's U.S. estate over the value of the deceased's worldwide estate (as determined under U.S. rules).

The proration of the credit means that Canadians are not subject to U.S. estate tax in 2020 if the value of their worldwide gross estate does not exceed US$11.58 million. It also means that wealthy Canadians who hold a relatively small proportion of their total estate in the United States are still subject to substantial U.S. estate tax. These Canadians should consider the planning options discussed in 19.4.5.

Your estate must file a U.S. estate tax return if your property within the United States is worth more than US$60,000 at the time of your death, even if no tax is payable. To access the treaty benefits, your estate must disclose all of your worldwide assets to the IRS on this return. The return is due nine months after the date of death, with the option to extend the time to file and pay (with interest) for up to one year.

19.4.3 Marital credit

A "marital credit" is available under the Canada-U.S. tax treaty if an estate tax marital deduction would have been available had the surviving spouse been a U.S. citizen. However, this credit is capped at the lesser of the applicable credit amount allowed to the deceased's estate and the U.S. estate tax payable after other credits. This effectively allows a minimum US$26,000 credit (i.e., 2 × US$13,000) where U.S. property is transferred to a spouse on death. Effectively, the marital credit almost doubles the exemption available when the deceased transfers his or her assets to a surviving spouse.

The executor of the estate must elect to take advantage of this provision and must irrevocably waive the benefit of any estate tax marital deduction that may have otherwise been allowable. In effect, the executor must either claim the treaty marital credit or create a qualified domestic trust (but not both). The deadline for the election and waiver is usually nine months after the date of death, unless you submit an extension of time to file the estate tax return.

19.4.4 Canadian credit for U.S. estate taxes

On death, Canada normally taxes the accrued capital gains in the deceased's estate (see 22.2.3). A foreign tax credit is available in Canada to offset foreign income taxes paid on foreign-source income. However, U.S. estate taxes are not income taxes. As a result, no foreign tax credit is available under Canadian domestic law to offset taxes on death.

Under the Canada-US tax treaty, Canada permits U.S. estate tax on U.S. assets to be deducted from a Canadian resident's Canadian tax otherwise payable for the year of death. The credit is limited to the Canadian tax attributable to the deceased's U.S.-source income for the year of death. U.S.-source income includes gains on U.S. real estate, U.S. dividends and rental income. For this purpose, the definition of U.S.-source income is expanded to include gains on deemed dispositions of U.S. securities. The CRA takes the position that the U.S. estate tax can only be credited against the Canadian federal tax and not the provincial tax.

19.4.5 Ways to reduce your exposure to U.S. estate tax

Leave U.S. property to your spouse or a qualified trust.

Once you have determined which of your assets are subject to U.S. estate tax and estimated your potential exposure, you may want to consider some strategies to reduce or eliminate your estate's potential U.S. estate tax liability.

When property is left to a surviving spouse who is a U.S. citizen, or to a qualified domestic trust (QDOT), the U.S. estate tax can be deferred until the death of the surviving spouse.

To qualify as a QDOT, the trust instrument must provide that at least one trustee be a U.S. citizen or U.S. corporation, and that no distribution of capital may be made from the trust without the U.S. trustee being able to withhold U.S. estate tax. Any capital paid out of a QDOT then becomes subject to estate tax. More stringent rules apply to QDOTs with assets exceeding US$2 million in value. A properly structured QDOT may be considered a "qualified spousal trust" for Canadian tax purposes (see 21.5.2). The deceased can use either a QDOT or the treaty marital credit but not both. Since the treaty marital credit produces tax savings of up to US$4,577,800 in 2020 and the QDOT only provides a deferral of estate taxes, there are few situations where establishing a QDOT is beneficial.

Another alternative is to transfer the property to a spousal trust in which the surviving spouse does not have a general power of appointment. This would not avoid estate tax on the death of the first spouse, but it would ensure that the assets in the trust are not included in the surviving spouse's estate for U.S. estate tax purposes.

Mortgage property (non-recourse) to reduce the value of your U.S. real estate.

A "non-recourse" mortgage is one that entitles the lender to have recourse only against the property mortgaged. That is, if you default on payment, the mortgagee can seize the mortgaged property but cannot sue you for the balance if the property is not worth enough to pay off the debt. A non-recourse mortgage outstanding on your U.S. real estate reduces your equity in the property and thus reduces the value of your taxable estate. The current lending environment generally limits the loan-to-value ratio to 60% with a non-recourse mortgage. As you repay the loan, the estate tax exposure increases.

Another way you can reduce your estate tax exposure is by acquiring U.S. assets jointly with your spouse (or another person). For this approach to work, you and your spouse each have to supply your own funds; you

> Acquire property jointly with your spouse or another person.

cannot simply give half of the interest in the property to your spouse or give your spouse the funds to invest, or you could be subject to U.S. gift tax. Where assets are jointly held and it can be proven that each joint tenant paid for their interest with their own money, on the death of the first joint tenant, each tenant is deemed to own their share of the property. If it cannot be proven that each spouse paid for their own interest, the first joint tenant to die is deemed to own 100% of the property for purposes of determining the value of the taxable estate for U.S. purposes.

For example, suppose you and your spouse each invested your own funds into a condominium worth US$400,000. On your death, only US$200,000 of that value would be included in your estate.

You can also acquire the property as tenants-in-common, but beware of potential gift tax if you transfer funds to your spouse for the purchase of the property. You also need to consider the Canadian attribution rules (see 5.2.2).

If your spouse's assets have a lower value than yours, consider having your spouse acquire full ownership of one or more of your U.S. assets, such as a vacation property. Seek professional tax advice before doing so,

> Split your worldwide assets with your spouse.

however, since the transfer could trigger the attribution rules or gift tax if your spouse does not use his or her own funds.

In some situations, it may be beneficial for U.S. estate tax purposes for you to split your interest in an asset with your child. In this strategy, you would acquire a life interest in the property and your child would

> Consider a split interest purchase with your child.

acquire a remainder interest with his or her own funds. The rules in this area are extremely complex for both U.S. and Canadian tax purposes—if you want to pursue this strategy, professional advice is a must.

A more obvious solution to U.S. estate tax is to hold any U.S. stocks and real estate in a Canadian corporation rather than personally. When you die, your corporation does not, and U.S. estate tax does

> Hold your U.S. property through a Canadian corporation.

not apply to U.S. holdings in a Canadian corporation. You have effectively converted the "location" of your assets from the U.S. to Canada. While this solution is often useful, it is fraught with pitfalls, and qualified professional advice should be obtained. Some possible problems that should be addressed include:

- Beyond the initial setup costs, there are ongoing costs to maintaining a corporation, including legal and accounting fees.

- The acquisition of the U.S. assets by the corporation must be legally complete, and all corporate formalities must be observed. If it is determined that the corporation was only acting as an agent or title holder for you, U.S. estate tax can still apply to the property on your death.
- Any income earned by the corporation on its U.S. assets (such as interest, dividends, rent) is subject to tax both when originally earned and when paid out to you in the form of dividends. The combined effect of the taxes is higher than the tax you would pay if you held the assets directly.
- If the Canadian corporation is a Canadian controlled private corporation, the passive investment income earned could decrease the small business deduction otherwise available (see 14.1).
- If you or members of your family will be using the real estate for personal purposes, you will be taxed in Canada as having received a taxable shareholder benefit from the corporation equal to the rental value of the property for all days it was available for your use.
- If the property is sold after death and the funds distributed, the total income tax cost may be higher than the potential estate tax cost in certain cases.

In 2004, the CRA changed its administrative policy of not assessing a taxable benefit to a shareholder of a "single purpose corporation", which is generally a Canadian corporation established for the sole purpose of holding residential real property in the U.S. for the shareholder's personal use and enjoyment. Single purpose corporations that existed before 2005 are exempt from this policy change until the property is sold or the shares of the corporation are transferred to someone other than a spouse or common-law partner. Because of this change, no new single purpose corporations should be established.

Hold your U.S. assets through a properly structured trust or a Canadian partnership that elects to be treated as a corporation in the U.S.

Instead of using a Canadian corporation, you might consider establishing a Canadian limited partnership (with a Canadian corporation as the other partner) to hold your U.S. assets and have the partnership elect to be treated as a corporation for U.S. tax purposes. On your death, your partnership interest and the underlying assets can be transferred directly to your beneficiaries. Since the U.S. will treat the partnership as a corporation, the assets held by the partnership should bypass your estate entirely for U.S. estate tax purposes. And since Canada will treat the entity as a partnership, you can avoid some of the negative Canadian tax implications discussed above of holding U.S. property through a Canadian corporation. This strategy is complex and should not be pursued without professional tax advice.

A properly structured trust where the settlor uses cash to settle the trust and has no retained interest or any right to the trust property may also be used to acquire U.S. assets. The trust must be established for as long as possible before an offer is made on any U.S. property to minimize U.S. gift tax exposure. Again, professional tax advice is essential.

Sell U.S. property before death.

You could plan to sell your U.S. assets (say, to a family member) before your death, and receive in exchange assets that are not "located in the U.S." (e.g., cash or a promissory note situated in Canada). Thus, you would have no U.S. assets left to form a taxable estate.

This step may be useful when death is anticipated within a short time. For example, property could be sold to a child to whom you intend to leave the property anyway, in exchange for a bona fide promissory note. The note might then be left to your spouse or to another family member. If the note were left to the child (and effectively forgiven), the sale may be treated as a gift and subject to U.S. gift tax.

On a sale of U.S. real estate, U.S. and Canadian income tax apply to any gain (the Canadian tax applying to one-half of the capital gain—see 6.2.1). A foreign tax credit is normally available in Canada to offset part or all of the tax paid. Canadian tax, rather than U.S. tax, applies to any gain on securities sold or gifted before death.

Be aware of the possible application of the Canadian attribution rules or the tax on split income (see Chapter 5) where you have transferred property to your spouse or to a family member who is under 18. Also, make sure you do not take back debt (such as a promissory note) from someone resident in the United States, since certain debts of U.S. residents are considered to be property located in the U.S. Before undertaking any transaction, be sure to compare the tax consequences that would arise on death to the tax consequences that would arise on a transfer before death.

If you anticipate that substantial estate tax will apply on your death, consider taking out life insurance as a way of funding the payment of the tax without requiring the sale of your U.S. assets. Life insurance proceeds would not form part of your estate on death, even if provided by a U.S. insurer (although they would be included in your worldwide assets for purposes of determining the applicable credit amount discussed in 19.4.2). Bear in mind that premiums paid on a life insurance policy are not deductible for either Canadian or U.S. income tax purposes. Also, if the policy is with a U.S. insurer, have your professional adviser review the Canadian income tax implications of holding the policy.

> Consider taking out life insurance to cover U.S. estate taxes.

If your will provides that your U.S. assets are to be transferred to a U.S. charity on your death, then you should not be subject to U.S. estate tax on those assets.

19.4.6 U.S. gift tax on real estate for Canadians

U.S. gift tax applies to the donor of gifts of U.S. real estate made by Canadians. The highest gift tax rate is 40% in 2020. The tax does not apply to gifts of U.S. securities by Canadians, even though U.S. estate tax applies to their value on death.

Gifts valued up to US$15,000 annually (US$157,000 for gifts to a spouse who is not a U.S. citizen) are exempt from U.S. gift tax. Gifts to a spouse who is a U.S. citizen are fully exempt from U.S. gift tax. The

> Be aware of drawbacks to gifting U.S. real estate.

Canada-U.S. tax treaty offers no additional relief. For U.S. tax purposes, the cost basis of the gifted property is transferred from the donor to the donee.

In Canada, gifts attract income tax if the gifted property has an accrued gain (unless gifted to a spouse). As we saw in 5.2, attribution rules apply to gifts to spouses and children under age 18. The tax on split income could also apply (see 5.2.4 and 5.2.5). No foreign tax credits are allowed in Canada for U.S. gift tax.

> **Example**
>
> Henry owns a home in California that he bought for US$200,000. The home is now worth $500,000. Henry decides to give the home to his adult son James.
>
> In Canada, Henry pays income tax on one-half of the US$300,000 capital gain. He also has to pay U.S. gift tax on the value of the home, less his US$15,000 annual gift tax exemption, or US$485,000. No foreign tax credit is available for the U.S. gift tax.
>
> The cost base of the property to James for Canadian tax purposes is $500,000, while his basis for U.S. federal and California purposes is US$200,000 (plus a portion of the gift tax). When James sells the property, he will have to pay U.S. federal and state tax on any proceeds over US$200,000. Henry's total tax would be much lower if he kept the property and transferred it to James on death because of the significant treaty benefits available for estate tax purposes. No treaty benefits are available for gift tax purposes.

As you can see, due to the different tax treatment of gifts in Canada and the U.S. and the double tax problems that may arise, gifting U.S. real estate is rarely advisable.

19.5 References

The CRA publishes information for Canadians who spend part of the year in the U.S. under the title "Canadian Residents Going Down South", available from the CRA's website at *www.canada.ca/en/revenue-agency.html*.

The following technical publications may be obtained by telephoning or writing to any office of the Internal Revenue Service (IRS). They may also be available at United States embassy and consular offices, or from the IRS website at *www.irs.gov*.

Publication 515, "Withholding of Tax on Nonresident Aliens and Foreign Entities"
Publication 519, "U.S. Tax Guide for Aliens"

Also, see the following selected topic on the IRS website:

"Individual Taxpayer Identification Number"

Chapter 20

Planning for your retirement

- Start planning and saving for retirement at least 15 years before you plan to retire (20.1)

- Consider topping up your RRSP and using the tax refund to pay down your mortgage (20.1)

- Prepare detailed cash flow forecasts to project changes in your expenses and sources of income as you get older (20.2.1)

- Reconsider your investment strategy as you near retirement (20.2.2)

- Split income by assigning CPP/QPP benefits to the lower-income spouse (20.3.1)

- Delay or defer income until 2021 where possible to minimize the OAS clawback (20.3.2)

- Aim for at least $2,000 of pension income annually for each spouse (20.3.5)

- File a joint election to split pension income with your spouse (20.3.6)

- Top up your RRSP before the end of the year in which you turn 71 (20.4.1)

- Convert your RRSP to a RRIF or annuity at the end of the year in which you turn 71 (20.4.6)

- Contribute excess after-tax RRIF or annuity income to your TFSA (20.4.7)

This chapter discusses some financial planning issues to consider as you plan your retirement. The decisions you make when planning your retirement can greatly affect your quality of life throughout your retirement and the financial resources you can make available to your heirs. We strongly recommend that you seek professional financial and tax planning advice. Since retirement planning and the estate planning issues discussed in Chapter 21 are closely related, you should consider developing your retirement and estate planning strategies at the same time.

20.1 Saving for your retirement

Most people can live comfortably in retirement on 70% to 80% of their pre-retirement income (adjusted for inflation). Meeting this target requires dedicated long-term planning. Generally, the principal sources of retirement income for Canadians are employer-sponsored pension plans, government pension plans, Tax-Free Savings Accounts (TFSA), registered retirement savings plans (RRSP) and other savings.

If you are a member of an employer-sponsored pension plan, you should consider this as one potential source of retirement income, not as your total retirement fund. Similarly, you should not plan to rely too heavily on Old Age Security (OAS) or the Canada and Quebec Pension Plans (CPP/QPP) since these government programs will not provide much more than subsistence level income.

Start planning and saving for retirement at least 15 years before you plan to retire.

Beyond these types of income, you'll probably have to develop resources on your own through other savings and investment strategies. If you don't start at least 15 years before you reach retirement age, you'll probably find yourself working longer than you had intended and/or unable to afford the retirement lifestyle you expect.

By your mid- to late-forties, depending on your circumstances, you should generally find it easier to put larger amounts of funds toward your retirement nest egg: you will be entering your peak income-earning years, your children may be nearing independence and most of your major lifestyle acquisitions (except maybe your home) will probably be bought and paid for. But don't wait until then—due to the exponential growth of your retirement investments through compounding, the earlier you can start saving for retirement, the better off you will be.

Your RRSP is one of the best available retirement savings vehicles. It allows you to set aside money and to defer the taxes you would otherwise pay on it. Try to contribute as much as possible, and do so early in the year so your contribution can earn tax-sheltered income for the entire year. In Chapter 3, we discussed the tax rules governing RRSPs and strategies for maximizing your RRSP's growth, along with registered pension plans (RPPs) and other deferred income plans.

Your TFSA can allow you to earn a significant amount of tax-free investment income for your retirement or other financial goals. Though your contributions to this type of tax-assisted savings account are not tax-deductible, the investment income and capital gains earned on investments in the account are tax-free. You can withdraw this income and your contributions to your TFSA at any time without tax consequences. See 4.1 for a detailed discussion of TFSAs and related planning ideas. TFSAs can continue to shelter your after-tax savings after you wind up your RRSP at age 71 (see 20.4.7).

Consider topping up your RRSP and using the tax refund to pay down your mortgage.

Building funds in your RRSP and TFSA and building equity in your home should be key components of your retirement savings plan. A commonly asked question is whether you would be further ahead in the long run to maximize your RRSP or TFSA contributions or to put the same funds toward paying down your mortgage (see 1.2.3). Since you gain no deduction for your TFSA contributions, if the amount you earn in your TFSA is less than your mortgage interest, it may make more sense to reduce your non-deductible mortgage interest as soon as possible. Regarding RRSPs, however, the answer depends on a variety of factors, including your mortgage's interest rate and remaining amortization period, your RRSP balances and types of investments, your marginal tax rate, the number of income-earning years you have left until you plan to retire, and the availability of other pension plan funds. To hedge your bets, consider making maximum annual RRSP contributions and using the resulting tax refund to make lump-sum mortgage payments.

20.2 Getting ready to retire

20.2.1 Assessing your financial situation

As you get closer to retirement, you will need to update your net worth statement (see 1.1.2) to get a clear picture of your potential retirement income resources. You will also need to prepare new cash flow forecasts to reflect the upcoming changes in your financial situation and to determine your monthly disposable income. As in preparing a budget (see 1.1.3), your cash flow forecasts should list the amounts you expect to receive and pay out monthly.

You should prepare several cash flow statements to take into account changes in your expenses and sources of income as you get older. For example, preparing a statement at retirement will show cash flow changes resulting from your loss of employment income and your receipt of pension income; it should

> Prepare detailed cash flow forecasts to project changes in your expenses and sources of income as you get older.

also reflect reduced employment-related expenses for items such as clothes and commuting to work and perhaps increased expenses for items such as travel and medical bills. Cash flow statements at ages 60 and 65 will reflect the impact of your CPP/QPP and Old Age Security benefits (see 20.3) on your finances. A further cash flow statement at age 71 or when you mature your RRSP should forecast TFSA, RRIF or annuity income you will receive.

These detailed forecasts will show whether your resources will be enough or whether you will need to reduce your planned spending or sell assets to help meet your cash flow needs (see 20.2.3). The projections will also give you the information you need to make decisions such as when you should apply to receive CPP/QPP benefits (see 20.3.1), when and how much to withdraw from RRSPs or TFSAs and whether you should opt for an integrated pension (see 20.3.7).

You should review your retirement projections every one or two years to take into account any changes in your personal circumstances or goals, tax or pension law amendments, economic events and changes to any other assumptions on which your plan is based.

20.2.2 Reconsidering your investment strategy

In 1.1.4, we discussed the importance of determining your objectives and risk tolerance in developing your investment strategy. As you enter retirement, your investment objectives will likely change: instead of building your asset base, your aim will be to preserve or draw on your capital gradually so it will provide a steady and dependable source of income throughout your own and your spouse's lifetimes.

The closer you get to retirement, the less able you will be to replace substantial investment losses and the less risk you should tolerate. Consider changing your investment mix in the years leading up to your

> Reconsider your investment strategy as you near retirement.

retirement so that a greater proportion of your wealth is invested in more secure, fixed income assets such as government or other high quality bonds, preferred shares and guaranteed investment certificates (GICs). Since your retirement could last 30 years or more, you will probably need to have some proportion of your portfolio invested in growth equities such as shares or other equities. (For a discussion of asset allocation, see 1.1.4.)

20.2.3 Planning for the sale of assets

On reaching retirement, you may need to reorganize your finances to meet your cash flow needs. This could involve selling some of your assets, withdrawing funds from your RRSP or selling your home. Before doing so, watch out for unintended tax consequences.

If you own (or previously owned) a business, you may have funds in an investment holding company. The best timing and method of withdrawing these funds should also be considered when you reach retirement. Although these funds generally will be taxable when you withdraw them, you may wish to seek professional advice in this area to determine whether tax-effective ways for extracting the funds may be available.

Many tax incentives and social programs are based on your net income for tax purposes (essentially your total income less certain deductions—see 2.1.1). The capital gains arising from asset sales or the income inclusion resulting from your RRSP withdrawals could significantly increase your net income and your tax bill for the year. If your net income is too high, some tax and social benefits will be reduced or eliminated. These include the federal age credit (see 20.3.4) and the Quebec age and pension income credits (see 17.5). You could also wind up having to pay back some of your Old Age Security benefits for the current year and receiving reduced OAS payments in July through June of the next year (see 20.3.2). A liability for minimum tax could also arise (see 7.6). Withdrawals from your TFSA do not have these adverse effects.

Before you sell your investments or dip into your RRSP funds, consider the following strategies for avoiding an unnecessary income inclusion:

- Consider using resources that do not affect your income for tax purposes first. For example, withdraw from your savings account (without using your emergency fund; see 1.3.1), TFSA (see 4.1) or certain fixed income investments before withdrawing from your RRSP.
- Spread your sales of assets such as shares and RRSP withdrawals over several years to avoid creating a large income inclusion in any one year.
- Instead of receiving any sales proceeds in one payment, consider making it part of the terms of sale that the proceeds are to be paid to you in equal instalments over five years. This will enable you to spread the income inclusion over the five years by claiming a capital gains reserve (see 6.5.1). Of course, you'll want to consider your cash flow needs and the risk of default of payment.
- Remember that selling your home or cottage will not affect your income for tax purposes if the property is eligible for the principal residence exemption (see 6.5.2).
- Instead of selling your home, consider a reverse mortgage whereby the lender pays you a fixed amount of money each month toward a mortgage

that the lender holds on your property. When your home is ultimately sold, the lender will get back the total amount of its payments plus interest and you or your estate will be entitled to the remainder of the sale proceeds. Since a reverse mortgage is not a beneficial strategy for everyone, be sure to consult an independent financial planning professional before entering such an arrangement.

20.2.4 Insurance coverage and other post-retirement benefits

As a retiree, your life insurance needs are somewhat different from those discussed in 1.3.2. While you will still want to be sure that funds will be available to cover your estate's tax liability arising on your death and to provide for your spouse and other dependants, you will likely have fewer debts to service and no need for coverage for loss of employment or self-employment income.

In reviewing your insurance needs, be sure to investigate the existing death benefit and survivor's benefits available on your death. Many employers provide life insurance to their pensioners, although the amount may decrease over time. Some employers also pay a death benefit (see 22.3), which may help your spouse financially.

You should also review your spouse's medical insurance coverage under your post-retirement benefits in the event of your death. Many survivors lose their entitlement to medical insurance coverage on their spouse's death, and you should consider alternate arrangements in advance to ensure your spouse will have coverage after your death.

Since life insurance fills many important roles in estate planning, your review of your coverage on retirement should take place in the wider context of the issues discussed in 21.7. For example, you may wish to consider purchasing life insurance to fund capital gains tax or other tax liabilities that may arise on your death.

20.2.5 Survivor's benefits

When you retire, if you are a member of a company pension plan, it will normally provide you with several choices regarding the payment of your pension after your death. These options may include a life-only benefit, a specified guarantee period, a surviving spouse benefit at amounts ranging from 50% to 100%, or a combination of these options.

If you choose a specified guaranteed payment period of, say, five, 10 or 20 years, your company guarantees it will pay your pension for that period. If you die before the period is over, your pension amounts will be paid to your estate until the period expires.

If you choose a 100% joint and last survivor guarantee, the company will pay you a pension until you die and continue to pay the same pension to your spouse until your spouse dies.

Under a 50% spousal benefit, your spouse will receive half of your pension on your death. Most provinces require that the surviving spouse receive 50% (60% in some cases) of your pension amount on your death, unless your spouse specifically renounces this entitlement in writing when you choose your pension option.

When you are assessing the various options, bear in mind that the longer the potential payout period, the lower the pension payment. For example, the monthly pension payment for a five-year guarantee period is usually much higher than payments under a surviving spouse benefit option.

20.2.6 Phased retirement under defined benefit pension plans

Employees in most provinces can receive pension benefits under defined benefit pension plans (see 3.5) while accruing further benefits at the same time under the same or another plan.

The rules are designed to allow older workers to continue working while at the same time receiving a partial pension and accruing further pension benefits for their part-time work. Employers can offer phased retirement programs that allow employees to reduce their work schedules and receive a proportionate mix of pension and salary income.

Employers can offer employees up to 60% of their accrued defined benefit pension, while incurring additional pension benefits. To qualify, employees must be at least age 55 and otherwise eligible to receive a pension under the plan. There is no requirement related to whether the employee continues to work full- or part-time.

This phased retirement option is not available to designated plans (generally, one-person plans or small plans for groups of executives) or to employees connected with their employer (generally, employees who do not deal at arm's length with their employer or who own 10% or more of the shares of the employer or a related corporation).

20.3 Government assistance for retirees

20.3.1 Canada Pension Plan/Quebec Pension Plan benefits

Between the ages of 60 and 70, you can apply to begin receiving your monthly pension benefits under the Canada Pension Plan or Quebec Pension Plan. You can receive benefits as early as age 60 without stopping work or reducing your hours.

The amount of your CPP/QPP payments will depend on how many years you have contributed to the plan, the amount of your contributions and the age at which you decide to start receiving your pension. CPP/QPP benefits are adjusted annually for inflation; the maximum monthly retirement benefit at age 65 is $1,176 for 2020. These benefits are taxable as income.

Although you can apply to receive pension amounts as early as age 60, you will have to pay a penalty in the form of reduced benefits for receiving these amounts early. In 2020, the penalty is 0.6% of your benefits otherwise payable at age 65 for every month (or 7.2% a year) before your 65th birthday that you collect CPP/QPP benefits and will apply to reduce your benefits for life.

Example Vanessa accepts an early retirement package from her company in 2020 and decides that she wants to start receiving her CPP/QPP benefits later in the year when she turns 62. Since she will begin receiving her pension benefits 36 months before her 65th birthday, she estimates her monthly CPP/QPP pension benefits at $1,176 less $254 ($1,176 x 36 x 0.6%), for a total monthly pre-tax pension amount of $922.

If you decide to wait and receive benefits after age 65, your CPP benefits will increase by 0.70% per month or 8.4% per year. As such, if you start receiving your benefits at age 70, you will receive 42% more than you would if you had taken your benefits at age 65.

To estimate your benefits, you may request a Statement of Contributions from Service Canada or the Régie des rentes du Québec.

Many factors will influence your decision about when to apply for your benefits. If you expect your expenses to be higher during the early part of your retirement, perhaps because you wish to travel, you may appreciate receiving benefits before age 65. By contrast, if you do not need the funds to pay your living or other expenses, you may be better off delaying your application since the benefits will be included in your taxable income. You may also want to consider your health status—if you expect to reach your late seventies and early eighties, you may benefit from starting to collect your CPP/QPP benefits at age 65 or later.

You will need to apply for your CPP/QPP benefits at least six months before you wish to begin receiving them. CPP applications are filed with Service Canada (see 20.6); QPP applications are filed with the Régie des rentes du Québec.

Working beneficiaries

If you are retired and receiving CPP pension benefits and you go back to work, you are not required to restart your CPP contributions as a working beneficiary, though you and your employer must still make CPP contributions if you are a working beneficiary under age 65.

If you are a working beneficiary age 65 or over, you can choose to make CPP contributions to build your pension. Contributions that you make after your 65th birthday will increase your retirement benefits. Additional benefits would be earned at a rate of 2.5% of the maximum pension amount ($14,110 in 2020) per year of additional contributions. As a result, your pension could be higher than the maximum monthly benefit.

If you change your mind about making these contributions, you can opt out of making them by completing an election form (CPT30). If you are considering opting out, you should weigh the benefit of your future CPP benefits against the cost of your current CPP withholdings. The election form can be submitted only once in a calendar year. If, for example, you elect to stop making CPP contributions and you give a copy of this completed form to your employer in 2020, you would have to wait until 2021 to file a new form to restart CPP contributions.

Death benefit and survivor's benefit

The CPP/QPP also pays a death benefit of $2,500; this amount is taxable to the estate or the survivor in the year received. The surviving spouse may also apply for a survivor's benefit under the CPP/QPP, which is a percentage of the deceased's benefits based on the survivor's age and other factors. For example, if the surviving spouse is 65 and not receiving other CPP benefits, the survivor's benefit is generally 60% of the deceased's CPP/QPP benefits.

Splitting CPP benefits between spouses

Split income by assigning CPP/QPP benefits to the lower-income spouse.

To help you save taxes through income splitting, you may direct that up to 50% of your CPP benefits be paid to your spouse, provided both of you are over age 60. If either of you does this, a portion of the other spouse's CPP is assigned automatically back to the first spouse.

If both spouses are eligible for maximum CPP benefits, assignment would not change anything, since each would assign half of the maximum to the other. But if one has high CPP benefits and the other has low benefits or none, the assignment can effectively transfer up to half of the CPP income to the lower-income spouse. The amount that can be split is equal to the retirement pensions you both earned while together, to a maximum of 50%.

The attribution rules discussed in Chapter 5 specifically do not apply to an assignment of CPP benefits. If you and your spouse are both over 60, and you have higher CPP benefits and are in a higher tax bracket, you should consider such an assignment in addition to the pension income splitting rules that allow certain other qualifying pension income to be split between spouses (see 20.3.6). Be sure to consider the effect of assigning CPP benefits on your spousal tax credit claim (see 2.2.1).

CPP benefits can be assigned by completing a form available from Service Canada; QPP benefits can be assigned by completing a form available from Régie des rentes du Québec.

If you are resident in the U.S. and you receive CPP/QPP benefits, see 20.3.3.

20.3.2 Old Age Security benefits and the OAS clawback

OAS benefits are a taxable pension available at age 65. Unlike CPP/QPP payments, which are based on prior contributions, your entitlement to the OAS benefit is based on your age and how long you have lived in Canada. To receive the maximum pension, you must have lived in Canada for 40 years or more after turning 18. Partial pension may be available if you lived in Canada for 10 or more years after turning 18. A social security agreement between Canada and another country may allow you to add your period of residence in the other country to your period of Canadian residence for purposes of determining your OAS entitlement.

OAS benefits are paid monthly and benefit rates are indexed quarterly for inflation. At the time of writing, the maximum OAS payment is about $614 per month. For high-income taxpayers, these payments are completely taxed back through a special tax, known informally as the "clawback". The tax reduces benefits for taxpayers whose net income (after most deductions such as RRSP contributions) is over $79,054. If your net income exceeds about $128,137, the clawback will apply to 100% of your OAS benefits. Spouses' incomes are not combined for purposes of the clawback; each taxpayer's income is considered separately.

The clawback tax on OAS benefits is deducted from your monthly benefits. The amount withheld is based on your income in the prior two years. For example, for the first six months of 2020, your tax withheld is based on your 2018 income while your tax withheld for the last half of 2020 is based on your 2019 income. If too much tax is withheld, the excess will be applied to reduce your income taxes otherwise owing or refunded to you after you file your return for the year. If the tax withheld falls short of your liability, you will have to repay the difference.

To minimize the clawback's potential effect, try to delay or defer recognition of income until the following year where possible. For example, if you are thinking about selling investments that have appreciated in value in 2020, consider waiting until 2021 to cash them in—preserving your OAS benefits may well outweigh the returns you'll forgo by waiting a few months for the proceeds from your appreciated investments (provided their value does not decline in the meantime).

> Delay or defer income until 2021 where possible to minimize the OAS clawback.

To start receiving your OAS benefits as quickly as possible after turning 65, you should file your application with Service Canada at least six months before your 65th birthday. If you make your application after turning 65, it may be approved retroactively for up to one year.

If you are resident in the U.S. and you receive OAS benefits, see 20.3.3.

20.3.3 Cross-border payments of CPP/QPP, OAS and U.S. social security benefits

Under the Canada-U.S. tax treaty (see 18.2.3), U.S. residents who receive CPP/QPP or OAS benefits are not liable for Canadian withholding tax on these amounts. These benefits received by U.S. residents are taxable only in the U.S.

Similarly, if you are a resident of Canada and you receive U.S. social security benefits, no U.S. withholding tax applies on these amounts; 85% of the benefits are subject to Canadian tax.

20.3.4 Age credit

If you are 65 or older by the end of the year, you get an additional federal tax credit of up to $7,637 (worth $1,146) for 2020. This credit is linked to your income and is phased out by 15% of your net income over $38,508. Thus, the credit completely disappears once your net income reaches $89,421. (Your spouse's net income does not affect this calculation.) The Quebec age credit is discussed at 17.5.

20.3.5 Pension income credit

You are entitled to a federal tax credit of 15% for 2020 of your qualifying pension income, up to $2,000 of pension income for the year. A similar credit is available in Quebec for up to $2,902 of pension income in 2020 (see 17.5).

Qualifying pension income does not include Canada Pension Plan, Old Age Security or Guaranteed Income Supplement payments. It basically means private pension income received through a life annuity. If you are 65 and over or are receiving payments as a result of your spouse's death, it also includes annuities out of an RRSP or deferred profit-sharing plan, payments from a RRIF (see 20.4.4) and the income portion of a regular annuity.

Aim for at least $2,000 of pension income annually for each spouse.

To make the most of this credit, you should aim to have at least $2,000 of qualifying pension income annually, plus another $2,000 for your spouse if possible.

20.3.6 Pension income splitting

File a joint election to split pension income with your spouse.

In Chapter 5, we described the potential tax savings you can achieve by splitting income with other family members so that the income is taxed at lower marginal tax rates (see 5.1). You may be able to split some of your pension income by transferring up to 50% of your income eligible for the pension income credit (see 20.3.5) to your spouse or common-law partner.

You and your spouse must jointly agree to the income splitting arrangement by each filing a joint election on or before the due date of your income tax return.

The amount of split pension income that will produce the most tax savings varies greatly among couples, depending on the income of each spouse. Be sure to consider the impact that the split pension income would have on the various personal tax credits such as the spousal, age and medical expense credits as well as the impact on each spouse's OAS clawback (see 20.3.2) and instalment requirements (see 9.2.2). You may want to consult a tax professional to help determine the split that is most advantageous for you.

20.3.7 Integrating government assistance with your pension benefits

Many pension plans offer the choice of an integrated or normal pension. An integrated pension takes into account the approximate amount of government assistance payments you will receive over the course of your retirement, providing higher payments in the early retiring years and lower payments when you become entitled to receive CPP/QPP payments (see 20.3.1) and/or OAS payments (see 20.3.2).

If you choose the integrated pension, you would normally have the same monthly income before and after age 65 (unless you decide to apply for CPP/QPP before then). Maintaining a consistent level of income before and after you start receiving your OAS and CPP/QPP benefits can help keep your income in a lower tax bracket and avoid having your government payments taxed back or reduced.

20.4 Maturing your RRSP

In Chapter 3, we discussed the tax rules and some planning ideas regarding RRSPs. This section discusses your options for maturing your RRSP. There are basically four routes for getting your money out of an RRSP—you must use one of the options described below by the end of the year in which you turn 71. Note that life income funds discussed in 20.4.5 are only available for locked-in retirement accounts.

Starting January 1, 2020, you can also transfer your RRSP funds tax-free to an Advanced Life Deferred Annuity (see 3.2).

20.4.1 RRSP contributions at age 71 and after

If you turn 71 and must wind up your RRSP in 2020, remember that you only have until December 31, 2020 (and not February 28, 2021) to contribute to your RRSP for 2020. You can continue making deductible contributions to a spousal RRSP until the end of the year in which your spouse turns 71, as long as you have earned income in the previous year or unused RRSP contribution room carried forward from prior years.

If you have earned income (generally salary and wages-see 3.1.3) in 2020, this will create new RRSP contribution room for 2021. But if you turn 71 in 2020, you must contribute both your 2020 and 2021 amounts before you wind up your RRSP at the end of 2020. If you have contributed your maximum amount for 2020 and your $2,000 penalty-free overcontribution, your additional contribution would attract a penalty tax of 1% per month. The penalty would only apply for the period between the date of the overcontribution and January 1, 2021—after that, your 2021 deduction room would be available.

> Top up your RRSP before the end of the year in which you turn 71.

20.4.2 RRSP maturity option #1—Withdraw the funds and pay the tax

The first, and easiest, way to cash out your RRSP is simply to withdraw the funds in a lump sum. The amount withdrawn from the RRSP is included in your income for the year in which you do so. It is taxed as ordinary income, just as if it were salary, even if some of the value of the RRSP represents capital gains (which outside an RRSP are normally only partially taxed and, in some cases, could be entirely exempt). A percentage to cover income tax is withheld at source by the financial institution and remitted to the CRA (and Revenu Québec if appropriate) on your behalf (see 3.2). You then report the income and the amount of tax withheld on your annual income tax return and either receive a refund or, if not enough tax was withheld, pay the difference.

20.4.3 RRSP maturity option #2—Purchase an annuity

The second method is to purchase an annuity, which will provide you with a steady income stream over the life of the annuity. The RRSP proceeds are not taxed immediately; annuity payments are taxed as you receive them. (As discussed in

20.3.5, up to $2,000 per year of the income may be effectively exempted through the pension income tax credit.)

There are three general kinds of annuities, each of which can be tailored through a variety of options to suit your needs: "term-certain", payable to you or your estate for a fixed number of years; "single life", payable to you as long as you are alive; and "joint and last survivor life", payable as long as either you or your spouse is alive. Other features may include a guaranteed term as part of a life annuity, indexing for inflation, reduction of payment on the death of your spouse, reduction of payment when Old Age Security payments begin, and so on. Unless you purchase a life annuity with a guaranteed period or a survivor option, your annuity dies with you and no residual balance is left to your heirs.

If you are interested in converting your RRSP to an annuity, you should discuss the available options, and their effect on the monthly annuity payment you receive, with your life insurance agent or trust company. Prevailing interest rates must also be considered to determine whether annuities alone, or a combination of annuities and RRIFs, might provide greater flexibility and returns.

20.4.4 RRSP maturity option #3—Convert your RRSP to RRIF

The third option for maturing your RRSP is to convert it into a RRIF. A RRIF is somewhat like an RRSP, in that you can have it invested in various kinds of securities. However, you must withdraw at least a "minimum amount" from the RRIF each year and report what you withdraw for tax purposes. (Again, currently up to $2,000 per year of such income may be effectively exempted through the pension income tax credit, as explained in 20.3.5.)

The amount that must be withdrawn from the RRIF is a fraction of the value of the RRIF at the beginning of the year that increases gradually each year based on your age, starting at 5.28% at age 71 and levelling out at 20% once you turn 95. You may use your spouse's age for the calculation of your RRIF minimum withdrawal amounts instead of your own. Doing so may allow you to extend the tax deferral on the funds in the plan if your spouse is younger than you are.

20.4.5 RRSP maturity option #4—Convert locked-in RRSP to LIF or LRIF

A life income fund (LIF) provides an alternative to a life annuity when certain individuals, who were formerly members of a registered pension plan, terminate employment or plan membership. The LIF is an option for individuals who have previously transferred pension funds to a locked-in retirement account (see 3.3.2).

A LIF is a RRIF for tax purposes (see 20.4.4) with additional restrictions. Generally, LIFs are available for pension and locked-in funds, subject to federal and provincial pension laws. Like any other RRIF, a minimum amount must be withdrawn each year. As well, under a LIF there is a maximum amount that can be withdrawn each year. In some provinces, the remaining balance of funds in the LIF must be used to purchase a life annuity by December 31 of the year in which the individual turns 80.

You may also want to consider a life retirement income fund (LRIF), now available in many provinces. If you hold a LRIF, you are usually not required to purchase an annuity at age 80, and the maximum amount available for withdrawal typically has some reference to the investment earnings remaining in the fund.

A LIF or LRIF can offer an attractive alternative to a life annuity option. The alternatives for accessing pension money and locked-in funds are evolving and changing in jurisdictions across the country. Contact your financial adviser to determine which options are available to you.

20.4.6 What's the best option?

By the end of the year in which you turn 71, you have to decide what to do with your RRSP. While your personal cash flow needs should be your primary concern, your decision should take into account your overall investment and estate planning goals. A straight withdrawal is rarely the best option, since you would be taxed on the total income in the current year—and none of it would be eligible for the pension tax credit (see 20.3.5).

Instead, if you wish to retain some control over the investment of your RRSP funds, you could purchase a RRIF (see 20.4.4). If you prefer simply to have a steady monthly income that you don't have to worry about, you could contact your life insurance agent and purchase an annuity (see 20.4.3).

> Convert your RRSP to a RRIF or annuity at the end of the year in which you turn 71.

A RRIF gives you more flexibility than an annuity in establishing the amount withdrawn each month, although you must still withdraw a monthly minimum. LIFs also offer flexibility within a range of minimum and maximum monthly withdrawals.

If you are maturing your RRSP, consider the effect of the tax brackets on your income. Your main goal, of course, is to ensure that you have enough income each month to meet your needs. If you can satisfy those needs with a longer-term payout that keeps your income below the high-tax brackets, you may be financially better off.

20.4.7 Using TFSAs in retirement

Tax-Free Savings Accounts (TFSA) are discussed at 4.1 and, together with your RRSPs, registered pension plan and other retirement investments, your TFSAs should be an integral component of your retirement plan. Although these plans are relatively new, the amount of retirement savings that you can contribute to your TFSAs will increase substantially over time and, unlike your RRSP, you can maintain your TFSA for your entire lifetime.

Once you are over 71 and you have wound up your RRSP, a TFSA can still offer a tax benefit if you want to save any of the income you receive once you are required to start drawing down your retirement

> Contribute excess after-tax RRIF or annuity income to your TFSA.

savings. For example, excess after-tax funds received from an annuity or RRIF can be invested in a TFSA, subject to your available contribution room.

If you have enough contribution room, consider transferring non-registered investments to your TFSA. Whatever your age, new contribution room will be created each year. You can make even more room for your most highly taxed investments with high growth potential by removing some of your existing TFSA investments that may attract less tax. If you wish to transfer investments with accrued gains or losses to your TFSA, you should seek professional advice beforehand as the transfer would trigger tax on the unrealized gains while unrealized losses would be denied (similar to the treatment of investments transferred to RRSPs discussed at 3.1.6).

Income earned in your TFSA does not affect your eligibility for federal income tested benefits and credits such as Old Age Security (see 20.3.2), the Age credit (see 20.3.4), or the Guaranteed Income Supplement and GST credit (see 2.9.3).

20.5 Cross-border retirement planning

If you have lived and worked in Canada and the U.S. (or in another country) and you are considering which country you want to live in after you retire, your retirement planning will be quite complex. In addition to two sets of income tax rules, you have to consider differences in your health care coverage, government assisted investment vehicles and how your assets will be taxed at death. Beyond your lifestyle goals, the taxation of your investment and pension income in Canada and the U.S. should be a key factor in your decision about where to retire.

If you have lived and worked in both countries, you may have built up retirement assets on both sides of the border. These assets can include RRSPs (see Chapter 3), U.S. Individual Retirement Accounts (IRAs) (see 18.3.3), Canadian company pensions (see 3.5), U.S. company pension plans (also known as 401(k) plans) and a variety of other types of plans. You may have paid into both the Canada/Quebec Pension Plan and "FICA", the U.S. social security plan.

Retirement planning in cross-border situations involves the same retirement planning steps discussed in 20.1: you need to assess your net worth, outline your goals and objectives, review your cash flow requirements now and in retirement and determine your sources of retirement income. You also need to consider the usual areas of risk management (including disability and life insurance), taxation, investment strategies and estate planning. Due to differences between the laws of the two countries, planning opportunities may be available to minimize your overall tax liability and maximize your retirement assets and cash flow. But without proper advice, double taxation can result, especially on death.

As we saw in 20.2, retirement planning typically involves the preparation of financial projections to incorporate outside sources of retirement income, such as government and employer pensions, and to determine which assets should be accessed and in what order to maximize your retirement income. Before these projections can be prepared, you need to review the rules for withdrawal of funds from the various Canadian and U.S. tax-sheltered plans. The tax treatment of withdrawals from these funds varies depending on their status under the tax laws of Canada and the U.S. The same income may be taxable in both countries and, if certain cases, a foreign tax credit is available to minimize or even eliminate double taxation (see 18.2.2).

When you are deciding whether to retire in the U.S. or in Canada and developing your retirement plan, you should address the following questions. The answers depend on your particular situation; professional advice is strongly recommended.

- What is your tax status in each country and how are you taxed as a result? Is this the best result from a tax perspective? Do you have any choices?
- How would your RRSP be taxed as a non-resident of Canada? Can you still contribute to your RRSP if you do not live in Canada? If you do not return to Canada, should you withdraw your RRSP in a lump-sum?
- Would your expenses be higher in Canada or in the U.S.?
- How would you pay for your health care coverage? How does your provincial health care coverage compare to your U.S. coverage, if any?
- How would your U.S. tax-deferred plans be treated for Canadian tax purposes if you are resident here?
- Can you transfer the funds in your U.S. plans to an RRSP? Would this be beneficial?
- How do the CPP and the U.S. social security pensions interact in your situation? Could you collect two separate pensions and when should you start collecting them?
- Would it be more advantageous to hold U.S. or Canadian-denominated investments? Should you adopt a different investment strategy depending on the country of retirement?

In creating your estate plan for the distribution of your assets on death, you need to review the laws of both Canada and the U.S. in detail. From a tax perspective, residing in the U.S. at death or simply holding U.S. property can be costly. For a detailed discussion of U.S. estate taxes on death, see 19.4.

20.6 References

Old Age Security and Canada Pension Plan application kits are available (in person or online) from Service Canada. You can apply for CPP online at *www.canada.ca/en/services/benefits/publicpensions/cpp/cpp-benefit/apply.html*.

You can apply for Old Age Security online at *www.canada.ca/en/services/benefits/ publicpensions/cpp/old-age-security/apply.html*.

You can apply for the Quebec Pension Plan and find related information online on Retraite Québec's website at *www.rrq.gouv.qc.ca/en/services/services_en_ligne/ regime_rentes_quebec/Pages/rente_retraite.aspx*.

The following publications and more information, including forms and brochures, can be obtained on the CRA's website at *www.canada.ca/en/revenue-agency.html* or by telephone request at 1-800-959-8281 for individual income tax and trust-related enquiries or 1-800-959-5525 for business and self-employed individual enquiries.

Fact Sheet RC4177, "Death of an RRSP Annuitant"

Fact Sheet RC4178, "Death of a RRIF Annuitant or a PRPP Member"

Guide RC4466, "Tax-Free Savings Account (TFSA), Guide for Individuals"

Guide T4040, "RRSPs and Other Registered Plans for Retirement"

Income Tax Folio S3-F10-C1, "Qualified Investments—RRSPs, RESPs, RRIFs, RDSPs and TFSAs"

Income Tax Folio S3-F10-C2, "Prohibited Investments—RRSPs, RRIFs and TFSAs"

Income Tax Folio S3-F10-C3, "Advantages—RRSPs, RESPs, RRIFs, RDSPs, and TFSAs"

Information Circular 72-22R9, "Registered Retirement Savings Plans"

Information Circular 78-18R6, "Registered Retirement Income Funds"

Chapter 21

Estate planning

- Make a will, or review your existing will (21.2)

- Take steps to minimize probate fees (21.4)

- Take action before the 21st anniversary of a trust's creation to manage the impact of a deemed disposition of all of a trust's capital property (21.5.3)

- Consider the advantages of establishing one or more family trusts (21.5.4)

- If you are 65 or older, consider setting up an "alter ego" or "joint partner" trust (21.5.5)

- Look into the potential benefits of an estate freeze (21.6.2)

- Make sure you have sufficient life insurance (21.7)

- Plan for the succession of your business (21.8)

- Consider a pre-paid plan to finance your funeral and cemetery arrangements (21.10)

Careful estate planning can help you manage the taxes arising on death and leave as much as possible to your beneficiaries. In this chapter, we provide some estate planning strategies that you may want to consider. Keep in mind that estate planning can be extremely complicated and depends very much on your personal situation and goals. It should be undertaken in conjunction with the development of your retirement plan, as discussed in Chapter 20. Professional advice is highly recommended. If you or your spouse are not Canadian residents, much of our commentary in this chapter will not apply to your situation. However, if one or both of you are U.S. citizens, see Chapter 18.

21.1 What is estate planning?

The goal of estate planning is to achieve the state of financial affairs you desire, either at your death or later in your life when you wish to transfer family property to others. Like your financial plan (see Chapter 1), your estate plan should not be something you do once, then file away. Rather, it is a continual process that should evolve to meet changing family circumstances and wishes concerning who inherits your estate. You should give serious consideration to your estate plan at least every five years and more often if the law in this area or your family situation changes significantly.

Estate planning may involve more than merely creating or changing the terms and features of a will. For example, you should also consider the way you hold assets. Whether you own your assets personally, through a trust or through a holding company has important estate planning implications. Like other aspects of estate planning that evolve with changing circumstances, you may wish to periodically consider whether the structure of your asset holdings remains appropriate for your estate planning goals.

21.2 The will

21.2.1 Purpose of a will

The will is a key element of estate planning. It allows you to provide for an orderly distribution of your assets in accordance with your desires and in a way that minimizes the tax burden on your estate and your beneficiaries. Depending on your circumstances, having more than one will may be advantageous—for example, multiple wills may help reduce probate fees (see 21.4) or facilitate the administration of your estate if you have assets in different countries.

Make a will, or review your existing will.

Your will's primary function is to specify to whom and when your assets are to be distributed. You may want to leave specific properties (e.g., jewellery, furniture or shares in your business) to specific beneficiaries. You may want to leave a stated sum of money to certain people or to named charities (make sure you get the correct legal name of the charity). You also want to specify a "residual" beneficiary, who will get everything left in the estate after your specific bequests are satisfied.

The way you choose to direct assets to beneficiaries is influenced by several factors. For example, you may wish to simply leave everything directly to your spouse (including a common-law spouse—see 2.2.1). Alternatively, you may want to use a "spousal trust" that, as we'll see in 21.5.2, can offer certain tax advantages and a measure of protection from potential creditors without any loss in flexibility for your surviving spouse. As discussed in 22.2.3, there will be no tax on the accrued capital gains on your property when the property is transferred to your spouse or a spousal trust, provided your spouse or spousal trust obtains ownership and unfettered rights to the property.

If you do not make a will, provincial law will determine how your assets are distributed. The result can vary significantly, depending on where you reside at the time of death. In Ontario, for example, the law provides that a surviving spouse gets the first $200,000 of an estate and divides any additional amounts with the deceased's children under a formula. However, in Alberta, the surviving spouse is entitled to all of the estate, unless the deceased had children from more than one relationship. In that case, the estate is divided among the surviving spouse and the deceased's children under a formula.

In some provinces, family law can effectively override the instructions in your will. In Ontario, for example, your spouse can elect to ignore the will and take the amount of money due to him or her under the "net family property" rules (see 21.3). If this is done, your estate may lose the benefit of the capital gains rollover described in 22.2.3.

If you have specific desires as to who should have custody of or guardianship over your children after your death and while they are under 18, you can put these desires into your will for consideration by the courts. However, in some provinces, this designation is not binding.

While in some provinces an entirely handwritten will may be valid, it is strongly advisable to have your will prepared or reviewed with the assistance of a lawyer, or a notary in Quebec, and a tax adviser to ensure it meets your wishes and takes tax and family law considerations into account.

Periodic reviews of your will are necessary to ensure that your estate plan is consistent with changes in the tax law, which occur regularly, as well as any changes in provincial family law and succession law.

Changes in your own personal circumstances such as the birth of a child or a change in marital status could also necessitate a change to your will. For example, in many jurisdictions, a will becomes void if you marry after making the will, unless it was made in contemplation of the marriage. By contrast, a will may not become void after a divorce.

If you do not make a will or if your will is invalid, the process of obtaining court approval for distribution of your assets may be cumbersome and expensive. Your representative or heirs must apply to the court to appoint an administrator (also called an "estate trustee") to administer and distribute the estate in accordance with a formula set out in legislation.

As discussed in 1.3.4, consider also executing powers of attorney in the event you become unable to act by reason of disability or mental incompetence—one for decisions related to your finances and one for decisions related to your personal care. If, for example, you become mentally disabled, the continuing powers of attorney would enable the named "attorney" to act in your stead. (In Quebec, you can designate such a person in a document called a "mandate in case of incapacity".) You may wish to give the powers of attorney to the same person you name as your executor, such as your spouse.

21.2.2 Choosing your executor and estate trustee

In your will, you should designate one or more persons as your executor(s) (also called estate trustee(s)). The person should be someone you can trust to take charge of your affairs and distribute your assets in accordance with your desires as set out in your will. The executor and estate trustee will normally apply to the court for "letters probate" (see 21.4), which will give court approval for the executor to take over your property, manage it and distribute it to your beneficiaries.

The responsibilities of your executor and estate trustee include determining the assets and liabilities of the estate, filing all income tax returns for you and the estate (including any foreign succession duty or tax returns) and paying the debts (including all taxes) outstanding at the date of your death.

Ideally, you should choose an executor and estate trustee who is familiar with your personal situation. Often the executor would be your principal beneficiary (such as your spouse). Sometimes this may not be appropriate, however, because of a possible conflict of interest with other beneficiaries.

You should consider naming an alternate executor and estate trustee in case your executor dies before you do. Otherwise your estate may be handled by the executor of your executor's estate. Naming an alternate executor and estate trustee is also important in case the named executor is either unable to or chooses not to act. This can avoid costly court proceedings.

If you are an executor and estate trustee yourself, see Chapter 22 for a discussion of your role and responsibilities.

21.2.3 Will planning to manage your estate's tax liability

There are many tax-oriented clauses that can be included in a will to help manage a tax liability at death. The will should include a provision granting executors and estate trustees broad authority to make or join in any election, designation or allocation under tax legislation. This will ensure that your executor can use benefits such as the principal residence designation and capital gains exemption. The following clauses should also be considered:

- forgiveness of certain loans made to family members
- a discretionary power permitting trustees to determine which assets are to form the trust property of spousal or other trusts
- a reminder to your executors that if you have not made your maximum RRSP contribution at the time of your death, one should be made by your estate to your spouse's RRSP before the required deadline.

In your will, you can name the beneficiary of your RRSP, RRIF, TFSA, deferred profit-sharing plan, death benefits and life insurance proceeds. Alternatively, these plans and policies usually allow for naming a beneficiary directly within the plan documents. While designating beneficiaries directly in the plan documents may reduce probate costs, there may also be implications for spousal rights under family law. You should also consider confirming these designations in your will and providing for the proceeds to form part of your estate if the designated beneficiary dies before you and no contingent beneficiary is named.

Note that your estate may have to pay tax on the full value of your RRSP or RRIF on your death if you designate as the beneficiary someone other than your spouse or, under a special election, your financially dependent children (see 22.4.1).

If you plan to make a charitable gift through your will, instead of donating cash, consider donating publicly traded securities, mutual funds or segregated funds of a life insurance company in order to help reduce taxes payable at death (see 8.2 and 8.2.2).

21.3 Family law

Provincial family law can have a significant impact on your estate planning. Every province has legislation to protect the interests of spouses on marriage breakdown. This legislation may apply on death as well. We'll use Ontario family law for purposes of this discussion. The laws of each province are different, however, and professional advice should be obtained.

On marriage breakdown, Ontario's *Family Law Act* provides for an equal division of "net family property", which includes almost all property acquired during the marriage and the increase in the value of property owned at the time of the marriage. Business assets, shares in a privately held or public corporation and investments are typically all included in "net family property". Each spouse's assets are totalled and an equalizing payment is required, so that each spouse ends up with half of the value of the net family property.

These above provisions apply on death as well. The surviving spouse may elect to take an equalizing payment for one-half of the difference in net family property rather than whatever has been left to him or her under the deceased's will. Clearly, such rules can interfere with estate planning, and they should be considered when making a will.

Spouses can agree to have these provisions of the *Family Law Act* not apply, or only apply to specific assets, by signing a "domestic contract". Separate independent legal advice for each spouse is required before signing such a contract.

21.4 Probate fees

Probate fees are charged by the courts in each province (except Quebec) to grant letters probate, which confirm that the deceased's will is valid and the executor has the authority to administer the estate.

Take steps to minimize probate fees.

The probate charge generally applies to the total value of the deceased's assets at the time of death, without any deduction for debts other than those encumbering real property. In some cases, the assets can be distributed and the estate wound up without probate, but probate is generally required before third parties such as financial institutions (e.g., banks, investment dealers) will release property to the executor or estate trustee. If there is no will, probate is still required because the court has to confirm that an administrator has been appointed to distribute the deceased's property as required by law.

Probate fees are highest in Ontario and British Columbia, where they are 1.5% and 1.4%, respectively, of the value of the estate over $50,000 (with no fees for an estate up to $50,000 in Ontario and lower rates applying to the value below $50,000 in B.C.). In Nova Scotia, the top rate is 1.695% of the value of the estate over $100,000 (with progressive flat rates applying to values below $100,000). In other provinces, the top rates are typically 0.4% to 0.7% of the value of the estate. Quebec levies a nominal flat fee that is not based on the estate's value. Alberta has progressive flat rates based on the estate's value to a maximum fee of $525. The probate fees for large estates in other provinces can be substantial as there is no maximum.

Property held by two people as "joint tenants" with right of survivorship (rather than as "tenants in common") is not subject to probate, since on the death of one joint tenant the property does not form part of the estate but simply becomes wholly owned by the other. Property is commonly held by spouses in this manner.

You may also hold property in joint tenancy with your adult children to reduce probate fee exposure (known as a "Pecore" joint tenancy arrangement, after the court case confirming the acceptability of this technique). In this case, your adult child holds the assets as bare trustee for you during your lifetime and, on your death the adult child is expected to transfer the assets to the beneficiaries under your will. Provided the will does not otherwise require probate, the value of the property is not subject to probate fees.

Example

Jonah, who lives in Ontario, dies in 2020. His estate consists of a house worth $1 million, with a $700,000 mortgage on it, $100,000 in personal effects, and the shares of his business, worth $1 million. He also owes $80,000 on a personal line of credit to the bank at the time of his death.

The value of Jonah's estate for probate purposes is $1.4 million. The house is counted as $300,000 (i.e., minus the mortgage), and his other assets are $1.1 million. The $80,000 debt is not deducted. The fee for probating Jonah's will is $20,250 (calculated 1.5% of the value over $50,000).

The following options can reduce the cost of probating your estate. Note, however, that any planning to reduce probate fees must take numerous other issues (such as family law, income tax effects, land transfer tax, GST/HST and other sales taxes) into account—professional advice is strongly recommended.

- If you are leaving property outright to your spouse (or another person), consider holding the property as joint tenants with your spouse (or that other person) with a right of survivorship. On your death, the property will pass automatically to the other joint tenant and not form part of your estate. Note that there may be immediate adverse tax consequences if you transfer the property to a joint tenant who is someone other than your spouse. Also, there are some situations where a joint tenancy will be severed on death by provincial legislation.
- If you are leaving property to a person subject to a Pecore joint tenancy arrangement (discussed above), properly documenting the arrangement is critical to ensure no immediate tax consequences arise.
- Try to keep certain assets out of the estate. This is quite practical in the case of life insurance, RRSPs, RRIFs and TFSAs, where beneficiaries (other than the estate) can be designated in the RRSP, RRIF or TFSA plan documents or in the life insurance policy. Also consider transferring property during your lifetime, either directly to your intended beneficiaries or to a trust for their benefit. Again, take care that this does not trigger premature recognition of accrued capital gains.
- If you own real estate with no mortgage and you also owe money (perhaps on a personal line of credit or on a debt secured by other assets) consider having the debt converted to a mortgage or charge on the real estate. Doing so may reduce the value of the real estate for probate purposes.

- If you have certain assets that can pass to beneficiaries without probate, such as shares in a private company, you may be able to reduce probate fees by making a secondary will that only includes these assets. Your executor would then apply for probate on the primary will but not the secondary one. This type of planning has become common in many jurisdictions and can be an effective way of reducing probate costs.
- If you are age 65 or over, two types of trusts—"alter ego" and "joint partner" trusts—can help you keep assets out of your estate and reduce its value for probate purposes without giving up your right to those assets during your lifetime (see 21.5.5).

21.5 Trusts

21.5.1 What is a trust?

A trust is an arrangement whereby one or more persons (the trustees) hold legal title to property (the trust property) for the benefit of other persons (the beneficiaries). The person who creates the trust and puts ("settles") property into it is called the settlor.

> Brian is leaving the country to work in Africa for several years. He gives Paul $120,000 to hold in trust for Brian's two teenagers, Dianne and Darryl. Brian draws up a trust agreement that allows Paul to use the trust funds to pay for Brian's children's education, to invest the funds not yet used, and to pay half of the capital of the trust to each child when they turn 23.
>
> *Example*
>
> In this example, Brian is the settlor, Paul is the trustee and Dianne and Darryl are the beneficiaries. Paul has legal ownership of the $120,000, but he is required to use it only for Dianne's and Darryl's benefit and not for his personal use. If the trust document permits, he can pay himself a fee for his services as trustee.

There is no legal requirement that the settlor and the trustee be different people. (In this example, Brian could simply declare and document that he is holding funds in trust for his children, and a trust would be created.) Similarly, the settlor and the beneficiary can be the same person. (This is what happens when you put funds into a self-directed RRSP, for example. You are the settlor and beneficiary, and a trust company is the trustee of your assets—see 3.1.6.) However, the choice of settlor, trustee and beneficiaries affects the taxation of the trust and its beneficiaries. For example, a number of attribution rules apply to trusts, including those outlined in Chapter 5. Careful planning is required.

Note that the mechanics and terminology of trusts are somewhat different in Quebec, which is governed by the province's *Civil Code* rather than by the common law that governs the rest of Canada.

Court cases involving trusts' legal constitution and residency highlight the importance of ensuring that trust arrangements are properly made, especially when the trust and its beneficiaries reside in different jurisdictions. Trustees should properly maintain the trust's accounting records and promptly document their decisions in trust minutes.

21.5.2 What kinds of trusts are there?

A trust can be set up during the settlor's lifetime (as in the example above). Such a trust is called an *inter vivos* (Latin for "among the living") trust.

A trust can also be created by the settlor's will, in which case it is called a testamentary trust.

A trust for the settlor's spouse that meets certain conditions is a "spousal trust". The principal conditions are that all of the income of the trust must be payable to the spouse during the spouse's lifetime and that none of the capital can be distributed to anyone other than the spouse during the spouse's lifetime. (After the spouse's death, however, the income and capital can be distributed to someone else, such as the settlor's children.) Such a trust can be either testamentary or *inter vivos*. A transfer of property from the settlor to a spousal trust does not trigger tax on any accrued capital gain; instead the property passes at the settlor's tax cost, and any capital gain is taxed only when the trust eventually disposes of the property or the spouse dies (see 22.2.3).

If your will creates a trust, that trust would be separate from your estate. The estate would be taxed as a trust for as long as it takes to wind up your affairs and distribute your assets. A trust set up in your will, on the other hand, could be designed to continue for many years beyond your death.

Many types of trusts are in use today. Each meets a purpose or addresses an aspect of tax or common law. For a discussion of two kinds of trusts called "alter ego" and "joint partner" trusts, see 21.5.5.

21.5.3 How is a trust taxed?

A trust is a separate person for income tax purposes. The trustee(s) must file a T3 trust tax return (and a TP-646 Quebec trust return in some cases) and pay tax on the trust's income. A trust is generally taxed as an individual but is not eligible for the personal credits (see Chapter 2). *Inter vivos* trusts pay tax at a flat rate—the top rate of combined federal and provincial tax for individuals (about 51%). Testamentary trusts paid tax at the same marginal rates as individuals (see 5.1) until December 31, 2015. Beginning in 2016, testamentary trusts (except certain estates, see 22.2.2, and qualified disability trusts, see below) also pay tax at the top rate.

A trust's income includes its income from carrying on business (see Chapter 11) from taxable capital gains (see Chapter 6) and from investments (interest, dividends, rent, etc.—see Chapter 7), calculated as if the trust were a living individual. Amounts that are payable or paid to beneficiaries are deducted from the trust income, and the beneficiaries report such income on their tax returns, subject to the attribution rules and the tax on split income discussed in Chapter 5

Certain kinds of income, such as capital gains and dividends, preserve their character when flowed through to a beneficiary. Thus, such income can be treated as capital gains (see Chapter 6) or as dividends (see 7.1.2) on the beneficiary's tax return. Other income loses its character as it flows through a trust.

A special election called the "preferred beneficiary election" may be available where a beneficiary is disabled (as defined for tax purposes in 2.5.1). This election allows the trust and the beneficiary to agree that the trust's income will be taxed in the beneficiary's hands so that, in a later year, the income can be paid out by the trust to the beneficiary free of tax.

Other special tax rules allow income and capital gains to be taxed in the trust even if these amounts have been paid out to the beneficiary during the year. For these rules to apply in 2016 and later years, the taxable income of the trust must be nil after making the designation to include the income in the trust. As such, these rules only apply if the trust has unused losses from other years that can offset this income.

If your will currently creates a separate testamentary trust for each beneficiary to allow each trust to benefit from lower graduated rates of tax for the income retained in such a trust, you may want to reconsider this arrangement because testamentary trusts are no longer entitled to graduated rates of tax for 2016 and later years.

However, if your will creates a testamentary trust for a disabled beneficiary, the trust may still be able to pay tax at graduated rates after 2015 rather than at the top rate. To qualify for graduated rates, one or more of the trust's beneficiaries must have a disability tax credit certificate (see 2.5.1). Further, the capital of such a qualified disability trust that was taxed at graduated rates must be paid to a disabled beneficiary. If such trust capital is paid to a non-disabled beneficiary, the tax savings previously realized must be repaid.

Every 21 years a trust (other than a spousal, alter ego or joint partner trust—see 21.5.2 and 21.5.5) is deemed to dispose of all of its property, so that accrued capital gains are taxed as if the assets have been sold. Before the end of each 21-year period, consult a professional adviser to determine whether steps can be taken to manage the impact of this deemed disposition.

> Take action before the 21st anniversary of a trust's creation to manage the impact of a deemed disposition of all of a trust's capital property.

21.5.4 The benefits of setting up a family trust

A trust offers tremendous flexibility in structuring your affairs and controlling the future use of your property. The powers of the trustees can be strictly limited and defined; or they can be given full discretion as to when and whether to pay income or distribute capital to the beneficiaries, how to manage the trust property and when to wind up the trust.

Setting up the trust while you are alive can provide several advantages:

- by making yourself a trustee, you can keep control of the trust assets (such as shares of your business)
- by getting the assets out of your estate, you can reduce probate fees (see 21.4)

- because the assets will not be in your estate, they will not form part of the public record that anyone can examine in the court office
- income splitting may be possible, depending on the application of the attribution rules and the tax on split income (see Chapter 5).

A trust can also be useful as part of an estate freeze (see 21.6). In many cases, you may not know at the time you set up the freeze how you want the future growth in value of the company allocated among your children. You may not want to give them direct ownership in the business yet. In such an event you should consider setting up a family trust and having the trust subscribe for the "growth" common shares (or have them gifted to the trust). If you are the trustee and have discretion as to how to allocate the income and capital of the trust, you can decide several years later (or even in your will) which of your children should inherit the business. This may also provide some flexibility for your children when dealing with family law legislation (see 21.3). If you have already established such a plan, ensure that its benefits will not be neutralized by the income-splitting tax on certain income received by family members (see 5.2.4 and 5.2.5).

An *inter vivos* trust can offer benefits over a power of attorney or applying to the court to appoint a guardian in the event of incapacity. As we saw in 1.3.4, a power of attorney allows you to designate a person who would take control of your financial affairs if you become incapacitated due to illness or injury. Potential advantages of trusts over powers of attorney include the following:

- Unlike a power of attorney, the trust agreement is a comprehensive document that sets out the trustee's specific duties and powers.
- A higher standard of fiduciary duty applies to a trustee than to a power of attorney.
- The trust survives death but a power of attorney does not.
- Property held under the trust agreement can be managed by the trustees in the event of incapacity without the settlor's involvement, thereby offering protection against third-party abuse, since the settlor does not have independent control of his or her assets.
- A power of attorney may not be adequate to manage assets outside of your own province—each province and state in North America has different legislation. The authority of a trustee acting on behalf of a trust would be more readily recognized by a foreign bank or other institution.

21.5.5 Alter ego and joint partner trusts

Two types of trusts, called "alter ego" and "joint partner" trusts, may be useful as substitutes for wills and powers of attorney and can produce significant benefits in terms of avoiding probate fees and reducing difficulties for your survivors or your business while your estate is being settled.

If you are 65 or over, an alter ego trust can help you keep assets out of your estate without giving up your right to those assets during your lifetime. Under the terms of such a trust, all of the income and capital of the trust property would be held and used for your benefit alone. No income tax is triggered when you put the property into the trust. Income and capital gains generated by the trust property would be taxable in your hands, as they would if you continued to own the assets personally. On your death, the alter ego trust document performs the same function as a will by setting out how the trust assets should be distributed.

A joint partner trust works the same way except that the assets are held for the benefit of you and your spouse. Spouses (provided they are also over 65) can also transfer assets to the trust without triggering any income tax, except that they would be taxed on all of the income and capital gains of the property they transferred during their lifetime.

If you plan to transfer qualified small business corporation shares or qualified farm or fishing property to an alter ego or joint partner trust, keep in mind that it may not be possible to use the lifetime capital gains exemption (see 6.4) for these types of property while you are alive.

On the death of the settlor of an alter ego trust or the second partner of a joint partner trust, the trust is deemed to have disposed of its assets at fair market value, and any capital gains are taxed in the trust's hands.

It is not possible to claim any unused lifetime capital gains exemption of the settlor or surviving partner to offset these deemed gains. As a result, you may want to elect out of the rollover provisions so you can trigger a capital gain and claim the lifetime capital gains exemption at the time the property is transferred to the alter ego or joint partner trust.

For alter ego and joint partner trusts, the deemed realization at fair market value discussed in 21.5.3 does not occur every 21 years; rather, as noted above, it occurs on the day on which the settlor or surviving partner dies. If the trust continues to exist, a deemed disposition will occur every 21 years after the death of the settlor (for alter ego trusts) or surviving partner (for joint partner trusts).

However, since alter ego and joint partner trusts are *inter vivos* trusts, they pay tax at the highest marginal rate for individuals. As such, trust income does not benefit from graduated rates of tax, and any capital gain that arises on the deemed disposition resulting from the settlor or surviving partner's death may bear more income tax in the trust than it would if taxed in the deceased's hands.

21.6 Estate freezing

21.6.1 What is an estate freeze?

"Estate freezing" is the term used to describe steps taken to fix the value of your estate (or some particular asset) at its present value, so that future growth will accrue to the benefit of others, such as your children (or a trust for your children) and not be taxed on your death. Several provisions of the *Income Tax Act* are designed to facilitate this type of planning.

Estate freezing is most often used when you own a business that your family will continue to own after your death and that you expect will increase in value in future years. Your children may be involved in running the business. Even if they are not, you may want them to own it after your death.

21.6.2 How do you freeze an estate?

There are many different approaches to an estate freeze, some of them very complex. The following example is one of the simplest types:

> **Example**
>
> Lucas owns all of the common shares of his business, X Corp. His original share investment in X Corp. was $100, and it is now worth $10 million. Lucas expects it to increase in value significantly over the next several years. Lucas has two children, both in their early 20s, who work in the business.
>
> First, Lucas exchanges his common shares of X Corp. for 10,000 new preferred shares (a step that can be taken without triggering any income tax). The preferred shares are voting shares. They are also retractable at any time, at his option, for $1,000 per share. In other words, Lucas can demand that the corporation pay him $10 million for his shares at any time.
>
> Each of Lucas's children then subscribes for 50 new common shares in X Corp., paying $1 per share. Since X Corp. is worth $10 million, and Lucas's preferred shares are retractable for $10 million, the common shares have negligible value at the moment.
>
> Over the next few years, the value of X Corp. rises to $10.5 million. Now Lucas's preferred shares are still worth only $10 million, but the common shares are worth $500,000. Lucas has thus transferred the post-freeze "growth" in the corporation to his children at no tax cost to him.
>
> Note also that since Lucas's preferred shares are voting shares, he has kept control of the corporation. Lucas has 10,000 votes and his children together have only 100.

The mechanics of an estate freeze are complex, and numerous income tax rules have to be considered. The basic concept, however, is generally as outlined above. Often you would set up a holding company and a family trust (see 21.5.4) as part of the freeze, rather than having your children subscribe directly for shares in the operating company.

Look into the potential benefits of an estate freeze.

An estate freeze can significantly reduce the tax payable on your death, if the value of your business is "frozen" sufficiently early. The value of the business is fixed at the time of the freeze, so the tax on the subsequent capital appreciation is deferred until your children sell the business (or until their deaths). You can also multiply the availability of the capital gains exemption for certain "small business corporation" shares (see 6.4.1), if it is still available when your children eventually dispose of the shares in certain circumstances. At the same time, you do not need to give up control of the business.

You can also continue to receive income from the corporation, either by declaring dividends on the preferred shares or by drawing a salary if you continue to work in the business.

If you use a trust to acquire the common shares, you can retain flexibility for allocating the shares of the business among your children later. However, you should consider the impact of the tax on split income if the shares are held through a trust (see 5.2.4 and 5.2.5).When you set up the freeze, you can trigger part or all of the accrued capital gain on your shares to date. This may allow you to use your lifetime capital gains exemption (see 6.4.1), for example. Be aware of the various restrictions on claiming the exemption (see 6.4.3).

Depending on how the freeze is structured, you may achieve income splitting (see Chapter 5) with your family in certain circumstances. Note that certain attribution rules do not apply if your corporation qualifies as a "small business corporation" (see 6.2.3) or your children have reached the age of 18 (see 5.2.6). However, existing arrangements may be affected by the relatively new income-splitting tax on certain income received by family members (see 5.2.5).

If you have carried out an estate freeze but the value of the frozen shares has gone down due to economic conditions (e.g., a pandemic), you may benefit from carrying out a "refreeze", which would fix a lower value on the business and your preferred shares. This lower value would further decrease the tax payable on your death and allow greater future growth for the common shares held by your children or a trust.

Whether an estate freeze or refreeze is useful to you depends very much on your business, your financial position, your future plans and your goals. You should obtain qualified professional advice before undertaking this type of planning.

21.7 Life insurance

Life insurance plays many roles in estate planning. For example, it can:

- provide replacement income for your dependants
- provide a fund for emergency expenses or children's education in future years
- pay for final expenses such as funeral costs
- assist in funding the succession of a business in a closely held corporation
- fund capital gains tax liability that arises on death (see 22.2.3)
- allow you to accumulate funds on a tax-sheltered basis to supplement retirement income (see 7.3.2).

Insurance proceeds received on the death of the life insured are not taxable. Similarly, the premiums you pay for your life insurance are generally not tax-deductible.

If your corporation is the beneficiary of a policy on your life, the corporation may be able to distribute the life insurance proceeds to your estate and other shareholders without any tax applying. Stricter rules apply for policy benefits received after March 22, 2016 to prevent what the government considers to be artificial increases in tax benefits.

Some business owners may own a holding company that owns an operating company. If you own such a holding company and it is the beneficiary of your life insurance policy but the operating company pays the premiums, the holding company may be assessed a shareholder benefit. You may want to consult your professional adviser about how to structure the ownership of the insurance policy to avoid the shareholder benefit.

Make sure you have sufficient life insurance.

Your need for insurance changes as factors such as your income, investment portfolio and dependants change. Therefore, a regular review of your coverage is important.

There are many different life insurance products available. These products can generally be divided into two types: term insurance and permanent insurance.

Term (or "pure") insurance policies usually have lower premiums at younger ages. You are paying the cost of insuring against the risk of your death in the current year and nothing more. As long as you continue to pay the premiums, your coverage continues; many policies guarantee renewal without additional medical evidence. However, the cost of premiums increases dramatically in later years for normal renewable policies. Most term policies terminate at age 70 to 75, which is lower than the current average life expectancy, though many companies offer "term to age 100"-type policies, which can be acquired for level premiums over life.

A permanent insurance policy (often called "whole life" or "universal life") combines pure insurance coverage with an investment fund. As a result, the cost of premiums is often much higher than term insurance though much of this cost forms part of the investment fund. Many permanent insurance policies offer fixed premiums for guaranteed maximum terms (say, 10 or 20 years). At the end of the term, the policy is often fully paid up. The policy can be designed so that the investment fund or cash surrender value accumulates tax-free. Such a fund can be borrowed against or "cashed out" in later years. However, doing so would have a tax cost.

Permanent insurance products are usually desirable for the following purposes:

- capital gains tax funding
- estate equalization (to allow for an even distribution of your estate, such as where you wish to leave business assets to beneficiaries active in a family business and non-business assets to those family members not active in the business)
- business succession planning
- long-term, tax-effective investment strategies.

When buying insurance, consider who should be the beneficiary. If your estate is the beneficiary, the insurance proceeds would form part of your estate on your death and be subject to any claims that creditors have on your estate. The proceeds would also be subject to probate fees (see 21.4). You may therefore want to have the insurance proceeds payable directly to your spouse, another beneficiary or an insurance trust, in order to bypass the estate. The investment fund or cash surrender value of a policy can also be protected from creditors during your lifetime where certain beneficiaries are named.

New rules affecting the taxation of whole and universal life insurance policies took effect January 1, 2017 (see 7.3.2). Policies in place before that date are generally not affected. You may want to consult your professional advisers to discuss how these changes may affect any estate planning with life insurance that you may be considering.

21.8 Business succession

If you own and manage a business, it could well be your family's largest asset. After your death, the business may be crucial for meeting your family's financial needs. Taking steps to ensure your business's ongoing profitability and management can be just as important as considering the planning opportunities available to reduce taxes on your death.

One of the first issues you must resolve is what will happen to the business when you die. You could plan for the business to be kept in the family, sold to a buyer outside the family or liquidated. The option you choose depends on things such as the nature of the business, the likelihood of its continued success after your death and the abilities of your family members and/or key employees to run the business's operations.

Plan for the succession of your business.

If the family is not capable or does not want to run the business, it may be in everyone's best interests to sell or liquidate the business on or before your retirement. If some family members are quite active in managing the business while others are not, dividing ownership equally among your family might seem fair but it could disrupt the business and create tension in the family. Often in these cases, you could use other family assets or life insurance to ensure fairness for all family members.

If you decide to keep the business in the family, you should seek professional advice to help you decide whether to transfer ownership during your lifetime or on death, who will receive the business's shares and in what proportion, whether the shares will be gifted or sold, and the most tax-effective way to structure the transfer. Note that the rules on intergenerational transfers of business may soon change, as the government has said it intends to develop new proposals in this area.

If you do not own 100% of your company's shares, the transfer of its legal control may be addressed by a carefully drafted shareholders' agreement (see 14.4).

Life insurance owned by you or your company can facilitate the sale of your shares of the company and help to fund any tax liability arising on death. The tax rules may allow you to maintain certain tax advantages associated with life insurance-funded arrangements if your company was the beneficiary of a life insurance policy held for this purpose on or before April 25, 1995, or if there was an agreement in place at that time relating to the disposition of your shares. These tax advantages would remain available if you cancel the pre-April 26, 1995 life insurance policy and replace it with another policy or you increase the amount of insurance coverage.

21.9 Planning for the succession of wealth

In some cases where a family business has been sold, the family's largest asset after the sale is the net sale proceeds. In other cases, wise investment decisions have resulted in the accumulation of significant wealth. Since the bulk of such estates may ultimately accrue to your children, you should assess the age at which you feel they should have access to this wealth and whether you should put controls or restrictions on the use of these resources for certain periods of time.

Inter vivos and testamentary family trusts (see 21.5.4) can facilitate the transfer of wealth to children over pre-determined ages. Such trusts are also useful in situations where the child is dependent by reason of mental or physical infirmity. They can also be beneficial if your children lack an appreciation for the value of money.

If you will be passing on a sizeable estate to your children, you should consult with your legal and tax advisers to develop a plan to transfer the wealth into their hands.

21.10 Pre-paid funeral and cemetery arrangements

Planning and paying for your funeral and cemetery arrangements in advance can go a long way toward easing the stress on your survivors at a difficult time. Many funeral and cemetery service providers offer plans through which you can deposit funds as pre-payment for their services.

Consider a pre-paid plan to finance your funeral and cemetery arrangements.

To help Canadians finance these arrangements, the tax rules provide a special tax exemption for the investment income earned on eligible pre-paid amounts. Like the deferred income plans discussed in Chapter 3, the sooner you contribute to a pre-paid funeral or cemetery arrangement, the longer your funds will benefit from the effect of tax-free compounding of income.

You can contribute up to $35,000 to an arrangement that covers both funeral and cemetery services. If the funeral and cemetery services will be provided by separate businesses, you can contribute up to $15,000 to an arrangement that covers only funeral services and up to $20,000 to an arrangement that covers only cemetery services. The funds in your account can be used to cover your own funeral and cemetery arrangements or those of anyone you choose; the limits only restrict the amount that any one person can contribute to such plans over his or her lifetime.

Although the amounts of your lump-sum or periodic contributions are not tax-deductible, any income earned on the deposited amounts is not subject to tax while they are in the plan. If you withdraw the funds and use them for other purposes, any amounts that exceed your total contributions are taxable in the year of withdrawal.

Any amounts left over after the funeral and cemetery expenses have been paid for will be refunded to the contributor or the contributor's estate. The tax payable on the refund is calculated with a formula that ensures that only the fund's investment income is subject to tax.

21.11 References

Estate planning can be complicated and every individual's case is different. Consult a qualified tax professional for advice.

Interpretation Bulletin IT-531, Archived – "Eligible funeral arrangements" is available on the CRA's website at *www.canada.ca/en/revenue-agency.html* or or by telephone request at 1-800-959-8281 for individual income tax and trust-related enquiries.

Chapter 22

If you are an executor or estate trustee

- Take steps to reduce the tax burden on the estate (22.1.3)

- Consider realizing selected capital gains and losses on assets left to a spouse or spousal trust (22.2.3)

- Consider filing separate income tax returns to multiply credits (22.2.4)

- Obtain a clearance certificate before distributing assets (22.2.5)

- Watch out for the effects of foreign estate taxes (22.5)

If you are an executor or estate trustee, your responsibilities for the deceased's estate include filing all tax returns required and ensuring that all taxes have been paid. To fulfill these responsibilities, you need to know about the tax rules that apply on death. In this chapter, we provide an overview of these rules and some steps you may be able to take to minimize the taxes owed by the deceased and the estate.

22.1 What happens on death?

When a person dies, the executor or administrator of the person's estate (also called the "estate trustee") is responsible for taking charge of the individual's affairs and distributing assets as set out in his or her will. The executor's responsibilities include determining the assets and liabilities of the estate, filing all income tax returns for the deceased and the estate, paying the debts outstanding at the date of the individual's death (including all taxes), and letting the beneficiaries know which of the amounts they receive from the estate are taxable.

If there is no will or the will is invalid, provincial law determines how the deceased's assets are distributed. The deceased's representatives or heirs must apply to the court to appoint an administrator to administer and distribute the estate according to a formula set out in legislation (see 21.2.1).

22.1.1 Applying for probate

The executor normally applies to the court for "letters probate", which will give court approval for the executor to take over the deceased's property, manage it and distribute it to the beneficiaries of the estate.

Probate fees are charged by the courts in each province (except Quebec) to grant letters probate. The probate charge generally applies to the total value of an estate's assets at the time of death, without any deduction for debts other than those encumbering real property. (See 21.4 for estate planning steps you may be able to take to minimize probate fees.)

22.1.2 Notifying government agencies

If the deceased received Canada Pension Plan (CPP) or Old Age Security (OAS) payments, the executor or legal representative should contact Service Canada to cancel the deceased's benefits and determine the death benefits due to a surviving spouse or the estate.

22.1.3 Post-mortem tax planning

Take steps to reduce the tax burden on the estate.

Tax planning does not necessarily stop on death. There may be many opportunities for post-mortem planning available to the deceased's estate to lessen the tax burden on the estate or the deceased taxpayer to the benefit of the beneficiaries. Post-mortem planning begins shortly after death and is usually complete within the first year.

For example, in certain circumstances, more than one income tax return may be filed for the deceased taxpayer (see 22.2.4). If the deceased has a surviving spouse, the executor may be able to make a contribution to a spousal RRSP before the deadline (60 days after the end of the year of death).

In more complicated situations, the deceased's representative may choose to wind up a corporation owned by the estate during the first fiscal period of the estate or make certain elections relating to capital losses arising in the estate (see 22.2.3).

If you are an executor and estate trustee, you should seek advice on how to manage the tax burden on the estate that has been left under your care. If you do not, you could be sued by the beneficiaries. The courts have found executors liable for failing to take active steps to structure the estate's affairs to reduce income tax.

22.2 Taxes on death

22.2.1 Tax payable by the deceased taxpayer

When a person dies, the executor must file a "terminal return" for the deceased to report income up to the date of death. Although the regular T1 and Quebec TP1 return forms are used, there are special rules for these returns. For example:

- charitable donations, which can normally be claimed for the year of donation or carried forward to future years (see 8.1), can be carried back and claimed in the year prior to death (subject to the limits discussed in 8.1) or, starting in 2016, claimed by the estate (see 8.2), if not of use in the terminal return
- medical expenses paid, which can normally be claimed for a 12-month period ending in the year (see 2.7.1), can be pooled for any 24-month period that includes the day of death
- the full amount of the deceased's RRSP (see 3.1) or RRIF (see 20.4.4) is brought into income for the year of death, unless the beneficiary of the plan is the deceased's spouse or certain dependants (see 22.4.1); if the funds are not transferred to the spouse's own RRSP or RRIF, the spouse must report the funds as income for tax purposes
- any balance borrowed by the deceased from an RRSP under the Home Buyers' Plan (see 3.3.6) or Lifelong Learning Plan (see 3.3.7) and not yet

repaid must be included in income unless an election is made to have the liability assumed by the surviving spouse

- the fair market value of the property held in the deceased's TFSA (see 4.1) at the time of death is not taxable to the deceased but any investment income earned in the TFSA after the holder's death is generally no longer tax-exempt (see 22.4.2)
- minimum tax (see 7.6) does not apply to the year of death
- capital property not left to a surviving spouse (either outright or through a spousal trust) is deemed disposed of at its fair market value, resulting in either a capital gain or a capital loss (see 22.2.3)
- capital losses, which are normally only allowed to offset capital gains (as discussed in 6.2.2), may be deducted from other income (except to the extent you have previously claimed the capital gains exemption)
- certain kinds of income earned but not received by the deceased before death can be reported on a separate return (against which the deceased's personal credits can be claimed a second time) (see 22.2.4)
- for deaths after 2015, the terminal return may include income deemed to have been received from certain testamentary spousal trusts (see 22.2.3).

The terminal return for the deceased is due by the usual deadline (see 9.1.1) or six months after death, whichever is later. For example, if the date of death is March 10, 2021, the deceased's 2021 return is due by April 30, 2022 (or June 15, 2022 if the deceased or spouse had self-employment income). Any balance of tax owing is due on April 30 of the year after the year of death or six months after death, whichever is later.

A similar extension is allowed for filing of the return for the year before the year of death if the individual dies before the return's normal due date. Continuing our example above, the deceased's 2020 tax return would be due by September 10, 2021 instead of the usual April 30, 2021 deadline.

If the deceased person was paying tax by instalments, no further instalment payments have to be paid after his or her death. The only instalments required are those that were due before the date of death.

Note that life insurance proceeds received as a result of an individual's death are not subject to income tax. Life insurance is discussed in more detail in 21.7.

If you are an active or retired partner of a professional partnership, see 16.2.6.

22.2.2 Tax payable by the estate

Any income earned after death is subject to tax as part of the estate. The estate is treated as a separate person that must file a return as a trust each year until all of the assets are distributed. (Sometimes this distribution can take several years, but some estates can be wound up within one year.)

An estate paying tax at graduated rates is only entitled to do so for the first 36 months of its administration. After that, the estate's income is subject to tax at the top federal and provincial rate.

Income earned by the estate on all of its assets (whether administered under one or more wills) is eligible to be taxed at graduated tax rates, whereas income earned by a testamentary trust created by a will is taxed at the top rate after 2015.

A graduated rate estate may use a non-calendar year-end for tax purposes during the first 36 months of its administration. Once the 36-month period ends, the estate must use a calendar year-end.

The estate trustee should ensure that the estate does not undertake transactions that could cause it to prematurely lose its graduated rate estate status during its first 36 months, for example, incurring certain debts owing to a beneficiary or certain other persons. If the estate loses its graduated rate estate status, it would prematurely lose the benefit of graduated income tax rates and other adverse tax consequences may arise.

Any income paid to beneficiaries of the estate may be taxed in their hands directly, instead of in the estate. Tax can generally be deferred on any capital distribution from the estate to a beneficiary resident in Canada. When an estate distributes property to a beneficiary who is not resident in Canada, different rules apply. The requirements for distributions to non-resident beneficiaries are complex—consult your professional adviser to ensure that you obtain proper tax advice before the distribution.

22.2.3 Capital gains on death

Canada has no federal estate tax or inheritance tax, nor do any of the provinces. To the extent you simply have cash in the bank and you leave it to your family, there would be no tax to pay at all (other than probate fees, discussed in 21.4).

Many people, however, have capital assets such as stocks, real estate and jewellery. As a general rule, capital assets are deemed for tax purposes to have been sold immediately before death at their fair market value, thus triggering a capital gain on all of the increase in value that has accrued since the assets were purchased. This prevents gains from accruing indefinitely without ever being taxed. The normal capital gains rules apply to this deemed disposition, together with the availability of exemptions, such as the lifetime capital gains exemption (see 6.4).

Example

Jane dies in March 2021. Her only capital assets are her house, which has a cost base of $50,000 and is now worth $600,000; a diamond ring, which has a cost base of $5,000 and is now worth $10,000; and a stock portfolio, which has a cost base of $10,000 and is now worth $100,000.

The house is deemed sold at fair market value just before Jane's death, but there is no capital gain because it was her principal residence. The ring and the stocks are also deemed sold at their current values, for a total gain of $95,000. One-half of the capital gain, or $47,500, is taxed as a taxable capital gain on Jane's terminal return.

Any accrued capital losses are also realized at death. If you own depreciable property, recaptured capital cost allowance or a terminal loss may also be triggered.

The main exception to the "deemed disposition" rule is where you leave assets to your spouse (including a common-law spouse—see 2.2.1) or to a spousal trust (a trust that meets certain requirements, as outlined in 21.5.2). In such a case, you are deemed to have sold your assets immediately before your death at their cost, so no capital gain results, as long as your spouse or a spousal trust obtains ownership and unfettered rights to the property. Your spouse (or the trust) then inherits that cost for tax purposes along with the assets. When your spouse (or the trust) sells the assets, or on your spouse's death, the full capital gain or loss from your original purchase price will be taxed.

If you establish a spousal trust, any capital gains on the assets in the trust at the time of your spouse's death would be taxed in the trust. It may be possible to elect to have the gains taxed in your spouse's estate in certain limited circumstances. A professional adviser can help you review your options in this area.

There is a special rule under which an estate executor may elect to realize a capital gain or loss on a property-by-property basis when assets are left to a spouse (or a spousal trust) on the deceased's death. This election may be beneficial if the estate executor elects to trigger a capital gain in order to use loss carryforwards or a lifetime capital gains exemption.

> Consider realizing selected capital gains and losses on assets left to a spouse or spousal trust.

Alternatively, triggering a capital loss may recover tax in the year prior to death, since capital losses in the year of death may be carried back to the immediately preceding year and used against any income, except to the extent that the deceased previously claimed the lifetime capital gains exemption (see 6.4).

Capital losses can also be carried back to offset capital gains in the previous three years.

If you transfer assets during your lifetime to an alter ego or joint partner trust, the assets pass to the ultimate beneficiaries according to the terms of the trust document and do not pass through your estate. Special rules apply to the trust on the death of the settlor of an alter ego trust or the second partner of a joint partner trust (see 21.5.5).

If you are an active or retired partner of a professional partnership, see 16.2.6.

22.2.4 Separate income tax returns

The executor or legal representative must file an ordinary income tax return reporting the income of the deceased from January 1 of the year of death to the date of death. In certain circumstances, the executor may exclude specific types of income from the ordinary return and report them on separate, optional income tax returns.

Certain tax credits such as the age credit, basic personal tax credit, spousal tax credit, wholly dependent person tax credit and caregiver credit that apply in the ordinary return for the year of death may

> Consider filing separate income tax returns to multiply credits.

also be deducted in each of the separate returns filed, making it advantageous to file these separate returns. Certain other tax credits and certain deductions may be used in either the separate returns or the ordinary return or split between the returns.

The executor may choose to file up to three separate returns aside from the ordinary return. These optional returns are for income from:

- rights or things
- a business as a partner or proprietor
- a graduated rate estate.

Rights or things are amounts that were not paid at the time of death and that, had the person not died, would have been included in his or her income when received. There are rights or things from employment and other sources such as certain investments—for example, uncashed matured bond coupons and unpaid dividends declared before the date of death.

If the deceased was a partner or sole proprietor of a business, business income may be reported on a separate return if the fiscal period of the business was not the same as the calendar year and the death occurred after the end of the fiscal period but before the end of the calendar year, among other conditions. The executor may use this return to report income for the time from the end of the fiscal period to the date of death.

Similarly, if the deceased was a beneficiary of a graduated rate estate and the estate does not report its income on a calendar-year basis, any income from the end of the estate's last fiscal period to the date of death may be reported on a separate return. Income from *inter vivos* trusts and, as of January 1, 2016, from testamentary trusts does not qualify for this special treatment.

22.2.5 Clearance certificates

Obtain a clearance certificate before distributing assets.

As executor or legal representative, you may want to get a clearance certificate from the CRA before you distribute all of the property under your control. A clearance certificate indicates that all taxes for which the deceased is liable have been paid. If you do not get a certificate, you would be liable for any tax the deceased owes. A final clearance certificate covers all tax years to the wind-up of the estate. A separate clearance certificate is needed for a trust such as a spousal trust, which is deemed to have disposed of its assets on the day of the spouse's death.

22.3 Death benefits

A death benefit is an amount paid in recognition of a deceased employee's service. Death benefits may be paid by the deceased's employer to the surviving spouse, other family members or to the estate. Up to $10,000 of such benefits may be received tax-free.

The first $10,000 of death benefits paid for any one employee is exempt from tax. The employee's spouse gets the exemption; to the extent there is no spouse or the spouse receives less than $10,000 and other taxpayers receive such funds, any remaining amount of exemption can be split among the other recipients. "Spouse" includes common-law spouses who meet the criteria outlined in 2.2.1.

Note that life insurance proceeds are completely different from death benefits, and are not taxed at all when received.

22.4 RRSPs, RRIFs and TFSAs on death

22.4.1 RRSPs and RRIFs

On death, a taxpayer is normally taxed on the entire amount of any RRSPs or RRIFs, except where the funds are left to the taxpayer's spouse or financially dependent child or grandchild, in which case they are included in the spouse, child or grandchild's income. To the extent the funds come from an RRSP, they can be transferred to the spouse's own RRSP or RRIF for a deduction that offsets the income inclusion. The spouse can also use these funds to acquire an annuity. To the extent the funds come from a RRIF, if the spouse is named as a successor annuitant to the RRIF, the payments under the deceased's plan would continue to be paid to the spouse. If the spouse is named as beneficiary of the RRIF, amounts under the deceased's plan can be transferred to the spouse's own RRSP or RRIF, or he or she can use the funds to acquire an annuity.

If the RRSP or RRIF funds are left to a financially dependent child or grandchild, the RRSP or RRIF funds can either be taxed in the hands of the child or grandchild or used to buy a term annuity to age 18. Other options are available for financially dependent children or grandchildren with mental or physical infirmities. The executor should obtain professional advice on these matters.

If the value of the RRSP or RRIF decreases after the taxpayer's death and before the assets are distributed to the beneficiaries, a deduction for the loss may be allowed on the taxpayer's terminal return, as long as the distribution is made by the end of the year following the year of death.

22.4.2 TFSAs

On the death of a TFSA holder, the fair market value of the TFSA is not taxable to the deceased, though other tax implications may arise.

The TFSA would continue to exist after the holder's death if the surviving spouse is named as the successor account holder. The successor would not have to pay tax on the TFSA's value on his or her spouse's death or on any future income earned in the account. This rollover of the account to the successor does not affect the successor's unused TFSA contribution room.

If no successor holder exists but the account holder has designated beneficiaries, these beneficiaries would receive the TFSA's value at the account holder's death tax-free. Any income earned in the account after the account holder's death would be taxable to the beneficiaries. If the beneficiaries have unused TFSA contribution room, they can roll over the amount received to their own TFSAs. If the beneficiary is the spouse, he or she may transfer the TFSA's value at the date of death (but not any subsequent income) to their TFSA without affecting their unused TFSA contribution room.

If the TFSA does not have a successor holder or designated beneficiary, the TFSA would pass to the deceased holder's estate.

22.5 Foreign estate taxes

If you own assets in other countries, estate, inheritance or succession taxes of those countries (or their states or provinces) may apply on your death.

Watch out for the effects of foreign estate taxes. Estate taxes and succession duties imposed by other jurisdictions are not normally eligible for a foreign tax credit in Canada, even though you may have a Canadian income tax liability as a result of the deemed disposition described in 22.2.3. Double taxation can result. You may need to plan for this possibility ahead of time.

If you are a U.S. citizen, see our discussion of U.S. estate tax in 18.8.3.

If you are not a U.S. citizen but own assets legally located in the U.S., including real estate, debts owed to you by U.S. citizens or shares in U.S. corporations, see the planning options to deal with U.S. estate tax discussed in 19.4.5.

22.6 References

The following publications and more information, including forms and brochures, can be obtained on the CRA's website at *www.canada.ca/en/revenue-agency.html* or by telephone request at 1-800-959-8281 for individual income tax and trust-related enquiries or 1-800-959-5525 for business and self-employed individual enquiries.

Guide T4011, "Preparing Returns for Deceased Persons"
Information Sheet RC4111, "What to Do Following a Death"

Also, see the following selected topics on the CRA's website:

"Final return"
"Optional returns"

Appendix I

Federal and Provincial Income Tax Rates and Brackets for 2020

	Tax Rates	Tax Brackets	Surtax Rates	Thresholds
Federal	15.00%	Up to $48,535		
	20.50	48,536–97,069		
	26.00	97,070–150,473		
	29.00	150,474–214,368		
	33.00	214,369 and over		
British Columbia	5.06%	Up to $41,725		
	7.70	41,726–83,451		
	10.50	83,452–95,812		
	12.29	95,813–116,344		
	14.70	116,345–157,748		
	16.80	157,749–220,000		
	20.50	220,001 and over		
Alberta	10.00%	Up to $131,220		
	12.00	131,221–157,464		
	13.00	157,465–209,952		
	14.00	209,953–314,928		
	15.00	314,929 and over		
Saskatchewan	10.50%	Up to $45,225		
	12.50	45,226–129,214		
	14.50	129,215 and over		
Manitoba	10.80%	Up to $33,389		
	12.75	33,390–72,164		
	17.40	72,165 and over		
Ontario	5.05%	Up to $44,740		
	9.15	44,741–89,482	20%	$4,830
	11.16	89,483–150,000	36	6,182
	12.16	150,001–220,000		
	13.16	220,001 and over		

	Tax Rates	Tax Brackets	Surtax	
			Rates	Thresholds
Quebec	15.00%	Up to $44,545		
	20.00	44,546–89,080		
	24.00	89,081–108,390		
	25.75	108,391 and over		
New Brunswick	9.68%	Up to $43,401		
	14.82	43,402–86,803		
	16.52	86,804–141,122		
	17.84	141,123–160,776		
	20.30	160,777 and over		
Nova Scotia	8.79%	Up to $29,590		
	14.95	29,591–59,180		
	16.67	59,181–93,000		
	17.50	93,001–150,000		
	21.00	150,001 and over		
Prince Edward Island	9.80%	Up to $31,984		
	13.80	31,985–63,969		
	16.70	63,970 and over	10%	$12,500
Newfoundland and Labrador	8.70%	Up to $37,929		
	14.50	37,930–75,858		
	15.80	75,859–135,432		
	17.30	135,433–189,604		
	18.30	189,605 and over		

Combined Federal and Provincial Top Marginal Tax Rates for Individuals[1]–2020

	Interest and Regular Income	Capital Gains	Eligible Dividends	Non-eligible Dividends
British Columbia	53.50%	26.75%	36.54%	48.89%
Alberta	48.00	24.00	31.71	42.30
Saskatchewan	47.50	23.75	29.64	40.37
Manitoba	50.40	25.20	37.79	46.67
Ontario	53.53	26.76	39.34	47.74
Quebec	53.31	26.65	40.11	47.14
New Brunswick	53.30	26.65	33.51	47.75
Nova Scotia	54.00	27.00	41.58	48.27
P.E.I.	51.37	25.69	34.23	45.23
Newfoundland and Labrador	51.30	25.65	42.62	44.59

Note

(1) The combined top marginal tax rate is the rate individuals pay on income that falls into the highest tax bracket in their province of residence. See the previous table for provincial tax brackets.

Appendix II

Federal and Provincial Non-Refundable Tax Credit Rates and Amounts for 2020[1]

	Federal	B.C.	Alta.	Sask.	Man.
Tax rate applied to credits	15.00%	5.06%	10.00%	10.50%	10.80%
Basic personal[2]	$13,229	$10,949	$19,369	$16,065	$9,838
Spousal/partner and wholly dependent person[3] (see 2.2.1)	$13,229	9,376	19,369	16,065	9,134
Net income threshold	–	*938*	–	*1,607*	–
Dependants					
18 and over and infirm	See Caregiver	See Caregiver	11,212	9,464	3,605
Net income threshold			*7,407*	*6,715*	*5,115*
Caregiver[4] (see 2.5.4)	7,276	4,792	11,212	9,464	3,605
Net income threshold	*17,085*	*16,215*	*17,826*	*16,164*	*12,312*
Child[5] (max)	–	–	–	6,094	–
Adoption[6] (max) (see 2.3.3)	16,563	16,563	13,247	–	10,000
Disability[7] (see 2.5.1)	8,576	8,212	14,940	9,464	6,180
Disability supplement[8] (see 2.5.1)	5,003	4,792	11,212	9,464	3,605
Pension[7] (max)	2,000	1,000	1,491	1,000	1,000
Age 65 and over[7,9]	7,637	4,910	5,397	4,894	3,728
Net income threshold	*38,508*	*36,552*	*40,179*	*36,430*	*27,749*
Medical expense threshold[10] (see 2.7.1)	2,397	2,277	2,504	2,268	1,728
Employment[11] (see 10.7.1)	1,245	–	Refundable	–	–
Canada Pension Plan[12] (max)	2,898	2,898	2,898	2,898	2,898
Employment Insurance[12] (max)	856	856	856	856	856
Children's fitness[13] and arts[14] (max)	–	–	–	–	500
Home buyers[15] (max) (see 2.7.3)	5,000	–	–	10,000	–
Home accessibility[16] (max) (see 2.5.5)	10,000	Refundable	–	–	–
Tuition fees[17] (see 2.4.1)	Yes	Yes	No	No	Yes
Education					
Full-time—per month	–	–	–	–	400
Part-time—per month	–	–	–	–	120
Charitable donations (see 8.1)					
Credit rate on first $200	15.00%	5.06%	10.00%	10.50%	10.80%
Credit rate on balance	29.00/33.00%	16.80/20.50%	21.00%	14.50%	17.40%

	Ont.	N.B.	N.S.	P.E.I.	Nfld.
Tax rate applied to credits	5.05%	9.68%	8.79%	9.80%	8.70%
Basic personal[2]	$10,783	$10,459	$8,481	$10,000	$9,498
Spousal/partner and wholly dependent person[3] (see 2.2.1)	9,156	8,882	8,481	8,493	7,761
Net income threshold	*915*	*889*	*848*	*849*	*777*
Dependants					
18 and over and infirm	See Caregiver	4,940	2,798	2,446	3,016
Net income threshold		*7,008*	*5,683*	*4,966*	*6,482*
Caregiver[4] (see 2.5.4)	5,082	4,940	4,898	2,446	3,016
Net income threshold	*17,388*	*16,869*	*13,677*	*11,953*	*14,741*
Child[5] (max)	–	–	1,200	1,200	–
Adoption[6] (max) (see 2.3.3)	13,155	–	–	–	12,818
Disability[7] (see 2.5.1)	8,712	8,468	7,341	6,890	6,409
Disability supplement[8] (see 2.5.1)	5,080	4,940	3,449	4,019	3,016
Pension[7] (max)	1,491	1,000	1,173	1,000	1,000
Age 65 and over[7,9]	5,265	5,107	4,141	3,764	6,063
Net income threshold	*39,193*	*38,019*	*30,828*	*28,019*	*33,226*
Medical expense threshold[10] (see 2.7.1)	2,441	2,367	1,637	1,678	2,068
Employment[11] (see 10.7.1)	–	–	–	–	–
Canada Pension Plan[12] (max)	2,898	2,898	2,898	2,898	2,898
Employment Insurance[12] (max)	856	856	856	856	856
Children's fitness[13] and arts[14] (max)	–	–	–	–	–
Home buyers[15] (max) (see 2.7.3)	–	–	–	–	–
Home accessibility[16] (max) (see 2.5.5)	–	Refundable	–	–	–
Tuition fees[17] (see 2.4.1)	No	Yes	Yes	Yes	Yes
Education					
Full-time—per month	–	–	200	400	200
Part-time—per month	–	–	60	120	60
Charitable donations (see 8.1)					
Credit rate on first $200	5.05%	9.68%	8.79%	9.80%	8.70%
Credit rate on balance	11.16%	17.95%	21.00%	16.70%	18.30%

Notes

1) The table shows the dollar amounts of federal and provincial non-refundable tax credits for 2020 (except for Quebec, see the table "Quebec Non-Refundable Tax Credit Rates and Amounts for 2020" in Appendix III). To determine the credit value, each dollar amount must be multiplied by the tax rate shown, which is the lowest tax rate applicable in the particular jurisdiction. For example, the Ontario basic personal credit amount of $10,783 is multiplied by 5.05% to determine the credit value of $545.

   Income earned by the taxpayer or dependant, as applicable, over the net income thresholds shown in the table reduces the availability of the credit on a dollar-for-dollar basis. The only exception is the age credit, which is reduced by 15% of the taxpayer's net income over the threshold.

2) The federal government proposed to gradually increase the federal basic personal amount to $15,000 by 2023. The basic personal amount is increased to $13,229 (from $12,298) for individuals with net incomes of $150,473 or less in 2020. The increase to the basic personal amount is gradually reduced for individuals with net incomes between $150,473 and $214,368 in 2020. Individuals with net incomes over $214,368 in 2020 will not be affected by these changes and their basic personal amount will remain at $12,298. These proposed measures have not been enacted into legislation but the CRA is administering the measures as though they are in force.

   Nova Scotia provides an additional basic personal amount of $3,000 where a taxpayer's income is $25,000 or less. This amount will decrease proportionately if the taxpayer's income is between $25,000 and $75,000.

3) The spousal/partner and wholly dependent person amounts are calculated by subtracting the spouse/partner and wholly dependant's net income from the maximum amount.

   The federal government proposed to gradually increase the maximum federal spouse or common-law partner amount and the eligible dependant credit to $15,000 by 2023. The maximum amount is increased to $13,229 (from $12,298) for individuals with net incomes of $150,473 or less in 2020. The increase to the maximum amount is gradually reduced for individuals with net incomes between $150,473 and $214,368 in 2020. Individuals with net incomes over $214,368 in 2020 will not be affected by these changes and the maximum amount will remain at $12,298. These proposed measures have not been enacted into legislation but the CRA is administering the measures as though they are in force.

   Nova Scotia provides an additional non-refundable credit for spousal/partner and wholly dependant person if the person's income is $25,000 or less. The amount for 2020 is $3,000. This amount will decrease proportionately if the person's income is between $25,000 and $75,000.

4) For Ontario and British Columbia, the caregiver credit amount is $5,082 and $4,792, respectively, for relatives who are infirm dependants, including adult children of the claimant or of the claimant's spouse or common-law partner.

5) Nova Scotia and Prince Edward Island provide a credit for children under age 6. If certain conditions are met, an individual can claim $100 per eligible month for up to $1,200 per year. Unused credit amounts may be transferred between spouses.

   Saskatchewan provides a credit for children under age 18 if certain conditions are met. Unused credit amounts may be transferred between spouses.

6) The adoption credit is available on eligible adoption expenses incurred in the year and not reimbursed to the taxpayer, up to the maximum amount shown in the table.

7) The disability, pension and age credits are transferable to a spouse or partner. The amounts available for transfer are reduced by the excess of the spouse's or partner's net income over the basic personal credit amount. The disability credit is also transferable to a supporting person other than a spouse or partner; however, the amount of the credit is reduced by the excess of the disabled person's net income over the basic personal credit amount.

8) The disability supplement may be claimed by an individual who is under age 18 at the end of the year. The amount in the table is the maximum amount that may be claimed, and it is reduced by certain child and attendant care expenses claimed for this individual.

9) Saskatchewan provides an additional non-refundable tax credit for individuals age 65 or older in the year, regardless of their net income amount. The amount for 2020 is $1,292.

   Nova Scotia provides an additional non-refundable tax credit for individuals age 65 or older in the year if their taxable income is $25,000 or less. The amount for 2020 is $1,465. This amount will decrease proportionately if the individual's income is between $25,000 and $75,000.

10) The medical expense credit is calculated based on qualified medical expenses exceeding 3% of net income or the threshold shown in the table, whichever is less. Medical expenses incurred by both spouses/partners and by their children under age 18 may be totalled and claimed by either spouse/partner.

   Taxpayers can also claim medical expenses for other eligible dependants to the extent the amount exceeds the lesser of 3% of net income of the dependant or the threshold shown in the table. Ontario is currently the only province with a maximum allowable medical expense for other eligible dependants. The limit is $13,155 for 2020.

11) The federal employment credit may be claimed by individuals based on the lesser of the amount shown in the table and the amount of employment income earned in the year.

   Alberta offers a refundable family employment credit for Alberta residents with children under age 18 who meet the income eligibility criteria. The credit is paid in January and July of each year. In July 2020, the Alberta child and family benefit replaced the Alberta child benefit and Alberta family employment credit. This benefit is non-taxable and is paid quarterly.

12) Self-employed taxpayers can deduct 50% of their Canada or Quebec Pension Plan premiums in calculating net income and claim the balance as a non-refundable tax credit. Self-employed taxpayers can also claim Employment Insurance premiums paid.

13) Manitoba is the only province that provides a fitness tax credit. Taxpayers in Manitoba can claim up to $500 for fees paid on registration or membership for an eligible program of physical activity for children under age 18 at the end of the year, for a spouse or common-law partner age 18 to 24 at the end of the year, and for themselves if they are under age 25 at the end of the year. For children or young adults eligible for the disability tax credit, taxpayers can claim an additional $500 if at least $100 is paid for registration or membership fees for a prescribed program of physical activity.

14) Manitoba is the only province that provide a children's arts tax credit. Taxpayers in Manitoba can claim up to $500 for fees paid relating to the cost of registration or membership in an eligible program of artistic, cultural, recreational or developmental activity for children under age 16 (or 18 if eligible for the disability tax credit) at the beginning of the year. For children who are under age 18 at the beginning of the year and eligible for the disability tax credit, taxpayers can claim an additional $500 if at least $100 is paid for registration or membership fees for an eligible artistic program.

15) Saskatchewan's First-Time Home Buyers Tax Credit provides a non-refundable income tax credit of up to $1,050 (10.5% X $10,000) to eligible taxpayers. Persons with a disability may also qualify for the purchase of more accessible homes, with eligibility rules similar to those for the federal first-time home buyers credit. The Saskatchewan credit generally applies to qualifying homes acquired after December 31, 2011.

16) The home accessibility tax credit provides a credit for qualifying expenses incurred for work performed or goods acquired for a qualifying renovation of an eligible dwelling of someone who is age 65 or older before the end of the taxation year or eligible for the disability tax credit. British Columbia and New Brunswick provide a refundable credit of up to $1,000 for similar expenses.

17) The eligible portion of the tuition tax credit is transferable to a spouse or common-law partner, parent or grandparent. Any amounts not transferred may be carried forward indefinitely by the student.

Appendix III

Quebec Non-Refundable Tax Credit Rates and Amounts for 2020

Tax rate applied to credits[1]	15%
Basic personal amount	$15,532
Amounts for dependants: (see 17.2)	
Child under 18 engaged in full-time training or post-secondary studies[2]	2,983
Child over 17 who is a full-time student[3]	See note
Other dependants over 17[4]	4,348
Person living alone or with a dependant:[5] (see 17.2)	
Basic amount	1,780
Single-parent amount (supplement)	2,197
Age 65 and over[5] (see 17.5)	3,267
Career extension (age 60 and over)[6] (see 17.10.8)	
Age 60 to 64	10,000
Age 65 and over	11,000
Pension[5] (max) (see 17.5)	2,902
Disability (see 17.9)	3,449
First-time home buyers (see 17.13.5)	5,000
Union and professional dues (see 17.10.4)	10%
Tuition fees (see 17.4.1)	8%
Interest paid on student loans (see 17.4.2)	20%
Medical expenses (see 17.8)	20%
Charitable donations (see 17.7.1)	
Credit rate on first $200	20%
Credit rate on balance	24/25.75%

Notes

1) To determine the credit value, each dollar value must be multiplied by Quebec's tax credit rate. For example, the basic personal credit amount of $15,532 is multiplied by 15% to determine the credit value of $2,330.

   The unused portion of non-refundable credits may be transferred from one spouse/partner to another, but only after all credits have been taken into account in calculating the individual's income tax otherwise payable.

   For details on these credits, see Chapter 17.

2) This credit is available for a dependent child who is under age 18 and is engaged in full-time professional training or post-secondary studies for each completed term, to a maximum of

two semesters per year per dependant. The credit is also available for infirm dependants who are engaged in such activities part-time.

3) An eligible student can transfer to either parent an amount relating to an unused portion of their basic personal credit amount for the year (transfer mechanism for the recognized parental contribution). Each taxation year, the amount that can be transferred must not exceed the limit for that year ($10,662 for 2020).

4) This credit is available if the dependant, other than the spouse, is related to the taxpayer by blood, marriage or adoption and ordinarily lives with the taxpayer. The taxpayer must not have benefited from a transfer of the recognized parental contribution from this dependant.

5) The total of the credit amounts for individuals age 65 or older, for living alone or with a dependant, and for receiving retirement income is reduced by 18.75% of the amount by which net family income exceeds $35,205.

6) Any unused portion of this tax credit cannot be carried forward or transferred to the individual's spouse.

Quebec Refundable Tax Credit Rates and Amounts for 2020[1]

	Tax Rate	Max expense	Max credit
Medical expenses[2] (see 17.8) Reduced by 5% of family income over $23,700	25%	only certain medical expenses qualify	$ 1,226
Child care expense credit (see 17.3.2)	26%–75%		
The lesser of expenses incurred or:			
For a child who has a severe or prolonged mental or physical impairment		13,445	
For a child under age seven		9,825	
For a child under age seventeen		5,170	
Adoption expense credit (see 17.3.4)	50%	20,000	10,000
Infertility treatment credit (see 17.3.4)	20%–80%	20,000	16,000
Tax credit for caregivers (see 17.6)			
Basic amount			1,250
Reducible amount			1,250
Reduced by 16% of eligible care receiver's income over $22,180			
Respite of caregivers (see 17.6)	30%	5,200	1,560
Reduced by 3% of caregiver's family income over $59,385			
Home support of elderly persons living alone (see 17.5.1)			
Not recognized as dependant seniors	35%	19,500	6,825
Recognized as dependant seniors	35%	25,500	8,925
Reduced by 3% of the individual's family income over $59,385			
Short-term transition of seniors in rehabilitation centre (see 17.5.1)	20%	costs incurred in maximum 60-day period	
Safety equipment for seniors (see 17.5.1)	20%	costs incurred over $250	
Residential waste water treatment system (see 17.13.3)	20%	costs incurred over $2,500	5,500

Notes

1) Quebec's credit rates, maximum expenses eligible and methods of calculating credits vary from one type of refundable credit to another. Quebec's credit rate is applied to the dollar amounts in the table to determine the maximum credit value. For example, the adoption expense credit amount of $20,000 is multiplied by 50% to determine the maximum credit value of $10,000. Some refundable credits are reduced when thresholds are exceeded.

   For details on these credits, see Chapter 17.

2) Quebec provides a refundable tax credit equal to the total of 25% of medical expenses eligible for the non-refundable credit (see the table "Quebec Non-Refundable Tax Credit Rates and Amounts for 2020") and 25% of the amount deducted for impairment support products and services. A minimum amount of earned income is required to claim the refundable tax credit; this amount is $3,135 for 2020..

Index